The PSYCHOLOGICAL BRAIN
A New Paradigm for Understanding How the Mind Works

Herbert J. Greenwald, PhD

INTRODUCTION

What makes us tick?

Imagine you are one of the first humans on earth. Did that bush move? What might be behind that tree trunk? Is an ambush waiting for you over the hill? You must be alert to very movement and sound because you could become some creature's dinner. Were we not wired to pay attention to what is observable, our species would have ended in that far distant past. Our senses and genes are geared for the kill-or-be-killed world in which our cave-men and women ancestors lived. The tension, violence, and wars that have existed since the advent of human history are more understandable in that context.

Everything humans do originates in the mind. If we had a better idea of how the mind works we might be able to create a better life for ourselves and others as well. This book offers a new understanding of mental processes and methods that might help us accomplish our worthy goals.

***

Key words:
Psychological Systems Theory, Psychological Roots, Hidden Sequences, state of uncontrollability, appealing forces, repelling forces, psychological homeostasis.

TABLE OF CONTENTS
INTRODUCTION
A BRIEF OVERVIEW

SECTION III. AUXILIARY INFORMATION

***

DISCLAIMER

The information in this book is from sources deemed to be reliable and accurate to the best of the author's knowledge. This book is provided to the reader for the purpose of education and does not take the place of medication or professional advice. If the reader or someone the reader contacts or advises uses any of the ideas, remedies, techniques, or other information in this book, that person should first consult appropriate psychological and medical professionals. If the reader or someone the reader contacts or advises uses any of the information, ideas, procedures, or therapies in this book, the reader agrees not to hold the author responsible for any damages, costs, and expenses, including any and all legal, psychological, or medical fees that result from the application of any of what is written or implied in this book. The author cannot be held liable for any errors or omissions in this book, nor guarantee the accuracy and validity of every aspect. This disclaimer applies to any damage or injury that result from any direct or indirect use of the information or advice in this book with regard to any issue, including implied contract, intent, injury, or any other aspect or action.

A BRIEF OVERVIEW OF THE PSYCHOLOGICAL BRAIN
A New Paradigm for Understanding How the Mind Works

Almost everything humans do originates in the brain, therefore if we want a better life and a better world we need to know more about how the brain operates. The biology of the brain and how it affects our physical body is substantially known in large part because the brain's structures and many of its tangible processes are visible, either with the naked eye or with the use of aids such as PET scans, CAT scans, functional MRIs, and blood analyses. However, the underpinnings of psychology are still largely unknown because they operate invisibly below the surface. This book is an attempt to describe many important missing pieces, bringing to light hidden factors, structures, and processes that explain important aspects of psychology. This new understanding clarifies misunderstandings and offers a blueprint and a vocabulary for what has previously been invisible. Psychology is now much less mysterious. One of the benefits is that previously difficult human problems now have effective practical solutions.

One of our core psychological systems is *Psychological Homeostasis,* which aids stability. However, exceeding a homeostatic extreme creates a major upheaval, such as depression, panic, ecstasy, addiction, or some other state of uncontrollability. How to prevent states of uncontrollability and exit from them are described in this book.

Another key psychological system involves *Psychological Roots,* such as needs, goals, beliefs, expectations, concerns, interests, and abilities. People know a small number of their Psychological Roots but are unlikely to know their importance, how many they have, how they operate, or that they enter life with some basic Psychological Roots pre-wired into them such as needs for safety, stability, closure, and interpersonal connectedness. A great many other Psychological Roots are acquired through experience.

Psychological Roots are not arranged haphazardly. The first Psychological Roots that are acquired link directly with a genetic root (e.g., need for safety). Then additional roots link with previously acquired roots, and so on. Psychological Roots continue to be added throughout life, which creates lengthy trees of roots that have large numbers of branches and clusters. The resulting webs of Psychological Roots and clusters facilitate thinking, problem-solving, and learning, and also create resistance to change. Some Psychological Roots foster pleasurable reactions while distress-prone roots (e.g., pessimism) contribute to down moods, tension, and irritability. Cognitions and emotions are connected, for example, a negative emotional reaction occurs when a cognitive Psychological Root, such as a belief, is opposed.

'Hidden Sequences' lead to internal reactions (such as thoughts and emotions) and overt behaviors. Those sequences begin with a Psychological Root itself or a root that has been impacted by a stimulus. Change – such as the result of successfully treating a psychological disorder – is more effective when pertinent Psychological Roots are satisfied and relevant stimulus conditions are coped with, compared to expressing feelings, medicating symptoms, or attempting to change behavior directly.

Another psychological system is executive functioning (e.g., evaluating and decision-making) and still another is thinking in absolutes (which can intensify behaviors, emotional reactions, and resistance). Appealing and repelling forces – which create positive or negative reactions, respectively – strongly affect social relations, communication, and persuasion. They factor importantly in conflicts, resolution of conflicts, and psychotherapy. Countervailing forces below awareness contribute to stability and resistance to change. A cumulative build-up of tension can reach a tipping point into a state of uncontrollability. Some other prominent systems are the relationship between goals and expectations, and the manner in which semi-automatic behaviors occur such as conditioning.

The many individual factors, processes, and systems constitute *'Psychological Systems Theory'* (PST). PST provides an understanding of how the subconscious parts of our mind function and leads to improved treatments for many psychological conditions such as depression, anxiety, obsessive-compulsive disorder, borderline personality, and addiction. The theory explains many hitherto puzzling aspects, such as the interconnection of cognitions, emotional reactions, and behavior. It also explains how seemingly irrational behavior, experimental evidence for which brought Thaler (2017) a Nobel-Prize, is nevertheless internally logical when the subconscious aspects that are involved are understood.

Psychological Systems Theory clarifies many other previously puzzling aspects of human behavior as well. For example, the theory explains how to lessen distress and improve the quality of life. It identifies the keys to effective teaching and learning, and provides a psychological explanation of the difference between short-and long-term memory. It also provides a new way to predict and prevent psychological disorders, and opens many new directions for scientific research. (Over 380 needed research studies are outlined at the end of Section II). In short, the author has found Psychological Systems Theory to be indispensable in understanding people, solving puzzling human problems, and treating psychological conditions.

This book has three Parts. Section I describes some particularly important systems and attendant implications. Section II describes some important practical applications (e.g., new approaches for psychotherapy, decision-making, creating win-win solutions, lessening prejudice, persuading, and teaching). Section III provides background information such as references and a glossary.

A Sampling of Questions That Psychological Systems Theory Addresses

1. What are major subconscious psychological processes?
2. How can subconscious processes be measured and tested scientifically?
3. What sub-surface path connects beliefs, thoughts, emotional reactions, evaluations, and behavior?

4. Is the potential for having mental disorders genetically wired-into humans?
5. Is there an underlying continuum between normal behavior and psychological disorders?
6. Is there a definable point at which what is abnormal diverges from what is normal? If so, is it measurable?

7. Is depression a normal phenomenon? Is the originating cause of depression a chemical imbalance?
8. Is depression caused psychologically? How can depression be lessened psychologically?
9. Are depression and anxiety connected? How can anxiety be treated effectively?

10. Can psychological disorders be predicted? Can psychological disorders be prevented? If so, how?
11. Do many psychological disorders have a common foundation? If so, what is it?
12. Can psychological causes of disorders be distinguished from biological causes?

13. Are emotions or thoughts the originating cause of behavior? Are cognitions and emotions connected?
14. Is expressing feelings an effective therapy? (Is feeling healing?)
15. What is the difference between the originating causes of behavior and proximal causes?

16. What goes on below the surface when conditioning occurs? Are beliefs involved?
17. Is it possible for operant conditioning to occur in one trial? With no trials?
18. How important are expectations, beliefs, and goals? Why is it important to know how expectations differ from goals?

19. How can the quality of life be improved?

20. What causes addiction? Is addiction normal? Can addiction be treated effectively?
21. Is the cause of criminal behavior acquired, genetic, or both?

22. Are the underlying psychological mechanisms of males substantially different than that of females or similar?
23. Does divorce occur because couples do not try hard enough to resolve their problems or for some other reason?
24. Why do childhood experiences and people's values last a lifetime? What causes long-term memory?

25. Is the basis for prejudice genetically wired-into humans? How can prejudice be unlearned?
26. How does a win-win solution differ from a compromise? What is the key to creating win-win solutions?
27. Is there a key to effective social relations? How does change occur? What is the key to persuasion?
28. How can thinking and problem-solving be improved? How can difficult decisions be easier to make?
29. What is the key to effective learning and teaching? What is the key problem with rote memorization?
30. Do children acquire knowledge in a similar way that adults do?

***

SECTION I. SOME MAJOR PSYCHOLOGICAL SYSTEMS[1]

A system consists of aspects that function together. Section I describes some major psychological systems, including Psychological Homeostasis, Psychological Roots, Hidden Sequences, appealing and repelling forces, goals and expectations, and semi-automatic behaviors such as conditioning. Some systems that have been substantially described elsewhere are not focused upon in this book, such as linguistic deep structure (Chomsky, 1957), intelligence (e.g., Guilford, 1967; Gardner, 1983), self-efficacy (Bandura, 1977), and creativity (e.g., Amabile, 1983; Sternberg, 1988).

***

[1] Some concepts in Psychological Systems Theory connect with concepts in other psychological theories. Some examples discussed in a later chapter include *linking* and Piaget's concept of *assimilation; flow-down effect* and Piaget's *accommodation; Psychological Root hierarchies* and Piaget's *schemas* (in Flavell,1966); *genetic Psychological Roots* and Murray's (1938) innate *needs; beliefs* and Adler's (1927) *beliefs;* also *countervailing factors* and Lewin's (1947) *quasi-stationary equilibrium.*

PROLOGUE

Tangibility

What we consider to be tangible is what we are consciously aware of that our senses detect. Our senses are remarkable and essential for survival, however they do not detect most of what exists in the world (e.g., radiation and tiny aspects such as atoms and molecules). As a result, it has taken humans over 325,000 years to become aware of aspects that are not directly detectable by us. For example, we cannot see our genes or the biochemicals that are present in our emotional reactions without using special equipment. Microbes provide another example. Humans have not known about them for almost all of the time our species has existed. It was only about 350 years ago that humans first became aware of microbes. It took another 60 years to realize that something invisible caused disease, but that idea was not believed at first. As a result, it took many more years to discover that some microbes cause sickness and death, still more years to discover which microbes caused what disease, and many more years to discover medicines that could kill harmful microbes inside humans (antibiotics). A lesson from this is that what is invisible to the naked eye does not mean that it does not exist.

Another example of invisibility is our inability to see thoughts or beliefs, although perhaps that possibility, too, might occur at some time. In the meantime, being effective in psychology (and many other fields, such as astronomy, physics, and chemistry) requires willingness to work with hidden aspects. The issues involved range widely, from personal distress to interpersonal conflicts, psychological disorders, poverty and war. Psychological Systems Theory offers a blueprint for understanding and developing solutions for many aspects related to those issues.

How much do we know about what goes on in the brain?

Humans did not know why we have a brain until a few hundred years ago. Initially, physicians believed that the brain's extensive blood supply meant that its purpose was to cool the body. People also believed that we consciously control what we do and many individuals still believe this idea, not realizing that our behavior is directed by factors below our awareness such as genetic needs for safety and stability. Evidence for the existence of sub-aware factors is that newborns can be happy, anxious, and have temper tantrums. Those capabilities are wired into our genes.

People are also unlikely to know that they have many thousands of acquired *'Psychological Roots'* (explained in forthcoming chapters). A little over 100 years ago, Freud startled the world by proclaiming that we are aware of only 10% of what goes on our mind ("the tip of the iceberg"; Freud, 1989). The largely hidden functioning of psychological processes is why it has taken a great many years for scientists to get beyond scratching the surface of what goes on psychologically. One result of psychological processes being largely invisible is that some people believe that psychology is not real, logical, important, measurable, understandable, or capable of being worked with effectively. This book offers a different perspective: that the mind functions logically and understandably, and that its processes can be measured and tested scientifically despite their subconscious operations. The considerable consequences of this understanding will soon be seen.

Psychology is not the only discipline that suffers from our senses' limitations, physics, chemistry, and biology also do. For example, our senses can detect only a small portion of the electromagnetic wavelength. We need special equipment to ascertain infrared and ultraviolet rays, microwaves, radio waves, X-rays, and gamma rays. This is not a trivial matter because some portions of that wavelength can be fatal, such as causing cancer. We cannot see expectations, evaluation criteria, psychological needs, and many other inner motivations, and we cannot see how subconscious psychological functions operate. As a result, people often do not know the actual reason for their behavior or that of other people, including their own counterproductive actions. (These issues will be discussed in the coming chapters, for instance, Chapters 3 - 9 explain *Psychological Roots.*)

Lack of knowledge about hidden psychological factors has led people to rely only on what is tangible to them, and therefore to conclusions that are incorrect. For example, Jon gives Mary advice, yet that advice – which seems correct to him – could be inappropriate for her. Sue might conclude that Rudy is inconsiderate because he was late for his date with her, not taking into account that he might have been detained unavoidably. Conflicts that seem impossible to resolve can often be successfully settled upon uncovering the hidden Psychological Roots that underlie those disagreements, as will be seen in Chapters 20 - 23.

There is a reason we lack awareness

Penfield (1975) found that the center of consciousness is in a small portion of a small organ deep in the brain (the amygdala). That discovery suggests that we are aware of far less than Freud's 10% estimate of what goes on in our mind, perhaps less than 1%. That speck of awareness is comparable to trying to understand the inner workings of a computer from a typical display on a monitor.

Why are we not wired to know our underlying psychological processes? Or know exactly what motivates others? A related question is why we are wired to be aware of only a tiny portion of the electromagnetic spectrum and not able to see electrons or disease-causing microbes. Why can we not see genes or how they work, or know how vast the universe is? In short, why are we not equipped to know many important aspects of life?

One possibility is that such issues were not a major concern for the first humans or any other any living beings. Rather, the creatures who survived were those who coped effectively with the substantial problems they faced at the time, which primarily were tangible issues such as finding adequate shelter and food and coping with predators. Moreover, if humans had been aware of the billions of subconscious activities that continually occur in the brain (Drachman, 2005), it would have interfered with their attending to surviving their harsh living conditions. Perhaps, therefore, if any creatures had developed super-perception they might not have survived.

Things are changing. We now have an opportunity to address aspects beyond what moment-to-moment surviving requires thanks to economic advances, schooling, inventions, science, think tanks, and the contributions of business and government. Our grasp of previously unknown aspects has taken great leaps. We are learning how to lessen anxiety, depression, poverty, and hopefully war. The more effective our knowledge of psychology is, the more we can accomplish. This book aims to help take the mystery out of psychology.

Chapter 1. PSYCHOLOGICAL HOMEOSTASIS

Biological Homeostasis

Biological Homeostasis helps the body maintain a steady state. For example, people shiver when they are cold because muscle activity creates warmth, which helps raise the body's temperature. An overheated body perspires, which helps lessen body warmth because evaporating moisture removes heat. Other well-known examples of biologically wired-in attempts of the body to return from an extreme to a more adaptive range include the body's automatic re-adjusting excessive levels of sodium, blood sugar, and blood pressure to sustainable levels. Another instance of homeostasis is a 'set point' in our body that helps maintain our weight at a steady level. That circumstance is a reason why almost everyone who uses commercial diets returns to their pre-diet weight in one to three years (e.g., Muller, Bosy-Westphal, & Heymsfield, 2010).

Life might not exist if our many internal biological operations did not function within their respective adaptive ranges, or did not function sufficiently close to those ranges for homeostatic processes to aid returning to effective functioning. Those biological functions operate automatically, below awareness. Since survival depends on returning to an adaptive state, it is likely that every biological process has an automatic homeostatic arrangement. The totality of homeostatic effects throughout the body generates a strong drive for stability and with it, creates substantial resistance to change (discussed in Chapter 13).

Exceeding extremes is disabling

There is an outer limit to homeostasis. Exceeding that limit causes a changed circumstance, the *opposite* of returning to an adaptive range, for instance, excessively low body temperature can result in hypothermia (e.g., frostbite), which can be fatal unless treated quickly. Excessively high body temperature can cause hyperthermia (e.g., burns) if not addressed appropriately. Those changes that occur when an extreme temperature limit is exceeded are differences in kind. This phenomenon of a quantitative change producing a qualitative change brings to mind the change of water to ice when the temperature drops below 32 degrees Fahrenheit and the change of water to steam when the temperature exceeds 212 degrees. Such circumstances are what physicists term 'phase transitions'. Other examples of phase transitions are the transformation of some liquids into gases (e.g., carbon dioxide) or solids (e.g., coconut oil), and some solids into liquids (e.g., iron).

With biological organisms, the qualitative changes that occur when homeostatic limits are exceeded are often debilitating. If those situations are not rapidly reversed they can be fatal. Examples of such biological changed circumstances that are *'states of uncontrollability'* are auto-immune diseases (an over-reaction of the immune system), inadequate immunity, cardiac arrest when heart blood flow is constricted, suffocation when air intake is diminished, and pain and disablement upon exceeding sensory continua (e.g., muscle spasms, blindness). The common denominator in those states of uncontrollability is that a sizable *quantitative* change creates a *qualitative* change.

Since a major function of homeostasis is maintaining health, it seems paradoxical that there would be a harmful effect when a homeostatic limit is exceeded. Perhaps this circumstance occurs because it would be seriously disruptive for the body's functions to not operate within an appropriate range.

The bottom line:
> When a homeostatic limit is exceeded, a qualitative change occurs that is not just a difference in amount. That changed circumstance can be extreme enough to produce debilitation, disablement, death, or other state of uncontrollability.

Psychological Homeostasis
Psychological Systems Theory assumes the following:
a) There is *'Psychological Homeostasis'* as well as biological homeostasis.
b) There is a psychological *'comfort zone'* (an adaptive range of optimal or highly effective functioning).
c) There are extensive individual differences within people (for example, for example, the same person can have a wide adaptive zone for some aspects and a narrow adaptive zone for other aspects, also the duration of a state of uncontrollability varies with individuals and varies at different times).
d) Exceeding a psychological homeostatic limit results in a changed circumstance, such as panic, depression, rage, ecstasy, addiction, or other psychological *'state of uncontrollability'.*
e) Extensive individual differences exist (for example, some persons can enter or resist entering a state of uncontrollability more readily than others, some people exit a state of uncontrollability more easily than others, and the duration of a state of uncontrollability varies from person to person and situation to situation).
f) A comfort zone is unlikely to exist along a negative emotional continuum.

Emotional states of uncontrollability

Examples of states of uncontrollability that can occur upon exceeding an extreme limit at the upper end of an emotional continuum include panic, rage, addiction, and ecstasy. At the lower emotional end, examples are apathy, anhedonia, and withdrawal. After entering a state of uncontrollability, it may be difficult to exit it, especially for some people.

High emotionality impedes cognitive functioning (e.g., Gutnik, Hakimzada, Yoskowitz, & Patel, 2006; Lowenstein, 2010), even though the ability to think well would be valuable at such times and could be critical. Some people can think clearly when intensely pressured, such as seasoned combat veterans and football quarterbacks, but most of us, not so much. Even individuals who do well with some kinds of stress might not function well with other types of stress, such as combat veterans or quarterbacks when they are in a domestic fight.

A moderate level of emotionality (e.g., 4 to 7 on a 0-to-10 scale) is likely to be more adaptive and comfortable for daily functioning than very high or very low levels of emotion. In some situations, very high or low levels of emotion would be appropriate and useful. Figure 1 shows continua and comfort zones for positive and negative emotions. The location and width of a particular comfort zone differ for individuals and circumstances.

Zones outside the adaptive range

Outside the optimal range, there are acceptable, tolerable, unacceptable, and intolerable zones. An 'acceptable range' can feel somewhat comfortable even though it is not ideal (see Figure 1). Just beyond the acceptable range is a 'tolerable range' – which is not particularly desirable but tolerated. With negative emotions, there is an 'unacceptable range' and an 'intolerable range' (see Figure 2). For some people in some situations there might be an unacceptable range with regard to some positive emotions, and tolerable or acceptable ranges with regard to some negative emotions. The number of these ranges and the breadth and location of each along a continuum varies with the circumstances, individuals, and emotional level. Some zones might not exist for some issues and persons.

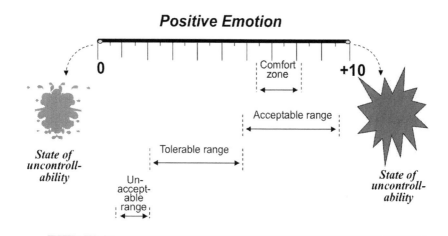

Fig 1. A representation of **positive** emotional homeostasis,
with comfort zone and ranges of acceptability & unacceptability.
(Emotional homeostasis is part of psychological homeostasis.)

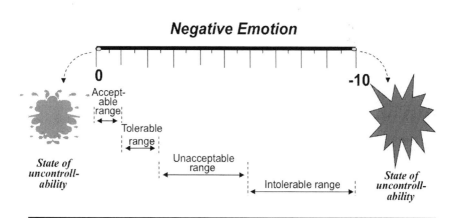

Fig 2. A representation of **negative** emotional homeostasis,
with ranges of acceptability, unacceptability, and intolerability.
(Emotional homeostasis is part of psychological homeostasis.)

Interpersonal comfort zone

There are interpersonal comfort zones regarding the level at which we accept other people. We consider some individuals particularly desirable, such as close family members and friends. Just beyond that comfort zone is an acceptable range – well-liked individuals who are not as close to us as those in our comfort zone. Still further is a tolerable range, which includes strangers (e.g., those near us when we shop, travel, or are at a theater). There is also a range of unacceptable people and a range of intolerable people. (Falvey, Forest, Pearpoint, & Rosenberg, 2000, discussed concentric social circles like those mentioned above.)

One of the implications of such interpersonal zones is that the further someone is from our comfort zone, the less acceptable he/she is to us. (The reason may be that such individuals possess different Psychological Roots than ours. Psychological Roots will be discussed in Chapter 3). Expecting other people to think or behave like we do can cause us to be disappointed in them when they do not do so, which can result in distancing ourselves from them, putting them in a distant zone. Having a narrow range of comfort, acceptability, or tolerance can make it difficult to accept others and to create compatible solutions when conflicts arise. (Conflict resolution is discussed in Chapters 20 - 23.) We have a desire to remain within our comfort zone and to return there when outside it, but our need for stimulation can lead us to seek new experiences and meet new people.

Tipping points

The end of a homeostatic continuum is a 'tipping point' into a changed circumstance that often is a 'state of uncontrollability'. A tipping point is somewhat analogous to the rim of a container at which water would spill over if more water enters than the container can hold.[2] Some highly reactive people might often be close to a limit so that only a little more intensity might put them over the edge (see Figure 3). A state of uncontrollability differs from the experience that exists before a tipping point occurs. For example, a person who had been functioning normally but crosses the tipping point into

---

[2] An extra boost or lack of energy may be required at the tipping point to put a person into a state of uncontrollability, akin to the "the straw that broke the camel's back", analogous to additional energy being needed to convert water to steam or a further lowering of temperature to convert cold water to ice. This conception of Psychological Homeostasis differs from that of Hull (1952), who focused on drive intensity, overt responses, and conditioned behavior.

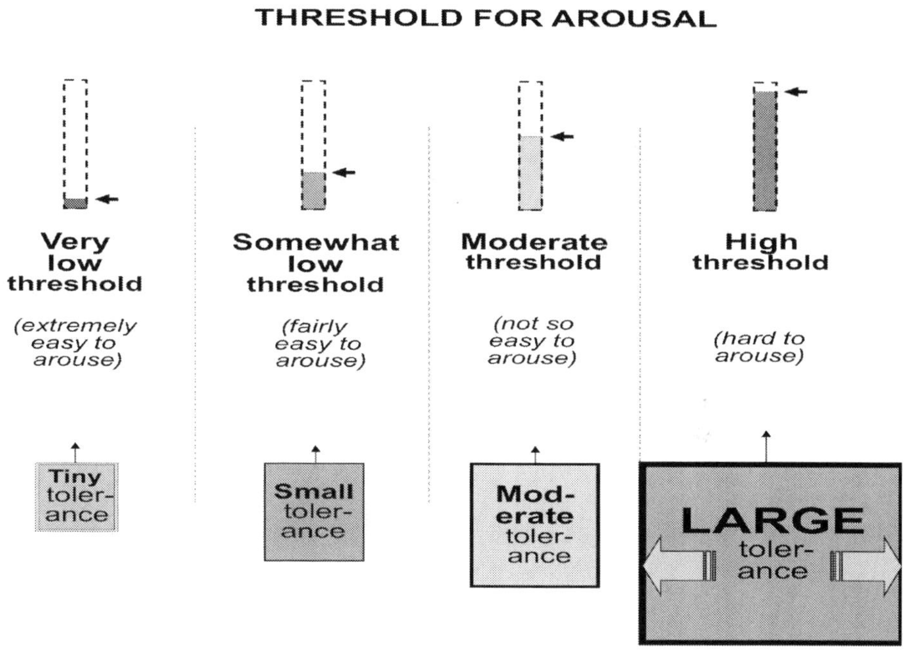

THRESHOLD FOR AROUSAL

Very low threshold	Somewhat low threshold	Moderate threshold	High threshold
(extremely easy to arouse)	*(fairly easy to arouse)*	*(not so easy to arouse)*	*(hard to arouse)*
Tiny tolerance	Small tolerance	Moderate tolerance	LARGE tolerance

Fig. 3. **Emotional sensitivity depends on the arousal threshold.**
• The *lower* the threshold for arousal the *more* emotionally reactive.
• The *higher* the threshold for arousal the *less* emotionally reactive.
• Raising the threshold for reactivity lessens emotional sensitivity.

a psychological disorder might become depressed, agitated, childlike, violent, or have a nervous breakdown or a psychotic episode. Such individuals might later say of themselves, "I was not myself", "I don't know what got into me", or "I wasn't thinking clearly". Some other expressions might be, "That is not me", "That was someone else", or "I didn't know I was capable of being like that". Extreme instances of such out-of-character behavior when in a state of uncontrollability include being highly agitated, suicidal, violent, or greatly withdrawn and silent.

A state of uncontrollability need not involve a psychological disorder, for example, the intensity of an attitude or an emotion can become strong enough to cross a tipping point into behavior. A biological need for food or water can become strong enough to drive a person to fulfill those needs. A desire to express an opinion can lead to speaking up.

A change into a state of uncontrollability can be noticed by others. For example, there is an observable difference between a down mood vs. being overwhelmed by depression, or being tense vs. being panicked or hysterical, or being irritated vs. being enraged. An implication of transformations like these is that quite different behaviors – such as severe depression vs. normal functioning – have the same underlying continua in common. The different intensities are due to the position along their respective continua. (How to treat states of uncontrollability is discussed in Section II.)

Success in society requires functioning within a socially acceptable range, however, the change that occurs at a tipping point can put a person beyond that range. In some circumstances, the change could be precipitous, like dropping off a cliff, and sometimes it can be explosive. It is difficult for a person in a state of uncontrollability to re-enter a normal homeostatic range, partly because doing so requires changing from one qualitatively different state to another. However, it is possible to have a 'short-term' or 'temporary state of uncontrollability', such as in the case of ecstasy and panic.

A psychological state of uncontrollability is unlikely to be a point of no return since people can return to normal functioning, even though doing so might be difficult and take some time. The author has found that correcting the conditions that contribute to a person's difficulties helps to bring about such reversals (e.g., by constructively modifying the distress-prone factors that led to that condition). (Strategies for accomplishing such changes are described in the chapters on psychotherapy in Section II.)

Tipping points at low and high extremes
There is a tipping point at each end of a continuum (e.g., 0 and 10 on a 0-to-10 scale). States of uncontrollability differ considerably, for example, ecstasy and rage (positive and negative states of uncontrollability, respectively). Instances of emotional states of uncontrollability past the high positive extreme of +10 include joy or excitement. Anxiety or depression are negative conditions that occur past the high negative extreme of -10. Apathy or anhedonia (in which there is an absence of emotion) occur past the low extreme of 0.[5] An implication of tipping points is that every person is capable of Jekyll and Hyde behavior.

---

[5] An answer of 'zero' on a bipolar questionnaire that assesses emotions may result from a lack of emotion or due to an about equal amount of positive and negative emotions neutralizing one another. Although these circumstances are different, they have some aspects in common, such as the person's neutrality about the issue and being indecisive.

Short-term states can last from a second to a few days (e.g., laughter, surprise, shouting, binging, a down mood).[6, 7] Medium-term states of emotional uncontrollability such as dysthymia (a strong down mood) can last from a week to several months. Long-term states of uncontrollability could last several months to a year or more (e.g., depression, addiction). Some personality traits involve long-term states of uncontrollability (e.g., hyperactivity, impulsivity, anger, immaturity).

A state of uncontrollability can occur when a particular stimulus triggers it, as in the case of phobias and obsessive-compulsive disorder. (Synonyms for a substantial psychological state of uncontrollability are psychological disorder and psychological condition, also see the glossary.)

Cumulative build-up

An increase in intensity can take place in increments (*'cumulative build-up'*, see Figure 4). A cumulative build-up is analogous to water entering a glass in stages. When the water level reaches the rim, even a slight amount of additional water will result in water spilling over the rim, comparable to "the straw that broke the camel's back". Thus, a down mood could intensify into dysthymia and still further increases could result in going past the tipping point into depression. A person's tension could intensify to anxiety and if it were to continue building, go past the tipping point into an anxiety attack (panic).

Emotional intensity – such as tension, gloom, feeling like a failure, and joy – can continue building until a tipping point is reached. At a tipping point, the person's emotions take over, impairing thinking and problem-solving ability. For example, a sense of failure can mount until it is overwhelming, leading to feeling hopeless and depressed. Irritation can increase to anger and further increases can lead to rage.

When there is a substantial build-up, even a tiny additional stimulus can trigger a big impact, as mentioned. Thus a major disorder such as depression

---

[6] Some states of uncontrollability can be short-term, some last for a moderate period of time, and some can be long term.

[7] Some emotional short-term states of uncontrollability include impulsivity, crying, hysteria, panic, rage, lethargy, and fugue states such as sleep-walking.

CUMULATIVE BUILD UP OF EMOTION

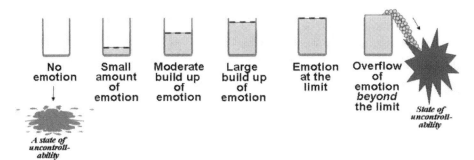

Fig. 4. **Unresolved emotions add up cumulatively.**
Exceeding a limit leads to a state of uncontrollability.
- Anxiety can build to panic.
- Failures can build to feeling overwhelmed, resulting in depression.
- Irritations can build and go out of control, resulting in rage.
- The last stimulus can be something minor, just enough to put a person beyond the limit.
- To observers, a state of uncontrollability can seem like an over-reaction or mental illness.

panic, or rage need not require a big incident to trigger it. Something trivial might be sufficient to do so when there has been a prior build-up.

As a result of feelings that have built to a strong level, people may feel a need to vent their pent-up emotion such as with words, tears, anger, or physical action. Other people might try to help the person solve his/her problem, however, a person in distress might want to solve the problem himself/herself. Or, someone who is venting may just want to air those feelings to relieve internal pressure, rather than seeking a solution to the underlying problem. Circumstances like those can be delicate and sometimes difficult to understand or respond to in a way that is acceptable to the person who is venting.

Taunting and bullying can generate a cumulative build-up of tension in the recipient, who might try to keep a lid on his/her pent-up feelings. That person's awareness of doing so and his/her attempt to avoid acting on that strong intensity (e.g., by counting to 10) suggests that it is possible for people to sense when they are near an internal tipping point. When a person "snaps", such as when an otherwise quiet person shoots people, a possibility is that the person had been sitting on accumulating internal tension, perhaps for a while. Quietness before shooting might have been due to keeping a clamp on those feelings, ignoring them, or not revealing them. As a build-up increases toward an extreme, the range of available alternatives can decrease. When a person is near or at a tipping point, only a tiny extra aspect might be enough to push the person over the edge into a state of uncontrollability, such as aggressive action against innocent people. (Synonyms: displacement, emotional spillover). Cumulative build-up may be involved when people have various types of "meltdown".

Common expressions

When people experience a cumulative build-up they might say: "I feel intensity building in me", "I'm sitting on a lot of tension", or "I'm full of suspense". Some other expressions are, "I'm trying to keeping a lid on my feelings", "My patience is at an end", "I've waited long enough", "I've reached the end of my rope". Still other things people might say are, "I'm at the edge", "I'm on the verge of ...", "One more thing and I'll explode", and "No rest for the weary". Following a cumulative build up, some of the things people might say are, "I couldn't keep it in any longer", or "It was just one thing after another until I couldn't take it anymore."

Manifestations of cumulative build-up

Cumulative build-ups can be involved in many behaviors, from obsessive-compulsive behavior and bipolar disorder to binges, panic, depression, rage, intermittent explosive disorder, and suicide. Cumulative build-up can lead some individuals to cope with their distress by using addictive substances such as alcohol, marihuana, and opiates.

Before a psychological disorder such as depression or rage is manifested overtly, a build-up of distressful disturbances might have been occurring below the surface in that individual. Outward indications of a build-up can sometimes appear before a person plunges into a state of uncontrollability ("coming events cast their shadows beforehand", "handwriting on the wall"). Such signs can be subtle, but a knowledgeable person might detect them. It may be possible to become trained in recognizing such signs.

Cumulative build-up can occur gradually over a period of time (a "slow burn") or rapidly (a "quick trigger"). Some individuals dismiss or deny signs of build-up in themselves or others (e.g., "He would never harm anyone", "She does that all the time, don't pay any attention to it"). A negative build-up does not meet the diagnostic criteria for a full-blown disorder so might not lead to identifying people who are at risk for disorders. Therefore, measures are needed to assess cumulative build-up and other pre-dispositions for disorders. (More on this topic in Section II.)

Mixture of components

A variety of different factors can contribute to a build-up. For example, a *'positive build-up'* can occur from having a good time with someone, a good day at work, and feeling especially healthy and in good spirits. Music can swell to a crescendo and comedians can string laughs together until the audience is engulfed in laughter. Pleasant feelings can build until a person experiences ecstasy, joyful hysteria, or an orgasm.

Stresses from work, disagreements, pain, worry, or feeling rejected can contribute to a *'negative build-up'* and from there carry a person past a tipping point into depression, anxiety, or rage. Some people who experience a build-up of irritability can unexpectedly explode into angry or psychotic-like episodes (e.g., persons with a borderline personality disorder). Such episodes could be set off by very little extra annoyance. That trigger might be noticeable to others, but when it is not, a person's sudden volatility might not make sense. People who sense irritability building up in someone might feel as if they need to 'walk on egg shells' when near that person.

People can be unaware of the contributors to the emotion building up in them or only vaguely aware of them. As a result, there might be many people who have a substantial amount of build-up, either positive or negative, without realizing it or knowing the consequences. Negatives are much stronger than positives (e.g., Cullen, Cullen, Hayhow, & Plouffe, 1975, also see Chapter 10), easily aroused and long-lasting. A major factor is the strength of genetic needs for safety and stability. As a result, cumulative build-up might be more likely with negatives. Negative reactions are especially important in psychological disorders.

Some aspects related to cumulative build-up

It might take very little for some people to reach a limit, such as those who have a low threshold for emotional arousal. (A threshold is a point at which a change takes place and can function as a criterion for action.) A person with a very low threshold for emotional arousal might frequently be emotional and also often experience a build-up of emotion. Such individuals might readily approach a tipping point and therefore be prone to states of uncontrollability.

Emotional build-up can occur in everyone, including people who have a high threshold for arousal. In such persons, build-up might not occur readily so they might only infrequently or perhaps rarely enter a state of uncontrollability. Nevertheless, even people with a high threshold for arousal have the potential to experience an emotional build-up and states of uncontrollability.

People can ignore or overlook cumulative build-up in themselves and others. Some people might intentionally put a clamp on building up tension in themselves, deny it, or disguise it, even when their tension is close to a tipping point. As a result, there might be quite a few people whose build-up does not show but who are nevertheless sitting on substantial tension, stress, anxiety, dysthymia, or irritation. Some of those individuals could be on the verge of tipping into a psychological condition even though it might not be apparent to others. In some cases, cumulative build-up could lead to vacillating moods, such as those who have bipolar disorder or borderline personality.

Marital breakups can occur after a long build-up of problems. In the author's experience, marriages suffer breakups when neither individual knows how to create compatible solutions rather than because they have not tried sufficiently hard enough to keep their relationship intact. (A method for creating effective solutions to conflicts is described in Chapters 20 - 23.)

Low threshold for emotional arousal can contribute to a cumulative build-up, as mentioned, and could generate a strong surge of emotion, impatience, impulsivity, or sudden mood swing. A low threshold for emotional arousal can also lead a person to be easily irritated, break the rules, not eliminate an addiction, or do unexpected or illogical things (e.g., sudden violence, fighting with police, or killing in a fit of passion). In such cases, the underlying causes can be hidden among many factors, which can make it difficult to identify the principal cause of the outcome. As a result, symptoms might be treated rather than the cause.

Tipping points along a continuum

On a bipolar scale (e.g., Figures 1 and 2 joined end-to-end), the midpoint separates the positive range from the negative range at the zero point. This circumstance creates three tipping points: one at each end of the scale and one at the midpoint, for instance, -10, 0, and +10 on the -10 to +10 scale. Each tipping point is a threshold (i.e., the locus at which a change takes place).

Cognitive states of uncontrollability

Cognitive states of uncontrollability can also occur. Examples of such states past the lower or upper cognitive extremes are rigidly absolute goals, beliefs, standards, and decisions. For example, a person might be implacably committed to an ideology, or completely believe that their problems are impossible to solve, or hold a prejudice to an unmovable extent. An example at the low cognitive extreme would be a complete lack of knowledge or interest, such as not being aware of certain information, historical events, or the cause of an illness. Some people are comfortable with a total lack of information ("No news is good news", "What you don't know can't hurt you"). The down-side of that circumstance is that they may be unaware of something important, not acquire valuable knowledge, be irrevocably locked into their viewpoint, be unable to make timely improvements, or deny that a significant problem exists ("Bury one's head in the sand").

Having an absolute viewpoint is a specific point on a continuum rather than a range of possibilities – for example, no acceptance or awareness of something (0 on a 10-point scale) or 100% acceptance (10 on a 10-point scale; see Figure 5). People who are committed to a particular viewpoint might find it difficult to comprehend anything that is inconsistent with their opinion, might not seek a solution, or might impede others who are trying to find a solution.[8] Signs of a person who is experiencing a cognitive state of uncontrollability are rigidity and use of absolutes (e.g., always, never, totally). Some other signs are considering something to be unquestionable and inviolate, or assuming that everyone knows a certain issue or should know it. Additional signs are intractably promoting or defending a particular idea, or believing something that is patently untrue. Indecision and dissociation can also be instances of cognitive states of uncontrollability. (Absolute thinking is discussed in Chapter 19.)

Absolute resistance is not uncommon when new ideas are presented, including information that subsequently is found to be correct or important, such as Galileo's astronomy discoveries, Columbus's idea about the world not being flat, Einstein's theory of relativity, and revolutionary technologies (e.g., automobiles and telephones).[9]

Non-absolute cognitions

Simultaneously holding opposing viewpoints, a mixture of cognitions, or degrees of liking or disliking can occur (e.g., being financially conservative and also socially liberal). On questionnaires, a moderate viewpoint is manifested as a mid-scale response (e.g., 3-to-7 on a 0-to-10 scale). Some

---

[8] Lack of understanding can result when nothing in a person's psyche allows a connection to be made. Connections are addressed in a subsequent chapter on linking.

[9] Total acceptance or absence of an idea is a single, extreme position. That can be a 'comfort spot' for some people who think in absolutes, but unlikely for people with a wide comfort zone.

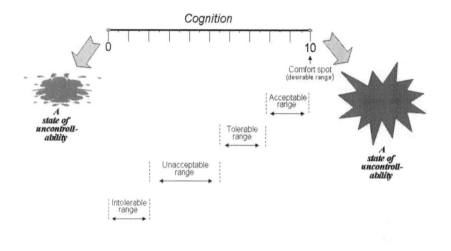

Fig. 5. A representation of **cognitive** homeostasis, with ranges of acceptability and unacceptability. (Cognitive homeostasis is an aspect of psychological homeostasis.)

questionnaires do not offer an opportunity for a person to respond moderately because they offer only two answer choices (e.g., True-False or Yes-No). Answering in degrees is not possible when there are just two choices and therefore could lead to false interpretations, for example, a moderate person who leans only slightly in one direction might answer yes to every question and therefore receive an inappropriately high score (e.g., 10 on a 10-item questionnaire). A moderate person who leans slightly negatively and answers every question 0 would receive a misleadingly low score (e.g., 0).

Extrication from a state of uncontrollability

Negative psychological states of uncontrollability have strong consequences (e.g., arguments, lost relationships, physical fights), yet it can be difficult to extricate oneself from them. People tend to be locked into in states of uncontrollability, whether those states are cognitive (e.g., a rigid belief, goal, or concern) or emotional (e.g., panic, depression, rage, or addiction). The factors that lead to such states often are not apparent (see Chapter 3 regarding the hidden nature of Psychological Roots). Even when the causative factors are known, some people are not resilient. In addition, people in a state of uncontrollability think in absolutes, which interferes with their considering other possibilities. Even if they are receptive, they may not be able to work effectively with alternatives. (Resistance to change is discussed in Chapter 13 and psychotherapy is discussed in Chapters 27 - 30. Methods that can help people become extricated from psychological states of uncontrollability are described in Section II.)

Open- and close-mindedness

Some people have wide zones of comfort, acceptability, and tolerability, with correspondingly narrow zones of unacceptability and intolerability. Such 'open-minded' individuals may be receptive to experiences, ideas, and people other than their own. They might also be inclined to be open to learning, have moderate opinions, and admit their errors. Some individuals have the opposite pattern – generally narrow zones of comfort, acceptance, and tolerance, together with correspondingly large zones of unacceptance and intolerance. Such 'close-minded' individuals might resist ideas other than their own, believe that they know everything they need to know, resist changing, and not tolerate others' viewpoints. Having a narrow adaptive zone could create stress since everyone encounters unexpected circumstances in life. Such individuals can also stress other people who interact with them.

Differences between Psychological and Biological Homeostasis

Biological Homeostasis occurs automatically, that is, the body's attempt to return to an adaptive range does not require a conscious intervention. There are some instances in which it is possible to consciously aid that process, such as intentional attempts to address hunger, thirst, pain, or elimination of wastes. Not needing to consciously choose when, where, and how to act is not just practical but important for survival. In Psychological Homeostasis, however, return to the adaptive range may not be automatic. Instead, there could be an internal warning such as malaise, tension, or a down mood. That warning offers an individual an opportunity to consciously decide whether or not to return to a more comfortable circumstance.

In such instances, effective action requires having appropriate skill. Many people in psychological states of uncontrollability might not have acquired such skills, or might not make good decisions about using the skills they have, or might be hampered for other reasons (e.g., because of beliefs, pessimism, fatigue, or drugs). When an extreme biological limit is exceeded, severe debilitation or death is a substantial possibility (e.g., hypothermia, hyperthermia). However, when a psychological limit is exceeded, there might not be physical harm or death, but harm could occur indirectly because of other aspects, such as impeded judgment, aggressiveness, inadequate problem-solving, insufficient prevention, or deliberate intention (e.g., suicide).

Some aspects related to Psychological Homeostasis

1. Phobias and binges (e.g., eating, drinking alcohol) are states of uncontrollability.
2. Addictions are states of uncontrollability that may have both Biological and Psychological Roots.
3. People can oscillate between low and high levels of activity, and between positive and negative moods. Children and people with volatile personalities or who are very emotional (e.g., due to a low threshold for emotional arousal) sometimes have such oscillations. Young children who do not get what they want sometimes cry as if they were being tortured. When adults have frequent up and down moods (cyclothymia), they may possess some distress-prone precursors that could lead to their experiencing a state of uncontrollability (e.g., bipolar disorder). (Precursors are discussed in the next chapter.)
4. Some people may not want to argue or be confrontational out of concern that they might say or do something harmful to another person and therefore help keep them from entering a state of uncontrollability.
5. It can be difficult to live with someone who is prone to experiencing states of uncontrollability.
6. Humans have a genetically wired-in need for stimulation, which leads to being bored when not stimulated or possibly slipping into lethargy (a state of uncontrollability). Boredom is a potent negative emotion that can occur when people are not engaged in things that interest them, for example, when they are not sufficiently challenged, do routine or repetitive things, do not feel a need to be alert, or are in the company of individuals they do not find interesting. For this reason, upon retirement, it would be wise to retire *to* something interesting and challenging, rather than retire *from* something that is disliked or boring.
7. Excessive stimulation (e.g., panic), as well as an excessive lack of stimulation (e.g., apathy), can be disturbing. Both are states of uncontrollability.
8. Human beings are likely to be effective when they operate in the mid-range of stimulation (e.g., Hebb, 1955; Fiske & Maddi, 1961). However, there are times when having very high or very low stimulation is desirable or appropriate.
9. Humans notice when they are not being stimulated ("sounds of silence"). Lack of stimulation can be aversive (see sensory deprivation experiments, such as Lilly, 1956). Reducing sensory input is sometimes desired to relieve excessive stimulation or other unpleasantness (e.g., stress, setbacks, hectic activities). Communicators, teachers, and parents should take into consideration their recipients' need for stimulation.

A practical application of this information

For many people, moderate positive emotionality (e.g., 4 to 7 on a 0-10 positive scale) is adaptive and facilitates daily functioning. It is especially helpful to have few or no negatives (such as stress, anxiety, down moods, annoyance, anger) and to try to avoid going off the deep end at either extreme. Extremes limit the number of possibilities and can contribute to tension and distress. It is possible for a person who worries a lot (which might correspond to -8, -9, or -10 on a 10-point scale) to become less distressed by developing an ability to consciously switch to just being concerned (e.g., -5, -6, or -7). A change of that sort would lower emotionality and might thereby somewhat lighten the mood and lead to better thinking and problem-solving. This example shows how it can sometimes be possible to consciously decide where along the scale we choose our emotional reactions and beliefs to be, rather than assuming that we have no control over the intensity of our emotional reactions or that being extreme is the only option. (Section II has practical applications related to the information in this chapter.)

Chapter 2. ALERTING THRESHOLDS AND PRECURSORS

Alerting thresholds

The previous chapter mentioned that crossing a homeostatic threshold might be noticed by people who are attuned to what is going on in them, perhaps an experience of tension, uneasiness, or an aura accompanying that transition. Those points are *'alerting thresholds'* (see Figs. 1, 2, and 5). When a threshold is crossed, it might not be noticed by other individuals since the indication is internal, unless the person in whom the signal occurs gives an overt indication of it, such as a strong reaction. The end of a continuum is a particularly important threshold because it is a tipping point into a state of uncontrollability. Crossing that threshold can be noticeable to both the person and others. Biologically, that change can be accompanied by pain, changed appearance, imbalance, or loss of appetite. Psychologically, that change can manifest itself as depression, panic, or rage.

Being aware of such signs offers an opportunity for a person to return from an unpleasant situation to a more congenial state, for instance by deciding to wrap oneself in a blanket when cold or to stop arguing when in a disagreement. When people are near a tipping point into a negative state, they might be able to keep themselves from going further in that direction to avoid entering a state of uncontrollability. Alternatively, when a state of uncontrollability would be desirable, such as laughter or joy, a person might want to facilitate experiencing that circumstance.

Intensity gradient

Intensity is postulated to accelerate as the upper emotional extreme of a continuum is approached (e.g., in the 8 to 10 range of a 0-10 scale; see the *'Intensity Curve'* in Figure 6). The considerable intensity at the upper end helps explain why the changed circumstance that occurs at the tipping point is likely to be a state of uncontrollability. For example, if emotional intensity is great, it might be difficult to resist engaging in the resulting behavior. That irresistibility helps explain why it is difficult to avoid being depressed, panicked, enraged, ecstatic, or addicted when an overwhelming amount of intensity pushes a person in that direction.

The increase in intensity as the extreme upper limit is neared is an *'accelerating gradient'*, a pattern that resembles the goal-approach gradient (Hull, 1952; Miller, 1944). Increases in positive emotional intensity might be heightened anticipation or elation, while with negative emotional intensity, agitation, frustration, irritation, or anxiety might be present (deBerker, Rutledge, Mathys, Marshall, Cross, Dolan, & Bestmann, 2016). That change in intensity is a signal that an extreme is being

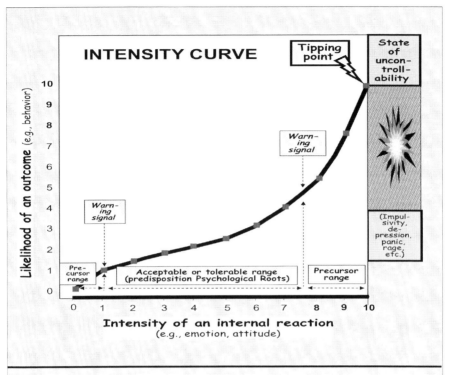

Fig. 6. Likelihood of behavior accelerates at the upper end of intensity continua and decelerates at the lower end.

(Note: Depiction of a state of uncontrollability at the lower end of the intensity continuum in this graph has been omitted to simplify the presentation.)

approached and might be noticeable to the individual and sometimes to others, especially if the reaction is strong.

Intensity is also postulated to decelerate as a lower emotional extreme is approached (e.g., 0 to 1 on a 0-10 scale; see Figure 6). The changed circumstance that results in a state of uncontrollability at the lower end is understandable because of the overwhelming absence of energy.

Lessened intensity related to that *'decelerating gradient'* might be noticed by observers as the lower end tipping point is approached (e.g., boredom, anhedonia, or lethargy). A 0-10 scale offers an opportunity to more substantially depict the graphing of accelerating and decelerating gradients compared to using shorter scales such as 1-5.

Some personality traits, such as those that are particularly distress-prone or pleasure-generating, can make it easier for a person to enter a range of a continuum that is a precursor to a state of uncontrollability or to enter a state of uncontrollability itself. Some individuals enter those states rapidly or frequently, while other individuals do so slowly, rarely, or never.

Speed at which the range of intensity is traversed

A person might remain at a particular range of intensity for a while, such as 4 through 6, or move from one level to another, such as from 4 to 7, or from 7 to 10. Moving from one level to another can take place gradually or rapidly. For example, a threat can cause a person's emotional intensity to jump from 3 to 10. People often change intensity levels unintentionally but sometimes do so purposely.

In some cases, a person might deliberately try to remain calm in the face of adversity and consciously clamp his/her emotionality. A person with a high threshold of emotional arousal might find it easier to bottle emotions than someone whose threshold is low. Someone with a very low threshold of arousal might move rapidly from low to high emotionality, as if there were only 2 or 3 positions along the intensity continuum rather than many (e.g., 10). Having a low threshold of emotional arousal is particularly important for people who suffer from anxiety because it might take very little for them to reach a high level of tension, agitation, or a state of uncontrollability (panic). The author has found that a low threshold for negative emotional arousal can also be a factor in depression because it can lead to feeling overwhelmed by failure more than in persons whose negative emotions are not easily aroused.

Is there a point at which what has been normal becomes abnormal?

The conception of Psychological Homeostasis described in these pages leads to the surmise that it is possible to identify the point at which normal psychological functioning becomes abnormal: the tipping point at the endpoint of a homeostatic continuum. The specific locations and other aspects that lead to crossing a tipping point vary with each person and issue. People with moderate temperaments might rarely or possibly never enter states of uncontrollability, and should those states occur, perhaps not experience a lengthy stay in them. By contrast, it might take comparatively little for people with a low threshold for arousal to enter states of uncontrollability and once there, remain in those states for a while. As long as a tipping point is not broached, emotions that are high or low are nevertheless in the normal range, even emotional reactions that are in a precursor range or are bothersome (e.g., tension).

Are some psychological disorders natural phenomena?

If Psychological Homeostasis is genetically programmed into everyone, every normal individual has the potential to go past a tipping point into a psychological state of uncontrollability (e.g., depression, panic, rage, addiction). This psychological susceptibility is akin to every normal person going beyond a biological homeostatic extreme and experiencing an abnormal physical condition as a result. This inference – that we are programmed by nature to experience extreme psychological states – would explain why depression occurs in substantial portions around the world. Up to 41% of the population experiences depression (Moffit, Caspi, Taylor, Kokaua, Milne, Polanczyk, & Poulton, 2010; Takayanagi, Spira, Roth, Gallo, Eaton, & Mojtabai, 2014). Taking into account methodological considerations that occur in such research – including many depressed persons not reporting being depressed or seeking professional help – depression might be present even more frequently than has been recorded. This inference is supported by data indicating that most people have a psychological disorder at some time during their lifetime (Schaefer, Caspi, Belsky, Harrington, Houts, Horwood, Hussong, Ramrakha, Poultin, & Moffitt, 2017).

Precursors to psychological disorders

An implication of the Intensity Curve in Figure 6 is that there is a 'precursor' to a state of uncontrollability as an upper extreme is approached, and also as a lower extreme is approached. Every normal person is genetically wired to experience precursors, such as anxiety before panic, dysthymia before depression, and anger before rage. Precursor states are a different experience than the states that precede them along the continuum or that follow them. For example, feeling tense is different than feeling anxious, which is still different than being panicked. Being in a down mood is different than being dysthymic, which is different than being severely depressed. Thus, a person with major depression will feel and look considerably different than someone in a down mood, but both conditions lie along the same *underlying* continuum.

When there is an emotional precursor state, such as anxiety, the emotional level is high, which diminishes thinking ability, but the person has some control over his/her behavior. Thinking becomes less and less successful as a tipping point is approached. When a person is in a state of uncontrollability (i.e., past a tipping point) his/her emotions take over, which severely impedes thinking (a "deer in the headlights" circumstance). A person who is panicked is controlled by that state, unable to think clearly, and feel a strong pressure to exit from that circumstance (which can be related to a "fight or flight" reaction). This severe effect might not be apparent in a summary statistical statement about emotionality and effective thinking having an inverse relationship (as has been found by Gutnik, et al., 2006, and Lowenstein, 2010).

In this perspective, tension, anxiety, and panic are part of the same continuum. A separate continuum exists for other emotional reactions, such as a down mood, dysthymia, and depression. Along a still other continuum are irritability, anger, and rage. The different experiences along a continuum – for example, tension, anxiety, and panic – feel and look different from each other but are nevertheless related. Someone who is in a down mood is substantially different than someone who is severely depressed, yet the same underlying continuum applies to both individuals. What matters is where along a sub-surface continuum an individual is.

Everyone is somewhere on various homeostatic continua, according to Psychological Systems Theory. Therefore everyone has a potential to experience any one of the conditions along those continua, including states of uncontrollability. Some people might never experience negative states of uncontrollability such as panic, depression, or hysteria because they have counteracting factors such as emotionally positive Psychological Roots that help them avoid being upset. Some people have techniques or external resources that help them solve their problems and some individuals might feel very down, anxious, or irritated only infrequently.

The theory assumes that every normal person is wired with the potential to experience common psychological disorders such as anxiety, depression, and rage if they go beyond their respective tipping points. In that sense, such disorders are "normal" occurrences when the conditions are ripe for those conditions to occur, analogically comparable to everyone's skin getting burned by fire or frost-bitten by severe cold.

People who are in a precursor range are near the end of a continuum and therefore close to a tipping point. Being in a precursor state, therefore, increases the possibility of entering a state of uncontrollability. Precursor states include dysthymia, anxiety, and irritability. This view of dysthymia, anxiety, and irritability differs from viewing those circumstances as being unrelated to major disorders such as depression, panic, and rage, respectively.

It was mentioned earlier that people who are highly reactive might more frequently enter a precursor range and therefore reach an extreme and a tipping point compared to persons who are not highly reactive. Extremes and states of uncontrollability are absolutes and it may be that people who think in absolutes might therefore be susceptible to entering states of uncontrollability. This possibility can be tested empirically.

Experiencing a negative precursor can be troublesome in and of itself even if a person does not enter a state of uncontrollability. For instance, people who are anxious, dysthymic, or angry can be considerably distressed by that circumstance, and some individuals can find that those conditions – such as high anxiety, strong dysthymia, and great anger – make it difficult for them to function effectively. When people experience those conditions they might upset others who, in turn, might not react well to them. As an example, someone with easily triggered irritability, as in the case of many persons with borderline personality disorder, can cause others to feel that they have to "walk on egg shells" when near those individuals.

Precursors can lead to impulsive or other counterproductive behaviors such as crossing interpersonal boundaries, losing a significant other's affection, becoming addicted, being stripped of a driving license, or getting fired. Those behaviors have long-term consequences. Nevertheless, some people minimize the problems that result from being in a distressing precursor range. For example, there are people who consider one or more of those conditions to be worthwhile (e.g., "Stress helps people accomplish things", "I like pressure", "I like people who say exactly what's on their mind"). Some people may blame others for their precursor circumstances ("It isn't my fault", "I don't know why bad things happen to me", "Others cause my problems so they should change, not me").

People in a precursor range and others who interact with those persons might be unaware that those individuals are in that range. Also, the importance of precursor circumstances might not be recognized, especially if those individuals do not manifest clear-cut symptoms. Some people consider a person's precursor behavior to be normal, for example, feeling tense, being in a down mood, or holding a grudge.

It helps to know about precursors when evaluating a potential mate or employee, especially when some anti-social aspects occur in connection with that condition since such aspects can affect other people's quality of life.

The consequences of being in a negative precursor range depend on such factors as the afflicted person's level of sensitivity, the intensity and frequency of the experience, the person's coping mechanisms, and the reactions of other people. Additional factors include the amount of cumulative build-up and the consequences of acting in accord with the precursor condition.

It seems likely that everyone has had positive and negative precursor experiences including positive instances such as pleasure, happiness, and delight, and negative instances such as irritability, anxiety, and down moods. It is also likely that many people have experienced short-term states of uncontrollability including such positive instances as laughter, joy, and euphoria, and negative instances like crying, blushing, rage, panic, and depression. Some people self-medicate their precursor conditions (and states of uncontrollability) by using alcohol, marihuana, opiates, cigarettes, or food. Hence, precursor states may be important in addiction.

It might be possible to keep oneself from reaching a tipping point by lessening the intensity of factors that lead to entering a precursor range. Contributing factors involve the same aspects that lead to full-blown disorders according to Psychological Systems Theory (such as Psychological Roots, discussed in upcoming chapters). Therefore, it is worthwhile for assessment specialists to evaluate the importance of precursors such as dysthymia, anxiety, agitation, and easily triggered irritability in addition to assessing full-blown psychological disorders.

Traits associated with depression

Poor ability to cope with failure is associated with depression (e.g., Beck & Ward, 1961; Warren & McEachren, 1977; Coyne & Gotlib, 1983; Billings, Cronkite, & Moos, 1983). The author's clinical practice and pilot studies support this finding. Some other distress-prone psychological factors the author has found to be important in depression include poor problem-solving strategies, difficult-to-meet expectations, low self-esteem, low confidence, counterproductive social beliefs and strategies, inappropriate personal rules, a low threshold for negative arousal, and believing that becoming extricated from despondency is unlikely. (Some examples and practical applications of this understanding for psychotherapy are discussed in Chapters 27 - 30.)

Before individuals become clinically depressed, they are part of the normal population. Those individuals possess some of the same distress-prone traits when they are in the normal range that they have when they are in a state of uncontrollability, albeit at a lower level. When depressed they are more extreme along those continua. Before their circumstance spills over into a major depression, they pass through a precursor state. Thus, people with such predisposing psychological factors are part of the normal population before they experience a clinical disorder. This surmise is consistent with Psychological Systems Theory's viewpoint that abnormality falls along a spectrum. That spectrum includes non-clinical and sub-clinical aspects.

Distress-prone personality traits

Mentioned above was that some of the same personality traits that contribute to a psychological disorder are present to a lesser degree in people in the normal range (e.g., distress-prone traits such as expecting the worst, having hard-to-meet expectations, and low self-esteem), from the standpoint of a Psychological Systems Theory. Whether or not full-blown depression occurs is related to the number and intensity of such traits. The occurrence of depression is also affected by how many counterbalances to distress-prone characteristics a person has such as positive traits like optimism, effective problem-solving strategies, and successful social strategies.

An implication of this perspective is that some depressed individuals who are severely disabled are in a state of uncontrollability because they are further along the same continua of distress-prone personality traits as some people in the normal population. This possibility might seem unlikely when viewing people from these two cohorts because they look considerably different. However, those surface observations do not take into account the psychological factors that operate below the surface. In this view, people who are hospitalized for severe depression are extreme along the same continua that people have who lead a normal life (e.g., some college students, office employees, and blue collar workers). The latter individuals may have some of the same distress-prone factors (e.g., pessimism or low self-esteem), but might be in the mid-range or at a low level along those dimensions.

The above hypothesis can be empirically tested by comparing underlying personality traits of individuals with a psychological disorder with those of people in the general population. If both sets of populations have some of the same distress-prone psychological traits, with those of depressed people at more extreme locations along those continua, it would: a) help explain why depression re-occurs in many previously depressed individuals (Monroe & Harkness, 2011), and b) why depression occurs so frequently.

If everyone can be depressed, should a great many people be depressed?

If everyone is capable of psychological disorders like depression, the potential exists for a great many people to have such disorders. However, some individuals do so only infrequently or perhaps might not get depressed, panicked, or enraged. One reason may be because they possess some positive personality factors that counteract the occurrence of negative states (e.g., Schaefer, et al., 2017). For example, some people are optimistic, have a high threshold for emotional arousal, and possess substantial problem-solving skills that enable them to take setbacks in stride. Also, some persons have less intense distress-prone traits than those with psychological disorders such as because they have a high threshold for negative emotional arousal, are not emotionally intense, and tend not to think in absolutes. There also are some people who have less stressful stimulus conditions than others and some individuals who have helpful resources to draw upon, such as friends, family, and professionals.

Stimulus conditions associated with depression

Some distressing stimulus conditions can make a person feel vulnerable, such as conditions that feel overwhelming or produce disturbing flashbacks. Such negative internal reactions can act as stimulus conditions that induce still further negative reactions, including states of uncontrollability.

Is a chemical imbalance the originating cause of psychological disorders?

A chemical imbalance, such as a decrease in the neurotransmitter serotonin, has been found to be associated with depression (e.g., Stockmeier, Shapiro, Dilley, Kolli, Friedman, & Rajkowska, 1998; France, Lysaker & Robinson, 2007). That correlation has contributed to a belief that the originating cause of depression is a chemical imbalance. (This belief has been challenged, e.g., by Lacasse & Leo, 2005, since correlations are associations and might not be causes.)

What causes the chemical imbalance is an important question. Might the cause be psychological? It is well-established that psychological circumstances produce biochemical changes (e.g., Brehm, Back, & Bogdonoff, 1964).[10] For example, situational stress can cause heart attacks and death. Danger – such as fire shouted in a crowded room – triggers powerful increases in adrenalin and blood pressure (the 'fight or flight' syndrome). When a danger ends, adrenalin and blood pressure levels decline. Perceived danger is a psychological phenomenon.

Displeasure, including unhappiness associated with loneliness, is in the same location in the brain as physical pain (Eisenberger, 2012). Severe pain can be effectively controlled by laughter (e.g., Cousins, 1981; Manninen, S., Tuominen, L., Dunbar, R., Karjalainen, T., Hirvonen, J., Arponen, E., Hari, R., Jasskelainen, I. P., Sams, M., & Nummenmaa, L., 2017). In addition, some intense medical disorders are caused psychologically, such as blindness and paralysis due to inability to cope with distress (conversion disorders, e.g., Akagi & House, 2001). Moreover, psychological stress is a major contributor to back pain, often more than physical aspects (e.g., Bigos, Bowyer, Braen, Brown, Deyo, Haldeman, Hart, Johnson, Keller, Kido, Liang, Nelson, Nordin, Owen, Pope, Schwartz, Stewart, Susman, Triano, Tripp, Turk, Watts, & Weinstein, 1994).

Addiction to video games and gambling produce alterations in biochemistry similar to what occurs in addictions that involve ingestion of substances (e.g., Kühn, S., Romanowski, A., Schilling, C., Lorenz, R., Mörsen,

---

[10] Some people do not believe that psychological aspects can have biological effects.

C., Seiferth, N., Banaschewski, T., Barbot, A., Barker, G. J., Büchel, C., Conrod, P. J., Dalley, J. W., Flor, H., Garavan, H. Ittermann, B., Mann, Know, Martinot, J-L., Paus, T., Rietschel, M., Smolka, M. N., Ströhle, A., Walaszek, B., Schumann, G., Heinz. A., & Gallinat, J. (2011).

Since psychology has powerful biological effects, a question arises about whether psychological distress produces brain biochemical changes similar to those found in depression. If so, perhaps such changes also occur in other psychological disorders as well, such as anxiety, addiction, bipolar disorder, and borderline personality. This inference raises the possibility that the cause of some major psychological disorders might be psychological. Brain biochemical and physical changes that result from psychological causes would be detectable (e.g., via blood tests, PET scans, and fMRIs).

If biochemical changes result from psychological causes, those changes are an intermediate step in a sequence of aspects that lead to disordered behavior. (Chapter 4 discusses this type of Hidden Sequence more fully.)

A practical application of this information

What might initially prompt many people to come for counseling is that they are in a state of uncontrollability or their intensity level may be in the precursor range (e.g., 8-10 on a 10-point scale). The author has found that it is possible to help people return from their psychological difficulties by helping them modify their distress-prone psychological traits and acquire skills that help them cope with distressing stimulus conditions (described in the discussion of psychotherapy in Chapters 27 - 30).

People with a psychological disorder (such as anxiety, depression, and addiction) have difficulty rebounding from their condition, and many feel socially stigmatized. Those stigmas might lessen if the idea was accepted that all of us are wired with the potential to experience states of uncontrollability.

Chapter 3. PSYCHOLOGICAL ROOTS

Imagine that your job is to instruct the waiters and waitresses at a restaurant how to interact effectively with patrons. Would you include in what you tell them, "Show everyone respect"? If you did, why would you? Might it be that you believe everyone wants to be respected? If that was the case, it would mean that everyone wants respect regardless of the society they came from or their biology, gender, parents, experiences, skin color, language, occupation, age, income, residence, or nation. When something occurs in everyone regardless of their circumstances, it may mean that it is genetically wired-into all humans. Examples include everyone's need for food, air, water, safety, and being connected with other humans.

Needs such as those just mentioned are intangible and invisible yet we know that they are universal because their power is seen in the drives they generate in everyone. As a result, we can infer the needs everyone requires even though we are not able to see, touch, smell, taste, or hear those needs. Scientific experiments can test those observations. We know, for example, that one set of universal needs is biological (e.g., needs for air and food) and another type of genetically wired-in needs is psychological (e.g., needs for safety and being connected with other humans).

Mentioned previously is that our senses are designed to identify tangible aspects (e.g., "Seeing is believing"), which makes it difficult to ascertain our biological and psychological needs directly. Therefore, we must infer the existence of those invisible factors. Among the many factors that exist despite their invisibility are desires, concerns, interests, and beliefs. We realize that those aspects strongly motivate us even though we cannot see, hear, or touch them. Some other inner motivations that strongly affect us even though their structures are hidden are expectations, abilities, and fears. In Psychological Systems Theory, those important psychological aspects and a great many others that operate invisibly below the surface are termed Psychological Roots. There also are Biological Roots such as those noted above (e.g., needs for air, food, water, and shelter).

Internal reactions and behaviors

When you feel good about something, such as upon achieving a goal or receiving an award, that emotion is an *"internal reaction"*. Some other types of psychological internal reactions are thoughts, ideas, evaluations, judgments, decisions, fantasies, and drives. The causes of psychological internal reactions are Psychological Roots, according to Psychological Systems Theory. Internal reactions involve the autonomic (involuntary) nervous system.

If you treat someone with respect, that behavior is observable. Observable behaviors involve the skeletal (voluntary) nervous system. According to Psychological Systems Theory, observable behaviors result from internal reactions. Thus, the sequence is that Psychological Roots lead to internal reactions, then internal reactions lead to overt behaviors. Such "Hidden Sequences" take place below awareness. Knowing Hidden Sequences is important if you want to understand yourself and other people. (Hidden Sequences are discussed in Chapter 4.)

Understanding human behavior

Psychological Systems Theory considers Psychological Roots to be *'inner motivations'* because they originate what we do, somewhat like the instructions of a director. Another term for Psychological Roots would be "*psychological guiding factors*" because of their influence on our thinking and emotional reactions.

There are thousands of Psychological Roots, some that are genetic and many that are acquired. Examples of genetic Psychological Root are needs for safety, stability, respect, and communication, also a need to connect with other humans, obtain stimulation, and have closure. Two other examples of wired-in Psychological Roots are a need to obtain positive experiences and avoid negative experiences.

Beliefs, that is what we consider to be true, are acquired Psychological Roots and there are many of them. For example, optimism is a belief that something good will happen whereas pessimism is a belief that something bad will happen. A concern is a belief that something bad could happen whereas hope is a belief that something good could happen. A value is a strongly-held belief that greatly guides thinking, emotional reactions, and behavior, while an expectation is a belief that something will or should happen. Confidence is a belief with different variations such as believing that success will occur regarding something. Self-confidence is a person's belief that he/she will personally succeed. Lack of confidence is a belief that failure will occur regarding something. And lack of self-confidence is an individual's belief that he/she will personally fail. Beliefs, values, confidence, optimism, and pessimism are Psychological Roots.

There are many thousands of Psychological Roots, including personal rules, problem-solving strategies, social strategies, and psychological thresholds. Some other Psychological Roots are self-esteem, ambition, philosophies, political ideologies, religious beliefs, and constituents of

Psychological Homeostasis such as comfort-zone, acceptable range, unacceptable range, and tipping points.[11]

People who speculate about "where a person is coming from" are trying to understand that person's Psychological Roots. Actors who endeavor to understand their character's motivation are attempting to unearth Psychological Roots. Instances such as these indicate that people have a sense that something inside a person causes that individual's behavior. That "something" is not obvious and can be difficult to articulate. The reason for people's difficulty in identifying Psychological Roots is that Psychological Roots operate almost entirely below consciousness. Their largely subconscious nature also means that many people do not realize that there is a deep cause of their thoughts, feelings, and actions.

The invisibility of Psychological Roots is a major reason why people's motivations, moods, decisions, and behavior can be puzzling at times. There is great resistance to change, which people might not realize (discussed in Chapter 13). For example, a person who frequently buys the latest electronic gadgets might think that he likes change, not realizing that he would stubbornly resist changing his deep Psychological Roots. A woman who frequently gets her hair done in different colors and styles might believe that she likes change without realizing that she would greatly resist changing characteristics of her personality. Those individuals do not realize that what they like is *surface* change. They also may not realize that the reason for their liking such changes is that they have a wired-in need for stimulation. Another hidden aspect they may not be aware of is that they and everyone else greatly resist changing their basic personality structure.

Despite Psychological Roots' hidden nature it is possible to identify them. (See Chapter 18.) It can be indispensable to do so when it is important to resolve people's problems since Psychological Roots constitute a major foundation of personality, thoughts, emotional reactions, attitudes, and behavior.

Genetically wired-in Roots

Mentioned earlier is that wired into everyone are genetic Biological Roots such as needs for air (oxygen), energy (food), water, and shelter, and also genetic Psychological Roots such as needs for safety, stability, closure, positive

---

[11] Synonyms for Psychological Roots are inner motivations, psychological driving Forces, psychological drivers, driving forces, psychological seeds, and guiding factors.

arousal, and avoidance of negative arousal. Everyone is born with the same overall set of genetic Biological and Psychological Roots, but there are widely ranging individual differences in the extent to which each particular genetic root exists. For example, some persons are biologically programmed to be taller or more athletic than others, and some individuals are psychologically programmed with substantially greater social or mathematical ability than others. Thus, while everyone has a psychological need for safety, some people have an extremely strong need for safety and therefore function with great caution, while other people have a relatively low need for safety and therefore might take many risks. Experiences can modify inherited levels of Biological and Psychological Roots.

Our inborn psychological differences, such as being highly artistic or verbal, gear us for much of what we become in life. Genetic Psychological and Biological Roots also guide the Psychological Roots we acquire through experiences, such as beliefs, expectations, and specific goals. Genetic Psychological Roots are permanent throughout a person's lifetime, however individuals differ in how those roots are applied in specific situations, how modified they become, and what acquired Psychological Roots link to them. (Linking is discussed in Chapter 7.)

One of many connections between psychology and biology is that everything psychological is ultimately biological, including Psychological Roots. However, much as a car is different than its metal, glass, and plastic components, Psychological Roots have particular structures and functions, which will soon be described.

People are more likely to be aware of Biological Roots (e.g., needs for food and air) than Psychological Roots (e.g., needs for closure and connecting with something larger than themselves). Nevertheless, the author has found that upon mentioning specific Psychological Roots, people are often likely to recognize them, such as their needs for stimulation and connecting with other humans. People are also likely to realize that some needs are wired into them, such as a need for safety.

Some Biological and Psychological Roots have similar labels, such as a need to maintain stability (e.g., homeostasis in biology and psychology), and a need for stimulation (e.g., "use it or lose it" in biology and avoidance of boredom in psychology). There also are countervailing factors in both biology and psychology (opposing hormones and muscles in biology, and opposing evaluation criteria and thoughts in psychology). There are many connections between Psychological and Biological Roots, for example, a person's desire for a particular food is initially motivated by a biological need to eat, and a desire to be effective in sports is possible because of the biological ability to acquire specific physical skills.

Needs for safety, stability, and communication exist in many species, even single-celled organisms (Bu & Callaway, 2011), indicating that psychological factors are not unique to humans. The existence of psychological factors in basic forms of life suggests that biological needs are not the only factors necessary for life and that psychological factors may be needed for survival (e.g., needs for safety, stability, communication, and avoidance of negatives). An implication of the genetic nature of some psychological aspects is that humans' psychology is a version of psychological factors that exist in other organisms. For example, needs for safety, stability, and communication appear to be present in microbes, which are single celled creatures.

Acquired Psychological Roots

Many Biological and Psychological Roots are obtained through experience. Examples of acquired Biological Roots are food preferences, the raising and lowering of sensory thresholds (habituation and sensitization, respectively), the acquisition of physical skills (e.g., dancing and typing), and the potential to become addicted. The longevity of some acquired Psychological Roots, such as life-long values that originate in childhood, provides evidence that acquired Psychological Roots are physically real. Thus, beliefs, goals, and expectations – even though not visible – are not just figments of the imagination, ephemeral, or "fluff" as some people believe, but rather are biological structures.[12, 13] There are far more acquired Psychological Roots than genetic roots (explained in a later chapter).

General and specific Psychological Roots

Everyone has psychological needs, for example, needs for safety, stability, and connecting with others. Everyone has expectations, for example,

---

[12] Values are strongly held beliefs that are part of a person's basic personality and function as a person's core principles that help guide thinking, reacting and behaving (e.g., believing in fairness, kindness, and being responsible).

[13] These long-lasting and powerful aspects contradict the idea that psychology is insubstantial or has little significance or effect. A major reason such mistaken ideas occur is because psychological systems operate below the surface and are intangible.

expecting others we know well to be true to their word, be trustworthy, and meet their responsibilities. Also, it is likely that everyone has a desire to live, acquire sufficient resources to maintain life, and be regarded well by others. These are *'general Psychological Roots'* in that they are likely to be held by a large percentage of the population.

There some Psychological Roots that are either specific to just one or a few individuals, or exist in only a small percentage of the population. For example, some people believe that they have a special system that can beat gambling odds, and an ailing person might want to stay alive long enough to see her children marry, or to see a child born, or to have grandchildren. Some people believe that the world will end at a soon-occurring date, or that aliens from another planet live among us. Some adults believe that they cannot succeed without depending on someone else in their life, whereas some other people believe that if they are to succeed it will be because of what they do without help from others. Those are *'specific Psychological Roots'* in that they are likely to be held by a small percentage of the population or are unique to just one person.

This distinction is important when doing scientific research because finding general principles requires identifying aspects that apply to many and perhaps all individuals, and therefore involves working with general Psychological Roots. Psychotherapy, on the other hand, requires identifying the particular Psychological Roots that create problems for each individual client and therefore involves working with specific Psychological Roots.

Significance of Psychological Roots

Our thoughts, emotional reactions, and behaviors are functions of both genetic and acquired Psychological Roots. When we evaluate something, the criterion we use to judge what is acceptable to us is a Psychological Root, such as a belief. Something that is evaluated positively generates a positive emotional reaction (liking). Something that is evaluated negatively results in a negative emotional reaction (disliking). Positive and negative evaluations are an example of how Psychological Roots affect emotional reactions. Another example is reacting in fear when our safety is threatened. Psychological Roots contribute to the perceptions we have and play a major role in shaping our frames of reference, opinions, and motivations as well as our emotions. Psychological Roots' cognitive effects include prompting the thoughts we have, what we desire to learn, and our decisions. Our behaviors and the social and problem-solving strategies we employ originate in our underlying psychology (e.g., Jones, Greenberg, & Crowley, 2015).

The Pygmalion Effect, a well-known study by Rosenthal and Jacobson (1968), offers an example of Psychological Roots. In that study, a grade school teacher was informed that some children in her class were exceptionally intelligent but "late bloomers", as indicated by an IQ test. However, that information was intentionally false; the children had low IQ scores. When those children were tested later in the semester, their IQ scores were higher than initially. That teacher was not aware that she had done anything differently. However, without her realizing it, her expectations appeared to have affected the way she engaged those children and that difference led to an improvement in those children's intellectual ability.

The effect of another person's expectations on someone else's intelligence is particularly noteworthy since it had been believed that intelligence is almost entirely due to a person's genetic inheritance. Subsequently, other studies found that intelligence is affected by many post-birth factors, including social skill (e.g., Goleman, 2005). (Expectations and social strategies are Psychological Roots.)

The Pygmalion study mentioned above is an example of a self-fulfilling prophecy in that what a person believes can occur subsequently because the person acts in accord with his/her belief. For example, if you believe that someone is nice, you might treat that individual well and therefore that person might be nice to you. Believing that someone is unpleasant can lead to your treating that person badly, leading that person to be unpleasant to you . As this illustrates, what we believe matters because we act on what we believe. (Beliefs are Psychological Roots.)

Expectations are beliefs – that is, a belief that something is going to happen and should happen – such as a child's potential to blossom, as in the Pygmalion study. From a Psychological Systems Theory perspective, what counted in that study is the teacher's belief that people can improve. It might not matter that the belief was acquired surreptitiously, as in the Pygmalion study. (The difference between goals and expectations is discussed in Chapter 11; effective teaching and learning strategies are discussed in Chapters 34 and 35, respectively).

Psychological Roots are involved in almost everything people do, including relationships. The author has found that the more similar a couple's deep Psychological Roots – such as their values, goals, and problem-solving strategies – the greater the opportunity for a successful relationship. Sub-surface Psychological Roots are therefore especially important for a good relationship, not just surface aspects such as appearance, personality, and sex appeal. (Deep and surface roots are discussed in Chapter 7).

In short, Psychological Roots are the foundation for almost everything we do including thinking, evaluating, and deciding, as well as our emotional reactions and behavior. Therefore, when we want to understand someone and ourselves, knowing the Psychological Roots that are involved is essential. Our becoming aware of Psychological Roots has been impeded because they are hidden, which makes it hard to visualize what they look like, much as microbes were unseen 700 years ago. Before microbes were known it would have been difficult to explain them and their potency, but their invisibility did not mean that they failed to exist. For humans to accept microbes' existence and effect required having the ability to detect them. That circumstance is akin to trying to understand Psychological Roots at this time.

Fortunately, much is known about Psychological Roots because people readily respond to questions about them (e.g., goals, beliefs, needs, and expectations), people's lives improve when distress-causing roots are modified, and scientific studies can be conducted on them. (The importance of Psychological Roots in thoughts, emotional reactions, and behavior are presented in the next chapter. Chapters in Section II describe how to use knowledge of Psychological Roots for practical purposes, such as solving conflicts, improving communication, persuasion, and psychotherapy, and treating psychological disorders, including depression, anxiety, and addiction. Other practical applications described in Section II are the key role of Psychological Roots have in teaching, learning, prevention, and lessening prejudice.)

The bottom line: Psychological Roots are the originating point for people's thoughts, emotional reactions, and behavior. There are many types of Psychological Roots that exist below awareness such as beliefs, expectations, abilities, and psychological needs. Since Psychological Roots are hidden, if something observable seems to explain a person's actions it is unlikely to be a Psychological Root. For example, stimuli, childhood experiences, and feelings are not Psychological Roots.

More about genetic Psychological Roots
Genetic Psychological Roots are comparable to computer hardware; acquired Psychological Roots are comparable to software. Some genetic Psychological Roots in addition to those mentioned previously, include wired-in needs for evaluating and being connected with something larger than themselves. Genetic Psychological Roots remain during a person's entire life.

Some genetic Psychological Roots oppose one another, for example, the need for autonomy conflicts with dependency needs, and the need to grow conflicts with resistance to change. Internal conflicts are consistent with Freud's theory (Freud, 1990), but some of humanity's most distressing problems are due to interpersonal conflicts (e.g., war). (Section II describes practical uses of psychological systems aspects such as Psychological Roots for helping to solve personal and interpersonal problems.)

More about acquired Psychological Roots

Mentioned earlier was that the vast majority of Psychological Roots are acquired, including some that have great importance, such as values acquired early in life. Cognitive Psychological Roots can generate emotional reactions, for example, a pleasurable emotional reaction results upon achieving a goal and an unpleasant reaction results when not meeting an expectation. Psychological Roots continue to be acquired during a person's lifetime and some remain throughout a person's life, such as those that are in an individual's basic personality structure (e.g., core values like believing in a strong work ethic, caring for others, and taking personal responsibility).[14]

Psychological Roots are inner motivations, while stimulus conditions are external motivations whose effect is due to their impact on Psychological and Biological Roots (described more fully later). Stimulus conditions include some physiological stimuli that originate inside the body, such as hormones, glandular secretions, and neurotransmitters.

People are internally logical

Since what people do involves their Psychological Roots, when a person does something that seems illogical to an observer, that action might nevertheless make sense when the person's Psychological Roots are known. For instance, a person might continue to do the same thing repeatedly despite being unsuccessful in doing so, such as when parents continue to demand that their child function in the way they dictate even when their child persists in disobeying. Even when what those parents do is obviously not succeeding, they continue to make the same demands in the same way. That persistent behavior occurs because people act in accord with their beliefs. Thus, their behavior makes sense to *them* (e.g., being controlling and speaking bluntly), even though it does not produce the results they desire. As this description illustrates, what individuals do is logical for *them* because it is consistent with *their* psychological framework – even when it does not produce a successful outcome, is counterproductive, or does not accord with other people's

---

[14] Some people believe that psychological aspects are not real, consequential, or long-lived.

observations or logic. (More on this topic in the discussion of the 'flow down effect' in Chapter 7.)

That someone might repeat the same behavior and expect something different is not uncommon since we are wired to resist changing (discussed in Chapter 13). Because unsuccessful repetitive behavior often occurs, such actions are therefore "normal" rather than constituting "the definition of insanity". Repetition is likely because resistance to change appears to be genetically wired-into us.

A few definitions (please see the glossary for other definitions):

A threshold is a point at which change takes place. As a result, a threshold can function as an evaluative criterion and a switch that turns something on or off. Examples are a tipping point into a state of uncontrollability at the end of a continuum, a criterion for evaluating success or failure, and the basis for judging what is acceptable and not acceptable, right or wrong.

A need is a necessity which, if not met, generates a negative reaction. Needs that are genetic are wired into organisms, such as biological needs (e.g., for air, food, and acceptable temperature) and psychological needs (e.g., for safety, stimulation, and connection with others). Some acquired Psychological Roots are reacted to as if they are needs such as responsibilities, standards, and expectations. Biological needs are Biological Roots; psychological needs are Psychological Roots.

A drive involves energy directed toward the achievement of a goal. Needs produce particularly strong drives. The drive to avoid negatives is especially intense and much stronger than the positive drive. Drives are internal reactions that result from Psychological Roots. (Chapter 10 discusses this further.)

A goal is what is aimed for and hoped to be achieved. When a goal is attained, that success triggers a positive emotional reaction. Thus, goals are criteria for judging whether or not success has taken place. This characteristic makes every goal a switch capable of generating a positive emotional reaction. A goal also provides a focus for what is to be accomplished and generates a drive to achieve it.

A belief is something that is assumed to be true or correct.

An expectation is a belief that something will happen and should happen. If what is expected does not occur, it is a failure that triggers a negative emotional reaction. This trait means that an expectation is a) a basis for judging whether or not a failure has occurred and b) a switch for arousing negative emotions. Since anything less than what is expected is unacceptable, expectations are criteria for failure and identify what the minimum goal is. Put another way, an expectation points to what is minimally acceptable and generates a drive to avoid failing to meet that criterion. By comparison, a full goal specifies what total success would be and generates a drive to attain that criterion.

Aspects that Psychological Roots have in common

Shared characteristics of Psychological Roots are presented in Box 1 in the next chapter, but it can be useful to note here that one thing that all Psychological Roots share is that they are thresholds and therefore evaluative criteria. A threshold is involved whenever a judgment is made or when something is evaluated, such as whether it measures up to a standard or does not. Psychological Roots – such as beliefs, personal rules, goals, expectations, and needs – are a major basis for making judgments and evaluating decisions, behavior, success, and failure. Such judgments affect our thoughts, emotional reactions, and subsequent behavior. Evaluation is going on all the time without people realizing it (discussed in Chapter 15). It is one of everyone's many hidden psychological aspects and therefore unlikely to be noticed by comparison to overt aspects such as differences between males and females, old and young, and successful and unsuccessful individuals.

Summary

Almost everything that humans do originates for psychological reasons or is greatly affected by psychology. Behavior might appear to originate from thoughts and feelings, but each of those aspects is an outcome whose origin is one or more Psychological Roots (described in the next chapter). Psychological Roots function almost entirely subconsciously. Each person possesses a large number of Psychological Roots, some that are genetically wired-in (e.g., need for safety, threshold for emotional arousal), while most roots are cognitive and acquired through experience (e.g., beliefs, goals, and expectations). Understanding behavior requires unearthing Psychological Roots that lead to thoughts, feelings, and actions. Hence, understanding why someone does something requires more than knowing that person's thoughts, feelings, actions, and the stimuli that impact that individual. (Methods for identifying Psychological Roots are described in Chapter 6.)

Psychological Roots have many characteristics in common, for example, all Psychological Roots are evaluation criteria. Psychological Roots – such as goals, beliefs, and expectations – constitute one of humans' major psychological systems. They are the metaphorical DNA of psychology.

A practical application of this information

Behaviors can be puzzling, with no outward indications that explain them or aid changing them. For example, no observable differences appear to exist between killers and other people (e.g., Fox & Levin, 2015). Nevertheless, there are likely to be differences in those individuals' Psychological Roots. Uncovering those Psychological Roots can offer an understanding of otherwise inscrutable behavior, and from that understanding, a constructive basis can be developed to generate improvement. This strategy can be essential when trying to cope with behavior that is difficult, disturbing, or puzzling.

When someone is not persuasive, that communicator's message may be inconsistent with the recipient's Psychological Roots and can turn off that recipient ("Don't confuse me with facts"). It would be better for someone who is trying to persuade to structure their message to fit the recipient's Psychological Roots. (Chapters 24 - 26 in Section II describe a practical method for doing so.)

Chapter 4. HIDDEN SEQUENCES

Knowing what drives behavior and internal reactions is invaluable. This chapter describes two types of Hidden Sequences that do so.

Root Sequences

Expecting good things to happen (optimism) creates a positive mood, as does having confidence and thinking well of oneself. The opposite, expecting bad things to happen (pessimism), generates negative moods. As this illustrates, Psychological Roots can generate moods and thoughts related to them. Those moods and thoughts are internal reactions in *'Hidden Sequences'*.

One type of Hidden Sequence is a *'Root Sequence'* in which an internal reaction originates from a Psychological Root without there being an external stimulus that triggers the sequence (See Figure 7). For example, a negative mood can result from distrusting others, believing that one is a victim, or having poor social strategies. (Strategies are Psychological Roots; tactics are behaviors.) Upbeat internal reactions can produce the opposite internal reactions such as being optimistic, trusting others, or having effective social strategies. (Later in this chapter another type of Hidden Sequence is described.)

Internal reactions

Cognitive internal reactions include perceptions, thoughts, ideas, mental associations, reasoning, evaluations, attitudes, judgments, attributions, conclusions, decisions, and intentions. Physiological internal reactions include emotional reactions, feelings, moods, drives, glandular responses (such as perspiration and digestive enzymes), biochemicals (e.g., hormones such as adrenalin, thyroxine, and insulin), and neurotransmitters (such as serotonin, norepinephrine, GABA, and acetylcholine). Emotional reactions, feelings, and moods can be positive (e.g., pleasure) or negative (e.g., fear, anger, feeling like a failure). A person's internal reactions are largely unobservable to others (e.g., unexpressed thoughts, evaluations, and decisions), but some internal reactions can be noticeable at times, such as those related to strong emotional reactions (e.g., anger, blushing, mood).

Attitude (an internal reaction) and behavior are sometimes strongly correlated, sometimes moderately correlated, and sometimes not correlated (Wicker, 1969, and Shuman & Johnson, 1976). An example of behavior that is in accord with an internal reaction occurs when a person who believes that he does not measure up to others associates with individuals less competent than he is to avoid feeling uncomfortable. A well-known example of people not acting in accord with their attitude occurred in a study conducted by LaPiere

(1934). In that study, a Chinese couple traveled to many places in the U.S. and were refused service only once. However, when the same establishments were asked by mail if they would provide service to that couple, 92% of them stated that they do not offer service to Chinese people.

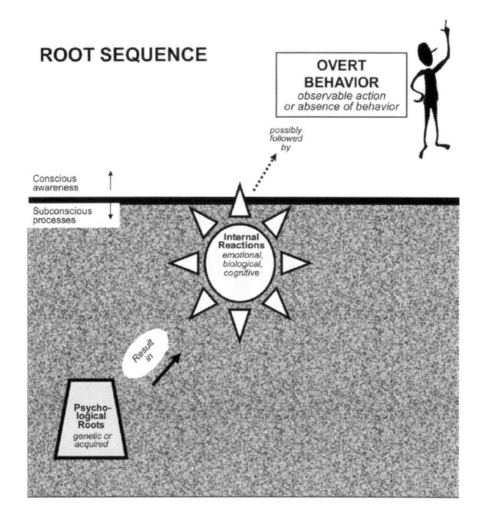

Fig. 7. **ROOT SEQUENCE** (a type of Hidden Sequence).
Major parts of this sequence are subconscious (below the dark line).
Observable aspects are above the dark line.

Hidden Sequences explains why wide variations occur between attitudes and behaviors: in Hidden Sequences, attitudes are internal reactions and therefore more directly affected by Psychological Roots than behavior, since behavior is at the end of Hidden Sequences and therefore somewhat removed from Psychological Roots. Behavior is also influenced by the positive and negative consequences for engaging in it, also the means and opportunity for that to happen. All other things being equal, the greater an attitude's intensity, the more likely a behavior related to that attitude will occur. A graph of that relationship would be similar to the Intensity Curve in Figure 6.

Since a mood can originate from a Psychological Root, an implication of Root Sequences is that people can be moody without having an external reason for that emotional reaction. People can be puzzled when there is no apparent reason for something. Moods, like other internal reactions, can lead to states of uncontrollability, therefore, a strong mood can be a precursor to a disorder and move a person toward a homeostatic tipping point.

A Root Sequence – in which a Psychological Root, in itself, produces an internal reaction – can be abbreviated as ***Psychological Root → internal reaction.*** An internal reaction can activate the autonomic nervous system and affect internal physiological structures such as the heart, lungs, gastro-intestinal tract, and circulatory system. Examples of Biological Root Sequences are the Krebs oxygen cycle, metabolism, and cell growth (e.g., creation of red and white blood cells).

Cognitions and emotions

Cognitive Psychological Roots can trigger internal reactions, including emotions, for example, a person who believes he is unworthy might feel distressed. Since many Psychological Roots are cognitive, many emotional reactions result from cognitions, even though many people might not believe that cognitions and emotional reactions are connected. Individuals who do not appear to be emotional (e.g., persons with flat affect or who are very cognitively-oriented) nevertheless have Hidden Sequences and emotional reactions.

Moods vs. emotional bursts

Emotional outbursts (e.g., laughter, anger) are strong, short-lived emotional reactions, sometimes just a few seconds long. Moods are longer-lasting emotional reactions. In some people, long-lasting moods and sometimes emotional outbursts occur so frequently that those actions seem to characterize those individuals (e.g., being joyous, serious, or unhappy).

When behavior results from a Root Sequence

Mentioned earlier is that an internal reaction might result in a behavior but not necessarily. In a Root Sequence, when a Psychological Root leads to a behavior it can be abbreviated as ***Psychological Root → internal reaction → behavior***.[15] When overt behaviors occur, an internal reaction activates skeletal muscles. The basis for a person's general cognitive or emotional characteristics depends substantially on the Psychological Roots that lead to those characteristics. The likelihood of behavior is related to emotional intensity among other things.

Stimulus-and-Root Sequences

An internal reaction can result when a stimulus impacts a Psychological Root, for example, being invited to a party can generate a happy feeling, and hearing "fire" shouted in a crowded room can create anxiety. When a stimulus triggers an internal reaction, the result is a *'Stimulus-and-Root Sequence'*, which differs from a Root Sequence in that it is initiated by a stimulus rather than a Psychological Root acting by itself (see Figure 8). Some other examples of a Stimulus-and-Root Sequence are sadness caused by the loss of a loved one, hurt feelings as a result of being put down, and disappointment triggered by failure (cf. Beck, 1972; Beck, Rush, Shaw, & Emery, 1979).

A stimulus that sets off a Stimulus-and-Root Sequence can originate from inside the body (e.g., from hormones or neuronal stimulation) or from the outside (e.g., what another person says or does). A Stimulus-and-Root Sequence can be abbreviated as ***stimulus condition + Psychological Root → internal reaction.*** (Synonyms for a Stimulus-and-Root Sequence are Stimulus Sequence and Stimulus-and-Psychological Root Sequence.)

When behavior results from a Stimulus-and-Root Sequence

A Stimulus-and-Root Sequence does not necessarily result in overt behavior. For example, experiencing a failure involves internal reactions such as thoughts or emotional reactions (e.g., disappointment), but a behavior might not result. However, when a strong negative emotional reaction propels a person past a tipping point into a disorder, some behaviors are likely to be associated with that disorder.

---

[15] Synonyms for Hidden Sequences are hidden processes, action sequences, and motivational sequences. A synonym for internal reaction is inner response.

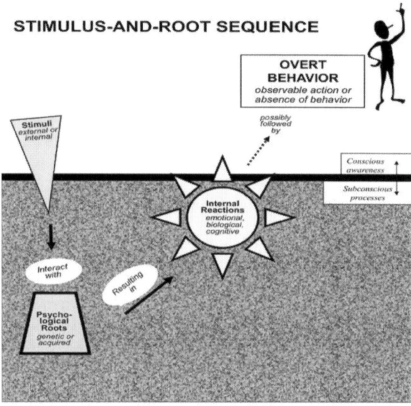

Fig. 8. **Stimulus-and-Root Sequence**. Major parts of this psychological process are subconscious (below the dark line). Observable parts are above the dark line.

Some Psychological Roots and internal reactions affect the likelihood that a behavior will occur. For example, a strong desire could increase the likelihood of a behavior, whereas concern about negative consequences might impede that likelihood. When a stimulus leads to a behavior in a Stimulus-and-Root Sequence, it can be abbreviated as *stimulus + Psychological Root* → *internal reaction* → *overt behavior*.

Experimenter-introduced independent variables and post hoc studies

When an experimental treatment introduced by a researcher in an *a priori* study produces statistically significant results it is because subjects' Psychological or Biological Roots have been impacted by that treatment. For example, a person might change his/her attitude after being apprised of a message from someone who has high credibility vs. receiving the same message from someone with low credibility. On the surface, the results may appear to be due to the communicator's credibility in and of itself. However, the result occurred because the stimulus (the message) impacted a sub-surface Psychological Root (e.g., the recipient's confidence).

As this analysis illustrates, the experimental treatment in *a priori* experiments is not the entire cause, but rather the treatment is a stimulus in a Stimulus-and-Root Hidden Sequence. The degree to which internal response-variables are involved, including Psychological Roots, can be assessed in pre- and post-study questionnaires. Hidden Sequences are involved in both *a priori* and *post hoc* studies.

A biological process is involved in Psychological Hidden Sequences

The internal reactions in psychological Hidden Sequences can involve biological aspects (e.g., neurotransmitters and skeletal-muscle behaviors), and psychological aspects (e.g., thoughts, evaluations, and decisions). For example, a Psychological Root impacted by the shout of fire in a crowded room (need for safety) can result in fear (an emotion, which is a psycho-physiological action) and a burst of adrenalin (a biological action). The level of adrenalin diminishes when the sense of danger ends. A stress-related heart condition is an example of a Stimulus-and-Root Hidden Sequence that affects a physiological organ directly.

If people *believe* that there is a danger, an adrenalin reaction can occur even if there is no physical harm, for example, a child might be upset by a clown or a strange noise at a carnival. A similar pattern occurs with psychological anxiety, even though the threat – such as an exam or job interview – does not create physical injury.

A Hidden Sequences explanation of the placebo effect is that a belief generates an internal reaction (e.g., something believed to be healing brings relief). In such cases, an acquired Psychological Root (a belief) generates an internal reaction (e.g., elevation of a pain threshold). It is an example of a cognitive stimulus producing a biological response.

Absence of a behavior

As mentioned, internal reactions might lead to observable behaviors such as speaking and moving. In the example of a Stimulus-and-Root Sequence involving fire in a crowded room mentioned above, some behaviors that might occur could be screaming, yelling for help, running to an exit, grabbing someone, asking questions, or battling the fire. The *absence* of behavior would also be observable, especially when people expect behavior to occur, such as when someone remains seated or standing when there is a fire.[16, 17, 18]

A person's behavior can trigger another Hidden Sequence in that person or other people. For example, people who run toward a door might ignite a Stimulus-and-Root Sequence in others who also speed to an exit upon seeing those individuals run. The skeletal nervous system and the cerebral cortex mediate overt behaviors.

Identifying the cause

Attempting to change behavior directly – such as by abstaining from an addictive substance or telling someone what to do – may seem to be an obvious thing to do in many circumstances and might change some behavior. However, Hidden Sequences suggests that such attempts are unlikely to have a long-term effect or perhaps any effect unless the pertinent Psychological Roots and stimulus conditions change. Trying to change internal reactions directly might be able to create some change and therefore, can be somewhat helpful, such as breathing exercises, relaxation, meditation, medication, and electro-cortico therapy (ECT, which disrupts internal mental communications). Medication and psychotherapy can be utilized jointly.

---

[16] Behaviors can result from a blend of inputs, especially in Stimulus-and-Root Sequences when various components of a complex stimulus impact different Psychological Roots. Internal reactions such as emotions, evaluations, conclusions and decisions can lead to overt behaviors depending on their intensity and other factors. This makes emotions an intermediary part of the process and a *proximal* cause of behavior, not the *originating* cause.

[17] An acronym for a Root Sequence is PIB (Psychological Root-Internal reaction-Behavior).

[18] An acronym for a Stimulus-and-Root Sequence is SPIB (Stimulus-Psychological Root-Internal reaction-Behavior).

A caution

   MEDICATION IS THE APPROPRIATE TREATMENT FOR SOME PSYCHOLOGICAL CONDITIONS AND MAY BE NECESSARY. FOR SOME PEOPLE, MEDICINE IS A NECESSITY.

   PEOPLE WHO USE PSYCHOTROPIC PHARMACEUTICALS SHOULD NOT STOP USING THEM UNTIL THEY HAVE A BETTER ALTERNATIVE.

   ENDING THE USE OF MEDICATION FOR A PSYCHOLOGICAL CONDITION SHOULD BE DONE WITH THE ADVICE AND THERAPEUTIC SUPPORT OF A CREDENTIALED PROFESSIONAL, PREFERABLY A LICENSED PSYCHIATRIST.

   WHEN MEDICATION FOR A PSYCHOLOGICAL CONDITION IS TO END, THE DOSE SHOULD BE TAPERED DOWN GRADUALLY RATHER THAN STOPPING ABRUPTLY.

   AFTER ENDING THE USE OF PSYCHOTROPIC MEDICINE, IT CAN BE IMPORTANT TO CONTINUE HAVING PROFESSIONAL PSYCHOLOGICAL TREATMENT.

Joint treatment

   Medicine and psychotherapy are often employed together for treating psychological conditions. This approach can be very beneficial even when the cause of a condition is psychological or primarily caused by psychological factors. If the cause of a psychological problem involves Psychological Roots and stimulus conditions, those aspects should be addressed appropriately in addition to medication.

Originating cause vs. proximal cause

   Internal reactions immediately precede behaviors, but the starting point for both typically is a Psychological Root. Hence, an internal reaction is likely to be a *proximal* cause rather than the originating cause of a behavior. When internal reactions (e.g., anxiety, anger, and other precursors) and behaviors generate still other reactions and behaviors, they act as stimuli.

   It is useful to assess behaviors and internal reactions, however, the key to treating the cause of an outcome effectively is modifying or overriding the pertinent Psychological Roots and stimulus conditions. Being able to do so is aided by identifying those originating causes.

   Many personality traits – such as being intuitive, extroverted, creative, or aggressive – are behaviors. A behavior is an outcome that occurs at the end of a Hidden Sequence. A behavior can trigger another behavior. A behavior that does so is a result of a previous Hidden Sequence and acts as a stimulus for a subsequent Hidden Sequence. When behaviors act as stimuli they interact with

Psychological Roots. Therefore, identifying the originating cause of a person's behavior requires going beyond personality traits that are observable. The underlying Psychological Roots need to be uncovered. (Techniques for identifying Psychological Roots are described in Chapter 6).

Genetic origin of psychological conditions

Some instances of depression and loneliness have a genetic origin (e.g., Gao, Davis, Hart, Sanchez-Roige, Han, Cacioppo, & Palmer, 2016). What percentage of depression and loneliness is due to genetics is an open question but appears to be quite small. When genetic biological factors have negative psychological effects such as depression and loneliness, a possibility is that they set the stage for acquiring distress-prone Psychological Roots. Then those acquired roots lead to psychological effects. In such instances, it is not just biological factors that are involved, Psychological Roots also are.

Who can change Psychological Roots?

The Hidden Sequences concept implicitly suggests that the only person who can change an individual's Psychological Roots is that person himself/herself. For example, when Mary tries to directly change Jon's behavior (such as his being overly critical or his addiction), her attempt might not alter the pertinent Psychological Roots that cause his behavior. The same holds for her trying to change his internal reactions (such as his emotional reaction or thought). Only Jon can make the change Mary wants. Therefore, a better way for Mary to try to influence Jon would be for her to motivate him to modify or override the *Psychological Roots* that contribute to his behavior. Hence, knowing the Psychological Roots that undergird his behavior would help. (How to do so is described in Chapter 6). There also might be some stimulus conditions that interact with his Psychological Roots that may also need to be changed. (See Chapters 25 and 26.)

Summary of Hidden Sequences thus far

There are two types of Hidden Sequences, Root Sequences in which a Psychological Root, itself, generates an internal reaction, and Stimulus-and-Root Sequences in which an internal reaction results from a stimulus condition having impacted a Psychological Root.

There are two types of outcomes in Hidden Sequences, internal reactions and observable behaviors. Internal reactions include thoughts, emotional reactions, feelings, fantasies, evaluations, decisions, and drives. Overt behaviors might result from an internal reaction, but might not, depending on factors such as the potency of the stimulus conditions, Psychological Roots, and the internal reaction (e.g., emotional or cognitive intensity). Behavior also depends on the potential consequences of the action, the person's memory of past success, failures, and degree of confidence, and the opportunity for a behavior to occur.[19]

A Psychological Root is the originating point of both types of sequences is (e.g., needs, beliefs, goals, and expectations), either alone or after being impacted by a stimulus. A mixture of stimuli or Psychological Roots can produce a combination of internal reactions and a complex behavior.[20, 21, 22]

Internal reactions and behaviors can act as stimuli that generate Hidden Sequences. (Synonyms for Hidden Sequences are *'subconscious sequences'* and *'underlying sequences'*). Hidden Sequences operate below awareness.

Overt indications of internal reactions can sometimes occur, such as when people are highly emotional.[23] The chances of successfully changing an overt behavior can be higher when Psychological Roots and stimulus conditions that originate that behavior are modified compared to trying to change an outcome directly.

---

[19] Psychological Roots in Hidden Sequences are analogous to germinating seeds that previously were dormant. Corresponding to a Root Sequence is the underground, unseen germination of a seed. Corresponding to a Stimulus-and-Root Sequence with an internal reaction is a watered seed that sprouts underground. Corresponding to a Stimulus-and-Root Sequence with overt behavior is a sprout that appears above ground.

[20] The frontal cortex and Psychological Roots might be limited or bypassed with some internal reactions and behaviors, such as biological reflexes, instincts, conditioned responses, and impulsive behaviors.

[21] When seeking to identify Psychological Roots it helps to know that internal reactions (e.g., feelings, thoughts) and behaviors either directly result from Psychological Roots or are due to a stimulus impacting a Psychological Root.

[22] In psychological matters, biological processes are always involved. Psychology is sometimes involved in biological processes and is often involved in motivation.

[23] Internal reactions are sometimes observable, such as a change in body, eye, face, or voice. Changes in such aspects can offer a non-verbal indication of what might be going on below the surface in a person.

Attempts to create change are aided by working effectively with the key components of Hidden Sequences, primarily the originating causes (pertinent Psychological Roots and stimulus conditions). Working with outcomes directly (such as internal reactions, which are proximal causes, and overt behavior), is likely to be a less effective way to create change than working with Psychological Roots.

Some additional aspects

Hidden Sequences take place rapidly, some evidence of which is the quick flow of thoughts and conversations. In Stimulus-and-Root Sequences, the impact of a stimulus on a Psychological Root is an *'initial interaction'*. Often, the stimulus conditions in Stimulus-and-Root Sequences are obvious or can be discerned easily. In contrast, Psychological Roots are hidden and unlikely to be readily identified, and their significance is often not understood. These aspects can make behavior difficult to change, such as intense interpersonal conflicts. Also unlikely to be realized is that stimuli have an effect because they impact a Psychological Root. Thus, when attempting to understand and change behavior, knowing about Hidden Sequences can be indispensable (as will be seen in the discussion of social influence in Chapters 25 and 26, and conflict resolution in Chapters 20-23).

When past experiences occurred, such as those in childhood, they were stimulus conditions at that time. Some of those experiences led to the creation of Psychological Roots in people (e.g., believing that one's parents can be depended upon, or feeling self-confident or vulnerable). However, people might believe that past experiences are roots because of their strong effect (e.g., childhood abuse or abandonment, which can lead to long-term psychological disturbances). Instead, some past experiences create Psychological Roots, for example, nearly drowning might create a concern about swimming or boating, an example of the powerful effect that stimuli can have. A stimulus or its impact might not be noticed at the time or remembered afterward, and its significance might be missed or not understood among the *mélange* of things that occurred at the time.

Demographic factors (e.g., gender, income, marital status, or other population characteristics) are observable aspects that can be stimuli, trigger internal reactions and overt behaviors, and lead to the formation of some Psychological Roots. Beliefs about social class, marriage, skin color, education, wealth, age, or residence can result.

An internal reaction may be the net result of many inputs. For example, a positive mood may mean that more positively-oriented Psychological Roots in a person are involved than negative ones. Conversely, a down mood may mean that more negatively-oriented Psychological Roots are engaged than positive ones. Since negatives are far stronger than positives (discussed in a later chapter), a single negative aspect or a small number of negatives can overshadow a large number of positives.

Different components of a stimulus condition might have an effect, with each triggering a separate Hidden Sequence. Hence a single stimulus condition could produce a variety of Hidden Sequences. A mixture of internal reactions and overt behaviors would result.

When there is a combination of internal reactions and behaviors, it can be hard to identify individual components, including which Hidden Sequence was the initial one. The complexity in such situations can lead to a variety of interpretations, an example of which is eye-witnesses whose reports are not in accord with one another.

Cognitive internal reactions

Internal reactions – such as feelings, thoughts, ideas, judgments, attitudes, conclusions, decisions, and drives – are based on Psychological Roots. For example, thinking about how to deal with a fire depends on a belief about how much danger there is. So does one's emotional reaction. A decision and then behavior can follow.

Internal reactions are further along the sequence than Psychological Roots and have a different role. Knowing the difference between a Psychological Root and an internal reaction has important consequences, as will often be seen in this book.

A cognitive internal reaction can generate a Psychological Root. For example, a person might develop low self-esteem after reacting negatively to being discriminated against or frequently being put down. Low self-esteem that originates in early childhood is a belief. That belief might be hard to change and could last a lifetime. Judging a person's success to be due to his work ethic or his political connections (an internal reaction) could lead to certain beliefs about that person.

Maslow's hierarchy of needs

Maslow (1954) postulated that genetically-wired-in needs are hierarchical, with physiological concerns being the first priority. Maslow believed that when those initial needs are satisfied, psychological needs can then be addressed, such as need for safety. After those needs are satisfied, other needs can be addressed, such as those for love, being with others, self-esteem, self-actualization, and at the pinnacle, self-transcendence (giving oneself to a higher goal than oneself). Strong motivations can alter that hierarchy as suggested by Maslow, some critics of Maslow, and the Hidden Sequences concept. For example, people have risked their lives running into a burning building to save someone, a behavior that runs counter to the need for safety. People's need for safety can also be overridden if they are impatient, angry, or have a strong need for stimulation. For instance, people can do risky things such as texting while driving or driving at an overly high speed. Also, the need to self-actualize – such as an artist's desire to finish a painting – can sometimes be stronger than that person's need to eat, seek shelter or safety, or be accepted by others.

Headaches can be caused psychologically

Headaches often have a biological cause, but some of them can be caused psychologically. For example, "Maura" had intense headaches that had been diagnosed as migraines and for which she was given medication. Unfortunately, despite being powerful, the medicine was not always effective. When the author looked carefully at the circumstances in which the headaches occurred, a pattern appeared. The headaches occurred a short time after Maura was strongly resisted by her teenage daughter. That resistance was a result of Maura's trying to impose her will to get her daughter to stop dating a low-level boyfriend. Frustration creates internal pressure and when relief of that pressure is blocked, one result can be a headache. Another can be an increase in blood pressure. (In Hidden Sequences, mental pressures and frustrations are internal reactions.)

The Psychological Roots that seemed to contribute substantially to Maura's frustration involved her strong sense of responsibility and her belief that pressuring her daughter would be persuasive. The author helped Maura understand her daughter's Psychological Roots, such as a strong resistance to being controlled. For Maura to have an effective solution, her sense of responsibility had to be satisfied – however, it had to be done in some other way than by Maura imposing her will.

It was hard for Maura to accept the idea of not controlling her daughter. Therefore, the author changed the focus to helping Maura reclaim her previously loving connection with her daughter, something of major importance to her. To help re-establish that connection, Maura was instructed to give her daughter permission to discuss everything freely with her without being criticized. For Maura to give her daughter permission to make her own decisions without being judged or pressured by Maura was difficult for Maura to accept. To her credit, Maura realized the benefit that could result and was willing to try.

A week after initiating this approach, Maura's daughter tested it by bringing up a sensitive issue. When they talked about it, Maura carefully avoided being controlling. Over the next few weeks, Maura's daughter talked increasingly frequently about many sensitive issues. The warmth between them returned. Three weeks later, Maura's daughter voluntarily dropped her boyfriend. When her daughter did that, Maura's headaches ended.

Six months later, Maura's headaches returned. This time it was because Maura was pressuring her daughter to go to college. Once again, Maura had to be persuaded to stop trying to control her daughter. When Maura stopped doing that, her daughter's obstinacy ended and so did Maura's headaches.

Some people do not believe that psychological factors can cause strong biological effects or medical conditions. One reason is that psychological factors are invisible ("Seeing is believing", "A picture is worth 1000 words"). Another reason is that there can be a sizable time difference between a psychological cause and its effect, which makes it difficult to see that connection, as in this case.

Dreams

Dreams are internal reactions. The meaning of dreams can often be puzzling. However, the author has found that they can often be understood upon identifying the specific internal reactions, such as emotional reactions, that the person experienced during the dream and then working backward from there to identify the stimulus condition that might have triggered a similar emotion in the person's waking life. Often the dreams that concern people are unpleasant. For example, "Thad" had a dream in which he was struggling to barely stay afloat in a rough, stormy sea at night. In the dream, he was desperately fighting to reach a rocky shore and no one was there to help. The struggle created a sharp pain in his heart and that pain awakened him. When he awoke he was gasping for air, shaking, and sweating profusely.

Rather than try to interpret the dream from the tangible aspects such as the ocean, a rocky shore, or the storm, the author sought the conceptual theme of that dream. It was that Thad was being severely threatened by something that was difficult to cope with. Was there something going on in Thad's waking life that might cause such strain? Yes, and when that conceptual theme – intense struggle – was mentioned it was easy to identify: he was about to take a do-or-die PhD exam that would determine whether he could continue in his chosen field. A substantial number of prior students had failed a similar test. Facing that school exam had nothing directly to do with a stormy sea at night, but he had a *similar emotional feeling* about it because of its extreme difficulty and if he did not succeed he would experience a type of death in that he had much to lose – three years of intensive study, the end of a career he loved, and the loss of a sizable amount of money in school loans. Also similar to that stormy sea struggle was that he had no one to help him. He was entirely on his own. Until that dream, Thad had not realized how much stress he had been experiencing and how significant that graduate program was for him. When he understood what that dream was telling him, he calmed down and focused his efforts on preparing for the exam. The situation ended well: he passed with a high grade, something he could not know when he had that dream.

The ability of a dream to cause intense struggle, stress, and heart pain (which might have been a transient spasm in a heart artery) as in Thad's case exemplifies the potency that psychological aspects can have. It illustrates that what exists in a person's mind is real for that individual, which is a reason why novels and movies are compelling. Some people have had a dream that their significant other was unfaithful and then believed that it was actually the case although it was not.

Thus, even though a person may be unaware of a dream's significance, dreams can provide clues about problems that bother that individual, particularly repetitive dreams. Understanding a dream often can help lessen a person's distress, as in Thad's case. The author has found that when the real-life problem is solved, a disturbing dream related to that problem no longer occurs.

A possible explanation of dreams' potency is that during sleep, internal reactions such as emotions, when strong enough, reach some level of awareness. However, there is only limited cognitive ability to make sense of those raw reactions. For this reason it is useful to focus on the emotions involved in the dream. Since negatives are stronger than positives, dreams are often likely to manifest strong negative emotions. Those emotional reactions are likely to originate in the person's waking life. Hence it should be possible to connect the emotional theme of a dream with a similar emotional theme in the person's waking life.

The foundation of feelings and behaviors

Feelings and behaviors might seem to arise by themselves or appear to be the result of a single stimulus. They might seem haphazard, or illogical, or the result of an overactive imagination. However, processes such as Psychological Roots and Hidden Sequences are at work, even though unknown. The effect that stimuli have is not obvious because they act below awareness on substrates such as Psychological or Biological Roots. Also not apparent is that what appears to be a single stimulus could be a mixture of stimuli, with each aspect impacting a different Psychological Root.

People are unlikely to realize that when they try to change feelings or behavior directly – such as by trying to squelch an action of theirs or by telling someone what to do – it might not work if the originating cause is not modified. Trying to change a behavior without tackling the cause is why New Year's resolutions are unlikely to have a long-lasting effect, such as when people pledge to diet or give up alcohol. It is also why many well-intentioned campaigns to end undesirable behaviors like smoking cigarettes and other addictions might not be effective, even though the intention is admirable.

Medications address internal reactions and therefore can lessen internal symptoms that result from psychological causes, but they do not change Psychological Roots. As a result, symptoms are treated and people may have to take psychotropic medications for a long time, sometimes without end. Hidden Sequences also suggests that if the reasons people use drugs are not changed, waging war on drugs is insufficient. Hidden Sequences also explains why prisons largely fail to rehabilitate criminals – jail is not designed to change Psychological Roots. Incarceration is also a turn-off that can generate defiance and opposition. (Chapters 27 – 30 in Section II describe a constructive method of psychotherapy.)

Modifiers

Internal reactions and overt behaviors can be affected by factors that amplify or diminish their effects. *'Modifiers'* can direct, redirect, or stop internal reactions and overt behaviors such as by shaping, overriding, or stopping Psychological Roots, internal reactions, and overt behaviors. As an example, an employee might put a clamp on his strong negative reaction to an unpleasant boss to avoid possible retaliation and losing his job. If his feelings remain bottled up, he might subsequently vent that pent-up pressure on an object or someone other than his boss, perhaps something safe to attack, such as a pillow, book, or an individual weaker than himself. Freud called this type of behavior displacement. (Another term for a releasing one's irritation on a substitute would be *'emotional spillover'*. When modifiers are beliefs – such as strategies – they are Psychological Roots.)

'Civilizing factors' (*'civilizing modifiers'* and *'civilizing Psychological Roots'*) are modifiers that foster civil behavior. Without civilizing Psychological Roots and modifiers that are acquired through training or accidental experience, humans would be savages. Some anti-social, violent, or sociopathic behaviors are due to not having acquired civilizing Psychological Roots or using them, or experiencing an emotional state that impedes using those restraints. Some aspects that interfere with using civilizing factors include experiencing intense emotions such as anger, having inadequate psychological modifiers, using inhibition-releasing substances (e.g., alcohol), and having brain damage.

Modifiers of Hidden Sequences

Modifiers can affect the various components of Hidden Sequences. A Hidden Sequence that has a modifier but not an initiating stimulus is a *'Modified Root Sequence'*. When a Modified Root Sequence does not eventuate in a behavior it can be abbreviated as **Psychological Root → internal reaction + modifier → modified internal reaction.** (See Figure 9).

A *'Modified Root Sequence'* in which overt behavior occurs can be abbreviated as **Psychological Root → internal reaction + modifier → modified internal reaction → observable behavior.** (See Figure 9.)

A Modified Hidden Sequence that is triggered by a stimulus is a *'Modified Stimulus-and-Root Sequence'*. When no behavioral outcome occurs, the sequence can be abbreviated as **stimulus + Psychological Root → internal reaction + modifier → modified internal reaction.** (See Figure 10).

A *'Modified Stimulus-and-Root Sequence'* in which overt behavior occurs can be abbreviated as **stimulus + Psychological Root → internal reaction + modifier → modified internal reaction → observable behavior.** (See Figure 10).

All Hidden Sequences have an internal reaction, however, overt behavior might not necessarily result. This leads to four prominent possibilities when Hidden Sequences occur:
- No observable behavior, with no modifying factors.
- No observable behavior, owing to modifying factors.
- Observable behavior with no modifying factors involved.
- Observable behavior that has been affected by modifying factors.

Some implications of modifying factors

Some modifiers can facilitate and heighten the effect of Psychological Roots, internal reactions, and behaviors, and some modifiers can dampen them or clamp their effect. Every component of Hidden Sequences can be affected by modifiers. Some modifiers can increase the likelihood that a person will enter a state of uncontrollability (e.g., because of absolute thinking or a high emotional level), while some modifiers can decrease that likelihood (e.g., because of using an effective problem-solving strategy or having a moderate emotional level). There are individuals who do not readily modify their internal reactions or overt behavior. Examples include people who are impulsive or who intentionally resist modifying themselves (e.g., criminals and extremists). Psychotherapy can be used to help people utilize modifiers.

Modifiers can also act as filters. Children are likely to have fewer modifiers than adults, a reason their statements can be amusing (see videotapes of Art Linkletter's TV show that featured children's unrehearsed statements).

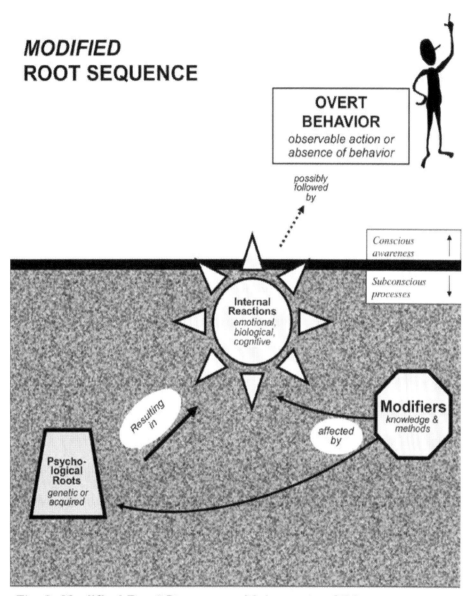

Fig. 9. **Modified Root Sequence**. Major parts of this psychological process are subconscious (below the dark line). Observable parts are above the dark line.

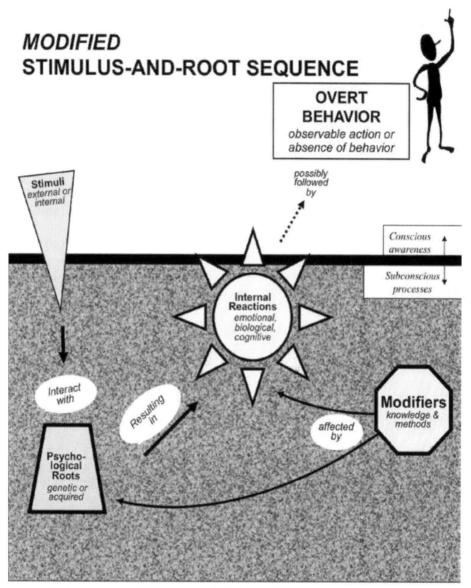

Fig. 10. **Modified Stimulus-and-Root Sequence**. Major parts of this psychological process are subconscious (below the dark line). Observable parts are above the dark line.

Components of Hidden Sequences can be stimuli that set off other Hidden Sequences, for example, Mary's behavior could be a stimulus for Jon's thinking or taking action. Internal reactions can be modified, so can non-verbal actions such as smiling and frowning. Those aspects, in turn, can affect other people and their behavior. Multiple internal reactions (e.g., thoughts) and overt behaviors can kindle multiple Hidden Sequences. Some behaviors are attempts to modify what has previously been said or done.

Predicting the likelihood of behavior

The ability to predict an observable behavior and its strength is affected by many factors. For example, predicting behavior increases when a person's internal reactions are known compared to just knowing the person's Psychological Roots, since internal reactions are closer in proximity to behaviors than Psychological Roots in Hidden Sequences. Predictability is still greater if both Psychological Roots and internal reactions are known. Awareness of a person's previous behavior pattern can also help. Knowing what the impinging stimuli are can also be useful, but much depends on knowing what Psychological Roots are impacted.

The degree of intensity is important. For example, a strong external stimulus is more likely to generate an overt behavior than a weak stimulus. A strong stimulus has a higher likelihood of eventuating in a strong behavior compared to a weak stimulus. Some internal reactions have a greater probability than others to generate an overt behavior, for example, a strong emotional reaction might be more likely to produce an overt behavior than a thought, evaluation, or cognitive decision. Some Psychological Roots have a greater effect than others. Some modifiers increase the likelihood that a behavior will occur while others diminish or block that likelihood.

A high level of emotion produces a strong pressure to act, such as by laughing, arguing, venting verbally, or acting physically. (A high level of emotion can be 8 or above on a 0-10 scale, see Figure 6). The lower the intensity of emotional reactions, the greater the opportunity for modifying factors to exert an effect.

Thus, the number and intensity of the various elements affect the occurrence of overt behaviors, and therefore predictability. The lack of a 1-to-1 connection among the constituents of Hidden Sequences makes predicting the likelihood of an overt behavior a matter of probability. (Such estimates are possible and are described in Chapter 32).

Mowrer's S-O-R formulation

A major reason for behaviorism's popularity is its ability to define, introduce, and measure stimuli (S) and responses (R) objectively, compared to the difficulty of working with subconscious processes and hypothetical constructs (Skinner, 1974). Mowrer (1950), despite being a behaviorist, recognized the importance of internal processes. In place of stimuli and responses alone, he employed an S-O-R frame of reference in which 'O' represented the organism. Hidden Sequences helps elucidate the intermediate 'O' aspect in S-O-R, expanding Mowrer's three-elements to four: S-P-I-B, in which S = stimulus, P = Psychological Root, I = internal reaction, and B = overt behavior. (Both I and B are responses.) Adding modifying factors produces a five-part sequence: S-P-I-M-B, in which M = modifying factors. This delineation of components inside the organism helps clarify what appears on the surface to be a simple S-R connection. The sub-surface elements in Hidden Sequences (Psychological Roots, internal reactions, and modifiers), and aspects that are observable (stimuli and overt responses) can be defined, measured, and studied scientifically.

Preparedness

Stimuli can only trigger responses an organism is capable of making. For example, humans can speak because doing so is biologically possible whereas other primates do not have that capability. A bird cannot speak because birds are not wired by nature with that capability (although parrots can imitate a few words), but birds have special abilities that humans do not have, such as flying. Seligman and Hager (1972) termed the ability to engage in a particular behavior, *'preparedness'*.

Preparedness is implicit in Mowrer's S-O-R conceptualization and in Hidden Sequences as intermediate aspects. Both biological and psychological aspects are involved. For example, humans have a wired-in need to connect with others, which drives relating to other humans. This perspective suggests that preparedness involves an *inclination* to behave in a particular way as well as a *capability* of doing so. For example, birds seem *inclined* to use their wings to fly, in addition to being *able* to fly, which would help explain why baby birds start using their wings immediately upon being pushed out of the nest by their parents.

An inclination to engage in a particular behavior helps account for why it is easier to condition some behaviors than others. For example, pigeons can readily learn how to play table tennis (Skinner, 1974) owing to their excellent eyesight and tendency to move their beak forward. Those attributes enable them to contact a ping-pong ball quickly coming at them. However, pigeons have great difficulty learning to bowl because they are not inclined to move their beak sideways, which would be required for them to hit a small bowling ball down a miniature bowling alley (Skinner, 1974). Humans may have both a biological and psychological *inclination* to speak, not just the *ability* to speak. Perhaps, therefore, both an inclination and a capability exist both biologically and psychologically. The psychological aspects include Psychological Roots and internal reactions.

Non-verbal aspects

Some internal reactions are observable, such as facial expressions and sounds. For example, a joyful person might smile or laugh. People experiencing fear might look tense, have a tight voice, vibrate, and focus narrowly on a fear-arousing stimulus. A person who feels like a failure might grimace, appear downcast, slouch, be irritable, or lack motivation. People can unintentionally reveal some of their internal reactions through non-verbal behavior, such as their body language and exclamations. Most of what is communicated is non-verbal (e.g., Burgoon, Guerrero, & Floyd, 2009) and, perhaps, is related to the strength of internal reactions.

How effective is it to try to change a behavior or a feeling directly?

The shortest distance between two points is a straight line so it can seem straightforward to try to change something in a direct way. That can work in geometry and with many material tasks but can be ineffective with psychological matters since trying to change a behavior directly would tackle the end portion of a Hidden Sequence. Hidden Sequences begin with Psychological Roots and a persuasive attempt that is not consistent with the recipient's roots can turn off the recipient. An example is Mary rejecting Jon's viewpoint because it conflicts with her beliefs, and Jon's being turned off by Mary's opposing his concerns.

It might seem counterintuitive that presenting facts might not persuade, especially since it would be hoped that people might prefer to be correct. However, it is well-known that giving people evidence is unlikely to persuade many individuals, for example, with regard to stopping smoking, using alcohol, or eating saturated fat. Trying to change behavior directly is also why arguing, detoxification for addiction, and will-power are less likely to be effective than satisfying people's underlying Psychological Roots. For example, giving people a constructive alternative way to satisfy their concerns can be especially useful when they resist direct attempts to persuade them. (More on this issue in Chapters 25 and 26 regarding social influence.)

People's resistance to change can also get in the way of trying to modify internal reactions directly. For example, telling anxious people to "get a grip on themselves" is unlikely to end their anxiety, and telling a depressed person to think positively is unlikely to resolve their down mood. Similarly, venting angry feelings might feel good at the moment but does not fix the problem and can alienate others and worsen the situation. Raising the serotonin levels of suicidal individuals might help lessen suicidal ideation (Mann, Arango, & Underwood, 1990; Arango, Huang, Underwood, & Mann, 2003), but if the primary cause of a person's suicidal ideation is a sense of hopelessness, then increased serotonin can offer only temporary relief. Relying on medication alone, such as taking an anti-depressant to end smoking or obsessive-compulsive disorder (OCD), would be a detour from treating the Psychological Roots that impel a person to smoke or have OCD.

In short, directly trying to change someone's behavior or thinking might seem like a good idea, but it is often insufficient and even antagonistic, and to that extent impractical. Identifying and satisfying Psychological Roots might seem to be indirect, slow, and counterintuitive because it requires the persuader to think abstractly before attempting to persuade. However, the author has found that doing so has a better chance of succeeding and often is relatively rapid, therefore is likely to be the method of choice, especially when other methods falter. If a persuasive attempt does not work, it is better to cease that attempt and try a Psychological Roots approach (see Spike's case in Chapter 18, and Chapters 25 and 26 regarding social influence).

There is a place for direct attempts to change behavior

Directly addressing behavior is useful when it is not feasible to work with Psychological Roots, such as when they are not known or hard to discern, or a situation is urgent, or a recipient is extremely resistant or unable to provide sufficient clues about his/her underlying issues.

Stimulus conditions

Internal reactions and behavior can be temporarily altered by changing relevant stimulus conditions. However, if the pertinent Psychological Roots are not changed and steps are not taken to prevent future difficulties, a similar outcome can occur. Hence, it is insufficient just to address current stimuli alone. (How to identify Psychological Roots is described in Chapter 6.)

Some well-known measures of Psychological Roots, internal reactions, and behavior

There are some well-established assessments of Psychological Roots such as measures of self-efficacy (Bandura, 1977), intellectual ability (e.g., Stanford-Binet/Terman & Merrill, 1960; Wechsler, 1981), and dysfunctional beliefs (Weissman & Beck, 1978; deGraaf, Roelofs, & Huibers, 2009). There also are many measures of confidence and self-esteem. Assessments of factors other than Psychological Roots, such as those listed below, can often provide useful clues for identifying Psychological Roots.

Assessments of internal reactions

Some well-established assessments of internal reactions include the galvanic skin response (e.g., Boucsein, 2012), anxiety (e.g., Taylor, 1953, Rorschach test (e.g., Exner, 2002), and the Holtzman Inkblot Test (Holtzman, Thorpe, Swartz, & Herron, 1961). Also word association (Jung, 1953), sentence completion (e.g., Lah, 1989), helplessness (Seligman, 1975; Abramson, Seligman, & Teasdale, 1978), and cognitive styles (e.g., Briggs Myers, McCaulley, Quenk, Hammer, & Mitchell, 2009).

Assessments of overt behavior

Some well-established assessments of behaviors include measures of alcoholism, depression (e.g., Beck, Steer, & Brown, 1996), and social desirability responses (Crowne & Marlowe, 1960). Some others include the California Psychological Inventory (CPI; Gough, 1987), angry behavior (e.g., Snell, Shuck, Mosley, & Hite, 1995), Dawson & Room, 2000), and aggression (e.g., Orpinas & Frankowski, 2001). Still others include emotional intelligence (Mayer, Salovey, Caruso, & Sitarenios, 2003), rumination (Feldman, Joormann, & Johnson, 2008), attention deficit disorder (e.g., Edebol, Lars, & Norlander, 2013), and couples' relationships (Gottman, 2015).

Joint assessments of internal reactions and overt behavior

Some measures assess both internal reactions and overt behaviors, such as the Thematic Apperception Test (Murray, 1943), the Minnesota Multiphasic Personality Inventory (MMPI; McKinley, J. C, & Hathaway, S. R. 1944), and the Rorschach Test (Choca, 2012).

Aspects that affect the outcome of Hidden Sequences

Many things affect the outcome of Hidden Sequences such as competing factors, modifiers (e.g., amplifiers and diminishers), and perception of consequences. Outcomes can also be affected by more than one Hidden Sequence occurring at the same time or immediately afterward. Obstacles to internal reactions and behaviors can be present, impeding some actions and triggering others. Much depends on the nature of the obstacles, the potency of the consequences, and the individual's Psychological Roots (such as goals, strategies, and skills).

Attempts to change behavior and stimulus conditions

People often try to change someone's undesirable behavior directly, such as by telling a person what to do or by using rewards or punishments. Another frequent strategy is presenting facts and logic. Many people argue or criticize, pressure, coerce, or threaten. Such efforts are unlikely to be as effective as satisfying or modifying the Psychological Roots involved. It is possible to employ a combination of Psychological Roots and behavioral methods (see the example involving "Spike" in Chapter 18.)

Common characteristics of Psychological Roots

Despite the extensive variation in Psychological Roots, many roots have a number of underlying characteristics in common, some of which have been described earlier. Some of the common characteristics of Psychological Roots are that they:
1. Act as thresholds (e.g., criteria for evaluating success and failure, what is acceptable vs. what is not).
2. Create a drive (e.g., a motivation that stems from a need, interest, or specific fear).
3. Can generate a Root Sequence (including an internal reaction and perhaps a behavior).
4. Can trigger a Hidden Sequence when impacted by a relevant, above-threshold stimulus.
5. Produce a positive emotional reaction when something is consistent with them.
6. Produce a negative emotional reaction when something is inconsistent with them.
(See Box 1, Items 1-83 for a more extensive list of common characteristics. Some of the aspects in Box 1 are addressed in later chapters.)

Durability of Psychological Roots

Some Psychological Roots exist for a lifetime, such as those at the core of an individual's personality structure. The durability of those Psychological Roots contributes to the stability of personality and behavior patterns. One of the reasons is that Psychological Roots that are basic to a person's personality are deeply embedded within Psychological Root structures (described in Chapter 8), and that circumstance reduces their likelihood of changing. As a result, it is often difficult to overcome aspects that remain from childhood.

Biological Hidden Sequences

There also are Biological Roots (e.g., needs for air, food, water, and shelter) and biological Hidden Sequences. The latter includes biological internal reactions (e.g., the Krebs energy cycle mentioned earlier) and overt biological outcomes (e.g., eating, breathing, and sleeping). Whether an overt outcome occurs depends on the factors involved.

Among the many associations of psychology and biology is that some Biological Hidden Sequences have a psychological effect, such as epinephrine's ability to heighten excitability, and serotonin's ability to lighten a down mood. Some Psychological Hidden Sequences have biological effects, such as when frustration and anger increase blood pressure, stress increases fatty acids in the blood stream, and fear triggers a large secretion of epinephrine (adrenalin). Whether biological or psychological aspects are the most prominent depends on the strength of the variables in a given circumstance.

Something biological is the most likely cause of biological disorders and something psychological is the most likely cause of psychological disorders. This understanding helps explain why trying to find the biological cause of some psychological conditions such as bipolar disorder has not borne much success thus far. It also explains why even though a chemical imbalance (an internal reaction) exists in depression, psychological treatments work as well or even better than medication (Lacasse & Leo, 2005; Kirsch, 2009). Also, symptom flare-ups can occur while a depressed individual is on a biological treatment regime such as medication or ECT. (More on this issue later.)

BOX 1. SOME CHARACTERISTICS OF PSYCHOLOGICAL ROOTS
A. Pertaining to all Psychological Roots
1. Psychological Roots are sub-surface factors that lead to internal reactions (e.g., thoughts, attitudes, decisions, and emotional reactions) and overt behavior, akin to the policies of a company or the constitution of a nation.
2. Psychological Roots are internal psychological factors that generate a drive (e.g., a drive to satisfy needs or to stay within comfort zones).
3. Psychological Roots provide a frame of reference for perceiving, understanding, and processing information.
4. Psychological Roots are guidelines for thinking, reacting, and behaving.
5. Psychological Roots act as thresholds, produce an internal reaction such as an emotion or thought (e.g., attaining a goal triggers a positive emotional reaction; not meeting an expectation triggers a negative emotional reaction; beyond a tipping point is a state of uncontrollability).
6. A positive emotional reaction occurs when something is consistent with a Psychological Root (e.g., aspects that fit a person's frame of reference are likely to be acceptable; attaining a goal elicits a pleasant feeling).
7. A negative emotional reaction occurs for aspects inconsistent with a Psychological Root (e.g., aspects not fitting a person's frame of reference are likely to be rejected; failure contradicts expectations, which produces disappointment).
8. Relevant stimuli impact Psychological Roots, triggering an internal reaction in a Stimulus-and-Root Sequence, which might lead to overt behavior, depending on attendant factors.
9. Everyone has genetically wired-in Psychological Roots (e.g., need for safety, need to be connected with other people, desire for pleasant stimulation, avoidance of negative arousal).
10. The extent and intensity of Psychological Roots vary in degree in different people, (e.g., widely different levels of need for safety and abilities such as music, athletics, & mathematics), as with genetic Biological Roots (e.g., needs for air, water, shelter). Hence, some people can appear to be extremely different from each other because of being at opposite ends on the same continuum).
11. Linking of Psychological Roots can occur when Psychological Roots are consistent with one another.
12. New information can be filtered out when it is inconsistent with an existing Psychological Root ("filtering").
13. Something inconsistent with an existing Psychological Root can link to a short term goal (e.g., remembering a phone number, rote memorization of information for an exam).

BOX 1. *(continued) CHARACTERISTICS OF PSYCHOLOGICAL ROOTS*

14. Linking of something new that is inconsistent with an existing Psychological Root can occur if it is pre-shaped to be consistent with an existing Psychological Root ("pre-shaping").
15. How genetic Psychological Roots are expressed is a function of a person's acquired Psychological Roots (e.g., need for safety may be satisfied by being with people an individual believes to be safe).
16. Psychological Roots provide a lens through which stimuli are comprehended and a frame of reference for perceiving, understanding, and processing information.
17. Psychological Roots provide orientation (e.g., goals focus an effort to solve problems).
18. Psychological Roots in one hierarchy can oppose roots in another hierarchy. That can lead to an internal conflict (e.g., desire to be independent can be opposed by strong dependency needs; desire to enlarge knowledge can be opposed by a need for stability).
19. Psychological Roots operate at a subconscious level, thus are hidden & largely unknown, making them amorphous, intangible, underestimated, abstract, and misjudged (e.g., their role in generating thoughts, feelings, and behavior; expectations' potency). Yet , people can often recognize Psychological Roots after they become known.
20. A Psychological Root can be overshadowed by a more dominant Psychological Root (e.g., will power can temporarily overcome a Psychological Root, such as need for safety).
21. Linked Psychological Roots form hierarchical chains of Psychological Roots.
22. Each Psychological Root hierarchy is founded in a genetic Psychological Root.
23. When a Psychological Root changes, roots further along a hierarchy align with that change (a "flow-down effect", cf. Piaget's assimilation concept, in Flavell, 1966).
24. Psychological Roots form clusters (connected groupings of related Psychological Roots), sub-clusters and categories (cf. Piaget's schemas in Flavell, 1966).
25. Each Psychological Root has a drive for it to be engaged.
26. The drives of related Psychological Roots are additive (e.g., each root adds to the intensity of a cluster, thus large clusters have a particularly strong impetus to be engaged, such as music ability).

BOX 1. *(continued)* CHARACTERISTICS OF *Psychological Roots*

27. Psychological Roots are physically real, not imaginary or ephemeral (e.g., values can be lifelong).
28. Psychological Roots can be empirically identified and measured.
29. Psychological Roots can be tested in scientific studies.

   B. *Pertaining to some Psychological Roots*
30. Genetic Psychological Roots are the foundation of root hierarchies.
31. Most Psychological Roots in root hierarchies, clusters, sub-clusters, and categories are acquired.
32. Initially acquired Psychological Roots link to genetic Psychological Roots (e.g., a child's belief that parents provide safety, comfort, and pleasure might be linked to safety and stability needs).
33. Psychological Roots other than those initially acquired, link with previously acquired roots, such as beliefs about acceptable customs (cf. Piaget's concept of assimilation, Flavell, 1966).
34. Strategies used for problem-solving include beliefs (hence are Psychological Roots, e.g., belief that there usually is a good solution, or that that tasks should be broken into parts, key aspects tackled first, & a variety of solutions sought).
35. The more effective a person's problem-solving strategies the greater that person's hardiness (ability to deal with difficult circumstances) and resilience (ability to rebound from setbacks such as states of uncontrollability). Some effective strategies are strong social skills, analytical ability, self-confidence, and desire to take the initiative in creating solutions.
36. A pertinent Psychological Root is one that is salient in a situation.
37. A Psychological Root that is not salient is a background Psychological Root. Most roots are in the background much of the time, awaiting being impacted by a stimulus or generate Response-Sequences.
38. The net mood from a number of Root Sequences is a net result of a combination of Psychological Roots.
39. When conditions are appropriate (e.g., high emotional intensity), internal reactions lead to skeletal muscle behaviors (e.g., speaking, athletic activity).
40. Genetic Psychological Roots (e.g., needs for safety and to be emotionally connected with others) generate especially strong internal reactions.

BOX 1. *(continued) CHARACTERISTICS OF PSYCHOLOGICAL ROOTS*

41. The closer an acquired Psychological Root is to a genetic root in a hierarchy, the stronger the internal reaction it is likely to generate (e.g., low self-esteem that is acquired in early life).

42. Stimuli that directly impact genetic Psychological Roots are likely to trigger especially strong internal reactions (e.g., need for safety, need to be emotionally connected with others).

43. Individual differences in Psychological Roots lead to people having different goals and using different methods to achieve goals.

44. The closer an acquired Psychological Root is to a genetic root in a hierarchy, the stronger its internal reaction is likely to be when that root is impacted.

45. Distress-prone (negative) Psychological Roots generate negative emotions, which are often strong (e.g., low threshold for negative arousal, intolerance of failure).

46. Eustress-prone (positive) Psychological Roots generate positive emotions (e.g., pleasure at achieving a goal).

47. A stimulus' effect can be very strong when it impacts a Psychological Root at or near the foundation of personality, such as genetic Psychological Roots (e.g., a need to be emotionally connected with others) and core acquired Psychological Roots (e.g., values).

48. Psychological Roots can be directly involved in generating an internal reaction or a behavior as part of a Root Sequence or Stimulus-and-Root Sequence. Those are pertinent Psychological Roots when that happens.

49. Acquired roots range widely (e.g., concerns, beliefs, knowledge), making everyone unique, even identical twins.

50. Individual differences range widely in genetic and acquired Psychological Roots, pre-shaping, and consistency or inconsistency with Psychological Roots. Hence, different people can have a different reaction to the same circumstance, and it is unlikely that anyone fully perceives actual reality (cf. Allport & Postman, 1948).

51. The result of stimuli that impact opposing Psychological Roots can be a mixture of their effects (e.g., a blend of positive and negative emotions) or a sequential effect (e.g., alternately liking or disliking another person).

BOX 1. *(continued)* CHARACTERISTICS OF PSYCHOLOGICAL ROOTS

52. Early Psychological Roots are likely to be more general than later roots (e.g., need for safety relates to a much wider range than believing in looking both ways before crossing a street).
53. Psychological Roots are increasingly specific and tangible the further removed they are from genetic roots at the foundation of a hierarchy (e.g., belief that matches are dangerous vs. need for safety).
54. The earliest Psychological Roots are genetically wired-in and together with roots acquired early in life, form the core structure of personality.
55. Later Psychological Roots are acquired after early Psychological Roots and are consistent with roots acquired earlier in life.
56. New Psychological Roots linked to early Psychological Roots can have broad effects on a person's thinking and personality (e.g., a philosophy of life or a scientific discovery that occur late in life).
57. The earliest Psychological Roots are genetically wired-in and form the core structure of personality together with roots acquired early in life.
59. New Psychological Roots directly linked to early Psychological Roots can have strong effects on a person's thinking and personality (e.g., a philosophy of life or a scientific discovery late in a person's life).
60. A change in a later Psychological Root must be consistent with the earlier Psychological Roots in its hierarchy. Adopting a position that is inconsistent with a pre-existing root will create internal pressure to backslide to the initial opinion.
61. Some clusters may be inconsistent with Psychological Roots in other clusters (e.g., a desire to retain some things vs. change other things; a desire to be moderate in some things vs. be extreme in other things).
62. Psychological Roots that are inconsistent with one another can operate in sequence (e.g., a desire for ice cream can dominate on one day, vs. a desire for pizza another day), or vacillation or indecision can occur (e.g., desire to be independent vs. desire to be dependent).
63. The result of stimuli impacting opposing Psychological Roots is a a mixture (e.g., a blend of positive and negative emotions) or a sequence (e.g., alternately liking or disliking another person).
64. Some aspects that are not Psychological Roots (e.g., attitudes, conclusions, past experiences) can convert to Psychological Roots, such as a belief.
65. Some Psychological Roots are long-term (e.g., genetic need for safety, acquired value to be diligent, and goal to have a successful marriage).

BOX 1. *(continued) CHARACTERISTICS OF PSYCHOLOGICAL ROOTS*

66. Some Psychological Roots are short-term (e.g., a soon-to-be-attained goal such as passing an upcoming exam), some are long-term (e.g., need for safety).
67. Short-term memory can occur when it is connected to a short-term Psychological Root (e.g., a goal that will soon end, like remembering a phone number or memorizing by rote for a coming exam).
68. Long-term memory can occur when it is connected with long-term Psychological Roots (e.g., genetic roots such as a need for safety, long-term such as a desire to be effective in an occupation).
69. An emotional reaction can aid long-term retention when it is related to a long-term Psychological Root (e.g., a liked party or disturbing incident during childhood).
71. Some Psychological Roots are permanent (e.g., genetic Psychological Roots such as need for safety) or semi-permanent (e.g., core personality roots such as basic values like a strong work ethic).
72. Psychological Roots can be modified to become short- or long-term.
73. People can have similar Psychological Roots (e.g., from the same sub-group) but different experiences mean that no two people have completely similar Psychological Roots, including identical twins, persons from the same neighborhood, schools, and religion.
74. Lower-order (later Psychological Roots) are more changeable than high-order (early) roots.
75. Genetic Psychological Roots (e.g., need for safety) are broad and affect a wider range of issues than acquired Psychological Roots (e.g., concern about being cautious when in a high crime area).
76. Unresolved issues are Psychological Roots (e.g., seeking emotional support owing to emotional deprivation in childhood, unquenched anger, and desire of adopted children to know their biological parents).
77. Psychological Roots are the origination of many behaviors since behaviors result from some internal reactions.
78. A stimulus can trigger a long-past memory that then generates a Hidden Sequence (e.g., as in a PTSD flashback).
79. Many Psychological Roots are absolutes (e.g., some Psychological Roots that are genetic such as a need for safety and some that are acquired early in life such as basic values).
80. A wide variety of Psychological Roots affect Psychological Homeostasis and are involved in emotional and cognitive states of uncontrollability.
81. Different levels of genetic Psychological Roots are inherited (e.g., a low threshold for emotional arousal, a strong need for safety, a strong need to be connected with others, a strong drive for closure).
82. The level of genetic Psychological Roots can contribute to psychological disorders (e.g., low threshold for arousal can be a factor in anxiety, depression, OCD, and borderline personality disorder.
83. Genetic Psychological Roots can be treated psychologically (see the relevant chapters in this book).

A practical application of this information

Problems can continue to occur if the cause is not dealt with successfully. Psychological Roots are the originating point in Hidden Sequences, therefore effectively treating a psychological problem is aided by directly addressing those roots and the stimulus conditions that impact those roots. Doing this is not obvious because of the hidden nature of Psychological Roots (e.g., a low threshold for negative arousal, a sense of vulnerability, and hard-to-meet expectations). Feelings are internal reactions and therefore proximal causes, not the originating causes of behavior. Therefore, when trying to create change, it would be better to modify Psychological Roots than to try to control or change feelings, thoughts, decisions, or behavior in a direct manner. Will-power and medicine can help to modify psychologically-caused issues at times, but often only temporarily.

When a diagnosis of a psychological disorder is made – such as depression, anxiety, obsessive-compulsive disorder, or addiction – that judgment tends to be about what is observable, such as behavior, rather than the hidden cause. (How to identify Psychological Roots and treat disorders is described in Chapter 6.)[24]

A Hidden Sequences perspective offers an understanding of what takes place below awareness. Understanding the separate roles of each component permits focusing on those elements that are particularly relevant in a given circumstance (e.g., Psychological Roots, such as beliefs and concerns, and Hidden Sequences). Thoughts and emotional feelings are internal reactions that are intermediate aspects of Hidden Sequences. Behavior, which may or may not occur, is an overt outcome. This perspective regarding sub-surface psychological aspects is particularly useful when complex phenomena occur such as psychological disorders and terrorism. For example, an effort to prevent terrorism would include identifying the Psychological Roots that contribute to it, the stages that lead to becoming a terrorist, the reasons people join terrorist groups vs. being lone wolves (cf. McCauley & Moskalenko, 2017), and strategies for modifying those roots to create more constructive behaviors.

---

[24] People are unlikely to know their Psychological Roots (e.g., their expectations, beliefs, and thresholds) since those roots are largely subconscious, or to know that they have many wired-in psychological needs (e.g., for stability, safety, and closure), or even some of their own subtle abilities, nor the significance of their Psychological Roots.

Summary of two basic types of Hidden Sequences:
1. In a Root Sequence, a Psychological Root (e.g., a need, goal, or belief) generates an internal reaction (e.g., a thought, evaluation, or emotional reaction), from which an overt behavior might result.
2. In a Stimulus-and-Root Sequence, a stimulus impacts a Psychological Root, producing an internal reaction from which an overt behavior might result.

In both types of Hidden Sequences, a behavior might or might not occur as a result of a variety of attendant factors such as the intensity of the internal reaction.

Chapter 5. MULTIPLE HIDDEN SEQUENCES AND MULTIPLE STIMULI

Hidden Sequences can occur soon after one another, sometimes rapidly so, such as when one thought leads to another or a comment by someone triggers a comment from another person. An example is probably not needed, but the following instance may be worthwhile knowing. "Troy" became upset when his teenage daughter, "Myra", canceled appointments and procrastinated in working on her assignments. When Troy reminded Myra to be on time for an upcoming situation, Myra felt guilty and in her ensuing resentment said unkind things to Troy. That upset Troy, who, in defending himself, reminded Myra that she had failed to meet many obligations in the past. His criticism angered Myra and she went ballistic. The resulting back-and-forth between them escalated to an extreme that neither could tolerate. The resulting strain between them led to their not speaking to each other for days. This pattern of anger and despondency kept recurring for years, with Myra feeling trapped and Troy feeling unappreciated. It was *'Multiple Sequences'* gone bad.

Despite Troy and Myra's high intelligence and years of counseling with a variety of therapists, they did not know about Psychological Roots nor that both of them were driven by the same Psychological Root, which was a strong sense of responsibility. That root explained why Myra procrastinated: she did not want to deal with issues that might cause her to fail to meet her responsibilities. It also explained why Troy was bothered about Myra's not meeting her obligations.

They had no idea about the underlying cause of their conflict or how to get their concerns satisfied. As a result, each considered the other to be unpleasant, unreasonable, and unkind. They were able to develop a compatible solution in part because the author explained that a key objective each of them had been trying to accomplish – getting the other person to be responsible – was already present without their realizing it. This case illustrates how Psychological Roots can be unseen, unknown, and overlooked by psychologists as well as non-psychologists. (A compatible method for resolving interpersonal problems is described in Chapters 20 - 23.)

Two other examples of multiple sequences are:
• "Clara" asked "Joan" a question that had several different facets to it and Joan answered each aspect separately. (Various parts of Clara's question

impacted a different Psychological Roots in Joan. Each of Joan's answers created a different Hidden Sequence.[25])

- "Sawyer" was hostile to "Reggie" (a behavior), regretted doing so (an internal reaction) and then apologized to Reggie (a behavior).

Sequential Sequences

A thought can trigger another thought in that same individual, and a comment made by one person can lead to thought or comment another person makes. In *'Sequential Sequences'* like these, one person's thought or comment is a stimulus that impacts Psychological Roots in that same individual or another person. Other examples of Sequential Sequences are repeated ruminating or worrying (due to the same Psychological Roots being continually impacted without there being an effective conclusion). The first Hidden Sequence in a Sequential Sequence is the *'initial sequence'*. That initial sequence might be difficult to discern when there are many back-and-forth sequences.

Simultaneous Sequences

A *'Simultaneous Sequence'* occurs when some Hidden Sequences take place at about the same time. Such simultaneous occurrences can happen when each aspect of a single stimulus condition impacts a different Psychological Root. For example, when Duncan compliments Celeste it might: a) generate a positive emotional response in Celeste by connecting with her desire for emotional support, but might *also:* b) create a negative emotional reaction in Celeste by her believing that the compliment might not be deserved. In addition, the compliment might: c) counter Celeste's desire to be self-effacing. This example shows how a single stimulus can engage different Psychological Roots because it can trigger separate Hidden Sequences. The result can be mixed feelings (internal reactions) and behaviors.

---

[25] Actors can create multiple Hidden Sequences in their performance by blending a number of Psychological Roots, internal reactions, and behaviors related to their character's multiple goals, beliefs, expectations, values, rules, etc. Synonyms for multiple Hidden Sequences are hidden cascades, multiple psychological sequences, multiple underlying processes, motivational cascades, and action cascades.

An implication of Multiple Sequences

Even a single statement or action can have more than one effect if it impacts different Psychological Roots (mentioned above). Multiple Sequences can impede being able to pinpoint the initial Hidden Sequence and the key Psychological Roots. That obfuscation and the hidden nature of subconscious processes can lead to treating symptoms of a disorder rather than the cause. If a symptomatic treatment provides some relief, it can be thought to address the originating cause and therefore, mistakenly, might be considered sufficient. Examples include people's attempts to lose weight by dieting when the actual cause of a weight problem is psychological, treating an addiction by abstaining from the addictive behavior, and treating tension and anxiety using relaxation and meditation. Those symptomatic treatments can have some success, and when they do, people can conclude that the cause is being addressed. An example of this is a belief that companions who drink are the cause of a person's alcohol problem, or that fear is the cause of addictions, or that low income is the cause of crime. An understanding of Multiple Hidden Sequences and Psychological Roots offers a more appropriate lens with which to understand complex behaviors.

Stimulus conditions

Stimulus conditions can be potent and therefore external stress can readily be believed to be the primary cause of a psychological condition such as anxiety, depression, and over-eating. Some stimuli can be so compelling that hidden aspects such as Psychological Roots can be overlooked. Focusing on current and past stimulus conditions can impede identifying the originating cause(s), especially when a variety of different Psychological Roots are involved.

When an outcome, such as an intense internal reaction or overt behavior seems too strong to have been caused by a mild stimulus, that mild stimulus might have been the "last straw" in a cumulative build-up. Sometimes what appears to be important might not be the key stimulus, but only what is salient. For example, "Ron" had an alcohol problem and believed that what triggered his recent binge drinking was being at home alone for several days. However, that circumstance was unlikely to have been the trigger since he had previously spent months alone without imbibing anything alcoholic. What turned out to be the stimulus for his serial drinking was his *belief* that he might not be an adequate parent, which happened when he learned that he was about to be given the primary responsibility for his children.

This example illustrates how an apparent stimulus (e.g., Ron's being alone) can be thought to be the cause of a behavior, yet the true cause can be something quite different and unapparent (in this case, Ron's lack of confidence for having sole responsibility for his children). Ron's being alone was a factor in his anxiety but not directly, because being alone gave him a great amount of time to worry about being inadequate. (Responsibility, confidence, and beliefs are Psychological Roots). Ron's desire to eliminate his stress connected with his belief that alcohol numbs unpleasantness. That combination of beliefs and multiple thinking sequences led to his being anxious (an internal reaction) and then imbibing alcohol (an overt behavior) to overcome his anxiety.

It seemed to Ron that his being alone at home caused him to drink, however being alone was not the originating cause of his drinking nor was his anxiety, rather they were *proximal* causes. The *originating* cause was a stimulus that impacted his sense of responsibility (a Psychological Root) after he was awarded primary custody of his children.

This distinction between the *originating* cause and the *proximal* cause is important because the key to ending Ron's drinking was finding a way to satisfy his sense of responsibility, which was not obvious. It might have appeared that Ron's abstaining from alcohol would be the key to solving his drinking problem, however it was not something Ron could accomplish because abstention did not address the cause of his anxiety, which was believing that he was going to fail to meet his responsibility. Ron was able to abstain from alcohol only after that Psychological Root was addressed successfully.

A practical application of this information

Overlooked stimuli can trigger Hidden Sequences, including Multiple Hidden Sequences. Salient stimuli can be mistakenly viewed as being important. Hence, it is important to identify the key stimuli and the pertinent Psychological Roots impacted by those stimuli. Identifying stimuli is often easier for people than identifying their Psychological Roots because those are almost entirely hidden. The sub-surface operation of Psychological Roots contributes to people's little understanding of them and their significance.

Chapter 6. HOW TO IDENTIFY PSYCHOLOGICAL ROOTS

Penfield's (1975) finding that the seat of consciousness is in a small part of the amygdala, itself a small organ (mentioned earlier), has informed us that we are aware of only a tiny fraction of what takes place in the mind at any given time. His discovery suggests that the center of consciousness is less than 1/100th of the brain.

We are unaware of almost everything that goes on inside the rest of our body as well. The hidden nature of our internal functions is a major reason why it has taken over 300,000 years to know what goes on in our internal organs (such as the thyroid, adrenal, and pituitary glands), as well as how our brain and psychology operate. To improve our effectiveness we need to know the hidden processes that affect and control us.

Our limited awareness

Our senses are not able to detect much of what goes on in nature. Even if we strained our senses as far as we could beyond our normal level of awareness, we would still not see oxygen, carbon dioxide, carbon monoxide, and nitrogen in the air, which is why it took so long for humans to realize that air has substance. Mentioned at the beginning of this book is that we cannot detect without aid almost all of the electromagnetic spectrum, such as radio waves, ultraviolet and infrared rays, X-rays, and cosmic radiation. We also cannot hear extremely high or low sounds, nor feel, smell, or taste what some other creatures can, which is why we have dogs sniff explosives and drugs. We cannot see atoms and how they connect with one another, and we cannot see the individual cells in our body without using a microscope. Thus, it is not just psychology that is beyond our sensory capabilities.

Trying to understand psychology is challenging, which becomes evident when people attempt to articulate their Psychological Roots such as their beliefs, expectations, values, and thresholds. The author has found that people can describe a few such aspects, such as some of their prominent goals, but are likely to be unaware of the huge number of Psychological Roots they have. (The reader is invited to test this issue with themselves and other people.) Also unlikely to be realized is that each person possesses a large number Psychological Roots that extend over a broad range, including evaluation criteria, subtle abilities, personal rules, and specific fears. People are especially unlikely to understand the role that their Psychological Roots have regarding their thoughts, emotional reactions, and actions. They might also not realize that they often think in absolutes or that their emotionality is a modifier of their internal reactions and behaviors, and that emotion can act as an amplifier or a diminisher.

Confronting human problems

Interpersonal conflicts, personality disorders, depression, anxiety, addiction, crime, violence, and war have most likely plagued humans from the inception. Psychological knowledge can help solve problems like these and can also facilitate effectiveness (e.g., in relationships, parenting, teaching, learning, health, and business). For example, knowing another person's Psychological Roots offers opportunities to adjust what we say before speaking or acting and thereby help avoid pitfalls. It would be ideal for people to understand how to apply psychology effectively at an early age and continue that learning at least throughout their schooling.

Where to begin?

Psychological Roots exist below awareness, like tree roots, and therefore require an understanding of how to identify them. Doing this can often start with the following question: "What hidden aspect currently existing in the person could cause him/her to act as he/she did in that situation?" This question inherently:

1. Seeks current hidden causes, that is, factors operating below awareness during the present. The current causes could have originated in the distant past.
2. Assumes that there is a logical explanation for people's behavior (e.g., Psychological Roots).
3. Opens the door for seeking core Psychological Roots (which are the foundation of roots that are acquired subsequently and which continue to exist).
4. Rules out readily observed aspects as the cause of people's behavior (e.g., statements, emotional reactions, decisions, and behaviors).
5. Bypasses easily noticed internal reactions (e.g., thoughts, emotional reactions, feelings, evaluations, and decisions).
6. Puts emphasis more on internal psychological aspects than current or recent stimuli (e.g., other people, sociological and demographic aspects, medicines, diet, and toxic agents).
7. Rules out the past as the direct cause of behavior (e.g., a person's history, such as childhood experiences and other past stimuli).

The above-mentioned aspects can help people realize that psychological aspects which operate below awareness are a major key to understanding behavior and that those aspects are identifiable. Among the most common types of Psychological Roots are goals, beliefs, expectations, needs, desires, concerns, interests, hopes, specific fears, personal rules, and evaluation criteria. Examples include needs for safety, stability, stimulation, closure, respect, pleasure, connecting with others, not being controlled, not experiencing unpleasantness, and a person's values and other beliefs. In addition to general Psychological Roots that exist in many people such as those mentioned, there are many Psychological Roots that are specific to each individual. Practical strategies for identifying Psychological Roots will be described shortly.

A starting point for estimating a person's Psychological Roots that are pertinent in a given situation can be derived from what the person says (e.g., about his/her thoughts, ideas, judgments, and decisions). It also helps to know other things about the person such as how he/she often acts and reacts (e.g., his/her emotional reactions and observable behaviors). An analysis of this kind can even be done with infants, for example, Brazelton & Sparrow (2006) view newborns' behavior as a kind of language from which their underlying needs and wants can be discerned. Questionnaires that assess Psychological Roots can help ascertain key aspects. Counselors who are experienced in the use of Psychological Systems Therapy can be a helpful resource.

Obstacles to unearthing hidden Psychological Roots
Mentioned earlier was that the likelihood of developing an effective solution increases if the cause of a problem is known. It is often easy but misleading to ascribe the cause of a problem to what is apparent, such as a symptom or a stimulus condition. Unfortunately, what shows on the surface can sometimes be so compelling that it might seem to be all that is needed to know. However, if the analysis is limited to just observable aspects it can be an obstacle to identifying the causes that exist below the surface. This is often the case when arguments occur and in disorders such as depression, anxiety, addiction, and borderline personality. Identifying the cause of behavior, including what is revealed in what people say, is often critical and requires unearthing Psychological Roots that operate below the surface. Ascertaining those sub-surface causes is hindered by assuming that what seems appropriate is correct or sufficient. Hence, testing hypotheses about what appears to be the cause of a behavior is important.

Seeking hidden causes requires patience and can seem to be an inappropriate delay. Thinking in absolutes and being locked into tangibles can interfere with being open to the real causes. Aspects such as these can also limit learning, an example of which is someone saying that a book does not apply to him/her "because the author doesn't know my situation". Another obstacle is automatically considering something to be wrong when it is inconsistent with one's own viewpoint, for instance, when people with different political opinions have opposite interpretations of the same fact. We also have perceptual filters that can keep us from recognizing when we are on the wrong track.

Another problem when attempting to discern Psychological Roots is not realizing that the same behavior can be generated by different Psychological Roots. For example, a person who runs from a theatre might be doing so out of a desire for safety, or concern about someone inside or outside the theatre, or desiring not to be late for an appointment. A person's aggressive behavior might be due to believing that he had been taken advantage of, or believing that the best defense is a good offense, or because of his/her anger being displaced from another circumstance (an emotional spillover). Anger could also be due to having a low threshold for irritability or hard-to-meet expectations.

Believing that the cause of a problem is a single factor can also get in the way since the problem could be caused by a number of Psychological Roots and often is. Another problem is believing something is important that actually has little significance. The most basic problems, the author has found, are not knowing about Psychological Roots, how to identify them, and how to create solutions even when the Psychological Roots are known. As a result, people pay attention to what others say and do, not realizing that the root cause of what is said and done is hidden.

Many obstacles to solving people-problems can be mitigated by first identifying the sub-surface causes of the problems, such as Psychological Roots, and then fashioning a suitable solution instead of trying to apply a solution before having that understanding. Identifying sub-surface causes requires patience, skill in recognizing the difference between symptoms and causes, and going beyond personal feelings and initial judgments. An analytical and tentative perspective that takes a variety of hidden factors into account is essential. Viewing conclusions as tentative hypotheses that need to be tested is also important, as is accepting the possibility of being wrong should a hypothesis not be correct. Starting over can be more effective than trying to justify an incorrect idea.

What are not Psychological Roots?

Since Psychological Roots are not readily accessible, people are not accustomed to seeking them. People who are unfamiliar with Psychological Roots might have difficulty with the idea that those factors are important since they are not tangible and operate almost entirely below the surface. Acknowledging the hidden nature of psychological causes helps having an appropriate mind-set for identifying hidden causes since it permits realizing that observable aspects are unlikely to be Psychological Roots. This realization rules out people's behaviors, emotional reactions, expressed feelings, and experiences. When seeking Psychological Roots, it can be counterproductive to focus on what is readily observable, or to be impatient, jump to conclusions, or use one's own experience as the major reference point. This awareness also leads to recognizing that inferences that immediately jump to many people's minds about the cause of a person's behavior should be thoroughly vetted.

People might believe that past experiences are Psychological Roots. However, past experiences are *stimuli* that occurred at an earlier time. It is also easy to be mistaken about what roots resulted from those circumstances. For example, it is understandable that "Dunwood's" harsh manner stems from the Psychological Roots he acquired from his extremely critical father. However, "Sanford" – who also had a harshly critical father – has the *opposite* Psychological Roots (which are a desire to be warm, caring, and supportive) because he wants to *avoid* being like his father. Another example of why it is important not to jump to conclusions about the effect of past experiences is that the majority of people who are abused do not become abusers or delinquent, despite a common belief otherwise (Widom, 1989).

Thus, even when a person's past experience had a powerful effect on him/her, it is important to discern just what the individual Psychological Roots were that resulted from past experiences. What counts are the person's current Psychological Roots, many of which resulted from significant past experiences and continue having a strong effect on the person. These examples illustrate why it is useful to be careful about deducing the Psychological Roots that resulted from a person's past experiences.

Memories, thoughts, evaluations, judgments, decisions, drives, feelings, and emotional reactions are *internal reactions* that result from Psychological Roots or the effect of stimuli on Psychological Roots. When feelings and other internal reactions generate overt behaviors or trigger Hidden Sequences they act as stimuli; they are not Psychological Roots. Overt behaviors also are not Psychological Roots. However, behaviors can be stimuli that impact Psychological Roots and thereby set off subsequent Hidden Sequences. Glandular secretions (such as adrenalin), and neurotransmitters (such as serotonin) are biological entities, not psychological aspects. (For a list of *general* types of Psychological Roots, see Box 2. For a list of many *specific* Psychological Roots, see Boxes 3a-d.)

BOX 2. SOME GENERAL TYPES OF PSYCHOLOGICAL ROOTS

Assumptions stored in long term memory	Motivations
Attitudes	Mottoes
Axioms	Necessities
Beliefs	Needs
Benchmarks	Normative procedures
Codes of behavior	Norms that are followed
Concepts	Objectives
Concerns	Optimism
Confidence	Personal rules
Corollaries	Perspectives
Creeds	Pessimism (expecting
Criteria	bad things to happen)
Customs	Philosophies
Dislikes stored in	Policies that are adhered to
long term memory	Postulates
Dogmas	Principles
Dreams	Proverbs
Ethics	Psychological boundaries
Expectations	Psychological limits
Faith	Reference norms
Flexible	Religious beliefs
Formulas that	(theologies)
people live by	Requirements
Frames of reference	Sayings that people
Frameworks	live by (e.g., proverbs,
Goals (sub- & partial	aphorisms, maxims)
goals, full &	Self-confidence
minimum goals)	Specific fears
Guidelines	Standards (high and low
Hopes	bars)
Hypotheses	Theorems
Ideas	Theories
Ideologies	Thresholds
Intentions	Values
Interests	Wants
	Wishes
	Worries

BOX 3a. SOME COMMON PSYCHOLOGICAL ROOTS *(in alphabetical order)*

Believe in a particular ideology
Believe in God
   Believe that: ...
a failure is permanently harmful
a good offense is the best defense
all prejudice is bad
a woman's place is in the home
ability to memorize indicates high IQ
addiction can be ended by will power
aggression is justified
an opportunity is once in a lifetime
an opposing viewpoint has no value
another political party will ruin the
   nation
anyone can be successful
being assertive is the key to success
being blunt and direct is persuasive
being blunt is a good way to talk
being book smart is a sign of high IQ
being intelligent is the key to success
being logical is the key to persuasion
being loud or yelling is persuasive
being pleasant is the key to
   persuasion
being popular is a sign of high IQ
being traditional is the best way
being very thin is attractive
being wealthy means being very
   intelligent
bombing wins wars
branding is the key to successful
   business
business people should be Presidents
cannot make a living by being an artist
changing someone's behavior is
   persuading
childhood experiences affect life
   permanently
college automatically produces higher
   income

college makes someone educated
compromise is bad
correcting people changes them
creativity refers to art or music
criticism works well
debates win arguments
demographic aspects cause behavior
discipline is a major key to success
doing the same thing will succeed
everyone can be depressed or anxious
everyone should be treated the same
   way
fast decisions indicates high intelligence
food has direct effects on health
giving facts or logic are the keys to
   persuasion
God has a plan for everyone
people transgressing rules should be
   punished
persisting is the key to persuasion
having material things brings happiness
holding children's attention requires
   moving fast
how others see things is incorrect
how a person sees things is the only
   correct way
it is easier to smile than to frown
it is good to be very competitive in
   all things
it is good to focus on tangibles
it is good to think in absolutes
it is important to be punctual
it is important to set others straight
it is more important to satisfy oneself
   than others
it is unlikely to have a good income
   as an artist
it is possible to be generally happy
it is possible to be happy much of
   the time

BOX 3b. *SOME COMMON PSYCHOLOGICAL ROOTS, continued*

knowledgeable people should be trusted
life is simple
love conquers all
love is the strongest emotion
love is all that a successful relationship requires
lying is the key to persuasion
making fast judgments indicates high intelligence
males cannot be trusted to be monogamous
marketing is the key to success in business
memorizing by rote produces comprehension
might makes right
mindfulness improves a person's psychology
moderateness is ineffective
money brings happiness
nagging works to change people effectively
negatives are stronger than positives
non-human creatures are dumb
normal can be defined
normal cannot be defined
normal people cannot have psychological disorders
once a decision is made it is final
one's own needs come first
only evidence-based treatments are worthwhile
ordinary people are not smart
others are at fault, not oneself
others are the cause of their problems
others are trying to take advantage

others should think as the observer does
parents should be obeyed by their children
people are addicted because they like being "high"
people from a particular ethnic group are good (or bad)
people from a particular sub-group are not human
people in authority are untrustworthy
people readily change
people who want something else than the observer are wrong
playing it safe brings success
poor short-term memory is the start of senility
positives are stronger than negatives
practice makes perfect
pressuring people is persuasive
professionals always know best
psychology is trivial, imaginary, or ephemeral
punishment changes behavior effectively
science has all the answers
self-promotion brings success
setting an example leads others to change
smart students do not need special education
some people are harmful
some people cannot be trusted
some people naturally rise to the top

BOX 3c, *continued*, COMMON PSYCHOLOGICAL ROOTS

Intolerance of:
what differs from one's own ideas
being controlled
disappointment
failure
injury
loss
people who differ from oneself
rejection
status that differs from one's own
values that differ from one's own

Low: self-confidence
low self-esteem
low threshold for physical aggression
low threshold for defensiveness
low threshold for negative emotional arousal
low threshold for psychological injury
low threshold for verbal aggression

Need for:
a loving and supportive mate
avoidance of negatives
being accepted by others
being liked
emotional support
getting things done quickly
having people in authority
making money
material support
perfection
positive experiences
problem-solving strategies
responsibility
respect
safety
shelter
simplicity
stability

BOX 3d. *SOME COMMON PSYCHOLOGICAL ROOTS, continued*

Concern:
Concern about health
Concern about the purpose in life

Desire:
for a strong connection with others
for attention
for protection
for quick gratification
to avoid confrontation
to be a grandparent
to be a follower
to be a leader
to be a part of a particular group
to be dominant
to be important
to have to be independent
to be married
to be obeyed
to be outstanding
to be part of something larger than
    themself
to be superior to others
to behave as their parents did
to do the opposite that their parents
    did
to emulate a role model
to excel at their occupation
to excel at their skill or sport
to grow intellectually

to have a family
to have children
friends
to have power
to make a contribution
to make a lot of money
dislike being controlled
disdain for whatever is not
    scientifically supported

Drive:
for closure
for power, be in control
not to be controlled
to achieve wealth
to achieve fame
to be highly competitive
to be important
to be respected
to dominate
to always be occupied
to succeed
to be very productive
to remain within the comfort
    zone
to survive
to have high standards
to have high expectations
to have high self-confidence

Aids for identifying Psychological Roots

Perspective: Psychological Roots are real and have powerful effects, but are hidden, so must be uncovered. When sought, Psychological Roots are readily found. Some strategies for doing so follow.

Strategy 1. Imagine being the person in question:
a. Role-play the person whose Psychological Roots are to be ascertained and imagine being that person in a pertinent situation. Try to get a sense of what that person is experiencing and why.
b. Try to articulate what Psychological Roots would explain why that person behaved as he/she did.
c. Try to specify the person's desires, beliefs, expectations, drives, concerns, interests, fears, hopes, and goals.

Strategy 2. Questions that can aid the search. Initially ask yourself:
a. What is causing the person to do something pertinent, react in a particular way, or continue doing something? Why might the person do something that stands out, such as being unproductive or having disturbing feelings, thoughts, concerns, interests, or recurrent problems?
b. What expectation might the person have that could explain his/her emotional reactions or behavior? For example, when a person is angry, what expectation of that person might not be met?
c. As in b, above, ask what possible desires, beliefs, concerns, or interests the person might have.
d. Ask what keeps the person from doing a particular thing? For example, why might the person not understand, remember, or change?
e. If a particular Psychological Root were to change, ask whether would it change the person's behavior or thinking. For example, would changing that root improve that person's life or make it worse?
f. Is a Psychological Root that you identified sufficient to explain the person's behavior or thinking? Would another Psychological Root be more explanatory?
g. Ask if the person's behavior might be due to a combination of Psychological Roots. For example, it is insufficient to explain bullying as due to low self-esteem alone since many people have low self-esteem but are not bullies. Other Psychological Roots that might be involved in bullying might perhaps be a desire to feel important, dominant, or powerful. Some other roots might be desires to look competent, exact revenge, displace anger, compensate for failure, or be stimulated. If other roots may be involved, what might those additional roots be?
h. Check to be sure that what has been identified is not a stimulus or experience, or a behavior, or an internal reaction (such as a memory, thought, judgment, decision, an evaluation, or an emotional reaction such as a feeling). If so, those are NOT Psychological Roots. If something is not a Psychological Root, search deeper.

Strategy 3. Start with an observable behavior

Work backward from an observable behavior, speculating about Psychological Roots that could have produced that behavior. For depression, might there be expectations or responsibilities that have not been met? Might there be an intolerance of failure, a low threshold for negative arousal, pessimism, or inadequate problem-solving or social strategies? Search for multiple Psychological Roots.

Strategy 4. Start with a stimulus

Work forward from a stimulus that impacted the person to hypothesize what Psychological Root with which that stimulus might have interacted. For example, what Psychological Root might an exam, job interview, or other circumstance have impacted to cause the observed outcome? Ask, "Might that circumstance have aroused a concern regarding safety, confidence, or fulfilling a responsibility?"

Strategy 5. Start with an internal reaction

Work backward from an internal reaction – such as distress or a dysfunctional thought – to speculate about what Psychological Roots could have produced that reaction. For example, if the person felt anxious, what might have threatened him/her? Might his/her anxious reaction stem from a threat to needs for safety, stability, or meeting an expectation? Use a similar process to hypothesize what Psychological Root could have led to a thought, evaluation, decision, memory, feeling, or strong emotional reaction.

Strategy 6. Start with a past experience

Ask what Psychological Root might have resulted from that experience. Then evaluate the resulting hypotheses to identify the Psychological Roots that most pertain to the present situation.

Strategy 7. Hypothesize possible Psychological Roots

Ask what the target person's desires, concerns, interests, beliefs, and expectations are. Expand this question to other possible roots, such as the individual's values, aspirations, wishes, specific fears, personal rules, threshold for emotional arousal, problem-solving strategies, and evaluation criteria.

Strategy 8. Hypothesize what the target person does NOT want

Ask what the target person does *not* want. The answers you come up with might provide a clue about what the person *does* want. Both what is desired and not desired are Psychological Roots.

Strategy 9. Note the other person's opinions and what the other person agrees and disagrees with

What the other person agrees and disagrees with offer clues about his/her Psychological Roots. Speculate about what those might be.

Strategy 10. Ask other people for clues regarding the target person's Psychological Roots

If appropriate and the target person agrees, ask other individuals their guesses about the target person's personality traits while being careful to respect his/her privacy. Ask about only one aspect at a time, such as goals, then another aspect after that topic is exhausted (e.g., beliefs, expectations, fears, etc.) Translate the answers into Psychological Roots.

Strategy 11. Ask other people about what the target person does NOT want

Ask other individuals their guesses about what the target person does *not* want, while respecting the target person's privacy (after obtaining the target person's agreement to do so). Ask about only one aspect at a time, such as goals then another aspect after that topic is exhausted (e.g., expectations, interests, concerns, fears, etc.). Translate the answers into Psychological Roots.

Strategy 12. List Psychological Roots of people who seem similar to the target person

List Psychological Roots that often are present in people who exhibit behaviors or who have psychological patterns similar to that individual. For example, the author has found that many people who are depressed have Psychological Roots such as a narrow comfort zone, low threshold for negative arousal, and inadequate problem-solving strategies.

Strategy 13. Interview the target person

Ask the target person about his/her interests, concerns, goals, beliefs, expectations, and background, and then derive hypotheses about possible Psychological Roots from what is learned. People are unlikely to identify their Psychological Roots, or if they have some idea, they may underestimate the significance of those roots and perhaps not mention them. It helps when the target person can tell you whether your hypotheses are correct, for example, the author has found that people often show immediate recognition when a Psychological Root applies to them. If a person hesitates to respond to some hypotheses or rejects some, it may mean that the hypotheses are not correct or that those hypotheses need to be revised. Sometimes the person might recognize a pertinent Psychological Root only after mentioning some variations of them. Be prepared for people to mention aspects other than Psychological Roots such as stimulus conditions (e.g., what others are currently doing to them or some past experiences), their feelings or thoughts (internal reactions), or their behaviors.

Strategy 14. Use an open-ended questionnaire
Ask the target individual to respond to an open-ended questionnaire (questions that invite them to answer in their own words), as distinguished from questions that can be answered with a number or a word from a list. Ask about only one aspect at a time. Inquire about the person's desires, concerns, interests, beliefs, and expectations. Respect the person's privacy in doing so. The person's answers can offer clues about his/her Psychological Roots.

Strategy 15. Obtain the target individual's answers to a fixed-alternative questionnaire
Ask the target individual to respond to a fixed-alternative questionnaire (questions or statements that can be answered with or a word from a list or a number, such as, "On a 0-to-10 scale, to what degree are you confident that you can manage difficult situations?"). The questionnaire items can inquire about Psychological Roots directly (e.g., "I have high expectations") or they can be indirect (e.g., "I react strongly"; "I think poorly of myself"). Respect the target person's privacy. Use a scale (e.g., 0-to-10, 1 to 6) rather than offering only 2 or 3 choices (e.g., true/false, yes/no, yes/no/do not know). A scale can help identify the degree to which each Psychological Root is important or unimportant to that individual.

Strategy 16. Rate the target person on a fixed-alternative questionnaire
Rate the target individual on a fixed-alternative questionnaire regarding items that directly or indirectly inquire about Psychological Roots (e.g., "She has high standards"; "When he does not solve a problem quickly, he stops trying"; "This person thinks highly of himself/herself"). Use a scale, such as 0-to-10, to help ascertain Psychological Roots that are particularly important to the individual.

Some additional aids for ascertaining Psychological Roots are offered in Boxes 4a-d.
When trying to figure out why someone (including yourself) did something, a way to quickly identify a Psychological Root would be to ask: What belief could have caused the person to do that? Then ask each of the following:
a. Is the answer to the above question a judgment, thought, conclusion, or emotional reaction? If so, it is an *internal reaction*, not a Psychological Root. What Psychological Root could have led to that internal reaction? There may be more than one pertinent Psychological Root involved.

b. Is the answer to the above question a stimulus or experience? If so, it is *stimulus*, not a Psychological Root. What Psychological Root could have resulted from that stimulus?

c. Is the answer to the above question a behavior? If so, it is an *outcome*, not a Psychological Root. What Psychological Root could have led to that behavior?

BOX 4a. ADDITIONAL AIDS FOR ASCERTAINING PSYCHOLOGICAL ROOTS

Some questions that can help sort out what is and is not a Psychological Root.

A. What is a Psychological Root?

1. Is the aspect in question an internal psychological factor that generates an internal reaction by itself or when a relevant stimulus impacts it? For example, is it a criterion for positive or negative arousal? If so, it is a Psychological Root.
2. Is a goal is a Psychological Root? Yes. A goal generates a drive to achieve that goal.
3. Is an expectation a Psychological Root? Yes. An expectation is a criterion for judging failure.
4. Is a belief a Psychological Root? Yes, it generates a drive for other aspects to be consistent with it and is a criterion for evaluating whether something is consistent with it (a positive reaction) or inconsistent with it (a negative reaction).
5. Is a desire for respect a Psychological Root? Yes, meeting it generates a positive internal reaction.
6. Is a rule, limit, or threshold a Psychological Root? Yes. They are criteria for thinking, evaluating, and behaving.

B. What is not a Psychological Root?

1. Is an emotion or feeling a Psychological Root? No. They are internal reactions. They can lead to overt behavior.
2. Is a behavior a Psychological Root? No, it is a skeletal muscle action. It can be a stimulus.

BOX 4b. ADDITIONAL AIDS FOR ASCERTAINING PSYCHOLOGICAL ROOTS

BACKGROUND INFORMATION

Psychological Roots (e.g., desires, expectations, and beliefs) start Hidden Sequences.

Root Sequences start with a Psychological Root (e.g., low self-esteem can generate a down mood).

Stimulus conditions, internal reactions, past experiences are not roots.

Stimuli interact with Psychological Roots, producing internal reactions and also overt behaviors.

Stimulus-and-Root Sequences start with a stimulus + a Psychological Root (e.g., being put-down can generate anger).

Stimuli can originate externally (e.g., what other persons do) or internally (e.g., hormones, feelings, microbes).

Past experiences are stimulus conditions that occurred at an earlier time (e.g., in childhood).

Internal reactions include physiological changes (such as emotions, neurotransmitters, hormones, enzymes), and cognitive processes (such as thoughts, evaluations, conclusions, and decisions). Some aspects of internal reactions may be observable, such as non-verbal expressions of emotion (e.g., crying, embarrassment, and anger).

Behaviors, such as skeletal muscle actions (e.g., talking, smiling, joking, laughing, working, disagreeing, arguing, and aggressing) result from internal reactions.

An internal reaction (e.g., an evaluation, judgment, or unstated attitude) might become a behavior such as when expressed as a statement of like or dislike, or a discriminatory act).

Attitudes and beliefs are often thought as similar, but occur at different places in a Hidden Sequence: beliefs are Psychological Roots that begin Hidden Sequences, while attitudes (likes and dislikes) are internal reactions.

A pre-formed attitude is a prejudice and an internal reaction. A discriminatory act resulting from an attitude is a behavior.

An attitude can become a longstanding concern or interest, and thus convert to a Psychological Root.

Psychological Roots are criteria for making evaluations (e.g., the basis for judging whether or not there is success or failure).

BOX 4c. ADDITIONAL AIDS FOR ASCERTAINING PSYCHOLOGICAL ROOTS

3. Is what someone says a Psychological Root? No, it is a behavior. It can be a stimulus.
4. Is a decision a Psychological Root? No, it is an internal reaction.
5. Is a judgment, evaluation, attitude, or a conclusion a Psychological Root? No, those are internal reactions. However, if they become part of a person's long-term problem-solving strategy they become Psychological Roots.
6. Is a drive a Psychological Root? No, it is an internal reaction stemming from a root and can lead to a behavior.
7. Is achieving a goal Psychological Root? No. A positive emotion that results is an internal reaction.
8. Is not meeting an expectation a Psychological Root? No. The resulting negative is an internal reaction.
9. Is pressure from someone a Psychological Root? No, it is a stimulus condition.
10. Are demographic factors Psychological Roots? No, they are external population characteristics that originate from Biological and/or Psychological Roots. They act as stimuli that can impact Psychological Roots (e.g., being elderly can foster a belief that the person is no longer useful), and can be behaviors (e.g., marriage; income level; a criminal record) that result from Psychological Roots. Psychological Roots provide more precise information about the cause of a person's behavior than demographic characteristics.
11. Are past experiences Psychological Roots? No, they are stimuli. They can generate Psychological Roots (e.g., having been put-down can produce low self-esteem). The Psychological Roots that resulted from that past experience can be identified (e.g., acquiring from an authoritarian father a belief that every rule must be rigidly obeyed).

BOX 4d. ADDITIONAL AIDS FOR ASCERTAINING PSYCHOLOGICAL ROOTS

12. Are personality traits Psychological Roots (e.g., those assessed by personality measures)? Not if they are behavior patterns. The Psychological Roots that generate such behaviors can often be discerned from knowing personality traits (e.g., such as having a wide adaptive range leads to being open-minded). Examples of personality traits are aggression, agreeableness, and anxiety.

Other examples personality traits include attention problems, close-mindedness, competitiveness, conscientiousness, considerateness, conventionality, creativity, depression, dutifulness, extraversion, friendliness, gloom, guilt, happiness, hardiness, hyperactivity, impulsivity, inquisitiveness, introversion, irritability, moodiness, neurosis, open-mindedness, passion, political conservativism and liberalism, religiosity, resilience, sadness, sociability, and traditional thinking.)

13. Is resistance a Psychological Root? No, resistance is a behavior. It stems from a Psychological Root (e.g., from a low threshold for negative emotional arousal or an unsatisfied Psychological Root).

14. Is frustration a Psychological Root? No, frustration is an internal reaction. It stems from a Psychological Root (e.g., from a low threshold for negative emotional arousal or an unsatisfied Psychological Root).

15. Is a perception a Psychological Root? No, perception is an internal reaction. It originates from a Psychological Root (e.g., from a belief or a Psychological Root that has been impacted by a stimulus).

Reliability and validity

When seeking Psychological Roots, those that emerge from the analysis should explain the behavior in question and fit what is known about the person. The author has found that when a root has been accurately identified, the person is likely to recognize it instantly and might have a noticeable reaction, perhaps by agreeing or by manifesting some non-verbal behavior such as an exclamation or a change in breathing, mood, appearance, or movement (e.g., leaning forward). Here is an example: "Trent" had been hospitalized for severe depression several times. When the author asked Trent whether a reason was that he had high standards and felt like a failure when he did not meet his standards, Trent caught his breath, felt faint, and had to take a break. That statement was difficult for him to handle because it turned out to be a major reason for his depression. His high standards had been drilled into him by his stern father. Strong reactions like Trent's are more likely to occur with issues that are sensitive.

When a hypothesized root is incorrect, the person is unlikely to agree with it. Some other possibilities are that the person might hesitate, equivocate, respond lukewarmly, look puzzled, or try to make a hypothesis fit. Incorrect hypotheses should be eliminated without challenging the person. Sometimes hypothesized Psychological Roots are just slightly off yet can be totally rejected by a target person. In some cases when a hypothesis is incorrect it may be rectified if modified. In such instances, asking the person to adjust or modify the hypothesis can sometimes succeed.

A Psychological Root that might seem correct may be only partly right, or play just a small role, or not be correct. Hence hypotheses should be tested such as by asking the person directly and by judging whether the analysis explains some of the person's other thoughts, emotional reactions, and behaviors.

The hypothesized Psychological Roots obtained from each method should be substantially consistent with one another. When similarities exist between the hypothesized roots but do not fully overlap, try to pin down the reason for those differences, such as nuances, or seek additional roots. If the roots derived from different analyses do not coincide, it may mean that there are other pertinent Psychological Roots that have not yet been identified.

A particularly useful test of a hypothesized root is whether or not the person improves as a result of modifying, over-riding or satisfying that root. For instance, when something is said or done that is consistent with that root, the person should relax, look happier, have less anxiety, feel relieved, have greater success with other people, or accomplish more with less effort. As an example, someone who is agitated might calm down when agreed with or given sympathy.

Multiple roots

Behavior can result from many Psychological Roots, some of which act in sequence, combine their effects, or affect some aspects but not others. Some roots emerge only after other roots have been identified, like peeling layers of an onion in a step-by-step process. (See Frank's example in Chapter 28.) If insufficient Psychological Roots are identified, further roots need to be discerned.

Key roots

Some Psychological Roots are more pertinent than others in a particular situation and therefore are especially important to identify. Since there often are multiple roots that contribute to the total effect, the search should not be limited to just one root.

A practical application of this information

Succeeding in life has much to do with being socially effective. Working with Psychological Roots can help, such as by aiding interpersonal relations and helping to create compatible solutions. (Suggestions for how to do so are presented in Section II.)

Chapter 7. LINKING, ROOT HIERARCHIES, AND CHANGE

We acquire Biological and Psychological Roots throughout life and those acquisitions do not occur by chance. What is acquired and how those aspects are arranged have important consequences for us in regard to our behavior, our resistance to change, and how change occurs, as this chapter explains.

Linking

Psychological Roots connect with one another (*'linking'*) when what is new is conceptually consistent with the root to which it links (similar to Piaget's concept of assimilation [Flavell, 1966]). For example, an infant's belief that its parents provide safety might link with that child's wired-in need for safety. A desire for a particular food might link with a person's desire for positive arousal. A concern about strangers might link with a need to avoid negatives. The first acquired roots link with genetic Psychological Roots, as in the above examples. Psychological roots can also link with Biological Roots, for example, a belief that parents provide food can link with the child's need for food.

Additional Psychological Roots attach to roots that were previously acquired. For instance, a belief that parents can be depended upon to take care of its needs might attach to a belief that parents provide safety. Also attached to that root might be a belief that parents will be emotionally and physically supportive (cf. Harlow, 1961, Bowlby, 1983, and Ainsworth, 1991). Each Psychological Root can receive and make multiple links.

Everyone develops many Psychological Roots throughout life. The larger the number of existing Psychological Roots, the greater the potential to acquire additional roots owing to the increased number of locations at which linking can occur. Individuals who are particularly open-minded, growth-oriented, curious, intelligent, and long-lived can acquire a particularly large number of roots.

Some roots obtained early in life last a lifetime, including much of what is acquired from parents such as their morality, values (e.g., work ethic, sense of responsibility), religious orientation, political ideology, expectations, and goals (e.g., having a suitable income, social acceptance, and marrying). Experiences contribute to the acquisition of Psychological Roots through observation, empathy, and instruction (such as from authority figures, role models, and peers).[1] Self-generated thinking also adds roots. Knowledge is what is believed, therefore involves Psychological Roots.

---

[1] Synonyms for linking are associating, connecting, attaching, adhering, bonding, binding, and absorbing.

This perspective explains the initial substrate to which acquired information attaches (genetic Biological and Psychological Roots) and helps clarify aspects Piaget had not fully elucidated. In addition to straightforward cognitive information, a variety of other psychological factors are capable of being linked (e.g., specific fears, psychological thresholds, goals, beliefs, expectations, concerns, and interests). Cognitions can also link with Biological Roots (such as needs for air, food, water, shelter, and moderate temperature), which further expands Piaget's ideas.

Having large numbers of roots facilitates the processing of information such as associations, reasoning, synthesizing, generalizing, and discriminating.[2] These and other processing abilities aid problem-solving, critical thinking, and being creative. The larger the number of Psychological Roots a person acquires, the greater his/her interest in acquiring further information and ideas, which further expands the person's knowledge. Intelligence is aided by the facility with which links are made, the drive to do so, the number of acquired Psychological Roots, and effectiveness in choosing relevant roots.

Psychological Root hierarchies

Each Psychological Root, including genetic roots, can be a foundation for many chains of acquired roots. The starting point for each chain is a genetic Biological or Psychological Root. The linking of acquired Psychological Roots creates lengthy chains, somewhat analogous to strings of railroad cars connected end to end (see Figure 11). The acquired roots in a hierarchy are aligned with the genetic root at the foundation of its hierarchy since each acquired root is automatically influenced by that genetic root. As a result, each hierarchy has a central theme related to its foundation root (e.g., a need for safety). That theme provides an implicit selective process as additional roots are acquired since potential roots must fit the theme of an existing chain. (More on the screening process later.)

---

[2] There is a drive to use whatever is genetically wired-in, including abilities, such as factors that contribute to intelligence (e.g., association, inductive and deductive reasoning, generalization, discrimination, synthesis, and problem-solving). There is also a drive to use what is acquired, stemming in part from the genetic Psychological Root at the foundation of each hierarchy.

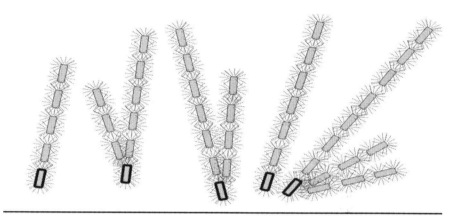

Fig. 11. LINKED PSYCHOLOGICAL ROOTS (like trains with the locomotive at the rear).
The 'cars' (with a light border) represent acquired psychological roots.
The 'locomotives' (with a dark border) represent genetic psychological roots.

As a result of this arrangement, people's Psychological Roots are systematically arranged rather than haphazard. So are internal reactions (e.g., thoughts, emotional reactions, and decisions) and overt actions (such as impulses and what a person says). As an example, a person might have a strong need to socialize because of her genetic need to be connected with others, and might be afraid of uncontrolled fire because it violates her genetic need for safety. The alignment of Psychological Roots in their respective hierarchies produces an internal consistency and logic to each individual's psychology even when an observer thinks someone's thoughts or actions are illogical. (More on this topic later.)

The genetic foundation of Psychological Roots
The hierarchical nature of Psychological Roots means that the impetus for a behavior originates from its foundation (a genetic Biological or Psychological Root). As a result, what shows on the surface – what a person says and does – is driven by genetic roots. While genetic roots are general in nature, specific behaviors eventuate from the Psychological Roots at the tangibly-oriented end of hierarchies. The overt behaviors that result can range from being simple, broad, and crude to being highly refined and complex such as the remarkable accomplishments of a professional violinist, mathematician, physicist, computer scientist, or inventor. A comparable biological arrangement exists, for instance, in the genetic need to eat and other genetic Biological and Psychological Roots drive the diverse creation of

a simple vegetable garden, the eating of an overloaded pizza, and the fashioning of an exquisitely elaborate dining experience.

Branches and hierarchical trees

Links to Psychological Roots can occur anywhere along the various hierarchies, therefore branches can spring up anywhere along the line (see Figure 12). For example, a person's interest in mathematics might lead to an interest in physics and then to an interest in a particular aspect of physics, then to an interest in a specialization of physics such as string theory. Links to Psychological Roots can occur anywhere along the various hierarchies and each root has a drive to link with still other roots. Each branch permits the acquisition of still other Psychological Roots that are conceptually aligned with it, and those roots and branches can then lead to acquiring still other branches. The increasing branches and sub-branches create an ever-growing forest of Psychological Roots. As a result, an aspect acquired early in a person's life occupies a position near the foundation of its hierarchy and can have a permanent effect in that person's life. Figure 13 offers a fictitious representation of a Psychological Root hierarchy.

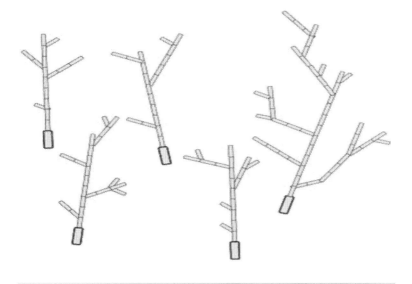

Fig. 12. **Branches** of psychological roots (analogous to trees).

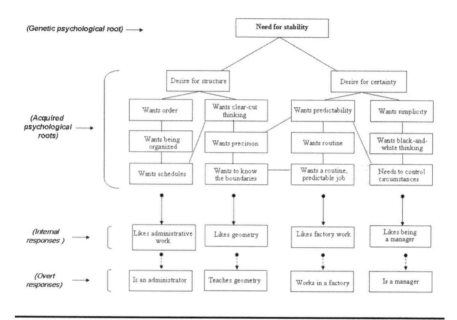

Fig 13. A fictitious representation of hierarchically organized psychological roots, with internal and overt responses.

Webs

Psychological Roots can also connect across different hierarchies, thereby producing multiple trunks, branches, groupings of branches, and connections among branches. Since Psychological Root hierarchies can grow and expand throughout life, huge *'webs'* of complex multi-faceted Psychological Root structures result resembling root systems in the plant world (see Figure 14).

The many connections within the various complex webs and sub-webs permit Psychological Roots to connect rapidly with one another. Stimuli also can connect readily with Psychological Roots in those webs. Those extensive communication networks help people quickly draw upon stored information, engage in chains of reasoning, find appropriate words and synonyms, combine disparate words to form effective sentences, connect ideas, and follow rules without being consciously aware of doing so. The more extensive the network, the greater a person's wisdom is likely to be, all other things being equal.

Experiences, problem-solving ability, effective evaluation, and desire to grow intellectually aid that outcome.

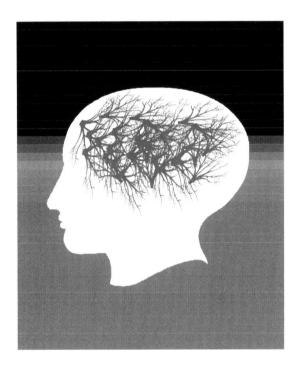

Fig. 14. Complex webs of interlinked psychological
roots, trees, and branches.

The ability of Psychological Roots to form substantial psychological hierarchies, branches, clusters, and webs illustrates how a simple beginning can blossom into a multifaceted array. A tangible example is the Wright brothers' air-foil, which led to a wide variety of aircraft from helicopters to rocket ships. The complexity of Psychological Roots' webs also illustrates how the individual components of complicated aspects can be relatively simple. Another example of complexity that is composed of simple components is the on/off digitalization that is the basis of complicated computer programs.

Core Psychological Roots, such as values, are hard to change, partly because of their deeply ensconced position in Psychological Root hierarchies.

That arrangement fosters stability, also resistance to change. Those aspects and the solidity of core roots help explain why it can take a long time for people from one culture to assimilate into another culture, sometimes a generation. Some other resistance-inducing factors involved in cultural assimilation include lack of confidence, initially incompatible skills, uncertainty, and fear, also the host culture's resistance and discrimination. Unpleasantness from individuals in the host culture occurs because of people in the majority reacting negatively to aspects that differ from their Psychological Roots, such as different religious and political beliefs. Those negative reactions might diminish as assimilated individuals acquire the Psychological Roots and behaviors of the host culture, especially if the host culture benefits from people who have assimilated (e.g., through jobs, discoveries, inventions, solutions to problems, or pleasing foods or art).

Early and Late Psychological Roots

Many Psychological Roots are acquired later than others. Those *'Later Psychological Roots'* align with *'Early Psychological Roots'* since Psychological Roots link to other roots that have something in common with them. As mentioned, this arrangement results in all Psychological Roots in a hierarchy aligning with the genetic root at the foundation of its hierarchy. Very Early Psychological Roots (*'deep Psychological Roots'*) are at or near the foundation of psychological hierarchies, roughly corresponding to tap roots in trees. Those roots furnish the major influence in a hierarchy and affect the Psychological Roots that are acquired at a later time. Later Psychological Roots are tributaries of early roots, similar to the roots that subsequently stem from tap roots. This aspect of hierarchies means that what is acquired early in life could have a lifelong effect, analogous to a change to a tree's beginning stalk affecting that tree's entire life. As a result, what happens in childhood, including the acquisition of values, expectations, and formal education, is extremely important.

Humans have many genetic Psychological Roots and a huge number of acquired Psychological Roots. The themes and related sub-themes of the various hierarchies contribute to the nature of the outcomes (such as feelings, thoughts, fantasies, and behaviors) and the uniqueness of an individual's personality. The hierarchical structure of Psychological Roots fosters continuity and stability of personality, interests, concerns, thinking, problem-solving style, and behavior. This arrangement helps explain why early childhood experiences matter a great deal and resist change (cf. Harlow, 1961, Bowlby, 1983, and Ainsworth, 1991).

'*Surface Psychological Roots*' (synonym: peripheral roots) are Later Psychological Roots that involve observable and tangible aspects, such as beliefs about what behaviors are socially appropriate and what material things a person considers to be desirable. Early Psychological Roots (synonyms: higher-order Psychological Roots, '*deep roots*') have a broader influence than Later Psychological Roots (synonym: lower-order Psychological Roots) because they affect a wider range of roots. A large number of '*Intermediate Psychological Roots*' exist between deep and surface Psychological Roots.

Are emotions illogical?

It is not uncommon for people to say that someone is illogical, that decisions are based on emotion, or that psychology is irrational. For example, a psychologist who specializes in politics said that "… psychology … is not rational … [viewpoints often are] an emotionally-based reaction rather than a more executive function reaction … [Someone said] that he did not agree with [a particular candidate] but liked his bravado and respected that and so, "I will probably vote for him." … [That voter] does not agree with [the candidate] but because he likes his style, that is enough" (Souter, 2016).

The psychologist quoted by Souter viewed that voter's decision as being based on emotion rather than logic. The idea that psychology or emotions are irrational contrasts with Psychological Systems Theory's perspective, which is that decisions are based on Psychological Roots, and therefore the above-mentioned voter's decision was logical to *him*. For example, that voter might have had an authoritarian philosophy (a Psychological Root) that led to his liking of autocratic leaders. Having a deeply-held concept like that would override aspects that were more peripheral to him, such as some opinions the candidate had with which he disagreed. The above-mentioned psychologist considered the voter's statements to be irrational because she did not know about Psychological Roots or their hierarchical nature and did not know that voter's Psychological Roots.

Something is logical when its aspects are consistent with one another such as when a conclusion follows from a premise. In Hidden Sequences, internal reactions like emotions and decisions result from the Psychological Roots that undergird them, which means that a person's emotions and decisions are logical for him/her. In this view, even impulsive, socially inappropriate, and obviously counterproductive behavior is nevertheless *internally* logical with regard to *that* individual's psychology even though it is not *objectively* logical and might even be harmful to that person. Counterproductive behavior includes the dangerous things that people do, their vibrating in fear instead of taking action ("deer in the headlights"), and employees who insult their boss.

It also includes partying instead of studying for an exam, driving at an unlawful speed despite having had many traffic tickets, feeling guilty about a *faux pas* they committed decades earlier, and compulsively obsessing about something without coming to a conclusion. This perspective, which derives from the theory, explains why people do things that are objectively irrational and why they might resist other people's pleas to do otherwise.

Below are three examples of counter-effective thinking, reacting, and behaving that seemed correct to the individuals who engaged in them since what they did was consistent with their Psychological Roots.

- "Edward" wanted his son to achieve at a high level, so he continually told his son how he was failing. However, that led to his son lacking confidence and resulted in his son's underperforming, including his son ending up working in an occupation far below his capability.
- "Ophelia" worried about things over which she had no control. However, her worrying brought her no objective benefits and instead, each worry added distress, which made her feel still worse.
- "April" was angry with "Brad" about not getting enough attention and affection from him. She expressed her anger about it to Brad. However, that irritated Brad, which created even greater emotional distance and still less closeness with Brad.

These examples illustrate that people behave in accord with their Psychological Roots, which is not always in their best interest and also might not be in accord with objective logic or other people's beliefs or norms. Circumstances like these illustrate why people may believe that love, anger, and other emotional reactions are inherently irrational.

Psychological Systems Theory suggests the following ideas about emotions:

1. An emotional reaction results from Psychological Roots in Hidden Sequences and is therefore internally logical for every individual.

Our internal reactions – thoughts, evaluations, judgments, decisions, and emotional reactions – seem appropriate to ourselves since those reactions are based on our Psychological Roots. However, those reactions and the behavior that follows from them might be counterproductive and other people might consider those reactions to be illogical or irrational. Nevertheless, that person's behavior is a logical result of his/her Psychological Roots. This perspective reconciles the difference between logic that is internal and subjective in an individual, and the logic that an observer has which might have an objective basis. This is a more accurate viewpoint than stating that "emotions are illogical", "people are irrational", or "psychology is not rational".

2. An emotional reaction can interfere with subsequent cognitive processing of information, especially if that emotional reaction is intense.

The interference of emotional reactions with thinking is why many mathematicians, engineers, philosophers, scientists, and military people prefer not being emotional when involved in their work. Other negative effects of strong emotions include intensified conflicts, heightened hostility, increased resistance to change, and an impediment to alternative ideas, and therefore can be an obstacle to growth and progress. Some positive effects of strong emotions are the experience of joy, love, enthusiasm, and energizing of desired behavior. This point of view allows positive aspects of emotion (e.g., empathy, caring, relationships, love, the arts, and decision-making) to be valued, and distinguishes such positive aspects from those related to negative emotions (e.g., counterproductive behaviors and thinking impediments).

Broad nature of Early Psychological Roots

Genetic Psychological Roots exist in many creatures and have broad effects, for example, the need for safety applies regardless of the environment, whether a person is in a jungle, desert, city, water, or outer space. The need for safety is broad and ranges from being generally alert (an Early Psychological Root) to a belief that one should look both ways before crossing a street and that one should be responsible with matches (which are Later Psychological Roots). Concern about fire is more general than later roots but less general than early roots and therefore is an Intermediate Psychological Root in a psychological hierarchy. As these examples illustrate, the closer a Psychological Root is to the genetic origin of its hierarchy, the broader the range of aspects associated with that root. Another way of putting this is that the further a Psychological Root is away from the foundation of its hierarchy, the more it is associated with something specific, tangible, or observable.

As mentioned earlier, what people do is connected with a large chain of Psychological Roots that stretches all the way back to a genetic foundation. It is important to realize this difference between early and later roots when addressing interpersonal problems, as will be seen in later chapters (e.g., when seeking to resolve conflicts, persuade, and conduct psychotherapy).

The generality or specificity of Psychological Roots is reflected in their labels. For example, the genetic needs for safety, stability, and social connectedness encompass a huge spectrum of possibilities. By comparison, liking a particular newspaper or video game is much more specific. This distinction does not mean that Later Psychological Roots are insignificant, for example, believing that matches can start a dangerous fire is important, so is the value of looking both ways before crossing a street. Whether a Psychological Root is general or specific has important practical implications, as will be seen in Section II's chapters regarding teaching, learning, persuading, doing psychotherapy, and resolving conflicts.

When someone is said to have his/her head in the clouds, be an "absent-minded professor", impractical, or lack "common sense", it may be because that person is pre-occupied with abstract thoughts that involve broad Psychological Roots. On the other hand, when someone "has both feet on the ground", is practical, likes working with material things, has "common sense', or is a "concrete" thinker, it may be because that person tends to focus on tangible things, which involve surface Psychological Roots.

It helps to be able to draw upon all hierarchical levels, both general and specific, when needed. An example of being effective at both levels is the Wright brothers who repaired bicycles for a living (a tangible level), and who discovered the secret of flight (an abstract level, see Figure 15). Benjamin Franklin operated a printing press for a living (a tangible activity) and contributed to concepts that led to creating the United States, also made scientific discoveries (abstract activities).

Can Psychological Roots be changed?

It is possible to change Psychological Roots, especially those that are not deeply embedded in a person such as Later Psychological Roots, especially roots that are close to the surface. A strategy for doing so (involving a *'flow-down effect'*) will be described shortly. Early Psychological Roots, such as those that are part of a person's core personality, can be hard to change. However, even genetic roots can be consciously overridden for a short time. Some common examples are engaging in behaviors that run counter to needs for safety, stability, and comfort (e.g., driving too fast, climbing a rickety ladder, eating strange foods, and associating with troublesome people). When a Psychological Root is overridden, that outcome might only last a brief time, hence would have to be repeated for a longer effect.

It is possible to consciously override Psychological Roots as a temporary therapy to overcome counterproductive thoughts and behavior, for example, with regard to depression, anxiety, and addiction. (The beneficial effect of having overridden a Psychological Root can sometimes be extended by shifting attention from that issue to something else of interest.) Described below are two aspects of Psychological Root hierarchies that foster resistance to change and two other aspects that contribute to change.

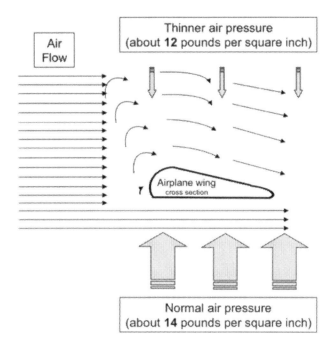

Fig. 15. The shape of an airplane wing (an 'air foil') **thins** the air
above a forward-moving wing, compared to below it.
As a result, **greater** air pressure **below** the wing pushes the wing up.
Therefore, an airplane wing's **natural tendency** is to move **upward**
when wind rushes over it. This makes flying **automatic**.
Flat wings won't work. This took humans 300,000 years to figure out.

1. Hierarchical alignment. Mentioned earlier was that the initial Psychological Root acquired in a Psychological Root hierarchy is conceptually in accord with the genetic Psychological Root at the foundation of its hierarchy, also that the next acquired Psychological Root will be conceptually in accord with the one before it, and so on. New aspects that are consistent with an existing Psychological Root are likely to be responded to positively. New aspects that are inconsistent with an existing Psychological

Root are likely to be responded to negatively. As a result, *'subsidiary Psychological Roots'* in a hierarchy are likely to be conceptually aligned with the foundation root.

The above-mentioned alignment produces: a) an automatic screening of additional roots so that they are in accord with that hierarchy's conceptual theme, and b) an automatic resistance to change from that theme. The resulting hierarchical alignment contributes to maintaining a person's existing personality structure, resistance to change, and stability.

One of the results of this alignment effect is that people with similar characteristics such as ethnicity, or beliefs such as religion or political philosophy, group together. Another is the mutual appeal of mates who have similar values.

2. Defense. When a Psychological Root is challenged, the above-mentioned hierarchical structure generates an implicit drive to maintain the *status quo.* Challenges to Psychological Roots can occur as a result of disagreements, errors, or failures. Overt efforts to support the *status quo* can include attempts to reinterpret an issue, obtain supportive evidence or logic, deny objections or problems, make excuses, blame others, and argue. A person might even defend negative aspects and a new idea might be rejected because it does not fit a person's existing frame of reference. An innovation might not even be understood because comprehension is partly related to a new aspect fitting with what previously exists in a person.

This defensive pattern helps people maintain their existing personality and information. Defensiveness also generates obstacles to innovation especially when accompanied by a commitment to tradition. For example, new theories often meet great resistance (e.g., ideas such as the world is round rather than flat, the earth is not the center of the universe, Darwin's theory of evolution, Einstein's theory of energy and matter, and the use of automobiles in place of horses).

Defensiveness can also lead to defending some unpleasant aspects that a person has who one is aligned with, such as a boss or political affiliate. Another instance occurs when people have trouble accepting others who differ from themselves, such as resisting the acquiring of homes in a particular residential area by people who have a different ethnicity or religion. Physical and cyber-bullying of people who are different are other examples of the defense effect. Genocide is a particularly vicious circumstance.

A result of this defensive effect is using a different criterion for evaluating others than oneself. For example, Mary might complain about what Jon does yet behave similarly. Having a double standard like that can be avoided by applying the same rules to ourselves as we do to others. Being defensive about failing can be lessened by viewing failure as an opportunity to learn.

3. *Ownership.* An ownership effect occurs when a Psychological Root is acquired. As a result, a sense of responsibility occurs for taking care of that root as it would for other important aspects in a person's life. In some instances, ownership might result in admitting a new Psychological Root into a particular cluster. In this way, a person's ownership of an idea and his/her sense of responsibility to it could lead to making personal changes in accord with the new idea. An example is a married couple taking care of one another or a family member becoming a caretaker of a disabled family member. Another example of ownership occurs when someone defends a friend who is being verbally or physically attacked. Still another example is becoming concerned only after one's own "ox is gored", not when bad things happen to other people.

4. *Flow-down effect.* When a Psychological Root is modified it creates an inconsistency among the Psychological Roots in its hierarchy. Consistency is restored when the Roots subsidiary to that root adjust so that they are in accord with that change. An adjustment then occurs all the way down the line from where the initial change occurred, resulting in everything subsidiary to a change becoming aligned with that initial modification.

A number of changes result from flow-down effects. One set of changes involves modification in all of the Psychological Roots that are subsidiary to the location of the initial change. Those changes then affect internal reactions such as thoughts, emotional reactions, intentions, decisions, and impulses. Some behaviors might also change depending on the circumstances. As a result, flow-down aspects can affect many psychological aspects and also some biological aspects (e.g., the placebo effect), not only a modification of informational aspects.[3]

---

[3] Further examples of the flow-down effect are adhering to a contract; monogamy after marrying; giving away possessions upon believing that the end of the world is near; and dissonance theory experiments in which attitude changes to be in accord with a decision (e.g., Festinger, 1957). Synonyms of the flow-down effect are trickle-down effect, domino effect, post-adjustment, and post-shaping.

Thus, the change that takes place when a flow-down result occurs is a domino effect in which more than a single modification can take place. A domino effect occurs because Psychological Roots change all the way forward from the location of the initial modification owing to subsequent alterations in subsidiary roots as they become aligned with the initial change. Thus, each effect can trigger Hidden Sequences which might themselves create other Hidden Sequences (see the Chapter 5 on Multiple Hidden Sequences, discussed earlier).

An example of the sequential *'flow-down effect'* occurs when there is a placebo effect in which a benign substance produces actual relief. Relief occurs when a person's internal reactions change to become in accord with believing that the placebo has a potent effect. (The ability of an abstract belief to create tangible healing illustrates the potency of Psychological Roots.) An instance of the flow-down effect occurs when a person who acquires a belief accepts negatives that accompany that belief. In constructive social influence, such as public health ads and psychotherapy, a flow-down effect can help create constructive outcomes. A conversion disorder, such as blindness when a person cannot tolerate distress, offers another example. It is a biological change that occurs for psychological reasons.

Irrational economic behavior

Richard Thaler won the 2017 Nobel prize in economics because of his research showing that humans make irrational economic decisions. For example, people are willing to pay more to *retain* something they own than to obtain the same thing which they do not own (the "endowment effect"). The endowment effect occurs even after having acquired an object just a few minutes previously so there is no apparent reason to evaluate something differently (the "valuation paradigm"). Related to this is people's ascribing more value to something they *own* than what they do not own, such as taking better care of a house that is theirs compared to one they rent. People may also be more careful about taking care of what they own compared to what they are promised or expect to get. People are also unwilling to exchange something they had been given for something else of equal objective value (e.g., a pen for a coffee mug, or vice-versa; "exchange paradigm", Kahneman, Knetsch, & Thaler, 1991). Carmon and Ariely (2000) found that the selling price people wanted for tournament tickets they owned was 14 times higher than the objective value of those tickets. These findings are also in accord with attachment theory (Morewidge and Giblin, 2015).

Psychological Systems Theory explains the endowment effect as being related to the ownership effect and sense of responsibility described above (# 3), also the much stronger effect that negatives have compared to positives. For example, taking something away is a negative experience, whereas the possibility of obtaining something desirable is positive. Need to avoid negatives, acquire positives, and take responsibility are genetic Psychological Roots. The ownership and flow-down effects related to Psychological Roots affect outcomes such as material things like tournament tickets, coffee mugs, and pens.

Thus, upon taking Psychological Roots into account, the endowment effect is logical on the basis of what takes place *internally* in an individual, yet the behavior that is seen by others can look irrational. Another way of saying this is that Jon might be functioning logically in regard to what leads him to take an action, but Jon's overt behavior can seem illogical to someone else who takes external aspects into account. It seems paradoxical that while a person's *subjective* psychological process can be logical, his behavior might be illogical from an *objective* standpoint.

Another economic behavior that appears to be irrational occurs when people expect a pattern to continue, such as a winning streak. Psychological Systems Theory's explanation for this "hot hand fallacy" is that there is selective attention to what is salient (e.g., a winning or losing streak), also a tendency to think in absolutes. *'Selective attention'* refers to focus on what is being attended to, with non-salient aspects fading into the background. (Chapter 19 discusses absolute thinking.)

Aversion to loss occurs when a loss has far more weight for a person than a gain of ostensibly equal value. This is another irrational economic behavior and Kahneman and Tversky's (1979) Prospect Theory offers an economic explanation. Psychological Systems Theory would ascribe people's aversion to loss to the greater potency of negative emotional reactions compared to positive reactions. Ownership and the genetic sense of responsibility add additional negatives to the experience of loss (e.g., how much distress a person has depends on "whose ox is gored".)

Thus, when people do illogical things, that behavior is judged on an *objective* basis. However, when people's *subjective* mental processes are taken into account, that behavior is seen to have an internal logic.

Change is not simple

One of the things that people may be concerned about when contemplating making a change is that they may have to cope with unknown consequences. That could cause them to be wary about making a change, which might be indicated by a person using phrases such as "fear of the unknown", "you never know what might happen", and "better to be safe than sorry". Since much of psychology operates subconsciously, people might not be able to articulate their concerns. When attempting to persuade someone, it may help to take into consideration the possibility that the other person may be concerned about possible negative consequences of changing.

Some practical benefits

Knowing that higher-order Psychological Roots are more general than lower-order roots is of great help when trying to resolve conflicts, as will be seen in chapters 20 – 23. As an example, a desire not to be controlled, disrespected, or taken advantage of (Psychological Roots that occur in some conflicts) are more general than issues in dispute such as feeling insulted by what someone said or feeling harmed by what someone did. The range of opportunities for creating a compatible solution are limited by protagonists' focus on tangible issues, for instance, two people claiming that a particular pen is theirs. It would be difficult to partition that pen, however viewing things from a Psychological Roots standpoint – such as each person needing an implement with which to write – provides a more general perspective that offers numerous options, which could lead to resolving the dispute. As another example, there are very few ways to satisfy someone's desire to get another person to retract a derogatory statement, or to get a refund, or to agree about something. However, if feeling disrespected is a reason for a particular conflict, there are many ways to satisfy that concern. Thus, when disagreements arise, it helps to realize that there are deep Psychological Roots (e.g., need for safety) which, because of their general nature, offer a large number of opportunities for creating solutions. The author has found that identifying the Psychological Roots involved offers the key to creating win-win solutions that can produce solutions even in conflicts that appear to be intractable. (A specific step-by-step strategy for resolving conflicts is described in Section II.)

Knowing about root hierarchies can be especially important when trying to correct a psychological disorder such as depression, anxiety, or addiction. For example, change that occurs in aspects close to or at the surface (e.g., some internal reactions, behaviors, or low-order Psychological Roots such as dysfunctional attitudes) might produce only limited gains if the origin of that disorder has not changed. The disorder's origin may be deep in the person's Psychological Root hierarchies. For this reason, a vacation might offer pleasant relief, but only temporarily. However, modifying the distress-prone expectations that fuel the condition can produce a much more powerful and long-term effect.

Opportunities for finding solutions increase greatly when high-order Psychological Roots are addressed because the broad nature of those roots can offer many solutions that would not be possible if only low-order aspects were addressed. Also, modifying or satisfying a higher-order inner motivation can have a wide-spread influence that spreads out to a great many Psychological Roots, compared to addressing lower-order Psychological Roots, internal reactions, and behaviors. Also, trying to change lower-order Psychological Roots can be difficult if those changes are not consistent with a person's deep roots.

'Filtering' and 'shaping'

'*Filtering*' occurs when new information is blocked from linking, such as by keeping new information from aligning with an existing Psychological Root. For example, people may refuse to accept ideas that counteract their viewpoint. '*Shaping*' occurs when something new is modified to facilitate or prevent linking, such as when incoming information is interpreted, altered, added to, or subtracted from so as to aid aligning with an existing Psychological Root. Filtering and shaping - by aligning new aspects with existing Psychological Roots or by rejecting them - may be some of the ways the brain tries to make sense of new things. Pre-shaping and post-shaping are described below.

- '*Pre-shaping*' is a process that modifies something before linking can take place. Some pre-shaping facilitates linking to make it consistent with a Psychological Root and thereby avoid having it screened out (synonym: pre-adjustment). However, there can also be pre-shaping that leads to non-linking, such as when someone intentionally refuses to be persuaded. An example of pre-shaping that aids linking occurs when a salesperson shows a shopper how a particular product can satisfy that customer's need. Pre-shaping is also operating when parents set limits on their children with the intent of training them to develop socially-acceptable guidelines. Another instance of pre-shaping occurs when a person with a strong religious conviction accepts Darwin's ideas by accepting the idea that evolution occurred after a supreme being created earth's living creatures.

- '*Post-shaping*' is a flow-down effect in which subsidiary Psychological Roots are altered after a root has been modified. (Synonym: '*Psychological Root modification*'.) An example of post-shaping occurs when a person moderates her negative perspective about an elected candidate to lessen her unhappiness about the defeat of the candidate she preferred. Another example of post-shaping occurs when a person adjusts his attitude to get along with a disturbing co-worker.

- *Concurrent shaping* occurs when new information changes during the process of being assimilated, as Piaget appears to have believed (Flavell, 1966). Such change might also be termed *'concurrent shaping'* or *'simultaneous shaping'*.

Shaping and filtering do not always occur

There are circumstances in which shaping and filtering do not occur. For example, a phone number can be remembered long enough for it to be dialed without modifying it. Another instance is retaining words that have been spoken long enough to maintain a conversation. In such instances, a person directly links new information to a short-term goal and does not need that information after the goal is achieved.

Memorizing by rote is another instance of linking new information to a short-term goal without shaping or filtering the information, such as when a student keeps information in memory long enough to pass an upcoming exam. There is a drawback to acquiring information via such memorization-by-rote in that after the objective is achieved, much of the information attached to that particular goal vanishes along with the goal. Hence, when a person's objective is to retain something in memory for a long time or to understand something, rote memorization would not be the preferred method. When the objective is long-term retention it would be better served by linking the new information with deep Psychological Roots. (More on this subject in Section II).

Algorithmic sequence

Taking the flow-down effect into consideration with filtering and pre-shaping produces the following algorithm when screening new information:
1. Evaluation of new information to ascertain if it aligns with existing Psychological Roots (YES or NO).
2a. If YES occurs at Step 1, the new information links to a Psychological Root.
3a. After linking, flow-down changes occur further along that particular Psychological Root hierarchy.

2b. If NO occurs at Step 1, the new information is rejected or shaped to align (REJECTED or SHAPED).
3b. If SHAPED after Step 2b, the new information links to a Psychological Root.
4b. After linking, flow-down changes occur further along that particular Psychological Root hierarchy.

3c. If REJECTED at Step 2b, another try at shaping might or might not occur (REJECTED or SHAPED).
4c. If SHAPED after Step 3c, the new information links to a Psychological Root.
5c. After linking, flow-down changes occur further along that particular Psychological Root hierarchy.

4d. If REJECTED at Step 3c, the new information is filtered out.
4e. If that rejection is challenged, a reason supporting the rejection may be created.

Uniqueness

Many genetic and acquired Biological and Psychological Roots can be involved when a behavior occurs, which contributes to the wide differentiation among individuals.

a) Genetic Psychological Roots: Although all normal persons have the same genetic Psychological Roots, the magnitude of each of those roots varies from person to person, with considerable variation. For example, some individuals' genetic threshold for emotional arousal could be extremely low, some extremely high, and some moderate. A similarly wide range exists for our other genetic Biological and Psychological Roots and thereby, itself, contributes to the large variation in personality that starts before birth and continues throughout life.

b) Acquired Psychological Roots: Acquired roots can differ qualitatively as well as quantitatively, such as in the many possible abilities, goals, values, expectations, beliefs, and personal rules that people have. As an example, religious people vary greatly in the importance and adherence ascribed to a religion's various tenets. Also, people absorb only some of the huge amounts of information to which they are exposed. Much depends on what aligns with each individual's Psychological Roots.

The huge differences in both genetic and acquired Psychological Roots result in such a large number of variations that it is unlikely that any individuals are exact replicas of one another, including identical twins. A common example of the differences among people is that some people might laugh at a joke, some might frown, some might take umbrage, and some might have little or no reaction to it. People's differences can be so extreme that it is possible for some people to understand a message to be the opposite of what the communicator intended or what the facts indicate, something that is not uncommon with people who have opposing political viewpoints. Sometimes what people perceive does not correspond to reality (e.g., Allport & Postman, 1948). Perceptions can differ across societies, with some societies viewing something to be beneficial that other societies consider harmful. Societies change, sometimes intentionally (e.g., support for or against particular abilities or public-health issues), sometimes unintentionally (e.g., as a result of revolutions, war, and technological advances). Sometimes change occurs when a scorned trait is transformed into a societal benefit, such as when law enforcement agencies use criminals to help thwart crime (e.g., bank-robber Willie Sutton [Moehringer, 2012] and con-man Frank Abnagale Jr. [Abnagale & Redding, 1980].

Longevity of Psychological Roots

The more significant an acquired Psychological Root is to a person the more salient and easily accessed that root is likely to be. Some roots have great importance for people, for example, a person who nearly drowns might develop a strong fear about being on boats, lakes, streams, and oceans. An intense concern about paying attention to hot objects can result from having touched a hot stove. Some acquired Psychological Roots can last a lifetime, for example, low self-esteem can occur from having been put down by parents or other authority figures, or from feeling like a failure, or from having been savaged by prejudiced individuals. A Psychological Root that is rarely utilized, or has low salience or relevance could have a low frequency of subsequently being drawn upon.

Since negatives are more potent than positives, low self-esteem is probably more prevalent than high self-esteem. Young children are especially likely to have strong reactions because of their tendency to think in absolutes. Hence, when a person acquires low self-esteem in early childhood, that negative self-regard might be extreme. Subsequent Psychological Roots that attach to that early root would then be consistent with that poor self-evaluation, which would further embed that person's low self-regard, perhaps for a lifetime (an example of the impact of early life experiences).

When positive traits are acquired in early childhood, such as confidence or optimism, such traits might also last throughout life. Individuals with high self-regard might feel good about themselves and have an upbeat perspective, and therefore have a lower chance of experiencing a psychological disorder such as depression or anxiety. The reverse can happen when traits acquired early in life are negative since that circumstance could prime a person to experience disorders (e.g., depression, anxiety, addiction, or criminality).

Predispositions acquired early in life can seem to be so fundamental to an individual that they might appear to be inherited genetically, especially if a parent or relative has similar characteristics. Deep Psychological Roots are difficult to change, which further underscores the importance of early childhood experiences.

Needs, desires, concerns, and interests

Biological and psychological needs generate strong drives to be fulfilled because they are necessities, hence not satisfying those needs can create emotional distress. For example, not having sufficient air to breathe is frightening, and not eating for two or three days can be extremely discomforting. Being alone produces sadness because it does not satisfy humans' genetically wired-in need for close emotional connections. As these examples illustrate, distress can result when Psychological Roots, such as needs, are not satisfied. Such strong negative emotional reactions are greater than the positive feelings that occur when roots are satisfied. A potential for experiencing strong distress occurs when people consider their acquired Psychological Roots to be necessities, such as when they believe that they must have a new device or a certain behavior is viewed as necessary, essential, required, or expected.

Freud (1990), Murray (1938), and Maslow (1954) described many genetically wired-in psychological needs. Some additional genetic needs are mentioned in Boxes 5a-b. Ability, talent, and giftedness are discussed in a later chapter. Listed below are some systems that have not been prominently discussed in this book (presented in alphabetical order).

Aggression	Here-and-now orientation
Anger	Ownership effect
Annoyance	Physical dependency
Centrality principle	Retaliation
Communication	Selective attention
Competitiveness (desire to win)	Successive insights
Contraction	Thematic analysis
Emotional dependency	Victim mentality
Growth (expansion)	Vulnerability

BOX 5a. SOME POSSIBLE GENETIC PSYCHOLOGICAL ROOTS
(in alphabetical order)

> *Desire:*
> for aesthetically pleasing sensory input
> for internal factors to be arranged hierarchically
> for quick closure (therefore impatient)
> for tangibility
> to be an individual
> to be aware of the limits
> to be caring, concerned, considerate
> to be creative
> to be unique
> to create clusters
> to engage in deductive reasoning
> to engage in inductive reasoning
> to focus
> to generalize
> to have challenges (e.g., wanting to engage problems)
> to have empathy, compassion
> to identify patterns
> to link with something larger than oneself
> to make an emotional connection with others
> to make discriminations
> to make evaluations
> to meet responsibility
> to mobilize effort in pursuit of a goal
> to not to be controlled
> to organize information, people, tasks
> to solve problems
> to synthesize
> to understand, know, make sense of input f
> use abilities, talents, and gifts
> use absolutes
> to win, be victorious, be competitive

BOX 5b. SOME POSSIBLE GENETIC PSYCHOLOGICAL ROOTS
(in alphabetical order)

Existence of:
a threshold level for emotional arousal
a threshold level for states of uncontrollability
comfort zone
criteria for failure, standards
criteria for goals, success, aspirations,
    objectives
ranges of acceptability and unacceptability
retrenching what is not used
strengthening what is used
utilizing what one has (genetic & acquired)

Need:
for autonomy, not be controlled
for closure, fill voids, make decisions
for respect, importance
for simplicity, non-ambiguity, directness
for stability
for stimulation
to acquire information
to attack back when hurt (retaliation)
to avoid negatives (e.g., failure, loss, boredom)
to be accepted by others
to communicate
to defend one's territory
to grow intellectually, explore
to have positives (e.g., pleasure, satisfaction)
to respond to stimuli (internal and external)
to set goals
to solve problems

Psychological Roots such as goals, aims, aspirations, objectives, and wants are desires. Fulfilling desires brings pleasure, for example, success, in itself, fulfills a desire to be effective, hence just satisfying a goal feels good even when without there being any material gain. A negative reaction can occur when a desire is not be satisfied, which could be substantial when that desire is considered a need. Desire automatically accompanies a need. However, the 'need' aspect is stronger than the 'desire' aspect because a strong negative reaction occurs when a need is not satisfied, and negatives are more powerful than positives (discussed in Chapter 10).

As a result, the drive to avoid failing to satisfy a need is likely to be stronger than the drive to achieve a goal (unless a person views a goal as if it were a need). Aspirations are not necessities, hence it should be easier for people to accept not achieving their goals than not having their needs met. However, as noted above, when people treat their goals and desires as needs, there is a double drive – a positive drive to achieve the goal and a stronger drive to avoid failing. In such instances, not achieving a goal can cause considerable distress. Children might not distinguish between goals and needs because they tend to think in sweeping absolutes, which would explain why young children have temper tantrums when adults refuse to give them something they desire, such as candy or a toy, because what they desire feels like a need to them. (More on this issue in Chapter 11 regarding goals and expectations, including how to lessen distress related to such aspects.)

A practical application of this information

The foundation for a better existence can start early in life by acquiring constructive Psychological Roots. Even minor opposition to Psychological Roots disturbs us, and we strive to maintain them, examples of which include having a strong reaction to being disagreed with, receiving unasked for advice, or having our boundaries transgressed (one of the reasons for our concern about privacy). Our ability to be interpersonally effective depends on connecting satisfactorily with others' Psychological Roots while simultaneously satisfying our roots. Understanding how to work effectively with Psychological Roots and their hierarchies can be learned. A society-wide effort to use these principles constructively might help people socially and perhaps also help solve many personal and interpersonal problems such as addiction, prejudice, bullying, and violence. (Section II offers aids for doing so, also for communicating, resolving conflicts, and constructive social influence.)

Chapter 8. CLUSTERS AND CATEGORIES

Why can we speak rapidly, readily draw upon correct words from tens of thousands of words in our vocabulary, easily create grammatically-correct sentences, and quickly recall long-past memories? This chapter offers an explanation.

Clusters

Linking, in addition to allowing Psychological Roots to form linear chains (hierarchies), also leads to *'clusters'* of conceptually related groups of roots (see Figure 16). For instance, a cluster connected to a person's interest in transportation might include interests, goals, and rules about many types of vehicles, from bicycles to boats. Clusters' themes are somewhat comparable to specific topic areas in a library such as American history, European travel, slow cooking, and back exercises. The existence of a cluster is illustrated by what happened to "Dorene" whenever she experienced a failure. Any setback, no matter how slight, instantly brought three troubling things to her awareness: her distressing childhood, her son's untimely death, and her unpleasant ex-husband. Those three aspects involved different times in her life yet were grouped together in her mind, associated with her believing that she was a failure. On the positive side, clusters can facilitate functioning effectively, including switching from one concern to another (e.g., from home, to travel, work, or hobby).[1] (Synonyms for clusters are Psychological Root clusters and root clusters).

Clusters are somewhat similar to Piaget's concept of schemas (Flavell, 1966). However, many different types of Psychological Roots are included in clusters, not just intellectual information (e.g., needs, interests, expectations, and specific fears; see Figure 16). Clusters also resemble groupings in schema theory (Young, Klosko, & Weishaar, 2006). (See Figure 17 for a representation of clusters). Clusters encompass a number of Psychological Roots and so are labeled with general terms, much as 'shoes' is a cluster that includes slippers, hiking boots, sneakers, sandals, and dress shoes. A particular Psychological Root can be especially salient within a cluster (e.g., especially painful concerns can come to mind when something distressing occurs, as with Dorene, mentioned above).

---

[1] There are *'sub-clusters'*, for example, a sub-cluster about airplanes might include beliefs and information ranging from small propeller planes to unmanned drones. Other sub-clusters might be groupings related to safety, speed, and knowledge about how an air-foil works to create flight.

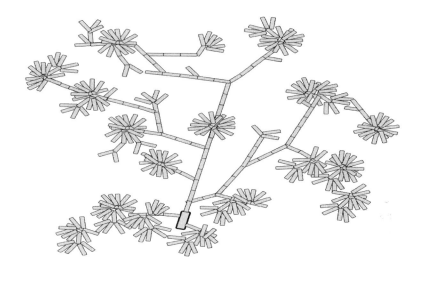

Fig. 16. **Clusters** of psychological roots
(analogous to bunches of grapes).

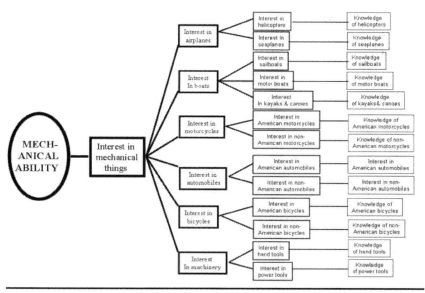

Fig. 17. A fictional representation of a psychological root cluster.

Categories

A group of clusters can have aspects in common, creating a *'category'*, somewhat like the broad topics in a library, such as history, travel, cooking, sports, and magazines. For instance, some clusters connected with different types of transportation might include cars, trains, boats, planes, and inter-stellar transports.[2] Category names are broader than those of individual clusters, for example, 'vehicle' encompasses all of the above-mentioned types of transportation, and 'clothing' involves clusters from shoes to hats.

When something new links with a Psychological Root it also connects with that root's cluster and category. Those links help explain why we readily connect many aspects, especially those with the same genetic Psychological Root. These associations facilitate verbal fluency, use of synonyms, thinking, reasoning, creativity, and utilization of examples, and is especially valuable in occupations and solving problems.

Abilities, talents, and gifts

An *ability* – such as a capacity to move one's muscles, to use language, or think – originates with genetically wired-in Biological and Psychological Roots. Some people have an especially strong genetic ability – a *talent* – for instance, a special facility with words, concepts, mathematics, art, social strategies, or athletics (see discussion of multiple intelligences in Gardner, 1983). Having a talent facilitates acquiring links related to it and those acquisitions can further develop that talent by creating a *'strong psychological-root complex'* containing extensive categories, sub-categories, clusters, and sub-clusters of Psychological Roots. Acquired Biological Roots also play a role. An ability is genetically wired in, whereas a skill is acquired.

A talent can be further developed by adding Psychological and Biological Roots through practice, information, and advances developed by oneself or others. Each acquired link adds further opportunities for increasing understanding, insight, and fine-tuning, expanding the breadth of that talent. Strong complexes are contributed to by motivation to grow, have questions answered, fill voids, and improve. Guidance and support from others can also help, as does having opportunities to use a talent, experiment with it, and creatively explore ideas connected with it. Such psychological growth can continue throughout life.

A *gift* is an even stronger genetically-endowed ability than a talent. Individuals with a gift have an extraordinarily strong Psychological Root

---

[2] There can be 'sub-categories' within categories that consist of multiple sub-clusters, for example, particular types of trains, boats, or planes.

complex with extensive Psychological Root clusters, sub-clusters, categories, and sub-categories.

Thus, while every normal person is born with some capabilities – such as ability with words, music, art, athletics, and reasoning – a relatively small number of people have a particular talent, and only a tiny number of people have a special gift. The difference between high ability, talent, and a gift might perhaps correspond to standard deviations of 1, 2, and 3 from the population midpoint. A person who is talented or gifted in one aspect might not necessarily be strong in other traits.

People who have a talent or a gift are likely to develop those abilities still further in part because Psychological Roots have a drive to be utilized. That drive is amplified by the number of roots in a root complex because the thrust of each of the various roots has an additive effect. As a result, each Psychological Root complex generates a particularly strong desire for a person to do things that are consistent with it (e.g., some starving artists would rather paint than earn a living at a routine job). Having a strong drive can lead to frequently using a particular talent or gift, which can produce still further expansion of knowledge and improved finesse ("practice makes perfect").

Facilitation

Noted previously were that the many associations among Psychological Roots facilitate thinking, talking, and planning. The greater the number of Psychological Roots, clusters, and links the greater the facilitation. Although associations occur below awareness, they can be utilized readily on demand, which usually makes it easy to retrieve relevant pieces of information as needed. For example, people can immediately name things that have a red color or are rectangular. This ability is especially present in people who previously developed a cluster related to the issue, such as one that relates to their occupation, hobby, or religion. Frequent use of information in a cluster also helps, while lack of use can lead to lapses in making connections and remembrance. Clusters also make it easy to recall experiences in the distant past, such as an early childhood incident. Such recall occurs without having to retrace the original sequence in which that information was acquired. Having the ability to go directly to a cluster also facilitates drawing upon aspects that a person might not realize he/she has, such as the ability to follow grammatical rules without consciously having to articulate them.

Clusters' rapid ability to make connections aids thinking, problem-solving, and communicating. Being able to instantly draw upon a substantial library of information that has been acquired over an extensive time is a special advantage possessed by experienced workers, seasoned team players, and military veterans. Despite their substantial experience, those individuals are unlikely to be aware of the complex sub-surface processes that have been involved in their having acquired and organized that knowledge. For example, young parents might not realize how much useful information they can give their children until they are called upon to do so.

People are unlikely to know that they have clusters or categories of Psychological Roots, or that those groupings enable them to quickly converse, do complex tasks, and draw upon varied aspects as needed. Should a person not have a cluster or piece of information, he/she can quickly acquire or create it by linking it to a Psychological Root related to it (e.g., learning something connected with their hobby). Learning can be slower and harder when there is no information or cluster related to that topic (e.g., when attempting to learn a new occupation or school subject). When Psychological Roots or links are no longer relevant, have not been used for a long time, or deteriorate (e.g., due to illness, poor nutrition, or aging), such skills and accessibility to them can diminish. An example is forgetting information with which one was fluent years before, such as someone's name.

Clusters and intelligence

Ability to acquire Psychological Roots facilitates creating clusters, which bolsters skill at solving problems related to those acquired roots. The more roots that are acquired, the greater the number of additional roots that can be attached to those that are acquired. Acquiring problem-solving strategies and additional information can improve intelligence. An expansion of the number of Psychological Roots and clusters is involved when people steep themselves in a particular skill area, such as music, graphics, logic, mathematics, kinesthetics, and social strategies (see Gardner's, 1983, multiple intelligences). If this pattern of acquisition of Psychological Roots and clusters also occurs in some other organisms, such as primates, then those creatures' intelligence would also improve accordingly. (Shettleworth, 2009, describes the intelligent behavior of many non-human creatures.)

Clusters and Psychological Root hierarchies

Clusters can branch anywhere along a hierarchical chain and can link to other clusters. A stimulus that relates to different aspects might be able to activate more than one cluster.

The totality of a person's various Psychological Roots, clusters, and categories are unique to each person, although many individuals have some roots, clusters, and categories in common with other people. There can be a commonality of some Psychological Roots in persons who grow up together. Commonality of some Psychological Roots is especially likely in people who are members of a particular sub-group, live in the same area, have a similar religion or political philosophy, or are engaged in the same occupation. Having similar clusters and particularly similar core roots such as values can aid compatibility when meeting people ("I feel as if I've known you for a long time"). Such aspects can be factors that contribute to relationships, military units that bond tightly, and sports teams whose members work well other. Conversely, having few Psychological Roots and clusters in common with other people could present obstacles for making close connections with other individuals, even with some people a person has known for a long time, including family members, neighbors, and school-mates. People whose clusters differ greatly from others can progress in different directions and can grow apart, such as marital partners who do not cultivate similar interests and individuals who leave a group or move to a different workplace or residence.

A person's Psychological Roots foster an interest in aspects related to those roots. The larger and more numerous the clusters related to something, the greater the interest in that topic. Great interest in something can contribute to a person being attentive to it when not interested in something else that is going on, such as school work. That distraction can create problems with attention. There is a benefit to being distracted when something is unpleasant (reframing).

Core personality structure

Core genetic and acquired Psychological Roots are integral to people's personality traits and some roots and clusters acquired later in life can become core roots. These include beliefs, goals, occupational and avocational interests, expectations of oneself and others, and specific fears. Knowing a person's core Psychological Roots and related root clusters can aid understanding that individual, relating to him/her, and being effective when attempting to help him/her when needed.

A practical application of this information

One reason we can reason and speak rapidly is that we can draw upon a huge amount of knowledge and vocabulary that exists in our many clusters. Tapping into one aspect can often trigger a connection with related aspects, which aids our ability to think and converse with others. The ability to discern another person's Psychological Roots is especially helpful when evaluating someone as a potential mate or employee, or when assessing that person's potential for creating disruption or danger. (Section II has practical applications related to the information in this chapter.)

Chapter 9. PERTINENT VS. BACKGROUND PSYCHOLOGICAL ROOTS

The *'centrality principle'* suggests that if you want to know what causes someone to do something or why a problem exists such as an addiction or a psychological disorder, it is essential to know the key aspects. This chapter discusses Psychological Roots that are pertinent and roots that exist in the background.

Pertinent Psychological Roots

A *'pertinent Psychological Root'* is one that is a prominent cause of a particular internal reaction or behavior. A number of roots can be pertinent in a given circumstance, with *'key pertinent roots'* having the strongest effect (synonym: *key roots*). Examples of pertinent roots are a necessity of escaping from danger, a need to pass an upcoming exam, and a desire to be victorious in a competition. Some *'non-salient pertinent roots'* can be pertinent but not key roots, for example, low self-esteem, which might generate a low amount of ongoing negative emotion or does so intermittently. A long-term goal that operates in the background can be a pertinent Psychological Root that is not salient. After a relevant internal reaction or behavior ends, such as after a goal has been achieved, the Psychological Roots that had been pertinent might no longer be so.

Background Psychological Roots

When a Psychological Root is not pertinent, it is a *'background Psychological Root'* waiting to be called upon, such as a belief that does not apply to a current situation. (Synonym: *'passive Psychological Root'*). In that un-involved status, a Psychological Root is passive and inactive, in effect, dormant. A currently passive Psychological Root can become a pertinent root in a different situation or when a stimulus impacts it. Whether a background root will or will not become a pertinent root depends on various factors, such as its threshold level and the strength of an impacting stimulus. (Stimulus-and-Root Sequences were described in Chapter 4 on Hidden Sequences). Some Psychological Roots are more easily triggered, accessed, or retrieved from their background status than others.

Only a small number of a person's vast store of Psychological Roots are pertinent at a time. Most Psychological Roots remain in the background, while some operate as non-salient pertinent roots (e.g., genetic needs for interpersonal connectedness and safety, and core acquired roots such as long-term goals and basic values).

Short- and long-term memory

Short-term memory exists as long as it is needed, often briefly, such as while conducting a conversation or completing a task. (Synonym: working memory.) Long-term memory can result when something significant happens to a person. Examples include an exhilarating circumstance, a special positive emotional connection with a loved one, or a particularly unpleasant emotional connection such as an injury or abuse. Since memory is connected to a Psychological Root, it can become active when a still higher-order root is impacted by a stimulus.

Memories are associated with background Psychological Roots and remain dormant until triggered. Being in the background lessens the chances of dormant roots and memories impeding or diluting attention to a current activity, such as decision-making, a task, reasoning, evaluating, or problem-solving.

Something that entered memory a long time before can be activated by a stimulus, such as a sound, odor, or scene. For example, living far from home can trigger a longing to be there (homesickness), and a past emotional experience such as an early romance can kindle a longing to re-engage that circumstance (nostalgia). Some stimuli that trigger long-term memories have a powerful impact (e.g., in Post Traumatic Stress Disorder).

(Reinforcement that is related to Psychological Roots is discussed in Chapter 18.)

A practical application of this information

When the Psychological Root to which new information attaches is a short-term goal – such as an upcoming school exam – much or all of what links to that goal vanishes after the goal ends. A better way to remember something would be to identify something that is particularly interesting related to the subject matter and then attach the new information to that aspect, preferably a deep Psychological Root. (*'Self-comprehension learning'* is discussed in Section II).

Chapter 10. APPEALING AND REPELLING FORCES

Some people have a knack for getting along well with other people, while other people have difficulties. A basis for each of these patterns of behavior is remarkably simple, as this chapter explains.

Emotions

There are two centers of emotion that are wired-into the brain, one positive, the other negative. Those centers are deep in the diencephalon, a part of the brain sometimes referred to as the "old brain" or the "reptilian brain". The centers for emotion originated many millions of years ago, in non-human animals. The emotionality of other creatures is readily seen, such as in our pets, who often are loving but can also aggress at times. The negative emotional center is far more defined and developed than the positive emotional center. The negative emotional center is located below the positive emotional center in the brain, indicating that it developed earlier than the positive center.

As a result, negative emotions are far stronger than positive emotions (also see Cullen et al., 1975). For example, if you have a great day then something bad happens, that unpleasant circumstance is likely to be what you are likely to focus on. The strength of negative emotions is seen in the powerful expressions of anger and the great destructiveness of violence. Negative emotions are easily aroused and therefore it might not take much for people to become irritated. Negative emotions are also likely to last longer than positive emotions and contribute to cumulative build-up, which often can set the stage for going past a tipping point more easily compared to positive emotions.

The characteristics of the emotional centers mentioned above suggest that as important as positive emotions are, strong negative reactions have been more critical for survival than positive emotions. Perhaps strong negative emotions were needed by the first *homo sapiens* on earth 325,000 years ago (and for earlier creatures including prior types of humans and non-human animals) because they aided coping with predators that strike powerfully and rapidly, such as wolves, lions, and bears.

In a civilized society, strong negative reactions can be counterproductive. Regulations, laws, police, and military forces do not change genetic wiring, therefore to avoid being savages, self-control is necessary. People who want effective interpersonal relations, a safe society and peace in the world recognize the need for people to moderate their negative emotional reactions and how people acquire effective self-control. Behavior that is criminal, disturbing, and non-cooperative works against maintaining a civil society. Having a constructive civilization depends substantially upon parents having the skill to raise children who contribute to civilizing behavior rather than impede it. Parents who know how to help their children acquire interpersonal skills and modify their Psychological Roots are benefiting society as well as their own family. A discussion of aspects that trigger positive and negative emotions is included in this chapter.

Appealing forces

We have a genetically wired-in desire to experience positive reactions such as pleasure, satisfaction, joy, and contentment. What produces a pleasing reaction are *'appealing forces'*, including aspects that are consistent with our Psychological Roots and therefore comfortable, such as cordial experiences with others, feeling appreciated, being agreed with, being loved, humor, and attaining goals. Unconditional positive regard (Rogers, 1951) and positive reinforcement (Skinner, 1974) are appealing forces, as is relief from unpleasantness (termed 'negative reinforcement', Skinner, 1974). A negative outcome that is averted or does not occur is an appealing force, such as when a tornado does not strike or when a remedy is found to be non-toxic. Being able to identify something positive when failures occur ("making lemonade out of lemons" or reframing) is an appealing force, such as when a divorce opens the opportunity for finding a better mate or losing a job leads to obtaining a better occupation.

Using sincere appealing forces increases the likelihood of obtaining positive reactions from other people in return. Identifying other people's Psychological Roots aids estimating what might constitute appealing forces for them. Aspects that satisfy genetic or acquired Biological and Psychological Roots can be positive reinforcers. Positive reinforcers need not be limited to aspects associated with Biological Roots, such as desires for food and avoiding pain. (Reinforcement that is related to Psychological Roots is discussed in Chapter 18.)

Repelling forces

A *'repelling force'* is anything that generates a negative emotional reaction such as distress, frustration, irritation, anger, loss, failure, fear, and discontent. We have a wired-in need to avoid experiencing such negative reactions. Repelling forces include being pressured, controlled, or insulted. Negative emotional reactions have a particularly strong effect, far stronger than positive emotional reactions (e.g., Cullen et al., 1975), and mentioned above. As an example, the New England Patriots football team accomplished something extraordinary, a streak of 21 straight wins. When they finally lost, the son of one of their coaches told him, "Your team is awful!" (The actual term was stronger). A common experience is that even after a day of good experiences, one small negative circumstance is likely to be what people are concerned about and remember. A possible reason for having such strong negative reactions is that when humans were first on earth, other creatures, including humans, were either friends or enemies and there were not many friends.

People are so sensitive to negatives that regaining acceptance from someone after using repelling forces with that person can sometimes be problematic, even when the prior relationship had been excellent. Love can be insufficient to sustain the strain that comes from arguing, criticism, putdowns, and yelling. Repelling forces are likely to be remembered for a long time and some people carry grudges to their grave. In the author's experience, a major reason for divorce is that couples do not know how to resolve their differences effectively. (A method for creating win-win solutions when conflicts arise is described in Chapters 20 - 23.)

The potency of negatives means that even a tiny repelling force can generate a disturbing reaction, even when accompanied by appealing forces. For example, something as simple as saying "Yes, but …" might create a problem because 'but' is negative and its effect could swamp the effect of having said 'yes' initially. It would be better to say 'yes', say something agreeable, omit 'but', then pause before introducing an opposing statement. This pattern may seem easy but can be hard to do. Smiling or nodding agreeably while presenting an opposing viewpoint might also help. (This behavior, too, is harder to do than it may seem.)

Unfortunately, people often use repelling forces. There are many such turn-offs, such as criticism, coercion, and punishment. People who complain or point out others' failings may feel justified but not realize the unpleasant effect they are having on the recipient. Another example is, "What have you done for me lately?", overlooking or forgetting the many positives the other person has done. The aversive nature of repelling forces is intuitively understood at times, such as when parents teach children to be polite to try to avoid their being inconsiderate to others, and when people avoid being unpleasant upon initially meeting others.

There are wide-ranging individual differences regarding the repelling forces people use, how often they use them, and how other people react to them. For example, Jon says something he thinks is funny but Mary reacts negatively to it. A cultural norm in one society can be a repelling force in another society (e.g., in Germany, direct and blunt speaking is valued, while the opposite occurs in China and Japan).

Using repelling forces greatly increases the potential for being disliked and has a high likelihood of generating a negative reaction in response, such as antagonism or rejection. It is especially important to try to avoid using repelling forces since negatives are far stronger than positives, which makes it hard to come back after having made a glaring *faux pas.*

Some people have the impression that being legally free to do whatever they feel inclined to do means that they can insult, put down, or intimidate other people, such as those who are disliked, disadvantaged, or in a minority group. Those individuals might intentionally want to harm others emotionally or may not be interested in avoiding doing harm. Using a self-statement of "Sticks and stones might break my bones but names will never harm me" might help a person who is pummeled by verbal repelling forces from someone, but emotional distress can result, nevertheless.

People who believe that others will forget negatives gamble against the odds. Since repelling forces have powerful negative effects, a particularly important social skill is the ability to realize in advance what is likely to attract or repel others and to try to prevent generating negative reactions with other people. Doing this can sometimes be difficult to accomplish even with good intentions, but it pays to make an effort to do so.

Something that is inconsistent with a person's Psychological Roots can be a repelling force unless there are extenuating circumstances (e.g., when it is acceptable such as some instances of comedy and satire). An out-of-control fire is an obvious repelling force because it conflicts with our wired-in need for safety and desire to avoid pain. Repelling forces can be intangible, such as withholding an appealing force (e.g., not keeping a promise, not selecting someone, not greeting someone, or not giving praise when it is expected). Profanity and retaliation may feel acceptable or justifiable to the person who uses them but can be repelling forces to others.

Negative reinforcement

Something that relieves discomfort is likely to be reacted to positively, allowing it to be used as a reward. The positive effect from ending something negative is termed 'negative reinforcement'. For example, a desire to avoid failing is a strong motivation for students to study for exams and therefore a negative reinforcement. Negative reinforcement is also involved when a mobster gives you "An offer you can't refuse" (i.e., no harm will come if you do what he demands). Blackmail is another instance of negative reinforcement ("Do this or else …").

Negative reinforcement is often confused with punishment since both involve negatives. However, negative reinforcement *relieves* discomfort and therefore its effect is positive, whereas punishment *induces* discomfort and therefore its effect is negative.

It is possible to use negative reinforcement as a constructive alternative to punishment, for example, some people who commit minor infractions can be given the opportunity to enroll in a diversionary program or provide community service in place of prison. The aim of those programs is to provide a step toward rehabilitation. Negative reinforcement can be effective when skillfully used in parenting, teaching, coaching, managing, legislating, diplomacy, and the criminal justice system.

Subtle appealing and repelling forces

People might use appealing forces without realizing the strong positive effect they have on the recipient, such as when they help others, show caring, step aside to let someone pass, and allow another driver to enter a driving lane. Something positive a person does without realizing it is a *'subtle appealing force'*.

Doing something negative without being consciously aware of its unpleasant impact is a *'subtle repelling force'*. Disagreeing is a subtle repelling force because, even when presented softly, it implies that the other person is wrong. Being condescending or not paying attention to someone is a subtle repelling force. Subtle repelling forces probably occur frequently, such as when people try to set someone straight about the facts, give unasked-for advice, or are egocentric. Examples of behaviors that can be subtle repelling forces in some circumstances are using unrefined language, speaking bluntly, and being loud or impolite. Some other subtle repelling forces include trying to change another person by persisting, pressuring, or using a "hard sell", since people do not like being controlled (cf. Brehm, 1966). Many ads and unsolicited phone calls are subtle repelling forces that produce the opposite effect than intended.

Compliments usually are appealing forces. However, a compliment could be a subtle repelling force if is perceived as false, phony, or manipulative. A negative reaction of that sort could happen when a compliment is perceived as contrived, if the recipient believes that he/she does not deserve it, or if he/she has low self-esteem. Even assisting someone can be a subtle repelling force if the recipient cherishes independence, as with some handicapped individuals.

Social strategies

Volumes have been written about effective social strategies, such as advice about relationships, communicating, and etiquette. A key social skill is an ability to use appealing forces appropriately and to keep repelling forces under control.[3] It helps to use appealing forces judiciously and to avoid using repelling forces, such as when presenting an opinion that opposes someone's viewpoint. In such instances, it can be useful to soften repelling forces, such as showing respect for other people with a soft preamble (e.g., "I have a different idea, would you like to hear it?"). It is also wise to not overdo using appealing forces because doing so may seem inappropriate or dishonest, and especially to avoid turning off people. It would be wise to stop using something that is thought to be an appealing force but does not succeed. Lessening a person's negatives, such as solving a problem for them can be welcomed by the person who benefits, but might not make that person happy since positive and negative emotions are governed by different emotional centers. In addition to using appealing forces effectively and not using repelling forces, other strong social skills include being able to create win-win solutions (described in Chapters 20 - 23), communicate well (described in Chapter 24), and apply social influence effectively (described in Chapters 25 and 26).

Active and passive appealing and repelling forces
Appealing and repelling forces can be active or passive depending on their intensity and intention. Praise is an active appealing force, while a comfortable atmosphere is a passive appealing force. Criticism and insults are active repelling forces, whereas not acknowledging someone is a passive repelling force. Passive appealing and repelling forces are often subtle rather than obvious.

A practical application of this information
The ability to engage others effectively is a major key to success in human life, something that Goleman (2005) termed emotional intelligence. Using even a few repelling forces can damage relationships and it can sometimes be hard to repair those connections afterward. Therefore, it pays to avoid using repelling forces as much as possible and to be judicious in using appealing forces. For example, expressing annoyance may seem justified, but if it is a repelling force, it can have the opposite effect on the recipient than what was intended and therefore be counterproductive.
There are many negatives in life so it may be impossible to completely avoid using repelling forces, especially since we often act spontaneously. When using a repelling force – such as criticizing, complaining, blaming, being self-

---

[3] The combination of using appealing forces and not using repelling forces could be termed an *'elixir of cordiality'*.

centered, being verbally provocative, being irritable, or using put-downs – an attempt should be made to soften it and try to avoid using that unpleasant behavior in the future.

One way to help avoid using a repelling force can be to ask oneself in advance, "Is what I'm about to say or do likely to be a repelling force in any way?" If there is even the slightest possibility that it might turn off someone, it would be wise not to use it. A way to criticize when it is necessary to do so would be to present it in a caring way, preceding it with a soft preamble, and then inserting the negative aspect between two appealing forces (a "communication sandwich"). (Section II presents some practical applications that use appealing forces and avoid the use of repelling forces, including methods for resolving conflicts and attempting to influence others in a constructive manner.)

Summary:
1. Use sincere appealing forces.
2. Avoid using repelling forces except when it is essential to do so.
3. When using a repelling force, try to soften it.
4. When someone resists, stop.

(When trying to getting a point across, the three-stage method for communicating and persuading described in Section II can be useful.)

Chapter 11. GOALS AND EXPECTATIONS

Goals and expectations may seem synonymous, but they are not the same. This difference is not trivial and the implications for distress and psychological disorders are substantial, as this chapter explains.

Goals

Goals generate a strong drive to attain them and activate psychological aspects that aid achievement, such as problem-solving strategies and stored information. The drive to attain a goal is so powerful it can even keep people from dying, such as generating a desire to stay alive long enough to attend a wedding or find out that a child has been born. Achieving a goal is satisfying, even when no material gain results from the achievement.

A person's major goals are one of the few types of Psychological Roots that he/she may be able to articulate. However, people are unlikely to be able to identify their subtle goals. The latter include many biological goals such as maintaining appropriate levels of glucose and electrolytes and keep their heart beating. There also are many subtle psychological goals such as achieving closure, having challenges, keeping one's mind occupied, and being connected with something larger than oneself. Some people think that a goal refers only to a large objective, such as an important project or a long-range aspiration, not realizing that they possess a large variety of small goals. People also might not realize that while they are striving to achieve a major goal, they have many other goals waiting in the background to be addressed such as aspects related to daily functioning. Synonyms for goals are aims, aspirations, objectives, desires, wants, hopes, wishes, dreams, and full goals.

Goals and distress

Goals facilitate getting needs and desires fulfilled, however people might not realize that they are in a failure zone until a goal is achieved. Being in a failure zone is especially likely when a person views not meeting a goal to be a failure. Since everyone always has goals, people who have that attitude give themselves extra stress. The more goals people have, the more important the goals, and the more difficult it is to accomplish them, the greater the amount of their stress. Affluent countries such as the United States have more stress than less affluent societies (Blanch, Shern, & Steverman, 2014) perhaps, in part, because of the opportunity to have many goals. A solution to this kind of stress will be presented after the preliminary discussion below.

Expectations

Many people view expectations to be the same as goals, but the two are different in that a goal is what is aimed for (the highest level targeted), whereas an expectation is the *least* that is acceptable. Thus, a full goal is somewhat like a ceiling while an expectation is somewhat comparable to a floor. Since an expectation is the smallest amount a person would settle for, it is the *'minimum goal'*. A goal, being the fullest amount that is sought, might be termed the *'full goal'*. The usefulness of this distinction will soon become apparent.

Achieving a goal produces a positive emotional experience such as pleasure, satisfaction, and contentment, while not meeting an expectation arouses negative emotions such as disappointment, failure, sadness, guilt, irritation, and a sense of loss (e.g., Abeler, Falk, Goette, & Huffman, 2011). Some examples of such negative reactions are:

• Feeling let down or angry when someone does not reciprocate your generosity.
• Being annoyed when a person does not do what you expect of him/her.
• Feeling guilty when you do not meet a personal responsibility you expect of yourself.

As these examples illustrate, expectations are criteria for evaluating failure. Even the expectation of a negative outcome can create distress (deBerker et al., 2016). Some other criteria for failure are standards, requirements, necessities, responsibilities, demands, needs, rules, laws, policies, shoulds, oughts, musts, high bar/low bar, what is minimally acceptable, and what has to be done. The arousal of negative emotions upon failing to meet those criteria is similar to the distress that occurs when a need is not met.[4] (Some displeasure comes from not achieving goals, in part because of goals being equated with expectations, and some pleasure comes from meeting expectations, in part because of expectations being equated with goals.)

Negative emotional reactions are stronger than positive reactions, which means that the drive to avoid failing is stronger than the drive to achieve a goal. The strong negative drive we have to avoid failing can go unnoticed because people tend to focus on goals and people often equate expectations with goals. The mind automatically connects an expectation with every goal just as it links other Psychological Roots that are thematically related to each

---

[4] The term 'expectation' has a number of meanings and nuances such as anticipation, probability, future prospect, hope, and belief. In the present discussion, the focus is on expectation as a criterion for failure.

other. (Linking of Psychological Roots is discussed in Chapter 7.) People are unaware of this connection because it happens subconsciously, although they are aware of the outcome including a concern about avoiding failure. People's tendency to think in absolutes further solidifies the association of goals and expectations. (Absolute thinking is discussed in Chapter 19.)

Another reason that people may think goals and expectations are synonymous and therefore inseparable, is that those two aspects are associated with the same objective. However, goals and expectations have different functions: goals are a criterion for evaluating success while expectations are a criterion for evaluating failure. These different functions do not have to be treated as a single indivisible unit; they can be separated in the same way that schools do. For example, the criterion in many schools for receiving a grade of 'A' on exams is 90% correct, while the criterion for total failure (a grade of 'F') is below 65% correct.

Low goals

Achieving a goal is a positive emotional experience. However, positive emotions often are only relatively brief. If the goal is low, only a small amount of pleasure might result, although that would be better than having no pleasure or a negative outcome. High goals are harder to achieve than low goals and may take longer to accomplish, but might generate more satisfaction because the sense of achievement is greater. Many people in third-world countries have low goals because they have few if any opportunities for achieving at a high level. Low goals also help avoid being disappointed because they are more likely to be achieved than high goals.

Some implications of expectations

The sense of failure when not meeting an expectation can be strong. Evidence of the potency of not meeting expectations includes revolutions, unruly mobs, riots, and the use of firearms and explosives that produce widespread death and destruction (Merton, 1963). Merton used the term *'relative deprivation'* to describe not meeting expectations because he found that people's rage did not stem from their actually being deprived but from their feeling deprived relative to what they expected. Relative deprivation explains why some middle-class individuals are intensely aggressive, violent, and join terrorist groups even though they are fairly well off in life, while many low socio-economic people who are deprived do not riot, are not violent, and do not join terrorist groups.

Relative deprivation occurs when people who expect to get promoted are upset when that expectation is not fulfilled, even when that expectation is not realistic or justified. Signs of unmet expectations are complaining, criticizing, and impatience, irritability, and anger. Individuals who react in those ways can create trouble when they are dissatisfied, such as quitting employers at a critical time, or suing, or returning to shoot some employees.

In short, frustrating a person's expectations can unleash strong negative emotions. Such reactions are seen in bitter divorces, lawsuits, customer complaints, and employee-management struggles. Even low distress from disappointed expectations can interfere with feeling contented. The author has found that people's unmet expectations contribute to dysthymia and depression, which further underscores the importance of expectations.

The up-side of the marriage of expectations and goals

The connection of expectations with goals generates two powerful drives to attain goals – one to succeed, the other to avoid failing. The drive to avoid failing is stronger since negatives are more powerful than positives. People's genetically wired-in need for closure further boosts the drive to achieve. The resulting focus on accomplishing goals, striving to achieve, and avoiding failure can generate a strong achievement drive and can bring substantial material success. This strong drive might have been a factor in our cave-man ancestors' ability to survive, obtain food and shelter, and cope with a variety of problems, predators, environmental dangers, and disasters.

The down-side of the marriage of expectations and goals

Since negatives are particularly strong, the drive to avoid failing may be much stronger than the drive to achieve goals. Such distress is especially likely when a person's goal is achieving 100% of the objective ("Total success or bust") since not fully achieving a goal – and therefore not meeting the full expectation attached to that goal – can still produce a strong sense of failure. In such instances, 90% attainment rather than complete success can seem like a huge failure. Losing a contest or a business account by one point is a total failure and for some people achieving 99% of their goal feels the same way. That kind of letdown can happen even with issues that are relatively trivial. If schools were to use total success as their standard, a student who achieved 99% would nevertheless fail. Having that stringent criterion would be like being required to get a base hit every time at bat, throw a basketball into the hoop every time, and never throw an interception in football. Those are things that not even gifted athletes can accomplish. No living being is perfect, and stress of that sort on students would be defeating. In short, an all-or-nothing standard is too extreme.

When expectations are the same as goals, people hold themselves to that absolute requirement. Hence, every goal brings the risk of feeling like a failure. As a result, anyone who expects perfection experiences some stress, such as employers with regard to their employees, parents with regard to their children, and married couples with regard to their partner. And the greater the consequences of an outcome, the greater the stress. Since everyone has many goals, including some with substantial consequences, this circumstance could be one of the reasons people do not smile as much as they might.

The down-side of expectations is illustrated by "Ned's" experience with a painful back, leading him to think that he might be handicapped for the rest of his life. Translation: he worried that he would never function at the level he *expected* of himself. Ned's distress was further intensified by his *expecting* that improvement should happen rapidly, which was not medically possible. Ned became more desperate, anxious, and depressed with each passing day.

The author suggested to Ned that he might be more comfortable were he to accept the idea of making small improvements over months rather than requiring that full health be restored immediately. However, he was unwilling to accept that perspective.

Ned is intelligent and realized that his expecting quick improvement was making him miserable, but he could not stop himself from holding onto that unattainable expectation. Ned's resistance is an example of how difficult it is for people to change their expectations and other strongly-held Psychological Roots even when they realize that not being flexible causes considerable distress for them.

The author then asked Ned if he would be willing to use his current rehabilitation period to modify his business in a way that might bring him greater personal satisfaction. That issue was important to Ned and he accepted the new goal with relish. His doing that immediately transformed his infirmity into something positive for him. The reason was that expectations accompany goals, therefore his having that new goal created a different expectation and was one that he was likely to attain. That new expectation permitted his previous expectation to fade into the background. His suffering diminished correspondingly.

Then something interesting happened. Ned's back improved greatly over the next few weeks. His having less psychological distress might have helped since research has found that psychological stress is a major contributor to back pain, often more than physical aspects (Bigos et al., 1994).

Expectations and distress
The difficulty that people have in separating expectations from their goals illustrates how strongly Psychological Roots link with each other, somewhat like powerful magnets. Since distress is harmful, it would be useful

for people who want to lessen distress to separate their expectations from their goals. An opportunity to do so often arises because we have many goals on a daily basis. The strong bond that holds expectations in place can be a major obstacle to lessening distress. It is important to try to lessen stress in general and especially when attempting to face difficult problems such as rebound from a setback or disorder, end an addiction, resolve a conflict, or surmount other major obstacles.

When we have a goal, the mind automatically attaches an expectation to that goal, in which case the expectation is the same as the goal. That instant arrangement immediately creates a zone of failure since attaining the goal is in the future and we have not yet met it nor the expectation attached to it. Thus, we instantly have some distress as a result of being in that circumstance.

We have many goals and therefore more stress than might be apparent. This problem becomes amplified with goals that are hard to achieve. Stress builds if we feel a need to achieve 100% of a goal, since achieving even 99% of the goal might be reacted to as if that was a failure. If there also are strong consequences for failing, still stronger distress would occur. Even when we fully achieve a goal, we eliminate only a portion of our overall stress because we have other goals and we keep adding more goals, piling up still more expectations and stress. Those stresses add up.

In short, having high goals can lead to substantial achievement and make life interesting, whereas the expectations that accompany goals heighten our distress. It would be better for psychological and physical health if, instead, we took conscious control of our expectations when appropriate to do so. How to accomplish this and also boost our level of accomplishment will be described in this chapter.

Procrastination and the drive to achieve

Many people like having high expectations because it heightens their drive to achieve. However, a problem with having such a strong drive is that high-powered striving is stressful and failing has powerful consequences. For example, failure is an important factor in depression (e.g., Beck & Ward, 1961; Warren & McEachren, 1983; Coyne & Gotlib, 1983; Billings, Cronkite, & Moos, 1983; and findings by the author). When failures pile up to the point of being overwhelming, people can become depressed. When people are depressed, their problems mount since the lethargy that accompanies depression makes it difficult for them to accomplish even small tasks. Their tension can increase if their standards are hard to meet.

One of the reasons that people procrastinate is to avoid dealing with unpleasantness such as potential failure. Avoidance increases as the potential for failure increases, and having difficult-to-meet expectations contributes to that possibility. The greater a person's anxiety, the less attention the person might give to other aspects of life, such as their cordiality, relationships, effectiveness, and creativity.

Must expectations be wedded to goals?

We might want to get a hit every time at bat when we play baseball, but we do not *expect* to do so. Golfers want to hit a ball onto the green (and ideally into the cup) every time, but do not *expect* such outcomes. Students want to get high exam grades, but do not *expect* to score 100% on every test (and in some courses, just hope to survive). The reason we do not expect a high outcome even though we have that level of accomplishment as a goal is that we realize that we cannot be perfect in those instances. At such times, we separate our expectations from our goals to avoid feeling like a failure when we are not superb. That separation is realistic and occurs automatically at a subconscious level.

Interestingly, motivation remains high after lowering expectations. The reason is that the goal remains the same. We intuitively realize that the goal is the key to achievement. We also realize that having a low expectation lessens distress. Thus, our subconscious has figured out that we can have high goals and low expectations at the same time.

Does having low expectations lessen achievement?

The afore-mentioned examples of baseball, golf, and school illustrate that high achievement can occur when the goal is high, and expectations are low. Here are five reasons why:
1. Examples in above paragraph illustrate that when the goal is high, it is possible to succeed at a high level, even when we do not expect to do so.
2. If you were in a situation in which you could not fail, then how high could you set your goal? You could then set your goal *even higher than usual,* because you cannot fail. Setting extremely high goals sets the stage for achieving far more than ordinarily.
3. When you cannot fail, your stress diminishes.
4. The mind works better when things are calm.
5. Efforts to achieve are more pleasureable when we are not tense than when we are distressed. ("If you like what you do you'll never work a day in your life.")

Thomas Edison, one of the world's greatest inventors, intentionally avoided thinking about failing. Although he had many unsuccessful attempts while trying to develop an electric light bulb, he said, "I have not failed. Instead, I learned thousands of things that do not work". That positive outlook allowed him to increase his potential to achieve by setting his goal higher than other people. Edison understood that achievement could be greater by avoiding being concerned about failure and can be accomplished by having low expectations.

Low expectations lessen irritability by making it easier to accept being wrong. That greater mellowness helps when we have setbacks, including the problems that others cause, due to being able to let minor disagreements fade into the background. Thus, a benefit of low expectations is that it can help us get along with others.

An interesting benefit of having low expectations is that it automatically produces many levels of success between an expectation and the full goal. Having different degrees of success permits having a partial gain if the full goal is not achieved. As an example, the Olympics has three levels of success – gold, silver, and bronze medals – not just one. Those multiple levels of success do not diminish the contestants' intense drive to achieve the top prize.

Life is more pleasurable when we experience success. When the floor is lower than the ceiling, partial success is possible all along the way. Having a gap between expectations and goals is somewhat like having the opportunity to experience many degrees of warm and cool water rather than having only very hot or very cold water.

Having several degrees of success is not the same as giving every student a prize for just being present. An award just for participating gives a reward for not having achieved anything toward attaining a goal, whereas having degrees of success emphasizes achieving the full goal and, at the same time, boosts students' confidence all along the way.

Is it always appropriate to lower expectations?

It is not always possible or appropriate to have low expectations, for example, situations in which it is critical to achieve a full goal. Neurosurgeons must try to be perfect, also engineers, draftsmen, and computer programmers. It is also counterproductive to have low requirements regarding societal laws, contracts, or the requests of a boss or a customer. We also would not have success if we did not keep our promises, or not follow company policies, or not be concerned about others. Some general circumstances in which it would be inappropriate to have low expectations are listed below. (Also see Figure 19).

It is important to have high expectations:

• When total success is essential and partial success is not acceptable (e.g., engineering standards).

- When intense motivation is required regardless of personal distress, frustration, or anxiety (e.g., in life and death matters and close athletic contests).
- When achieving a goal in steps would be counterproductive, undesirable, inappropriate, or take too much time (e.g., in emergencies).
- When innovation and creative problem-solving would be counterproductive, undesirable, inappropriate, or take too much time (e.g., when meeting tight deadlines and rigid criteria).
- When less than total success is very costly (e.g., regarding time, expense, resources, or reasonableness).
- When it is not feasible or appropriate to set one's expectations (e.g., when required to meet others' expectations or there are established minimum criteria).

The best of both worlds

Distress is harmful, such as struggling to meet a high goal or a difficult deadline, deal with an unpleasant boss, make ends meet, or put pressure on ourselves to avoid failing. Distress often is unavoidable when attempting to achieve our goals. Nevertheless, there are times when it is possible to achieve goals, even high goals, and yet have little distress, the best of both worlds. This positive approach can be achieved by intentionally setting goals high and expectations low. This strategy should be used only when it is appropriate to do so.

An example

A. Jon wants to earn $50,000 in the coming year, with only that amount or more acceptable to him. Therefore, anything less than $50,000 would seem like a total failure to him, perhaps even earning $49,999. Hence Jon might have to strain for an entire year to reach $50,000 and might have considerable distress during the entire year.

B. Suppose that Jon has the same goal, $50,000, but calculates that the minimum he needs to meet expenses is $35,000. Therefore, any amount between $35,000 and $50,000 would be somewhat acceptable to him. Ending up with less than $35,000 would upset him, rather than anything less than $50,000 as in A, above.

     Jon would still have a strong drive to earn $50,000. The closer to $50,000 that Jon achieves the better he would feel. The difference between $35,000 and $50,000 gives Jon some breathing room and permits him to be more relaxed, happier, less stressed and therefore even healthier than feeling do-or-die pressure throughout the year to earn $50,000 in order to avoid feeling like a failure.

As Jon works toward earning $50,000, he might reach a point when he realizes that his chance of earning at least $35,000 is quite likely. At that point, perhaps 6 to 9 months into the year, he might also feel that he could actually reach his full goal of $50,000. The author has found that when people reach that point they feel a substantial lightening of their burden. They may also experience greater confidence and less stress. Positive reactions like this contrast greatly with feeling pressure and stress all the way to the full goal.

C. Now suppose that Jon decides to set his full goal still higher, say $60,000, while keeping his criterion for failure at $35,000. Jon might then gear himself to earn more than $50,000 and work accordingly. Jon *would not be additionally distressed* because anything above $35,000 would provide partial success. This strategy gives Jon the best of both worlds – a high goal (with the possibility of higher achievement than he might have had otherwise) with relatively low stress from having set his goal high.

The bottom line:

The author has found that people can lessen their stress by taking conscious control of their expectations. They can do this by setting their minimum goal lower than their full goal. Having less stress allows them to set higher goals and achieve more than otherwise, when circumstances permit doing so. The result can be that they achieve much more than they ordinarily would while simultaneously lowering their stress.

Goals are a major key to achievement

It was mentioned earlier that having a goal gets things done because the mind focuses on that goal and directs us to accomplish it. (This circumstance is an instance of selective attention). As a result, what people attain depends substantially on how high their goal is. If a person's goal is low, his/her mind will focus on that low level and function accordingly. However, when a goal is high, the mind gears itself for that high level. Thus, the higher the goal, the more the mind sets itself to accomplish.

Also helping us accomplish goals is our drive for closure. (The need for closure, which is genetically wired-into us, is discussed in the next chapter.)

To some people, it may seem illogical that goals can be separated from expectations. It might help those individuals to realize that goals and expectations have different functions. Knowing that goals and expectations are different sets the stage for working with each aspect separately.

People who separate their expectations from their goals in circumstances when it is appropriate to do so can lower their stress to some extent, in the author's experience. Taking conscious control over expectations is particularly important for people who are anxious, depressed, or irritable.

Creativity, innovation, and problem-solving

Negative emotions are powerful and no one handles failure well. If we had no expectations, there would be no criterion for failure, and that would greatly lessen tension, for example, imagine being largely free of distress while taking an exam or when in an intense contest. When tensions are low, we think better, which facilitates problem solving and helping to achieve goals.

Having low expectations also decreases pressure on us to obtain immediate gratification, and that improves our patience. Patience helps free the mind to explore possibilities, make associations, and generate new ways to achieve goals, such as by using *'mental incubation'* [5]. Patience also permits widening the zone of acceptability, which opens us to exploring new possibilities. These aspects, along with not being plagued by concerns about failing, can facilitate thinking, solving problems, and taking constructive risks. They also aid creativity, inventiveness, and innovation, and thereby contribute to progress.

Would lowering expectations make people lazy?

People who try to achieve high goals are the opposite of being lazy. When we have no expectations we are free to set far higher goals that we would otherwise do since we cannot feel like a failure no matter what happens. Goals set the objective. High goals boost motivation and lead to higher achievement than low or moderate goals (see Figure 18). Having this outlook allows people to set goals that are way out of reach. That way, even if an impossible goal is not attained, far more can be accomplished than otherwise. A bonus is that failing is not a concern, which lessens distress.

People who have high standards can feel like failures when they fail. An example is the severe depression experienced by Martin that is described in Chapter 28.

---

[5] Having patience (in addition to lessening premature closure and tension) aids in obtaining time for *'mental incubation'* (subconscious mental processes that can aid in finding solutions to problems among other things).

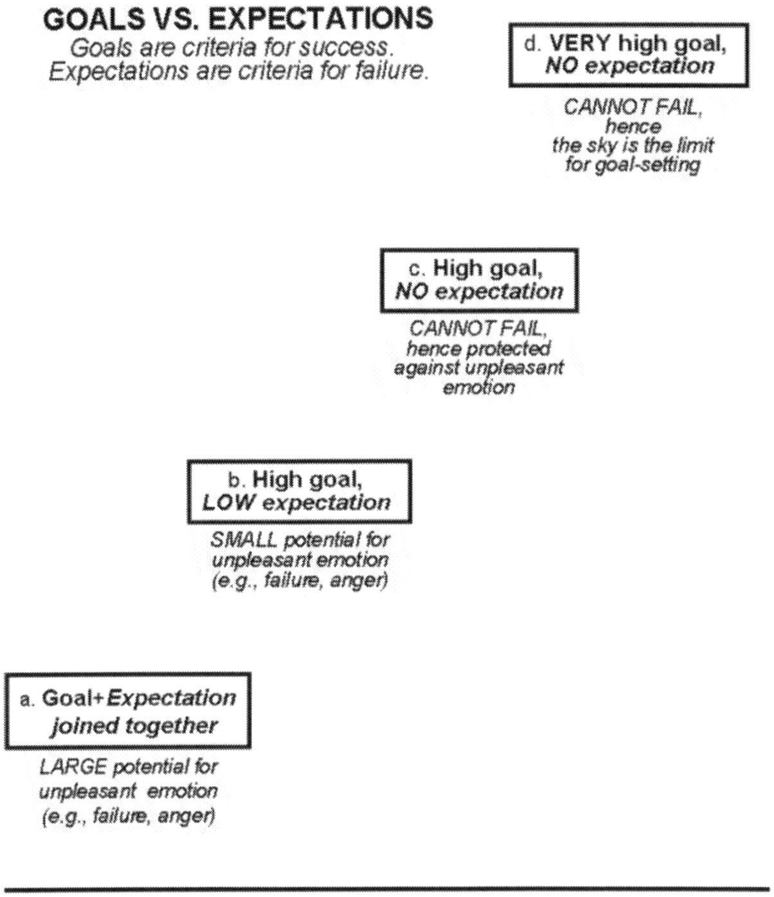

GOALS VS. EXPECTATIONS
Goals are criteria for success.
Expectations are criteria for failure.

d. VERY high goal,
NO expectation

CANNOT FAIL,
hence
the sky is the limit
for goal-setting

c. High goal,
NO expectation

CANNOT FAIL,
hence protected
against unpleasant
emotion

b. High goal,
LOW expectation

SMALL potential for
unpleasant emotion
(e.g., failure, anger)

a. Goal+*Expectation*
joined together

LARGE potential for
unpleasant emotion
(e.g., failure, anger)

Fig. 18. **High goals** with **low expectations** produces
high motivation to achieve with little distress.

Many people who have high standards are concerned about failing to meet those standards. To avoid experiencing failure, many people whose standards are high purposely set low or moderate goals. An unfortunate result of doing this is that they may end up with a life filled with regret because they did not achieve as much as they might have been able to accomplish.

In addition, the possibility of failing can generate tension and anxiety, which is not only stressful, it can decrease problem-solving ability, creative thinking, and willingness to take risks. This, too, can decrease achievement.

It is counter-intuitive that people's achievement can be greater when their expectations are low than when expectations are high. As in the case of Thomas Edison, the accomplishment can be far greater than for people who cannot readily diminish the impact of failure. For many people, the value of this perspective has to be experienced to be understood.

Does having no expectations mean settling for less? Or never achieving the full goal?

Goals can be achieved in stages ("A journey of 1000 miles begins with a single step") and creating a gap between goals and expectations aids doing this. For instance, if the goal is to paint a 10-room house and two rooms have been finished, the full goal remains and the task is readily understood as something to be achieved in stages. It is easy to see accomplishing the full goal over a period of time rather than rather than needing to achieve the full goal all at once. Having this perspective also allows viewing each small increment as a positive step toward the full objective in which every accomplishment, no matter how small, is a pleasant achievement. This way of structuring tasks improves patience, reduces pressure, lessens frustration, and avoids settling for less. Also, every small step boosts enthusiasm and confidence for continuing the effort. By contrast, allowing expectations to be the same as the goal puts us in a failure zone until the full goal is achieved. For example, finishing two rooms would feel like a failure. Having a stressful reaction like that could lead to procrastinating.

Another benefit of breaking goals into small steps is that each step can receive careful attention, which boosts quality. Accomplishment in stages is reflected in AA's (Alcohol Anonymous) saying, "One day at a time".

Is a series of sub-goals the same as lowering expectations?

Having a number of sub-goals is different than having low overall expectations. The reason is that every sub-goal has its own expectation, with a possibility that a sub-goal might not be achieved. A person could feel especially inadequate if he/she did not accomplish a low sub-goal. Most importantly, the expectations related to the full goal are not changed and remain high. High expectations set the stage for experiencing failure and that stress remains throughout the effort to achieve the full goal.

When there are a number of sub-goals, lessening distress requires that: 1) the expectation for *each* sub-goal must be lowered, and 2) the expectation for the *full goal* must also be lowered. If the expectations for *both* the full goal and the sub-goals are not lowered, there is a high potential to feel like a failure throughout the entire effort, creating stress all along the way. If the full goal is not lowered, then when the last step (the full goal) is ready to be addressed, the expectation and the full goal are the same.

Thus, having a series of sub-goals can be a formula for distress if expectations are not lowered for *each sub-goal* and *also* the overall objective for the project as a whole. The steps for accomplishing both are outlined below.

1) Eliminate the *overall* expectation associated with the full goal.
2) Articulate each sub-goal.
3) Purposely eliminate any expectations for *each sub-goal*.
4) After achieving a sub-goal and moving on to the next sub-goal, consciously remind yourself to have *no* expectations for that new sub-goal.
5) Continue to have no overall expectation *about the full goal* throughout the effort.

How about lowering expectations just a little?

Lowering the criterion for failure might lessen stress a little and therefore offer only a small buffer against feeling like a failure. Having less distress is aided by setting very low expectations or none when feasible.

Is there an easy way to lower expectations?

A simple way to lower expectations is to consider anything above zero to be a plus. Doing this eliminates the possibility of feeling like a failure. A similar way to accomplish this is to consider something to be better than nothing.

Is it possible to change other people's expectations?

Sometimes it can be possible to modify other people's expectations. For example, many vendors give customers a window of time in which to expect a delivery, for instance, between 9 AM and Noon, rather than giving them a specific time, such as 10 AM. The range of time helps to avoid disappointing a customer if delivery does not occur exactly as expected. Workers can sometimes set supervisors' expectations regarding when they are likely to accomplish a project.

Does having no expectations eliminate failing?

Having no expectations does not prevent actual failure. However, having no expectations when a failure occurs offers a softer landing because it lessens some negative emotionality. It allows a person to realize that, "Even though what I did was not successful, *I'm* not terrible." Lowered expectations also make it easier to admit mistakes, lessen defensiveness, not blame others, be open to improving, and learn from errors.

Is it strange to have high goals with low expectations?

High goals and low expectations may seem strange at first. Experiencing the relief that results from having less stress can help make it easy to get used to doing so.

Can being in a 'zone of failure' be avoided?

The possibility of feeling like a failure could be eliminated if there was no criterion for failure. It is possible to consciously eliminate all expectations by accepting the idea that "anything above zero is a plus" when it is reasonable to do so. A benefit of this perspective of "something is better than nothing" is that each small achievement can be seen as a partial success even when it is tiny. This philosophy avoids feeling like a failure if the total goal is not accomplished. Having some positives also lessens distress from unpleasant endeavors because it allows a half-filled drinking glass to be considered to be "half full", rather than "half empty".

Is it possible to permanently eliminate feeling like a personal failure?

The brain automatically links expectations with goals and creates a powerful negative reaction when we fail. These aspects are genetically wired-in and therefore it is impossible to permanently eliminate feeling like a failure. It would not be desirable to do so since it is important to know when we are not effective and then make corrections. There also are times when expectations should be high (described earlier). Thus, it is likely that a conscious decision will always be required by every person regarding whether to lower the criterion for failure. (See Figure 19.)

Are expectations strong enough to cause disorders?

Yes. No one handles distress well, and some types of distress result from failing to meet expectations, including anxiety, malaise, anger, headaches, and high blood pressure. Violence is also possible (described earlier in connection with relative deprivation.) The power of psychological factors to cause serious problems should not be under-estimated.

Why should I lower my expectations when another person caused the problem?

Other people can make mistakes and do disturbing things, such as being irresponsible, untruthful, and harmful. Since we do not have control over what other people do, we can lessen the frustrations that other people cause us by having no expectations when it is appropriate to do so. Doing that can permit us to remain calm when people cause problems, something that is much healthier than being irritated, anxious, angry, or letting their actions impede our functioning. Not struggling with people who cause problems can avoid compounding problems for ourselves.

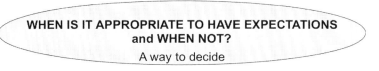

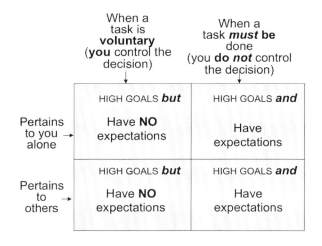

Fig. 19. Expectations often are necessary.
However, expectations create undue stress when they
are *not* necessary.

Some examples of people who did not separate their expectations from their goals:

1. *Refusal to accept the potency of expectations.* "Walter" used liquor to medicate his depression and, as a consequence, had a serious alcohol problem. Nothing else had worked for him – not the many professionals he had seen, nor the many prescription medications he took, nor the many rehabilitation and detoxification programs he had been in over the years. He was through with therapists and twice attempted to kill himself. When he began thinking about taking his life again, his wife came for counseling to

help her find a way to deal with the situation. She was then able to talk him into coming for a session by himself.

The author tried to help Walter understand that he felt inadequate because he had unattainable expectations about everything. His sense of failure had been building day by day, plunging him ever deeper into his self-made dungeon. Suicide seemed to him to be the only way out. Alcohol could not cure his depression because it did not eliminate the psychological cause of his problems and it was toxic, which made his situation worse.

Walter refused to believe that anything psychological could have the strong effects he experienced. Instead, he believed that he had a biological condition such as a chemical imbalance or bad genes, even though medical treatments had never helped him.

Walter used his intelligence to find ways to deny that his expectations had anything to do with his problems. That thinking put him in a trap from which he was unable to extricate himself. He refused to be counseled and spiraled further downward. Suicide seemed to him to be the only way out, and he almost succeeded in trying to kill himself again. His unwillingness to recognize the potency of psychology was more important to him than using a psychological method that might have helped him.

2. *Never enough.* "*Angie*" grew up in low-level rent districts and had always wanted to own her own home. After marrying and becoming the proud owner of a house, she was delighted to work at getting her home to be just the way she envisioned it. Her husband was central to her renovation plans, ranging from his installing brick paths and patio borders to replacing doors, windows, door-panes, cabinets, molding, and storage shelves, not to mention creating flower and vegetable gardens, climbing trees, fixing furniture, etc., etc. In her hyper-attention to tasks, every moment her husband was not at his day job she had him working on projects. Those tasks engulfed him so much that he had no time to unwind from his stressful occupation nor opportunity for recreation. What especially got to him was that before he was able to finish any task, Angie gave him orders about his next assignment. Her doing that made him feel that whatever he did was never good enough. He concluded that he could never succeed, that the house was more important to her than he was, and that her demands would never end. He felt controlled, manipulated, and disrespected, and believed that his interests would never be met.

After a year and a half of this distress, Angie's husband insisted that they go for counseling. The author explained to Angie that she made him feel like a failure because her never-ending chores, demands, and expectations caused him to think that he could never succeed. She could not believe that possibility since she was delighted at converting their house into something fulfilling. Angie was so involved in her dream that she could not comprehend that her husband was not on the same page with her or that her marriage was in danger, despite his many discussions with her about it.

There were times during counseling that Angie seemed to be on the verge of realizing that her sky-high expectations were undermining her husband's well-being. However, those glimmers of comprehension did not last long. Instead, she was so engulfed in her goal and her mind was so full of chores that they crowded out any other considerations. The many tasks that she had in her mind melded into a single overpowering mountain of necessities. Angie's intense internal pressure to create a dream house prevented her from offering a breathing space between tasks for herself or her husband. Not letting up made sense to her and prevented her from accepting the author's explaining that she could lose her husband's affection if she did not modify her expectations. However, she never fully accepted lessening her intense effort to achieve her goal.

Angie's husband decided to visit his parents in another State to create a brief break from Angie's tidal wave of chores. There he met a woman who did not make demands and fell in love with her. That ended his marriage with Angie.

Angie could not understand this. From her standpoint, the goal of creating a dream house was correct, noble, appropriate, and overshadowed everything else. She thought in strictly black-and-white terms about her objective, which kept her from grasping that her husband did not have the same dream she did. Her thinking in absolutes prevented her from separating her expectations from her goals. As a result, Angie's drive captured her so entirely that the idea of lessening the crushing pressure she put on herself and her husband seemed illogical to her. As a result, she strained her marriage past the breaking point. Relationships require nurturing.

3. *Yelling.* "Phoebe" frequently screamed at her husband, "Marvin", who defended himself by trying to straighten her out with facts. His attempts to correct her statements only made things worse because Phoebe then turned up the volume, sometimes for hours at a time.

Phoebe blamed Marvin for their conflicts because he did not meet her expectations. She thought her expectations were reasonable and more than that, essential, and demanded that others meet them. When the author tried to help her understand the role that expectations played, she did not believe that it made sense to separate them from her goals. Instead, she believed that she would not accomplish her many objectives if she were to lower her expectations. So, rather than modify her beliefs, she converted the therapy sessions to opportunities for venting her many disappointments. She did not succeed with other therapists as well.

Marvin expected that he would persuade Phoebe by showing her that her harsh criticisms were wrong. That strategy never succeeded and worse, always inflamed her because she could not tolerate being wrong. His resistance dramatically escalated their arguments.

Three years later, Phoebe and Marvin divorced, despite still loving each other.

Two examples of people who separated their expectations from their goals:

1. *Distress and marihuana.* "Ralph" was the owner of a company and that business stressed him continuously. He dealt with his distress by smoking a great deal of marihuana, but that created problems at home because he lay stoned on a living room couch until bedtime, unavailable to his wife or children. When he did communicate, he was irritable and often criticized his wife, telling her that she was incapable. Her resentment continued to build, which led to intense arguments. After three years of this, their marriage was in shreds.

Ralph's high standards were a major part of his problem since he applied high standards to everything he did, including his personal life. The author helped Ralph understand how to lower his criterion for personal failure while still retaining his extreme goals. He began to make that transformation, which led to his allowing some emotional leeway for his employees as well as himself. He did this while maintaining his high goals, which permitted him to continue to produce excellent results at work. He did the same at home and that allowed him to stop demeaning his wife and children, and to meet his goals for his family much better than before.

His lessened distress made it easier for Ralph and his wife to communicate more effectively, decrease their use of repelling forces, and create win-win solutions. Ralph felt less need to use marihuana and that led to his being a more effective family person as well as employer. He continued to taper off marihuana and eventually stopped using it entirely.

2. *Tension.* "Van" had been tense all his life. He was easily frustrated and quick to berate people. That behavior turned off others including his wife and children. Whenever his children got poor grades at school, his anger overpowered him and he administered strong punishment, such as using harsh words. Without warning, he would suddenly take away things that mattered a great deal to his children such as their art materials, books, music,

cell phones, and TV privileges. They considered him explosive, overly harsh, and not someone with whom they could talk or feel close. That behavior clouded their relationship with him.

Van's high expectations were a major part of the problem. Van is intelligent and used his intellect to make the case that strong demands were essential for success in life. He put especially great emphasis on task performance and applied his high standards to everyone, his family as well as his business. When people did not meet his standards, which often occurred, he openly criticized them for their poor workmanship.

Van had not realized that he was in an intense zone of failure continually in part because of his numerous goals. As a result, Van was always distressed and caused others to be distressed others as well. His tension built up cumulatively and he sometimes went ballistic. Those explosions were states of uncontrollability.

The solution for Van's tension and outbursts was easy and occurred remarkably quickly. Van quickly understood how his extremely high expectations contributed to his tension and to the distress of people around him. Van learned when it was useful and appropriate for him to lower his expectations, for example, he learned to lower his expectations about *people* while maintaining his high expectations about *tasks*.

All of the individuals in these five examples – Roger, Van, Walter, Angie, Phoebe, and Marvin – are highly intelligent. Roger and Van used their intelligence to understand the role that expectations had in creating problems and were willing to modify their expectations to prevent further difficulties. However, Phoebe, Angie, and Walter used their intelligence to reject the idea that expectations were important or caused problems for them and others. They considered expectations to be synonymous with goals so were unable to separate them from each other (an example of how thinking in absolutes can cause problems). Marvin was willing to change his belief that facts and logic would persuade Phoebe, but when Phoebe verbally attacked him, he had an automatic tendency to defend himself and that behavior took over.

These examples illustrate why improving oneself requires being open to new ideas and the importance of psychological factors. Angie's circumstance shows how powerful the drive to accomplish goals can be, and Marvin's inability to stop defending himself shows how powerfully rooted expectations can be.

(Some practical applications related to this chapter are presented in Section II. As a side note, Thibaut and Kelley's, 1959, conception of 'comparison level of alternatives' has some relevance for understanding relative satisfaction.)

Strategies and methods

A strategy is a belief about what to do. A method (such as a tactic, tool, technology, or behavior) is a means of accomplishing something. Beliefs are Psychological Roots that are at the start of Hidden Sequences while behaviors are outcomes at the end of Hidden Sequences. Some people are wedded to a particular strategy or method and may believe that no other way is acceptable or even possible ("What else can I do?"). Some people's reasons for not changing a method can be due to their believing that it is the best or only way, or not knowing any other way to proceed. Some other reasons are focusing only on tangible aspects or thinking in absolutes ("If I do not do X, am I supposed to do the opposite, which is unacceptable?"). Thinking in absolutes impedes being flexible.

Summary

Expectations constitute a criterion for failure and the mind automatically creates an expectation for every goal we have. Therefore, when a goal is not completely achieved it can feel like a total failure. For some people, even 99% attainment can feel like a failure. That perspective causes stress. Stress also occurs because people are in a zone of failure as soon as they have a goal. Fortunately, it is possible to give ourselves a margin for error by lowering our expectations, sometimes by having no expectations, when it is reasonable and appropriate to do so.

Having no expectations prevents feeling like a failure, even when we have an objective failure. ("What I did failed, but I'm OK.") When it is not possible to feel like a failure, the goal can be set much higher than usual and we can persist until we find a way to succeed (as Thomas Edison did). High goals boost achievement while less tension reduces impediments to thinking and problem-solving (see Figure 18). Setting a high goal while having no expectations permits achieving at a high level while reducing tension, a strategy that produces the best of both worlds – high achievement with low distress.

Expectations can be eliminated entirely by telling oneself, "Anything above zero is a plus" and that "Something is better than nothing". Having a gap between expectations and goals permits experiencing degrees of success and thereby permits even tiny accomplishments to have merit. Doing so helps maintain confidence.

Some practical ways to lessen distress

When traffic snarls and long waiting lines cause delays, impatience can be lessened by changing expectations about how long the wait will be by extending the time frame, for example, by changing the expected wait time to be 30 minutes instead of 5 minutes. We can then turn our attention to something more interesting or productive instead of being impatient, fuming, or complaining. We can also tell ourselves, "Don't get caught up in this" and "I can handle this". Irritation can also be avoided by telling ourselves, "Don't take this personally". We can also avoid expecting that other people must reciprocate what we do for them.

Chapter 12. NEED FOR CLOSURE

Have you ever wondered why people are impatient, feel driven to climb mountains, and have a strong drive to answer questions asked of them? Or why we experience suspense and feel a need to solve problems that arise? Our sub-surface genetic need for closure is at work, as this chapter explains.

Impatience, suspense, and our drive to complete tasks

We have a wired-in *need for closure* that generates pressure in us to finish what we start. This need closure adds to our drive to accomplish goals and complete tasks, and also drives us to fill voids, solve problems, answer questions, and dislike leaving things unfinished. Subtle aspects of the need for closure include a desire to obtain clarification, understand puzzling phenomena, clarify ambiguity, and explore unknowns. Our drive for closure may be one of the reasons we have curiosity. Desire for closure may contribute to our preference for having things clear-cut, simple, and absolute (discussed in a later chapter), and many people's disdain for middle-of-the-road viewpoints because those seem too "wishy-washy". The drive for closure is at work when we want to find out how a story ends, what a decision will be ("I can hardly wait"), and feel suspense. Some experimental evidence for the existence of a drive for closure is that unfinished tasks are remembered better than completed tasks (Zeigarnik, 1967).

A desire for rapid closure ("I want it now") contributes to being impatient and wanting instant gratification, and can lead to impulsive behavior without our considering the consequences. Preference for quick results is at work when businesses focus on quarterly earnings rather than multi-year plans, or when abstinence is prescribed as the primary treatment for addiction versus addressing the cause, and when criminals are punished rather than employing more complex attempts to rehabilitate them. The desire for closure might also contribute to settling for simple beliefs such as assuming that rote memorization produces effective learning and society's putting ill, infirm, homeless, and disordered people into out-of-sight enclosures.

The need for closure operates without our realizing it

Mentioned above is that a need for closure accompanies every goal, which increases our motivation to attain it. The intensity of the closure drives varies depending on the consequences of the outcome and the level of emotionality, concern, and interest. The less time available for an outcome to occur, the stronger the drive for closure. As with other necessities, if our need for closure is not satisfied or when delays occur there is a strong negative emotional reaction, such as frustration. That negative psychological reaction could be accompanied by biological effects (e.g., headaches or high blood pressure). An unfulfilled drive for closure may be involved in some psychological conditions such as obsessive-compulsive disorder, anxiety, depression, bipolar disorder, and borderline personality disorder.

Premature closure

Striving can end before reaching a desired conclusion such as when people refuse to consider other possibilities or believe that they have tried everything. Such *'premature closure'* occurs when a couple decides that nothing more can be done to avoid their divorcing, not realizing that they have been addressing tangible aspects rather than the underlying psychological causes of their discord. (See Chapters 20 - 23 on how to resolve conflicts.) People who are impatient, hyperactive, or frustrated may be prone to pressing for premature closure.

A practical application

Stress can result from not having one's desired outcome occur quickly. Jumping to conclusions (premature closure) can increase the likelihood of making a poor judgment. Clamping a desire to act is an attempt to avoid closure. Some people believe that when they try to keep their desire for closure under control, they are being patient. However, patience is feeling comfortable with the time it takes for closure to occur. Putting a clamp on impatience or annoyance only temporarily controls the issue and can build tension rather than decrease it. One way to increase patience would be to extend the amount of time for an outcome to occur, for example by allowing extra time when stuck in a slow checkout line or traffic, then revising the estimated time for closure as necessary.

Chapter 13. RESISTANCE TO CHANGE

Do you know someone who is especially stubborn? Or people who hold fast to their viewpoint in the face of evidence, logic, and facts? Resisting change is not an accident.

Why do people resist making personal changes?

We have a wired-in drive to remain as we have been owing to our genetic need for stability and Biological and Psychological Homeostasis, which also contribute to stability. In addition, the interlocking of Psychological Roots in extensive webs of hierarchies, trees, branches, and clusters can foster resistance in order to avoid numerous additional changes that would have to be made if a Psychological Root is changed, especially if it is a deep root. (Also see the discussion of hierarchical alignment and defensiveness in Chapter 7.)

Needs for safety, stability, and attempting to avoid negative reactions also contribute to resisting change ("The devil you know is better than the devil you don't know"). The closure drive also fosters remaining in place. Some other factors that help maintain the *status quo* are counterbalancing factors such as positive vs. negative emotional reactions (discussed in the next chapter). Some Psychological Roots, internal reactions, and behaviors that heighten resistance to change include believing that others need to improve rather than oneself, liking routines or tradition, defensiveness, refusing to admit being wrong, blaming others rather than oneself, and not having effective coping mechanisms. A subtle cause of resistance occurs when new information is rejected because it is not in accord with existing Psychological Roots (discussed in Chapter 7).

As a result of aspects such as those described above, everyone is stubborn to some extent, and some people are particularly unreceptive to new ideas. Some people resist change in general, while others resist change in particular aspects (e.g., their livelihood or certain beliefs). Resistance to change impedes learning and therefore improving, which can be a disadvantage since no one is perfect. Resistance also impedes keeping up with societal changes, which have been occurring in society with increasing rapidity. Resistance to change can lead to repeating previous patterns, including unsuccessful behaviors.

Core Psychological Roots

Psychological Roots that are at the core of personality – such as genetic roots and acquired roots that are attached to genetic roots – especially resist changing. In part, their resistance occurs because of their deep entrenchment as part of the foundation of Psychological Root hierarchies, clusters, webs, and personality. It would also be disruptive to modify many of the huge number of subsidiary roots, branches, and clusters that contribute to a person's basic personality structure. (See the flow-down effect in Chapter 7). The stability of core Psychological Roots, both genetic and acquired, is a reason that major personality traits, style of thinking, emotional reactions, and behavior patterns remain relatively constant throughout life. Will-power can temporarily override Psychological Roots including core roots.

Later Psychological Roots

Psychological Roots that are acquired later in life, such as a person's recent interests, are more readily modified than deeply ensconced roots that are at the foundation of root hierarchies. As an example, people can readily change what they eat, wear, and other later Psychological Roots but resist changing their early roots such as basic values, family connections, religious beliefs, and political ideology. Flow-down effects partly account for the relatively greater elasticity of later roots. Even when people intentionally try to make deep changes (such as when attempting to cope with especially challenging personal circumstances), they are likely to return to their basic personality after making such changes.

Some people are especially resistant

Some aspects increase resistance to change such as thinking in absolutes, preferring simplicity, having a narrow acceptability range, and being highly emotional because those aspects limit possibilities. Some people resist changing because they fear the unknown or feel inadequate about coping with change, and some people like being provocative or "devil's advocate". Some people cannot tolerate being wrong, and some individuals have personality traits that foster resistance, such as pessimism, a narrow adaptive zone, or a lack of self-confidence. Some persons accept ideas only if they are from an authoritative source and some people believe that their thinking or behavior is the way it is, period. Some individuals believe that they are too old to change or that it is too late to alter something.

Resistance to change has some drawbacks

Being cautious can be wise, but people who often resist change impede their adopting useful advances, putting them at a disadvantage in today's world of accelerating change. Resisting change can contribute to stagnation, which can lead to decline and impede other people's growth and effectiveness.[6]

Signs of substantial resistance to change

Some signs of people who are especially resistant to change are an unwillingness to consider viewpoints other than their own, disdain for other people's opinions, unwillingness to accept being wrong, and frequent arguing. Some other signs are the use of such phrases as, "I'm rarely wrong", "Things are good the way they are", and "Things were better in the old days". Some other signs of resistance to change are, "If it was good enough for my grandfather, it's good enough for me", "The devil you know is better than the devil you don't know", and "If nature intended us to fly we'd have wings". A sign of resistance to making personal changes occurs when a person says, "Other people should change, not me". Knowing that a person is especially stubborn can help when trying to avoid arguing with that individual.

When it is important to try to persuade someone to change it is especially important to avoid using repelling forces (e.g., pressure, criticism, arguing). (Section II has strategies for communicating, persuading, and creating win-win solutions that might be able to help lessen a person's resistance to an opposing viewpoint.)

Why do innovations occur if humans are so resistant to change?

Innovations occur for many reasons, such as a need to solve problems. People also have many goals and seeking to fulfill those objectives can lead to new challenges and open new paths. Advances can accidentally occur while working toward a goal, such as the discovery that microwaves can cook food. We also have genetic drives to grow, acquire information, make links, seek challenges, and explore. Our ability to make associations and desire to grow helps counterbalance our natural resistance to change. In addition, we need stimulation, evidence of which is our disliking boredom and the same foods, music, clothes, and messages ("Some things get old quickly"). A boring or

---

[6] Resistance to change creates difficulties when change is needed. People who are especially resistant – such as traditionalists and persons with certain physical, intellectual, or psychological conditions (e.g., depression) – may find advances difficult. Those individuals can limit their effectiveness by resisting new developments.

monotonous job can lead to mistakes, being disgruntled, and quitting.[7] Some activities such as science, business, art, entertainment, and problem-solving are particularly likely to generate innovations.

A change that is consistent with our Psychological Roots and is within our zone of acceptability is more likely to be accepted than a change that is outside that zone. Changes have a better chance of being accepted when they are familiar to us, tangible, and seem likely to satisfy a need of ours. For example, we might be more inclined to buy a new product if the packaging is the same and proclaims that it is *"IMPROVED"*, versus being in a different package and labeled *"NEW"*.

Openness to change

Some people are especially open to innovation, such as creative individuals, while some people are open to certain types of change (e.g., new fashions or gadgets) but not other changes (e.g., changes in traditions or deep personal changes). Personality traits of people who are largely open to innovation are likely to include being accepting of making errors, being flexible, and being interested in innovations and ideas. Some people make personal changes when faced with the possibility of a strong negative outcome if they do not change. Some people are naturally creative and inventive, and some people rebel against the *status quo*.

Being open to new ideas contributes solutions, provides alternative possibilities and can aid being compatible with other individuals. Some employers seek workers who are open to change. People who are receptive to change might say such things as, "I like creativity", and "There is always a solution, we just have to find it".

When contemplating making a change, it may help consider these questions:

- Is this change useful or necessary?
- Will this change help others?
- Will this change help me be more effective?
- Will this change lessen distress?

---

[7] There are negative consequences for people who do not adjust to changes in their lives. Offspring have an opportunity to be better adjusted to environmental circumstances because they have less interference from prior circumstances than their parents. Kurzweil (2005) suggested that human functioning in the future will be complemented by computers that can readily adjust to environmental changes and many of their deteriorated parts can be replaced.

• How much gain might result from this change compared to the effort, time, and cost?

A practical application of this information

Living creatures often resist change because of homeostasis, countervailing forces, and needs for stability and safety. Hence, finding that someone resists a new idea or does not do what we expect should not be a surprise.[8] One of the reasons that logic or facts might not be successful when trying to persuade is that the communicator's logic and facts are not in accord with the recipient's Psychological Roots. People whose circumstances require them to persuade others to change – such as leaders, parents, and teachers – should not be surprised when they meet resistance. The strategies for change and conflict resolution described in Section II can help, a central theme of which is to present new ideas in a way that is consistent with the recipients' Psychological Roots.

---

[8] When people change, it is may be in degree rather than in kind (i.e., a change in magnitude on one side of a bipolar scale, rather adopting an opposing viewpoint on the other side of the midpoint). People can enlarge their homeostatic ranges up to the outer limit, which is likely to be easier when they do not start with a strong opinion. This perspective offers a possible explanation of Fisher & Lubin's (1958) finding in which subjects changed their opinion moderately in the direction of a vastly different viewpoint, yet did not reject that viewpoint or change beyond a moderate amount.

Chapter 14. COUNTERVAILING FACTORS

Life might not exist without stability. One of the systems that helps maintain stability consists of opposing factors that balance each other to some extent, as this chapter explains.

Countervailing Factors
There are inhibitory and excitatory nervous systems in biology, also counteracting muscles (e.g., biceps and triceps), male and female hormones in both sexes, and prostaglandins that heighten inflammation vs. those that lessen inflammation. A balance of opposing factors also occurs in inanimate objects, such as electrons vs. protons in physics, positive vs. negative magnetic poles, and gravity vs. centrifugal forces. Opposing valences are present in chemistry, also acids and alkalines have opposite effects. This chapter describes some psychological factors that have opposing actions.

Concurrently opposed factors
Some countervailing factors oppose one another simultaneously (*'concurrently opposed factors'*). For example, positive emotions oppose negative emotions, a desire to be independent opposes a desire to be accepted by others, and a drive to grow opposes resistance to change. There are many psychological factors that oppose one another in a concurrent fashion, such as positive and negative emotional reactions, also conflicting thoughts, overt behaviors, and Psychological Roots.

Factors that push on one side of the balance point add their effects to the total force pressing in that direction. The net result is affected by the number, type, and intensity of the underlying elements on each side. What is observed on the surface is the net outcome of many opposing aspects that operate below the surface. Lewin (1947) used the term 'quasi-stationary equilibrium' for such opposing factors because the outcome of each such arrangement shifts as the number and intensity of the underlying factors varies (see Figure 20).

It is useful to realize that a behavior can appear to be straightforward yet be the outcome of a dynamic interaction among countervailing factors that operate below the surface. Such hidden countervailing factors are among the many sub-surface systems that strongly affect us.

When an outcome involves a number of countervailing factors it is difficult for a single underlying factor to dominate. That circumstance also creates resistance to substantial changes and thereby helps maintain stability and homeostasis.

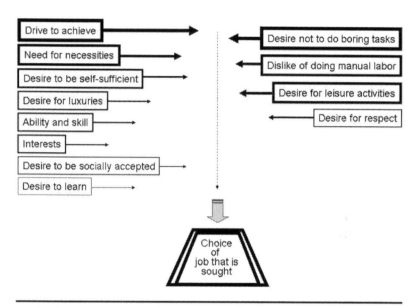

Fig. 20. An example of sub-surface countervailing factors with an observable outcome.

An outcome can be changed by introducing one or more countervailing factors or by intensifying, de-intensifying, modifying or eliminating some countervailing factors. For example, the length of time that a down mood exists can sometimes be shortened by adding pleasantness (as in the psychotherapeutic technique of reframing). When a strong negative outcome occurs – such as depression, anxiety, or anger – a substantial amount of positives would be required to counterbalance the negatives involved (but even then might not be sufficient or long-lasting). The tension in an interpersonal conflict might be lessened by each protagonist respecting one another.

The balance point of countervailing factors depends on the potency of each underlying factor. Since negatives are much stronger than positives, it may be that balance points often lean in a negative direction. A neutral person who appears to have no opinion or no emotional reaction regarding an issue (0 on a -10 to +10 scale) might have an equal balance of between his/her underlying negatives and positives.

Sequentially opposed factors

Another type of countervailing balance occurs when opposing factors occur in sequence rather than simultaneously ('sequentially opposed factors'). In biology, for example, the biceps muscle moves a person's arm inward and then the triceps muscle moves the arm outward, and vice-versa. Conversations and many contests occur in a back and forth manner (e.g., tennis, soccer, card games, and board games). People can be cooperative at one time and competitive at another time. Some musical compositions have point-and-counterpoint sequences.

A practical application of this information

Many sub-surface aspects contribute to what people say and do. When people try to influence someone to change they are likely to address only what they observe, but there can be resistance from hidden factors. Identifying sub-aware factors can be important, such as when attempting to cope with opposition from someone. An example of this occurred with newly-trained factory workers who, puzzlingly, were less productive after their training period than while they were being trained (Coch & French, 1948). Attempts to improve the workers' performance by explaining the situation to them did not succeed. Careful interviewing led to discovering that the workers believed that the managers had arbitrarily assigned them to deal with more difficult tasks than those workers believed was reasonable. That concern of the workers was corrected by allowing them to be involved in decisions about work assignments.

This study illustrates the existence of subsurface factors, in this case, beliefs, and the value of constructively addressing aspects that operate below the surface rather than trying to change behavior directly such as by using logic. (From a Psychological Systems Theory perspective, the workers no longer felt inappropriately controlled.)

Knowledge of countervailing factors helps us understand that:

• Change can be resisted due to sub-surface factors (e.g., unspoken or unknown beliefs).
• It is difficult to dislodge an opinion that is linked to deep Psychological Roots.
• Pressuring people to change is a repelling force and can be resisted.
• Having an absolute opinion can lead to rejecting even slightly different viewpoints.
• People might be willing or able to change to only a small degree.
• Change might exist only temporarily due to subsequently acquired sub-surface factors.

Knowing that observable behavior is due to hidden factors such as Psychological Roots points to the importance of underlying aspects when meeting resistance. It helps to identify those aspects and then use that knowledge constructively. (A method for creating constructive change is described in chapters on social influence and win-win solutions in Section II.)

Chapter 15. EVALUATING AND DECISION-MAKING

The way we evaluate has big effects on our thinking, judgment, emotional reactions, decisions, and behavior. This chapter explains how and some practical applications of that knowledge.

Sometimes we can make a conscious choice about how we evaluate

Much of how we react depends on whether we evaluate our circumstances in a positive or a negative way. For example, as people age, some individuals find something positive to focus on such as their still being alive, enjoying their family, feeling good about their career, or continuing to be active. That positive evaluation makes it easier to accept some of the drawbacks of aging such as wrinkles, aches, and sagging skin. A negative evaluation makes aging distressful. It is often possible to consciously decide whether to evaluate something in a positive or a negative way.

Imagine that Mary gets an A on an essay and Joan gets an F. That grade was determined by the particular criterion the teacher used. Had the teacher used a different criterion, perhaps Mary might still get an A, but Joan might get a C, and therefore a passing grade rather than a failing grade. Thus, the criterion people use to evaluate makes a considerable difference.

We can consciously decide some of the criteria we use. As a result, we have an opportunity to increase the number of positive emotional reactions, moods, decisions, and behaviors, and decrease the number of negative ones. This chapter describes some aspects related to evaluation and decision-making.

The executive function

The executive function includes thinking, evaluating, prioritizing, sorting, strategizing, and decision-making. Those largely subconscious processes are internal reactions in Hidden Sequences. All Psychological Roots are evaluative criteria because a circumstance is either consistent with a Psychological Root, only partly consistent with it, or not consistent with it. Thus, the executive function operates in part by drawing upon Psychological Roots such as needs, goals, expectations, interests, concerns, beliefs, personal rules, and specific fears for making evaluations. This chapter discusses evaluating, one of the executive functions.

Evaluation is often involved without our realizing it, such as our reaction when a goal is achieved, and whether something is emotionally satisfying or displeasing. People who believe that humans should treat people kindly unless there is good reason not to, negatively evaluate the harming of innocent people such as children, the elderly, refugees, or pets. The emotional reactions that result from evaluations mean that the negative and positive emotional centers are engaged, indicating that the evaluation process connects with those centers.

The above description highlights the following points:
a) Beliefs are evaluative criteria.
b) Emotional reactions can result from Psychological Roots such as beliefs.
c) Meeting a positive psychological criterion stimulates the positive emotional center.
d) Inconsistency with a psychological criterion stimulates the negative emotional center.

The bottom line: We can change our emotional reactions, thoughts, and behavior by changing the criteria we use for evaluating. Psychological Roots are evaluative criteria.

Evaluating occurs subconsciously

There are times when maintaining an evaluation is critical, such as when survival is on the line, and effectiveness is impeded if we do not evaluate effectively. As an example, imagine that you are driving on a two-lane road, calmly listening to the radio. Suddenly you become alert without knowing why. You look further up the road and see why: a car is heading toward you in your lane. You swing into action: you slow down, move your car closer to the road's edge, look for a place to pull off the road and get ready to sound the horn. When you again look up the road you realize that the reason the other car entered your lane was to pass another car. You stay alert to be sure that the driver moves back to the correct side of the road. When that car does re-enter its proper lane, it just misses your car. You heave a sigh of relief and realize that you might have had a head-on collision had you not slowed down and moved over. The realization of what might have happened causes you to tremble. This circumstance, which has happened to the author and perhaps to the reader, illustrates how the evaluative process is always at work below awareness.

The executive function evaluates constantly, day and night and is involved in decisions from the mundane to the momentous. Evaluating occurs not just for important situations but about almost anything, including trivial aspects. Examples include judging whether something is harmless, pleasure-filled, disturbing, or dangerous, and what the distance and speed are of aspects that are approaching us or moving away from us. Our subconscious mind also evaluates success and failure, how effective we and other people are, and who our competition is, among many other things.

Harm evaluation

When there is a danger of being harmed, the evaluation process triggers awareness and relevant emotional reactions. Some people are especially reactive, for instance, individuals who have a low threshold for negative emotional arousal can be upset by circumstances that others take in stride. Some other distress-prone Psychological Roots include having a pessimistic outlook, a narrow range of acceptability, weak problem-solving strategies, poor social skills, a belief about being vulnerable, and a strong need for safety. Distress-prone roots increase the likelihood of experiencing states of uncontrollability. The effect of those roots can be intensified in individuals who are highly emotional and think in absolutes (see the intensity curve in Figure 6).

Conscious selection of criteria for evaluations and decisions

Some evaluations, decisions, emotional reactions, and behaviors are primitive and counterproductive in much of today's circumstances, such as anger, ranting, and vengeance-seeking. Not taking conscious control of evaluations allows natural impulses like those mentioned to have a strong effect on people. Such impulses are geared for a kill-or-be-killed existence such as that of our cave-man ancestors. In some circumstances, responding ultra-aggressively is beneficial but in a civilized society doing so can often be detrimental. As a result, it is important for us to acquire civilizing modifiers that modify our evaluations and other reactions, including skill in creating compatible solutions when difficulties with other individuals occur. In a civilized society, effective social and problem-solving skills can help when conflicts arise, including strategies for helping to change our own and others' beliefs and habits. Having analytical skills can also help.

Negatives

Negative emotions – such as distress, frustration, and anger – can lead to acting harshly such as disparaging others and worse, having harmful personal and interpersonal effects. Strongly negative emotional reactions can eventuate in states of uncontrollability that have negative characteristics such as panic, depression, and rage. Such states can be difficult to rebound from and their damage hard to repair. Therefore, it would help to acquire effective skills for controlling such actions, including the ability to raise one's threshold for negative arousal when it appropriate to do so.

Conscious control of negative evaluation criteria

When negative emotional reactions occur, the ability to prevent unconstructive outcomes is aided by knowing the Psychological Roots that are involved and how to modify them constructively. For example, one way to raise the threshold for negative emotional arousal is to tell oneself, "Don't get caught up in this". A self-statement like that might have only a momentary effect, but that effect can be extended by repeating the statement until enough self-control has been acquired to act constructively. Another way to lessen negatives would be to introduce positives to dilute their effect, such as by finding something worthwhile in unpleasant situations (reframing). Yet another way would be to increase confidence by viewing difficult circumstances as being manageable. Another method for modifying negatives would be to modify or override distress-prone Psychological Roots constructively or to acquire problem-solving skills that can lessen feeling vulnerable. Lowering expectations can also help avoid becoming distressed (discussed in Chapter 11). These examples illustrate how it is possible to obtain some conscious control, albeit brief, over some subconscious operations.

When we are highly emotional, such as when we are stressed or angry, it is hard for us to adjust our evaluative criteria and control our actions. Some individuals believe that it is not possible to modify their subconscious functions, such as their evaluative criteria, or that when they are negative or aggressive it is justified, and some people resist change for other reasons (discussed in Chapter 13).

Decision-making

In the discussion to follow, decision-making (a topic of special interest to cognitive psychologists, economists, and game theorists) is limited to a particular technique. Selecting an alternative can be hard when the alternatives seem equally attractive or when strong consequences exist for making a poor decision. In such instances, a rating scale might uncover a slight difference between the choices, for instance, imagine using a 10-point rating scale to rate two attractive choices and evaluating them as 9 and 8, respectively. In that case, the slightly more attractive alternative might be chosen. If both alternatives receive the same rating (e.g., 9), decimals might detect a difference, such as 9.3 vs. 9.2. The 9.3 alternative would then be chosen. If one decimal place is insufficient to identify a difference, two decimal places might do the trick (e.g., 9.24 vs. 9.23).

When a choice is to be made between unappealing alternatives, a 0 to -10 scale might be able to identify "the lesser of two evils". For example, -6 triumphs over -7, and -9.1 wins over -9.2.

The author has employed this simple procedure to help people make decisions that had handcuffed them. This method also reduces the time required to make a choice when there are many alternatives such as when needing to select a few people from a large number of job applicants.

The author has found that a single overall rating for an alternative produces an outcome comparable to conducting a substantial analysis that takes into account each relevant component (such as credentials, cost, compatibility, durability, and consequences). If this inference is correct, it would mean that a single all-encompassing rating automatically takes into account many factors that subjectively and objectively affect the decision. An empirical study would be needed to test this hypothesis (see the list of possible studies in Chapter 38).

Subconscious evaluations and decisions can be overridden

Evaluations and decisions are internal reactions that occur subconsciously, yet it is possible to override some evaluations and the actions that flow from them. Being able to make conscious evaluations can help limit impulsive urges and counterproductive behaviors. It is also possible to ask oneself before acting, "Is what I'm about to say or do likely to have negative consequences?" If the subjective answer is "Absolutely not!", the action in question can then be taken. However, if there is even a slight chance that negative consequences might occur, it may be wise to avoid taking action.

The bottom line:

Much failure can be avoided by not acting when an evaluation suggests that a high chance of failure is possible. Feeling like a failure can be avoided by lowering expectations when making a decision.

A practical application of this information

Below are a few self-statements that may be useful for aspects presented in italics below (in alphabetical order):

- For *absolute thinking* – "There are other worthwhile possibilities", "There are likely to be many aspects".
- For *high expectations* – "Anything above zero is a plus", "Something is better than nothing", "I'm grateful".
- For *impatience* – "Expand the time frame", "Provide time for mental incubation".
- For *low self-esteem* – "I'm worthwhile", "Some people like me a lot", "Everyone doesn't have to like me".
- For *low threshold for negative arousal* – "Don't get caught up in this".
- For *narrow comfort zone* – "It is win-win to expand the number of possibilities".
- For *pessimism* – "I can handle this", "There is a solution, I just need to find it".

- *For one's own resistance to change* – "No one is perfect", "Improvement aids effectiveness".
- *For others' resistance to change* – "Show how my viewpoint solves a problem of that person".
- *For problem-solving* – "Break the problem into parts", "Find the key issue and solve it first", "Finish working on something before tackling something else".
- *For social strategy* – "Use appealing forces", "Avoid using repelling forces", "Seek win-win solutions".
- *For unwillingness to be wrong* – "I learn from mistakes", "There's something good in things that go wrong".

(In Section II, a win-win approach is presented that can generate solutions to interpersonal difficulties.)

Chapter 16. CAUSE AND EFFECT

It can be indispensable to know what is causing a difficult problem. Many psychological issues are difficult to understand because the underlying causes are invisible. This chapter discusses the difference between an apparent cause and the real cause, and how to distinguish between them.

The cause is often invisible

Not knowing the cause of something can readily lead to making incorrect guesses about what that cause might be. For example, some people think that airplanes fly because they have wings and a powerful motor. That seems reasonable on the surface, however, some people have lost their lives because they did not realize that the wing must be shaped in a special way. Flat wings do not work. A powerful motor can help but is not the major key since gliders fly without a motor. It took hundreds of thousands of years until the Wright brothers figured out the secret (see the air-foil design in Figure 15).

It is often possible to believe incorrect ideas. For example, many people believe that jail is a good way to rehabilitate addicts and criminals. The idea that imprisoned individuals will change themselves does not take into account that those individuals do not know the powerful internal and external factors that cause them to be the way they are, nor how to create the deep changes that are needed. The Psychological Roots that are involved have yet to be identified. Once those roots are known, inmates who want a better life would have a better opportunity to improve than at present.

Another example of an incorrect idea about cause-and-effect occurs with phobias. Many people believe that facing up to a fear or purposely experiencing it is what is needed. However, many people would be traumatized by experiencing what distresses them rather than get better. Also, a phobia is likely to remain if what causes it is not rectified. Many phobias (perhaps a large majority) are caused by hidden aspects that people are not aware of, such as subconscious beliefs (see Nell's bridge phobia described in Chapter 28, which was not due to bridges).

The cause of many problems is hidden, such as disease-causing microbes and distress-prone Psychological Roots. So, although the tendency to focus on tangible aspects is understandable (discussed earlier), doing so can be an obstacle when trying to identify the cause of a psychological internal reaction or behavior. Appearances can also be deceiving, for example, observing that birds flap their wings can lead to the idea that any type of wing would be sufficient for flight (mentioned above). Another example of an incorrect belief about causation is reflected in overly simple advice that some people give to others, such as telling depressed people to cheer up, anxious people to calm down, and low self-esteem individuals to feel good about themselves.

A major difficulty with not knowing the cause of a problem is that it can lead to treating symptoms. For example, a crack in a wall can be plastered over but if the cause is a foundation that is settling, a crack will continue to appear no matter how many times it is plastered. Similarly, believing that an addiction to drugs will end when a person abstains from using drugs or that a war on drug traffickers will end addiction problems, does not address the cause of the problem. The proximal cause of people's addiction to drugs often is their need to lessen great distress, which might originate with distress-prone Psychological Roots or a harsh stimulus that impacts such roots.

Mastering an addiction requires modifying the Psychological Roots that contribute to it. Therefore, successfully addressing the problems caused by addiction requires that the psychological aspects of addiction be tackled effectively. Addressing externally observable aspects – such as drugs, distributors, suppliers, and behaviors associated with addiction – would be unlikely to succeed. (Treatment of psychological conditions is discussed in Chapters 27 - 30.)

Treating symptoms is understandable when the cause is not known, but doing so can permit problems to persist or worsen. Biased ideas about what the cause is can arise in such instances, something that is often seen in politics. If the condition continues and flare-ups occur it can be a sign that symptoms are being addressed rather than the cause (see the examples in Chapter 28 with regard to people who were medicated for anxiety, depression, or addiction when the cause of those problems was psychological). In short, it is important to identify the cause and to realize when symptoms are being treated instead.

Identifying the cause

It is difficult to treat a problem effectively when the cause of a circumstance is not known. The importance of subconscious aspects can be overlooked because those aspects are hidden. Conversely, it is easy to assume that an observable aspect is the cause. For example, "Lyman" was frustrated by what "Iona" said and angrily told her off. What appeared to cause Lyman's outburst was what Iona said. However, Lyman's frustration had been building before that circumstance due to prior altercations he had been having with various people. Lyman had been keeping a lid on those annoyances but they kept building up to the point at which almost any additional frustration could have triggered an angry outburst. What Iona said was "the straw that broke the camel's back" and therefore a *'precipitating factor'* or *'proximal cause'* of Lyman's anger, not the *'originating cause'*.

Lyman's outburst relieved his irritation for that moment but did not solve his underlying frustrations because it did not change the originating cause. The origin of his frustrations involved his unduly high expectations of others, which people were not meeting. Lyman's outburst illustrates how the originating cause can be hidden and how a proximal cause can readily be mistakenly assumed to be the originating cause. It is also an example of how venting does not solve the cause of a person's problem.

"Claire" and "Frank" had money problems so their frequent arguments about money would seem to be entirely about finances. However, a major reason for their discord was that Claire felt disrespected and Frank felt controlled. That is why their discord continued after they solved their money issues. Their quarreling subsided only after counseling assistance helped them resolve their hidden psychological issues.

The discovery that a chemical imbalance in serotonin is associated with depression is important. That knowledge led to the belief that a chemical imbalance is the originating cause of depression. A chemical imbalance is an internal reaction in a Hidden Sequence, as an intermediate part of that sequence, therefore a proximal cause rather than the originating cause.

This understanding raises a question about what the originating cause of that chemical imbalance is. That cause could be something biological or physical, but many researchers have found that psychological aspects cause chemical imbalances (e.g., Brehm, Back, & Bogdonoff, 1964; Bigo, Baowyer, Braen, et al., 1994; Ciompi & Panksepp, 2005; and anxiety causing an increase in adrenalin). In Psychological Systems Theory, distress-prone Psychological Roots and the stimulus conditions that impact those roots are major causes of chemical imbalances.

It is possible to obtain some salutary effect by treating an intermediate aspect but doing so does not address the originating cause of the problem. Often the positive effect is modest or temporary. As a result, people continue to be depressed while taking medication and for some people, such medicines have little effect. People who use alcohol, cigarettes, marihuana, heroin, cocaine, or food to deal with their problems are also treating their symptoms rather than the cause.

Many people have some obvious difficulties such as problems involving money or family disturbances, and some of them might obtain improvement by treating their internal reactions and overt behaviors. In such instances, it can seem counterintuitive to seek hidden psychological factors. However, there can be hidden causes, such as distress-prone Psychological Roots that unpleasant stimulus conditions impact. If those underlying aspects are not corrected, problems can continue and possibly worsen. Treating proximal causes and symptoms can divert attention from addressing the originating cause and thereby allow problems to become still more entrenched.

Thus, when behavior occurs, it is to be expected that a chemical imbalance is involved because there are internal reactions that precede it. Knowledge of Hidden Sequences leads to identifying the originating cause: Psychological Roots (see Chapter 4). There may be more than one Hidden Sequence involved and therefore more than one Psychological Root, stimulus condition, internal reaction, and behavior that need to be modified to produce improvement (see Chapter 6). In many situations, it is possible to treat symptoms, internal reactions, and Psychological Roots with medication as well as strategies derived from Psychological Systems Theory (e.g., psychotherapy).

The bottom line:
Seeking hidden Psychological Roots might seem indirect especially when there are clear-cut stimulus conditions, internal reactions, and behaviors, however, the author has found that doing so is highly practical.

Distinguishing between psychological and biological causes of psychological disorders
Determining the best treatment is aided by ascertaining the cause, which might be psychological, biological, societal, or physical. The author has found that distress-prone Psychological Roots and stimulus conditions often cause or significantly contribute to psychological disorders such as depression, panic, bipolar disorder, obsessive-compulsive disorder [OCD], addiction, and eating disorders. (See the list of distress-prone Psychological Roots at the end of this chapter.)

Precursors to psychological states of uncontrollability – such as dysthymia, anxiety, compulsivity, cyclothymia, and high reactivity – can progress to full-blown disorders. For instance, feeling like a failure can create a down mood, then progress to dysthymia, and then to depression. There are some psychological conditions in which psychotherapeutic methods are not the primary treatment or appropriate, such as in the case of biologically-caused disorders like autism, age-related dementia, genetically-caused schizophrenia, and brain injuries (e.g., due to concussions or toxins). In such cases, biologically-based methods are the treatment of choice, such as medication, surgery, or electro-cortico therapy (ECT). In some of those instances, psychotherapy might offer adjunctive treatment.

194

In some circumstances, both biological and psychological treatments are useful. Biologically-based methods can provide valuable adjunctive treatment for some psychologically-caused disorders and vice-versa, psychologically-based methods can provide valuable adjunctive treatment for some biologically-based methods. Societal factors (e.g., bullying, social media, or gangs) can cause psychological conditions and need to be addressed. Physical aspects, such as environmental pollutants, unsanitary conditions, and overcrowding may also need to be changed. Some individuals, such as very young children and individuals with limited intellectual development, might benefit from tangibly-oriented psychotherapy.

Ascertaining whether the cause of a psychological disorder is or is not psychological
How to ascertain whether the cause of a psychological disorder is psychological or biological might be aided by applying the following questions:
1. Are non-psychological aspects likely to be the cause (e.g., biological, physical, or societal)?
   If yes, those causes should be addressed.
2. If psychotropic medicine is being taken, must it continue to control the symptoms?
   If yes, the originating cause might not be biological, and another cause should be sought.
3. Do Psychological Roots and stimulus conditions completely explain the condition?
   If no, another cause should be sought. If yes, the originating cause may be psychological.
4. Does modifying Psychological Roots and stimulus conditions correct the situation?
   If yes, the originating cause is likely to be psychological. If not, another cause should be sought.
5. After the initial condition has been corrected, does a similar condition re-occur?
   If yes, the changes have not been sufficiently long-lasting, and the diagnosis and treatment may need to be re-examined.

A repeated caution
MEDICATION IS THE APPROPRIATE TREATMENT FOR SOME PSYCHOLOGICAL CONDITIONS AND MAY BE NECESSARY. FOR SOME PEOPLE, MEDICINE IS A NECESSITY.

PEOPLE WHO USE PSYCHOTROPIC PHARMACEUTICALS SHOULD NOT STOP USING THEM UNTIL THEY HAVE A BETTER ALTERNATIVE.

ENDING THE USE OF MEDICATION FOR A PSYCHOLOGICAL CONDITION SHOULD BE DONE WITH THE ADVICE AND THERAPEUTIC SUPPORT OF A CREDENTIALED PROFESSIONAL, PREFERABLY A LICENSED PSYCHIATRIST.

WHEN MEDICATION FOR A PSYCHOLOGICAL CONDITION IS TO END, THE DOSE SHOULD BE TAPERED DOWN GRADUALLY RATHER THAN STOPPING ABRUPTLY.

AFTER ENDING THE USE OF PSYCHOTROPIC MEDICINE, IT CAN BE IMPORTANT TO CONTINUE HAVING PROFESSIONAL PSYCHOLOGICAL TREATMENT.

The appearance of normality can impede identifying the psychological cause

Psychological disorders and precursors vary in intensity and frequency, and many people with such conditions enter and exit states of uncontrollability or precursor conditions rather than remaining continuously in them. As a result, when people who have a disorder are not experiencing symptoms they are in the normal range of the population. They are not disordered at that time. Perhaps many or even most people with common psychological conditions – such as anxiety, depression, and borderline personality disorder – are in the normal range of the population much of the time and manifest substantial symptoms of their condition only when they cross a tipping point into a state of uncontrollability.

People can appear to be normal when they disguise their symptoms. Some people's symptoms show only when they are stressed. Some individuals do not appear to have symptoms because of self-treatments that disguise their issues such as alcohol, marihuana, or another person's medication. Some people deny their condition or refuse to accept the idea that they could benefit from professional help. Doing such things can delay obtaining appropriate treatment.

Some aspects that mistakenly can be believed to be the originating cause

Below are some aspects that have been mistaken for the originating cause. These aspects include salient stimuli, past experiences, internal reactions, overt behavior, and demographic characteristics. In such instances, the originating cause can remain undetected and unattended.

Stimulus conditions

Relevant stimuli are often noticeable, such as deadlines, financial problems, and problems with other people. The prominence of an observable stimulus can lead to believing that the originating cause is solely that stimulus.

196

However, stimuli have an effect because they impact a Psychological Root, according to Psychological Systems Theory. On this basis, a successful treatment calls for constructively modifying the pertinent Psychological Roots in addition to coping with the relevant stimulus condition.

Past stimulus conditions

Past stimulus conditions are earlier experiences, such as significant experiences that occurred in childhood. Some past stimulus conditions can affect an individual throughout life, for example, having been sexually abused, beaten, disparaged, bullied, or discriminated against could lead to acquiring a strong belief of being vulnerable.

Sometimes past experiences produce Psychological Roots different than what would be expected. For example, "Al" grew up in a criminal family but had the *opposite* personality traits. That unexpected effect resulted from his not wanting to be like the people in his family, so he intentionally developed a strong work ethic and a concern about being honest. In another case, "Sanford" grew up with a harsh father, but was warm, caring, and supportive because he specifically rejected his father's style. Many people believe that the majority of abused individuals are abusers or delinquent, however, research has found that not to be the case (Widom, 1989).

Thus, counter to common sense, a person's past experiences do not always provide an accurate understanding of their personality, just as some aspects of a tree's current appearance can differ from how it existed at an earlier time. When trying to understand a person's present behavior, what counts are the individual's *current* Psychological Roots. This viewpoint is consistent with Rotter's (1966) opinion that the effect of a stimulus is related to the meaning that an individual ascribes to it.

Cumulative build-up

Successive stimulus conditions can contribute to a cumulative build-up and thereby set the stage for a substantial reaction such as a state of uncontrollability (e.g., rage, panic, or depression). In such instances, a minor stimulus can trigger a major episode. That stimulus might appear to be the cause, but it is a precipitating cause, not the originating cause. (See the example of Iona and Lyman earlier in this chapter). It can help to identify the Psychological Roots that are involved and any cumulative build-up that has occurred.

Cumulative build-up can also occur biologically, such as in dementia, in which distinct signs appear after the condition has been considerably advanced. A biological build-up also occurs with regard toxicity from cigarettes, alcohol, fatty foods, asbestos, and cancer. A build-up can be hidden and therefore delay treatment sometimes to a point where it can be too late to turn things around.

Thoughts

A thought, according to Psychological Systems Theory, originates from a Psychological Root (with or without having been impacted by a stimulus condition). It is a cognitive internal reaction in a Hidden Sequence and can trigger other internal reactions (e.g., emotions such as happiness or sadness) and behavior (e.g., skeletal-muscle action). Changing a negative thought to something positive can be beneficial even when the originating cause has not been modified.

Feelings and other emotional reactions

Feeling guilty, impatient, irritated, anxious, angry, happy, contented, and other emotions are internal reactions in Hidden Sequences and can trigger other internal reactions (e.g., sad or desperate thoughts) and behavior (e.g., aggression or attempted suicide). Some people believe feelings are the originating cause behavior, especially strong feelings, but they are proximal causes of behavior.

Some internal reactions such as feeling annoyed or anxious are so bothersome that direct relief of them is sought. In such instances, treatment may be addressed to those aspects, but they are symptoms.

Emotional reactions and other internal reactions are important but are not Psychological Roots. Rather, emotional reactions stem from Psychological Roots (or an interaction of stimuli with Psychological Roots). A person's pent-up emotional intensity can be temporarily relieved by expressing feelings, but doing so is unlikely to change the causative Psychological Roots. To change feelings and other emotional reactions requires changing the pertinent Psychological Roots or the stimuli that impact those roots.

Biological and biochemical aspects

A chemical imbalance in neurotransmitters such as serotonin and dopamine has been thought to be the originating cause of psychological conditions such as depression, anxiety, and suicide. (Some other neurotransmitters that might be involved in psychological conditions are norepinephrine, GABA, and acetylcholine). Neurotransmitters are internal reactions in Hidden Sequences and so are proximal causes of psychological conditions, not the originating cause, according to Psychological Systems Theory (discussed earlier). The originating basis of many common psychological conditions is a Psychological Root or a stimulus condition interacting with a Psychological Root. From this perspective, neurotransmitter medications treat an intermediate part of Hidden Sequences rather than the originating cause of behavior, which helps explain why medication can have little or no effect and why flareups can occur while a person is taking medication.

Genetics

Some people are born with psychological disorders such as autism or schizophrenia, or precursors that lead to psychological disorders, such as a low threshold for negative emotional arousal. Some people with an addiction to alcohol have predisposing genes, however, experiential influences appear to be an even stronger factor (Gordis, 1992). When a person exhibits a psychological condition similar to that of another family member – such as anxiety, aggression, or addiction – it is easy to believe that the trait has been genetically inherited ("It runs in the family").

However, people frequently acquire traits similar to those of family members. For instance, adopted children can have their adoptive family's belief systems and philosophies, such as a strong drive to achieve, high standards, or belief that punishment is the disciplinary method of choice. It is even possible for children to have their parents' characteristics at an even stronger level and therefore can be even more competitive, accomplishment-driven, perfectionistic, prejudiced, or aggressive than a parent or a peer. Children's tendency to think in sweeping absolutes may be one reason.

Ignoring the potency of acquired characteristics can result in a person's behavior being ascribed erroneously to genetics. (Technically, doing so views a phenotype as if it was a genotype). A person's acquired traits, especially later Psychological Roots, might be somewhat more malleable than genetic traits at times.

Incorrectly believing that genetic inheritance causes behavior is abetted by:

• Being unaware that strong psychological behaviors can be acquired from experiences
• Being unwilling to accept the idea that behavior patterns can be acquired experientially.
• Focusing on tangible aspects (discussed earlier).
• Thinking in absolutes (discussed in a later chapter).
• Not believing that strong behavior patterns can be changed.

Behavior

Some behaviors are particularly troublesome, such as addiction, crime, and violence, and it is understandable that people try to stop those problems directly. Examples are people's using will-power to try to control their behavior (for example, forcing themselves to abstain from using drugs) and punishing others to try to squelch their behavior (for example, putting people in prison). Doing such things treats the bothersome behavior as if it was the cause, however it addresses the outcome, not the cause. Reining in disturbing behavior is understandable and needed, but it does not target the cause.

If the cause is not treated, stopping a behavior directly might work for a short time but it is not surprising that the behavior can return. Treating symptoms without treating the cause explains why efforts to control disturbing behavior have had only limited success. It would be better to identify and modify causative aspects, such as Psychological Roots.

A version of addressing a symptom as if it was the cause occurs when a synonym is stated as the cause, such as saying that a person is a narcissist because he is egocentric, or that a person's tension is a result of stress, or that a skin rash is due to dermatitis. Another example is a coach saying, "We lost because we didn't score enough points" or "I made that decision because I considered it to be in the best interest of the team." Still another example is proclaiming that being overweight is caused by ingesting more calories than the amount expended. In such instances, the reason for the outcome is not stated. For example, in the case of being overweight, the reason for a person's excessive intake of calories might be a person's attempt to counteract distress by obtaining pleasure from eating sweets. That reason may be overlooked or not realized, but can be the cause of the weight problem.

Treating symptoms instead of the cause is not infrequent, such as therapies for anxiety involving relaxation, meditation, medication, hypnosis, guided imagery, deep breathing, and breathing into a paper bag. In addiction, examples of treatments that treat symptoms rather than the cause include abstention, methadone, restricting the number of opiate prescriptions, criminalizing drug use, and warring against drug dealers. And while it is necessary to isolate criminals, prison or ostracism are not effective rehabilitation aids because they do not treat the causes and can worsen criminal behavior. Not directly addressing the cause of a behavior can result in not changing the behavior or only minimally affecting the situation. This helps explain why the relapse rate after treatment for alcohol addiction can be as high as 80% (Moos & Moos, 2006). Criminal recidivism is also high (e.g., 75%, Bureau of Justice, 1994). As high as these figures are they appear to under-estimate the problem since they do not take into account all instances of subjects' recidivism, subjects who died, and subjects who had temporary lapses.

When the cause of a problem is not known, it is understandable that symptom-oriented efforts may be used. For example, psychologically-caused anxiety or depression is often treated with medication, which often can lessen symptoms but treats outcomes rather than causes, according to Psychological Systems Theory. Many attempts to lose weight focus on diet or exercise, not the causative psychological factors. Criticism is commonly used when trying to get someone to change rather than constructively addressing the reason for that person's viewpoint. Many treatments for physiological conditions such as headaches, backaches, and sleep problems address symptoms rather than causes.

Treating symptoms is better than doing nothing. However, it should be understood when doing so that the cause is not being treated and that the relief that is provided is likely to be temporary. When what is treated is what is observable on the surface rather than the underlying cause, the temporary relief that occurs can lead to a mistaken belief that the cause is being treated and that the treatment is effective. It might therefore be concluded that the treatment is all that is needed or even that such treatments should be the standard. Accordingly, there should be awareness that: a) symptoms are being treated, b) efforts are needed to identify the cause, and c) the ultimate objective should be treating the cause. (See Spike's case in Chapter 18, win-win solution examples in Chapter 21, and psychotherapy examples in Chapter 28.)

The bottom line:

When treating symptoms does not provide substantial relief – for example, when a person's symptoms return unless medication continues to be taken – the cause should be sought and that cause should be treated appropriately.

Demographic aspects

Demographic data – such as statistics about gender, age, ethnicity, and income – provide interesting and useful information about observable characteristics of the population. For example, more females are diagnosed with depression than males, and more high-income business-owners vote for conservative office-seekers than blue-collar workers do. However, demographic aspects are externally-observable characteristics rather than the actual causes of behavior. For instance, demographic information does not explain why blue-collar workers vote differently than business owners, or why females are diagnosed with more depression than males. The underlying causes of demographic characteristics are hidden, such as concerns, interests, goals, beliefs, expectations and other Psychological Roots.

An example of the reason for females' greater incidence of depression is that they may be more concerned than males about their health and obtaining professional help. (Concerns are Psychological Roots.) It might also be noted that many demographic aspects have relatively low correlations with outcomes. One reason is that there are wide-ranging individual differences within demographic groups (e.g., only *some* women do 'X', and only *some* low-income people do 'Y').

In 2016, demographic data did not offer a suitable explanation of Donald Trump's election as President of the U.S. For example, he received only slightly greater support from low-income white males than from other voter cohorts. A much better explanation for Mr. Trump's success had to do with voters' psychology: many Trump voters had authoritarian beliefs and wanted an autocratic leader (Hetherington & Weiler, 2009; Taub, 2016).

In sum, psychological aspects are more likely to indicate the cause of behavior than demographic characteristics.

Treating the cause

It can be indispensable to identify the psychological cause of internal reactions and behavior, such as the distress-prone Psychological Roots noted at the end of this chapter. It is understandable that when a person's Psychological Roots are not known, other aspects are likely to be treated instead, such as emotional responses, attitudes, serotonin levels and other internal reactions. (See Chapter 4's discussion of Hidden Sequences.)

Possible treatments for aspects mentioned in this chapter are presented below.

- *For originating causes*: Constructively modify pertinent distress-prone Psychological Roots (e.g., change expectations, raised the threshold for emotional arousal, acquire effective problem-solving strategies), and change the stimulus conditions that impact those Psychological Roots.

- *For proximal causes and internal reactions:* Change or remove distressing stimulus conditions, or modify those conditions by reframing the person's perspective, or modify the reaction by using relaxation or medication.

- *For overt behavior:* Use behavior modification to change goals and methods, also hobbies, sports, hypnosis, and constructive distraction. Punitive treatments and other repelling forces often are counterproductive, such as criticism, physical attacks, incarceration, aversive therapy .

Summary

Problems are more likely to be solved when the cause of a problem is appropriately addressed. The cause may be hidden and require special understanding to uncover it. With psychological disorders, there often is a subconscious cause, such as Psychological Roots. In cases where a person's Psychological Roots are not known or addressed, treating symptoms is better than doing nothing, yet concomitant efforts should be made to identify the cause.

Some indications that the cause is not being treated occur when the symptoms continue, flare up, or increase or the treatment is required over a long period of time. In such cases, rather than treating the underlying cause, what is being addressed often is what is apparent such as emotional reactions, dysfunctional thoughts, or counterproductive behavior. Emotional reactions and dysfunctional thoughts are internal reactions in hidden sequences and therefore proximal causes, not the originating cause. Counterproductive behaviors are overt outcomes rather than causes. Therefore, methods such as relaxation, meditation, medication, venting of feelings, dieting, and exercise treat symptoms rather than the cause and therefore are likely to provide only temporary relief.

When symptoms or the behavior itself are being treated there is a hope that the mind or body will correct itself in some unknown way. It would be better to identify the cause and address it directly, such as Psychological Roots and the stimulus conditions that impact them. (See Chapter 6 for methods of identifying Psychological Roots and Chapters 20 – 30 for strategies to help change Psychological Roots.)

Deeply-rooted Psychological Roots are difficult to change, but they can be modified or overridden. Memories of past stimulus conditions such as traumas may remain, but the Psychological Roots that resulted from them can be adjusted. People can experience internal pressure to return to the original Psychological Roots so there may be a need to reinforce changes from time to time.

The bottom line:

When trying to solve a problem, it is best to identify the cause and correct it. We should be aware that treating symptoms is less effective and therefore try to find the cause. An indication that symptoms are being treated is that progress is slow or non-existent, the symptoms keep returning, and flareups occur. In psychological conditions, the causes often are Psychological Roots and the stimulus conditions that impact those roots. Substantial improvement requires appropriate modification of those aspects.

Quantitative assessments

Scientific measures of psychological aspects are useful and can be essential. Most such measures that currently exist assess outcomes, such as behavior (e.g., addiction, aggression, attention disorder, alcohol use) and internal reactions (e.g., anxiety, anger). Relatively few measures of Psychological Roots are currently available (e.g., self-efficacy and self-esteem) and more are needed, such as standardized measures of distress-prone Psychological Roots.

A practical application of this information

When a psychological intervention fails or has only a limited effect, it may be that the originating cause is not being addressed or not being treated effectively (e.g., Psychological Roots). Something that may seem to be an obvious cause, "common sense", or promoted by experts, might not be the actual cause. Aspects that might be mistakenly considered causes are childhood experiences (which are past stimulus conditions), emotional reactions or thoughts (which are internal reactions), behavior (which are observable outcomes), or someone else's behavior (which is a stimulus). It can help to seek hidden distress-prone Psychological Roots such as those listed at the end of this chapter. If an intervention based on an analysis of Psychological Roots does not work, a more extensive analysis may be required, including seeking a cause that is biological, sociological, or environmental.

Some distress-prone Psychological Roots

. Belief one's problems cannot be solved
. Belief that abstract ideas are not useful
. Belief that being controlling persuades
. Belief that criticism is effective
. Belief that directness is effective
. Belief that facts and logic persuade
. Belief that negativeness is appropriate
. Belief that oneself is a victim
. Belief that oneself is helpless
. Belief that oneself is highly vulnerable
. Belief that oneself is unworthy
. Belief that persistence persuades
. Belief that retaliation is appropriate
. Belief that theories are not useful
. Desire for autonomy

. Desire for retaliation or revenge
. Desire not to be controlled
. Desire not to be taken advantage of
. Desire not to surrender or give in
. Desire to be independent
. Desire to be oppositional
. Desire to be provocative
. Desire to be unpredictable
. Desire to control other people
. Desire to dominate or win
. Disregard of others' boundaries
. Disregard of others' resistance
. Generally thinking in absolutes
. Hard-to-meet expectations or standards
. Intolerance of being controlled

. Intolerance of being wrong or failing
. Low confidence or self-esteem
. Low threshold for for irritability
. Low threshold for negative arousal
. Much distrust of others
. Narrow range of acceptability
. Need for attention, support, or love
. Need for respect or importance
. Need for safety, stability, or stimulation
. Need to defend oneself
. Pessimism, expect bad things to happen
. Poor problem-solving strategies
. Poor social strategies
. Strong focus on tangible aspects
. Want unrestricted personal limits

Chapter 17. SHORT- AND LONG-TERM MEMORY
(The present chapter describes some aspects related to this broad topic.)

Short-term memory, sometimes called working memory, helps us remember where the house and car keys are and what has just been said. In other circumstances, long-term memory is important, for example, when we draw on a skill or a vocabulary word we acquired years ago, or create a sentence that obeys grammatical rules we learned in childhood.

Here is a paradox: some of our deliberate attempts to generate long-term memory are unsuccessful, such as what we memorized for an exam, yet some things that we did not intentionally try to remember can remain with us for a lifetime, such as certain childhood experiences. This chapter explains this paradox and how to use that understanding to help memory serve your needs.

Short and long-term memory

Short- and long-term memory are valuable for different reasons. When short-term memory is impaired its importance becomes apparent, such as when individuals cannot remember what occurred just minutes before and lose their train of thought. This circumstance is extreme with Alzheimer's patients (Jannis, 2017) in which afflicted individuals might not recognize important people in their life, the names of those individuals or the day, week, month, or year it is. Impairment of short-term memory can be dangerous if those individuals forget their destination, get lost, and do not know how to return.

Interestingly, the long-term memory during the early stages of many individuals who suffer from loss of memory might be largely unaffected at first, which can sometimes lead to their functioning somewhat as they did at a much earlier time in their life (a kind of "second childhood"). An inference from this circumstance is that short- and long-term memory are different operations, have different processes and are in different locations in psychological hierarchies or other structures.

Short-term memory

Short-term memory – also called working memory – lasts as long as a person needs it, permitting people to remember the steps they have taken while working on a project, what is said during a conversation, and remembering a phone number long enough to dial it. Short-term memory is what students draw upon when they memorize by rote, that is when they try to remember something by reading it repetitively or by using flash-cards. Students in that circumstance have a goal that soon will be achieved, such as passing an upcoming exam. When that exam is over, the goal ends and with it, much of the information linked to that goal disappears. As a result, much of what is memorized for school tasks is forgotten. Teachers in subsequent classes might believe that the material had never been taught to students by previous instructors and might not have sufficient time to help students acquire what they were supposed to have retained.

Rote memorization does not require understanding the material. Hence, students who memorize by rote can pass exams and even get high grades without comprehending what they memorized, nor add to their knowledge or wisdom, nor change their thinking. Therefore, obtaining good school grades and "book learning" are more likely to reflect a student's perspicacity and diligence than his/her intellect, comprehension, problem-solving ability, or creativity. Memorizing by rote is tedious and therefore can contribute to disliking school.

Long-term memory

Mentioned earlier was that long-term memory could be generated by linking new information to long-lasting inner motivations such as high-order Psychological Roots (e.g., a strongly held belief, a long-term goal, values, or a desire for social connectedness). As an example, a phobia caused by a single incident might last a lifetime if the threat involved links directly to the person's genetic need for safety. What people acquire in childhood from their parents (e.g., values, religious affiliation, and work ethic) can last a lifetime in many people when those aspects become part of their basic personality. Since high-order Psychological Roots are likely to have a great deal of significance for people and last longer than low-order roots (such as short-term goals and surface roots), comprehension and long-term retention are more likely when new information links with deep roots.

Emotional significance

'Emotional significance' refers to whatever arouses a substantial positive or negative reaction, such as an incident that was especially pleasurable (e.g., a birthday party) or particularly disturbing (e.g., a serious injury). Some early childhood memories remain for a lifetime because the emotional reactions were directly associated with a deep Psychological Root, such as the need for safety or acceptance. The greater the emotional significance a circumstance has, the greater the likelihood that it is connected with a deep Psychological Root and being remembered for a long time. However, extremely intense emotional reactions (such as panic or rage) can impede cognitive processing. Thus, some experiences might not register or may be too negative for a person to want to remember. For example, childhood sexual abuse might not be recalled or not become available for recall until an individual feels capable of coping with that memory. (Also see Nell's phobia in Chapter 28).

Cognitive significance

How long a memory lasts depends in part on its cognitive significance. Something is *'cognitively significant'* when it is of particular interest or concern to a person, such as when it pertains to a long-term goal, major relationship, or occupation. Examples include knowledge, thoughts, ideas, proverbs, and poems that have special relevance, importance, or meaning. Some long-term memories can last a lifetime, such as significant childhood experiences. For something new to link with a long-term Psychological Root it must be thematically consistent with the root to which it links, for example, all the roots in a hierarchy related to need for safety must be in accord with that need. What is new may have to be modified to render it capable of linking (see pre-shaping, discussed in Chapter 7). It is possible that the changes involved in pre-shaping might deviate from reality, such as who was present, what was said, and what the person's racial identity was (see Allport & Postman, 1948).

A *'meaningful experience'* is something that is either cognitively or emotionally significant (e.g., something that is particularly interesting or of considerable concern).

Stimuli can trigger memories

When a stimulus connects with a cluster, aspects related to aspects in that cluster, such as memories of past experiences, can be triggered. For example, a traumatic remembrance, such as a post-traumatic stress disorder (PTSD) flashback, can be elicited by a loud sound, distinctive occurrence, or special odor. When a stimulus triggers a soldier's anxiety-producing flashback, a Stimulus-and-Root sequence is involved. Such PTSD reactions can sometimes be diminished by lessening the threat involved, or by using a desensitization procedure (which employs a series of related stimuli ranging from bland to intense, Wolpe, 1958). Eye movement desensitization response (EMDR) can sometimes help, as can reframing to identify positive aspects.

Additional memory aids

It is paradoxical that some things a person intentionally tries to remember (such as what is memorized by rote) might remain only briefly in memory, while some aspects that were not intentionally remembered (such as potent childhood experiences) can be retained for a long time, sometimes a lifetime. A Psychological Systems Theory explanation is that: a) what a person intends to recall for a short-term purpose largely disappears after that short-term goal is accomplished, and b) aspects that have cognitive or emotional significance might be retained for a long time because of their having linked with a long-term Psychological Root.

Memory can often be aided by linking with something appealing or striking (i.e., an aspect that has cognitive or emotional significance), such as a pleasant rhyme, alliteration, or mnemonic (e.g., "Columbus sailed the ocean blue in 1492"). Remembrance can also be bolstered by certain information having substantial long-term value and also by its usefulness (such as when it is frequently used over an extended period). Different aspects of what is remembered can link with different Psychological Roots and clusters, which may be why pieces of memory return at different times after having been lost due to a brain injury.

A practical application of this information

Using flash-cards or continually repeating or re-reading something may seem to be an effective way to remember something, however doing so is likely to produce short-term memory, especially if it links to a goal that will soon end, such as a current task or an upcoming appointment. When it is important to remember something for a long time, a useful strategy would be to link it to an important issue such as a long-term concern. A way to do so would be to use the new information to solve an important problem or to make the information interesting. (Section II has practical applications related to this topic, such as how students can better understand what they are learning, retain it for a long time, and make school subjects more enjoyable.)

Chapter 18. AUTOMATIC AND SEMI-AUTOMATIC BEHAVIORS
(The present chapter describes some aspects related to this broad topic.)

We are programmed with some automatic behaviors (e.g., biological reflexes that are genetically wired-into us) and the ability to acquire some semi-automatic behaviors (e.g., conditioned responses). Some of those actions can occur without conscious attention, deliberate cognitive analysis, or intentional decision-making. Having semi-automatic behaviors is practical in situations that are urgent, routine, or simple. However, in circumstances that are complicated, unusual, difficult, intricate or require creative thinking, automatic behavior can be counterproductive.

This chapter offers a new perspective on semi-automatic behaviors such as conditioning.

• *Some biological reflexes have a connection with Psychological Roots*
In biological reflexes, a sensory neuron connects directly with a motor neuron, hence when that sensory neuron is stimulated, the motor neuron linked to it reacts, unless the circuit is blocked. Should that automatic reaction not accomplish its function – such as when an automatic eye blink does not sweep away an eye speck – considerable discomfort can result. That discomfort or pain might arouse needs for safety, stability, and escaping from that negative situation. Those needs are genetic Psychological Roots.

• *Instincts have a connection with Psychological Roots*
An instinct differs from a biological reflex in that there is an intermediate neural connection present between a sensory neuron and a corresponding motor neuron. That intermediate neural connection permits a cognitive process to be engaged that could affect the resulting reaction. For example, an employee might decide not to aggress against an unpleasant boss. That modified behavior might include assessing the situation and intentionally changing what might otherwise have been an automatic action such as aggression. That cognitive assessment and the decision that results draws upon Psychological Roots, such as a desire to avoid confrontations and a concern about consequences. Concerns and desires are Psychological Roots.

The above example of a person keeping himself from aggressing against a boss runs against that person's internal pressure to aggress when injured, something that is genetically programmed (see the animal experiments conducted by Azrin, 1967) and explains why people seek revenge. Our internal pressure to aggress when injured might seem to be a reflex, however, it is an instinct since weaker animals control their aggression so as not to attack animals stronger than they, and humans can control their aggression, as in the above example. Another example is provided by Spike's circumstance, mentioned later in this chapter.

Being able to control one's aggressiveness upon being injured does not necessarily end the situation at that point since both humans and non-human animals can displace their reaction onto a safer object (which Freud termed displacement, a synonym for which is emotional spillover). For non-humans such as laboratory rats to choose something safer to aggress against suggests that they evaluate the situation and engage in reasoned decision-making. Those are executive function operations. Thus it would appear that instincts have both Biological and Psychological Roots.

• *Sensitization and habituation have a connection with Psychological Roots*

People can be particularly sensitive to a stimulus in a positive or negative way. For example, someone can become hyper-alert upon entering a dangerous area or have an especially strong interest in something he/she likes. Those are instances of sensitization in which the threshold for arousal lowers as a result of beliefs about what is dangerous and what is interesting.

When someone 'gets used to something' – such as when taking safety for granted or not feeling one's clothes after putting them on – he/she believes that the circumstance is neither a threat nor particularly interesting. Those are instances of habituation in which the threshold for arousal rises as a result of beliefs about what is dangerous and what is interesting. Beliefs are Psychological Roots.

• *Mirror neurons*

Some neurons in the brain mimic observed behavior, such as permitting someone else's skills to be copied or being able to model oneself after an admired person (e.g., Cattaneo & Rizzolatti, 2009; Iacoboni, 2009). We copy what we believe is worthwhile and are unlikely to copy what we believe is not worthwhile. For many people, what is not worthwhile to copy are behaviors that we believe are counterproductive, dangerous, or destructive. Beliefs are Psychological Roots.

• *Classical conditioning/respondent conditioning has a connection with Psychological Roots*

Salivating is a genetically wired-in reaction to food, however, Pavlov (1927) found that if a bell had been sounded each time just before food appeared, when the bell was sounded dogs salivated even when food did not appear. Thus the dog's system began the process of digesting the food upon receiving a signal that food was about to arrive. Prior to that conditioning (i.e., salivating upon hearing the bell), that bell had been a 'neutral' stimulus with regard to salivating (i.e., the bell had been an unconditioned stimulus). The dog's developing a conditioned response to the bell meant that the bell's sound had acquired a new significance for the dog.

Salivation is genetically wired to occur when food arrives, and therefore is an unconditioned response. However, after the bell became paired with food, the bell became a conditioned stimulus in the dog's mind. (This experiment of Pavlov's was the first recorded experimental evidence of classical conditioning, synonym: respondent conditioning). Salivating is an internal reaction in a Hidden Sequence (see Chapter 4).

Many instances of classical conditioning occur in life, such as becoming tense when a car suddenly comes at us, or a person who previously had painful dental experiences reacting anxiously when a dentist gently touches her tooth with a cotton-tipped applicator. Another instance of classical conditioning occurs when a pet that previously had an unpleasant veterinary experience, aggresses against individuals who wear a uniform. Phobias (e.g., fear of flying, insects, or snakes) are also classically-conditioned responses.

When a stimulus and a response that previously were not connected become associated with one another, what takes place in the mind? Consider a person who smiles in anticipation of having a good time at a party, a date, or a concert. That person expects to have a pleasant occasion. When a car speeds directly at us, we believe that it could hit us. The closer that car comes, the more we expect that to occur. Anxious dental patients believe that they are about to experience pain and expect it to happen. People who fear traveling on airplanes or crossing bridges believe that they are in danger. A dog who salivates upon hearing a bell believes that food will immediately follow the bell and expects food. Pets who become anxious at the sight of someone in uniform believe that they will be harmed.

Expectations and beliefs are Psychological Roots. The point of view expressed above assumes that dogs are capable of having beliefs and expectations. The idea that non-human animals might have beliefs and expectations may seem a stretch, but pet dogs and cats appear to believe that they are safe with their owners, not with some strangers. Watch-dogs seem to believe that they should protect their owners, and many animals seem to expect that they need to protect their territory. There are many experiences in which animals alert their owners to unsafe conditions, which suggests that they believe that their owners are in danger and also believe that they should protect their owners. (More on this topic later.)

In this perspective, classical conditioning starts with a biological Hidden Sequence that subsequently becomes a psychological Hidden Sequence, as when Pavlov's dog acquired a belief and an expectation that food would follow immediately after the bell sounded. The resulting salivation is an internal reaction (the amount of which was measured by a tube Pavlov had attached to the dog's salivary gland). A similar psychological Hidden Sequence may be at work when a dentist's touching a patient's tooth with a cotton-tipped applicator connects with a patient's previously formed belief that pain is about to arrive. Anxiety then follows. If a patient flinches or groans, those reactions are observable behaviors related to the patient's expectation of pain.

Beliefs and expectations are Psychological Roots. Feeling anxious is an internal reaction in a Hidden Sequence. Flinching and groaning are overt behaviors that follow an internal reaction. Touching someone with a dental instrument is a stimulus.

Classical conditioning starts with a genetically programmed reflex in which a stimulus automatically produces a wired-in response. (Technically, an unconditioned stimulus elicits an unconditioned response, such as when food triggers salivation or when air blown into an eye triggers an eye-blink.) This pattern is a biological Hidden Sequence (a stimulus-and-root sequence): **unconditioned stimulus + Biological Root → internal reaction.** In some cases, an internal reaction may be observable, such as salivating and eye blinks.

Applying technical terms to Pavlov's experiment:

• The bell initially was an **unconditioned stimulus** (i.e., initially unrelated to salivating).

• The bell became a **conditioned stimulus** when it signaled that food was about to arrive.

• The need for food is a **Biological Root.**

• Food was an **unconditioned stimulus** that automatically elicited salivation.

• Salivating is an **internal reaction** (although Pavlov made it observable).

• Believing that the bell is a signal that food is about to arrive is a **Psychological Root.**

Thus, classical conditioning appears to be a Stimulus-and-Root Hidden Sequence: **conditioned stimulus + Biological Root + Psychological Root → internal reaction.**

Classical conditioning starts with an involuntary internal reaction. The ears of the dog may have perked up when the bell sounded in Pavlov's experiments and if so, that ear movement would be an overt behavior in a separate Hidden Sequence. (If Pavlov did the same experiment with a human, the person might be consciously aware of the association of the bell with food. Perhaps the dog might also be aware of that connection.)

To an observer, what happens in classical conditioning may seem simple: a response is elicited by a stimulus that ordinarily is not capable of triggering that response, such as a bell that elicits salivation (a traditional stimulus-response [S-R] conception). However, in the perspective of Psychological Systems Theory, a belief and an expectation have been created in the organism's mind regarding that stimulus. It should be possible to test this understanding of classical conditioning with human subjects.

For conditioning to occur, repetition is often required, yet classical conditioning sometimes occurs after a single experience, such as with some phobias (e.g., fear of insects, snakes, rodents, and deep water). (More on this topic later.)

The creation of a belief would be facilitated if the neutral stimulus is readily discernible, the organism perceives a logical connection between the neutral stimulus (a bell) and the unconditioned stimulus (food), and the organism's response (salivating) is strong. When those conditions are met, classical conditioning should be able to occur in a single instance or with very few repetitions, not just with regard to phobias. This possibility should be able to be tested experimentally.

Classical conditioning may involve a goal (e.g., with regard to aiding survival, experiencing pleasure, or avoiding discomfort). Satisfying that goal produces an emotional reaction, for example, eating food is accompanied by a positive emotional reaction. When discomfort is involved, such as a phobia, a negative emotional reaction is involved. Goals, beliefs, and expectations are Psychological Roots. Emotional and physiological responses are internal reactions in Hidden Sequences.

• *Preparedness and conditioning*

Sometimes it is not possible to condition a connection between a stimulus and a previously unrelated response. For example, Garcia and Koelling (1966) found that rats did not connect light or sound with nausea regardless of the number of times those two stimuli were presented immediately before the rats became nauseous from radiation. By contrast, those researchers readily conditioned rats to react negatively to sweet water after that water was paired with radiation.

One hypothesis offered to explain this phenomenon is that it is difficult to pair internal stimuli with external responses, and external stimuli with internal responses. However, are times when an external unconditioned stimulus can generate an internal conditioned response (e.g., when a bell elicits salivating by a dog, as Pavlov showed).

Seligman and Hager (1972) suggested that organisms must have the biological capability of associating a particular stimulus and response with one another. It is unclear what might produce such *'preparedness'*. The discussion of Hidden Sequences in Chapter 4 raised a question about whether preparedness might involve an inclination to engage in a particular behavior as well as a capability of doing so. If there is a biological inclination and also a biological capability, Biological Roots such as physical ability are involved. If Psychological Roots are involved – such as goals, expectations, beliefs, and strategies – there is a psychological inclination and a psychological capability as well. When psychological linking occurs, what is new to an organism must be consistent with a previously existing Psychological Root (see Chapter 7).

These assumptions suggest the following with regard to Garcia and Koelling's findings:

1) Both sweet water and nausea directly engage the gastro-intestinal tract, so perhaps the rats could readily believe that sweet water produced nausea.
2) Light (a visual stimulus) and sound (an auditory stimulus) are unlikely to be connected with deeply internal aspects of digestion and therefore might not readily be associated in a rat's mind with nausea.
3) Perhaps lab animals can readily believe that certain stimuli can be a cue signaling forthcoming food, but they might not readily believe that all stimuli furnish that kind of cue.

The above hypotheses assume the following two possibilities, mentioned earlier:

a) Conditioning involves a belief and an expectation regarding the association of a stimulus with a response, and
b) Some non-human animals have beliefs and expectations.

Memory and conditioning occur in animals that do not have a cerebral cortex, such as the sea slug, *Aplysia californica* (Kandel, 2006; Shettleworth, 2009). When conditioning occurs, what has taken place is that a creature anticipates that a particular stimulus (a cue) will be followed by a different stimulus. Conditioning and memory involve association, anticipation, and expectation. Expecting that something will occur involves a belief that it will happen. Beliefs have been considered cognitive phenomena that originate in the frontal cortex, however, the ability of sea slugs to be conditioned raises a possibility that beliefs or expectations can occur in parts of the brain other than a cerebral cortex. (Some possibilities might be glial cells, certain types of neurons, or the hippocampus.)

The possibility that associations, anticipations, expectations, and beliefs exist in a variety of non-human creatures is consistent with the common observation (mentioned earlier) that pets such as dogs and cats feel safe in the presence of their owners (*'learned safety'*, Kandel, 2006). Those pets might not feel safe with some human or non-human creatures. An interesting example of a non-human creature being comfortable with humans appears in a videotaped documentary of a lion in Africa named Christian who, for a time, was partly cared for by two missionaries (Adamson, 1972). When those two men returned years later, they were told not to expect that Christian would remember them, especially since Christian had been living in the wild for some time. Later, when Christian emerged from the surrounding area, he remained at the top of a hill overlooking the compound for a while, appearing to be unsure about the two men. Then Christian slowly came down toward them. Then he picked up speed and upon reaching the men he embraced them in a strong display of affection. After that, Christian's mate and his two cubs – none of whom had previously seen those men – came down and engaged the two men in a similarly warm and friendly way. Christian's mate had not been reared by humans, nor had the cubs. All four lions then settled down for a lengthy stay in a calm, cordial, relaxed, and playful manner with the two men and the person who ran the compound. That circumstance could be construed as those animals' believing and expecting that they were welcome and safe with those particular humans. (As well as considering the men to be friends and not prey.)

There are many stories of pets whose behavior seems to involve acquired beliefs and goals (e.g., Hare & Woods, 2003; Horowitz, 2009). Such instances include attempts by pets to save their owners from danger, pets calling attention to someone who is in danger, pets being depressed and then deteriorating and sometimes dying when their owner dies, and pets being protective of the young children with whom they live.

There is now a substantial amount of evidence that many non-human animals have considerable thinking ability (see Shettleworth, 2009). This evidence includes birds' ability to solve difficult, novel problems and hens passing along what they have learned to their chicks (e.g., Smith & Zielinski, 2014). These findings run counter to Morgan's (1903) canon advising against ascribing anthropomorphic attributes to non-human animals. It appears that this canon needs to be revised, especially since the largest bulk of our DNA (80% to 98%+) is similar to that of other living creatures whose forebears existed long before the *homo* species. This evidence raises a possibility that humans have a version of earlier creatures' cognitive abilities and emotions, including goals, beliefs, expectations and perhaps other acquired Psychological Roots as well.

When all of this is considered together, a prediction might be made about when classical conditioning is likely to occur or not occur:

a) Classical conditioning is likely to occur when an individual can readily believe that a response is associated with a particular stimulus, and

b) Classical conditioning is unlikely to occur when an individual does not readily believe that a response is associated with a particular stimulus.

• *Is preparedness circular reasoning?*

Schwartz (1974) suggested that the preparedness hypothesis constitutes circular reasoning, illustrated by the following questions and answers: "Why did conditioning occur? Because of preparedness."

"How is it known that conditioning was due to preparedness? Because conditioning occurred."

In circular reasoning, a proposition is given and attempted to be justified without independent evidence to substantiate it. In this case, the preparedness concept was promulgated after conditioning occurred with no empirical evidence to substantiate it. To avoid circularity, there must be independent empirical evidence that preparedness is present before conditioning occurs.

If Hidden Sequences exist as postulated in Psychological Systems Theory, evidence for preparedness in humans would be that Psychological Roots (e.g., beliefs and expectations) and internal reactions (e.g., thoughts, decisions, and emotional reactions) are precursors to conditioned responses. Carefully designed time-sequenced questionnaires can provide empirical evidence regarding such Psychological Roots. There also are ways to assess internal reactions such as functional MRI (fMRI) and Positive Emission Tomography (PET), perhaps focused on the hippocampus, frontal cortex, and limbic system. (More on this matter in the coming paragraphs). PET scans and fMRI can also be used with non-human animals.

• *Decisions, evaluation of alternatives, and cognitive dissonance*

The above discussion about preparedness brings to mind a question regarding whether there is a change in the evaluation of alternatives before or after an overt decision is made. The next few pages discuss pre-and post-decisional changes.

Pre-shaping

Mann, Janis, and Chaplin (1977) found empirical support for their hypothesis that evaluating the alternatives in a decision situation changes before a decision is made with regard to the alternatives. A change that occurs before a decision is consistent with the concept of preparedness (Seligman and Hager, 1972). It is also consistent with Psychological Systems Theory's concept of pre-shaping that facilitates linking or non-linking with a Psychological Root (discussed in Chapter 7).

Post-shaping

In cognitive dissonance theory (Festinger, 1957), dissonance is a type of psychological discomfort that results after a decision is made. According to this theory, people cannot tolerate disagreement with their decisions because inconsistency with a decision would create dissonance for them. Thus, there would be dissonance after choosing between two similarly attractive choices because the person would have acquired the negative features of the chosen alternative and would have lost the positive features of the unchosen alternative. In that case, dissonance could be lessened by elevating the value of the chosen alternative and decreasing the value of the rejected alternative. That change might be subconscious without the person realizing it. As an example, if a person were to choose between two alternatives that he/she previously rated 8 and 7 on a 1-15 scale, the rating of the chosen alternative should rise (perhaps to 9), and the rating of the unchosen alternative should decrease (perhaps to 6). This type of change was found when tested by Brehm (1956) who used equally-attractive alternatives, and by the author (Greenwald, 1969) who used almost equally-attractive alternatives.

Jarcho, Berkman, Lieberman, (2010) and Sharot, DeMartino, & Dolan (2009) conducted fMRI assessments of internal reactions involved in decision-making and found that physiological changes occurred after a decision. (The activated locations in the brain included the anterior cingulate cortex, anterior insular cortex, right-inferior frontal gyrus, medial fronto-parietal region, and ventral striatum.) Piaget's concept of assimilation and accommodation (Flavell, 1966) is consistent with the idea that change occurs after acquiring new information and with the author's flow-down principle (post-shaping, described in Chapter 7).

A possible explanation other than dissonance theory for the spreading apart of similarly rated choices is that the selected alternative becomes salient and the competing alternative recedes into the background (i.e., an instance of selective attention). If so, the change in the ratings would occur immediately after the decision is made.

Mentioned about above is that dissonance theory expects that the difference between the ratings of similarly-rated alternatives will spread apart after a decision because that wider gap would lessen dissonance. What should not happen according to the theory is that the gap in ratings will diminish after a decision because that would increase dissonance. Yet, the author found that ratings that initially were widely separated came *closer* together after a choice was made between them (Greenwald, 1969). That result is the opposite of what the theory expects.

If the explanation offered by dissonance theory is incorrect, a question arises about what might cause the ratings of decision choices to come closer together. A possibility might be that initially disparate decision choices (e.g., 10 and 5 on a 15-point scale) become more similar (e.g., 9 and 6) because the act of choosing between them might make them seem more equivalent to each other than initially. That is, the attractiveness of the higher-rated alternative diminishes a bit and the attractiveness of the lower-rated alternative increases a bit. If so, these changes would be made prior to the decision. Selective attention would be involved in that the higher-rated alternative remains salient while the lower rated alternative recedes into the background.

Preparedness may also be a factor that affects the situation because preparedness would be present before a decision is made during the time that competing alternatives are being evaluated.

An obstacle in ascertaining what occurs immediately before and after a decision is that decisional changes happen instantaneously and subconsciously, making it difficult to pin down whether the evaluations of the alternatives change before, during, or after a decision. Also unclear is what causes those changes. If all of the aspects that have been mentioned here take place (pre-shaping, post-shaping, preparedness, the flow-down effect, and selective attention), then it is possible that a number of changes might occur before and after a decision and when Psychological Roots link. Here are some possibilities:

1. Pre-shaping might occur before a decision in order to make a decision.
2. Pre-shaping might occur before Psychological Roots link in order for linking to occur.
3. Post-shaping might occur after a decision is made in order to solidify the decision by elevating the chosen alternative.
4. Post-shaping might occur after a decision is made in order to allow unchosen alternatives to fade into the background.
5. Post-shaping might occur after a decision is made in order to permit related Psychological Roots to be brought into alignment (a flow-down effect).
6. Both pre-and post-shaping might take place.
7. Pre-shaping might take place without any post-shaping in some circumstances.

8. Post-shaping might take place without any pre-shaping in some circumstances.

It is useful to learn how psychological processes work, such as whether both pre- and post-shaping occur when decisions are made or whether one type of shaping occurs at some times and the other at different times. It would also be interesting to know what conditions lead to pre- and post-shaping and how decisions occur. Of particular importance is knowing how Psychological Roots link, what causes Psychological Roots to link, how internal reactions occur, how internal reactions lead to behaviors, and what triggers each aspect. These and many other research possibilities are noted in Chapter 38. (Chapter 4 discusses Hidden Sequences and Chapter 7 discusses linking).

• *Salience of the stimulus*
Seligman (1972) developed a phobia about *Sauce Bearnaise* after he became sick at a restaurant. Why did Seligman not become phobic about other aspects related to the meal, such as the steak, vegetables, wine, restaurant, or his trip to the restaurant? Seligman suggested that it was because *Sauce Bearnaise* was salient in his mind since that sauce had been a special favorite of his. A stimulus that is especially salient would facilitate its linking with a belief, in accord with Psychological Systems Theory's concept of selective attention (that is, what is focused on is salient, whereas what is not salient recedes into the background.) (For an example of a phobia that did not appear to have a logical basis see Nell's bridge phobia in Chapter 28).

• *Operant conditioning/instrumental conditioning has a connection with Psychological Roots*
Someone tells Stella that the jacket she's wearing enhances her appearance after which she wears that jacket more frequently. In this example of operant conditioning, Stella's behavior (wearing that particular jacket) was strengthened after she received a compliment (a positive reinforcement). Another example of positive reinforcement strengthening a behavior is a waitress's increased willingness to provide good service after receiving tips for doing so.

The effects of reinforcing behavior have been studied extensively, such as by giving hungry laboratory animals a pellet of food after they behave as the researcher desires (e.g., press a lever or peck at a disk). When food stops arriving the animals continue their conditioned behavior for a short time afterward (e.g., lever-pressing) despite no longer being rewarded for that behavior. Some people might deride a parent's rewarding a child for good behavior as just being a bribe, but the child's good behavior might remain after it no longer receives a reward, as with the above-mentioned laboratory animals.

Complex voluntary behavior – such as selecting and putting on a particular item of clothing, engaging in behavior that is socially approved, or pressing a certain lever – is not pre-wired into an organism. Such non-wired-in behavior does not have a single external stimulus to trigger it as with salivating or an eye blink. Rather, the organism must coordinate a number of voluntary (skeletal) muscles in a particular sequence when and if the organism decides to do so. Hence, for a complex voluntary behavior to be conditioned, the initial response must be voluntarily generated by the organism. (A way to facilitate this behavior with humans is described in a later part of this chapter.)

By contrast, in classical conditioning, an initial behavior can be elicited directly by a single external stimulus. The reason is that classical conditioning occurs with behaviors that initially were automatic (because of genetically pre-wired connections between certain sensory and motor neurons). Therefore, when a stimulus impacts one of those particular sensory neurons, the reaction is automatic. Examples include a biological reflex such as salivation when food appears, and an eye blink when a puff of air touches an open eye. Thus, a pre-wired automatic response exists that can be triggered readily, setting the stage for classical conditioning to occur.

A further complication with operant conditioning is that if a reward does not arrive immediately after a particular behavior, when the reward eventually arrives it can reinforce a different behavior.

Whether or not a behavior is conditioned can be tested by observing whether that behavior continues after it is no longer reinforced. Why would a complex pattern of skeletal-muscle behaviors continue to occur? From a Psychological Systems Theory standpoint, a particular behavior is conditioned when an individual believes that the behavior will be followed by an expected outcome. For example, Stella continued to wear a particular jacket because she believed that it made her look good, even when she did not continue receiving compliments for doing so. A child believes that he will get a material reward and praise for doing what his parents want him to do. A waitress believes that she will be rewarded for having provided good service. Similarly, a lab animal might believe that pressing a lever will be followed by food.

On this basis, operant conditioning should last as long as the individual believes that it will bring satisfaction. As an example, were Stella to no longer receive compliments for wearing that jacket or if she is criticized for wearing it, she might relegate the jacket to a dustbin or give it to charity. If a lab animal's pressing a lever no longer brings food pellets, its pressing a lever will gradually extinguish as the animal realizes that pressing that lever will no longer be followed by food. Thus, operant conditioning should continue as long as pertinent beliefs and expectations remain. According to Psychological Systems Theory, a belief that is newly acquired might be retained for a long time after reinforcement ends if that belief is connected with a long-term root.

It might be thought that a child rewarded for engaging in parent-approved behavior might not continue that approved behavior after he no longer receives a material reward for doing so. However, there is more to that situation than simple bribery: the child also receives parental approval, which is rewarding. Emotional support from his parents might continue after the material reward ends. Also, the child may feel pleased about having mastered the target behavior successfully. If mastering a behavior boosts the child's confidence or self-esteem it would be self-reinforcing. Something like this might happen when a child is praised for not wetting his bed.

A waitress might continue to provide good service even if she gets small tips or no tips if she has a strong work ethic, desires to please people, or believes that she has a responsibility to be effective. Confidence, self-esteem, work ethic, beliefs, and desires for pleasure, emotional support, parental praise, and meeting responsibilities are important add-ons beyond tangible rewards. Each of those positive aspects has a strong effect. A combination of those aspects could have a considerable impact on the recipient.

A person's belief about being rewarded can occur in a variety of different ways. For instance, a person might know what the salary and benefits will be before applying for a job and might be motivated to apply for that job as a result. Thus, people who have an idea about what a reward will be for doing something might engage in that behavior *before* they obtain a reward. If they then receive a benefit because of having engaged in that behavior, it would boost the chances of their continuing to do what they did.

The hypothesis offered here is that an operantly conditioned individual believes that engaging in a certain behavior will bring satisfaction. If satisfaction actually occurs, the likelihood of the person repeating that behavior would increase. Satisfaction is an internal reaction in a Hidden Sequence. If a person's engaging in that particular behavior continues to bring satisfaction, he/she might acquire an expectation that satisfaction will continue.

A reward need not be a material substance. The requirement for something to be a reward is that it be pleasing, for instance, emotional support (such as praise, a compliment, or a success), or a decrease in unpleasantness (such as ending distress, pain, or failure). A conditioned behavior could be satisfying in itself, such as singing, dancing, skiing, or speaking. In a Hidden Sequence, satisfaction results from a positive internal reaction or a favorable outcome (e.g., food satisfies a psychological desire for pleasantness and the biological need to eat).

This discussion suggests that operant conditioning is a Stimulus-and-Root Hidden Sequence: **stimulus + Psychological Root → internal reaction → overt behavior**.

In operant conditioning, the behavior that eventually becomes conditioned, initially was made voluntarily. Viewed by an observer, the connection between a reinforcement and a conditioned behavior appears to be simple and straightforward: just reward a target behavior, and the organism repeats that behavior (a traditional S-R conception). Stella's frequently wearing a jacket because of having been complimented for doing so is an example. However, if the present analysis is correct, a subconscious process occurs in which a reward for a behavior provides pleasure or relieves discomfort and creates a belief and an expectation that such satisfaction will continue to occur. This process can take place below conscious awareness, but awareness of what is going on or aspects of it may occur. Some associated internal reactions might be overtly noticeable, such as joy or relief.

The likelihood of creating an operantly conditioned response might be increased if the stimulus, reward, and the connection between them are readily discernible and logical to the organism, and if there is a strong positive internal reaction. The quickness with which a belief and an expectation are created – and therefore the speed and strength of conditioning – is related to how quickly a behavior is rewarded and the amount of satisfaction it brings.

• *Is repetition required for operant conditioning to occur?*

Operant conditioning typically requires many repetitions of reward to establish a new behavior. However, the above discussion raises a question about whether operant conditioning of humans could happen after just a single reinforcement. (Single-experience instances of classical conditioning occur, such as some phobias). Perhaps the possibility of one-trial conditioning might occur if the target person were to anticipate becoming satisfied before receiving a reward, such as hearing that a particular job pays well and thereby believing that the job will bring satisfaction. The stronger the expectation of a reward, the higher the likelihood that operant conditioning might occur. Perhaps connection with a particularly important goal (e.g., to aid survival, avoid discomfort, or experience pleasure), might increase the likelihood of such conditioning. When an idea of a forthcoming reward is presented before the person engages in a new behavior it is an attempt to persuade (see Chapters 25 and 26).

Taking this a step further, might operant conditioning be possible without there being an actual reward? That is, might just having a belief be sufficient for conditioning to occur? If this is possible, then reward and repetition would strengthen the behavior but not be necessary for conditioning of humans to occur. The possibility that a belief has this kind of power is supported by observing the counterproductive behaviors that people continue to do despite the failure of those behaviors. People often continue doing unsuccessful things because those derive from their beliefs.

Whether conditioning can occur due to just having a belief could be tested by observing whether a target behavior can occur and if it does, whether it resists being extinguished (that is, whether the target behavior continues without there being an objective reward for doing so).

• *Learned helplessness*
Dogs that were prevented from escaping painful electric shock did not escape by leaping a barrier when given a chance to do so (Seligman and Maier, 1967). *'Learned helplessness'* also occurs with humans, for example, people who are told that they will never be good at a particular school subject (e.g., mathematics) may subsequently feel helpless about coping with that subject and avoid it throughout life. Seligman (1975) suggested that depression is an instance of learned helplessness in which people feel a lack control over circumstances that affect them.

From a Psychological Systems Theory standpoint, learned helplessness is a state of uncontrollability in which a belief exists that it is not possible to extricate oneself from that state. Such individuals might feel so overwhelmed by failure or so irredeemably incompetent that they believe that they cannot stop being in that state (e.g., Klein, Fencil-Morse, & Seligman, 1976). This inference raises a question about whether the dogs in Seligman's studies that seemed to be helpless were experiencing a state of uncontrollability (described in Chapter 1).

• *Negative reinforcement*
Something that lessens unpleasantness brings relief and therefore is rewarding and can be used to reinforce behavior. Examples of such *'negative reinforcement'* include superstitions, such as believing that a particular action will prevent something bad from happening (e.g., by throwing salt over a shoulder, worrying in the hope that doing so will prevent a bad event, and not walking on sidewalk cracks). Thus, negative reinforcement's ability to lessen unpleasantness can increase the likelihood of a behavior, even if there is just a belief without direct evidence to support that belief.

By contrast, punishment brings unpleasantness and therefore might decrease the likelihood of a behavior recurring. Punishment and negative reinforcement both involve negatives, but have *opposite* effects owing to the different way their negative aspects are applied. (It might be noted that the use of punishment to control behavior is often resented and that some individuals react in the opposite way to punishment than might be expected, such as by being rebellious. As a result, it can be counterproductive to use punishment as a method for controlling behavior.)

• *Intermittent reinforcement and extinction*
De-conditioning and extinction occur when an individual no longer has the beliefs, hopes, desires, and expectations that contributed to a conditioned response. Being rewarded intermittently delays ascertaining when the reinforcement actually ends and therefore realizing that having a particular belief, hope, desire, or expectation is no longer appropriate. That delay in recognition helps explain why it is harder to extinguish a conditioned response that had been intermittently reinforced than a response that had been continuously reinforced.

When a newly acquired Psychological Root is connected with a long-term root, it might be retained for a long time. If a connection of that sort occurs, it would support Allport's (1937) concept of functional autonomy that a motive and behavior could continue to occur on their own without further reinforcement, even when the original reason for that motive or behavior no longer exists.

• *Partial reinforcement*
Preferred activities can be utilized as reinforcers (e.g., Premack, 1959) because a person likes what is consistent with his/her Psychological Roots. A weakly satisfying activity would be only mildly pleasurable and therefore only mildly be rewarding. Non-preferred activities might not satisfy Psychological Roots and therefore would not be useful as reinforcers. Activities preferred by some persons might not be preferred by others owing to each person having different psychological roots.

• *An example of how satisfying Psychological Roots can foster acceptable behavior*
"Spike", a violent resident at a mental institution, terrorized everyone. None of many therapies or other efforts employed over many years had lessened his intense aggressions, disruptions, and explosions. Those methods included a variety of medications, types of behavior modification, and

psychotherapies, as well as efforts to reason with him, cajoling, criticism, and punishment.

When the author visited that institution as a psychological consultant, it seemed to him that prominent among Spike's pertinent Psychological Roots were strong desires to be important and not be controlled. (It was unlikely that Spike had an unfulfilled need for attention since his destructiveness brought him continual attention.) If Spike had the afore-mentioned roots of wanting to be important and not controlled, those aspects would have been violated by his years of having been in a locked ward, disdained, pressured, and punished.

Based on the Psychological Roots mentioned above (strong desires to be important and not be controlled), the author created an opportunity for Spike to satisfy those hypothesized desires. Doing so would provide Spike a brief opportunity for a pleasant activity outside the institution, under heavy guard. A staff member presented the offer to Spike on the condition that Spike was calm and cooperative for two weeks. Spike turned down the offer, which was understandable since he had been behind bars from childhood, he could not be certain that he would receive the reward, and the benefit was small. The author prepared the staff member to respond to Spike's expected negativity by telling Spike that since he rejected the offer, another resident would be given that opportunity. Spike then accepted the offer and asked for details.

As he did, something dramatic happened. Suddenly Spike was calm. He was also pleasant, peaceful, and accommodating, something that had never characterized him in all of the years he had been at the institution and perhaps beforehand as well. For the next two weeks, Spike continued being cordial and cooperative. The staff found Spike's pleasant behavior hard to believe and remained highly skeptical and guarded. When the trial period ended, Spike received the prize he was promised and was delighted and grateful for it. He was pleasant and cooperative throughout the experience, for example, he gave no resistance or trouble when the time came for him to return to the institution. The staff found it hard to believe that Spike had changed and waited warily for him to explode in an unexpected way.

The next part of the plan called for Spike to be told that he could have the same privilege again if he continued his good behavior for another month. As a bonus, he could choose one resident to enjoy it with him. (The purpose of doing this was to give Spike a further sense of importance and control, and to begin to repair his relationship with the other residents.) Spike continued being a model citizen. That reward arrangement was renewed every month together with a stipulation that he choose a different resident to join him. Spike continued his good behavior, stunning the other residents and the staff.

Spike's case illustrates the power of satisfying pertinent Psychological Roots and especially that problems occur when those roots are not satisfied or countermanded. From the standpoint of Psychological Systems Theory, previous therapies did not work, perhaps because they had not satisfied Spike's Psychological Roots. Also, some methods caused Spike to feel demeaned and controlled, the opposite of his feeling important and obtaining some autonomy. Thus, without the staff realizing it, the way Spike had been treated had violated his Psychological Roots, which helps explain why he had not responded favorably. The rewards that had been given to Spike for good behavior, such as sweets, did not work perhaps because they seemed demeaning and ordinary rather than special enough to satisfy his need to feel important, and did not address his desire not to be controlled.

Spike's example also illustrates how trying to change behavior directly – such as using logic, criticism, pressure, or punishment – can be counterproductive. It also shows how ineffective it can be to use rewards that do not relate to pertinent Psychological Roots. In Spike's case, the rewards that the staff used (sweets) may have insulted him. In contrast, it shows how strong the positive effect can be when satisfying a person's Psychological Roots by even a small amount.

Spike's demeanor changed the moment he agreed to the plan, illustrating how quickly a flow-down effect can occur. That instant turn-around raises a question about whether Spike had known all along what appropriate behavior was and his unwillingness to cooperate might have been due to his resentment. Spike's subsequently maintaining socially acceptable behavior might also have been aided by his having acquired some civilizing modifiers.

Spike's case shows how working with Psychological Roots can improve extreme behavior, even long-term disruptive behavior that had never been under control before. It also illustrates that a Psychological Roots approach can work with people of limited intellectual ability, as in this case. The author has found that Psychological Roots exist at basic levels of functioning (concerns, interests, desires, and beliefs, including a need for respect and not being controlled). Spike's improvement is one of many in which the author has found that a Psychological Systems approach is effective when other approaches have not succeeded.

• *Making use of Psychological Roots in conditioning*
A Psychological Systems Theory approach extends the range of possible reinforcers that can be used for conditioning by including aspects that relate to intangible subconscious factors such as desires for respect, acceptance, not being controlled and other Psychological Roots. Examples of intangible

reinforcers include emotional support, solutions to problems, opportunity to fulfill responsibilities, and competitive success. Cults and terrorist groups successfully use non-material reinforcers to recruit members by providing acceptance, emotional support, and a perceived opportunity to right the wrongs that concern those recruits. As this illustrates, positive reinforcers need not be material rewards and can be even more powerful than tangible rewards. The potency of reinforcements can be bolstered by using rewards that connect with pertinent Psychological Roots that are identified which, in Spike's case, made the difference in succeeding with him. Psychological Systems Theory provides behaviorists with a way to predict what type of reinforcers are likely to succeed and offers another way of connecting behaviorism with clinical and social psychology.

Personality traits and non-verbal behavior

Some people have personality traits that seem to characterize them, for example, generally being upbeat, friendly, irritable, or rigid. Such characterizing traits might be based in a particularly strong cluster of Psychological Roots, such as positive social skills (e.g., social and problem-solving strategies, optimism, a wide comfort zone, and low expectations). An opposite set of Psychological Roots might be present in someone who is often difficult to get along with, irritable, grouchy, or unpleasant. When such characterizing traits exist they are likely to be accompanied by strong internal reactions, some manifested verbally and some non-verbally.

Can Psychological Roots be conditioned?

In addition to behaviors, internal reactions can also be conditioned. Examples include conditioning of salivation (a glandular reaction described earlier in this chapter), blood pressure, headache control, and body temperature (internal physiological reactions). It seems likely that emotional reactions can be conditioned (e.g., readiness to laugh, cry, be tense, anxious, or have an upbeat or down mood). Recurring thoughts might also be conditioned, such as when ruminating occurs. Perhaps conditioning is also possible with some decisions (e.g., generally accepting or rejecting new ideas of opposing viewpoints). Internal reactions are intermediate aspects of Hidden Sequences.

It might also be that some Psychological Roots can be conditioned such as goals, beliefs, and expectations. For example, some people are trained from early childhood to be responsible for others, as well as themselves. Conditioning might also be possible with regard to a desire to lead, control, exert power, be analytical, or remained focused on tasks or other tangible aspects.

A related question is whether conditioned Psychological Roots and internal reactions contribute to personality traits that seem to characterize a person (mentioned above), such as an individual who typically is upbeat, generous, caring, impatient, in a down mood, or irritable. Perhaps there might also be a conditioned tendency to enter some states of uncontrollability (such as panic, depression, apathy, ecstasy, or rage), and to enter precursors to those states. This possibility that there might be conditioned patterns involving Psychological Roots should be capable of being tested empirically, also as a factor in psychotherapy.

Acquisition of automatic and semi-automatic patterns

A repeated pattern can become semi-automatic, which is reflected in phrases such as "second nature" and "practice makes perfect". Self-statements – for example, "I'm a good person", "I can handle this", and "There is always a solution" – are used in some therapies. When those statements help it may be because they temporarily modify some Psychological Roots and internal reactions (see Chapter 4). Negative self-statements – for example: "I can't do this", "There is no solution for my problems", and "I expect bad things to happen" – can foster a down mood. Frequent use of self-statements might lead to those aspects becoming semi-automatic.

A practical application of this information

Acquiring some automatic behaviors is useful, such as when greeting others, being polite, engaging in routine behaviors, and acquiring constructive habits. Such patterns, including self-affirmations, can sometimes help people get through difficult times. For example, confidence might be bolstered and anxiety lessened by using self-affirmations such as "I can handle this", and "Don't get caught up in this", followed by using effective problem-solving strategies. Other examples include using sincere appealing forces (e.g., cordiality, considerateness), attempting not to use repelling forces (e.g., lessened arguing, reduced criticizing), and developing win-win solutions when disagreements occur. The stronger a person's belief that self-affirmations are useful, the more likely they are to help that person.

When trying to eliminate an automatic pattern such as a phobia, superstition, addiction, or bothersome habit, it helps to constructively satisfy or change the underlying belief that powers that behavior. (Section II has practical applications related to this chapter.)

CHAPTER 19. THINKING IN ABSOLUTES

Why are some people extreme? Why do some people commonly use words such as 'the greatest', 'the worst', and other hyperboles? Or words such as always, never, and other black-and-white terms? Is such all-or-none thinking constructive? This chapter discusses absolutes, which has considerable implications for behavior.

How common is thinking in absolutes?

When a newborn feels content, its entire body is serene and when it is upset its whole body vibrates in angst. Those are global reactions in which the infant's entire being is engaged.[37] Those actions and others that are all-encompassing include laughter, despair, and hysteria. Such behavior can occur at any age and constitute psychological states of uncontrollability. Psychological disorders such as panic, depression, and rage also involve thinking in black-and-white terms, including viewing things as all-or-nothing, either-or, friend or enemy. Hyperbole is another of many types of absolutes (e.g., always, never, best, most, terrific, sensational, fantastic, terrible, awful, helpless, disastrous).

We become more differentiated as we mature, which helps us understand nuances and fine details, combinations of factors, and complex thoughts. Nevertheless, ability to make differentiations does not prevent adults from using absolutes such as words like definitely, totally, finally, and completely. Adults, including some highly learned individuals, make sweeping statements at times such as, "I can never count on you". Some sports broadcasters have said "That baseball player can't hit" and football coach Vince Lombardi is reputed to have stated, "Winning isn't everything, it's the only thing."

---

[37] It may be that newborns have digitalized (on/off) wiring that can subsequently develop into multiple on/off combinations producing intricate cybernetic webs perhaps somewhat similar to complex human-created computer programs (see Chapters 7 and 8). Some people who prefer to operate in absolutes may have an especially strong need for certainty, structure, stability, or safety. Some aspects of society might foster absolute thinking (e.g. affluence offers opportunities to acquire exactly what is desired; being a tiny fraction better can produce victory), while other societal aspects might foster non-absolute thinking (e.g., poverty or weak skills can require moderation or settling for less).

Newborns' global actions and adults' use of absolute statements suggest that there may be a general predisposition to think in a broad, sweeping manner. If so, thinking in absolutes is a genetic Psychological Root. A tendency to think in absolutes can be bolstered by the situation, such as when there is a desire to simplify something or when there is a lack of knowledge. Having extensive knowledge about a subject can contribute to not thinking in absolutes, including recognizing that there are multiple aspects and making tentative conclusions.

The upside to thinking in absolutes

There are times when it is appropriate and constructive to be absolute, such as when attempting to help make messages understandable and when being humorous. Other positive uses of absolutes include being true to one's word, trustworthy, and supportive of others. Being absolute can also aid focusing, boosting energy, speaking rapidly, producing firm decisions, and constructing a general overview of something that is complex.

Thinking effectiveness

A person with substantial knowledge of a subject can perceive nuances and make differentiations that might escape others. A person who understands multiple points of view has a more substantial comprehension than someone who sees things from only one perspective. Flexibility aids adaptation. Ability to operate at different levels of intensity aids effectiveness compared to being locked into extremes. Ability to think in degrees facilitates rebounding from states of uncontrollability. Someone who accepts being wrong and makes improvements is likely to be more effective than someone who does not.

Focus and distraction

The author has found that when people are engaged in a task, their attention focuses on that particular issue and that other tasks fade into the background (*'selective attention'*). A multi-tasker might seem to focus effectively on several activities at the same time, however doing so diminishes effectiveness (Rubinstein, Meyer, & Evans, 2001). It has been found that multi-taskers shift their focus from one task to another (termed *'serial tasking'*). Multi-tasking is easier when tasks are routine or simple, such when listening to the radio while driving. It would be difficult, however, to do multiple things while intensely involved with a challenging task or deep in thought. In a tense driving situation, even an avowed multi-tasker might opt to focus fully on driving rather than simultaneously listening to the radio.

Ability to focus on a single aspect and ignore other things offers a strategy for coping with unpleasantness by intentionally being distracted with work, social interaction, or sports rather than on loss, rejection, failure, or pain. Hypnosis can also help people be distracted beneficially such as when an airplane-phobic person who, while traveling in the air, puts herself into a hypnotic state in which she imagines relaxing at a tropical beach. A negative side of being distracted is that it shifts attention from a task at hand to less important aspects, which can impede accomplishing more important tasks. That kind of distraction is a common experience for people with attention deficit disorder (A.D.D.) and people who procrastinate. Distraction can be amplified by thinking in absolutes.

Interestingly, A.D.D. individuals can often focus for long hours on something that holds their interest, such as aspects consistent with their deep Psychological Roots and strong Psychological Root clusters. Ability to focus raises a question about whether a reason people diagnosed with A.D.D. are distracted is that they lack interest, such as with routine jobs, lectures, and school subjects. Those individuals might be more attentive if the issue was connected with their major root clusters (such as hobbies or their relationship) or there is a particularly potent stimulus (e.g., an interesting visual or video game, or a disturbing personal situation).

Our wired-in drive for closure helps us complete tasks but also contributes to thinking in absolutes. Being single-minded can lead to being negative about viewpoints other than one's own and thereby contribute to conflicts and impede finding compatible resolutions (e.g., gridlock in Congress). Expecting the absolute worst can impede the ability to think effectively about possible solutions. Individuals in a state of uncontrollability think in absolutes, which can lead them to believe that their situation is impossible to repair and impede their ability to rebound from conditions such as depression, panic, rage, or addiction. Extremists and violent people think in absolutes – they believe that their way is the only way.

Some instances in which thinking in absolutes is unconstructive
Burns (1989), Linehan (1993), and Otis (2007) have described ways in which absolutes create difficulties. Below are some prominent instances in which absolutes work against being constructive:
- Blanket perspectives such as all-or-nothing, friend-or-enemy.
- Sweeping generalizations such as entirely, completely, everyone, cannot, total disaster, final.
- Unrestrained ideas such as "expect the worst", "I just want to be happy", "everything is predetermined".

• Superstitions such as "breaking a mirror brings seven years of bad luck", "stepping sidewalk cracks causes something bad to happen", "my wearing something special helps my team win".

• Hyperbole such as occurs in advertising messages (e.g., "the best", "the only", "the finest").

• Broad judgments such as "you never help out", "men are …"; "women are …".

• Non-empathic advice such as telling someone that they "will get used to it" when something bad happens, or that they should "get over it" or "forget it".

• Proverbs, which may seem correct until realizing that another proverb may say the opposite, such as:
  . "Haste makes waste", *but* "A stitch in time saves nine".
  . "Too many cooks spoil the broth", *but* "Two heads are better than one".
  . "Absence makes the heart grow fonder", *but* "Out of sight, out of mind".

• Some beliefs, such as:
  . Believing oneself to be unworthy (low self-esteem) that could last a lifetime
  . Believing that being asked to have a lab test for cancer means that they
                            have cancer
  . Believing that things cannot get worse
  . Believing that another person's viewpoint is completely wrong

Why spotlight absolute thinking?

As the above list indicates, absolute thinking can lock people into an overly narrow perspective that impedes their ability to respect other possibilities or consider other viewpoints to have credibility, or even to view other people's opinions as having any value at all (see Figure 21). Eliminating possibilities due to thinking in absolutes can reduce the potential to improve by heightening resistance to change. Absolute thinking can also lead to using stereotypes, incorrectly viewing complicated issues as being simpler than they are, and deriding people who differ from oneself. Such thinking can also lead people to believe that only their viewpoint is correct and that complicated things are simpler than they are. Thinking in absolutes can diminish the ability to make fine distinctions, work with complexity, and value thinking in degrees and combinations of factors. Such aspects can lessen the chance of being successful interpersonally and with difficult problems, and can also contribute to impatience, impulsivity, frustration, and anger.

High expectations contribute to stress (described in Chapter 11). Thinking in absolutes increases the chances of being stressed due to having expectations that are the same as goals. Disrespect – especially absolute disrespect – harms relationships (see the example in Chapter 11 in which Angie's pressuring her husband to make their home her dream house led to a divorce). Thinking in absolutes lessens opportunities to bolster problem-solving effectiveness and supports having prejudices and being hostile. Autocratic people and governments are likely to be absolute rather than to employ a balanced perspective.

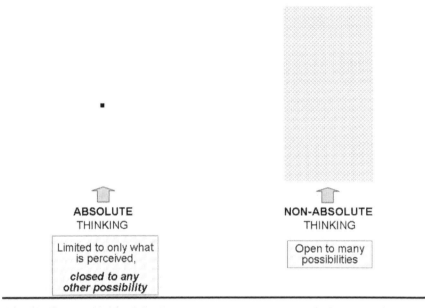

Fig. 21. Absolute thinking limits the perspective and shuts out all other possibilities. Non-absolute thinking is open to other possibilities and aids rapport with people.

Some people are so black-and-white that they believe that nothing can solve their problems, or that they are doomed to not accomplish much in life, or that they are no longer useful, or that they are a total failure. People can believe to an absolute extent that they have heart disease, cancer, or Alzheimer's disease, or that they will die much sooner than their health or statistics suggest. Having a negative perspective can be a self-fulfilling prophecy that generates unpleasantness. When a negative perspective is absolute, it could be one of a number of factors that, when in combination, contribute to dysfunctional moods, or precursor conditions such as dysthymia or anxiety, or even states of uncontrollability such as depression or panic.

Thinking in absolutes can make it easier to enter a state of uncontrollability and make it harder to exit from such states.

An absolute perspective can lead to overlooking details, impede taking combinations of factors into account, and coping with complexity. Problems can feel overwhelming and possibilities can be reacted to globally rather than considering them as aspects that lie along a continuum. Problems can be denied and differences can be ignored. Aspects like these can impede effective thinking, problem-solving, and decision-making. Absolute thinking can also narrow a person's range of acceptability and limit horizons (tunnel vision, termed 'encapsulation' by Royce, 1964).

Thinking in absolutes increases the likelihood of interpersonal conflicts and gridlock. Divorce is an example, political paralysis is another. Absolute thinking can increase resistance to change and impede learning and growing. Thinking in black-and-white terms can also make a vague possibility seem like reality, or make reality seem inconsequential. It can also exacerbate problems and intensify negatives. In short, there is a large downside to thinking in absolutes, especially with subtle or complicated issues.

Non-absolute thinking

The more knowledge a person has about a topic, the more aware that individual is likely to be with regard to nuances and complexities related to that issue. Hence, thinking in absolutes is more likely when things are unfamiliar than when a great deal is known about them. Not thinking in absolutes aids being able to work with shades of gray, combinations of factors, and complex perspectives. Thinking in relative terms can help avoid being single-minded. There are many times when it is useful to be tentative rather than inappropriately rigid. Non-absolute thinking can be especially helpful when dealing with aspects that have many components or are subtle or ambiguous. Non-absolute thinking can aid being tolerant of alternative viewpoints. Tolerance aids democracy, intolerance aids autocracy. Not being absolute can also be useful when patience is required.

The individual systems in Psychological Systems Theory become more complex with time as they grow, combine, and intertwine. A similar pattern occurs in other disciplines, including biology, chemistry, physics, economics, politics, and computer science. The need to think in non-absolute ways is likely to increase as knowledge advances, also as the need to resolve conflicts increases.

It may have made a great deal of sense to view things in absolutes 325,000 years ago when *homo sapiens* first appeared on earth since other creatures were either friends or enemies and there were a lot of enemies. People did not know the many hidden aspects and extensive combinations of factors that underlie what is observable. We frequently see absolute thinking in today's world such as when people argue about who was the greatest this or that, or believe that voting for a particular candidate will destroy our way of life, or whether the football coach or the quarterback is responsible for competitive success. (The answer to the latter question is both and further, it takes an entire team working together in an effective manner.)

The bottom line: Skill in coping with a wide range of aspects is aided by being able to think in a variety of ways as needed, rather than automatically thinking in absolutes.

Summary

Newborns' global reactions and adults' frequent use of generalities such as always or never suggest that there may be a genetic tendency to use absolutes. Thinking in absolutes can aid focus and simplify communications but on the negative side, can lead to inaccurate generalities and overlooking important details and nuances. States of uncontrollability – such as psychological disorders, extremism, and violence – involve thinking in absolutes. Using qualifiers can help avoid errors when desiring to be accurate. It can help to choose when to be absolute and when not to, be moderate, and try to avoid making sweeping and judgmental statements. (For a list of some psychological systems in addition to those already discussed, see Box 6.)

A practical application of this information

States of uncontrollability are absolutes, including depression, anxiety, OCD, borderline personality disorder, and addiction. Not thinking in absolutes might help lessen such negative states, shorten their duration, and facilitate exiting from them. However, it can be difficult to modify the tendency to be extreme because there is a wired-in tendency to be absolute.

When people feel tense, down, irritable, frustrated, or angry, they may be better able to rebound by purposely thinking in degrees. For example, they might ask themselves, "Do I have to be absolute?". Also helpful can be telling oneself, "There is likely to be another way, I just have to find it." It is possible to soften making absolute statements by adding a caveat, such as, "Using generalities makes talking about this issue less complicated" or "Generalities omit details, gradations, and exceptions."

Some people recognize when someone is inappropriately absolute, such as making sweeping generalizations that overlook important exceptions, or requiring total compliance with their demands when doing so is not reasonable. When another person's thinking in absolutes is an impediment, it might help to considerately ask the person, "Is there a way to look at this other than black-and-white?"

BOX 6a. SOME ADDITIONAL PSYCHOLOGICAL SYSTEMS
(in alphabetical order)

ALGORITHMS. Criteria that provide a series of decisions based on evaluations at each step, such as "if A occurs, then go to B; if C occurs, then go to D".

AMPLIFIERS. Aspect that increase an effect (e.g., high emotionality, optimism; cf. augmenter, Petries, 1978). Some aspects (e.g., absolute thinking, emotionality) can either amplify or diminish, depending on the factors.

CLUSTERS. Groupings of conceptually related aspects, such as beliefs.

CONSCIOUSNESS. Awareness. The seat of consciousness is a small portion of a small organ (the Amygdala; Penfield, 1975), providing us little awareness of our sub-surface functioning.

CREATIVITY. A drive to develop something new.

CYBERNETIC PROCESSES. Self-adjusting processes using feedback to produce adjustments.

CYCLES AND REPETITIONS. Repetition of prior behaviors (e.g., conditioning, ruminating).

DIMINISHERS. Aspects that lessen an effect (e.g., low emotionality, pessimism; cf. reducer, Petries, 1978). Some aspects (e.g., absolute thinking, emotionality) can either amplify or diminish, depending on the factors.

DOMINANCE. The overshadowing of one aspect over another, which permits at least temporary change.

BOX 6b, *continued.* SOME ADDITIONAL PSYCHOLOGICAL SYSTEMS
(in alphabetical order)

FOCUS. Attention to one aspect, which causes other aspects to fade from awareness ("Out of sight, out of mind"), aids problem solving. Inappropriate focusing (e.g., when ruminating, procrastinating, or being in a state of uncontrollability such as depression, panic, or rage) can impede effective problem-solving. Changing a focus from something disturbing to something pleasant (distraction) can lessen distress temporarily.

GRADIENTS. An increase or decrease over time (e.g., intensity of emotionality). A gradient in one direction graphs monotonically; a gradient that changes direction graphs non-monotonically.

HIERARCHIES. Linked elements in which higher-order aspects exert influence over others (e.g., Psychological Root hierarchies, executive function, authoritarian rule, & some social relationships).

INTELLIGENCE. Ability to solve problems. Some thinking skills involved can be generalization, discrimination, analysis, synthesis, deductive and inductive reasoning, associations, causality, and pattern perception

MENTAL INCUBATION. A subconscious attempt to solve problems that occurs when attention is not focused on another task (e.g., during sleep, while showering, during vacation, or taking a break).

NETWORKS. Linked aspects, hierarchies, or clusters. Large networks can form extensive webs.

PATTERN RECOGNITION. Identifying something systematic example repetitive, linear, cyclical.

BOX 6c, *continued*. SOME ADDITIONAL PSYCHOLOGICAL SYSTEMS
(in alphabetical order)

PATTERN SEEKING. Seeking to identify something systematic in an attempt to make sense out of something.

PERMANENCE. Long lasting aspects (e.g., values, long-term goals), some of which can remain throughout life.

PROBLEM SOLVING. An attempt to attain a goal, resolve a difficulty, or eliminate an obstacle.

SALIENCE. Having more prominence than competing alternatives. Aspects that are more salient than others are more likely to be selected than those that are less salient.

SEQUENCE. When one aspect follows another (e.g., gradients, stages, development, Hidden Sequences).

SEQUENCE. When one aspect follows another (e.g., gradients, stages, development, Hidden Sequences).

SUBCONSCIOUS. Below awareness, which applies to almost everything in the brain (Penfield, 1975) and blocks knowledge of psychological & biological processes, allowing a focus on tangible aspects without interference.

THRESHOLDS. Points at which change occurs (e.g., a tipping point into a state of uncontrollability such as rage).

UNDERSTANDING. Making sense out of circumstances (e.g., finding patterns, making associations, comprehending cause and effect, and solving problems).

SECTION II. SOME PRACTICAL APPLICATIONS OF PSYCHOLOGICAL SYSTEMS THEORY

This section describes some practical applications of Psychological Systems Theory such as methods for resolving difficult conflicts, conducting psychotherapy, constructively influencing others, lessening distress, and facilitating communicating, teaching, learning, prevention, and improving the quality of life. Included in this section are over 380 needed research studies to help advance knowledge about how the mind functions psychologically and use that knowledge constructively.

***

Chapter 20. CONFLICT RESOLUTION

The arguments that occur when disagreements arise can lead to intense conflicts. The options at that point – struggle, yield, or compromise – are likely to be unsatisfying. A much better outcome is possible: creating a win-win solution that satisfies everyone. That possibility might seem unlikely but some of the following chapters show how knowledge of Psychological Roots can help make it happen. To facilitate the discussion, this chapter and those that follow focus on disputes between two humans, although the same principles apply to an individual's internal conflicts and to conflicts between large groups such as organizations, businesses, neighborhoods, societies, and nations.

Interpersonal conflicts are inevitable

People's opinions vary because everyone is different, including identical twins. There are many reasons for such differences, among them the large number and diversity of Psychological Roots that people possess. Some disagreements among people are particularly intense and some can seem impossible to resolve, reflected in terms such as gridlock, deadlock, at loggerheads, and "Mexican standoff". Sometimes relationships are strained to the breaking point because only a certain amount of negativeness is tolerated. Conflicts intensify when protagonists are stubborn and danger can result when people are aggressive, hostile, or destructive. Not creating compatible solutions can have severe outcomes, such as lawsuits, physical fights, and even murder.

This chapter describes a strategy for resolving conflicts in which everyone's concerns are satisfied without anyone feeling that they made a sacrifice. An outcome like this may not seem to be realistic, but it is often possible, as will be seen. The key is satisfying the Psychological Roots of both individuals that are the basis for the conflict.

The underlying cause of conflicts

Conflicts arise when one alternative among competing alternatives is to emerge as dominant. Therefore, every decision involves conflict because at least two alternatives are involved, even in situations where it may appear that there is only one alternative since there is a possibility of that alternative not being chosen. Even when one alternative is heavily favored, strongly dominates, and the outcome never seems in doubt, conflict nevertheless exists because there is a possibility that the leading choice might not be accepted and there always is at least one other alternative. Conflict is technically present even when a decision is instantaneous since a conflict existed immediately before that decision was made. Therefore, conflict is involved whenever there is a competition or a personal choice.

As a result, a conflict existed before every decision that has ever been made and will be present before every decision that will be made. In typical conflicts, one alternative emerges as dominant, however, there might not be a single winner in some circumstances such as a draw, a win-win solution, a withdrawal of all the choices, or a nullification of the situation.

In Hidden Sequences, decisions are internal reactions that originate with Psychological Roots. Hence, when two people conflict it is because they have different Psychological Roots that led to their divergent viewpoints. Since everyone's Psychological Roots differ, there will always be conflicts within each person and between individuals. Hence, ability to resolve conflicts effectively is an important skill, especially when peaceful relations are desired.

Conflict does not exist until a decision must be made

Having to make a decision creates a conflict because a choice has to be made among competing alternatives. For example, possessing a large collection of tunes does not create a conflict. However, a conflict arises when a tune is to be selected. It is an intrapersonal conflict if one person does the selecting, and it is an interpersonal conflict if two or more people are engaged in selecting a tune. As this example suggests, a conflict can be calm and pleasant without involving aggression.

The selection of an alternative ends a conflict. A subsequent conflict can result within oneself (e.g., remorse about a decision) or with another person (e.g., public protests after an election).

Human decisions depend on the Psychological Roots involved, the emotional intensity of the protagonists, the difficulty of making a decision, and the consequences of the outcome. A decision is more difficult the more similarly the alternatives are evaluated. The difficulty of making a decision is also affected by the consequences and the ambiguity of the situation. Additional factors include the familiarity of the choices and the relationship between the protagonists.

Some conflicts are more interesting than others, such as those that pertain to oneself (e.g., related to one's goals or personal life) and how difficult the struggle is. The need for closure creates suspense until a decision occurs and also makes us impatient for quick resolutions, especially with bothersome issues.

Conflicts that do not involve humans

Non-human organisms can have conflicts, such as when predators attack prey and when creatures fight among themselves for food, the opportunity to mate, or to protect their territory. Non-living aspects also have conflicts, such as when waves crash against a shore and earth's tectonic plates move against one another. Scheduling that requires being in different places at the same time is a conflict (and an example of a conflict that does not entail aggression).

Conflicts between individuals

Psychological Systems Theory assumes that interpersonal conflicts originate with the Psychological Roots of the individuals involved. Hence, a compatible solution can result from satisfying each of those individuals' Psychological Roots. A *'win-win solution'* results when each person's roots are satisfied without either individual experiencing a sacrifice (synonym: *'positive solution'*). Some win-win solutions have minor negatives that the protagonists readily accept. By contrast, a *'negative solution'* occurs when one or both individuals give up something they are reluctant to do or are bothered by the outcome.

When both individuals are negative about an outcome, such as when both give up something they did not want to, it is a *'lose-lose solution'*. Compromise typically is a lose-lose solution, which is why compromise is often resisted. A *'win-lose solution'* is also negative because one person or group involved in the conflict is unhappy with the outcome, such as the result of a court case or a sports contest.

Many people in business and sports have a win-lose perspective about life, which may seem appropriate to them but can produce tension, distress, and poor interpersonal relations. A win-lose approach to life can also lead to ignoring other people's ideas, concerns, and contributions. By comparison, win-win solutions allow everyone to feel good about the outcome, cooperate, get along well, and contribute.

When a conflict involves groups, the Psychological Roots of the members need to be satisfied for there to be a win-win solution. Satisfying the predominant Psychological Roots of the people who represent the groups (e.g., the leader, board members, consultants, or lawyers) can produce a win-win solution with other groups.

When a solution cannot be worked out with Psychological Roots that have been identified, additional Psychological Roots may need to be uncovered. Sometimes a person will not accept a reasonable win-win solution or work toward obtaining a mutually satisfactory solution yet a solution might be possible when the underlying reason for that resistance is addressed satisfactorily. If it does not seem possible to resolve a conflict, it may be wise to postpone seeking a solution until a more propitious opportunity occurs for creating a resolution. When either of the protagonists is absolute or antagonistic, it may be wise to end the effort and cordially agree to disagree. An attempt to achieve a solution might be possible at a later time.

Arguing is counterproductive

It is natural for people to present logic, facts, and evidence to support their viewpoint when differences of opinion occur. There may be an expectation that doing so will be convincing. However, facts and logic of one person might not satisfy the underlying concerns of the other person, even when well-founded. For example, forensic evidence might not convince some parents that their son is a threat to society, and scientific evidence does not persuade some individuals who want to believe that human activity does not affect the earth's climate.

In addition, disagreement implies that the other person is wrong and is a strong repelling force because no one wants to be wrong. Repelling forces turn off people and shut down receptivity, the opposite of obtaining the other person's acceptance. Also, people dislike losing or surrendering. In addition, presenting opposing facts and logic implies that the other person's viewpoint lacks credibility and is inappropriate. As a result, we should not be surprised when people adhere to their initial viewpoint despite being presented with contrary compelling evidence ('confirmation bias', e.g., Nickerson, 1998). Still more repelling forces are introduced if Jon tells Mary that she is wrong or is disrespectful, or if Mary tries to impose her viewpoint on Jon. Aspects like these can escalate arguments rather than persuade. In short, it is hard to win arguments.

When one person feels good about the outcome but not the other, it is not a compatible solution. When no attempt is made to satisfy the other person, it is hard to create a solution with which both individuals can agree. However, a win-win solution is possible when the protagonists satisfy each other's Psychological Roots.

Five ways to resolve interpersonal conflicts
1. Eliminate the need for a decision.
2. Withdraw from the situation.
3. Split the difference between the alternatives (a lose-lose compromise).
4. Select one protagonist over the other (a win-lose situation, such as a sports contest).

5. Satisfy both protagonists without there being rancor or a sacrifice (a win-win solution).

An overview of the process for creating win-win solutions
   A three-stage process for seeking win-win solutions is summarized below. Details of this procedure are spelled out in Chapter 22.
- In the first stage, the other person's receptivity is obtained, the Psychological Roots of both individuals are identified, and a possible solution is constructed that might satisfy both parties.
- In the second stage, a possible solution is presented in a way that seems likely to be accepted by the other person, perhaps when subsequent modifications are made.
- In the third stage, an attempt is made to solidify the agreed-upon solution to help lessen the likelihood of either person backsliding.

   A win-win solution may seem impossible when both people do not believe that a solution is possible, or resist being compatible, are angry, or fight tooth and nail. Nevertheless, the author has helped create compatible solutions in many hundreds of difficult conflicts and has found that it is almost always possible to create a solution that satisfies everyone even when the protagonists have strong doubt, resistance, or rancor. (Chapter 22 provides details of the method for accomplishing this.)
   It should be noted that some people are unwilling to accept a reasonable solution and some individuals may not want to work toward obtaining a compatible solution. Among such individuals are persons who are competitive, extreme, absolute, resistant, hostile, or violent. (Being competitive, extreme, and using other repelling forces is counterproductive when attempting to create peaceful resolutions and should be avoided when possible.)

Is compromise a win-win solution?
   Some people think that a compatible solution necessarily entails compromise. It is possible for compromise to resolve many conflicts when people are willing to do so. However, compromise is not a win-win since at least one person, and often both must give up something they desire. Also, many people view compromise as surrender and reject doing so even when compromising is worthwhile and could be accomplished readily. Even when compromise can provide a compatible solution, it might be resisted since it is not a win-win. Nevertheless, there are times when both parties are pleased to seek a compromise, such as when compatible couples settle minor differences

and when negotiators compromise willingly such as in the purchase of a house or car, or in other circumstances in which bargaining is expected.

The author has found that people are unlikely to realize that win-win solutions are possible. Some people believe that it is not possible for everyone to benefit when a conflict occurs ("If his needs are satisfied, then mine will not be."). For people to accept the idea that win-win solutions are possible requires a different perspective than what people generally believe, the author has found.

A win-win approach requires a different outlook and strategy than what is needed for creating a compromise. Win-win solutions are facilitated by working in a compatible way with the hidden Psychological Roots that underlie the protagonists' opposing viewpoints. By comparison, creating a compromise involves making a sacrifice about what is apparent and tangible.

The up-side to compromise

It is often possible to create a compromise by splitting the difference between competing alternatives. That possibility is facilitated when the disputed positions lie along the same continuum (one of the reasons that money has largely supplanted bartering). Some people are prone to seek ways to compromise when disagreements arise and there are situations in which it is customary to compromise, mentioned above, such as when negotiating to buy a house. Marriages, business partnerships, organizations, and democracies would find it hard to succeed without compromising. When compromise is possible, and people are willing to do so, it can provide effective solutions.

The down-side to compromise

Some people prefer no solution to compromising ("I will not compromise my principles!"). Some people refuse to give in ("I never give up"), and some people do not want to provide another person any satisfaction ("I would never give anything to that snake"). Still other people cannot tolerate losing ("Failure is not an option", "I'm never wrong") and some people demand that their view prevail ("No other possibility is acceptable").

There also are some people who blame others rather than seek a solution ("Why should *I* compromise when *he's* causing the problem?"). For some people, the negatives related to compromise can be especially off-putting, such as needing to give up something, feeling controlled by the circumstances, or not completely being able to achieve their objective.

Many people are so negative about compromising that they view it as unacceptable or as a last resort. Some people easily feel taken advantage of ("I will not be a victim"), and some people are locked into their viewpoint ("I know I'm right"). Some highly competitive individuals refuse to compromise because they need to win ("My viewpoint is correct", "I cannot accept any viewpoint than mine"). Some people believe that holding strongly to their position is a badge of honor and resist giving an inch.

When individuals such as those mentioned do compromise, they may fight to the end, feel forced into the solution, and resent the outcome. As a result, the author has found it wise to avoid using the term 'compromise' when helping people resolve their differences.

There are some circumstances in which a compromise is not possible or easy to achieve. An example is King Solomon's dilemma described in the Bible, in which two women claimed to be the mother of a child. To resolve that dispute, the King ordered that the child was to be cleaved in half, giving each woman half of the child. One of the women was extremely distraught at this prospect and the King awarded the child to her. That drastic method was used to determine the rightful mother since compromise was not appropriate or feasible.

Some types of compromise

It may be possible to fashion a type of compromise even when there is no quantitative middle ground. One method is a *'combination solution'* in which opposing alternatives are stitched together. As an example, the founding fathers of the United States were faced with determining whether every State should have the same number of representatives (e.g., two each) or whether the number of representatives should be proportionate to the size of a State's population. This dilemma was solved by doing both: creating a Senate (in which every State had two Senators) and a House of Representatives (in which States with larger populations would have more Representatives). A combination solution that is viewed negatively by one or both protagonists is a negative solution.

Sometimes a *'sequential solution'* is possible in which the protagonists take turns, such as Mary and Jon do what Mary wants first, then do what Jon wants. In the case of Thanksgiving dinner, for example, a couple can visit one set of parents early in the day, and the other set of parents later that day, or visit the two sets of parents during alternate years. (Synonym: *'alternation solution'.*) If a sequential solution creates unhappiness, it is a negative solution rather than a win-win. For example, Jon might be unhappy about waiting to be satisfied or Mary might be unhappy about having to be patient while Jon gets his turn.

A *'tradeoff'* occurs when each party surrenders qualitatively different things. For example, Joan agrees to control her spending if Brian agrees to stop criticizing. Reggie agrees to give up cigarettes if Samantha relinquishes alcohol. Tradeoffs have inherent negatives since both people must give up something, yet a tradeoff can be positive if the outcome is strongly desired by both individuals.

Is compromise always possible?
Mentioned above is that there are some circumstances in which it is difficult to fashion a compromise, such as:
• There is no apparent middle ground or other ways to compromise such as opportunities to combine solutions, create tradeoffs, or develop sequential solutions.
• Each party claims total ownership, is unyielding, demands that the other party accept their terms (e.g., gangs, tribes, and extremists), or kills opponents (e.g., criminals and wars).
• Negatives such as hostility or obstacles such as physical barriers interfere with the ability to create a compromise.
• Trying to work out a difficult situation would take a long time, perhaps years.

In short, there are some circumstances in which compromise may not be reasonable or feasible. Even when compromise is easy to accomplish it might not be accepted and in such instances would be a negative solution. Some compromise solutions – such as splitting the difference, integrating both parties' viewpoints, sequential arrangements, and tradeoffs – can be positive if both persons are pleased to do what is decided upon without either of them feeling that they made a sacrifice.

Is there such a thing as a win-win solution?
Some people believe that win-win solutions are not possible, or that win-win is another term for compromise, or that their needs will not be satisfied. Those individuals might resist trying to develop a win-win solution or accept it only after it becomes a reality. Some people might reject a reasonable win-win solution because they want their view to predominate.

Focusing on what is observable (e.g., the conflicted alternatives) can interfere with finding a win-win solution. People who think in absolutes might not believe that both individuals can be satisfied. It is also common for people not to realize that there are hidden causes of conflicts such as Psychological Roots or that win-win solutions are possible when those underlying aspects are satisfied. (The next chapter provides some examples of how win-win solutions were created in conflicts that seemed impossible to resolve.)

Does a win-win solution mean surrendering or caving in?

With win-win solutions, surrendering or caving in does not occur because both persons are satisfied.

Knowing Psychological Roots offers an advantage

People's conflicts often are about surface aspects, a circumstance that limits the options for creating a compatible solution. For example, a dispute about who owns a pen would be hard to resolve by alternating its use and would not be solved by breaking the pen in half. However, when the deep Psychological Roots of both individuals are identified, many opportunities for a solution open up because of the broad nature of those roots. For example, there are many ways to satisfy people's needs for respect, stability, social connectedness, and autonomy.

Identifying Psychological Roots is often easier than many people might believe (see Chapter 6). One reason is that some roots – such as needs for respect, not being controlled, and not feeling taken advantage of – are involved in many conflicts. Another reason is that clues about Psychological Roots are often present in what the individuals say and do. Still another reason is that the protagonists may be willing to help find a solution when they see some progress being made or because they like the calm and cooperative atmosphere that exists when seeking a win-win solution. Much gridlock and rancor might be avoided if people understood Psychological Roots and applied that knowledge to seeking a win-win solution when disagreements occur.

A problem with the term 'win-win'

There is a logical problem with the term 'win-win' since 'win' implies that someone is victorious and therefore the other individual loses. It would be cumbersome always having to spell out what a win-win solution means (e.g., that everyone obtains what they want with little or no unpleasantness). Another problem is that some people construe 'win-win' to mean a tie or a circumstance in which both individuals' concerns are not satisfied.

Some possibilities for a suitable shorthand term – such as a "positive solution" or a "mutually beneficial solution" – can be unclear because those phrases might be interpreted by some people to mean compromise. Hopefully, a more satisfactory term will be developed, perhaps by the reader. In the meantime, "win-win" and 'win-win solution' are the terms that are employed in this book.

The bottom line: A win-win solution can be created when everyone involved feels good about the outcome without anyone feeling that they made a sacrifice. Win-win solutions are possible when the Psychological Roots of both protagonists are satisfied. Negative solutions, on the other hand, are those that are unpleasant to one or both of the protagonists, including lose-lose situations (e.g., typical compromises) and win-lose situations (e.g., sports contests).

Chapter 21. EXAMPLES OF WIN-WIN SOLUTIONS
The instances cited below are real. Names and some identifying details have been changed to protect privacy.[38]

This chapter describes three examples of interpersonal conflicts that seemed impossible to resolve yet were easily ended in a positive way using the win-win approach described in detail in Chapter 22.

Situation 1. Driving Debacle. A man in his late 80's was a terrible driver but refused to admit it and insisted that he drive himself and his wife to Florida for the winter from their home in the Northeast. His children objected, explained the danger to him and his wife, and pleaded with him not to drive. He was unbudgeable, however. The more they tried to persuade him the more adamant, testy, irritable, and resistant he became. His family's great frustration increased day by day. As the departure date drew near, they crossed a tipping point from intense concern to desperation.

One of the family members sought help from the author. Among the man's hypothesized Psychological Roots was his wanting to feel competent, intolerance of appearing to be wrong or inadequate, and believing that admitting his driving incompetence might bring him a step closer to a nursing home. He also might have had a strong aversion to being controlled and losing his independence. Perhaps the man realized that he was an inadequate driver and was unwilling to admit it.

If this analysis was correct, then the family's attempts to persuade him were violating his Psychological Roots, therefore turning him off and having the opposite effect than they intended. Therefore, the author asked the family to stop trying to change his mind. Instead, the author sought a solution that would be consistent with the man's Psychological Roots and also those of his family. That solution could not include even a slight repelling force because of the man's strong resistance, hyper-irritability, and easily aroused anger. Hence, nothing that even hinted at his inadequate driving could be part of the solution.

A safer way to get the man and his wife to Florida would be for someone reliable to drive them there, but the man had refused that. The author asked if there was someone in the family who had not been associated with the

---

[38] The author has successfully employed the win-win strategy such as those described in these examples with a wide variety of individuals, couples, groups, and organizations in many hundreds of instances.

conflict, a person the man liked and who could drive them to Florida safely. There was: an 18-year old grandson who had a great relationship with his grandparents. When that grandson was asked, he said he would be happy to do the driving and would be available because he had a school break at that time.

The family was not concerned about the man driving while he was in Florida because he rarely drove while he was there, knew the streets well, and usually walked to nearby shops on safe sidewalks in a self-contained community in which there was little traffic.

The author's instructions were for the grandson to ask his grandparents if he could accompany them on the ride. They said that they were delighted to have his company. On the day of departure, after the luggage was loaded and they were about to start, the grandson was to ask his grandfather if he could get them started by beginning the driving. The man readily agreed, as hoped. The grandson was instructed never to relinquish the wheel. It worked. The grandson took an airplane back. This method was repeated on the return trip. Once again, there was no problem.

This solution satisfied the man's Psychological Roots since he made his own decision, did not feel pressured by others, and did not have to admit that he was an incompetent driver. He was in control because he gave his grandchild permission to drive and was pleased because he enjoyed his grandson's company. The man's children obtained safety for their parents and accomplished what they wanted without getting any pressure, rancor, or resistance from the man. They stopped fighting with their father and were no longer frustrated. This solution was a win-win because everyone got what they wanted without any unpleasantness or giving up anything they did not want to.

This situation demonstrates the value of being compatible with the target person's Psychological Roots and how it is also possible to be compatible with everyone else's concerns at the same time. It also illustrates why trying to directly change someone's behavior by using logic, facts, and evidence may not work when it goes against the target person's Psychological Roots. In short, it pays to seek a solution that works with the person rather than against that individual.

Situation 2. Dock Dispute. "Joe" and his wife were blue-collar people who loved vacationing at a popular lake during the summer. After scrimping for years, they finally saved enough for a down payment on a small cottage a short distance from the lake. Soon after moving in they met "Maurice" and his wife, a wealthy couple who owned a well-equipped home on the lake. The two families became fast friends. That led to Joe and his family spending many summers enjoying Maurice's lake house and all of its amenities, including a beach, deck, dock, and boat.

Then a brutal, icy winter wrecked the dock. Maurice asked Joe to split the cost of repairing the dock so that they could continue having the fun they had enjoyed for years. Joe refused. Worse, Joe was incensed to have been asked. He criticized Maurice bluntly, including harshly saying, "You expect me to put *my* money into *your* dock? You've got to be crazy!"

That enraged Maurice, who used strong profanity. He angrily told Joe, "You ungrateful #@$&! After all that I've done for you? I'll never speak to you again." Maurice was so infuriated that he refused to repair the dock, keeping it that way as a permanent reminder of Joe's perfidy. Those bad feelings both families had about each other did not end there. When the two families came across each other in town they screamed profanities at each other and their children spat on one another. Their anger continued expanding and exploded into a major feud. It became a huge scandal in that small town.

A friend of the two families sought advice from the author. Analysis of Joe and Maurice's possible Psychological Roots suggested that they both believed the other person was trying to take advantage of them. Each also felt disrespected by the other person. Most importantly, Maurice expected that he should get something in return for his generosity, while Joe believed that it was unfair for him to put his scarce funds into what was not his.

If there was to be a win-win solution it would have to meet the expectations each family had about what was fair and right, eliminate each family's feeling that they were taken advantage of, and restore respect for one another. Unfortunately, each protagonist was absolute, as often happens in conflicts. For example, Maurice believed that the *only* way for him to be satisfied would be for Joe to pay part of the cost of repairing the dock, and Joe believed that he should not give *any* money, not even a dime. Each of them believed that they were totally right and would not budge from their principles.

From a Psychological Roots standpoint, the key for Maurice was his wanting to be reciprocated for his generosity, and the key for Joe was his not spending any money on something that was not his. Might there be something that Joe could do to reciprocate Maurice that Joe would accept? If so, it would have to be something other than money. An answer quickly suggested itself: what if Joe were to repair the dock using materials purchased by Maurice? That would provide a relatively equivalent arrangement for both of them.

That solution might have worked before things got out of hand. However, now they were not talking to one another, were explosive, had vowed to be enemies forever, and their feud was public, with everyone in town talking about it frequently. The situation appeared to have gone beyond a point of no return and it seemed to be too late to try to arrange the above solution or even for them to communicate rationally with one another.

There was a possible remedy for their not talking to one another: perhaps they might be able to communicate through the mutual friend who contacted the author. The author asked her if she would be willing to be a *'welcome intermediary'* and she agreed to do so.

The plan called for her to contact them in sequence, first asking Joe whether he would fix the dock if Maurice were willing to buy the materials. Joe told her, "Yes, but that #@$&! Maurice would never agree to it." The intermediary then quickly contacted Maurice and asked if he would agree to that arrangement. Maurice said, "Yes, but that #@$&! Joe would never agree to it." The welcome intermediary then told him that Joe had already agreed and immediately contacted Joe to nail down the agreement and get things to the next stage.

The materials needed for the repair had to be identified and the only way to do so was for the two families to meet at the dock and discuss it. That meeting had the potential to blow the solution out of the water. The atmosphere was so highly charged when the two families met at the dock that the air seemed to crackle with electricity. The two families expected fireworks and stood far from each another. Anticipating this, part of the plan called for the welcome intermediary to ask the members of both families other than Maurice and Joe to remain silent throughout and the children to be respectful. Fortunately, no one did anything untoward.

The work was to start early in the morning on the day scheduled for the repair. Prior to that event, the welcome intermediary once again asked the families to be silent. When Joe and his family pulled up in his truck, tensions were sky-high. The families stood far from each other. No one said a word as Joe and his son unloaded the materials. Everyone expected an explosion. The silence was intense, like the quiet before a storm.

Joe and his son worked steadily, speaking to each other in whispers when they had to communicate. At mid-morning, Maurice's wife distributed lemonade and some snacks. Her doing so eased tensions a bit, which the welcome intermediary noticed despite no words having been spoken. Two hours later, Maurice's wife served lunch without any words being spoken between the two families.

Near the end of lunch, one of the children said something cordial across the gulf that separated the families. Some time later, Maurice went to the dock to make some suggestions. Still later, Maurice returned and offered to help. As the day wore on, small conversations between the two families started to occur.

Their talking gradually increased and became more friendly. The children started playing together. As daylight waned, the last part of the repair was in place.

And then, surprise! The two families were friendly. Joe and his family stayed late into the evening. Maurice invited Joe's family over for the following day. Everything resumed where it left off. After that, the families continued spending every summer together and enjoyed one another's company as they had before.

This solution was a win-win because both parties' Psychological Roots were satisfied. Everyone felt respected and not taken advantage of, and no one gave up anything they did not want to relinquish. No one brought up anything about the past.

This situation illustrates how a welcome intermediary who has credibility with both parties can help resolve conflicts. If she had not been willing to be a go-between, that dispute might never have been resolved. This circumstance also illustrates how creating a win-win solution can lead to a complete cessation of hostilities and that seemingly irreparable breakups can be stitched together, despite intense anger that seems impossible to resolve.

Situation 3. Gun Safety. "Brenda" refused to allow her fiancée, "Randy", to store his guns in her house, fearing that her 12-year old daughter or her daughter's friends might get them. Randy's pledge to put the guns into a special locked chest did not persuade her. Their arguments about this issue became increasingly frequent and agitated. After three years of intense wrangling about this concern, they were on the brink of breaking up. As a last resort, they sought counseling.

The author speculated that the primary cause of their problem was that Brenda had an intense sense of responsibility and need for safety that would not be satisfied by Randy's locking up his guns. She thought in black-and-white terms about the issue and therefore might need to feel that there was *absolutely no chance* that her daughter might get the guns. One way for her to have that guarantee would be for Randy to store his guns elsewhere. However, Randy refused to put his guns in someone else's house because he often used his target pistol. The author's discussion with him about this possibility bore fruit, however, because during the conversation, Randy revealed that he hunted only once or twice a year. The author then asked Randy if he would be willing to store his hunting rifle and its ammunition at the house of the person with whom he hunted. Randy agreed to do so.

One gun down, one to go. The author then asked Randy if his target pistol could be taken apart. It could. Would he be willing to dismantle the gun and put its various parts and ammunition in different locked boxes? Yes. Would Randy be willing to distribute the various boxes in different locations in the house, each in a place that was unlikely to be accessed by Brenda's daughter? Yes. The author then asked if there was a place in the house that Brenda's daughter might not be likely to come upon the various boxes, perhaps an attic space whose only access was through a small ceiling panel in a closet. Yes. As a bonus, that particular closet was in Brenda's bedroom, which would give Brenda additional oversight and control, and therefore even greater assurance.

Brenda had been silent during this conversation between the author and Randy. The author asked Brenda whether that solution was acceptable to her. Astonishingly, Brenda was enthusiastic. She explained that her daughter feared dark places, especially attics, and had poor mechanical skills. Hence, even in the unlikely event that her daughter entered the attic, located the various boxes, and found a way to open them, she would not be able to put the pieces of the gun together.

This solution instantly ended Brenda and Randy's intense three-year argument and potential split. They walked out holding hands. It was a win-win solution since both people's Psychological Roots were satisfied without either of them surrendering anything they did not want to. Brenda felt absolutely assured of her daughter's well-being because her concerns regarding safety and meeting her responsibility were totally satisfied. Randy was able to keep his target gun at the house and have access to his rifle when he needed it, and he felt comfortable with both aspects.

This case illustrates how thinking in absolutes can get in the way of finding a solution. Nevertheless, even then and even when a conflict has been going on intensely for years and people believe is impossible to solve, as in this case, a solution can often be found by working with the Psychological Roots involved.

These are just three examples of many hundreds of conflicts the author has helped resolve that seemed impossible to repair. People often tell the author that they have tried everything or that a compatible resolution is not possible. However, they do not know about the Psychological Roots that underlie their issues, or how to create a range of suitable alternatives, or how to use that knowledge to create compatible solutions. Many people also may not believe that both individuals can be satisfied when a conflict arises.

The next chapter describes how to create win-win solutions. Accomplishing a solution often does not take long, which sharply contrasts with the length of time some conflicts can last (15 years in one instance brought to the author). In the above examples, discerning the Psychological Roots involved and creating a plan that solved the conflict took 10 to 25 minutes.

Why do people have trouble resolving conflicts?

Mentioned earlier is that a major reason for people's difficulty in resolving interpersonal conflicts is that they focus on the tangible aspects of a conflict. They are unaware that they have Psychological Roots and that those hidden aspects are causing their struggle. When people try to make their viewpoint prevail, they introduce repelling forces that lessen the chances of a compatible solution. The longer a conflict escalates, the more emotional, absolute, and rigid they may become. People also do not realize that their attention to tangible aspects limits their opportunity to expand the range of potential solutions. For example, if both Beth and Mitzi claim they own a particular umbrella while it is raining, finding a solution that satisfies both of them would be difficult. However, if the issue is broadened to their finding a way to protect each of them from the rain, a variety of possibilities open up.

The bottom line: Interpersonal conflicts can be difficult to resolve since each protagonist's viewpoint does not satisfy the other person's concerns. However, the tangible aspects that people are conflicted about are based on underlying aspects such as Psychological Roots that can be identified. Working with each person's Psychological Roots, such as needs for respect and not feeling disadvantaged, aids finding a solution because the broad nature of those roots expands the range of alternatives. Satisfying both individuals' Psychological Roots produces a win-win solution.

Chapter 22. A THREE-STAGE METHOD FOR CREATING WIN-WIN
SOLUTIONS

Prepare, Present, and Solidify are three stages the author has found
useful when creating win-win solutions in interpersonal conflicts. To simplify
the presentation below, this topic is addressed as if there are only two people
involved in a hypothetical argument.[39] However, the general principles
underlying this procedure apply to groups of people and internal
psychological conflicts as well.

1. PREPARE.
   The most important aspects of this stage are obtaining receptivity,
identifying the Psychological Roots that explain why each person holds
his/her viewpoint, and then developing a plan that might satisfy both
individuals' Psychological Roots.
   Without receptivity, each protagonist might not cooperate sufficiently,
provide sufficient information to identify their pertinent Psychological Roots,
nor accept a reasonable solution. Receptivity is aided by using appealing forces
judiciously, avoiding the use of repelling forces, and having confidence that an
outcome will be found that can satisfy both individuals.
   It helps to identify two sets of Psychological Roots in each person, one
that directly pertains to the overt conflict (surface roots) and another set that
is at the foundation of those roots' hierarchies (core roots), since both sets of
roots must be satisfied. (See Chapter 4 regarding Hidden Sequences.)
Effective interviewing techniques help uncover hidden Psychological Roots.
Core roots offer a broad range of opportunities from which to create solutions
compared to surface roots because they encompass a wide range of
possibilities, hence are particularly helpful in creating a resolution. There are
times when it also helps to identify intermediate Psychological Roots.
   After the pertinent Psychological Roots of each individual are discerned,
a potential solution should be developed that seems likely to satisfy both
people. Creating more than one solution can be useful.
   When one of the individuals is more of an obstacle to a solution than the
other person, it can often help to start by focusing on that person's concerns
(as happened in all three of the examples in Chapter 21, the Driving Debacle,
the Dock Dispute, and Gun Safety).

---

[39] Various solutions are often possible when conflicts arise because, as
   mentioned earlier, deep Psychological Roots are general, which opens
   many opportunities for finding a satisfactory solution.

2. PROPOSE A SOLUTION.

Present a solution in a way that both individuals might accept, which requires being consistent with each person's Psychological Roots. A good way to begin would be for one person to ask the other, "Help me find a solution that might satisfy both of us". It would be ideal if the individuals were to do this as soon as a disagreement starts, especially before hostility occurs.

Use appealing forces (e.g., be caring and calm) and especially avoid using repelling forces (e.g., do not argue, be forceful, or condescending). Be confident that there will be a win-win solution, also be helpful, caring, and brief. Expect objections and do not get sidetracked on side issues a protagonist introduces. Expect each person to hold tightly to his/her initial viewpoint until a good solution is perceived to be possible.

Do not expect the protagonists to be effective at developing a good solution or to be optimistic about creating a win-win solution, or even believe that a win-win is possible. Remain calm and focused on problem-solving. Do not argue or be highly emotional, and try to avoid letting anyone's bias interfere with finding a compatible solution.

If a protagonist does not accept what appears to be a good solution, ask that person if he/she can adjust it to meet his/her concerns. If that does not succeed, develop another solution. If that does not work, develop yet another solution or seek other Psychological Roots, then develop a new solution that addresses the newly found roots as well as the roots that had been identified previously.

If no solution works, it may be that some key Psychological Roots have not been identified or that one or both individuals are extremely resistant for hidden reasons. If so, it might be wise to stop, identify further Psychological Roots, develop yet another solution, and perhaps present that new solution later. If nothing works, the protagonists may be too rigid to accept a resolution. In such (hopefully rare) circumstances, the individuals might be better off agreeing to disagree, preferably in a cordial manner.

3. SOLIDIFY THE ACCEPTED SOLUTION.

After a solution has been agreed upon, try to strengthen the accepted solution in order to lessen the chances of a protagonist backsliding to a previous viewpoint. Solidifying can involve giving emotional support such as praise, clarifying ambiguities, resolving misunderstandings, presenting additional information, and expanding the solution's usefulness, doing each when and if it is appropriate to do so. Be considerate and responsive to each person, and be open to questions.

***

The author has found that possibilities for win-win solutions often spring to mind soon after identifying the underlying Psychological Roots. If one person agrees to a solution but the other person does not agree, some progress may have occurred nevertheless because there will be fewer remaining aspects to address and the atmosphere may have improved. When a person does not accept a reasonable solution, there may be more to that situation than meets the eye and therefore a deeper understanding may be required. For example, some other reason may exist such as an outside influence. Sometimes it is beneficial to take a temporary break and agree to return to the issue at a later time. If nothing works, it may be wise for the protagonists to remain cordial and just agree to disagree.

The bottom line:

When people disagree, there is no need to fight, despair, stop communicating, pout, or give up since there often is a good chance to create a win-win solution. The three-stage approach described in this chapter may help when trying to create win-win solutions.

Stage 1 (Preparation): Obtain the receptivity of both protagonists, identify the Psychological Roots of each person, and develop a possible solution.

Stage 2 (Presentation): Propose the possible solution to both protagonists in a way that is comfortable to each of them.

Stage 3 (Solidifying): Strengthen whatever constructive aspects the protagonists agree upon. Give both persons emotional support, review the solution, offer additional information as needed, clarify possible misunderstandings, and bring up other ideas for how the solution can be used.

***

The next chapter addresses some subtle aspects related to resolving conflicts.

Chapter 23. IMPEDIMENTS TO WIN-WIN SOLUTIONS
This chapter extends some previous issues.

When trying to create a compatible solution, many obstacles can arise and being aware of impediments in advance can help to mitigate them. It also helps to know how to solve problems that arise. This chapter describes how.

Not developing compatible solutions is counterproductive

When a disagreement between people occurs, each individual may believe that he/she is entirely right and the other person is completely wrong, and some people attack the other person's viewpoint. Doing so harms everyone. Fighting has much to do with desire to be victorious, unwillingness to lose, focus on tangible aspects (which can impede realizing the hidden psychological cause of the conflict), and a tendency to think in absolutes. Those aspects originate in our genes that are more appropriate for a kill-or-be-killed world that existed more than 300,000 years ago. It was not reasonable in that world to seek a mutually satisfactory solution with non-humans, predators, kidnappers, or thieves.

When people argue they are likely to be addressing surface aspects, such as what a person said or did rather than the underlying reasons for the conflict. As a result, arguing is unlikely to succeed and is a repelling force since no one likes to lose. Trying to persuade using facts, logic, and criticism implies that the other person is wrong, which can decrease that other individual's receptivity, the opposite of what is desired. The longer a conflict continues and the more emotional and agitated the protagonists become, the further they move from a compatible solution. Escalations can spiral out of control and lead to damaged relationships, divorce, lawsuits, violence, and even killing.

Some impediments to win-win solutions

It is worth repeating that repelling forces can lessen a protagonist's willingness to find a compatible solution, including disagreeing, which implies that the other person is wrong. Some other common repelling forces are using facts and logic (which implies that the other person's viewpoint lacks credibility), pressing a point of view (which can come across as controlling), raising one's voice (which can be grating), and being inconsiderate (which is disrespectful). Insults and profanity are particularly strong repelling forces. Demanding an apology is a repelling force because people do not want to admit being wrong. Even if an apology were given, it would not resolve the cause of the conflict.

There are many subtle repelling forces such as body language or tone of voice that unintentionally imply that another person's viewpoint is unacceptable. Another subtle repelling force is a protagonist's belief that his/her viewpoint is the only acceptable possibility. Some other repelling forces are being impatient, irritable, or rigid, not being open to a compatible solution, or telling another person that he/she is obstinate, selfish, or unintelligent.

People may find it incredulous upon being told that the issue about which they are quarreling is based on hidden aspects. That reaction is understandable because we focus on tangible aspects, like other creatures. This is why a dispute about money might substantially be about feeling controlled, disrespected, taken advantage of, or pressured to give in (all of which were present in the Dock Dispute example in Chapter 21). In many instances, the underlying aspects are not ancillary, but key.

Two types of repelling forces that impede resolving conflicts are:
1. Direct repelling forces such as those mentioned above, including overt insults, resisting, arguing, being condescending, and trying to control the other person.
2. Indirect repelling forces such as implying that the other person is wrong or focusing on one's own concerns (which interferes with valuing the other person's concerns). Some other indirect repelling forces include being locked into what the other person said or did, trying to persuade rather than seeking a compatible solution, and persisting with the same argument.

The above-mentioned behaviors are unlikely to succeed for several reasons, such as:
1. No one handles failure well nor many other negatives.
2. A person who is not satisfied by what another individual says may feel that he has no reason to agree with it.
3. Overt aspects, while important, often are not the major key to resolving disagreements. Sub-surface Psychological Roots are likely to be significant factors.
4. Conflicts are likely to continue or worsen if the protagonists continue to promote their viewpoint or attack the other person's viewpoint.

What might succeed
What might be effective is a new solution that has the potential to satisfy both individuals. Creating a compatible solution is aided by at least one of the protagonists knowing how to identify Psychological Roots and use that

understanding to create win-win solutions. The following aspects might help if you are in a conflict with someone:

1. Present your viewpoint only one time.
2. Stop when a disagreement occurs.
3. Assume that the disagreement is because your viewpoint is inconsistent with the other person's Psychological Roots.
4. Do not argue.
5. Although your viewpoint seems logical and correct to you, it does not satisfactorily address the other person's underlying concerns.
6. Recognize that resolving the disagreement requires that both you and the other person must be satisfied, not just yourself.
7. Do not try to persuade, justify your viewpoint, or believe that your logic will prevail.
8. Change the focus to seeking a compatible solution rather than trying to promote your viewpoint.
9. Accept the legitimacy of the other person's viewpoint even when that person is wrong since that viewpoint is based on his/her Psychological Roots.
10. Assume that the person does not realize what the Psychological Roots are that are the basis of his/her viewpoint.
11. Ask the other person to help you find a solution that might satisfy both of you.
12. Ascertain the other individual's underlying concerns and other Psychological Roots. (See Chapter 6 for how to identify Psychological Roots.)
13. Develop a solution that might satisfy the *other person's* concerns as well as yours.
14. Present your solution in a supportive and caring way. Be moderate, careful, and tentative rather than forceful or controlling.
15. Try to use appealing forces throughout (e.g., respect the other person, and be considerate and cordial).
16. Try to avoid using *any* repelling forces. Do not be impatient, oppositional, frustrated, angry, or try to win. If you are irritated, let that feeling pass over you and out.
17. If an idea is not accepted by the other person, modify that idea or ask the other person to help modify it.
18. Do not expect the other person to create a solution. Not having that expectation could help you avoid being upset if the other person does not contribute a solution.

19. If the person does not have a constructive alternative, seek another solution that might more appropriately address both the other person's underlying concerns and yours.
20. Continue to try to find a solution that both of you can accept.
21. Remain calm and cooperative throughout.
22. If a win-win solution does not arise, consider the possibility of presenting a different solution at a later time.
23. If no solutions work, agree to disagree and do so cordially.
24. Consider your relationship with the other person to be more important than finding a compatible solution to the current issue.

Solving people-problems

Some people excel at solving material problems yet are not effective with interpersonal issues. Objective logic, defending one's viewpoint, or being rigid might not persuade another individual if it does not address that person's subjective concerns and it could antagonize that person. Trying to force a viewpoint on someone else is a strong repelling force. It helps to know how to discern the aspects that are hidden, particularly Psychological Roots (see Chapter 6). Knowing how to work constructively with that knowledge, using appealing forces, and not using repelling forces are important social skills.

Do people usually know how to resolve their differences?

The author has found that people are unlikely to have a good way to resolve their disagreements other than by compromising, yet they may be reluctant to compromise because they do not want to give in. People may also focus on observable aspects, such as what they or the other person says or does. Using repelling forces diminishes the chances of developing a compatible solution.

Couples

The author has found that couples typically try hard to solve their problems but do not know how to create win-win solutions. If they criticize or put down their partner, their problems worsen. Their disagreements can escalate out of control if they harm their partner or are unfaithful.

Relationships require special nurturing, yet some people do not seem to realize that they must satisfy their partner's needs if they want their needs to be fulfilled. Relationships are also undermined by a lack of trust, hence truthfulness is necessary and promises should be kept. Putting one's own needs, tasks, or material things ahead of the relationship can exacerbate emotional distance and contribute to conflicts. What one person says and does has special weight because of that person's importance to his/her partner. Complaints and statements such as, "What's wrong with you?", "You never help", "Can't you do anything right?" can be remembered for years by the other person. Special effort should be made to avoid repelling forces, which requires self-control, avoiding attempts to control the other person, and not trying to win arguments. Unilateral decisions should be avoided unless both people agree in advance about when that should occur. As soon as a disagreement occurs, win-win solutions should be sought to avoid escalating disagreements.

Maintaining a relationship requires patience, skill, and effort. The relationship should be paramount and it is wise to be flexible and to consider compatible solutions to be more important than holding fast to a viewpoint. Creating a positive atmosphere is aided by having a win-win perspective and viewing conflicts as opportunities to obtain still better solutions than those of either person alone. It is easier to create win-win solutions when both individuals value each other's concerns and are considerate of one another. If an idea is rejected, it helps to keep searching until a compatible one can be found. The author has helped a great many couples by using these guidelines.

A way to help avoid disagreements is to ask oneself, "Will he/she like what I'm about to say or do?" If you sense that the answer is not a strong "Yes!", then what you contemplate should not be said or done except in unusual circumstances. It would be better to find something to agree with or say nothing and work toward finding a win-win solution than to introduce yet another repelling force.

As soon as a disagreement starts, it can help to immediately seek a win-win solution. If that attempt does not bear fruit, it can help to postpone addressing the issue until a more propitious opportunity arises.

The work-place

Disagreements can arise for many reasons between co-workers, supervisors, employees, and customers. When conflicts are not resolved the result can be stressful, time-consuming, disruptive, and costly. Employees or managers who do not resolve disagreements can develop a reputation for being difficult to work with and harm their relationships, raises, and promotions. It can help them to address the underlying causes (e.g., concerns, interests, beliefs, and other Psychological Roots) and seek win-win solutions.

Present a viewpoint only once

Mentioned previously was the value of presenting a viewpoint only once. When an idea does not seem to be heard by the other person, it might not be because he/she failed to hear or understand what was said. Rather, it might not fit that individual's Psychological Roots. A good start when trying to resolve a difference of opinion can be, "Help me find a solution that could satisfy both of our concerns". A negative atmosphere can sometimes be lightened by mentioning something with which the other person agrees, such as a common goal.

Tangible aspects
A sticking point between people can become unbudgeable when people limit themselves to the overt issue. A solution can often be found upon pausing to identify the Psychological Roots that underlie the other person's resistance such as their concerns, interests, beliefs, goals, expectations, needs, and desires, then seek a win-win solution based on that awareness.

Thinking in absolutes impedes finding a good solution
Rigidity is an obstacle to obtaining a solution that could satisfy both individuals. Being flexible can help, especially if both persons are not rigid.

Conflict with a disliked person
It is understandable that someone might not want to satisfy an individual he/she dislikes, distrusts, or finds annoying, or who seems devious or dangerous. However, developing compatible solutions might help avoid future problems. In such cases, most of the problem-solving might be done by oneself. It does not pay to be resentful about doing so or to take setbacks personally because doing so can add distress. It helps to settle issues quickly rather than let them drag on. If a bad situation lasts a long time or the person is particularly difficult, unpleasant, or harmful, it might be wise to drop the issue and lessen or avoid future connections with that person when doing so is possible.

A caution
The conflict-resolving strategy presented in this book is not a panacea because some people resist effective solutions. Some individuals are committed to their viewpoint or interpret a compatible solution to mean losing, or are very competitive, hostile, rigid, negative, provocative, or combative. Some people strongly resist admitting being wrong, do not tolerate viewpoints different than their own, are unwilling to change their thinking, or like being provocative or punitive. Sometimes someone not directly involved in a conflict – such as a relative, friend, or boss – can interfere with developing

a reasonable solution. Impediments of that sort are more likely with people who are antagonistic, easily irritated, very emotional, or think in absolutes. As a result, there are times when it is wise to end a conflict by agreeing to disagree and then dropping the issue.

A solution can dramatically change the mood
Mentioned earlier was that the author has often found that when a solution is acceptable to both parties, tension and strife end, sometimes abruptly. Such positive outcomes can be surprising when there previously had been substantial friction, frustration, or anger. Also surprising is that relationships often can pick up where they were before as if there had never been a problem (see the examples described in Chapter 21). Such positive re-connections attest to the importance of relationships and the benefit of addressing conflicts constructively.

How to start
A good way to begin to resolve a conflict, mentioned earlier, is for one person to ask the other individual to work with him/her to find a solution that can satisfy both persons. Working together to find a solution automatically puts both people on the same side of the fence and helps lighten the atmosphere since both individuals seek the same objective. Even partial cooperation can help diminish negatives and might lessen rigidity. In some instances, full cooperation between protagonists might not happen until a solution is close or after a solution is found. Some solutions quickly happen while others require some time or effort. When rancor or another obstacle impedes communicating, a welcome intermediary's assistance might help (as in the Dock Dispute example in Chapter 21).

Identifying Psychological Roots
The techniques for identifying Psychological Roots described in Chapter 6 can help unearth the Psychological Roots that underlie the cause of disagreements. Ascertaining Psychological Roots can often be accomplished quickly after familiarity with the process. Sometimes clues about the Psychological Roots of the protagonists can be provided by people who know those individuals.

What if a dispute involves many aspects?
Conflicts that involve a variety of issues require a solution for each aspect, as in the gun-safety example in Chapter 21. Sometimes a single solution is possible if all the issues revolve around a single Psychological Root (e.g., need

for autonomy or need for safety) since satisfying that deep root can produce a flow-down effect that automatically modifies many subsidiary Psychological Roots. (See Chapter 7 on psychological hierarchies and the flow-down effect.)

What if a solution is rejected?

A solution might be rejected by a protagonist when some of the pertinent Psychological Roots are satisfied but not all of them. When that happens yet the analysis seems to be correct, it may be that nuanced modifications are required for some or all of the identified roots. If that adjustment does not work, additional Psychological Roots may need to be unearthed. A protagonist's willingness to accept a solution can sometimes be aided by inviting that person to adjust that proposed solution to fit his/her concerns. Sometimes providing a fuller understanding of a solution can help, or offering people more time to process the circumstances, or giving social support. There are times that providing concrete examples, anecdotes, or visual aids can help. There also may be occasions in which a protagonist has to experience the solution to accept it or needs encouragement from a trusted person. Sometimes it helps when the protagonists are reminded of the consequences if a solution is not found. If a solution is rejected because of anger, competitiveness, or rigidity, the strategy described in the chapters on social influence might help.

Expect everyone to want to be respected and not controlled, also expect questions and objections. Encourage everyone to voice their concerns, recognizing that some people especially need to vent their feelings and concerns. Questions and other issues should be answered in a calm, helpful, considerate, and uncontroversial manner.

Chapter 24. EFFECTIVE COMMUNICATION

The three stages described in this chapter are related to the stages of resolving conflicts described in Chapter 22. For simplicity, the present discussion often refers to a single recipient although the same principles apply to groups of people.

Communication is essential in life – it is not an accident or limited to humans. Being able to communicate effectively requires special skill, as this chapter explains.

The nature of communication

Communication occurs widely in nature: dogs bark warnings, tigers and bears mark their territory, birds and crickets chirp when seeking mates, bees dance to indicate where pollen is, termites transmit messages through their saliva, and even trees and microbes send and receive messages. There also are communications within organisms, such as via neurons, blood, and lymph. Since the ability to send and receive communications within and between organisms seems to be genetically wired into all living creatures and has important purposes that range from aiding functioning to avoiding danger, it may be that communication is vital to survival.

Communicating in a positive way to others frequently is reciprocated by positive reactions from the recipients, whereas negative communications and not communicating are often reacted to negatively. Non-verbal communications (such as body language, tone of voice, and eye contact), often convey much more information than verbal statements (e.g., Burgoon, et al., 2009). Dogs, cats, primates, and other creatures also pay attention to non-verbal cues, not just humans (Hare & Woods, 2003; Horowitz, 2009; Shettleworth, 2009).

We expect others to comprehend what we say, yet our messages can be misunderstood and reacted to differently than we intended. One reason for misunderstanding is that incoming messages are filtered and shaped in recipients' minds to align with their Psychological Roots, including their needs, goals, expectations, beliefs, concerns, and interests. Thus, misunderstandings can occur even with people who speak the same language, are from the same family, or have similar cultural backgrounds.

Some of the reasons for misinterpretation are many nuances, interpretations, and meanings of words and phrases that are possible, such as with colloquialisms, acronyms, technical jargon, and idioms. Communication can also be hindered by complicated wording, lengthy sentences, and involved logic. Other complications occur from omission of words, inappropriate grammar, and unfamiliar accents. Recipients might understand only part of a message, misunderstand it, or reject it. Some recipients have hearing or vision problems. Many recipients comprehend or retain only part of what is communicated based on the particular Psychological Roots with which the message connects. Also, some well-intentioned and carefully crafted messages nevertheless might contain repelling forces that turn off recipients. As a result, it is readily possible for people to obtain a different meaning than what a communicator intended.

When attempting to communicate, the recipient's receptivity is critical. If a recipient is not receptive, a message's potential to benefit a recipient can be lost even if the communicator has good intentions. In such instances, it may not matter that the communicator uses well-formed sentences, correct verbiage, clear-cut logic, or strong facts. A lack of receptivity can occur even when a presentation is objectively clear, important to the recipient, and well-founded. Resistance can occur even when a communicator has high credibility, good will, positive intentions, humor, showmanship, attractiveness, and vigor, although those might help. Hence, it is especially important not only to obtain and maintain recipients' initial receptivity but also to try to present messages that are accord with the recipients' Psychological Roots while conveying the intended message.

Obtaining receptivity

Noted earlier was that repelling forces can shut down recipients, therefore communicators should try to avoid using them. Appealing forces can help obtain recipients' receptivity and partially mitigate the deleterious effect that repelling forces can have. Appealing forces include being caring, concerned, believable, trustworthy, likable, and interesting. However, appealing forces may not be sufficient to overcome every negative, therefore it is important for communicators to pay attention to the social and emotional aspect of presentations even when factual information is being conveyed.

When recipients do not respond to a message, it is advisable to change the presentation. Some non-verbal signs of unresponsiveness include recipients' lack of attention, a shift in their attention to something else, a glazed appearance, and yawning. Some of the reasons for recipients' unresponsiveness might be:

1. The communicator is substantially involved in his/her own perspective.
2. The communicator is not connecting well with the recipients.
3. The communicator does not know how to connect with the recipient's interests.

Some reasons for the above communication difficulties are:
1. The recipients' interests are not being met, resulting in disinterest.
2. The communicator or the communication turns off recipients.
3. A communicator's not being flexible can make things worse.

Comprehension

A message is more likely to be accepted and understood the more closely it aligns with a recipient's Psychological Roots. Cues about when such alignment does not occur can be obtained by paying attention to the recipients' non-verbal behavior. It helps for communicators to use words, phrases, examples, and visual aids with which the recipient is familiar. Knowing the recipients and their experiences can be obtained by talking with recipients, being genuinely interested in them, and discerning their Psychological Roots. Messages should be adjusted to align with the recipients' interests and concerns.

Recipients' understanding is aided by examples, especially tangible aspects that are familiar to the recipients. The more interesting, familiar, and concrete the examples are to the recipients, the greater the chances of their grasping and retaining the message. A recipient with little or no experience with the examples a communicator uses might not comprehend what is being presented, misunderstand it, or even reject it.

Self-comprehension

When someone acquires new information, it is a unique experience for that person. Recipients' ability to understand is aided by their working with the information their own way (*'self-comprehension'*, also termed experiential learning [Dewey, 1938/1997] and self-directed learning, [Gibbons, 2002]). Examples include recipients solving problems for themselves or imagining themselves in a situation connected with the message. The opportunity to process information in their own manner increases the likelihood of it linking with their Psychological Roots. Such self-linking aids understanding because it automatically fits each person's individual framework.

A three-stage method for communicating
1. PREPARE.

Receptivity is critical because a message is unlikely to be accepted by a turned-off recipient. It is often better not to continue until receptivity can be obtained. Receptivity is aided by linking with the recipient in a positive way. Plan how to link the message with the recipient's Psychological Roots since understanding and retention requires that linking. (See Chapter 7 regarding Psychological Root hierarchies.) Hence, identify some of the recipient's core, surface, and intermediate roots to which to connect the message in a positive manner and avoid opposing those roots. It may be useful to prepare answers to possible questions and objections.

Communicating vs. persuading

Successful communicating occurs when recipients comprehend a message, even if the recipients do not agree or change their minds. By comparison, persuading occurs when recipients change their viewpoint to agree with a message. As an example, recipients might understand a communicator's political viewpoint yet remain opposed to it, yet the objective would have been met if the purpose was for the recipients to understand that viewpoint. Situations like this occur with impartial radio, TV, and print journalists. If a communicator's aim is just to provide knowledge, he/she might not be unhappy if the recipients do not change their viewpoint.

A person's attempt to persuade would benefit from using a more elaborate strategy than just presenting information clearly. Persuasion is discussed in the next two chapters for people who want to persuade for constructive reasons, such as parents who want their recalcitrant children to obey reasonable guidelines. Examples of other constructive purposes of persuasion include bosses who need their employees to improve, politicians who try to win votes for new programs, and health care professionals who want people to employ a healthy life-style.

Some communicators believe that recipients should accept what they say or change and if that does not happen, disdain the recipients as being inattentive, resistant, hostile, or unintelligent. A communicator's negative reactions might be detected by recipients and diminish recipients' receptivity. To avoid having negative feelings about recipients, it can help communicators not to expect recipients' agreement with the message.

A three-stage method for communicating

The following version of the three-stage approach discussed earlier can help when communicating. This method can be especially useful when a message is difficult to grasp, or is complicated, abstract, or unpleasant, or when recipients are resistant. Some components of this method have been described earlier related to resolving conflicts.

1. PREPARE.

Receptivity is critical because a message is unlikely to be accepted by a recipient who is turned-off or tuned-out. If a recipient is unreceptive, it is often better not to continue until receptivity can be obtained.

Receptivity is aided by linking with the recipient's Psychological Roots in a positive way (see Figs. 8 and 9). As an example, some politicians begin talking to a local community by saying, "I'm delighted to be here, one of the greatest places in the world." Woe be it to politicians who get the name of the town wrong.

Teachers who believe that their subject matter is the most important aspect of students' education might inadvertently turn off some students who disagree with that opinion or believe that the instructor is not concerned about them. It would be better for teachers to show that students are their top priority and how the subject matter connects with their students' interests.

2. PRESENT THE INFORMATION.

Recipients are more likely to grasp a message they welcome therefore it is important to maintain receptivity all the way through the presentation. Maintaining receptivity is aided by respecting and caring about the recipients, and by not using repelling forces (e.g., pressure, criticism, or condescension).

Examples that are familiar to the audience and tangible can help recipients understand the presentation. When talking to groups, it helps to talk with the audience, not at them, as if the communicator was speaking personally to them in their home. Lecturing, shouting, or being shrill are repelling forces.

A message might not be understood if it is inconsistent with beliefs the recipients have. If a communication does not seem to be working, try to modify the message or the style of delivery before proceeding further.

The communicator should make it easy for recipients to raise questions. Answers should be cordial, caring, and succinct. If need be, an answer can be postponed until a later time, such as via email. Following through on promises made to recipients is important.

Communicators can avoid being surprised and reacting negatively by expecting objections and resistance. The communicator should respond cordially and briefly, without being irritated or displaying any other repelling forces. If a recipient in a group speaks too long, that person can be asked to continue the conversation with the communicator after the presentation, citing a necessity to move to another part of the presentation.

3. SOLIDIFY THE PRESENTATION.

The communicator should accept the potential for negative eventualities such as recipients' misunderstanding, being confused, or forgetting. Solidifying the message can help. Solidifying is aided by reviewing the main points, adding information, answering questions, and suggesting additional ways that the information might be used (e.g., for solving problems that might come up or other constructive uses). It can help to give the recipients emotional support, such as by complimenting them. In classrooms, solidifying is aided by the tasks that students do such as projects, homework, test preparation, and class discussions, including reviewing of the answers to the tests questions after exams have been graded.

The bottom line: Communicators should try to obtain recipients' receptivity before presenting the message, endeavor to maintain that receptivity throughout, and connect their message with the recipients' Psychological Roots and the way they process information. Connecting in a positive way with recipients is aided by communicators connecting the message with what interests the recipients, caring about the recipients, and not using repelling forces. After presenting the message, communicators should try to solidify what the recipients have acquired from it.

274

Chapter 25.   CONSTRUCTIVE SOCIAL INFLUENCE

This chapter presents a method that can aid obtaining agreement from another person. The three stages described in the present chapter are related to the three-stage method for communicating and resolving conflicts described in the previous chapters.

People try to persuade others more than might be realized. This chapter provides a background for the method that is spelled out in the next chapter.

Is it insidious to try to persuade another person?

For some people, attempts to influence people have an unsavory reputation, conjuring up images of slick talkers who try to take advantage of others, are manipulative, or lie. Some individuals believe that people who are persuaded are gullible ("A sucker is born every minute"). However, many persuasive efforts are constructive, such as when parents, teachers, coaches, and health-care professionals try to help someone be healthier or avoid being harmed. Such attempts occur frequently. The strategy described in the following chapter can be useful in such instances.

Some considerations

It was noted earlier that change in behavior stems from Psychological Roots and the only person who can change those roots is the target individual himself/herself. Trying to change behavior directly, such with a New Year's resolution is unlikely to have a lasting effect unless the person's Psychological Roots change. Hence, an effective persuasion strategy is to arrange for recipients themselves to change the Psychological Roots that contribute to their behavior. As an analogy, turning off a valve inside a house is more effective at stopping water gushing from a garden hose than placing a hand over the end of the hose. If a recipient yields without his/her deep roots having been satisfied or modified, such as when someone is coerced or bribed, change might not last long. Thus, when substantial or lasting change is desired, the message should be consistent with the recipient's deep Psychological Roots.

Expect resistance

Resistance should be expected because of factors that push for us to remain largely in place, such as homeostasis, countervailing forces, and the genetic need for stability. Moreover, Psychological Roots are well ensconced and largely hidden, and opposing a person's viewpoint is a repelling force. Resistance to change is wired-in even for beneficial messages and is especially likely to occur when there is minimal receptivity on the recipient's part. (See Chapter 13 also Figures 14 and 16). In short, persuading is more difficult than people realize.

Repelling forces

It is easy to introduce repelling forces without realizing it, such as just by telling someone that he/she is wrong, criticizing, or persisting.

Noted earlier was that the only person who can change a person's Psychological Roots is that individual himself/herself. Hence, an effective persuasion strategy is to arrange for recipients to change their own Psychological Roots. A possible analogy would be stopping gushing water from a garden hose by turning off a valve inside a house, rather than by trying to stop the flow by placing a hand over the end of the hose.

Changing a recipient's internal reactions and overt behavior is aided by:

a) The recipient satisfying, modifying, or overriding the Psychological Roots that originate his/her internal reactions or behavior,

b) The recipient obtaining Psychological Roots that can modify the roots that affect his/her internal reactions, or behavior, and/or

c) The recipient, someone else, or circumstances changing the stimulus conditions that impact the Psychological Roots that affect the recipient's internal reactions and behaviors.

Some methods that many people use to persuade – such as presenting logic, facts, evidence, and "common sense" – can be ineffective if the recipient's pertinent Psychological Roots are not changed or satisfied. Worse, such attempts to persuade can introduce repelling forces, such as implying that the person is wrong or there is an attempt to pressure, control, or coerce, use fear messages or threats, be lofty or condescending, or argue. Pitfalls like these can be avoided by using constructive methods. Some ideas for doing so are presented in this chapter and the next one, after the following discussion.

Major obstacles to persuasion

Modifying a person's Psychological Roots can be difficult because the roots may be well ensconced and hidden. Also, opposing a person's Psychological Roots is a repelling force. Resistance to change is wired-in even for beneficial messages and is especially likely to occur when there is minimal receptivity on the recipient's part. (See Chapter 13 also Figures 14 and 16). Change might not last long if a recipient yields without his/her deep roots having been satisfied or modified, for example, when someone is coerced or bribed.

Expect resistance

Resistance should be expected because it normally occurs owing to such aspects as the genetic need for stability, homeostasis, and countervailing forces. People also are concerned about the consequences of changing (e.g., fear of the unknown and an abhorrence of being wrong), have networks of tightly bonded Psychological Roots, and a tendency to think in absolutes (see or even not being in accord with the way a recipient thinks. Hence it is not surprising that people resist persuasive attempts and also resist new ideas. Communicators who understand resistance might be less frustrated when encountering it.

Sometimes it is possible to change someone's behavior by nagging, coercing, threatening, or giving ultimatums, however those are repelling forces. Therefore, if a change occurs it is unlikely to last, especially when a repelling force directly impacts a recipient's deep Psychological Roots. In short, repelling forces are a major impediment to persuasion.

Presenting a different viewpoint is a subtle repelling force in that the communicator is unaware that doing so implies that the recipient is wrong. Another subtle repelling force is telling people to change, as often happens with parents vis-à-vis children, teachers vis-à-vis students, managers vis-à-vis employees, and couples with one another. Other subtle repelling forces are giving unasked for advice, making demands, pointing out mistakes, making disparaging observations, and being irritated upon meeting resistance from someone.

For these reasons, "Telling it like it is" or "Telling truth to power" are unlikely to persuade, even though doing so might seem appropriate and make the communicator feel good. Also unlikely to persuade is shouting, telling people to "just get over" something, persisting, pleading, complaining, arguing, or making threats. Being blunt, forceful, or aggressive also are repelling forces.

Fear messages
A fear message attempts to persuade by heightening recipients' anxiety. Examples are: "You'll suffer if you ….", "Your brain will look like a fried egg if you ….", "The nation be in terrible shape if you vote for …", and labels that proclaim "Hazardous to Your Health". It is not uncommon for fear messages to be used when trying to get people to relinquish their addiction or to change their food, health, and driving habits (see the Driving Debacle example in Chapter 21). Communicators may believe that fear messages persuade because those messages align with their own viewpoint, not realizing that recipients might respond differently.

It would be better if communicators realized that making recipients anxious is a repelling force and that fear messages do not satisfy the underlying basis for the recipient's behavior (e.g., Psychological Roots). Fear messages can work some of the time with some individuals, for example, in the heat of an election campaign, however, it is generally preferable for people to avoid using fear messages with one another (see Janis & Feshbach, 1953).

Trying to persuade someone to dislike something

This chapter and the next address how to persuade someone to accept something, however, a simpler strategy might work when trying to influence someone to dislike something. The reason the process is simpler is because negatives have great potency. For example, an effective strategy would be to show how a viewpoint, reaction, or behavior violates a major Psychological Root the recipient has (e.g., needs for safety or respect). The deeper the root that is violated, the more effective the negative effect is likely to be.

Negative advertisements attempt to get recipients to dislike a particular aspect or person, which often occurs during political campaigns. The thinking behind negative campaign ads is, "If we can get you to dislike the other candidate, you might vote for our candidate or else not vote. Either way, our candidate gains."

The more credible, familiar, and tangible a negative statement is, and the more readily it fits a recipient's Psychological Roots, the more likely it is to be accepted by the recipient. Perhaps these aspects are among the reasons that some people are prone to accept conspiracy theories.

It is more difficult to influence someone to be for something than against something, for example, when attempting to persuade someone to agree with a viewpoint with which they currently disagree or to adopt a healthier life-style than their current one. How to accomplish positive influence constructively is the focus of this chapter and the following one.

Do facts straighten out people who are wrong?

Trying to set a person straight when not invited to do so by that individual is a repelling force since the communicator implies that the recipient is wrong. Even were such a message to work to some small extent (Fisher & Lubin, 1958), the recipient's viewpoint might not change from one side of an issue to the opposite point of view (Greenwald, 1964). This lack of success is especially likely when a recipient holds a strong viewpoint since beliefs are what people consider to be true. In such cases, an opposing viewpoint can be experienced by the recipient as a violation of his/her Psychological Roots and helps explain why they might say, "Don't confuse me with the facts". For this reason, when trying to persuade it would be better for a communicator to show how the message can satisfy a recipient's underlying concerns better than the recipient's current viewpoint. Doing so would have a greater chance of succeeding than telling the recipient that he/she is wrong or implying it by presenting a contrary view, evidence, facts, ideas, logic, or "the truth".

Common mistakes when attempting to persuade

A mistake that communicators make when trying to persuade is that they do not realize the underlying reasons why people hold their current viewpoint. For example, "Laurel's" parents told her to get more sleep rather than staying up late to study. However, that persuasive attempt did not work because it did not change the reason Laurel kept late hours. The reason was that she was afraid of failing and strongly desired to succeed. Adding to Laurel's problem was that her parents told her not to be concerned about her grades. However, that led Laurel to believe that she was not measuring up, which caused her to feel even more like a failure.

When people tell addicted individuals that their addiction harms them, they may not understand that those individuals may be dealing with a disturbing issue that they may feel unable to cope with without their "fix". Telling low self-esteem individuals that they should recognize their good qualities does not correct the underlying reasons for those persons' low self-regard, which can be deeply embedded in them. Being blunt because of thinking that "the shortest distance between two points is a straight line" may seem efficient, but it can feel harsh or controlling to the recipient, and therefore a repelling force that can lessen the person's willingness to change.

Trying to change oneself – such as by making resolutions, counting to ten, and venting feelings – might work for a short time, but the original behavior is likely to return unless the Psychological Roots are changed. For example, almost every diet works at first, including various commercial programs, but almost all of the lost weight returns within two to three years (e.g., Jeffery, Epstein, Wilson, Drewnowski, Stunkard, & Wing, 2000). The reason is that those individuals resume their prior eating patterns, possibly because the psychological causes of their counterproductive eating have not been changed (e.g., a need to lessen distress). Tension can be lessened by relaxation, and anxiety can be diminished by medication, but those methods might only work temporarily if they do not change the underlying Psychological Roots or stimulus conditions that contribute to those conditions. (See the example of Lily's anxiety in Chapter 28.) The social influence method to be described has a better chance of persuading because it provides a constructive way to satisfy the recipient's Psychological Roots.

Does logic persuade?

The logic a communicator typically uses when trying to persuade comes from his/her own frame of reference, which could have little or no connection with how the recipient thinks (e.g., Nyhan & Reifler, 2006). A lack of connection with the recipient's underlying psychology is also likely to be the case with the logic and facts the communicator uses to support his/her point of view. Worse, a communicator's logic implies that the recipient is wrong, which makes the communicator and the message repelling forces that can shut down the recipient's receptivity. As a result, trying to change someone's mind by using logic and facts to directly contradict their viewpoint is somewhat like trying to push a heavy boulder uphill with bare hands. That boulder is likely to remain as it was.

Presenting an opposing viewpoint can shut down a recipient if it runs counter to that person's Psychological Roots, especially if those roots are deeply embedded and repelling forces are used. Trying to directly change a person's internal reactions or behavior by presenting opposing logic and facts can be a repelling force. Doing so also addresses tangible aspects rather than the hidden and often subconscious causes of the recipient's outward behavior.

Advice, sermons, and proverbs

Advice, even healthful advice – such as parents telling their children not to be wasteful and ministers preaching caring – are attempts to influence people. If the message is not in accord with the recipient's deep Psychological Roots, should a change result it is unlikely to last. This circumstance especially applies to advice that is not requested. Also, attempting to use proverbs to persuade, such as "Make hay while the sun shines", ignores alternative proverbs that state the reverse, such as "Everything comes to he who waits".

Is setting an example a good way to get another person to change?

Modeling exemplary behavior is worthwhile, but it is an indirect attempt to persuade since it does not attempt to change the recipient's Psychological Roots. Also, modeling's effectiveness is related to the importance the communicator has for the recipient and how resistant the recipient is. For many recipients, modeling is not a major way to create change.

Does intelligence affect willingness to change?

For people who are willing to change, their intelligence can aid their ability to comprehend and accept a new idea. However, for people who are resistant, their intellectual competence can be used to support their not changing. People's Psychological Roots substantially determine how they use their intelligence.

If a message is resisted is it worthwhile to continue presenting it?

When a message is resisted, the likelihood is that it does not satisfy one or more of the recipient's Psychological Roots. If so, persisting in presenting that message is unlikely to succeed and could be a repelling force. Some communicators persist in the hope that they will eventually overcome the recipient's resistance, or that the recipient will finally realize the value of the message or be worn down ("If at first, you don't succeed, try, try, again"). If a badgered recipient changes to appease a communicator, that change might not last long.

It can help to present a message only once and then develop a message or a way to communicate the original message that satisfies the recipient's Psychological Roots. If that attempt and others fail, it may be better for the communicator to focus on maintaining the relationship and drop the issue.

Self-comprehension

People acquire new aspects when information links with their Psychological Roots such as through personal experience, for instance, some drivers become more patient with pedestrians and cyclists after having had harsh experiences as pedestrians or cyclists. Self-comprehension can happen automatically and subconsciously, and can be bolstered with examples, visual aids, representative models, imagined scenarios, and role-playing.

What might work?

The reason that people purchase goods and services is to obtain a benefit. Similarly, a message has a better chance of being accepted when the recipient benefits from it. For change to occur, the gain needs to be substantial enough to overcome resistance. A particularly strong benefit occurs when what is suggested alleviates a disturbance because of the great impact that negatives have. As an example, a person might give up cigarettes only after contracting lung cancer, or stop drinking only when alcohol use threatens his relationship. (Also see Spike's case in Chapter 18). Cults and extremist groups (e.g., ISIS) win recruits by claiming that they will solve the recruit's frustrations (see Hoffa, 1951). As a result, public health officials who want to promulgate a healthy lifestyle might show how it relieves a current problem that greatly bothers recipients rather than by presenting a general message about health, prevention, or longevity.

Persuasive attempts also have a better chance to succeed when they align with recipients' deep Psychological Roots such as their needs and values. The deeper the Psychological Root with which a message connects, the broader the flow-down effect on subsidiary Psychological Roots (see Chapter 7). If a recipient reacts negatively to a communicator, a welcome intermediary may help (as in the Dock Dispute example in Chapter 21).

A difference between attempts to persuade and attempts to generate operant conditioning

Persuasive attempts are presented before a recipient employs an intended change. Attempts to create operant conditioning entail presenting a positive reinforcement after a recipient acts. (See Chapter 18 for a possible exception that involves persuasion).

The bottom line: Persuasion is harder to accomplish than it might seem. Persuasive attempts are aided by showing how a new idea can resolve a problem that bothers the recipient.

Eight ways to generate constructive change (some of which overlap)

1. Provide an acceptable alternative for satisfying pertinent Psychological Roots.
2. Modify pertinent Psychological Roots (e.g., through self-discovery, experimentation, being open-minded, willingness to accept exceptions).
3. Override a bothersome Psychological Root (e.g., with self-statements, will-power).
4. Link the desired change with a deep Psychological Root to thereby create a flow-down effect.
5. Offer a positive benefit for changing (a potential positive reinforcement).
6. Offer a solution for a bothersome problem (i.e., a potential negative reinforcement).
7. Change an impinging stimulus to a stimulus that can generate an outcome desired by the recipient.
8. Remove obstacles that impede the occurrence of a desired behavior.

Summary of steps when attempting to persuade

1. Identify a problem the recipient has.
2. Discern the recipient's Psychological Roots.
3. Obtain receptivity, which includes not using repelling forces.
4. Identify a problem that bothers the recipient.
5. Show how the new idea solves the recipient's problem in a way that the recipient finds acceptable.
6. Stop trying to persuade when resistance occurs.
7. Eliminate possible repelling forces.
8. If a persuasive attempt does not work, create a new solution, identify a different problem, or address other Psychological Roots.
9. If the recipient resists, stop. View your relationship with the recipient to be the primary consideration.

Chapter 26. A THREE-STAGE METHOD FOR SOCIAL INFLUENCE

This chapter spells out the procedure at each of the three stages in this method of social influence - Prepare, Present, and Solidify. The key is to provide a strong benefit for changing, especially a solution to a problem that bothers the recipient. Arranging for the recipient to self-comprehend the benefit can help.

Some considerations. The previous chapter indicated that persuasion could be facilitated by describing a strong benefit for changing to the recipient, especially by showing how to solve an issue that bothers the recipient. If the recipient accepts that idea, his/her Psychological Roots related to its acquisition will automatically modify to be in accord with it, according to Psychological Systems Theory. A flow-down effect might then produce changes in the recipient's subsidiary roots, internal reactions, and behavior (see the discussion of Psychological Roots in Chapter 3, Hidden Sequences in Chapter 4, and Psychological Root hierarchies in Chapter 7). As an example, using hypnosis to try to change a person's behavior is aided by having the person imagine being in a circumstance in which the person changes himself/herself, rather than by the hypnotist trying to change the person's behavior directly. For instance, if a hypnotist were to tell you to perspire, your body might not do so or the effect would be very slight. However, if the hypnotist were to ask you to imagine being in the Sahara desert and then describe the details (the sun slowly rising in the sky and the air becoming hotter and hotter until you feel heat like being in a furnace), you are more likely to perspire. Thus, your belief that you are experiencing heat can lead to your perspiring. (Technically, a Psychological Root leads to an internal reaction). Hypnosis as an aid for stopping cigarette smoking would be greatly aided by correcting the distress-prone Psychological Roots and stimulus conditions that underlie a person's smoking habit. Correcting those causes would be ideal and perhaps essential in many (and perhaps most) instances of cigarette smoking.

This chapter describes a procedure that can help a recipient accept a different viewpoint by proposing a solution for a disturbing problem that is consistent with that person's Psychological Roots. The three general stages are Prepare, Present, and Solidify, as in earlier chapters.[40]

---

[40] Lewin (1947) suggested that change occurs in three phases: unfreezing of the initial viewpoint, change to a different viewpoint, then freezing of that change. Lewin did not explain how to accomplish each stage. The three-stage approach in this book suggests what some of those procedures might be with some differences, such as an automatic unfreezing of the initial viewpoint when change occurs.

1. PREPARE. Much rests on a successful preparation.

A. *Create receptivity.* Establish rapport with the recipient using appealing forces and especially avoiding introducing repelling forces. Proceed to the other stages only if you have receptivity.

B. *Identify the person's Psychological Roots*

Discover a problem that the person has and identify the relevant Psychological Roots involved. Two sets of Psychological Roots are particularly helpful to know: pertinent surface roots (e.g., the person's specific concerns and interests), and relevant deep roots (genetic and acquired) at or near the base of the hierarchies of those surface roots. (See Chapter 7 regarding Psychological Root hierarchies.) Some deep roots include needs for safety, respect, connecting with others, meeting responsibility, protecting a loved one, stability, and not being controlled, also long-term goals. There are times when it also helps to identify intermediate Psychological Roots as well. Deep roots offer a particularly broad range of opportunities for compatibility.

C. *Prioritize the recipient's problems.*

Rank-order the problems and choose the most important one if possible.

D. *Develop a solution*

Create a solution to the problem in 2 C in a way *that incorporates your message or is consistent with it.*

E. *Construct the message*

Construct a message that:

1) Presents the solution to the recipient's problem identified earlier,
2) Satisfies your objective (e.g., incorporates your message),
3) Is consistent with or satisfies the person's Psychological Roots, and
4) You believe that the recipient will readily accept.

The eight ways to create change in Chapter 25 may be useful.

F. *Anticipate resistance*

Expect that the recipient might resist changing. Identify possible objections the person might have and develop constructive responses to those objections. Avoid using repelling forces.

G. *Be patient*

Be considerate, understanding, and patient, and do not pressure the recipient to change since change can be difficult for people. It can help to develop an outline in advance.

2. PRESENT THE MESSAGE.

A. Offer a strong benefit

Make it easy for the recipient to change by showing how your message can help solve the problem you identified. Explain how the problem can be solved in a way that appeals to the recipient, is consistent with his/her Psychological Roots, might satisfy the person better than his/her present arrangement, and conveys the message you want the recipient to accept. Some of the ways to create change mentioned at the end of Chapter 25 might also help.

B. It may help to explain the cause of the problem

The chances of persuading might increase if the recipient is willing to understand the cause of the problem and how your solution addresses that cause.

C. Use appealing forces

Present the message only if the recipient is receptive because the message may be resisted if receptivity is not present. Employ appealing forces throughout, such as by helping the recipient feel comfortable and by being caring, considerate, sympathetic, patient, cordial, on the recipient's side, and goals you have in common. Listen sincerely and be respectful, agreeable, sincere, truthful, trustworthy, and helpful. Try to maintain rapport all the way through, including after Stage 3 ends.

It may help to precede the message softly such as by saying, "A possibility occurs to me." If the person is then receptive it can be followed with, "Here's a thought". Consider asking, "What do you think about …?", or "Would you consider …?", "How about this possibility …?".

It may also help to show how the message connects to something the recipient said at a prior time if it is truthful to do so. For example, "As you've mentioned, …". Or, "You said that 'X' is a concern. I've been thinking about it, and an idea occurred to me: ….". Or, "I have an idea about something you brought up. What about if …?"

D. Link the message to a relevant high-order Psychological Root the recipient has

Linking to a recipient's high-order Psychological Root can help people accept a new idea. Doing so also can create a flow-down effect that changes lower-order roots as they come into alignment with the change in the deep root (see Chapter 7 regarding Psychological Root hierarchies). Mentioned earlier are deep roots that everyone is likely to have (e.g., a need for safety, respect, connecting with others, meeting responsibility, protecting a loved one, stability, not being controlled, and a long-term goal). When new information is linked to core roots, the person's surface roots may also change owing to a flow-down effect.

E. Know where you are along the person's Hidden Sequences path as you proceed

Focus on supporting the recipient's pertinent Psychological Roots rather than directly trying to change the person's feelings, emotional reactions, thoughts, opinions, reasoning, decisions, or behavior.

F. Avoid using repelling forces

Try not to use repelling forces since doing so can be a deal-breaker. For some recipients, just being apprised of a different viewpoint is a repelling force. Try to use facts or logic only once; if the recipient does not accept what you are presenting, stop and move on because that message may run counter to that person's Psychological Roots. (Save facts, logic, and evidence for Stage 3, in which those aspects can help to solidify constructive changes that the recipient has made).

Avoid adding negatives, for example, do not tell the recipient what he/she should or should not do, that he/she should change, nor that he/she is wrong. Do not try to persuade when you are irritated and do not contradict the recipient unless he/she invites you to do so. Do not be blunt, demanding, persistent, dominating, controlling, or harsh. Also, do not pressure, argue, or criticize, or use guilt, fear, threats, or punishment. Avoid being condescending, assertive, or controlling. Also do not be impatient, try to win, or be inattentive to the recipient's concerns and non-verbal cues.

G. Use a self-comprehension approach if useful

It may help to provide examples, visual aids, or activities that help the recipient comprehend the issue for himself/herself, such as opportunities for to experience the issue (e.g., through role-playing or imagining a particular scenario). There are times when broad statistics are useful but it can help to describe a single individual's emotional experience because doing so is more tangible and compelling than generalities. Another method would be to ask the recipient open-ended questions in a calm, cordial, and considerate manner. When doing so, allow each question to slowly lead the person to arrive at the desired conclusion on his/her own.

Sometimes it can help to ask questions that widen the person's range of acceptability. For example, "Are there other possibilities that you might consider?" or "Might there be other explanations?"

Another strategy – used with caution and not in a controlling manner – would be to give the recipient an opportunity to choose between alternatives. For example, "Which would seem better to you, '___' or '___'?". When this approach is employed, it should be done in a considerate and non-condescending manner.

If your message is complicated or difficult to understand, consider presenting it in small steps ("successive approximations to the goal", Skinner,

1974). If you do so, start with an aspect that is simple, tangible, and easily understood, then gradually progress from there, with pauses to allow the person to process the information and raise questions.

H. Stop if things are not going well

Be alert to *any* indication of resistance, including those that are not verbal. If the recipient does not appear to accept your message it may be that his/her concerns are not being addressed or are inappropriately being addressed. Should that happen or if the recipient is otherwise not receptive, *stop*. It is possible that pertinent Psychological Roots have not been identified and a thorough and deeper analysis is needed. Try to identify the recipient's issues and concerns, and make adjustments accordingly.

I. Change direction if need be

If nothing seems to work, identify another problem the person has and show how your message solves that problem, or try to connect with a different Psychological Root. If the person still does not accept your viewpoint, identify other problems that trouble the person and other Psychological Roots and consider trying to persuade at another time.

J. If nothing succeeds

If nothing succeeds, end the persuasive attempt and try to lessen tension. Always be cordial and avoid using repelling forces. Change the primary concern to maintaining the relationship, such as by cordially agreeing to disagree.

Consider attempting to persuade at another time. If so, start a new Stage 1 (preparation), including identifying still other Psychological Roots and an even more disturbing problem the recipient has. Develop a plan for how your message can solve that problem. Present your new message in a way that is in accord with the recipient's pertinent Psychological Roots.

K. If the renewed attempt does not succeed, stop

If the attempt at persuading does not succeed, try to create a win-win solution. Doing this is can be more effective than trying to persuade (as in the 'Driving debacle' example in Chapter 21 in which a family was asked to stop trying to convince a person not to drive).

3. SOLIDIFY.

A person who is persuaded might return to a previous viewpoint ('*backsliding*'). Backsliding can sometimes occur at a later time because an inconsistency occurs with a Psychological Root somewhere in the recipient's vast network of root hierarchies and clusters. Also, the person might have received only part of the message, has misunderstood some aspects, or some ambiguities are attached to it. Therefore, try to clarify and strengthen whatever gain has occurred.

A. Give social support

Sincerely compliment the recipient for something, such as his/her having raised an interesting question, helping you clarify the issue, having noticed something special, or for being a good conversationalist. Do not take credit for the recipient's acceptance of the message and do not be condescending.

B. Review

If appropriate, useful, and accepted by the recipient, it might help to review the main points. Be careful, since repeating what has been said before is not always necessary and might be overkill that could turn off the person.

C. Clarify misunderstandings.

Expect that the recipient might have some misunderstandings and that some aspects of the message, presentation, or grasp of the circumstance might contain ambiguities, errors, or other undesirable aspects. Ask the person if he/she has questions if it is appropriate and useful to do so. Be open to objections and answer cordially and patiently without any repelling forces. Address every aspect in a way that is acceptable to the recipient.

D. Provide additional information

If helpful, add evidence, facts, logic, or new information that supports the change that the recipient has made. (If facts and logic had been presented initially it would have opposed the person's viewpoint at that time and therefore could have been a substantial repelling force.)

E. Forget the past

Avoid putting the recipient in the position of wanting to defend his/her initial position because that could lead him/her to reconsider or even return to that viewpoint. Hence, do not mention the recipient's previous viewpoint and do not even imply that the recipient was mistaken to have held that viewpoint.

F. Support using the new idea

Invite the person to use the new idea, such as by asking the person how he/she might do so. Suggest some ways that the person could use the new perspective, if appropriate and useful to do so. Consider giving the recipient written self-reminders, but only if it is acceptable, useful, desired, and appropriate.

The bottom line:

The above-mentioned three-stage method of social influence – *Prepare, Present,* and *Solidify* – offers the recipient a way to solve a bothersome problem in a way that the recipient comfortably accepts. The solution that the communicator suggests includes the change the communicator would like the recipient to make. The chance of the recipient being persuaded is related to his/her perception of benefit – the greater the benefit compared to the perceived drawbacks the greater the likelihood that the recipient will accept making the desired change.

The communicator should be prepared for the possibility that persuasion might not occur. Persuasiveness is aided by the communicator being sincerely caring, helpful, and sensitive to the recipient and his/her concerns. This method is one in which everyone gains and can lessen the amount of frustration, energy, and time that might otherwise occur.

Chapter 27. PSYCHOTHERAPY
(The glossary may be useful for some of the terms that appear in this chapter.)

Psychotherapy might seem mysterious, but Psychological Systems Theory offers an understanding of it that is readily grasped. This chapter discusses some of the basic issues, often drawing upon depression and anxiety for examples. The focus is on helping the person change the subconscious causes of his/her problems rather than on what he/she did, felt, or thought.

The puzzle

People with psychological disorders can be a puzzle to themselves and others. A person may be anxious without knowing why, or depressed and not know how to pull out of it, or enraged without being able to control his/her anger. A major reason people are unlikely to understand their condition is that the causes of their internal reactions and behavior occur at sub-aware levels. As a result, what people do may seem inappropriate, irrational, or unjustifiable, sometimes even to themselves. Thus, a depressed individual might remain in bed – yet realize that his not being employed worsens his problems. An anxious student might procrastinate in studying for an exam – yet understand that her not studying increases the likelihood of her doing poorly. Addicted persons might continue their counterproductive behavior – while recognizing that doing so worsens their life and does not solve their underlying issues. Also puzzling is that people with psychological disorders can be normal and well-adjusted much of the time, yet disordered at a few other times. For example, many people with a borderline personality disorder can look normal, intelligent, attractive, and effective, so cannot understand why many people dislike them.

Behavior can be illogical when viewed objectively, yet the author has found that an *internal* logic exists. That logic becomes clear upon uncovering the sub-surface Psychological Roots that are involved. For example, a depressed person's remaining in bed might be due to his believing that there are no solutions to his problems. An anxious student might procrastinate because she postpones addressing problems she feels inadequate to address and dreads. An addicted individual might believe that he cannot function without his 'fix'. People with a borderline personality disorder may believe that they are justified in being irritable and hostile because of the way they were treated. Beliefs are Psychological Roots. Behavior that results from a person's beliefs is not always socially appropriate, effective, or task-efficient.

People's thinking, emotional reactions, and behavior stem from their Psychological Roots. Thus, from a Psychological Systems Theory perspective, behavior is internally logical. When the relevant subconscious processes are unearthed, such as pertinent Psychological Roots, the chain of elements that stems from that originating point also becomes clear. The author has always found that there is an internal logic that underlies objectively irrational or counterproductive behavior, which can be understood when the Psychological Roots and other hidden aspects that led to that behavior are unearthed, including stimulus conditions. Psychological Systems Theory therefore considers behavior that is objectively illogical to be the outcome of a rational process operating below the surface.

This perspective makes a distinction between internal logic that is hidden from observers because it takes place below the surface, and the logic of observers who consider a person's reactions or other behavior to be irrational from an objective standpoint. This understanding explains why objective logic is not always in accord with an individual's subjective logic. When a person's subjective processes are sufficiently understood, the logic that underlies that person's behavior should explain instances of puzzling thinking or behavior perceived by other people. This realization does not mean that the person is correct or effective, nor that his/her errant behavior should be accepted, only that the cause of that behavior is a logical process based on the person's Psychological Roots and other sub-surface aspects.

Distinguishing between subjective and objective logic is important because treating psychologically-caused behaviors can be more effective when important hidden aspects are uncovered, compared to focusing on symptoms, behaviors, emotional reactions, and people's verbal statements. There also are some psychological outcomes that stem from hidden biological processes such as genetic anomalies, brain damage, glandular problems, microbial disease, nutritional deficiency, chemical poisoning, medicinal side effects, and severe fatigue.

This point of view – that a person's underlying psychological processes are logical even when his/her overt behavior is illogical or counterproductive – contrasts with a belief that emotions are irrational and that humans act illogically. Having a rationally-based perspective sets the stage for addressing psychological conditions systematically and logically rather than haphazardly or without a blueprint. Thus, Psychological Systems Theory views common psychological disorders – such as depression, anxiety, and rage – as being understandable and capable of rational treatment. (See Spike's violent behavior in Chapter 18 and the psychotherapy cases described in Chapter 28.)

A paradigm for understanding some psychological disorders
Mentioned previously is that everyone – not just an individual with a psychological disorder – has trouble with negatives such as failure, insults, criticism, and threats. Also, according to Psychological Systems Theory, everyone is capable of states of uncontrollability. Those states can be predicted since they are normal occurrences that result from certain extreme conditions. For example, tension-inducing circumstances can generate anxiety, and when anxiety becomes overwhelming, it can spill over into a state of panic. Feeling like a failure can lead to a down mood, which can progress to dysthymia, and, if a person feels sufficiently overwhelmed, he/she could tip over into depression. Annoyance can build to anger and from there to rage. Cumulative build-up frequently occurs.

From the standpoint of Psychological Systems Theory, the above-mentioned circumstances are predictable and have the potential to occur in everyone. In that sense, common psychological disorders like depression and anxiety are a normal outcome when the type of conditions that lead to them are sufficiently extreme.

Psychological disorders can involve cognitions, emotions, physiology, and behavior including aspects such as dissociation, confusion, dysthymia, tension, rage, and anti-social behaviors. Preceding those outcomes are internal reactions (see the discussion of Hidden Sequences in Chapter 4). The stronger an internal reaction, the greater the likelihood that overt behavior associated with that reaction will occur. As a result, some people who often feel very tense or anxious are likely to panic more frequently than others who are not frequently prone to those reactions. Some people who often have strong depression, anxiety, borderline personality disorder, bipolar disorder, PTSD, eating disorders, phobias or other dysthymic feelings are likely to become depressed more frequently than others who do not have those experiences. Also, some people who are easily irritated are likely to be enraged more frequently than others who are not readily annoyed.

Medications that treat biological aspects of disorders, such as serotonin levels, can lessen symptoms. However, pharmaceuticals do not change Psychological Roots such as beliefs and expectations. In Hidden Sequences, biological reactions are an intermediate aspect (see Chapter 4), but those reactions can be caused psychologically. In such instances, psychologically-caused conditions can be treated by modifying the Psychological Roots that originate those disorders, also the stimulus conditions that impact those roots. Thus, pharmaceuticals can be a helpful adjunctive treatment for psychologically-caused conditions, but not necessarily the primary treatment.

Similarly, psychological therapy can be an adjunctive treatment for biologically-based conditions, but not be the primary treatment.

Overview of Psychological Systems Therapy

Psychological Systems Theory views psychological processes as being systematic, logical, and understandable. Viewed through this lens, everything psychological must make sense, a perspective that greatly helps when trying to decipher puzzling behavior. (See Nell's bridge phobia in Chapter 28 that seemed to arise out of nowhere, also see Spike's violent behavior in Chapter 18 that had not yielded to many years of traditional therapies, including medication). When a behavior is not explained by what has been uncovered in a thorough psychological analysis, other causes should be sought, such as those that are biological, sociological/societal, chemical, or environmental.

Since Psychological Roots are considered the starting point for internal reactions and overt behaviors in Hidden Sequences, a major focus in Psychological Systems Therapy is ascertaining what the pertinent Psychological Roots are and then modifying them, also changing the stimulus conditions that impact those roots or learning how to cope with them. There are times when complications arise because of the extensive number of Psychological Roots, the complexity of root hierarchies and clusters, and a client's difficulty in making effective changes. (See the discussion of Psychological Roots' hierarchical alignment in Chapter 7.)

Resistance might be encountered when trying to directly change some elements, such as surface and intermediate roots, internal reactions, and overt behavior. As a result, it can help to identify deep roots and attach improvements to them because doing so effectively can create substantial flow-down effects on other elements such as those mentioned above. Flow-down effects are related to the *'centrality principle'* which states that one or a few core aspects are at the foundation of what is observed on the surface.

Mentioned earlier was that in psychotherapy it is not sufficient to know general Psychological Roots that pertain to many individuals, rather it is essential to identify the specific Psychological Roots that create problems for each individual client. The author has found that understanding some pertinent Psychological Roots can often be obtained quickly. Hence, it is often rapidly possible to construct an initial therapeutic strategy for common psychological problems. The author has found that when clients understand the hidden nature of the processes that explain their problems, their tension lessens and their receptivity for change increases. Understanding the subconscious processes involved typically points to a solution about what might be done, such as what particular distress-prone Psychological Roots need to be modified (e.g., expectations and emotional thresholds), also the stimuli that need to be addressed.

Clients' concerns can be prioritized, which permits the most salient issues to be addressed quickly, often starting in the first session. Past stimulus conditions are important but an extensive examination of them is typically not needed if the most pertinent Psychological Roots that stemmed from them are identified. Those roots often can be addressed as soon as they become clear.

Among the aspects addressed in therapy are strategies the client can use for solving his/her problems such as how to lessen distress, create win-win solutions, and avoid turning people off. Doing these things gives clients an opportunity to obtain control of aspects that previously had been unknown to them and out of their control. The author has found such knowledge to be invaluable to clients. (Some frequently occurring distress-prone Psychological Roots are listed at the end of Chapter 16. See Box 7 for Psychological Roots that the author has frequently found in psychological disorders.)

Durability of psychotherapeutic changes

There is a varied length of time that the constructive changes made in psychotherapy last. For some people, the changes last a lifetime or are able to remain in place because the client reviews them frequently or periodically. For other people, a change exists for just a short time or is applied to just an immediate situation rather than being incorporated into their general lifestyle.

Some changes in psychotherapy might not last long because of the following:

1. A general resistance to change that is wired into everyone.
2. Deep Psychological Roots that remain in place for a long time, perhaps a lifetime.
3. A person might want to obtain relief only for a specific circumstance.
4. The changes made for one circumstance are not applied to other circumstances.
5. The person may need to return to previously existing psychological aspects (e.g., having extremely high standards may be needed in some circumstances).
6. The person might associate with people or other circumstances for which his/her earlier psychological patterns are the norm or are required.

Receptivity

Change is often difficult for people, especially for deeply embedded aspects. Since only the target person can make changes in himself/herself, it is essential that the client be willing to improve. Therefore, it is important for the therapist to have rapport with the client. The three-stage approach to social influence (described in Chapter 26) can help, also the other three-stage methods related to communicating and resolving conflicts (see Chapters 24 and 22, respectively). For couples, strategies for resolving conflicts, communicating effectively, and persuasion are especially important.

Stimulus conditions

It is important for clients to obtain effective methods for understanding and coping with distressing stimulus conditions. Sometimes a particular stimulus can be so strong that it might seem to be the culprit. However, Psychological Systems Theory suggests that the reason stimuli have their effect is that they impact Psychological Roots and thus fall on fertile ground. Hence, even when a stimulus is powerful, it is often wise to search for the pertinent Psychological Roots the stimulus impacts. In this perspective, psychological problems are not entirely situational. (See Amory's case in Chapter 30 and the discussion of situational vs. chronic depression a little later in this chapter.) Therefore, in addition to the value of addressing harmful stimulus conditions effectively, healing is likely to require modifying some Psychological Roots as well. It is also useful to know that a stimulus condition can have multiple aspects and therefore more than one Psychological Root might be important to identify.

BOX 7a. SOME FACTORS HYPOTHESIZED TO RELATE TO PSYCHOLOGICAL DISORDERS
(In alphabetical order by condition)

Addiction – A strong habit with physiological and psychological craving, often due to a desire to lessen distress.
Some distress-prone Psychological Roots may be (e.g., difficult-to-meet expectations, poor problem-solving strategies, pessimism, a low threshold for emotional arousal).

Anxiety attack/panic – Being overwhelmed by threat. Some distress- prone Psychological Roots are a low threshold for emotional arousal, belief of vulnerability, difficult-to-meet expectations, pessimism, and poor social or problem-solving strategies.
Some internal reactions include tension, impatience, ruminating, and worrying.

Bipolar disorder 1 – Extreme and sometimes sudden mood swings between depression and manic behavior. Some Psychological Roots contributing to volatility include low arousal threshold, and strong drive for closure.
See depression for relevant Psychological Roots and behaviors.
Some internal reactions include feeling overwhelmed by failure, disappointment, or rejection, compartmentalization, impatience, rigidity, extremeness, thinking in absolutes, and a lack of interest in life.

Bipolar disorder 2 – Symptoms and Psychological Roots are similar to borderline personality disorder (see next panel) and there is a debate about whether this may be the same condition as that disorder.

***

* Intensifiers that can heighten psychological conditions include thinking in absolutes, focusing on tangibles, emotion, and need for closure.

297

BOX 7b, *continued*. SOME FACTORS
HYPOTHESIZED TO RELATE TO
PSYCHOLOGICAL DISORDERS
(In alphabetical order by condition)

Borderline personality disorder – Easily triggered irritability with counterproductive interpersonal behavior that can seem immature.

Some distress-prone Psychological Roots include a low threshold for negative emotional arousal, difficult-to-meet expectations, intolerance of being controlled, distrust of others, unwillingness to admit being wrong, poor social skills, poor problem-solving strategies, believing that there is no solution to their problems, weak ability to understand or empathize with other individuals, strong drive for closure, and believing that retaliation is appropriate.

Some internal reactions include feeling abandoned, emotionally deprived, victimized, and taken advantage of.

Some behaviors are strong resistance to change, narcissism, externalizing when injured (such as complaining, blaming others, being retaliatory, and treating others harshly) because of feeling helpless and overwhelmed by negatives.

Some internal reactions include feeling overwhelmed by failure, disappointment, or rejection, belief that they are vulnerable, impatience, rigidity, extremeness, and a lack of interest in life.

Some overt behaviors include lethargy, staying in bed for long periods, inability to hold a job, and not acting preventively.

Some past stimulus conditions include abuse and abandonment.

Depression – Inability to cope and function normally because of feeling helpless and overwhelmed by negatives.

Some distress-prone Psychological Roots include difficult-to-meet expectations, strong drive for closure, poor social and problem-solving strategies, strong need for closure, and believing that there is no solution to problems.

Some internal reactions are feeling overwhelmed by failure, disappointment, or rejection, impatience, rigidity, extremeness, feeling vulnerable, and a lack of interest.

Some overt behaviors include lethargy, staying in bed, inability to hold a job, and not acting preventively.

298

BOX 7c, *continued*. SOME FACTORS
HYPOTHESIZED TO RELATE TO
PSYCHOLOGICAL DISORDERS
(In alphabetical order by condition)

Depression – Inability to cope and function normally because of feeling helpless and overwhelmed by negatives.

Some Psychological Roots include difficult-to-meet expectations, strong drive for closure, poor problem-solving or social skills, and believing that there is no solution to their problems.

Some internal reactions include feeling overwhelmed by failure, disappointment, or rejection, feeling vulnerable, impatience, rigidity, extremeness, and a lack of interest.

Some overt behaviors include lethargy, staying in bed for long periods, inability to hold a job, and not acting preventively.

Obsessive-compulsive disorder – Adherence to a counterproductive thought or behavior, often doing so repetitively.

Some Psychological Roots are difficult-to-meet expectations, low threshold for emotional arousal, poor problem-solving strategies, and belief that doing a particular behavior wards off unpleasantness.

Some internal reactions include perfectionism, ruminating, and worrying.

Rage – Extreme hostile behavior that sometimes is violent.

Some Psychological Roots include difficult-to-meet expectations, a low threshold for emotional arousal, intolerance of being controlled, unwillingness to be wrong, poor social and problem-solving strategies, and belief that aggression and use of power are appropriate.

Some internal reactions include easily feeling hurt, unwillingness to accept being wrong, belief that others are the cause of their problems, thinking in absolutes, and strong resistance to change.

Some overt behaviors include externalizing when injured (e.g., blaming others, treating others harshly, retaliating).

Feelings and thoughts

People's feelings (e.g., anger, frustration, disappointment) and dysfunctional thoughts (e.g., "There are no solutions to my problems", "People don't like me") are internal reactions in Hidden Sequences. Thoughts and feelings are intermediate aspects in Hidden Sequences and therefore proximal causes rather than originating causes.

People can often experience some relief by venting their intense thoughts and emotions, however doing so does not solve the originating causes of their problems and therefore can provide only temporary relief. A further concern is that a client's venting of negative feelings and thoughts – such as anger, frustration, disappointment, and complaints – can upset other people, which could worsen a client's problems. So, although venting is understandable as a release, the idea that "feeling is healing", is insufficient.

Understanding the Psychological Roots that lead to dysfunctional thoughts and feelings offers a basis for changing thoughts and feelings. Modifying, satisfying, or changing the causative Psychological Roots and stimulus conditions is a major way to lessen a person's distress.

Constructive beliefs sometimes can become dysfunctional

It is possible that a constructive belief can be dysfunctional at times. For example, taking responsibility is worthwhile, but when people believe that they have not met that standard, they can experience guilt, anxiety, and dysthymia. Such negative reactions are especially possible when a person's sense of responsibility is absolute. High expectations are another example of aspects which are constructive at times but can be inappropriate when perfection is counterproductive, such as when Mary demands that Jon should adhere to her expectations without taking his concerns into account.

It is not easy for people to solve psychological issues

People with psychological problems can resist addressing their difficulties, sometimes because they believe that nothing can help them or that psychology cannot understand, cause, or treat their problems. Some people resist counseling because they believe that their problems are strictly biological and some resist because they are concerned about being stigmatized if they receive psychological help. Some people refuse to admit being inadequate or wrong or are concerned that they might be embarrassed or controlled. Some people believe that they can solve their problems and improve without depending on others, and some people believe that certain other people cause their difficulties. Some believe that they know themselves better than anyone else or that no one else can understand their issues, and some people have no confidence in psychology. Some people begin counseling but do not persevere.

It is understandable that people want to solve their problems by themselves. However, as in every discipline, special knowledge can be indispensable. The author has found that it is often essential to understand the subconscious psychological systems involved and how to create effective change (e.g., using Psychological Systems Therapy), which is not easily done even by professionals. The more people know how the mind works, such as the concepts in Psychological Systems Theory, the more effective they can be in solving their problems. It takes more than ability to identify the Psychological Roots involved because it can be difficult to change those roots. Even if a person successfully modifies his/her Psychological Roots at Time 1, he/she may not be able to do so at Time 2.

Psychotherapeutic skills

Psychotherapists are concerned about their clients' welfare and tend to be empathetic, caring, non-judgmental, and often able to provide explanations of abstract psychological aspects. They are frequently are good at helping people overcome their resistance to change, confront their issues, and cope with distressing stimulus conditions. Many counselors are flexible, eclectic, and have a good "bedside manner". Employing Psychological Systems Therapy requires additional abilities, such as skill in identifying Psychological Roots and knowing how to help clients modify those factors. Other skills include using the three-stage approach for constructive change, psychotherapy, win-win solutions, and not using repelling forces.

Are biological factors the originating cause of psychological reactions?

For some psychological disorders there are biological causes, such as autism (a genetic disorder) and brain damage (due to traumas, toxins, infections, or nutritional deficiencies). Neurotransmitters (e.g., serotonin) play an important role in psychological disorders as biological internal reactions in Hidden Sequences. Evidence that depressed individuals who committed suicide had decreased serotonin levels (Stockmeier, Shapiro, Dilley, Kolli, Friedman, & Rajkowska, 1998), has led to a belief that a chemical imbalance causes depression, although that idea has been challenged (e.g., by France, Lysaker, & Robinson, 2007). In Psychological Systems Theory, a changed serotonin level is an internal reaction in a Hidden Sequence and thus a proximal cause of psychologically-caused depression rather than the originating cause.

Psychological Systems Theory suggests that many psychological conditions – such as anxiety, depression, obsessive-compulsive disorder, and borderline personality disorder – are often caused psychologically. In a psychological Hidden Sequence, the starting point is a Psychological Root. Genetic Psychological Roots (e.g., needs for safety and avoiding negative arousal) are always involved because they are foundations of root-hierarchies. Acquired Psychological Roots (e.g., beliefs, goals, expectations, concerns, and interests) contribute to the formation of those hierarchies. Some acquired roots that are deep roots include a person's basic values that are attached to or near a genetic root. Some acquired roots at the end of a root hierarchy are near the surface. Intermediate roots are situated between deep and surface roots (see Chapter 7 for a discussion of Psychological Root hierarchies).

Some people consider psychological factors to be too insubstantial to cause disturbances such as anxiety attacks, depression, and addiction, yet there is considerable evidence of their potency. For instance, psychological aspects can produce substantial biological outcomes (e.g., Ciompi & Panksepp, 2005). Examples include heart attacks and death from distress, a powerful increase in adrenalin due to fear, and an increase of fatty acids in the blood stream that result from stress (Brehm, Back, & Bogdonoff, 1964). Psychological stress (e.g., due to anger) is a major cause of severe back pain, even more than many physical causes (Bigo, Baowyer, Braen, et al., 1994). Depression is associated with failure (e.g., Beck & Ward, 1961; Klein, Fencil-Morse, & Seligman (1976); Warren & McEachren, 1977; Coyne & Gotlib, 1983; Billings, Cronkite, & Moos, 1983).[41] Also, psychotherapy has often been found to be equal in potency to medication or even more effective (e.g., Butler, Chapman, Forman, & Beck, 2006). In short, there is substantial physical evidence that psychological aspects can produce strong biological and biochemical effects.

Medications, including antidepressants and anti-anxiolytics, have an important role in health care and are especially important for treating acute situations and biologically-caused disorders such as dementia. Medications can also help people who do not desire psychotherapy or who are not able to obtain or make use of it. In such cases, medical interventions are the preferred treatment. However, in cases where medicines provide only temporary relief of a psychological disorder or do not work, or when symptoms exacerbate while a person is taking medicine for that condition, consideration should be given to the possibility that the originating cause is not being addressed. In such

---

[41] The author has also found that failure often is a key factor in depression in his clinical practice and pilot research studies.

instances, what is being treated may be an internal reaction rather than the originating cause, which might be psychological. Believing that medication is treating the originating cause of a disorder when it is treating an intermediate aspect can delay, impede, or prevent receiving more effective treatment. Medications can also have side effects and medicines can lose effectiveness after a while, some interfere with the body's defenses, many have strong side effects, and some have a potential for addiction.

The treatment of choice for common psychological disorders

When a problem arises it is important to address the cause, especially when harm occurs, such as happens with addiction, criminality, and violence. When Psychological Roots are the key causes, non-psychological interventions such as drugs are unlikely to correct the situation since they do not address psychological aspects such as beliefs, goals, concerns, or expectations.

A question arises about some frequently occurring psychological disorders such as anxiety, depression, and obsessive-compulsive disorder. Is the originating cause biological (e.g., a chemical imbalance) or psychological (such as Psychological Roots or the impact of stimulus conditions on Psychological Roots)? This issue comes down to the question of what causes a chemical imbalance in the brain. Also, why would huge numbers of humans around the world have a biological anomaly? The answer to that question is not known, however, biochemical changes occur during an intermediate stage of psychological Hidden Sequences. Therefore there is a possibility that chemical imbalances – such as in serotonin, dopamine, and norepinephrine neurotransmitters – could be due to something psychological. Perhaps a similar circumstance occurs in other psychological conditions especially with those in which there are strong emotional reactions such as anger, bipolar disorders 1 and 2, borderline personality disorder, and post-traumatic stress disorder.

If psychological Hidden Sequences are involved, then using medication for those psychologically-caused conditions treats symptoms rather than the cause. (Discussed previously was that medications treat internal reactions in Hidden Sequences, according to Psychological Systems Theory). Appropriate treatment will be delayed or prevented if the treatment is medical but the cause is psychological.

Here is an abbreviated list of some biological circumstances that result from psychological causes:

. Biochemical effects of psychological aspects (e.g., Brehm, Back, & Bogdonoff, 1964; Ciompi & Panksepp, 2005).
. Medical disorders due to stress such as heart attacks, death, blindness, and paralysis (e.g., Akagi & House, 2001, regarding conversion disorders).

. Psychotherapy's equal or greater effectiveness than medication in treating depression (e.g., Butler, Chapman, Forman, & Beck, 2006).

. The role of failure in depression (e.g., Beck & Ward, 1961; Warren & McEachren, 1977; Coyne & Gotlib, 1983; Billings, Cronkite, & Moos, 1983).

. Flare-ups in psychological disorders that occur while people take medication for those conditions, which should not occur if the medicine is treating the cause.

Psychological Systems Therapy has been successful with some conditions that are considered to require medical treatment but in which medical therapies have not worked well. (See Spike's violent behavior in Chapter 18 and cases of depression and anxiety in Chapter 28). For example, in the case of depression and anxiety, clients have improved with Psychological Systems Therapy, often rapidly, when their distress-prone Psychological Roots are modified, such as hard-to-meet expectations and standards, pessimism, a low threshold for negative emotional arousal, expecting that their problems cannot be solved, and believing that there is no hope for them.

The bottom line: Some common psychological conditions such as depression, anxiety, and anger may be due principally to psychological causes and therefore can benefit from treatment that is psychological. Medication might help lessen symptoms in such cases, and be the primary therapy in conditions that are caused biologically or do not yield to psychological intervention.

Signs of some psychological conditions

Anxiety and panic: being extremely anxious, agitated, feeling threatened easily, worrying, thinking poorly, high sensitivity, and high reactiveness. A major cause is having a low threshold for negative emotional arousal, according to Psychological Systems Theory. Pessimism and having expectations and standards that are not easily met can also contribute to anxiety.

Bipolar disorder: Extreme mood swings that range from being manic or extremely joyful to being depressed. Depression is much more common than upbeat moods. A major cause is a low threshold for negative emotional arousal in combination with the major cause of depression (feeling overwhelmed because of distress-prone Psychological Roots are not being satisfied, such as pessimism, hard to satisfy expectations and standards, and poor problem-solving strategies), according to Psychological Systems Theory.

Borderline personality disorder (BPD): counterproductive interpersonal behavior that makes a person difficult to be with and feel a need to "walk on egg shells" when with them. (The term 'borderline' refers to explosive episodes that sometimes happen in someone who appears to function normally otherwise.) Many borderlines feel highly vulnerable, victimized, emotionally deprived, and defensive (sometimes due to abandonment or other traumas such as sexual or emotional abuse). They may take things personally, complain frequently (e.g., saying "why me?" or "woe is me"), and be egocentric. Many BPDs do not trust others, have suspicions about others' intentions, and easily-triggered irritability. They often have great difficulty accepting being wrong, blame others rather than taking responsibility for their actions, and cannot tolerate feeling abandoned

   Their not accepting being wrong leads them to resist changing and improving. Many of them have difficult-to-meet expectations, are impatient, act impulsively, want to control others, and cross others' boundaries. Some readily point out others' flaws, are verbally aggressive, hold grudges, and remain irritated for long periods. They can be vindictive and create turmoil, and some are explosively angry and physically aggressive. Many BPDs lack empathy and understanding of other people, and do not reciprocate support given them or why others dislike them. Many borderlines feel entitled to express their irritation and criticize someone, lie or cheat, but do not accept anyone acting that way to them. Some BPDs are oppositional, paranoid, or have multiple lawsuits and court cases. As a consequence, many people with borderline personality are disliked and have few close friends

   Borderlines might not be diagnosed as having a borderline personality disorder but rather as depressed, bipolar, suicidal, or as having PTSD, OCD, or oppositional defiance disorder. They might have several such disorders. The Diagnostic And Statistical Manual (DSM V) calls for at least five of the following nine aspects for a diagnosis of BPD: Extreme emotional swings, explosive anger, intense fear of rejection/abandonment leading to frantic efforts to maintain a relationship, impulsiveness, self-harm, unstable self-concept (not really knowing who they are), chronic feelings of emptiness (often leading to excessive drinking/eating, etc, to fill the vacuum), dissociation (feeling disconnected from reality), and intense, highly volatile relationships.

Many BPD individuals resist improving and obtaining counseling because they cannot accept being wrong and view other people as the problem rather than themselves. Some BPDs who obtain counseling use it to vent extensively about what other people do to them, have difficulty accepting their faults and resist making personal changes. However, those who make constructive change in themselves greatly improve their lives and the lives of others.

Some of the characteristics of BPDs mentioned above occur in people who are diagnosed with bipolar-2 disorder, which has led to the hypothesis that the two conditions are the same. A question also arises about whether the factors that contribute to chronic depression are easily triggered distress-prone Psychological Roots and few eustress-prone (pleasure-producing) Psychological Roots to counteract those negatively-oriented roots.

Dysthymia and depression: feeling overwhelmed because distress-prone Psychological Roots are not being satisfied, such as pessimism, hard to satisfy expectations and standards, and poor problem-solving strategies), according to Psychological Systems Theory. Depression is manifested by a long-lasting down mood and somber perspective, being lethargic with very little energy to accomplish things that they might otherwise readily do, having ineffective solutions, quickly giving up on problems, complaining a great deal, and being pessimistic. From a Psychological Systems Theory perspective, reasons for depression are distress-prone Psychological Roots that are easily triggered, with few or no eustress-prone (pleasure-producing) Psychological Roots to counteract the effect of those negative roots.

Obsessive-compulsive disorder (OCD): Having a narrow tolerance for some things and not deviating from an idea even when there is no objective reason for holding onto it. The person might experience a need to perform every element of an exercise routine every time in the same order with the same number of repetitions (an instance of thinking in absolutes). If that routine does not happen, the person feels uncomfortable and anxious. Other examples of OCD behavior are frequent worrying, ruminating, or obsessing. (See the prior discussion regarding anxiety.)

Post-traumatic stress disorder (PTSD): The re-experiencing of a powerful negative experience, such as fear or abuse. For example, an unrelated stimulus can suddenly trigger remembrance of a past trauma. Sometimes a traumatic memory can occur by itself without any apparent external stimulus. PTSD symptoms can include anxiety, panic, hyper-vigilance, startle responses, sleeping problems, concentration difficulties, irritability, and social or occupational impairment. (See the prior discussion regarding anxiety.)

Situational depression vs. chronic depression

'Situational depression' is a type of depression thought to be caused by an external stimulus. In Psychological Systems Theory, the reason a stimulus has an effect is because it impacts at least one Psychological Root in a Stimulus-and-Root Hidden Sequence. If so, situational depression does not act alone, rather it is a combination of a stimulus with at least one Psychological Root.

'Chronic depression' is a type of depression thought to be caused by intrinsic psychological factors. That circumstance is a Root Sequence in Psychological Systems Theory, that is, no external stimulus is involved.

In Psychological Systems Theory, Psychological Roots are affected by stimulus conditions. If so, it may be that a person diagnosed with chronic depression could at times become depressed because of a stimulus. If this possibility is correct, chronic depression can provide the basis for a Stimulus-and-Root Sequence. (See Amory's example in Chapter 30.)

This perspective suggests that distress-prone Psychological Roots might be involved in both situational and chronic depression. If so, stimulus conditions might generate depressive episodes in people who have chronic depression, and people who have situational depression might experience chronic depression at times. Thus, whether a person's depression is primarily situational or chronic might be related to whether or not stimulus conditions are involved at the time.

The number and intensity of distress-prone Psychological Roots would also be a factor. For example, a distressing situation might be strong enough to cause some people to become depressed but not strong enough to cause others to be depressed.

In short, situational and chronic depression may be the same condition. Whether a situation stands out as the cause or the chronic aspect is the primary issue may depend on the circumstances. An implication of this inference is that when people seem to have situational depression, distress-prone Psychological Roots in those individuals should be identified and treated nevertheless. Also, when people appear to have chronic depression, distressing stimulus conditions that might contribute to depression in those individuals should be identified and addressed nevertheless.

Post-partum depression

Depression that some mothers experience might be due to a substantial change in their hormone levels after giving birth. However, every mother experiences such substantial hormone changes after a child is born, therefore if post-partum depression was caused largely or entirely by hormones, the rate of that occurrence should be far higher than 10 to 15% (CDC, 2008). This perspective suggests that additional factors may contribute to post-partum depression.

The author has found that some new mothers with post-partum depression believe that they might fail at parenting, do not feel adequate to meet the responsibilities required or are reluctant to do so, or do not believe that they have much to offer their child. Some women feel overloaded by the tasks involved, and some are upset about changes in their lifestyle or appearance. Sometimes problems occur in their relationship with the man in their life or with their families. Feeling overwhelmed by negatives can trigger depression, according to Psychological Systems Theory. (See the discussion of Psychological Homeostasis and states of uncontrollability in Chapters 1, 2 and 3.)

Some women with post-partum depression were depressed, greatly distressed, or possessed substantial distress-prone Psychological Roots before they were pregnant. Some mothers are cigarette smokers, which may be because they had been dealing with distress before they became pregnant.

Therefore, post-partum depression might seem to be purely an instance of biologically-caused situational depression, but the hormone changes often might be an additional factor that pushes women who are depression-prone past their tipping point into depression. Since psychological factors are always present they should be part of the analysis.

Dual diagnosis and common distress-prone roots

A person can have two or more disorders simultaneously. A possibility might be that a disorder acts as a stimulus that triggers another disorder. For example, some depressed individuals might feel threatened by the prospect that their depression will continue, which creates anxiety. Some anxious individuals' inability to cope with their circumstances might lead to their feeling sufficiently overwhelmed to be depressed.

Another possibility is that some of the same distress-prone Psychological Roots underlie more than one psychological condition (e.g., a low threshold for negative arousal, hard-meet-expectations, poor problem-solving strategies, and pessimism). Also, some distress-prone factors are more salient than others, depending on the individual and the circumstances. For example, in depression, hard-to-meet expectations and pessimism may be particularly important, whereas, in anxiety, a low threshold for negative arousal and a strong need for safety may be key. In bipolar disorder, low threshold for negative arousal and hard-to-meet expectations might have a strong presence, while in obsessive-compulsive disorder, poor problem-solving strategies, pessimism, and a belief that the person is vulnerable might be substantial as well as hard-to-meet expectations and a low threshold for negative arousal. Thus, while some of the same Psychological Roots might be present in different conditions, different outcomes result because:

a) Some factors are not present in some conditions,
b) Some Psychological Roots exist at different strengths,
c) Different stimulus conditions trigger different reactions,
d) The diagnosis might shift when the Psychological Roots change (e.g., when some are added, subtracted, intensified, or diminished), and
e) The diagnosis might shift when the stimulus conditions change (e.g., when some stimuli are added, subtracted, intensified, or diminished).

As an example, some often-occurring Psychological Roots in borderline personality disorder include strong sense of vulnerability, inability to accept being wrong, and believing that anger is appropriate. Some depression-prone Psychological Roots, mentioned earlier, might also exist in those individuals. If so, Psychological Roots would help explain why people with borderline personality disorder s are depressed at times.

Psychological disorders other than those mentioned here also might have some Psychological Roots in common. Perhaps that circumstance is why mass murderers and Jihadist killers appear to have some similarities (see Hauslohner, Achenbach, & Nakashima, 2016). (A list of distress-prone Psychological Roots are at the end of Chapter 16. See Chapter 2 for a discussion of precursors and Chapter 32 for a discussion of predicting and preventing disorders.)

Addiction
Addictions generate a powerful demand to be satisfied, giving the appearance of having a life of their own. Addictions can originate for biological or psychological reasons. Examples of biological circumstances include some prescribed medicines (e.g., benzodiazepines for anxiety and opiates for pain), and some non-prescribed substances (e.g., marihuana and alcohol). An example is a newborn's addiction to alcohol due to its mother's drinking during her pregnancy or during the period in which the infant is

breast fed. Psychological causes include methods used by people to cope with distress such as heroin, marihuana, cigarettes, and food. Biological and psychological causes are often intertwined, for example, biologically-addictive substances such as opiates and marihuana can relieve psychological distress, and psychologically-addictive behaviors such as video games and gambling can distract a person's attention from pain.

Internal biological aspects of addictions occur when the cause is psychological, even for aspects that do not involve ingesting substances. Examples include video games, gambling, and nail-biting (e.g., Conrad, Ford, Marinelli, & Wolf, 2010; Navarro, Quiroz, Moreno-Delgado, Sierakowiak, McDowell, Moreno, Realize, Cai, Aguinaga, Howell, Hausch, Cortés, Mallol, Casadó, Lluís, Canela, Ferré, & McCormick, 2015). Biological craving occurs even when a substance is not ingested, such as addictions to video games and gambling. Relapses are contributed to by both the biological and the psychological aspects of craving (Leshner, 1997). Relapses are internal reactions in Hidden Sequences.

Craving can be so powerful that it controls a person, an internal demand comparable in some ways to the strong need for food or water after not having either for a lengthy period. Addicted individuals feel that they do not have a choice and cannot say 'no'. Non-addicted individuals may have difficulty understanding the power of addictions. People can relapse even when they believe that their addiction is over, such as when need a way to cope with distress. Relapses even occur with individuals who proudly believe that they have conquered their addiction. The frequency of relapses and the lifelong need to adhere to 12-step programs attest to the tenacity of addictions.

12-step programs (e.g., Alcoholics Anonymous [AA] and Narcotics Anonymous [NA]) have been helpful. Also helpful have been symptom-relieving drugs, group therapy, and support groups. Addiction substitutes (e.g., methadone, Suboxone, Vivitrol/naltrexone), detoxification programs, and ceasing to associate with enablers have also been useful. Trying to persuade addicted people to relinquish their counterproductive behavior by presenting them with facts, logic, or serious consequences such as jail has been much less effective.

A problem with many approaches is that they do not address the cause of addictions, which is somewhat like using over-the-counter cough medicine to heal a serious lung disease. Methods like jail, logic, criticism, and abstinence have an inherent drawback in that they address symptoms and behaviors, rather than the originating causes. As a result, addicted individuals who have some success in various current programs must faithfully adhere to a symptom-controlling protocol for many years. Even then, relapsing can occur (a "revolving door").

In Psychological Systems Theory, a major contributor to addictions consists of Psychological Roots and the stimulus conditions that impact those roots (see Chapters 24 - 26). An example is provided by "Martha", who was addicted to cigarettes and overeating. Martha decided to end both addictions and chose to stop smoking first because of its greater harm. Knowing that nicotine is highly addictive, she expected to engage in an intense struggle when trying to eliminate cigarettes. To her surprise, she found that she had no difficulty stopping smoking. As a result, she expected that her ability to end overeating would be even easier but that brought another surprise: she could not stop overeating. When her great effort to stop overeating failed, she came for counseling.

Martha wanted to know why she ended smoking easily yet could not stop over-eating. There was a simple explanation: she had two ways to relieve her distress, cigarettes and food. That circumstance allowed her to divest herself of one stress-reliever readily because she still had the other one. Had she initially chosen to eliminate overeating, she might have found that easy to accomplish, but then relinquishing cigarettes would have been very difficult to do.

The author helped Martha understand the Psychological Roots that caused her distress, such as her hard-to-meet expectations, low threshold for negative emotional arousal, and intense sense of responsibility which she had difficult satisfying. Those roots caused Martha to feel like a failure. In counseling, she was able to modify those distress-prone Psychological Roots. When she stopped feeling like a failure, she was able to control her eating.

As Martha's case illustrates, people turn to methods that lessen their distress, including self-therapies that are addictive, in her case, cigarettes and food. Such self-therapies tackle symptoms rather than the cause (which are distress-prone Psychological Roots from the standpoint of Psychological Systems Theory). Some self-therapies – such as alcohol, marihuana, and opiates – are especially addictive, both biologically and psychologically. Some self-treatments are addictive primarily for psychological reasons, including video games, nail-biting, and hobbies. An addiction that begins for psychological reasons can acquire biologically addictive effects as well (e.g., Conrad, Ford, Marinelli, & Wolf, 2010; Navarro, Quiroz, Moreno-Delgado, Sierakowiak, McDowell, Moreno, Realize, Cai, Aguinaga, Howell, Hausch, Cortés, Mallol, Casadó, Lluís, Canela, Ferré, & McCormick, 2015).

It appears that addictions' power is due to both biological and psychological aspects, regardless of how the addiction starts. A combination of the two generates a particularly strong addiction. As a result, regardless of how an addiction starts or continues, both the biological and psychological aspects of addictions need be addressed successfully. In short, addiction is not just a medical problem.

The desire people have to relieve distress helps explain why people become addicted. It also explains why fear messages, punishment, and aversive therapy are unlikely to succeed since those methods do not eliminate the distress that people have. Those methods are repelling forces as well, which turns off people who are addicted and lessens their motivation to continue using them. Jail, ostracism, and a war on drugs have similar drawbacks when they are used to try to rein in addictive behavior. Unfortunately, those methods are not focused on changing people's Psychological Roots. When pertinent Psychological Roots are not changed, ending an addiction is particularly difficult, even when an individual is motivated to end his/her addiction, makes resolutions to abstain, and tapers off.

It is important to treat the distress-prone Psychological Roots that contribute to addiction (e.g., hard-to-meet expectations and a low threshold for negative emotional arousal) and the distressing stimulus conditions that interact with those roots. People who are addicted need constructive ways to modify their pertinent Psychological Roots, also coping strategies and often a change in contributing social factors (such as not associating with certain individuals). It is often difficult to end addictions abruptly, therefore gradually tapering off is likely to be necessary.

There are other circumstances in which treating behavior or internal symptoms is insufficient. Examples include criminality, extremism, and violence. In homelessness, for instance, some aspects other than having a shelter include psychological issues, society's attention to the homelessness problem, and homeless individuals' needs for food, medicine, income, and social services such as job training.

Opioid and alcohol antagonists

Opiates can be countered by some medications, such as naloxone (brand name Narcan), naltrexone (brand name Vivitrol), and buprenorphine (brand name Subutex). Alcohol can also be countered by Naltrexone. Suboxone is a combination of naloxone and buprenorphine. Methadone (brand name Dolophine) is an opiate that is used as a substitute to wean people from the use of illicit opiates such as heroin. The medical effects of those substances are extremely valuable and have saved lives.

The medicinal effect of substances such as those mentioned above treats internal reactions in Hidden Sequences, not the psychological reasons why people use opiates and alcohol. Unfortunately, those medicines also can be addictive.

Fear of dying does not appear to be sufficient to prevent some people from using harmful substances. There are powerful psychological reasons for using addictive substances, especially a felt need to counteract great distress. If medicinal substances are needed, they can be administered in conjunction with appropriate psychological treatment of addictions.

Some alcohol treatments create an aversion to alcohol, such as disulfiram (brand name Antabuse) and paraldehyde. However, the unpleasant nature of aversive treatments makes them unpopular with people who have an alcohol problem, many of whom reject that treatment. Using an aversive treatment is not a good fit with Psychological Systems Therapy, which attempts to create change in a positive way.

Does an addict have to reach 'rock bottom' to be motivated to change?

The idea that addicts must be devastated by their habit to be sufficiently motivated to change might not always be the case. There are many instances in which "hitting rock bottom" does not always prompt people to change, for example, the author has found that some addicted individuals relinquish their habit without having suffered, some end their habit without help, some even end it without tapering off ("quit cold turkey"). Some addicted people put themselves on a schedule to end their addiction substantially before their circumstances become harsh or upon seeing others suffer. Some people improve when a significant other gives them an ultimatum, and some quit their addiction after having an epiphany. Some persons replace one addiction with another. Some individuals can stop immediately after resolving to do so, while others end their habit gradually. There also are people who do not end their addiction despite suffering greatly.

In addition to effective psychological and biological therapy, some other aspects that can help a person end his/her addiction include having a strong commitment for doing so, having excellent emotional support, not being judged or criticized, and having a committed schedule for tapering off.

The bottom line:

The key to ending an addiction is to treat the cause. As with other psychological disorders, not correcting the distress-prone Psychological Roots and stimulus conditions that underlie addiction is unlikely to produce substantial improvement.

313

Post-traumatic stress disorder (PTSD)

From a Psychological Systems Theory standpoint, PTSD originates from a powerful threat to a person, such as to his/her genetic needs of safety and stability. Two prominent results that can result from such experiences can be a person's acquiring a belief that he/she is vulnerable and a low threshold for negative arousal. There can be especially powerful effects if the person initially had a very low threshold or a belief that he/she was particularly vulnerable. Those Psychological Roots can produce intense reactions and in some cases last a person's entire life. Some people with PTSD also feel taken advantage of and angry, and as a result, have a low threshold for irritability. Those individuals can be easily irritated and that annoyance can build up cumulatively, a circumstance that can result in their having angry episodes that are easily triggered. Repeated traumatic incidents can be especially troublesome and unfortunately happens in many cases of social, physical, and sexual abuse. Disturbing flashbacks can also occur. Such disturbing emotional reactions like these can bother people throughout life. People who are connected with a traumatized individual can also be affected by that person's reactions.

Trauma may be a contributing factor in many instances of borderline personality disorder and phobias, and can be present along with PTSD. As a result, some people with PTSD also have characteristics of borderline personality disorder.

Desensitization techniques such Wolpe's or EMDR can help some people cope with the horrific memory of their past experiences. Changing the Psychological Roots of people with PTSD can be especially important.

A three-stage treatment of PTSD using Psychological Systems Therapy is outlined below.

1. PREPARE:
    A. Identify the person's problems (e.g., stress, anxiety, depression, failure, or rejection).
    B. Rank-order the problems and choose the most important problem to work on initially.
    C. Ascertain the Psychological Roots and stimulus conditions that cause the problem (e.g., not meeting high expectations, low threshold for negative arousal, needs for social acceptance, safety, or stability).
    D. Develop a strategy for helping the client understand the subconscious process that explains their condition.
    E. Develop a strategy to help solve the client's problems.
    F. Develop a strategy for presenting the solution to the client in an effective way.

2. PRESENT

A. Help the client understand the subconscious processes contributing to their condition (e.g., a low threshold for negative emotional arousal, unmet expectations, and absolute thinking) and how they can be helped. Present the message in a way that is comfortable for the client.

B. Give the client a method of solving his/her problem (e.g., raising his/her threshold for negative emotional arousal and adjusting his/her distress-prone expectations). Include aids as needed such as deconditioning (e.g., desensitization and other forms of behavior modification), focus on positives, creation of a positive long-term goal, deliberate relegation of the trauma to the past, and self-affirmations.

C. Build the client's confidence (e.g., by providing problem-solving techniques, methods for succeeding with material and conceptual tasks, making decisions, understanding puzzling aspects about themselves, and win-win solutions for interpersonal conflicts).

D. Begin a tapering-off schedule when the client is ready to do so.

3. SOLIDIFY

A. Briefly review some of the key aspects above.

B. Identify ambiguities, misunderstandings, and questions the client has and answer them in a way that is comfortable for the client.

C. Invite the client to apply what he/she has learned to new situations.

Borderline personality disorder (BPD)

Some characteristics of borderline personality disorder were described earlier in this chapter. Some people with a borderline personality disorder were traumatized earlier in their life. Trauma can lead people to feel very vulnerable and have a low threshold for negative arousal, which can cause them to be highly reactive emotionally. Some have a low threshold for irritability, feel taken advantage of, and a built-up irritability, with even slight irritations triggering a strong angry reaction. People who interact with them might feel that they have to "walk on egg shells" when near them.

They may have a particularly strong reaction to negatives, such as failure, and may resist responsibility for being wrong. They may blame others for their problems, making it difficult for them to improve ("Why should I change when they're the cause?"). Their anger is a repelling force, as are many of the other characteristics mentioned above. They may think in absolutes, which exacerbates their distress and unpleasantness. As a result, people with a borderline personality disorder often have trouble with relationships. Yet, despite having a distressing inner life, they might be attractive, intelligent, superb at their occupation, and earn a substantial income.

Some people with borderline personality can feel hopeless and attempt suicide when no solution seems possible. Therefore, some people with borderline personality disorder can be diagnosed as having depression, dysthymia, bipolar disorder, PTSD, anxiety, OCD, relationship problems, anger, antisocial behavior, oppositional defiant disorder, parent-child problems, or addiction. Consequently, there may be many more people with a borderline personality disorder than has been recorded.

Therapy for borderline personality disorder might include aspects related to treating PTSD, depression, and anxiety, also training in social skills (e.g., empathy, win-win solutions, constructive social influence, and not using repelling forces or taking things personally). Maintaining rapport with them can be difficult because of their sensitivity to implications that they might be wrong or need improvement. Many people with a borderline personality disorder do not seek counseling and when they do, they might seek ways to get other people to change rather than themselves.

Intensification of psychological disorders

PST suggests that psychological disorders might intensify and be prolonged because the negative outcomes continue occurring (e.g., depressed people with failure, anxious persons with feeling additional threat, and borderline with more rejection from others). This hypothesis can be tested empirically and if correct, would underscore the importance of early detection and treatment.

Some prominent methods of psychotherapy Psychological Systems Theory aspects that apply to some well-known therapies are noted below in italics.

Freud (1990) recognized that people did not know what caused their behavior and that early childhood experiences *(past stimulus conditions)* can have lifelong effects. He postulated the existence of some subconscious factors such as the superego (conscience) in conflict with the id (unfettered raw drives), and resolved by the ego (rational decision-making). In Psychological Systems Theory, these elements somewhat correspond to elements in *Hidden Sequences*, such as *acquired* and *genetic Psychological Roots*, and *internal reactions* such as decisions. Freud's therapy called for clients talking without reservation about whatever comes to mind *(often internal reactions, behaviors, and past stimulus conditions)*. Freud thought that the sex drive was often the cause of people's difficulties and that healing occurred by understanding the cause of problems and expressing feelings and fantasies *(internal reactions)*. Freud's theory and therapy focus primarily on intermediate and end portions of *Hidden Sequences*.

Jung (1953) was intrigued by how some symbols throughout history occur in people who do not know one another and interpreted symbols of people's thoughts and feelings (internal reactions). Jung was interested in personality traits such as introversion and extraversion (internal reactions and overt behavior). His therapy focuses primarily on intermediate and end portions of *Hidden Sequences*.

Adler (1927) recognized that people's beliefs were important *(acquired Psychological Roots)* and was instrumental in establishing social services. His therapy includes attention to the originating, intermediate, and end portions of *Hidden Sequences*.

Behavior-modification therapies (e.g., Skinner, 1974; Wolpe, 1958) employ conditioning and de-conditioning such as desensitization *(overt behavior)* and intentionally avoid working with subconscious causes in the belief that those are hypothetical and difficult to verify empirically.[42] This therapy addresses the end portion of *Hidden Sequences*.

Cognitive therapies (e.g., Rational-Emotive Behavioral Therapy, Ellis & MacLaren, 2005; Gestalt therapy, Perls, 1973) assume that problems stem from dysfunctional thoughts and judgments *(internal reactions)*. The therapy focuses on trying to get clients to behave more rationally by showing them the illogicality of their thoughts and actions *(internal reactions, overt behavior, intermediate* and *surface Psychological Roots)*. These therapies focus primarily on intermediate and end portions of *Hidden Sequences*.

Rogers (1951) asked his clients a series of questions in a gentle, warm, and empathic manner to allow them to solve their problems themselves (non-directive therapy using unconditional positive regard). This therapy focuses primarily on *behavior, internal reactions,* and *surface Psychological Roots*.

Berne's (2015) transactional analysis views interpersonal relations *(overt behavior)* as the key to people's difficulties. Therapists try to help clients improve how they perceive themselves and others *(internal reactions)*, and thereby be more interpersonally effective *(overt behavior)*. This therapy focuses on the end portion of *Hidden Sequences*.

---

[42] Mindfulness lowers the threshold of awareness for what is focused on (*'sensitization'*), and raises the threshold for other aspects (*'habituation'*). An example of habituation is not being aware of the clothing one is wearing even though it was felt when it was put on initially. Another example is no longer sensing an odor that was noticeable at first. Selective attention occurs when something that holds one's attention (e.g., a pleasurable distraction) blocks from attention thoughts that are bothersome. A caveat here is that problem-solving is aided by focusing on aspects that are bothersome.

Beck's (1991) cognitive behavioral therapy (CBT) addresses some readily knowable aspects in psychological disorders such as *stimulus conditions* and dysfunctional thoughts and emotional reactions *(internal reactions)*. It tries to help clients change beliefs such as a notion that their problems cannot be solved and that there is nothing positive in their life. (This therapy focuses primarily on *internal reactions, behavior,* and *intermediate* and *surface psychological roots*).

Greenwald's (2017) Psychological Systems Theory addresses hitherto hidden aspects of psychology and helps explain normal behavior. The therapy derived from this theory is a three-stage strategy for changing the causes of disorders, such as distress-prone Psychological Roots and the stimulus conditions that impact those roots. Common psychological disorders such as depression and anxiety are viewed as states of uncontrollability that occur when homeostatic extremes are exceeded. (This therapy focuses on the *Psychological Roots* and stimuli that originate *Hidden Sequences*.) The theory's many applications include normal circumstances such as how to resolve interpersonal conflicts, and improve communication, persuasion, teaching, learning, and interpersonal relations.

Assessment of psychotherapy's effectiveness

Hard evidence about the effectiveness of psychotherapeutic interventions can be obtained by comparing the outcome of people who receive treatment with people who are not treated therapeutically, after a non-biased selection of participants for the two groups from among people who have been diagnosed with a particular disorder. Standard tests can be used to measure changes in behavior, beliefs, thoughts, attitudes, and reactions. Multiple assessments and studies provide evidence of validity and reliability. Some examples of measures that contribute to assessing outcomes are listed below, in alphabetical order:

. Addictive behavior
. Biochemical assays
. Blood pressure
. Blood tests
. Breathing tests
. Electrical skin transmission (galvanic)
. Evaluations by independent observers
. Hospital records

. Journal entries by clients (e.g., daily)
. Medications (type, frequency, amount)
. Muscle tension (electromyograph)
. Positive emission tomography scan
. Pulse rate
. Questionnaires
. Records (e.g., attendance, work)
. Self- and family reports

Summary of Psychological Systems Theory's Approach to Psychotherapy
Psychological disorders and psychotherapy are not mysterious. The author has found that people's difficulties are often due to distress-prone Psychological Roots and distressing stimulus conditions, and often can be treated successfully. Depression, for example, can be lessened by helping clients to no longer feel overwhelmed by failures, such as by lowering their hard-to-meet expectations, acquiring problem-solving methods, not thinking in absolutes, and coping with harsh stimulus conditions. Practical applications derived from Psychological Systems Theory help clients make constructive changes, such as methods for creating win-win solutions and other social skills.

Chapter 28.   EXAMPLES OF PSYCHOLOGICAL SYSTEMS PSYCHOTHERAPY

These examples are real. Some identifying details, including names, have been changed to protect privacy.

This chapter illustrates how Psychological Systems Therapy was utilized in seven difficult cases. The specific procedure this therapy employs is provided in Chapter 29.

1. Inability to stop drinking alcohol.

'Ted' made numerous attempts to stop drinking but could not stop despite strong efforts to do so. Alcoholics Anonymous meetings gave him strategies and support but he still could not stop drinking, which puzzled him. Ted was not knowledgeable about psychological matters, but when his alcohol use cost him his driver's license and also his job, he came for counseling.

The author soon realized that Ted's drinking was related to his dysfunctional marriage. Ted had begun to use alcohol heavily when his wife cheated on him. That was the last straw for him after years of her verbal abuse, severe neglect of their two children, and impossible demands. She screamed at him to make more money – which required that he work still more hours – yet also spend more time with her. She became even more problematic after he filed for divorce, including frequently threatening to go to the police and accuse him of abusing her. She told him that she would get him sent to prison and get total custody of their children.

Ted sometimes drank in binges that he could not control but did not know why. When the author examined the stimulus conditions for those circumstances a recognizable pattern emerged. Ted binged when his wife particularly distressed him, such as when he discovered yet another instance in which their children were harshly dealt with by her or by the low-life men with whom she was sleeping. He also binged after each major threat she made such as legal actions against him, manipulative behavior such as bringing him to court, and attempting to get custody of their children.

Ted also drank large amounts of alcohol every time he discovered one of her various schemes to kidnap their children. Another trigger was each discovery of the many ways she was trashing his house. (She was living in his house while he temporarily stayed in a rented apartment.) Particular triggers for Ted's binging occurred when his children complained to him about her, which frequently happened. Ted did not see the underlying theme of these circumstances.

Whenever Ted told the judge his concerns and his children's problems with their mother, the judge did nothing to improve things. Instead, the judge continued to allow her to remain in his house, which now was long past the time she had agreed to leave.

Analysis:

Ted did not know how to be effective with his wife. Whatever he did with her made things worse. As a result, he felt helpless, anxious, and depressed. Alcohol tranquilized his anxiety. Ted did not understand what was going on because he paid attention only to tangible aspects such as his wife's behaviors and had no grasp of psychological aspects. As a result, he was continually unaware of why harsh things happened to him and he often reacted spontaneously, aggressively, and inappropriately. Put succinctly, Ted was a walking repelling force without realizing it.

For Ted to become more effective required that he understand his wife and her concerns. She appeared to have a low threshold for negative arousal, an intense need for emotional support, and inappropriate expectations. She also seemed to consider herself a victim who was being taken advantage of by Ted. In addition, she could not accept being wrong and believed that whatever bad things happened to her were Ted's fault. Her behavior also suggested that she was narcissistic, vengeful, angry, and could not tolerate his attempts to bring her behavior under control. She may also have had a narrow comfort zone. (These aspects are some of the characteristics of borderline personality disorder.)

Treatment:

The author helped Ted grasp the above hypotheses about his wife's Psychological Roots and gave Ted strategies that might satisfy the concerns both of them had. The plan included Ted's ceasing to be immediately reactive, argumentative, resistant, and aggressive. The author showed Ted how to create compatible solutions that could satisfy both of them rather than his continuing to ignore her concerns. Ted also learned how to avoid using repelling forces, including how to avoid being confrontational.

Ted began to use appealing forces such as being sympathetic to his ex-wife's complaints when she caused problems. He learned how to speak calmly and softly to her rather than harshly, and how to create win-win solutions. Ted also acquired methods for counteracting some of the harm his ex-wife and her male companions caused his children. He lessened his strong emotional reactions to her hostile actions and learned how not to feel personally attacked by the outrageous things she said and did to him.

Ted's wife's hostility and harshness lessened with each positive step he took. Those successes boosted Ted's mood and supported the above-mentioned Psychological-Root hypotheses about her. As Ted's success increased, his confidence about coping with her improved and he became less agitated and more patient. His increasingly cordial manner and newly-found skill in avoiding confrontations led to improving the way she treated the children. (She may have been taking out her frustrations on the children.) As her disruptions of Ted's life and his court appearances diminished, Ted's alcoholic binges decreased. His many positive changes and his wife's ceasing to complain against him led the judge to decide that it was now appropriate for her to leave his house.

Ted's anxiety greatly decreased when he returned to his disheveled home and cleaned it. Soon after that, his distress diminished to a point where he no longer felt a need to use alcohol. That success and his improved ability to cope with his wife led to his being able to re-acquire his driver's license and get re-hired. Some weeks later, the judge awarded him principal custody of his children.

2. Major depression.

'Martin' was extremely weak and looked as if he would soon die. He could hardly talk, had not been eating, was not interested in living, and was pale and fragile. He was pathologically depressed, often thought about suicide, and attempted to kill himself several times. He had long since lost his job, had no motivation, lacked energy, rarely got out of bed, and had given up looking for work. No treatment had helped him, including a variety of therapies he received while he was a patient at different mental hospitals. His anti-depressant medications had not ended his depression nor even lessened his symptoms. The medicines had strong side effects, such as fogging his thinking, making him feel drugged and causing him to be uninterested in his wife. He found those aspects intolerable.

Martin was very intelligent but could not figure out why he was depressed or how to pull out of it. His thoughts ran together in his mind, keeping him from thinking coherently. He believed that his condition was too extreme to be due to anything psychological so he had refused further counseling. His wife managed to get Martin to go to a session with the author, during which he spoke haltingly and in short whispers. After ten minutes, the author summarized in a few words a key problem Martin had. His finding that someone understood and could succinctly articulate some of his issues perked him up a bit.

322

It is common for depressed individuals to feel overwhelmed by multiple problems so the author encouraged Martin to talk about all of his issues and then succinctly summarized each difficulty he brought up. Sixteen problems came to light. The author asked Martin to rate each problem on a 10-point scale, which Martin now felt capable of doing. The author then briefly outlined how each of the 8, 9, and 10-rated problems could be managed, starting with Martin's top-rated problems. The reason for beginning with the most troublesome problems is that if those are not addressed the person will continue feeling overwhelmed. (Refer to the Intensity Curve, Figure 6, in Chapter 2.)

When Martin realized that his problems were capable of being solved, he began to look somewhat hopeful and even slightly smiled a few times. When the author asked him if he was ready to try to start coping, he said was willing to do so. By the time he left that first session, he had a more upbeat appearance and behavior, which contrasted sharply with his appearing to be near death at the beginning of the hour.

Analysis:

Martin's most pressing problem was his believing that he had not met his responsibility to his family owing to having lost his job. That circumstance devastated him because he viewed it as having failed to meet his responsibility to his family and therefore that he failed his major role in life. He had also failed to meet many other expectations he had of himself. As a result, he considered himself a total fiasco who did not deserve to live.

Treatment:

The author helped Martin understand many subconscious factors that had been controlling him, such as his extremely strong sense of responsibility and hard-to-achieve expectations and standards. The author gave him strategies for solving each situation. Martin was willing to use those strategies, such as lowering his expectations, and he improved with each change he made. His feeling like a failure gradually began to decrease. Each success lessened Martin's guilt feelings and he slowly began to allow himself to believe that he was not the awful person he thought he was.

There was a point at which he made a distinctly observable change and looked more relaxed. That change occurred when he finally stopped punishing himself. At that point he stopped being depressed. (Technically, he had returned from his previous state of uncontrollability, see Figure 6 in Chapter 2). The author continued to help Martin acquire problem-solving strategies for the other distressing circumstances that previously had seemed unsolvable to him. With that further progress, he was able to relinquish his remaining dysthymia.

A major reason that Martin was able to succeed was that he was willing to adjust his expectations. That adjustment included reconfiguring his understanding of what it meant to be the head of his family, what his actual obligations were, how to put in perspective the role of an employee and understand the culture of the work place, and what was realistically expected of him by his supervisors and co-workers. He improved a step at a time as each distressing issue was solved. His down mood ended substantially only after all of his major distress-prone Psychological Roots, stressful stimulus conditions, and subsidiary issues were dealt with constructively. He had not been able to solve his problems because they were caused by subconscious aspects that were not known to him. Understanding his Psychological Roots made sense to him and, with guidance, allowed him to apply his considerable intelligence to solve them.

The reason that Martin had extreme feelings of guilt is that the unpleasant things that been happening to him fell on fertile ground: his distress-prone Psychological Roots. It turned out that he had been plagued by guilt since early childhood and that he had been punishing himself for many years. His down mood had built to the point that it impeded his effectiveness at work and contributed to his having lost his job. Thus, paradoxically, his high standards had worked against him by adding to his anxiety and lessening his effectiveness at work. Losing his job was the last straw that pushed him over the edge into a severe state of uncontrollability. His depressed appearance and diminished reactions worked against him when he applied for other jobs.

Martin's experience illustrates how failure can contribute to a person's feeling overwhelmed to the point of becoming depressed. The author has found that solving the issues that overwhelm people helps lessen depression and frequently ends it, as in Martin's case. Improvement often can begin to occur as soon as people have a credible basis for hoping that their condition can be addressed successfully, open themselves to understanding the subconscious causes of their circumstances, and start making constructive changes in those factors.

3. Defiance

21-year old 'Ira' was explosive and had been violent since childhood. His intensely destructive temper tantrums put his family continually on edge. They never knew when he would suddenly explode. Ira had received many treatments in his young life, including anti-psychotic medications, psychiatric hospitalizations, extensive counseling, police emergency visits, and jail. No therapy had improved him.

Ira was difficult in many other ways as well – he was irritable, moody, depressed, and sometimes suicidal. He did not tolerate being in school, had completed only a few high school courses, and could not hold a job, nor did he want to. Ira slept during much of the day, stayed up nights playing computer games, was uncooperative at home, and refused to help with household chores.

Ira had rejected receiving any further therapy and his family felt helpless to do anything with him. They considered him to be so seriously mentally ill as to be beyond hope and had given up any possibility that he might improve.

Ira's father, 'Al', grew up in a dysfunctional, drug-using, criminal family whose members were nasty, unpredictable, manipulative, untrustworthy, and violent. Al was fiercely determined to avoid being like them and left home at age 14. At that point he was on his own but despite being young, unskilled, and alone, he somehow supported himself. Succeeding took great perspicacity and sacrifice on his part. That tremendous effort paid off. Al became the only one in his biological family to get a college education, hold a steady job, own a house and two well-maintained cars, and marry a high-quality spouse. He was the only person in his family of origin who was honest, hard-working, dependable, faithful, and financially successful. Al is intelligent, cordial, respectful, an interesting conversationalist, and makes a great appearance.

Analysis:

Al was intensely driven to make sure that his children would not be like anyone in his biological family. Therefore, he put strong pressure on his two sons to be responsible, upright, and have a strong work ethic. Al's younger son readily accepted his father's pressure, but Ira resisted defiantly. The more Ira resisted, the greater Al pressured him. That led to frequent arguments, some of which were so intense that they escalated to the afore-mentioned explosions. Neither Al nor Ira knew any other way to function.

Treatment:

Since Ira had refused psychological counseling, improvement had to come entirely from Al. The author helped Al understand how his Psychological Roots had led to problems with Ira and that Ira's explosions occurred when Al applied especially strong and unrelenting pressure. Despite Al's intelligence, it had not occurred to him that his behavior could cause problems because he was convinced that he was doing the right thing. Al was well-intentioned and could not imagine that his intense commitment to doing what he believed was right could trigger dysfunctional behavior in his son since his being intensely committed and persistent had brought him success.

The author helped Al understand Ira's hypothesized Psychological Roots and showed Al how he might be able to meet his objectives with Ira by interacting effectively with him without clashing. That strategy called for Al to modify his beliefs about what it takes to persuade and learn how to create win-win solutions. Al also had to lower his expectations, raise his threshold for negative arousal, and lessen his drive for closure. Of special importance was that Al had to avoid using all repelling forces, get his points across calmly and constructively, and recognize non-verbal signs of Ira's resistance. As soon as those signs of resistance occurred, it was critical for Al to stop attempting to change Ira instead of pushing even harder as he had done before. As Al changed in that direction, the less the home situation spun out of control.

Ira's interactions with his family slowly improved. Explosions became a thing of the past. Ira surprised them a few times by being unexpectedly kind and caring, behaviors that had occurred only rarely before. After a while, Ira changed his sleep pattern to coincide with the rest of the family. He enrolled in a few courses, worked with a tutor, sought a job, and began to think of how to create a constructive future for himself.

4. Puzzling phobia.

'Nell' suddenly found herself extremely fearful of traversing bridges. That fear came out of nowhere and made no sense to Nell since she had never had an unpleasant experience with a bridge. When she could not end her panic about bridges despite her great effort to do so, she came for counseling.

Phobias (including fear of snakes, insects, or flying) are instances of classical conditioning in which anxiety is triggered by a stimulus that, in many instances, is something about which many other people do not have a strong negative reaction. (Classical conditioning is discussed in Chapter 18). Nell was very intelligent and if there was something about bridges that disturbed her, it might be assumed that she would have at least some clue about what that something was. However, Nell had no idea why she suddenly became afraid of crossing bridges.

Her having no clue about suddenly being afraid of something she had never been fearful of raised a question about whether her phobia might be due to something other than bridges. However, despite Nell's strong determination to understand what was going on and her high intelligence, Nell had no idea whatsoever about anything that could even be connected in a remote way with her phobia. If something else was going on but was not known, it created a problem for treatment since Psychological Systems Therapy is substantially based on ascertaining the cause.

When the cause is not known, an alternative treatment would be to treat the behavior or internal reaction. One way to do this would be to try to de-condition her phobia using a desensitization method (Wolpe, 1958). In Nell's case, she would be presented with a series of aspects related to bridges, starting with bland objects that only vaguely resembled bridges such as stuffed toys and Lego constructions, then moving in very gradual steps to the real thing. At each step in the process, Nell would be coached to relax, creating a conditioned response in which she would relax whenever she had anything to do with a bridge. The reasoning behind this procedure is that it is not possible to be afraid when relaxed. The process is lengthy, but at the end of it Nell should be able to relax when crossing a bridge.

Desensitization assumes that the problem is what the person is afraid of – bridges, in this case. However, Nell had never been bothered by bridges before. Since her phobia appeared suddenly, seemingly out of nowhere, what if bridges were not the issue? If there was something that greatly bothered Nell but was not addressed in therapy, she might continue being fearful even if she was desensitized to bridges. Upon discussing this dilemma with Nell, she opted to try to discover the cause. If that did not happen fairly quickly, the plan was to employ the desensitization technique mentioned above.

Accordingly, Nell and the author redoubled their efforts to understand what was going on. If something other than bridges caused Nell to panic, most likely it was something that aroused strong fear. For something to be that intense, Nell would probably have some awareness of it. However, no matter how hard she tried she could not identify anything that caused her to be afraid.

The author then broadened the effort by asking Nell to examine many aspects of her life. She was a somewhat tense person and was experiencing a variety of stresses, such as her demanding occupation and the courses she was taking for an advanced degree. She also had substantial stress trying to balance her family, work, and college tasks. She had a strong sense of responsibility and high standards, which prodded her to be very effective at whatever she attempted and that caused her to be stressed about almost everything she did. However, none of the various aspects she mentioned were connected to bridges. Moreover, all of those aspects had strong positives that made the distress worthwhile, for example, she was delighted with her husband and their two children, loved her occupation, and was optimistic about her future.

That lack of obtaining deeper understanding led to further probing to try to uncover some clue about why she panicked about bridges. Some additional tensions came to light. Her husband had recently lost his job, which was causing them much difficulty with regard to meeting mortgage payments. Nell was very concerned about her children's health. Also, she had an unpleasant work supervisor, which was particularly bothersome to her. However, none of those issues frightened her nor had anything to do with bridges. In short, none of the tensions that came to Nell's mind were likely to be the culprit.

This circumstance was a test of Psychological Systems Theory's assumption that psychology is logical. If the theory is correct, Nell's bridge phobia must be connected with something that frightened her. Since Nell had no idea about what that could be, might the theory be wrong about psychology being logical?

There was another possibility: perhaps something was so disturbing to Nell that her subconscious mind was blocking it from her awareness. To try to find out, the author continued to probe gently in an ever widely-ranging discussion. At some point, Nell mentioned something that disturbed her: one of her professors ranted about racism. In her once-a-week classes with him, he used strong language and blamed the students for society's anti-black attitude. He was big, burly, abrasive, loud, and crude. He also was explosive, erratic, and unpredictable, and at times seemed out of control. Nell was sensitive and refined, and he bothered Nell a great deal. One day he brought a gun to the class and pointed it at each of the people in the classroom, which scared each of them as he intended. Then he slammed the gun on his desk loudly. Nell shook with fright.

The next week she found herself afraid to cross a bridge.

Analysis:
Did her fear of crossing that bridge have anything to do with that out-of-control teacher? Yes. That bridge was on the route she took when driving to that professor's class. Now it was understandable why Nell was anxious about crossing the bridge to her class.

The reason that Nell did not realize the significance of that out-of-control professor was because her subconscious mind had kept her from being aware of that angry professor – except when she was in that classroom. One of the reasons was that she had a philosophy about thinking positively, which blocked out unpleasant things.

Why did she not connect that angry professor with the bridge? First, because she had blocked him out of her mind when she was not in class. Second, the bridge was more than a mile from the college so was not directly associated with her class. Third, she had no obvious reason to associate the bridge with that professor. That association occurred below her awareness, in mental processes that took place subconsciously. (A way of understanding this is that the mind follows its own processes.)

A question arises about why Nell's subconscious mind did not associate something other than the bridge with the terror that her angry professor generated, such as the school, the road she took to go to the school, other professors, the students, or her school-work. It was because the bridge stood out during an otherwise routine car trip to the school (see Seligman, 1971) and therefore could provide a clear signal that she was approaching danger. (Technically, the bridge had become a conditioned stimulus and fear was a conditioned response to that stimulus.)

Why was Nell anxious about all bridges? Because the brain is wired to generalize and Nell's being afraid of all bridges provided her with a warning that she was approaching something dangerous. (Technically, Nell had a Psychological Root cluster related to danger that now included bridges. The foundation of that cluster was her genetic need for safety.)

Why was Nell unaware of this? It was because almost all of what goes on in the brain occurs without awareness. (See the Prologue regarding the biological structure that explains this phenomenon). Also, Nell had a strong propensity for viewing things positively and ignoring negatives. In addition, the bridge on the way to her class did not stand out during the rest of the week.

Why could Nell not squelch her anxiety about bridges despite her strong attempts to do so? Because her safety was involved. Need for safety is a powerful Psychological Roots that is genetically wired-into everyone. Her consciously-applied will power was not able to overcome the danger with which her mind was concerned.

Treatment:

The author's therapy did not involve bridges, which might seem counter-intuitive on the surface. Instead, a major focus of the treatment was the powerful stimulus that caused Nell's panic – her out-of-control professor. Nell did not want to drop that professor's class. It was a required course and she thought that she might get the same professor the next time if she ended that class. She also did not want a negative mark on her transcript, did not want to lose her sizable tuition payment for that course, and did not want to feel that she failed her responsibility. Since Nell wanted to remain in the course, she had to feel safe there. Included in this aspect of the treatment was an attempt to lessen her strong need for safety in that situation, helping her raise her low threshold for negative emotional arousal, and lessening her concern about the classroom situation being out of control.

A second aspect of the treatment addressed Nell's ongoing tension because, from the standpoint of Psychological Systems Theory, she had a considerably large build-up of tension to which her out-of-control teacher added a huge further amount. Nell had been considerately tense before she entered that fateful classroom because of her demanding life and some Psychological Roots such as her strong sense of responsibility. The agitated professor's pointing his gun directly at her pushed her over the edge into panic. That teacher's extreme act was the last straw that had caused her to tip into a state of uncontrollability.

A third aspect of this part of the treatment addressed the unpleasantness and tension that Nell's work supervisor caused her.

Accordingly, the following three aspects guided the author's plan to diminish her fear of bridges:
1. Mitigate her fear of that irate professor.
2. Reduce the stresses related to her many responsibilities.
3. Lessen the distress her unpleasant supervisor caused her.

These objectives led to the following three-part therapy:

Objective 1. *Calm Nell's strong need for safety.* Nell was advised to never be alone in that classroom. The author suggested that she sandwich herself in among other students as she entered and left that classroom, and sit as far from the instructor as possible (behind some tall male students, rather than at the front of the class as she usually did). Nell was also asked to avoid eye contact with the instructor and to keep a can of pepper spray and a whistle within reach to bolster her sense of safety,.

Objective 2. *Raise Nell's threshold for negative emotional arousal.* The author gave her strategies help lessen her emotional reactivity and thereby lessen the degree to which she became upset. For example, she was to repeatedly tell herself not to get caught up in the professors' rants or any of his other disturbing actions. Nell was also given methods to help bolster her confidence and lessen her anxiety about that instructor, including constructive ways to cope with her concerns about his harmfulness.

Objective 3. *Help Nell get the other tensions in her life under control.* The most important of the additional tensions in Nell's life was her unpleasant work supervisor. The author helped Nell acquire effective methods for coping with that person, such as how to create win-win solutions and some methods for solving problems. The author also helped Nell address other issues that bothered her, including ideas about how to create an effective budget to help her meet her mortgage payments, how to help assure the health of her children, and how her husband could obtain a new job.

As each of the above three objectives was met, Nell's anxiety about bridges lessened. Progress occurred in stages. When the last of the above aspects came under control – coping with her difficult supervisor – what remained of Nell's fear of bridges ended abruptly and entirely.

The success of this procedure meant that:

a) Part of the strong reaction Nell had to that professor was due to the cumulative build-up of many prior tensions in her.

b) Nell's phobia regarding bridges was primarily related to the anxiety the professor created in her. The bridge she had to cross to go to her classroom had become a signal that she was approaching that out-of-control professor, who she considered to be dangerous.

c) Bridges had generalized in Nell's mind to become a sign that she was approaching something dangerous.

d) Nell was unable to exit from her state of uncontrollability all at once. Instead, she had to make progress a step at a time.

e) Nell's anxiety had to get below the precursor range related to her panic before her concern about bridges completely ended, which required substantially diminishing many of her other tensions.

f) All three of the objectives mentioned above had to be met for Nell to fully exit from her state of uncontrollability and her precursor range adjacent to that condition.

5. Anxiety

'Lily', a 20-year old college student, had always been anxious, which her parents thought was caused genetically since a number of family members were anxious. Her parents viewed her condition as being biological so they obtained medical treatment for Lily, which led to her taking anti-anxiety medication for many years. The medicine lessened her symptoms initially. However, Lily's anxiety began to worsen. That led to her being given larger and larger doses of medicine. Nevertheless, despite being heavily medicated, Lily began having panic attacks. When those attacks increased in frequency yet various medical treatments and consultations did not provide a solution nor explain what was happening, her parents decided to see if there might be a psychological basis for her anxiety.

Analysis:

Lily was a perfectionist who was intensely driven to achieve at a high level, a pattern that characterized her family. She was conscientious yet nevertheless had difficulty getting high grades. Her not getting high grades occurred in part because her anxiety about avoiding failure impeded her ability to think effectively. Lily also lacked effective strategies for studying, writing papers, and doing well on exams. She also was poorly organized, had difficulty paying attention in class, and procrastinated. Those obstacles got in the way of her studying, writing term papers, doing class projects, and answering exam questions effectively.

The reason Lily's condition had gone from anxiety to panic and why her panic attacks were now occurring with increasing frequency was that the pressure she was receiving from school had been heightening as she progressed from grade to grade. She was also falling further behind in her projects and papers and was intensely worried about meeting deadlines. Exams made her especially anxious. Those difficulties started to traumatize her and there was no relief in sight. Her anxiety had now built to an extreme level and her panic attacks occurred whenever her anxiety exceeded a tipping point.

Lily looked frail and was always worried, causing her to lack sleep. Sleep was also elusive because she stayed up late to get her school work done. Her worrying lessened the amount and quality of whatever sleep she got. Some of her inadequate academic skills added to her travail. In short, Lily's psychology was undermining her.

Treatment:

The author helped Lily understand the psychological reasons for her anxiety, such as her difficult-to-meet expectations, her low threshold for emotional arousal, and her limited academic skills. Showing her how she could lower her expectations while retaining her high goals reduced the pressure she put on herself. Her distress lessened and her high goals allowed her to continue aiming for high achievement.

The author also gave her strategies for getting better organized, prioritizing her tasks, addressing a single issue at a time, and using a step-wise method for accomplishing her goals. He also gave her strategies for studying effectively and methods that helped her focus her attention, write more cohesively, complete each task before moving on to a subsequent task, and answer exam questions more effectively. Each strategy boosted her confidence, improved her ability to cope, and lessened her procrastinating. Lily's panic attacks ended, and her tension dropped substantially.

6. Aging and depression

'Frank' was in his mid-80's and looked much older. He had difficulty walking, his mind had slowed to a crawl, and he frequently dozed off during the day. He could barely bring himself to tolerate the activities in which his wife involved him. He disliked doing new things and making decisions. Even choosing what restaurant to go to or where to go on vacation were long, convoluted processes for him that often did not end with a conclusion. He wanted things done the 'right' way and was cranky when things were 'not done correctly', which created hassles with other people as well for him. Frank had been much more active in earlier years, so his dragging through each day puzzled everyone, including his wife. She was full of life and mourned the loss of the characteristics she had loved in him when he was younger. Frank had not improved despite taking medication and seeing a variety of therapists.

Initial analysis:

Frank's Psychological Roots included a desire that everything be done at an extremely high level, which explained why everything in which he engaged plunged him into a lengthy and ponderous decision-making process that often was inconclusive. His difficulty making simple decisions, often not making them at all, greatly frustrated his wife. He was irritable when his high standards were not met and he often said, "People don't do what they should", and "Things used to be a lot better". Frank's thinking in absolutes kept him from tolerating any viewpoint different from his. His frequently telling people that they were wrong was ruining his relationships. Frank also resisted making any changes in his thinking.

Frank focused almost entirely on tangible things, which impeded his ability to comprehend aspects that he could not see or touch, including subconscious psychological processes. He believed that psychology had no substance or significance and was just something that people made up. As a result, he did not understand himself, his wife, or anyone else. His tunnel vision and resistance to change kept him from improving.

Initial treatment:

Frank was willing to accept written reminders the author gave him and he agreed to review them every day. Those reminders helped keep his marriage intact and were necessary because Frank forgot what was discussed shortly after he left the office sessions. A problem arose when one of the reminders asked him to identify psychological aspects that occur below the surface, something that had been discussed in the office. That request was more than Frank could manage and he balked at even attempting to try doing it.

Subsequent analysis:

Upon talking with Frank about his resistance, the author discovered that Frank believed that he was near death. Frank had concluded that since he was more than eight years beyond the average life expectancy of 78 years, he had long since outlived his usefulness in life. He believed that he would soon be entering a grave, so felt "What's the use" about almost everything.

Frank's belief that he was near death led to his behaving in accord with that concept and being gloomy (a self-fulfilling prophecy). Having that belief had considerable behavioral consequences for him, for example, Frank believed that he must conserve what little energy he believed he had left. That belief was a major reason Frank avoided being active and explained why he functioned at a bare minimum and had no interest in anything. Also, why he did not mobilize any motivation to do anything that was out of the ordinary, especially the energetic things his wife wanted him to do with her. Trying to grasp anything psychological was too much for him.

Frank had concealed all of this from his wife and the various counselors, physicians, and psychiatrists he had seen. Frank's case is an example of the power of beliefs and potency of the flow-down effect that results from those beliefs (discussed in Chapter 7).

Subsequent treatment:

Frank believed that his usefulness in life primarily involved aspects related to his earning a living. He had not been doing that for many years and did not feel up to doing it again. The author helped Frank understand that earning money was not his only usefulness in life; he was very significant to his wife, children, and grandchildren. The author also encouraged Frank to engage in interests he used to have and to do so with people whose interests were similar to his. As he did so, each activity perked him up, a little bit here and a little bit there. His wife helped.

Frank began to discover that he was healthier than he thought. He gradually returned from looking like he was almost a candidate for intensive care to being more absorbed in life, having more energy, and looking healthier and more alive than before.

7. *Sex addiction*

'Roger' had been unfaithful to the women in his life and, not surprisingly therefore, had a history of ruined relationships. He came for counseling because he did not want to lose 'Darlene', who he loved, yet he could not stop feeling compelled to be with other females. He did not know why he was unfaithful to Darlene nor the other women who had been in his life.

Roger is intelligent and motivated. He had a powerful drive to conquer obstacles, which affected everything he did. For example, he frequently took on extreme challenges and chose dangerous occupations.

Analysis:

When things did not go well for Roger, his desire to surmount challenges intensified. His intense need to find difficult tests and cope with them started in his early childhood when he strove to win the affection of his emotionally distant father. He never succeeded in obtaining his father's affection and was continually striving to achieve it.

When a woman in his life did not take the lead in being affectionate with him, his mind automatically connected that circumstance with his father's not reaching out to him. In Roger's mind, a woman's not taking the initiative in love-making indicated that she did not love him. That angered him, and he reacted by seeking love from someone else.

Roger had not been aware of this process in him despite his being very insightful, having tried to understand what was going on for years, and having seen a number of counselors. The problem for Roger was that subconscious processes can be inscrutable and what had been going inside Roger was not intuitive.

Treatment:

The author helped Roger understand the connection between his father's lack of demonstrativeness, his anger toward women who did not take the initiative regarding affection, his intense efforts to overcome challenges, and his womanizing.

The author also presented some possible reasons for his father's unfortunate withholding of affection, such as a male cultural norm that men not be demonstratively affectionate. Roger began to realize that it might be possible that his father did not disdain Roger, rather felt restrained from being emotionally supportive and showing affection because of societal norms and his particular subjective psychological perspective.

Roger's tensions began to diminish upon understanding that it was possible for his father to have some unfortunate beliefs about being demonstrative and that those were present at a subconscious level in his father and that his father had never expressed them to him. Roger increasingly pondered the possibility that his father cared for him yet felt prohibited from expressing his caring for his son. As this idea began to sink in, Roger's requirement that he receive overt affection from his father began to diminish.

During these discussions, Roger realized that his intense drive to win loving attention from his father was also why he sought strong challenges. That understanding helped Roger lessen his need to overcome difficult obstacles. The author also helped Roger understand why Darlene might not take the lead in being affectionate, even though she loved Roger.

This understanding made sense to Roger and the more it did, the less irritated he was with Darlene when she did not initiate affection. Roger stopped being absolute about requiring that anyone show that they cared for him. His changed attitude greatly improved his emotional connection with Darlene. In turn, her emotional connection with him improved. She no longer felt required to be something that she was not. When everything came together for Roger, his desire for sex with other women vanished.

Chapter 29. DISCUSSION OF THE PSYCHOTHERAPY EXAMPLES

The examples in the previous chapter illustrate how people can be unaware of what takes place in their subconscious. The author has found that there is no substitute for understanding subconscious psychological processes and treating those processes when difficult psychological problems occur, rather than focusing on symptoms and behaviors. This chapter elaborates on some aspects related to the examples described in the previous chapter.

Ted

Ted could not stop his binge-drinking because he did not know any other way to relieve his distress. He did not understand why he was anxious. Ted did not realize that the way he interacted with his dysfunctional wife aggravated the situation for both of them. What he did seemed to be correct to him and did not know how to function differently.

When Ted understood what was going on psychologically, he was able to acquire more effective ways of relating to his wife and protecting his children. Ted's improvements produced better relations with his ex-wife, which altered his belief that his situation was hopeless. As Ted's life improved, his anxiety decreased and his lessened need to relieve his distress led to his no longer needing to medicate himself. That allowed him to relinquish alcohol.

Ted's case illustrates that mitigating distress temporarily, such as by using alcohol, does not solve the underlying problem. Such situations can become worse, especially when a toxic or addictive behavior is employed. Counterproductive methods like using alcohol might relieve symptoms temporarily but have severe consequences that create more problems, often with other people, and are a detour from obtaining more appropriate solutions. It is important to tackle the underlying cause of problems, which often involves modifying pertinent Psychological Roots, coping with distressing stimulus conditions, and acquiring effective problem-solving strategies.

A question arises about why Ted drank in binges rather than in moderate amounts or only occasionally. It was because his anxiety kept building in stages until a tipping point into a state of uncontrollability occurred. To quell that distress required that Ted imbibe copious amounts of alcohol. The more alcohol he drank, the more it interfered with his ability to control his actions, think effectively, and develop effective solutions. Those negatives made his situation worse and trapped him in a vicious cycle: counterproductive interpersonal behavior, blowback from his wife, anger, anxiety, alcohol use, more counterproductive interpersonal behavior, more blowback from his wife, etc. (Binge drinking is a state of uncontrollability.)

Ted's success in getting his ex-wife to behave more civilly illustrates how it is sometimes possible to improve another person's behavior without providing that distress-causing person with counseling. Stimulus conditions count.

Martin

Martin had been battling guilt feelings throughout his life. His feeling guilty built-up cumulatively and eventuated in his being completely overwhelmed by a sense of failure upon losing his job. His lack of income and losing a respected position was the precipitating cause of his depression because of its great significance for him, causing him to be convinced that he was a failure in meeting his responsibility to his family. That circumstance accelerated his long downhill slide until he went far past the tipping point into abject depression.

The key to Martin's improving was his learning how to achieve conscious control over the criteria he used for evaluating himself. Counseling helped Martin understand that he had the ability to change the subconscious rules he used to judge himself. He gradually accepted the idea that he did not have to employ the rules he had always used to evaluate himself. The more he was able to do so the more he relinquished considering himself to be a total failure. That change took place gradually.

As Martin's depression began to lift, his mind began to clear up and his confidence about his ability to cope improved. His thinking became still clearer with each step he made in modifying the absolute expectations and beliefs that had been plaguing him, including some erroneous ideas about work and what was expected of him. That progress allowed him to lessen the amount of his medication, further helping clear his foggy mind and allowing him to feel closer to his wife. As his clarity improved, he understood more about himself and what was required of him as a family person and employee. That improved perspective helped him function better, seek another job and obtain it, and perform well in that position. When it became clear that his new job was stable, his down mood lightened even more. That stability allowed him to relinquish much of his remaining dysthymia.

Martin's case illustrates the potency of Psychological Roots such as people's belief about what their role in life is and the importance of expectations and sense of responsibility. What made Martin's psychology particularly troubling for him was that his beliefs were absolutes and therefore gave him no margin for error. The author has found that the above-mentioned Psychological Roots are among common contributors to depression. So although the upside of high standards and expectations is a strong drive to achieve, the downside can be extreme unhappiness when failures occur which, when overwhelming, can lead to depression.

Medication is not likely to change Psychological Roots, although it could have an indirect effect because it acts on biological factors that may affect them. Hence, when medicine does not help a person improve in a substantial way, something else such as psychological factors may be causing the problem, as in Martin's case.

Ira

Ira's low threshold for negative emotional arousal and extreme reaction to being controlled led to his being a volatile missile waiting to explode, like a ticking time bomb. His explosions illustrate how it is possible for irritations to build-up until reaching a flash point. His family did not recognize the signs of Ira's irritability building up, which explains why his explosions made Ira seem psychotic and took them by surprise. Ira's attempt to keep a lid on his annoyance illustrates how a person can have intense internal reactions without other people being aware of what is going on in that person.

Ira's violent outbursts led to his being diagnosed as psychotic and treated accordingly. Misdiagnosis can occur when people are unaware of the potency of psychological factors. The hidden nature of psychological processes is a factor in such misunderstandings, also lack of awareness of the potency of those hidden processes. When a person has flare-ups despite taking medication for a condition, as in Ira's case, the cause might not be biological.

Neither Ira nor Al, his father, had a constructive way to deal with the explosive situations or preventing them. Al's method of dealing with problems was to passionately push against the odds until positive things occurred. That strategy had often worked for him in the past, which made it hard for him to use a softer approach such as raising his threshold for negative arousal and acquiring alternative ways to engage Ira instead of increasing the pressure he gave Ira. Understanding win-win solutions and using them were especially hard for Al to do. An important aid for avoiding blow-ups was Al's stopping himself upon noticing some subtle non-verbal cues in Ira before Ira exploded. Al was willing to do what the author asked him because Ira's altercations decreased. Al deserves much credit for being willing to make those modifications that ran counter to some of his strong Psychological Roots.

As time went on, Al's willingness to avoid engaging in conflicts with Ira lessened tensions. Al was rewarded when Ira's rages ended and Ira occasionally helped with family chores. Ira believed that other people and circumstances, including his father, were the entire cause of his problems. He did not realize how difficult he was.

Ira's case highlights people's needs to be respected and not controlled. (Also see Spike's case in Chapter 18.) Al's interacting constructively with Ira is another example of how it is sometimes possible to improve another person's behavior by changing what one does with the other person. As with Ted's wife, mentioned at the beginning of this chapter, stimulus conditions count.

Nell

How could Nell suddenly be afraid of crossing bridges without ever having had an unpleasant experience with a bridge? How could someone have intense anxiety without knowing why? The reason is that people are unaware of almost everything that goes on in the mind (mentioned in the Prologue of this book). The cause of Nell's phobia needed to be uncovered because it would have been hard to lessen her underlying panic if the cause was not known. Even when the cause is known it can be difficult for people to change.

Uncovering the cause was guided by Psychological Systems Theory's assumption that internal reactions and behavior have a logical cause that can be identified despite its being hidden in subconscious processes. In Nell's case, the most likely genetic Psychological Root was her need for safety. Anxiety would not suddenly occur unless it was aroused by a stimulus in a Stimulus-and-Root Hidden Sequence. Whatever that stimulus was would have had to have been extremely threatening. (See the discussion of Hidden Sequences in Chapter 4). Since Nell could not think of what caused her to be panicked, either the theory was wrong about the logic of psychological processes or her mind was blocking the cause from her awareness. Blocking of that sort can happen at times, such as when a person does not remember a severe trauma until he/she is ready to consciously address it, for example, having been sexually abused in early childhood. Therefore, probing was needed and had to be done delicately, without turning off Nell, who was very sensitive, or making things worse for her.

Initially, the author's probing to identify the presumed missing stimulus did not elicit pertinent clues from Nell, which was mysterious. After the stimulus was identified, a reason for her being blocked from awareness appears to have been her strong desire to think in positive terms and avoid negatives which, if so, would offer another example of how powerful Psychological Roots can be.

Nell's focus on bridges was another factor that kept her from being aware of the importance of the angry professor in that bridges received her attention while other aspects associated with bridges faded into the background (an instance of selective attention). Nell's selective attention also contributed to her not realizing that the bridge was a *signal* that she was approaching danger rather than the *cause* of her panic. Her inability to know what was going on was not her fault because those aspects took place below her awareness and beyond her conscious control. The hidden nature of psychological processes and the way the mind can work on its own kept her from using her considerable intelligence to solve her problem.

When bridges became a sign that Nell was approaching danger, it was an instance of classical conditioning. That conditioning is somewhat related to the conditioning that took place in Pavlov's experiment which a bell signaled the arrival of food (see Chapter 18). That bell did not cause salivation, just as bridges did not cause Nell to be in danger. To Nell, however, bridges appeared to cause her to be intensely anxious. Had bridges been the focal point of the therapy and had desensitization been employed, Nell's situation would not have been adequately resolved.

Using a desensitization technique might seem to be a way to deal with Nell's bridge phobia directly. However, desensitizing Nell to bridges would have been *indirect* because bridges were not the actual cause of her problem. Satisfactorily addressing the originating cause – that out-of-control professor – and the cumulative build-up of her background tensions permitted her panic about bridges to end. From a behavioral standpoint, Nell's no longer being concerned about bridges was somewhat similar to Pavlov's dogs ceasing to salivate when food no longer followed the bell.

Hypnosis was another way that Nell's anxiety about bridges might have been addressed. Hypnosis can help many circumstances, such as solidifying the Psychological Root changes that people make. However, using hypnosis to lessen Nell's anxiety directly without addressing the cause might have only reduced her anxiety, not eliminate it, because the cause would not have been addressed (the threat caused by the professor). As a result, hypnosis, like desensitization, was not a preferred method.

Since the cause was the hostile teacher, the therapy did not address bridges directly and instead, focused primarily on helping her feel safe in that professor's classroom. Bridges did not cause her condition, however they were important in understanding the situation.

Nell's case is an example of why focusing on observable aspects can be misleading (bridges, in her case) and why it is often essential to obtain clues about the powerful psychological processes that operate below people's awareness. When sub-surface processes are not understood, symptoms might be addressed rather than the cause. Understanding the psychological processes involved helps when developing an appropriate therapy. Theories provide guides and the author has found that Psychological Systems Theory is particularly helpful in this regard.

Disguised and hidden causes also occur related to biological aspects. For example, some migraine headaches are caused by a knotted back or neck muscle (an instance of referred pain). Some headaches are due to frustration, such as problems involving a clash with another person (see Maura's case in Chapter 4). A person's digestive system can be upset because of an infection in an ear if that ear's semi-circular canals are disturbed. Before disease-causing microbes were known, some serious illnesses were not treated effectively.

Even though Nell's feeling safe from her raging teacher was addressed, that issue was not sufficient to eliminate all of her concern about bridges because other tensions that had contributed to her state of uncontrollability had become attached to that circumstance. As a result, Nell's other tensions had to be treated, not just her concern about the professor, including a way for her to cope with her unpleasant work supervisor and unresolved family issues.

Nell had ignored the tensions caused by other things in her busy life. Those tensions had built-up cumulatively, which set the stage for a 'perfect storm' that was triggered when that raging teacher entered the scene. It was not intuitive that for Nell's bridge phobia to end it was also essential to bring those other tension-producing aspects under control. This aspect of Nell's situation was not immediately apparent since apart from bridges, she initially talked only about positive aspects.

Nell's panic about crossing bridges illustrates how potent the wired-in need for safety is and also how people can be unaware of aspects that can nevertheless generate strong emotions. Nell's phobia also offers an indication of how the mind makes associations on its own without being consciously directed to do so and without providing any conscious indication of what is taking place. In addition, Nell's phobia illustrates that what goes on inside a person's brain can remain hidden even when that individual attempts to discern it, and the person is intelligent and highly motivated to find out. Nell's case also illustrates how surprised an individual can be upon discovering the cause. Knowing about psychological processes and having effective strategies for working with those processes can be indispensable.

Nell's concern about the professor and her phobia about bridges illustrate how experiences can generate Psychological Roots, in her case, a belief that she was in danger from that professor. Nell's experience also shows why intelligence can be insufficient when attempting to solve some difficult problems; it helps to know the underlying processes involved and having effective problem-solving strategies.

That hyper-aggressive professor seemed to believe that rage, shock, and fear messages change people's minds. He apparently did not know that ranting, trying to induce fear and guilt, and being aggressive are repelling forces that turn people off, the opposite of being persuasive. Hence, instead of his winning converts to his cause he frightened Nell and probably turned off others as well. Misunderstanding of that sort is an example of the lack of knowledge many people have about psychology. Perhaps even if he knew more about psychology he might not use a softer approach. Another question is whether his raging was a way to vent his pent-up feelings and therefore was more about his interests than those of the students and the curriculum.

Lily

The anxiety of some of Lily's family members led her parents to believe that her anxiety was due to her genetics and led to giving her strong medication for many years until her parents realized that something else might be going on. Many people are not aware that anxiety often occurs for psychological reasons. A sign that the cause of a psychological condition is not being treated effectively is when a psychological disorder continues or increases while a person is taking medication for it. It took many years of Lily's ingesting large doses of anti-anxiety medications and having frequent panic attacks before Lily's parents realized that the cause might be something other than biological. The medicine had been addressing Lily's physiological reactions, which is an intermediate part of Hidden Sequences and therefore a proximal cause, rather than the originating cause of her anxiety.

Lily's procrastinating about doing her school work puzzled Lily's parents since it did not seem logical to them that she would procrastinate if she were motivated. They thought that Lily was not sufficiently motivated, the opposite of what was going on. They did not realize that Lily delayed addressing school work because she did not want to work with aspects that would increase her anxiety. Lily's strong anxiety was substantially due to the huge demands on herself. Therefore, paradoxically, her strong motivation *heightened* her procrastinating. Her parents frequently prodded Lily to do better at school because they did not understand subconscious processes. Their doing so unintentionally aggravated Lily's anxiety and *diminished* her academic effectiveness. As a result, Lily's parents were surprised that Lily's procrastinating decreased after she *lowered* her expectations.

Lily improved because her low expectations lessened the tension-filled demands she made on herself, reduced her anxiety about failing, and permitted her to feel better about her efforts. She remained strongly motivated because she kept her goals high (see Chapter 11). Fortunately, Lily grasped this understanding even though her parents did not fully comprehend it. Understanding psychological processes, such as in this case, can be counter-intuitive unless there is some understanding of those subconscious processes. Psychological Systems Theory can help people understand some of those otherwise puzzling aspects of human behavior and lessen counterproductive actions.

Anxiety about avoiding failure can diminish students' performance because high emotionality impedes cognitive processes. This result is counterintuitive because many people believe that people perform better when they are motivated, regardless of how they are motivated. However, attempts to motivate students by emphasizing the need to avoid failure (a fear message) can backfire and reduce cognitive effectiveness, as Lily's problems illustrate. School anxiety can also cause students to dislike school, make learning painful, and lessen creativity. Positive strategies for teaching, learning, and school achievement can be highly effective. (Teaching and learning, including interesting self-comprehension activities, are discussed in Chapters 34 and 35).

Frank

On the surface, Frank's debilitated physical state seemed to be due entirely to his age. However, some of it was caused by Frank's believing that he had no further reason to live and was preparing to die. His hard-to-meet expectations and narrow comfort zone created a negative perspective that was further amplified by his thinking in absolutes. His focus on tangible aspects made it hard for him to understand hidden psychological aspects. Frank's downward spiral illustrates how potent beliefs are, also some of the drawbacks of knowing little about psychology and its potency, and being unwilling to learn.

Frank realizing that he had a reason to live (his family) helped him become more alert, active and alive. Another aid in bringing him back from his physical decline was his realizing that there were interesting things in which he could still become engaged. Coinciding with those realizations was grasping that he probably had many good years ahead of him. Having a purpose in life can be a strong motivation. Frank's acquiring a more positive outlook and related behavior illustrate how people can improve even when they start out highly resistant and do not have a psychological perspective. The power of beliefs should not be overlooked.

Roger

Roger was addicted to sex, not because of an intense sex drive, or a biological or hormonal quirk, or because he was deviant. The cause was not intuitive: his intense need to be loved by his emotionally distant father.

Without his realizing it, that need had generalized and had been modified to become a requirement that he be loved by important people in his life. Whenever a woman he loved did not initiate affection, Roger interpreted it as a sign that she did not love him and turned to other women out of anger. That unfaithful behavior of his began to end when he stopped thinking that he would succeed in obtaining overt affection from his father. It was also important to him and morale-boosting to realize that his girl friend loved him even though she did not initiate making love.

Roger's situation illustrates the powerful emotional impact that fathers have on their children, the life-long impact of childhood experiences, the potency of subconscious drives, and the non-intuitive nature of some behaviors.

The potency of psychological factors

The problems of depression, anxiety, addiction, and infidelity mentioned above involving Martin, Ted, Ira, Lily, Frank, and Roger appeared to be caused biologically but were due to psychological factors. Ted's alcohol addiction was not a medical disease, Frank's diminished interest in living was due to believing that his life was ending, and Roger's addiction to sex was not due to an overactive sex drive. These cases illustrate that some maladies that appear to be biological can have psychological causes and therefore require psychological treatment.

These situations also provide examples of how beliefs, expectations, and other Psychological Roots can have powerful emotional and behavioral effects. Despite those effects and the substantial education, professional background, high intelligence, strong problem-solving ability, and other counseling of many of the author's many hundreds of clients over 30+ years, none of them knew what caused their psychological issues. However, unearthing the Psychological Roots that were involved led to solutions.

Psychological Systems Theory has been indispensable in the author's helping people, which is consistent with Kurt Lewin's concept that "There is nothing as useful as a good theory". The next chapter provides specific details of Psychological Systems Therapy.

Chapter 30. THE THREE-STAGE METHOD APPLIED TO
PSYCHOTHERAPY
(Prepare, Propose a solution, then Solidify constructive changes.)[43]

This chapter describes the three-stage method as it applies to
Psychological Systems Therapy. During Stage 1 (Preparation), distress-prone
Psychological Roots and the stimulus conditions that impact those roots are
identified (techniques for which are described in Chapter 6).[44] Obtaining the
client's receptivity also occurs during Stage 1 as well as identifying his/her
concerns, thoughts, feelings, beliefs, reactions, behavior patterns, childhood
experience, and relationship issues.[45] In Stage 2 (Present the message), an
attempt is made to help clients understand and modify their distress-prone
Psychological Roots and stimulus conditions, and acquire coping strategies. In
Stage 3 (Solidifying), an attempt is made to strengthen the constructive
changes a client makes.

Stage 1. PREPARE
A. Receptivity
Modifying Psychological Roots and behavior can be challenging.
Accomplishing those changes is aided by the client having a positive
connection with the counselor and being motivated to improve. Even slight
negatives can inhibit a client's motivation. The therapist must earn the client's
cooperation and should employ soft attempts to influence the client rather
than apply pressure, and not respond negatively should a client resist. Clients'
receptivity is bolstered by their believing that a good solution is possible and

---

[43] The author has found that this therapeutic approach can often produce
substantial progress in the first few sessions, helping even when other
counseling approaches or medication have not.

[44] Employing a seek-and-solve approach is consistent with Nezu & Wilkins
(2005).

[45] Beck's (1991) cognitive behavioral therapy (CBT) considers beliefs to
important, but views them as having a role similar to that of attitudes. In
Psychological Systems Theory (PST). Beliefs are Psychological Roots and
attitudes are internal reactions (see Chapter 4). CBT is a therapy of
psychological disorders, whereas PST is an overall theory of human how
the psychological mind works.

feeling comfortable with the therapist. Rapport is aided by judiciously using appropriate appealing forces, including putting the client's interests first and being caring, emotionally supportive, respectful, empathic, comforting, and on that person's side. The counselor must be sincere, respectful, truthful, trustworthy, agreeable, and offer hope (without a guarantee) when it is reasonable to do so. Sincere listening, patience, and helping the recipient feel comfortable are musts. Occasional humor when appropriate can lighten the atmosphere.

Repelling forces should be avoided or softened in the rare instances in which such aspects might be appropriate. Special care should be employed when disagreeing with a client since it implies that the recipient is wrong and therefore can be a repelling force. Arguing should be avoided.

B. Interview

Each client requires an individual plan that addresses his/her particular issues and concerns. Discovering those aspects requires special interviewing in which the primary emphasis is on uncovering the Psychological Roots and stimulus conditions that contribute to the client's current problems. Significant past experiences are important to know, primarily to discern the Psychological Roots that resulted from those circumstances that currently affect the person. The client's early experiences are past stimulus conditions rather than Psychological Roots. All hypotheses should be checked to increase the chances of being accurate.

Effective psychological interviewing requires having skills for identifying Psychological Roots (See Chapter 6). The therapist must be open to clues that can come from any number of directions, such as the client's concerns, emotional reactions, memory, and hypotheses about the cause of his/her problems. Some of the types of problems that often are important to identify are:
1. The client's internal psychology, such as his/her distress-prone Psychological Roots.
2. Pertinent current external stimulus conditions, particularly those that distress the client.
3. Background circumstances affecting the client (e.g., regarding family, work, school, and significant past stimulus conditions).
4. The client's interpersonal difficulties (e.g., regarding relationships).
5. Significant people in the client's life.
6. The client's problem-solving strategies, particularly strategies that do not solve his/her problems or make them worse.

Maintaining rapport is essential and offers opportunities to connect warmly with the client. Miller and Rollnick's (1991) motivational interviewing strategy may be useful.

C. Rate the client's problems

After the client's problems are identified, it can help to evaluate the relative importance of each, ideally with the client's assistance (e.g., by using a 10-point scale to rate the issues). The most important problems should be addressed first because of their impact on the client. (Solving problems of low importance might provide only little relief for the client, see the Intensity Curve in Chapter 2.)

D. Identify the causes of the person's negative reactions

Since negative reactions are a major basis of people's psychological difficulties, it is important to discern what those are and their causes, such as distress-oriented Psychological Roots and stimulus conditions. Then rank order their importance or the sequence in which they will be addressed in counseling.

E. Identify the client's Psychological Roots

It is unlikely for clients to know the causes of their problems since those are hidden and it is difficult to change what is not known. Effective interviewing techniques can help understand sub-surface mental processes and unearth hidden causes such as distress-prone Psychological Roots that generate difficulties for the client (see Chapter 6). It is particularly helpful to identify two sets of Psychological Roots: pertinent surface roots (such as the person's material concerns and interests) and relevant core roots (abstract genetic and acquired needs, concerns, beliefs, and expectations) that exist at or near the foundation of Psychological Root hierarchies. Some core roots include needs for safety, respect, connecting with others, meeting responsibility, protecting a loved one, stability, and not being controlled, also important long-term goals. There are times when it also helps to identify intermediate Psychological Roots.

It helps to know the difference between Psychological Roots (such as beliefs and expectations) and past stimulus conditions that led to the creation of Psychological Roots. Psychological Roots can often be gleaned from limited information and might not require extensive recounting of details related to a person's past. It also helps to know that a person's surface roots, internal reactions, and behaviors can be modified by flow-down effects that can take place when new information is linked to deep and intermediate roots.

Psychological Roots should be addressed in a way that makes the client feel comfortable. Examples of distress-prone roots (such as those listed at the end of Chapter 16) include hard-to-meet expectations (which can lead to feelings of failure, loss, anger, and embarrassment) and a low threshold for negative arousal (which can lead to feeling vulnerable, agitated, anxious, and reactive). Two other examples are pessimism (expecting bad things to happen) and a strong sense of responsibility (which can lead to feeling guilty, tense, and irritable).

"Amory" provides an example of three Psychological Roots that often contribute to psychological conditions, in the author's experience – high standards, low threshold for emotional arousal, and a strong sense of responsibility. Amory appeared to have situational depression due to the difficulties his work supervisor caused. However, closer examination of the circumstances revealed that Amory was stressed by almost any task because of his extremely high standards. Seven consequences of his high standards were:

1. Amory put inordinate personal pressure and strain on himself because he always tried hard to succeed, for example, he put in many extra hours at work.
2. Amory never felt that he had done enough and therefore could never feel that he had sufficiently succeeded at any task. That feeling of failure was especially happening at his job because his supervisor gave him tasks that were inappropriate, without adequate support, and then repeatedly put him on other projects before he could finish any task successfully.
3. Amory was frustrated because he could never complete a task.
4. Amory was anxious about his future at that job because he felt that whatever assignment given him by his supervisor would eventually become a failure in some way.
5. Amory had been clamping his feelings out of loyalty to the company. When his bottled-up emotions were close to a tipping point, he came for counseling.
6. Amory was frustrated because of his inability to solve his dilemma.
7. Amory was angry about the unpleasant things that had been happening to him at work.

Amory did not realize that his feeling overwhelmed by failure, frustration, anxiety, and anger had much to do with his rigid standards and sense of responsibility. He also did not realize that it did not take much for him to feel unhappy because of his low threshold for negative emotional arousal. Hence, what appeared to be depression caused by his situation, was primarily due to his psychology. His Psychological Roots provided a breeding ground for his becoming distressed. As a result, Amory had been experiencing a cumulative build-up of distress for a while. What his manager did pushed him beyond his tipping point.

On the positive side, the distressing circumstances with his supervisor led to Amory's seeking help. When the hidden causes of Amory's problem were explained by the author, Amory quickly understood and was ready to accept making changes in himself. He raised his threshold for arousal, such as by using self-statements such as, "Don't get caught up in this" to give him immediate relief. Longer-term relief resulted from lowering his criterion for failure (while not relinquishing his high goals) and putting his overwhelming sense of responsibility into perspective. He improved quickly, starting in the first session. Subsequently, Amory learned how to speak constructively with his bothersome supervisor about issues that concerned him. Those discussions went well.

During the counseling sessions, the author realized that one of the reasons Amory had been frustrated was that the work he was doing was not in accord with his talents. Amory agreed and sought a more appropriate job with a better boss. Amory also changed his after-work activities to be in accord with his talents. Those modifications also improved his circumstances.

If a client does not provide much information, has difficulty doing so, or resists, it is wise to stop and try an alternative approach. It is important to identify the Psychological Roots that are pertinent to each problem a client wants to address. The deeper those roots are, the broader the range of opportunities to help the client accept solutions because deep roots offer more chances of acceptance than roots closer to the surface. Mentioned earlier is that everyone's desire to be respected can be satisfied in many ways, whereas a client's desire to be promoted at his workplace might be satisfied in only one way.

Constructive changes linked with the client's deep roots can flow down through a hierarchy and have a widespread effect on subsidiary roots, an example of which is when people's low expectations lessen their stress related to work, home, and relationships. (See the discussion of deep roots in Chapter 7 regarding Linking, Psychological Root Hierarchies, and Change). Examples of core roots are needs for safety, stability, closure, connecting with other people, autonomy (a desire not to be controlled), abilities, and avoiding negatives.

Concerns about being disrespected, controlled, vulnerable, and victimized are some other commonly occurring distress-prone Psychological Roots. For couples, some often-occurring problem roots are a desire to set one's partner straight and believing that it is good to tell the other person what he/she does wrong. Other roots that can cause troubles include believing that facts, logic, bluntness, persistence, and criticism are persuasive. Some other problem-causing aspects are disdain for compromise, unwillingness to accept less than one's full objective, intolerance of being wrong or controlled, and believing that win-win solutions are not possible.

Starting points for understanding a client often are his/her problems, statements, opinions, emotional reactions, and behaviors. Among those are habits, defenses, tensions, moods, difficulties with people, and problem-solving strategies. It also helps to understand and be sympathetic to the client's internal reactions, including her feelings, thoughts, judgments, and decisions, especially aspects that foster down moods such as rejection, loneliness, anxiety, guilt, anger, and depression. (Chapters pertaining to these issues include Chapter 6 [identifying Psychological Roots], Chapter 4 [Hidden Sequences], Chapter 11 [goals and expectations], Chapter 15 [executive function], and Chapter 7 [Linking, Psychological Root hierarchies and clusters], also Boxes 3, 4, and 5, and Figs. 13, 14, and 19. Psychological-Root questionnaires can also help identify Psychological Roots.)

F. Identify the actual issue

There are times when the key issue differs from what the recipient believes it is. For example, Nell believed that her problem was fear of bridges although the real problem was her out-of-control teacher, Al believed that Ira was psychotic rather than recognizing his role in Ira's violent reactions, and Ted believed that his ex-wife was entirely at fault without realizing that his behavior triggered strong reactions in her (see Chapter 28). The cause can be thought to be biological, although the cause can be psychological. For example, Maura's headaches were due to her getting resistance from her daughter (see Chapter 4), Martin's depression was due to his feeling that he failed to meet his responsibilities, and Roger's philandering was due to his belief that the woman he loved did not love him (see Chapter 28).

G. Develop solutions

Create possible solutions to the client's problems that align with the person's Psychological Roots and can be presented in a way that might readily be accepted by the client. (It may also help to construct a message related to one of the eight ways to create change described at the end of Chapter 25.) The solutions should include ways the client can make constructive changes in aspects that pertain to him/her personally and might include changes that affect others.

The creation of solutions is aided by understanding the client's Psychological Roots, not just their feelings and behaviors. It is not always easy to develop a way to present solutions in a way that is consistent with the client's Psychological Roots. For example, a client might refuse to stop strongly trying to control his children or spouse (e.g., demanding absolute obedience from a child despite the child's rebelling against being controlled). When a solution is not readily accepted by a client, alternative solutions should be developed (see the example involving Ned's back pain in Chapter 11).

Below are ideas that might help clients cope with their distress-prone Psychological Roots.

- **For hard-to-meet personal expectations,** standards, demands, goals, needs, necessities, desires, responsibilities, and requirements, tell yourself, "Anything above zero is a plus," or "Something is better than nothing" when doing so is appropriate.

- **For inadequate problem-solving strategies:**
  . Break problems into parts, identify key parts, tackle those aspects first, try to complete each part before tackling any other aspect, and avoid attending to ancillary issues while tackling an important task.
  . Use a quantitative scale to evaluate the alternatives in difficult decisions.
  . Give yourself a long time frame to solve problems.
  . Acquire problem-solving strategies during therapy sessions.

- **For low self-esteem:**
  . Acquire social strategies, realize that you are important to someone, and do not think in absolutes. Remind yourself of your positive qualities.

- **For low threshold for negative emotional arousal:**
  . Tell yourself, "Don't get caught up in this", and "Don't take things personally". Distract yourself with something pleasant that absorbs your full attention. Acquire effective problem-solving strategies and improve your confidence about ability to cope with difficult situations.

- **For a narrow adaptive zone:**
  . View an opposing viewpoint as a step toward developing a more effective perspective. Consider failures as opportunities to learn.

- **For pessimism and low self-confidence:**
  . Tell yourself, "There is always a solution"; imagine the worst and assure yourself that "I can manage whatever occurs". Acquire effective problem solving and decision-making strategies.

- **For weak social strategies:**
  . Acquire effective social skills, including ability to ascertain people's concerns, emotional state, and Psychological Roots. Develop skills in creating win-win solutions and communicating. Stop if you meet resistance to your viewpoint and seek a compatible solution. Use appealing forces judiciously and try to avoid using repelling forces.

H. Be prepared and be flexible

After a client understands the cause of the problem, he/she may immediately want a solution. Having a plan that was developed in Stage 1 can help. Expect the possibility that obstacles can arise, such as a difficult-to-understand issue, a client's inability to understand something, or his/her resistance to some solutions. Be cordial and supportive throughout, and avoid using repelling forces.

I. Joint effort

Effective therapy is a cooperative effort between the client and the counselor. The therapeutic strategies and the examples employed to convey information vary with different issues and clients. Some clients need additional services, such as medical treatment, psychiatry, legal and financial advice, job training, academic assistance, or relocation. In such instances, community agencies can be a helpful resource.

J. Stimulus conditions

Distressing stimulus conditions need to be identified and addressed, such as problems with other people (e.g., a significant other, relative, boss, acquaintance, or a particularly bothersome individual), or with issues that involve occupation, school, health, finances, or the law.

K. Amplifiers and diminishers

Amplifiers and diminishers that affect the client's condition should be identified, such as absolute thinking, emotional level, the threshold for emotional arousal, and hyperactivity.

L. Anticipate resistance

Anticipate objections. It may help to prepare some constructive ways of addressing resistance and objections without taking offense.

The bottom line: Establish rapport, identify the Psychological Roots and stimulus conditions that contribute to the client's negative reactions or distress, and develop a plan to help the client modify those aspects constructively.

Stage 2. PRESENT THE MESSAGE

A. Explain the cause of the problem to the client

Help the client understand the cause of his/her difficulties. It can help to use tangible explanations, concrete examples, visual aids, and role-playing especially about abstract issues. (The author often uses examples related to the person's experiences and also draws upon the diagrams in this book.)

B. Develop solutions

Try to engage clients in developing solutions to their problems, one problem at a time. Even when a client is not very effective at doing this, their attempt can help them grasp some of the subtle and sub-surface aspects involved. This approach can help get clients grapple with their issues constructively, learn what is going on inside them, "own" the solutions and then use those strategies. Some aids for comprehension include tangible examples to which they can relate, brief pertinent stories, effective answers to their questions, and the use of their own words when articulating the issues.

C. Start with the most important problem

Addressing the client's most pressing problem first helps the client realize that his/her seemingly overwhelming issues are manageable, illustrates what can be accomplished, boosts clients' receptivity, and sets the stage for making further changes. Addressing issues of low importance initially delays getting to the major issues and might provide the client with only a small benefit. Progress can begin immediately upon identifying key Psychological Roots, often in the first session.

D. Present solutions carefully

In a supportive and caring manner, help the client understand that the major way to create effective long-term change is by changing his/her relevant Psychological Roots or by using constructive ways to satisfy those roots. It is not helpful to pressure the client to change. Trying to change a client's behavior directly can be insufficient because it is an outcome of Hidden Sequences, not the origin. The client needs support and understanding especially about invisible aspects below the surface such as Psychological Roots. The counselor should not be lofty, condescending, or controlling when communicating.

It is difficult for people to change, especially their deep Psychological Roots. The therapist should be patient, careful, and flexible when making suggestions, and not be surprised if the client is resistant at times. Some clients need a considerable amount of emotional support, understanding, confidence-building, and concrete explanations or demonstrations.

E. The client's problems with other people

Helping the client succeed with other people is often essential. Succeeding is aided by having skills for understanding others, communicating, persuading, and resolving conflicts.

F. Clients' venting of their feelings

Clients need to feel free to present their concerns and may want to express strong feelings as a way of obtaining some relief. However, for them to vent at length can be unproductive since doing so does not solve their problems and can lose time in the session that could be used to develop solutions. If the person who is the object of the venting is present or if the client continues venting to others outside the session, those could be strong repelling forces that worsen the client's circumstances, especially if the venting is angry or involves complaints. Instead, the focus of the session should be about what the client can do to improve himself/herself and develop effective solutions.

In instances in which a client complains at length or argues, the therapist should develop an alternative direction in a constructive manner, such as by trying to move the client toward understanding the cause of his/her problems and the creation of solutions that have a reasonable chance of resolving his/her difficulties. With couples, successful counseling may require having some separate sessions with each person. If a client frequently or vociferously vents about feeling put upon and shows very little improvement as well, it may be a sign that the person is resisting making constructive changes or might have a borderline personality disorder. In such instances, the therapeutic direction should shift to identifying the pertinent underlying Psychological Roots and helping the client make constructive changes in those roots.

G. Types of change

There are various types of substantial change (see Chapters 25 and 26). A particularly helpful type of improvement occurs when a client's high-order Psychological Root is modified because doing so can produce a widespread flow-down effect. Also helpful is a client's acquiring modifiers that moderate his/her internal reactions and behavior.

H. Understand Hidden Sequences

Knowing about Hidden Sequences helps the counselor know what aspect in the sequence is being addressed and what aspects should receive attention. For example, a client may want to dwell at length on an experience but doing so is not likely to be as productive as understanding the Psychological Roots that resulted from that experience or led to it. Also, trying to change a current internal reaction (e.g., an emotional response or a dysfunctional attitude) is less likely to be effective than modifying the Psychological Roots that contribute to that reaction. Clients probably do not realize aspects like these and may try to directly change their own or someone else's overt behavior such as aggression or an addiction. Having a Hidden Sequences perspective can help avoid giving undue attention to unproductive aspects, such as a client's extensive venting of feelings or overly focusing on background details. Effectiveness is aided by focus on key aspects, such as key Psychological Roots and stimulus conditions.

I. Avoid the use of repelling forces

Since the primary objective in counseling is to lessen tensions and difficulties the client has, the therapist should try to avoid adding unpleasantness. For example, it helps for the therapist to not be impatient, blunt, critical, argumentative, controlling, persistent, guilt-inducing, or inattentive to the concerns the recipient considers important. The author allows the client to be in control and is attentive to the issues that the client considers important. It helps for the therapist to be understanding about clients' lateness, cancellations, and fees. (See Chapter 10 regarding appealing and repelling forces.)

J. Resistance

The counselor should expect resistance from clients since people find it difficult to understand aspects that are abstract and invisible to them, and to change. Improving can be impeded when clients think in absolutes, which often accompanies states of uncontrollability such as depression, anxiety, and personality disorders. The counselor should not be critical or focus on what the client does wrong and should not be surprised when a client has objections or misunderstands. The counselor should also be prepared that changes made by clients might not last long.

Clients' questions should be answered to their satisfaction and explanations presented in a manner that helps them understand and accept the information. Examples are often needed, sometimes many examples. Those aspects should ideally relate to the client's experiences, such as their occupation or hobby. It might help to ask reluctant clients if they would be willing to try an idea for several weeks to see if it helps.

Clients should not feel that they are being judged or are wrong. Repelling forces should be avoided. The therapist should not take offense, use pressure, argue, or criticize when clients are negative, disagree, or break appointments. The therapist should be graceful and take those occurrences in stride because rapport is more important than being right or introducing repelling forces. There are times when the therapist needs to change strategies or pace, eliminate some aspects, or connect the client with another therapist.

K. Additional psychological analyses and interventions

As counseling proceeds, additional Psychological Roots and stimulus conditions may need to be addressed, or a different approach may be needed. The therapist should be knowledgeable about other approaches and willing to use those strategies.

L. Physical health

Everything psychological rests on a biological foundation, therefore clients' physical health is important, including their life-style, pain, illness, injuries, nutrition, exercise, sleep, and other medical issues. Respect should be given to a client's desire for their health issues to not be discussed.

M. Addiction

It is critical to treat the cause of addictions. A client might not be able to abstain from an addictive behavior without addressing the cause, which often contributes to attempts to relieve substantial distress. Some therapists do not want to counsel anyone who is using an addictive substance, however many such individuals may be unable to relinquish their addiction without emotional support or having a constructive way to cope with their issues. The author has found that requests for counseling offer a window of opportunity to help clients with an active addiction. The key is how willing an addicted person is to make progress.

N. Slow or no progress

When a client makes little or no progress, some Psychological Roots may have been overlooked. For example, a depressed person might have low self-confidence or inadequate problem-solving techniques, or may have strong dependency needs. In such instances, more progress might be accomplished by the therapist searching for additional Psychological Roots that explain the slow pace and then and working patiently and constructively with the client to help him/her achieve more substantial improvement.

O. Setbacks

Some clients forget what they learn, misunderstand, have difficulties using what they are learning, continue to engage in counterproductive behaviors, or miss appointments. The counselor should adjust cordially and seamlessly, be patient, and support whatever constructive improvements a client makes. It is particularly important for the therapist to be accepting and cordial, and to avoid using repelling forces, such as not being impatient or irritable. Sometimes using a different approach or explanation can help a client understand or resolve an issue and sometimes visual aids, written statements, or hypnosis can help. Sometimes presenting information in small steps can help, or using self-comprehension methods (e.g., role-playing, imagined scenarios, or self-discovery [Rogerian] questions), or a different therapeutic style.[46] If progress does not look promising or if rapport between the client and the therapist greatly diminishes, the client can be guided to another therapist.

The bottom line: Helping clients solve their problems often requires helping them modify their deleterious Psychological Roots, cope with their distressing stimulus conditions, and acquire effective task and social skills.

Stage 3. SOLIDIFY CONSTRUCTIVE CHANGES

It is possible for people to misunderstand some aspects, use only part of what they learn, or revert to earlier behaviors. Therefore, it is useful to try to solidify the positive changes a client makes. Solidifying can be aided by the following aspects.

A. Emotional support

Praise the client for making progress such as being willing to move forward, making changes, having a good attitude, and achieving successes. The therapist should not take credit for the changes the client makes, allowing clients to conclude for themselves that they have made progress and that the therapist helped them.

B. Additional information

Provide additional explanations, facts, evidence, logic, and examples that support the main or other aspects if it seems appropriate, useful, and acceptable to the client.

---

[46] Clients are likely to have difficulty solving their own problems, especially people who have limited understanding of psychology. The author has found that self-comprehension learning, such as Rogers' (1951) non-directive counseling, works better when clients understand their hidden sub-surface psychology.

C. Review

Review some of the main points if appropriate, useful, and acceptable to the client. Do not overdo the review unless the client requests doing so. Hypnosis or guided imagery can be used to help solidify what the client has learned, if the client wishes it and if doing so is useful and appropriate.

D. Hypnosis

Hypnosis can help strengthen a behavior, reaction, or idea in people who are receptive to its use and who have already accepted that particular behavior, reaction, or idea, such as after having been engaged in a therapeutic process like that mentioned in this chapter. A reason that hypnosis works may be that what is presented is not automatically screened out by the person's evaluative process while that individual is in a hypnotic state. That state aids what is presented to be readily accepted, believed, and incorporated into a person's Psychological Root system. Therefore, if a client is willing to accept using hypnosis, it can help solidify the changes a client has made. For individuals who are willing to allow that to happen, perhaps because they have a strong desire to eliminate an undesirable habit such as smoking, hypnosis can work well.

The client must feel that the hypnotist is trustworthy and be receptive. Some people are especially ready to accept hypnotic suggestions. However, some individuals do not feel comfortable when things are not under their control or are conflicted about giving up a deeply held habit (such as overeating, smoking, or alcohol use). Some people do not believe hypnosis can work, are turned off because of what a stage hypnotist has done, or do not believe that they will benefit from it.

Hypnosis might not change behaviors that are deeply embedded in a person's psyche, such as phobias acquired in very early childhood (e.g., claustrophobia, fear of falling, or abuse). Hypnosis also might not work if the cause of an internal reaction or behavior has not been modified since the origin of those outcomes will remain. Hypnosis is not a panacea and is unlikely to work in instances such as those described above. No attempt should be made to persuade individuals who resist the idea of using hypnosis. **If a person does not readily accept being hypnotized, hypnosis should not be used**.

E. Address the client's future

Clients can be invited to identify additional circumstances to which they can apply the skills they have acquired. The therapist might suggest additional applications if appropriate.

Chapter 31. STRESS

Everyone has problems and experiences stress. It is useful to know some of the aspects of stress touched upon in this chapter.

Distress and eustress
    Stress is often considered to be unpleasant, yet some stresses are pleasing, healthy, helpful, and needed, such as a positive emotional connection with a significant other or a strong interest in a hobby. Selye (1955) referred to positive experiences as 'eustress'. Psychological health is aided by experiencing positive emotions and low distress. Some positive experiences are physical (e.g., functioning effectively within an adaptive zone) while some are psychological (e.g., upbeat thinking and positive emotions). Appealing forces foster eustress and contribute to feeling comfortable, thinking effectively, and general health. Repelling forces, on the other hand, contribute to distress and ill health, both physically (e.g., inflammation and a compromised immune system) and mentally (e.g., malaise and impeded thinking and problem-solving). (See Chapter 10 for a discussion of appealing and repelling forces.)
    Psychological and biological health can be aided by having Psychological Roots and stimulus conditions that foster eustress and lessen distress. Some suggestions for lessening distress are given below.
• Avoid using repelling forces, such as in social situations. Use appealing forces when feasible such as making people feel comfortable. Use a win-win approach when disagreements arise (described in Chapters 20 - 22).
• Help manage difficulties by acquiring effective problem-solving strategies. Assume that there is always a reasonable solution and try innovative ways to find it. View failures as learning experiences to help counteract down moods, pessimism, or a lack of confidence.
• Counteract low self-esteem by recognizing your competence, worth, value, and usefulness, and realize that other people care about you. Also, realize that you do not have to be outstanding, be accepted by everyone, or change the minds of people who do not agree with you.
• For an especially difficult task, split it into parts, identify the most difficult aspect, and tackle that key element first. Retain what you learn for future use.
• Widen your comfort range. If you have a narrow acceptability zone, consider enlarging it if circumstances are appropriate for doing so.
• When difficulties arise, tell yourself, "I can handle this", "There is always a reasonable solution", and "Don't get caught up in this".

• If you are feeling distressed, ask yourself whether you have hard-to-meet expectations or if your expectations are too high. If so, lower your expectations if it is reasonable and feasible to do so. After lowering your expectations, consider keeping the same goals or raising your goals still higher. (See Chapter 11.)

Relaxation and medication

Methods that can help temporarily lessen symptoms include breathing exercises, relaxation, and meditation. Temporary use of some professionally prescribed medications may also help.

A practical application of this information

Lessening distress aids mental, social, and physical well-being. Ability to create win-win solutions when disagreements arise can help. Distress can often be lessened by constructively modifying distress-prone Psychological Roots (e.g., raising one's threshold for negative arousal and lowering expectations). Being preventive can often help avoid stress.

Chapter 32. PREDICTING AND PREVENTING PSYCHOLOGICAL DISORDERS

It is often possible to identify potential problems and correct them before substantial damage occurs ("An ounce of prevention is worth a pound of cure"). This chapter provides a way to predict and prevent psychological conditions.

Prediction

It is possible to assess the degree to which distress-prone Psychological Roots are present in people by comparing the Psychological Roots of people who have a psychological disorder with those of people who do not have that disorder. Some of the disorders with which this method could be employed include depression, anxiety, obsessive-compulsive disorder, borderline personality disorder, bipolar disorder, PTSD, phobias, addictions, and eating disorders. Some Psychological Roots that the author often has found to be distress-prone were listed at the end of Chapter 16. Those roots included a low threshold for negative emotional arousal, pessimism, narrow zones of acceptability, hard-to-meet expectations, low self-esteem, and weak problem-solving strategies.

Eustress-prone Psychological Roots of psychologically healthy people are also possible to identify. Eustress-oriented roots (often the reverse of distress-prone roots) include a high threshold for negative arousal, optimism, a wide range of acceptability, high confidence, moderately high self-esteem, easy-to-meet expectations, and effective problem-solving strategies (such as an ability to create win-win solutions and skill in identifying key aspects). Aids for boosting eustress can be useful to people and their effects should be empirically testable.

Predictive studies can also assess internal reactions (e.g., tension, stress, failure, worrying, anger, gloomy thoughts, and down moods) and overt behaviors (e.g., argumentativeness, aggression, retaliation, quality of coping strategies, use of addictive substances, and suicide attempts). Overt behaviors can be quantitatively assessed with standard questionnaires (e.g., Beck, Steer, & Brown, 1996). A questionnaire assessing frequent types of distressing stimulus conditions might also be possible (e.g., regarding relationships, family, peers, work, health, and societal circumstances).

Statistical analyses of results can be aided by using self-report questionnaires that are responded to numerically (e.g., with a 0-10 scale). In addition to assessing the probability of a person subsequently experiencing a psychological disorder, it would be useful to know the relative strengths of the distress- and eustress-prone Psychological Roots that are related to psychological disorders, also the intensity of internal reactions, relevant modifiers, and distress-prone stimulus conditions.

Some distress-prone factors might exist early in life hence age-appropriate measures would be needed for children.

Analysis of such data, including aspects that relate to internal reactions and behaviors, could lead to creating a numerical index regarding the risk an individual has for a psychological condition, ideally well before he/she experiences a full-blown disorder. In some instances, distress-prone factors might exist in early childhood. If so, child-oriented assessment methods might be useful to create in addition to methods suitable for later years such as questionnaires.

People in a precursor range – such as those experiencing dysthymia, anxiety, or annoyance – might have a high risk for entering a state of uncontrollability (e.g., depression, panic, or borderline personality disorder) compared to other individuals.

Prevention

People who are at risk might be able to avoid a full-blown disorder if they receive appropriate treatment. Preventive methods include skills for solving task and social problems, lessening distress, modifying distress-prone Psychological Roots, and coping with distressing stimulus conditions. Preventive programs might thereby lessen major stresses and the likelihood of experiencing a psychological disorder. Increased eustress might also be possible.

It might be possible for people to improve their lives and be more productive in many ways, such as by programs on smart phones, the Internet, TV programs, tapes, and in books and workshops. There could also be educational programs starting in grade school and continuing through college and graduate school. Some preventive programs might be designed for special circumstances such as particular industries, educational institutions, and government agencies.

The ability of preventive programs to reduce personal and family turmoil, unhappiness, and costs of living and running businesses could be measured. Improvement in productivity, employee motivation, and absentee rates could occur with some programs more than others. Lessened divorce, addiction, crime, violence, and a saving of lives are other possibilities.

A preventive psychological approach would be analogous to preventive medical and life-style programs that have successfully lowered the incidence of strokes, heart attacks, and diabetes. The cost of prevention would be far less than treating psychological disorders after they occur.

People who are not at risk nevertheless might benefit from preventive programs if the general quality of life improves for society as a whole. Preventive programs, research, and societal improvements might be a result.

Chapter 33. PREVENTION IN GENERAL
(The present chapter presents some highlights related to this broad topic.)

We are not perfect. Everyone makes mistakes ("To be human is to err"). Therefore, identifying potential problems and fixing them before serious consequences occur can be beneficial. This chapter describes a prevention perspective that might help.

Benefits of being preventive

Taking preventive action on foreseeable problems can help avoid troublesome problems, such as some railroad crossing incidents, inappropriately labeled poisons, and terrorist activities. Advice about doing so comes from many sources, including well-known proverbs and sayings such as "Look both ways before crossing a street", "Look before leaping", and "Safety first". A reason that there are many such sayings may be that being preventive requires special effort and motivation. This issue is examined in this chapter, including why prevention does not readily occur and what might be done about that.

Obstacles to prevention

There are hindrances to being preventive. One is a strong need for closure that can make a person impatient, be concerned about the present rather than the future, or focus on tangible aspects. Need for stability, desire to avoid unpleasantness, and being conditioned can contribute to wanting to remain with what one has. People also dislike being wrong, which impedes their willingness to admit errors and correct them. We are also concerned about cost, time, and effort, which can lessen our willingness to put resources into preventing something that might not happen. Thinking in absolutes intensifies these tendencies and can keep us locked into existing patterns.

Resistance to being preventive manifests itself in many ways. For instance, many persons do little or nothing to rein in their harmful behaviors such as their use of toxic substances (e.g., alcohol, cigarettes, and illegal drugs). Many people lack sufficient sleep, and eat unhealthy foods (e.g., fast foods, toxic ingredients such as preservatives and artificial sweeteners, and over-use of saturated fat, salt, and sugar). Action to prevent a future danger might occur only after serious events such as fatalities. Many individuals ignore warnings related to pesticides and safety devices ("They are just suggestions"). Some people are incautious when driving, for example, doing so while inebriated, even after their license has been taken away. Some people take chances when boating, diving, biking, skiing, climbing mountains, or engaging in contact sports. Many people bet in lotteries and at casinos even though they know that the odds are against their winning. Also, impulsivity and overspending are not uncommon.

Perhaps for reasons like these, there are many proverbs and other sayings that support the value of being preventive in addition to those mentioned above. Examples include, "A stitch in time saves nine", "Marry in haste, repent at leisure", "A penny saved is a penny earned", "The early bird catches the worm", and "Don't eat your seed corn". On the other hand, some proverbs promote not being preventive, such as "He who hesitates is lost", "Damn the torpedoes, full speed ahead", "Analysis paralysis", and "All talk and no action".

The bottom line: Humans often are not good at thinking preventively.

Some preventive behaviors

Some people have a preventive philosophy. For example, some individuals eat a carefully designed diet. Many people change the oil in their car on a regular schedule. Many business people try to make carefully calculated, conservative decisions. Insurance companies exist because they offer people a bulwark against negative contingencies. Many people recycle waste products such as paper, metal, plastic, and glass. Some individuals consult psychics to try to peer into the future.

Forward-looking strategies include acquiring formal education, saving for emergencies and retirement, bathing and other hygienic activities, paying attention to sanitation and other health needs, being concerned about one's appearance, careful selection of clothing to wear, and the use of perfume and cosmetics.

Some non-human creatures are genetically wired to be preventive. Birds build a nest before laying an egg, some creatures warn others not to enter their territory (e.g., barking dogs), and some poisonous snakes and fish give warnings such as rattling, hissing, or displaying a bright color.

The bottom line:

Being preventive is aided by having a preventive philosophy.

Psychological Roots that might bolster thinking preventively

Philosophies are Psychological Roots. Some Psychological Roots that might support being preventive are noted below, in alphabetical order.

- Ability to identify problems
- Abstract thinking ability
- Analytical thinking ability
- Concern about danger
- Concern about the future
- Confidence in prevention
- Desire to avoid failure
- Desire to learn from mistakes
- Low threshold for negative arousal
- Sequential thinking ability
- Strong need for safety
- Willingness to expend effort & resources

The opposite of the above-mentioned Psychological Roots foster resistance to prevention, for example, over-confidence in existing circumstances, poor problem-solving strategies, over-confidence in the present and past, and low interest in abstract thinking.

A three-stage model to aid prevention
A version of the previously described three-stage model provided below might help when attempting to be preventive.

1. PREPARE
A. Have a preventive perspective.
B. Identify problems might occur in the future.
C. Use effective problem-solving strategies. For example, have confidence that a solution will be found and work to develop a good solution. Consider the potential consequences of that solution and make improvements in it. Try to make the solution cost-effective and capable of being accomplished reasonably rapidly.

D. Anticipate getting resistance from other people regarding a solution, then develop win-win solutions to help resolve possible disagreements.

2. PRESENT THE SOLUTION OR APPLY IT
Anticipate getting resistance from other people regarding a solution, then develop win-win solutions to help resolve possible disagreements.
E1. If only you are involved in the situation, apply the preventive solution.
E2. Evaluate the outcome.
E3. Make modifications to the solution as needed.
E4. If other people are involved, present your preventive solution to them. Offer your viewpoint calmly, without arguing. Accept the possibility that your idea might run counter to other people's viewpoint and rejected by them.
E5. If the solution is not accepted by other people, try to identify the Psychological Roots of the individuals who do not accept it and find a way to make it consistent with those roots (e.g., by showing how your idea might solve a problem that the person has).

F. If the new solution is accepted (2-E4, above), apply the solution.
G. Evaluate the outcome.
H. Make modifications to the solution as needed.
I. If what you presented is not persuasive (2-E5, above), identify the

reasons for the resistance, including Psychological Roots, and
create a win-win solution that attempts to satisfy everyone.
J. If the new solution is accepted, apply the solution.
K. Evaluate the outcome.
L. Make modifications in the solution as needed.

M. If the solution in 2-I, above, is not accepted, do a further analysis of the
Psychological Roots underlying that resistance and develop a different
win-win solution accordingly.
N. If the new solution is accepted, apply the solution.
O. Evaluate the outcome.
P. Make modifications to the solution as needed.

Q. If the solution in 2-M, above, is not accepted, do not argue. Assume that
the solution is inconsistent with the resisters' Psychological Roots. Then
cordially agree to disagree and temporarily end your effort.

R. Think about the issue and discuss improvements and alternative
possibilities with others.
S. Return at a later time with a more thoroughly thought out solution.
T. If your new solution is not accepted, end your efforts until the idea can be
better received.

3. SOLIDIFY THE SOLUTION
A. After a solution is implemented, continue to evaluate the outcome.
B. Expect problems to occur with the solution and be alert to those problems.
C. Specify the problems and mistakes.
D. Correct the problems and mistakes.

E. If the solution does not work, create a new solution that addresses the
problems satisfactorily.
F. It may be useful to evaluate the outcome regularly.
G. Learn from what has occurred and apply that knowledge to other
circumstances.

Chapter 34. TEACHING
(The present chapter addresses some aspects related to this broad topic.)

Teaching may be one of the oldest human behaviors, such as parents instructing their children, peers doing so with peers, and elders teaching younger people. Humans know much about educating others, yet there still are important things to know about effective teaching. The reason is that communicating and learning, like many other human endeavors, involves psychological processes, and much about psychology is not known. Psychological Systems Theory offers a perspective on some hidden aspects of effective teaching, which are described in this chapter.

What is the key to effective teaching?
There are many views about what the essential ingredients are for teaching effectively. Some people believe that the key to effective teaching is knowledge of the subject, having high standards, or creating a well-formulated curriculum. Some other beliefs are that effective teaching requires strong classroom discipline, rigorous testing of students, audio-visual aids, organized presentations, parental support, or an appropriate budget. All of these factors are relevant, although according to Psychological Systems Theory, the core issue is that learning occurs when new information links with a learner's long-term Psychological Roots (similar to Piaget's concept of assimilation, Flavell, 1966). Since every person is different, effective teaching requires that the teacher create opportunities for new information to link successfully with each student's Psychological Roots.

The deeper the Psychological Roots to which new information is linked, the more likely a student will understand, absorb, and retain it *('deep learning', a 'meaningful learning experience')*. Linking is a fundamental way that cognitive learning occurs and can take place in every person at every age.

In this point of view, effective learning involves self-comprehension (mentioned in earlier chapters.) Therefore, the key skill for teachers is being effective in facilitating learners' ability to link new information with their own Psychological Roots, such as interests and concerns. Other teaching skills include the ability to shape new information to fit their students' intellectual level, background, and interests. Many other factors affect a student's learning such as his/her ability to comprehend, desire to grow intellectually, and regard for the information. Some other factors that affect learning are the student's level of intellectual development, prior experiences, cultural background, gender, occupation, and amount of external emotional and material support.

Every subject matter has a central core about which it revolves (*the centrality principle*). Examples include physicians' awareness that microbes cause important diseases, Einstein's theory of energy and matter, the Wright brothers' discovery of the air foil (see Figure 15 in Chapter 7), and Freud's recognizing that most psychological processes occur subconsciously. If a practitioner in a discipline does not know the key aspects in his/her field, it diminishes his/her effectiveness. When the core aspects of an issue are known, much is understood about a phenomenon and much can be derived from that understanding. Hence, a thorough grounding in how to identify and teach core aspects should be a major part of teaching and learning.

Students' linking of new information with their Psychological Roots can be aided by each student actively working with the subject matter in his/her own way. Doing so automatically facilitates aligning new information with each learner's Psychological Roots. Such experiential ("hands-on") learning has been espoused by many educators (e.g., Dewey, 1938; Gibbons, 2002). An example of experiential learning occurs when people acquire another language upon living in a foreign country (immersion learning). Experiential learning also occurs during role-playing, for example, when students imagine themselves being Neville Chamberlain trying to convince Hitler not to start World War II. Self-comprehension learning also occurs when students attempt to answer open-ended questions such as, "What can we learn from past wars that might help avoid future wars?" Questions generate strong motivation because of the drive for closure, which is genetic. Some teachers use experiential learning methods extensively.

In a self-comprehension activity, each student works on tasks in his/her unique way. In some instances, students have to develop their own solution to a problem or to find out for themselves how to obtain the information they need.

There are many ways to generate self-comprehension, such as by using case studies, 'what if' questions, 'what's wrong?' scenarios, the Socratic method (successive questions that permit students to arrive at an answer themselves), and problem-based learning (in which students develop solutions to ill-defined problems). It helps when teachers connect educational tasks with their students' interests ("Teach students what they need to learn through what they want to learn", Nina Greenwald, 1999). It also helps to use tangible examples and to give students tasks that they have sufficient skill to master ("Teach through a student's strength", a maxim in Special Education.) Working in groups can also help, also using demonstrations that hold students' attention.

Self-comprehension activities can be constructed to fit every intellectual level and are a particularly effective way to teach basics, as is done in

Montessori and Waldorf schools. Such active learning also helps students enhance their self-directed problem-solving skills, personal responsibility, and creativity, compared to more passive methods such as rote memorization, didactic presentation of what other people have accomplished, or routine homework. An advantage of self-comprehension activities is that teachers do not need to identify students' Psychological Roots (although doing so can be useful when a student lacks comprehension or is a disciplinary problem).

Teachers using self-comprehension activities:

1. Establish objectives, starting points, and guidelines for each activity.
2. Create interesting self-directed activities that meet the criteria in Item 1, above.
3. Explain to students at least some of the importance of the information that is to be acquired from an activity.
5. Provide some introductory information before students start to work on a task.
6. Be a background resource and guide, help students stay on track, and assist when students have difficulties, offering small hints at propitious times.
7. Explain complexities in understandable and bite-size quantities, and provide helpful examples.
8. Create a cordial, accepting, and positive classroom atmosphere in which students feel comfortable in presenting ideas that differ from those of other students or the teacher.
9. Be patient, caring, provide emotional support, and avoid being harsh (in short, use applied psychology such as appealing forces rather than repelling forces).
10. Create opportunities for students to think critically about their efforts and those of others.
11. Support students' creativity and innovative efforts.
12. Help students feel comfortable with the possibility of there being more than one right answer or method when it is appropriate to do so.
13. Help students feel comfortable about discussing theoretical concepts.
14. Create cordial solutions when difficulties arise (e.g., win-win resolutions when conflicts occur between students).
15. Have advanced students help slower students.
16. Ask each group of students to present its results to the class
17. Know how to elicit effective answers.
18. Teach students how to organize information, identify major themes (*extraction ability*), and articulate core concepts.
19. Teach students how to study effectively rather than to memorize by rote.
20. Review key aspects periodically.

Effective and interesting self-comprehension methods can increase students' interest in school, lessen discipline issues, and create an upbeat classroom in which students take intellectual risks, think complexly, learn at a deep level, and enjoy doing those things. Self-comprehension activities that interest students are a way for teachers and schools to succeed. Learning need not be painful.

The concept of self-comprehension and the centrality principle shifts the focus in teaching from presenting information to facilitating recipients' acquisition of information, teaching how to identify essential concepts, being able to think with that information, and skill in solving novel problems.

There are other issues as well. Teachers who are skilled at creating a positive atmosphere can help students acquire a positive attitude about learning and may be more effective than teachers who do not pay attention to such aspects. This perspective shifts the criteria for hiring teachers in the direction of those who lead students to accomplish their own learning of core concepts and do so in a positive, thoughtful, and considerate way.

Hidden psychological factors

Minds are not blank slates. Students, like everyone else, have a large number of Psychological Roots. For example, some students believe that school is boring, restrictive, controlling, or has little relevance for them. Some students do not want to participate because they believe that they might be embarrassed, are concerned about being evaluated, or want to avoid conflicting with the teacher or other students. Also, some students have problems with authority figures, rote memorization, or grades, and some are especially discomforted by failure. (See Lily's problem with anxiety in Chapter 28.)

An advantage of using effective self-comprehension methods is that students' active involvement is inherently part of those activities. That positive engagement also makes it useful for teaching students who have attention problems or who are impatient, hyperactive, or have difficulty with abstract issues. Varying the types of self-comprehension activities employed makes every class fresh and appealing.

Tests

It is essential to assess what students learn, yet tests create anxiety in students and contribute to schooling being a negative experience. It is possible to transform that circumstance by making learning, itself, the primary motivation for students rather than anxiety about avoiding failure. The unpleasantness of tests can be somewhat offset by giving students a second opportunity to improve their grades and by giving students academic and emotional support. Interest in education can be created by actively engaging students in interesting activities that are appropriately challenging.

Tests can contribute to learning when the solving of new problems are included, which can be solved by applying the general principles that have been learned, rather than by relying on what has been memorized. Types of challenging questions that are new to students include:

"According to the concept of ..., what is wrong with Jon saying ... ?"

"If chemicals ... and ... were mixed, what would result?"

"The ... war between ... and ... had much to do with what concerns?"

Both multiple-choice and open-ended formats can be used. Doing so makes tests part of the instructional process, especially upon reviewing the answers and the way they are solved after tests are over. Doing so extends the use of tests beyond evaluating and motivating students.

Preparing students for the future

Effective formal education is an important pathway for creating a better world. The forthcoming increases in complexity of ideas and devices in the world will require having a great many individuals who know how to learn effectively, and are able to develop and apply effective problem-solving skills in new circumstances. Individuals with such skills are likely to have a greater chance of success and make more contributions to society than persons who do not have those skills. Accordingly, teachers should help their students learn how to think critically, abstractly, and creatively. Students' skill in thinking can be helped by being given training in being analytical, flexible, innovative, and self-evaluative. Teachers should also help students learn how to function independently and work well with people whose personalities and viewpoints differ from their own. Students can also be taught how to identify key aspects in a large amount of information *('extraction ability')* and how to use problem-solving strategies when coping with difficult challenges.

The three-stage method applied to teaching

Teachers might not view their role as that of persuading students to learn, however, there are some connections between teaching and social influence, such as:

a. Students are more likely to understand and retain information when it fits the way they think and process information.

b. Students are more likely to be receptive when the subject matter interests them, especially if what is presented helps them solve a problem they consider to be important. When something that does not interest students they might not comprehend what is taught or might reject it. Examples include students saying, "Why should I learn this, I'll never use it" and "What relevance does this have for my life?".

c. Students are more likely to be cordial and cooperative when the teacher uses appealing forces and avoids using repelling forces.

The following version of the three-stage approach described earlier can help teachers facilitate their students' participation, cooperation, information acquisition, comprehension, and memory. Some highlights of this approach are presented below.

1. PREPARE.

A. Identify aspects that particularly interest students.

B. Identify problems that concern students, especially problems that bother them.

C. Create ways to connect what is being taught with what interests the students such as things that can intrigue them or help them solve problems with which they are concerned.

D. Develop self-comprehension activities for students that will interest them and allow them to solve problems on their own, with teacher-guidance as needed.

E. Create examples that can be used to help students grasp concepts. The more tangible and familiar the examples are to the students the better.

F. Ascertain how students can use what they are learning in their personal lives.

G. Obtain students' receptivity. Use appealing forces (e.g., by being caring and supportive) and avoiding using repelling forces (e.g., by not being critical or harsh).

H. Anticipate objections and resistance and develop constructive ways to deal with those aspects.

2. OFFER THE INFORMATION.

A. Establish a positive atmosphere. Be encouraging and give hints when needed.

B. Use strategies for effective communication, persuasion, and teaching (see Chapters 24 - 26). Be patient with students who are slow to comprehend complex or abstract ideas. Pay attention to non-verbal cues.

C. Provide tangible examples and use audio-visual aids.

D. Employ self-comprehension activities in which students generate their own solutions to problems.

E. Provide limited teacher input and give feedback in small doses. Limit didactic presentations to a minimum.

F. Keep things interesting by varying the format, activities, tempo, subject matter, group membership, and group size (e.g., groups of two, three, and five). Modify activities if students show disinterest, boredom, or a lack of understanding.

G. Invite questions and comments from students.

3. SOLIDIFY WHAT HAS BEEN LEARNED.

A. Ask individuals and groups to inform the class about their solutions to the problems with which they have been working.

B. Review answers to questions, activities, and exams.

C. Help students discuss their own thinking about the issues ('meta-cognitive activities')

D. Invite students to apply what they are learning to other situations, such as their personal life, sports activities, current jobs, and possible future occupations.

E. Ask students to report the experiences of their applying what they learned.

The bottom line: A major key to effective teaching is arranging for students to link new information with their Psychological Roots. The deeper those roots, the better. An effective way for students to link information with their Psychological Roots is for teachers to engage students in self-comprehension activities.

Chapter 35. LEARNING

(The present chapter addresses some aspects related to this broad topic.)

Learning is the reciprocal of teaching and a skill that can be acquired. Knowing those skills can make a huge difference in comprehension, retention of what is learned, ability to use what is learned, and ability to enjoy the process. Psychological Systems Theory offers some ideas about how to accomplish these things, some of which are described in this chapter.

The key to effective learning

Mentioned in the previous chapter was that the primary issue in effective learning suggested by Psychological Systems Theory is for new information to link with the learner's Psychological Roots, the deeper those roots, the better. Connecting information to core roots provides "deep learning". The theory also suggests that self-comprehension, which is a personal matter, helps in acquiring knowledge, and also supports the use of learning activities that foster self-comprehension. Learners who actively work with the subject matter in their own way automatically connect new information, ideas, problem-solving skills, and understanding with their Psychological Roots. Examples that involve aspects with which students are familiar can help. It can also help students to understand the key aspects of a topic and to know how to ascertain those often abstract and non-obvious aspects *('extraction ability')*.

Some personal traits that aid learning include having appropriate discipline and responsibility, having a high regard for education, and having supportive parents, teachers, peers, and opportunities to concentrate without distraction while studying. Students' learning is also aided by their motivation to grow intellectually and by being willing to be wrong, accept criticism, and make personal changes. This perspective differs from a belief that learning is painful or that the key to effective learning is memorizing by rote, being verbally competent, possessing test-taking skill, coming from a high socio-economic status background, going to a prestigious school, or using the latest educational technology.

Another inference from Psychological Systems Theory is that when something new is attached to an upcoming goal, that new information might last only as long as the goal exists. Thus, when students study for an exam by using flash-cards or by reading repetitively (memorizing by rote), what they attempt to remember attaches to their objective of passing a test. After that short-term goal is over, their need for much or perhaps almost all of that information no longer exists, therefore they forget much, almost all, or all of what they had memorized.

By contrast, long-term learning occurs when what is new links to long-lasting Psychological Roots such as genetic needs (e.g., need for safety) or other core roots (e.g., acquired high-order roots such as values and other strongly held beliefs, and deep concerns and interests). Information that has special cognitive or emotional significance for an individual has a substantial chance to be retained. Such significance can occur when new information is useful or particularly pleasing to the recipient, for instance, when it answers an important question or solves an important problem the student has. (See the discussion of short- and long-term memory in Chapter 17.) Some aspects that are memorized by rote can be long-lasting if they link with a student's deep Psychological Roots, something that can happen with aspects that interest the student.

Psychological Roots have a built-in drive to link with other roots, according to Psychological Systems Theory, therefore the more Psychological Roots and root clusters a person has, the greater the opportunity for associations to occur. The drives in a cluster are additive, so the larger the cluster, the stronger the drive to acquire information related to that cluster. As a result, having a particularly strong interest could lead to developing a large cluster of roots related to it. That cluster, together with related clusters, sub-clusters, and drives can lead to a person acquiring still more links that connect with them. Discomfort can result if a strong root-cluster's drives are not satisfied, and that dissatisfaction can increase motivation to acquire appropriate information. Psychological Roots continue to link with clusters throughout life and create new clusters, which increases the size and number of clusters as a person acquires new interests and experiences. A learner's specific interest therefore offers a strong opportunity to bolster learning, comprehension, and retention of aspects associated with that interest. In essence, people are learning machines about what they want to learn.

These principles related to learning are fundamental and universal, and apply to all ages, both genders, and a wide range of subject matters, regardless of whether the learning is formal or informal and whether the person is an infant, kindergartener, graduate student, in a professional occupation, or learns through experience. At the same time, variations in presenting the subject matter to the learner are required to match the ability and interests of the learner (e.g., related to differences in age, maturity level, experience, prior knowledge, and receptivity).

A learner who wants to boost his/her comprehension and retention can use a version of the three-stage approach, such as:

1. PREPARE
A. Identify your interests and concerns, especially those that are particularly strong in you.
B. Ascertain how to connect what you want to learn to those interests and concerns.

2. LEARN
C. Create a foundation for substantial learning by initially skimming the subject matter. Skimming can help generate clusters and categories in the mind to which information can be linked. Skimming or scanning is facilitated by reading headings, topic sentences, graphs, and summaries.
B. Translate new information into your own words and create examples, mental associations, and diagrams that aid your understanding. Those will be consistent with the particular way you process information.
C. Summarize the new information in your own words.
D. Identify the key themes in the information (i.e., the core aspects)
E. Coordinate the core aspects of each topic to generate a composite understanding of the entire subject matter.
F. Raise your own questions about aspects related to the subject.

3. SOLIDIFY
A. Find a way to make the new information personally relevant to you.
B. Actively engage the new information by thinking about what you have learned, talking to others about it, and trying to explain puzzling issues with it.
C. Apply what you have learned to other situations (e.g., your personal life, jobs, sports).
D. Review the new information periodically.

Chapter 36. PREJUDICE
(The present chapter describes some aspects related to this broad topic.)

Prejudice has a bad reputation, which is justified for many negative prejudices that create much suffering. However, there are some negative prejudices that are constructive, such as dislike of unsanitary conditions and disease-carrying creatures. There also are positive prejudices, such as liking a particular person, although that aspect of prejudice does not get much attention. For reasons that this chapter explains, it may be impossible to avoid being prejudiced, and therefore everyone may be prejudiced in some way.

Prejudice defined
Prejudice is a shortened version of 'pre-formed judgment' and can be with regard to anything, from a specific material object to a complex abstraction, including people, food, or ideas. Therefore, even if a person has a logical reason or constructive basis for prejudging something, a pre-formed judgment automatically is a prejudice.

There are positive and negative prejudices, for example, a person might love pepperoni pizza while another might abhor it. Some people's negative prejudices that hurt or upset other people or have other unpleasant consequences may be disdained by those who do not have those prejudices.

When a prejudice is a belief or an expectation, it is Psychological Root. When a prejudice is an attitude, evaluation, or thought it is an internal reaction. When a person acts on a prejudice, that action is a behavior (the term for which is discrimination).

Acquisition of prejudice
A prejudice can arise without a person having had a direct experience with the object of that prejudice and can even occur about something that does not exist, such as non-existent people like "Wallonians", "Piraneans", and "Danerians" (Hartley, 1946). A person can acquire a prejudice from hearing what someone says (e.g., a parent, clergyman, or political leader), or from reading or watching television, Facebook, Twitter, or the Internet. It might be easier to form pre-judgments about something that is readily identifiable and stands out compared to aspects that do not, such as something unusual about a person's appearance, speech, ethnicity, skin color, residential area, national origin, religion, or political ideology.

Positive and negative prejudices

Mentioned above is that there are positive prejudices as well negative prejudices, for example, someone can have a pre-formed idea about what kind of pizza, ice cream, or steak to order at a restaurant. There are many instances in which emotional reactions occur and therefore everyone is likely to have some prejudices. For example, a positive emotional reaction can attach to something that is consistent with a Psychological Root, and a negative emotional reaction can result with regard to something that is inconsistent with a Psychological Root. Even though some individuals might believe that they have no prejudices, nevertheless, they are likely to have some prejudices since everyone has a huge number of Psychological Roots and emotional reactions. It is understandable that some people might believe that they have no prejudices because humans know very little about what takes place in their mind.

It may be that there are more negative than positive prejudices since negative reactions are stronger than positive reactions (e.g., Cullen et al., 1975; also see Chapter 10). Perhaps for the same reason, strong negative prejudices often get attention because of their great intensity and impact. Negative reactions are also likely to be easily aroused and last longer than positive emotions, and therefore perhaps negative prejudices might have a particularly long life.

Generalizations

Prejudices can be about a single aspect, however, there are many broad prejudices because the brain is wired to create generalizations (e.g., dislike of an entire group, such as spiders [arachnophobia] or cohorts of humans [xenophobia]). Some prejudices serve a worthwhile purpose, such as having a positive prejudice about one's significant other, family, and friends, and having a negative prejudice about unsanitary conditions, dangerous locales, and disease-carrying insects.

A generalized prejudice about an entire group of people implies that everyone in that group thinks, reacts, and behaves alike. However, such uniformity is extremely unlikely because each individual is unique and everyone has a huge number of Psychological and Biological Roots. For comparison, the number of vocabulary words an average 12-year old child possesses has been estimated to be about 10,000 words and an average college graduate about 20,000 words (Nation & Waring, 1998).

The number of Psychological Roots is hard to estimate, possibly in the many tens of thousands of Psychological Roots or more. The large amount of such roots suggests that it is unlikely that anyone is identical to anyone else.

This likelihood would explain why some identical twins have dissimilar personality traits and why some people who have the same political affiliation differ on some issues and candidates. For example, some Democrats are financially conservative, and some Republicans are socially liberal. Some males have a strong feminist ideology, and some females reject a feminist ideology. It is also possible that included among people's large number of Psychological Roots are those that some people have in common. For instance, many Democrats and Republicans support democracy, have a strong work ethic, and value education.

A hostile prejudice toward a person or a group of humans can lead to active aggression toward them (e.g., Nazis killing Jews, gypsies, and homosexuals, Stalin's killing opponents of communism, Islamic extremists' killing people who do not agree with their cause, and the Ku Klux Klan killing African-Americans). Killing that stems from prejudice continues to roil the world.

Psychological factors underlying negative prejudice against a group of people

The problems caused by negative prejudice against groups of people makes it important to identify the Psychological Roots that undergird those prejudices. Studies are needed to identify the Psychological Roots involved, possibly including a strong need for safety, a low threshold for emotional arousal, and a belief about being personally vulnerable. There might also be a narrow acceptability range, a desire for closure, and an unwillingness to create compatible solutions. Perhaps generalized, fervent, and rigid prejudices are particularly strong in individuals who often think in absolutes, desire simplicity, and have strong emotional reactions. There are times when sweeping generalizations (e.g., "the government", "the left", or "the right"), facilitate thinking and communicating. However, a possibility is that often using absolutes might facilitate acquiring generalized prejudices about people and philosophies.[47]

Some people who are prejudiced against a group of people might feel threatened by that group, believe fictitious notions of that group's wrongdoing, and focus on isolated negative instances involving that group. A

---

[47] Some politicians, like other people, have prejudices, such as White supremacists George Wallace and David Duke. New Orleans' Mayor Ray Nagin said, "This city will be a majority African-American city. It is the way God wants it to be", claiming that Hurricane Katrina occurred because "God is mad at America" (Martel, 2006).

person's prejudice can be supported by associating with individuals who have a similar prejudice and by cherry-picking information that supports a prejudice (confirmation bias), also by disregarding aspects that contradict a prejudice ("Don't confuse me with facts"). Ominous behaviors that can result from negative prejudices include scapegoating, verbal aggression, discrimination, persecution, and genocide. The impact of negative prejudices in human history has been staggering.

Can bigotry and xenophobia be changed?

A prejudice can be modified or ended by modifying the pertinent Psychological Roots which contribute to that prejudice, however it is not easy to do so if the prejudice is a deep root or directly attached to a deep root. For example, if a person's xenophobia is directly connected to a person's need for safety, stability, or other deep Psychological Roots, that prejudice is likely to strongly resist being changed. Replacing xenophobia with peaceful co-existence might take centuries of many concerted world-wide efforts before humans' genetics are sufficiently overshadowed by civilizing Psychological Roots. It may be that such efforts will be aided by having strong defenses to rely on in case of need, keeping in mind that negatives are stronger than positives.

Those efforts can be aided by some aspects that are already known such as strongly positive interactions of xenophobic individuals with disdained persons. For example, Sherif (1958) successfully modified prejudices of people who disliked one another when they worked together to obtain common goals. The most effective strategy involved an issue they perceived to be related to their survival. Also effective but less powerful was when they worked together in other ways, such as playing on the same sports team. The more serious the issue that was involved, especially when it was perceived as urgent, the greater the benefit and the more positive the change that occurred. (The author was the evaluator of a successful experiment involving this principle and found results similar to those of Sherif [1958], which Sherif termed the effect of a 'superordinate goal', that is, a circumstance in which when all the people involved work together to achieve the same goal.)

1. *'Compelling common goals'* - Prejudice can sometimes change when prejudiced people of different backgrounds work well together in combat, sports, and industry. Mentioned above was that the more important the circumstance the greater the effect, for instance, when a member of a disdained group rescues a prejudiced individual from danger or receives assistance in fighting a foe ("The enemy of my enemy is my friend").

2. Self-comprehension – Some prejudiced persons' negative perspective alters when they have positive experiences with a disdained group. Such

experiences include discovering that those individuals have values and behaviors similar to their own (e.g., a strong work-ethic, societal contributions, being well-spoken, caring about others, helpful, safe, and trustworthy). Some milder positive experiences include liking the disliked group's pleasing music, food, entertainment, and important advances (such as medical aids, life-saving electronic devices).

3. Endorsements – Some persons' prejudice against groups they disdain might lessen when advised against it by people they regard highly (e.g., celebrities, sports stars, Nobel prize winners, religious leaders, college presidents, physicians, columnists, and world leaders).

4. Widen the person's acceptance range – Some persons' prejudice can diminish when their range of acceptance widens. Sometimes this is a result of receiving income, emotional support, or pleasing actions from people in a disdained group. Activities that provide opportunities to broaden people's experiences might also help.

5. Psychological understanding – Provide information that gives prejudiced people important positive information about people they disdain. For example, helping them:
   . Become aware that people in a disliked group have many Psychological Roots similar to theirs, such as values and goals.
   . Become aware that prejudices against entire groups involve surface attributes, rather than deep traits.
   . Become aware of the personal benefits that diversity provides (e.g., jobs, medical advances, foods, entertainment, and inventions).
   . Become aware that no-one knows who will create ideas that will advance society (e.g., it could be from 1st, 2nd, or 3rd generation immigrants).
   . Learn how to create win-win solutions in which everyone's concerns are met in place of a win-lose attitude.
   . Become aware of the benefit of taking into account gradations and complexities compared to the disadvantages of thinking in absolutes.
   . Become aware of how repelling forces can backfire against the person who uses them.
   . Create circumstances in which people in a disdained group are caring, supportive, respectful, trustworthy, and responsible with regard to people who are prejudiced against them.
   Create circumstances in which from people in a disliked subgroup reciprocate aid that they might receive from others.

6. Public service announcements
   . Present frequent public service requests for people to work together for the benefit of society and connect those requests with patriotism.
   . Devote resources to acquainting prejudiced people with the above-mentioned aspects.

Chapter 37. SOME IMPLICATIONS OF PSYCHOLOGICAL SYSTEMS THEORY (PST)

This chapter provides a summary of some implications of psychological Systems Theory (PST) for readers who would like to have it.
(The numbers are for convenience and do not signify importance.)

1. PST describes important subconscious psychological processes (e.g., Psychological Roots, hierarchies, clusters, Hidden Sequences, and psychological homeostasis) that previously were hidden or not substantially understood.
2. PST permits subconscious processes to be measured and scientific studies to be conducted on them.
3. PST indicates hidden psychological processes to be logical, systematic, important, potent, predictable, and real.
4. PST explains the connection between surface observations and their hidden psychological causes.
5. PST explains how emotional reactions and Psychological Roots are connected.
6. PST suggests why humans focus on tangibility (e.g., sensory abilities, conscious awareness, drive for closure), rather than hidden aspects.
7. PST explains why common observations and admonitions (e.g., proverbs) are likely to be overly simple and inaccurate.
8. PST explains the role of Psychological Homeostasis in both stability and instability (states of uncontrollability).
9. PST facilitates understanding the role of multiple factors in internal
10. PST describes powerful effects from even small negatives.
11. PST explains why different behavior can result from apparently similar causes.
12. PST explains why similar behavior can result from different causes.
13. PST describes how some different aspects (e.g., goals, beliefs, and thresholds) have certain characteristics in common.
14. PST describes substantial ways to improve mental and social functioning.
15. PST suggests ways to improve critical thinking (e.g., thinking in relative terms rather than absolutes).
16. PST suggests ways to improve creativity (e.g., by widening the acceptability range and improving problem-solving).
17. PST explains how information is acquired by linking to Psychological Roots (e.g., beliefs, goals, and genetic needs).
18. PST can improve learning by helping to identify key aspects to which new information can link.

19. PST explains how self-comprehension can improve learning and long-term retention.
20. PST suggests keys to effective teaching.
21. PST suggests aspects of applied psychology (e.g., win-win solutions) that could be taught starting at an early age.
22. PST describes factors that foster resistance to change and oppose such resistance.
23. PST explains why surface actions ("Just do it", will-power, telling others) are unlikely to create substantive change.
24. PST provides a way to improve communication involving linking a message to Psychological Roots.
25. PST provides a new understanding of how effective change can be created.
26. PST explains why facts, logic, and evidence may not persuade people.
27. PST explains why trying to control overt behavior directly may not be an effective way to create change.
28. PST explains how to generate win-win solutions by satisfying the protagonists' Psychological Roots that underlie interpersonal conflicts.
29. PST provides an understanding of how to improve interpersonal interactions.
30. PST opens new paths for understanding some complex social issues (e.g., prejudice, crime, extremism, violence,)
31. PST describes important connections between psychology and biology.
32. PST explains the psychological origin of some psychological disorders, including some that seem biological (e.g., depression, anxiety, bipolar disorder).
33. PST postulates that everyone is wired to experience depression, panic, rage, and some other disorders.
34. PST explains how much depression and anxiety originate from distress-prone Psychological Roots.
35. PST explains why chemical imbalances in depression and anxiety result from psychological causes.
36. PST explains why biochemicals can be proximal causes of psychological behavior rather than originating causes.
37. PST offers a salutary psychotherapy approach that identifies and modifies Psychological Roots, such as those that are distress-prone.
38. PST offers a new approach to understanding addiction.
39. PST explains why abstinence is not the key to effectively treating addictions.
40. PST explains why aversive treatments (e.g., criticism, punishment, jails) are unlikely to be effective rehabilitators.

41. PST offers a method of predicting the risk of psychological disorders (e.g., by identifying distress-prone Psychological Roots).
42. PST offers a way to prevent some psychological disorders (e.g., by modifying distress-prone Psychological Roots).
43. PST provides a logical explanation of irrational economic behavior.
44. PST opens new directions for psychological research.
45. PST points the way to obtain important information from pilot studies, role-playing, psychotherapy, and personal experiences.
46. PST suggests paths that might possibly lead to creating a better world.

Chapter 38. FUTURE ADVANCES

Almost everything that humans do originates in people's minds, therefore knowing what goes on in our subconscious psychological processes is worthwhile and at times necessary.

Research strategies

There is a long list of problems for which knowledge of psychology can help, including alleviating suffering, illness, poverty, homelessness, refugee crises, interpersonal conflicts, psychological disorders, oppression, gangs, terrorism, and war. Solving challenging problems such as these can be aided by perspectives and research that are coming, such as through research and practical applications related to Psychological Systems Theory. New knowledge and insights will come from both scientific and non-professional sources related to social-psychology (e.g., via experiments, self-evaluations, and role-playing), clinical-psychology (e.g., via analyses, therapies, and self-reports), sociology (e.g., via group and geographic measures), anthropology, archeology, economics, philosophy, history, biology, chemistry, physics, and perhaps from other sources as well, including thought experiments (as Einstein did).

The author has found that accurate information about subconscious aspects can be obtained from fixed-alternative questions even when respondents are unable to articulate effective answers to open-ended questions (e.g., regarding Psychological Roots and other aspects related to Psychological Systems Theory).

Needed research studies

Below are over 380 potential studies needing to be accomplished. Background information for each of these issues can be found in this book. (The numbers associated with the following research possibilities do not represent priorities.)

Basic research related to Psychological Systems Theory and Therapy

1. Test the structure and function of the concepts in Psychological Systems Theory (e.g., psychological homeostasis, Psychological Roots, internal reactions, overt behavior, and Hidden Sequences [Root Sequences and Stimulus-and-Root Sequences, including whether Psychological Roots alone or in combination with stimulus conditions lead to internal reactions and then to overt behavior]).

2. Test the cause-and-effect implications of Psychological Roots, Hidden Sequences, internal reactions, and initial interactions in Stimulus-and-Root Sequences.

3. Ascertain if there are postulated ranges in Psychological Homeostasis (comfort, acceptable, tolerable, unacceptable, and intolerable), wide and narrow comfort zones, states of uncontrollability, and alerting and tipping point thresholds.

4. Ascertain whether the end of a homeostatic continuum is a tipping point at which abnormal behavior diverges from normal behavior. And if so, what states of uncontrollability occur (e.g., depression, panic, rage, hysteria, obsessive-compulsive behavior, addiction).

5. Ascertain the characteristics of short-, medium-, and long-term states of uncontrollability.

6. Ascertain whether some states of uncontrollability are primarily Root Sequences (e.g., some instances of chronic depression, generalized anxiety, and generalized PTSD). Also ascertain whether some states of uncontrollability are primarily Stimulus-and-Root Sequences (e.g., situational depression, specific phobias, and situational PTSD). Also, ascertain whether there are some states of uncontrollability in which Root and Stimulus-and-Root Hidden Sequences are about equally present.

7. Ascertain whether Psychological Roots have a drive to link with other Psychological Roots (and therefore whether linking takes place between Psychological Roots), also determine whether Psychological Roots form root hierarchies, clusters, sub-clusters, and categories.

8. Ascertain whether acquiring Psychological Roots is facilitated when new aspects are conceptually aligned with prior Psychological Roots. Also, ascertain whether information is likely to be rejected if it is inconsistent with a Psychological Root. Also, ascertain other factors that contribute to acquisition and rejection of Psychological Roots.

9. Ascertain whether the postulated drive for Psychological Roots to link is additive and therefore that clusters of Psychological Roots have a correspondingly large combined drive. Also, ascertain whether the drive to acquire information about a topic is greater the larger the number of Psychological Roots in a cluster because of the postulated additivity of Psychological Roots' drive to link with other roots.

10. Ascertain whether building a cluster of Psychological Roots by acquiring still more information generates a still stronger drive to acquire additional information.

11. Ascertain if people who have a particularly strong interest may have a large cluster of roots related to that interest and therefore a strong drive to

acquire information related to it and also engage in aspects related to that cluster.

12. Ascertain whether discomfort results if a strong root-cluster's drives are not satisfied. Also, ascertain if that postulated discomfort is partly relieved y acquiring additional aspects and whether that drive produces still motivation to grow.

13. Ascertain the specific mechanism involved when roots, clusters, and categories link with existing Psychological Roots, including biological and biochemical changes.

14. Ascertain whether genetic Psychological Roots are foundations of Psychological Root hierarchies.

15. Ascertain whether Psychological Roots are in alignment with the genetic root postulated to be at the foundation of each Psychological Root hierarchy.

16. Ascertain whether a defense effect occurs in which a Psychological Root is defended against a challenge (e.g., when a root creates a problem, a mistake, or a disagreement with someone).

17. Ascertain whether a flow-down effect occurs that modifies subsidiary Psychological Roots along a Psychological Root hierarchy, thereby creating substantial change.

18. Ascertain whether the flow-down effect occurs rapidly.

19. Ascertain whether change resulting from a flow-down effect is more widespread when a Psychological Root close to a genetic foundation is modified than when modification of a more peripheral root occurs.

20. Ascertain whether a subsequent trickle-down effect or other changes might occur following a flow-down effect.

21. Ascertain whether Piaget (Flavell, 1966) was correct in theorizing that new information necessarily changes the process of assimilation.

22. Ascertain whether pre-shaping of new information sometimes occurs before linking with an existing Psychological Root to make that information consistent with existing Psychological Roots and thereby facilitate linking.

23. Ascertain how information that does not quite fit with existing Psychological Roots is pre-shaped to link with existing Psychological Roots. Also, identify the range of individual differences involved in the degree to which people make such adjustments.

24. Ascertain whether pre-shaping occurs in the evaluation of alternatives to thereby facilitate making a decision (an internal reaction).

25. Ascertain whether post-shaping occurs after a decision is made in order to solidify the decision by elevating the chosen alternative (a selective attention phenomenon).
26. Ascertain why post-shaping occurs in the evaluation of alternatives after a decision is made in which the evaluations of the alternatives spread apart (an internal reaction) perhaps due to selective attention in which the unchosen alternative recedes into the background.
27. Ascertain whether post-shaping occurs after linking to thereby align subsidiary Psychological Roots with that change (a flow-down effect).
28. Ascertain whether both pre- and post-shaping occur when decisions are made, or whether each type of shaping occurs selectively. What conditions cause each type of shaping to happen? Are there circumstances when neither pre- nor post-shaping occurs?
29. Ascertain how closely problem-solving ability is associated with intelligence and what Psychological Roots are particularly associated with intelligence.
30. Ascertain the Psychological Roots involved with intelligence, problem-solving, and creativity (e.g., the width of the acceptability range, a desire to grow psychologically, and having extraction ability [the ability to identify key aspects in a large amount of information]).
31. Ascertain whether intelligence and wisdom are related to the ease with which links are made, the drive to do so, the number of acquired Psychological Roots and clusters, and ability to evaluate.
32. Ascertain whether linking capability is related to the higher rate of intellectual growth in very intelligent people compared to those of lesser intelligence.
33. Ascertain if openness to new information contributes to intelligence, inventiveness, and creativity.
34. Ascertain whether a strong ability to pre-shape new information contributes to intelligence, inventiveness, and creativity.
35. Ascertain if different types of intelligence (Gardner, 1983) can be improved by expanding relevant Psychological Root clusters.
36. Ascertain whether making associations and problem-solving is facilitated by the linking of Psychological Roots within different hierarchies and between them.
37. Ascertain whether absolute thinking and emotionality affect intelligence and problem-solving ability.
38. Ascertain whether filtering takes place in which new information that is inconsistent with existing Psychological Roots is screened out.
39. Ascertain whether achieving a goal is satisfying even where there is no material gain.

40. Ascertain whether the drive to achieve a goal automatically generates a drive to achieve it.

41. Ascertain whether the drive to achieve a goal is the same as the drive for closure, or whether the drive to achieve a goal and the drive for closure are similar or closely linked to each other.

42. Ascertain whether having a goal engages a person's internal ability to help achieve that goal, such as automatically drawing upon his/her stored mental information, strategies, and methods.

43. Ascertain factors that contribute to the intensity of the drive for closure (e.g., the amount of time available for an outcome to occur, the consequences, and the level of emotionality, also Psychological Roots such as expectations, concerns, and interests).

44. Ascertain the Psychological Roots that contribute to impatience (e.g., need for closure, expectations).

45. Ascertain whether expectations automatically link with goals. Also, ascertain why it is difficult for people to conceive of having high goals simultaneously with possessing low expectations or no expectations.

46. Ascertain whether high goals can generate high achievement when expectations are low.

47. Ascertain how expectations generate distress and how separating expectations from goals might lessen distress.

48. Understand why people are reluctant to lower their expectations, even when they are aware that failing to meet their high expectations causes them distress.

49. Ascertain whether Psychological Roots such as beliefs, expectations, and goals play a role in classical and operant conditioning (which, if correct, would thereby help explain and expand the present S-R conceptualization).

50. Ascertain whether a behavior such as classical conditioning occurs in an organism because of 'preparedness' involving capability and inclination, psychologically and biologically.

51. Ascertain whether operant conditioning can occur after just a single reinforcement (see Chapter 18).

52. Ascertain whether beliefs and expectations about a behavior generate resistance to extinction (see Chapter 18).

53. Ascertain whether an acquired Psychological Root that is linked with a long-term root might be retained for a long time (long-term memory). If so, ascertain whether that circumstance is consistent with Allport's (1937) concept of functional autonomy (that motives and behavior can continue

to occur on their own without requiring additional reinforcement or the original reason for having engaged in them).

54. Ascertain whether repeatedly modifying a deep Psychological Root can make that change semi-automatic (the equivalent of a conditioned response).

55. Ascertain whether linking new information with deep Psychological Roots – such as roots in people's core personality structure – produces long-term memory.

56. Ascertain whether linking new information with surface Psychological Roots – such as short-term goals (e.g., immediate tasks and rote memorizing for exams) – produces short-term memory.

57. Ascertain whether long-term memory is stored in glial cells in parts of the cerebral cortex related to the type of memory (e.g., frontal cortex for cognitive information, or visual or auditory cortex, etc.)

58. Ascertain if salient stimuli are stored in memory as quick reference points that connect with certain Psychological Root clusters (e.g., those that have particular significance to people such as phobias, recollection of important concepts and events, and recognition of people, material things, and ideas).

59. Ascertain if a newly acquired Psychological Root that connects with a long-term root might be retained for a long time even when there is no reinforcement or if there is no further reinforcement.

60. Ascertain if deconditioning/extinction occurs when an individual no longer has the beliefs, hopes, desires, and expectations (Psychological Roots) that support a conditioned response (see Chapter 18).

61. Ascertain whether a warning signal is experienced when a psychological alerting threshold is crossed and what the nature of such experiences is (e.g., malaise, tension, discomfort).

62. Ascertain whether thinking in absolutes is an amplifier of internal reactions, and non-absolute thinking is a diminisher.

63. Ascertain whether emotionality amplifies internal reactions, and low emotionality diminishes them.

64. Ascertain whether a low threshold for emotional arousal (and therefore emotional reactivity) is an intensifier, and a high threshold for emotional arousal is a diminisher.

65. Ascertain whether cumulative build-up occurs (e.g., of tension).

66. Ascertain whether only a small aspect added to a build-up might be sufficient to trigger a substantial reaction including a state of uncontrollability ("the straw that broke the camel's back").

67. Ascertain whether cumulative build-up is an intensifier.

68. Ascertain whether acquired Psychological Roots link with genetic Biological Roots.
69. Ascertain whether Psychological Roots have biological effects.
70. Ascertain whether Biological Roots have psychological effects.
71. Ascertain whether there are biological Hidden Sequences.
72. Ascertain the degree to which absolute thinking is correlated with emotionality.
73. Ascertain whether there are differences in absolute thinking related to education and gender.
74. Ascertain whether absolute thinking is related to age (e.g., perhaps a bell-shaped curve)
75. Ascertain whether there is a tendency for adults to think in absolutes and whether that tendency is related to childhood thinking in absolutes.
76. Ascertain whether absolute thinking is more likely with negatives than with positives.
77. Ascertain whether thinking in absolutes contributes to resistance to change.
78. Ascertain whether absolute thinking is inversely correlated with intellectual ability and complexity.
79. Ascertain if absolute thinking is especially likely regarding aspects with which people are unfamiliar.
80. Ascertain whether there is a tendency for children to acquire their parents' behaviors, values, and beliefs in an absolute manner, such as their parents' religion and political beliefs, and therefore possess those acquired aspects even more strongly than their parents.
81. Ascertain whether the more Psychological Roots and clusters a person has the greater the number of associations that person can make.
82. Ascertain what Psychological Roots contribute to inventiveness and creativity.
83. Ascertain how genetic and acquired Psychological Roots are encoded in the brain psychologically, biologically, and biochemically; how Psychological Roots are acquired; also how and why new Psychological Roots can be acquired quickly.
84. Ascertain where in the human brain Psychological Roots, root hierarchies, and clusters reside.
85. Ascertain whether some ongoing individual differences are due to relatively stable weightings of Psychological Roots and other factors that favor a particular set of counterbalancing factors (e.g., the relative strength of needs for safety and stability; the degree of flexibility vs.

rigidity regarding the acquisition of new information, change, and creativity).

86. Ascertain whether Root Sequences and Stimulus-and-Root Sequences occur as postulated (see Chapter 4).

87. Ascertain whether emotional reactions are connected with cognitions (such as Psychological Roots) in Hidden Sequences, and therefore cognitions and emotions are connected, despite each being distinctively different from the other and functioning differently.

88. Test the causal role of Psychological Roots using experimenter-introduced interventions.

89. Ascertain whether states of uncontrollability include anhedonia, apathy, astonishment, crying, ecstasy, hysteria, impulsivity, indecision, laughter, lethargy, and mania.

90. Ascertain if the tipping point into abnormal behavior is the extreme limit of emotional continua.

91. Ascertain whether curiosity is generated by drives for growth, linking, exploration, and closure.

92. Ascertain whether psychological growth is more general in early childhood than in later years, partly because of the broad nature of early Psychological Roots compared to later Psychological Roots.

93. Ascertain whether communicating is a necessary aid for the survival of living beings.

94. Identify factors and processes that facilitate change and factors that counteract resistance to change.

95. Ascertain if attempting to use facts and logic to cause some people to be even stronger in their initial viewpoint ("boomeranging" or "backfiring") might stem from recipients' need to defend their viewpoint.

96. Ascertain the degree to which deep Psychological Roots can be changed or modified, or whether those deep roots are unchangeable.

97. Ascertain whether overriding deep Psychological Roots is a substantial way to modify internal reactions and overt behavior, also whether such overriding can become a semi-automatic (conditioned) behavior.

98. Ascertain whether directly trying to change behavior or internal reactions is less effective than modifying or overriding Psychological Roots.

99. Ascertain whether solving an important problem that relieves discomfort is an effective way to persuade (and modify or override internal reactions and overt behavior), compared to providing the recipient with a purely positive benefit.

100. Ascertain whether a repeated modification of a deep Psychological Root can make modifying that root a semi-automatic occurrence.

101. Ascertain whether change is easier to achieve with peripheral Psychological Roots than with roots close to the genetic foundation of Psychological Root hierarchies.

102. Ascertain whether opinion-discrepancy study results (e.g., Fisher & Lubin, 1958, and some dissonance theory studies are due to a widening of subjects' range of acceptability or tolerability.

103. Ascertain why alternatives initially rated widely apart (e.g., 10 and 5 on 1-15 point scale) are re-rated to come closer together (e.g., 9 and 6) after people make a decision between them (see Greenwald, 1969). For example, might choosing between alternatives create a perception that they deserve more similar evaluations?

104. Ascertain what effect *a priori* stimulus interventions have on Psychological Roots (e.g., via questionnaire assessments in mixed factorial designs).

105. Ascertain whether valid causal data can be obtained by using experimenter-introduced stimulus variables in which subjects engage in role-playing for circumstances that do not readily lend themselves to *a priori* studies (e.g., parenting, criminality, war).

106. Ascertain whether the postulates in Psychological Systems Theory apply about the same extent to both males and females.

107. Ascertain whether the same Psychological Systems Theory concepts apply to the acquisition of information throughout the range of ages from young children to elderly individuals.

108. Ascertain how the postulates in Psychological Systems Theory apply to children and adults of various ages. Also ascertain what differences, if any, exist between the way Psychological Systems Theory applies to very young and very old people.

109. Ascertain whether people have a large complex web of Psychological Roots with many hierarchies and many links among the Psychological Roots in those hierarchies.

110. Ascertain whether Psychological Roots, clusters, and webs continue to expand throughout life.

111. Ascertain whether there is an inverse correlation between emotionality (positive or negative) and cognitive functioning (such as problem-solving) and if so, what the cause of that inverse correlation is (e.g., decreased blood supply to the prefrontal cortex).

112. Ascertain if the likelihood of behavior heightens as increases occur in the intensity of internal reactions. Also, whether a graph of that relationship results in an *'intensity curve'* in which there is an accelerating gradient at the upper intensity levels as the upper extreme is approached, and a

decreasing gradient at the lower intensity levels as the lower extreme is approached.

113. Ascertain whether the intensity of emotion outside an adaptive zone accelerates as the extreme upper end of the continuum is approached.

114. Ascertain whether the intensity of emotion outside the adaptive zone decelerates as the extreme lower end of the continuum is approached.

115. Ascertain whether increases and decreases in emotional intensity along homeostatic continua are accompanied by internal changes (e.g., changes in tension, malaise, agitation, or neurotransmitters).

116. Ascertain whether some non-monotonic graphs might be due to a cumulative build-up that in which a tipping point into a different (perhaps qualitative) state occurs.

117. Ascertain whether people are aware of when a cumulative build-up occurs in them, when they are in a precursor mode, and when they are at a tipping point to a state of uncontrollability.

118. Ascertain whether cumulative build-up can contribute to constructive change and, if so, what the determining factors for such build-up and change are.

119. Ascertain whether being consistent with a Psychological Root (e.g., satisfying a goal) stimulates the positive emotional center.

120. Ascertain whether being inconsistent with a Psychological Root (e.g., not meeting an expectation) arouses negative emotions (and therefore the negative emotional center).

121. Ascertain whether generalization is related to making a connection with a Psychological Root hierarchical theme and a Psychological Root cluster.

122. Ascertain whether discrimination is related to making a distinction between a different Psychological Root hierarchical themes and Psychological Root clusters.

123. Ascertain whether Psychological Homeostasis might provide only a warning (e.g., malaise, tension, or a down mood), leaving it to the individual to decide whether or not to return to the comfort zone.

124. Ascertain whether exceeding a psychological limit might not directly result in death. Also ascertain if death or disablement related to Psychological Homeostasis occurs it is due to something indirect, such as inadequate problem-solving, lack of prevention, or an associated illness.

125. Ascertain whether biochemical changes occur when Psychological Homeostasis thresholds are crossed, such as at the end of homeostatic continua.

126. Ascertain whether psychological aspects affect neurotransmitter levels (e.g., serotonin in depression) and hormone levels (e.g., adrenalin in anxiety).

127. Ascertain whether pertinent Psychological Roots (e.g., beliefs, expectations) and internal reactions (e.g., thoughts, evaluations, and emotional reactions) change immediately before decisions, after decisions, or both. Also, ascertain where in the brain those changes occur.

128. In decision situations, ascertain whether a single rating of the competing alternatives (e.g., on a scale of -10 to +10) automatically takes into account the evaluation of myriad underlying factors (e.g., subjective, hidden, and objective factors such as cost, attractiveness, and Psychological Roots).

129. Ascertain if the degree to which non-verbal cues are picked up by others is correlated with the strength of a person's internal reactions in Hidden Sequences.

130. Ascertain whether threats generate negative emotional arousal because they impact the recipient's genetic need for safety, possibly the genetic need for stability as well.

131. Ascertain whether there is a genetically wired-in need to connect with something larger than oneself.

132. Ascertain if it is sufficient to indicate whether the cause of a condition is psychological, rather than biological, when Psychological Roots and stimuli seem to explain a condition and when changing those factors corrects the condition.

133. Ascertain the role of stimulus conditions in interacting with Psychological Roots. Also, ascertain what aspects of stimulus conditions and Psychological Roots are involved.

134. Ascertain whether the various steps in different Hidden Sequences follow the hypothesized pattern for Hidden Sequences, and whether that pattern changes when there is a mélange of internal reactions and behaviors.

135. Ascertain whether people who have a strong tendency to focus on tangible things have difficulty grasping psychological concepts and using such concepts effectively.

136. Ascertain whether a strong emotional reaction means that a Psychological Root has been impacted.

137. Ascertain whether Psychological Systems Theory's concepts are universal and apply to people all around the world.

138. Ascertain whether psychology is logical rather than haphazard or irrational (see Chapters 4 and 5).

139. Ascertain the degree to which overt behavior is predictable (see Chapter 32).
140. Ascertain whether the ability to predict behavior is greater knowing the likelihood of particular internal reactions compared to knowing what Psychological Roots exist.
141. Ascertain whether the stronger an internal reaction, the more likely an observable behavior will result.
142. Ascertain whether emotional reactions are more likely to lead to overt behavior than thoughts, evaluations, or cognitive decisions.
143. Ascertain whether the lower the intensity of emotional reactions the greater the chance that modifying factors will affect the outcome.
144. What changes occur regarding each type of internal reaction (e.g., thoughts, evaluations, emotional reactions, and decisions), how those aspects are triggered, what specific effects they have, and how they generate those particular effects.
145. Ascertain how Psychological Roots are stored, how they are located when called upon, how their information is retrieved, and what the mechanism is that affects thinking, emotions, and behavior.
146. Ascertain whether there are genetic drives to acquire information and to create links.
147. Ascertain whether there is a genetically wired-in need to solve problems and have challenges.
148. Ascertain whether people's beliefs carry more weight than objective facts (e.g., when people say, "Don't confuse me with facts", they put aside aspects that run counter to their Psychological Roots).
149. Ascertain whether Psychological Roots exist in people around the world regardless of their culture, also what Psychological Roots people often have in common.
150. Ascertain whether focusing on one aspect causes other aspects to fade into the background.
151. Create mathematical models based on Psychological Systems Theory and related research findings.
152. Ascertain whether some non-human creatures have genetic Psychological Roots (e.g., needs for safety, communicating) and acquired Psychological Roots (e.g., goals, beliefs, expectations). If so, what creatures are they, how early in the phylogenetic chain does it take place, and what is the location of those aspects in those creatures?
153. Ascertain whether some non-human creatures possess some acquired Psychological Roots (e.g., goals, beliefs, expectations).

154. Ascertain whether Psychological Root clusters exist in non-human mammals and some non-mammalian creatures, hence whether other creatures may have various types of intelligence (Gardner, 1983).

Practical applications of Psychological Systems Theory
155. Ascertain the Psychological Roots involved in psychological conditions and disorders that occur frequently (e.g., addictions, anxiety, phobias, PTSD, OCD, shyness, depression, suicidal ideation, borderline personality disorder, bipolar disorder, attention disorders, hyperactivity, mania, and anger).
156. Ascertain the Psychological Roots related to eating disorders (e.g., anorexia, bulimia, being overweight).
157. Ascertain the Psychological Roots involved in extreme antisocial behavior such as rage hate, violence, psychopathy, and sociopathy.
158. Ascertain whether psychological disorders have an understandable logic (see Chapters 4 and 32).
159. Ascertain the Psychological Roots involved in psychological conditions thought to be due to biological causes such as schizophrenia and other psychoses.
160. Ascertain whether constructively modifying distress-prone Psychological Roots lessens the frequency with which such disorders recur in the population (a test of the postulated causal effect of Psychological Roots).
161. Ascertain whether a core set of distress-prone roots Psychological Roots exists in some psychological conditions (e.g., depression, anxiety, addiction) (e.g., the distress-prone Psychological Roots listed at the end of Chapter 16).
162. Ascertain whether precursors to depression, anxiety attacks/panic, and rage are dysthymia, anxiety, and irritability, respectively.
163. Ascertain whether extremely high levels of emotional intensity are precursors to states of uncontrollability (e.g., tension, dysthymic mood, irritability).
164. Ascertain whether extremely low levels of emotion are precursors to states of uncontrollability (e.g., anxiety, irritability, dispassion, apathy, boredom, lethargy, anhedonia).
165. Ascertain whether eustress-prone Psychological Roots and a relative weakness or absence of distress-prone Psychological Roots are precursors for happiness.
166. Ascertain whether the Psychological Roots that contribute to precursors are similar to the Psychological Roots that contribute to states of uncontrollability.

167. Ascertain whether distress and distress-prone beliefs can be precursors to the development of superstitions and phobias.
168. Ascertain whether negative precursor conditions (e.g., irritability, anxiety, and dysthymia) and short-term negative states of uncontrollability (e.g., rage, panic, and depression) exist to a substantial extent in the population.
169. Ascertain the extent to which distress-prone conditions are present in the normal population and whether they are precursors to psychological disorders (e.g., dysthymic mood regarding depression; easily triggered counterproductive social behavior such as in borderline personality disorder; and emotionality and absolute thinking regarding bipolar disorder).
170. Ascertain whether there is an under-diagnosis of borderline personality because many of the accompanying behaviors overlap with other conditions such as depression, PTSD, bipolar disorder, anger, relationship problems, parent-child problems, and addiction.
171. Ascertain whether the amount of borderline personality disorder in the population is much larger than statistical tallies suggest because of its overlap with other conditions such as those noted above.
172. Ascertain whether easily-triggered counterproductive social behaviors are related to borderline personality disorder.
173. Ascertain whether the intensity of states of uncontrollability is due to the number, type, intensity, and duration of psychological factors such as Psychological Roots and situational aspects.
174. Ascertain whether depression, panic, compulsivity, violence, addiction, and are states of uncontrollability associated with Psychological Homeostatic continua.
175. Ascertain if cumulative build-up contributes to binging behavior on addictive substances.
176. Ascertain whether a cumulative build-up of stress can lead to going past a tipping point and eventuate in states of uncontrollability such as depression, panic, rage, addiction, suicide, and psychotic episodes.
177. Ascertain whether people who have psychological disorders are especially likely to have trouble coping with negatives such as failure, insults, criticism, and threats.
178. Ascertain whether extrication from states of uncontrollability can occur by modifying, overshadowing, or satisfying distress-prone Psychological Roots can aid ability for people to extricate themselves from a state of uncontrollability. Also, ascertain other skills that can aid such extrication.

179. Create effective methods for extricating people from a variety of states of uncontrollability (e.g., by utilizing effective problem-solving strategies).

180. Ascertain whether some people who are in psychological states of uncontrollability might not have acquired effective extrication skills or are hampered in the way they use such skills.

181. Test the postulated causality of Psychological Roots to ascertain whether distress-prone Psychological Roots pre-date particular psychological disorders (e.g., depression, anxiety, and addiction) such as by employing longitudinal studies of the normal population.

182. Test a treatment for anxiety which includes helping clients raise their threshold for negative emotional arousal and their confidence, lower their expectations, acquire problem-solving techniques, and avoid thinking in absolutes.

183. Test a treatment for depression which includes helping clients raise their threshold for negative emotional arousal and their confidence, lower their expectations, acquire problem-solving techniques, and avoid thinking in absolutes.

184. Test a treatment for PTSD which includes helping clients raise their threshold for negative emotional arousal and their confidence, lower their expectations, acquire problem-solving techniques, avoid thinking in absolutes, and receive deconditioning.

185. Test a treatment for BPD which includes giving clients a combination of treatment for PTSD, depression, and anxiety (e.g., raise their threshold for negative emotional arousal and their confidence, lower their expectations, acquire problem-solving techniques, avoid thinking in absolutes, and receive deconditioning).

186. Test a treatment for OCD which includes helping clients raise their threshold for negative emotional arousal and their confidence, lower their expectations, acquire problem-solving techniques, and avoid thinking in absolutes.

187. Test a treatment for A.D.D which includes helping clients prioritize, remain focused on each task until it is finished, find something interesting in boring tasks, raise their threshold for negative emotional arousal, plan, acquire problem-solving strategies, and make careful judgments before taking action.

188. Develop and refine the treatment of psychological disorders (such as those mentioned above) using the principles of Psychological Systems Theory (including stimulus conditions and Psychological Roots).

189. Assess the effectiveness of Psychological Systems Therapy in psychological disorders.

190. Develop therapeutic methods that help people successfully prevent entering states of uncontrollability.
191. Develop programs based on Psychological Systems Theory to help prevent psychological disorders such as depression, anxiety, rage, OCD, borderline personality disorder, bipolar disorder, PTSD.
192. Ascertain whether some people in the normal population have a lower level of some of the same distress-prone personality characteristics as people with major depression (precursors).
193. Ascertain whether many or even most people with common psychological conditions – such as anxiety, depression, and borderline personality disorder – are in the normal range of the population much of the time and manifest substantial symptoms of their condition only when they cross the tipping point into a state of uncontrollability.
194. Develop programs based on Psychological Systems Theory to help treat addiction.
195. Develop programs based on Psychological Systems Theory to help prevent addiction.
196. Assess the role of Psychological Roots in conflicts, win-win solutions, communication, social influence, teaching, learning, and psychotherapy.
197. Identify factors and processes that contribute resistance to change and persuasibility.
198. Ascertain whether the three-stage approach addressing Psychological Roots aids communication.
199. Ascertain whether effective communicators employ the precepts of Psychological Systems Theory, such as those related to the three-stage approach of communication.
200. Ascertain whether the three-stage persuasion approach and satisfying recipients' Psychological Roots aids persuasion such as by solving a bothersome problem the recipient has.
201. Ascertain whether a reason that facts and logic may not persuade is because they run counter to the recipient's deep Psychological Roots and therefore are repelling forces.
202. Ascertain whether people often have difficulty persuading others.
203. Ascertain whether the presentations of effective persuaders (e.g., salespeople) coincides with Psychological Systems Theory concepts.
204. Ascertain the Psychological Roots and modifiers that contribute to commonly occurring uncivil interpersonal behavior (e.g., angry, retaliatory, and hostile actions).
205. Ascertain the Psychological Roots that contribute to criminal behavior.

206. Develop programs that help prevent and correct criminality based on Psychological Systems Theory.

207. Ascertain whether thinking in absolutes can lead to overlooking details and thereby impede understanding of degrees, combinations of factors, and complexities. Also, whether absolute thinking contributes to a narrowing of the range of acceptability and thereby limits horizons (termed encapsulation' by Royce, 1964).

208. Ascertain whether absolute thinking contributes to a denial of problems and ignoring differences and nuances and thereby results in less effective thinking and decision-making especially with complicated issues and troublesome problems.

209. Ascertain whether thinking in absolutes makes it more likely for people to have conflicts with others, including gridlock (e.g., in divorce and political paralysis).

210. Ascertain whether absolute thinking increases resistance to change and thereby interferes with learning and growing, makes it easier to enter a state of uncontrollability, and causes difficulty in exiting from that state. (In short, ascertain whether thinking in absolutes a substantial source of human problems.)

211. Ascertain what is required for people to learn how to think in non-absolute terms and to do so readily, rather automatically employ absolute thinking.

212. Ascertain whether teaching students to think more complexly than in absolutes improves their lives and thinking ability (e.g., in problem-solving, social interactions, and avoiding disturbing conflicts).

213. Ascertain whether Psychological Roots that underlie negative prejudice toward groups of people include strong needs for safety, closure, and focusing on tangibles; beliefs about being vulnerable and retaliating when injured; a narrow acceptability range, an unwillingness to create compatible solutions, and modifiers such as a low threshold for emotional arousal, and tendency to think in absolutes, use generalizations, prefer simplicity, and focus on solitary aspects.

214. Ascertain if negative prejudices can be lessened by modifying Psychological Roots that pertain to those prejudices.

215. Develop effective methods for acquiring Psychological Roots and modifiers that aid civil behavior and are potent enough to counteract uncivilized, antisocial, angry, hostile, or violent behavior.

216. Ascertain whether the more overt and salient a group's trait, the easier it is to acquire a prejudice against them as a group (e.g., because of appearance, skin color, gender, religion, viewpoint, or social class).

217. Ascertain whether people become more flexible and open to improvement after acquiring skills derived from Psychological Systems Theory and Therapy.
218. Ascertain how the postulates and processes of Psychological Systems Theory can aid practical applications of psychology.
219. Ascertain Psychological Roots that foster resistance to medication, prevention, and healthful living.
220. Ascertain whether satisfying the Psychological Roots of people helps generate win-win solutions. Also test whether the three-stage approach for resolving conflicts does so effectively.
221. Ascertain whether giving business managers and employees training in how to create compatible solutions (e.g., win-win solutions based on satisfying Psychological Roots) might lessen conflicts, improve morale and productivity, and avoid strikes.
222. Ascertain whether giving every person training in how to create compatible solutions (e.g., win-win solutions based on satisfying everyone's Psychological Roots) and respect for others (e.g., providing respect and delimiting the use of repelling forces) might lessen divorces, social conflicts, and riots.
223. Ascertain whether couples' lack of knowledge about how to resolve their conflicts compatibly is a major contributor to divorce rather than their not trying hard enough.
224. Ascertain whether some people who have been diagnosed with A.D.D. are distracted because they lack interest in some activities, such as school tasks and routine tasks, and instead, are attentive to things that they are interested in or concerned about, such as hobbies, relationships, or disturbing personal situations.
225. Ascertain whether some people who have been diagnosed with A.D.D. are able to focus for long hours on aspects related to their Psychological Roots and not to other aspects. Also ascertain whether people with A.D.D. would be more effective in school and other tasks when they find something in the subject matter that interests them.
226. Ascertain whether people with attention deficit disorder are distracted largely because they lack interest in aspects not connected with their Psychological Roots (e.g., many school tasks and routine jobs), but would be drawn to aspects related to such roots (e.g., their hobbies, relationships, or jobs), hence would be much less distracted if that strategy were employed.
227. Ascertain the Psychological Roots that contribute to effectively managing and leading people.

228. Develop effective programs that help contribute to effective leadership and managing people based on Psychological Systems Theory.
229. Ascertain whether giving diplomats and governmental leaders training in how to create compatible solutions (e.g., win-win solutions based on satisfying everyone's Psychological Roots) might improve international relations, lessen conflicts and the likelihood of war, and increase the chances of peace.
230. Develop programs to help avoid homelessness based on Psychological Systems Theory.
231. Ascertain the role of eustress-prone (positive) Psychological Roots in contributing to contentment and happiness (e. g., easy-to-meet expectations, a high threshold for negative arousal, effective problem-solving strategies, and good social strategies).
232. Ascertain if cumulative build-up is a factor in some psychological reactions, such as quick or unpredictable changes of mood (e.g., in bipolar disorder and borderline personality disorder).
233. Ascertain whether cumulative build-up can lead to a tipping point into a psychological disorder.
234. When a person "snapshot scenario" (e.g., suddenly engages in violent or chaotic behavior), ascertain what distress-prone Psychological Roots have been involved.
235. Ascertain if there has been a cumulative build-up before a person "snapping". Also ascertain what distress-prone Psychological Roots have been involved.
236. Ascertain if the instances of a person "snapping" can be reduced by constructively modifying distress-prone Psychological Roots.
237. Ascertain if constructively modifying Psychological Roots has more effective long-term effectiveness in lessening counterproductive behavior and psychological disorders than directly treating internal reactions or behavior. Also, whether treating internal reactions lessens counterproductive behavior and psychological disorders for a longer period than treating behaviors directly.
238. Ascertain if a narrow adaptive range, low threshold for negative arousal, belief about being vulnerable, need to have things under control, and absolute thinking are present in obsessive-compulsive disorder (OCD).
239. Ascertain if constructively modifying Psychological Roots can lessen OCD.
240. Ascertain the Psychological Roots that contribute to binge drinking of alcohol.
241. Develop effective methods for helping resistant individuals' willingness to improve the psychological reasons for their circumstances.

242. Ascertain whether learning about precursors (see Chapter 2) and how to deal with them can help people avoid entering negative states of uncontrollability (e.g., panic, rage, addiction).

243. Ascertain whether learning about precursors and what to do about them (see Chapter 2) can help people avoid experiencing negative states of uncontrollability (e.g., panic, rage, and addiction).

244. Identify psychological and biological aspects that lower the threshold for negative emotional arousal (e.g., danger, prior trauma, hormones, medications, fatigue, illness, caffeine, and nutritional deficiencies).

245. Develop effective methods to raise the threshold for negative emotional arousal (perhaps medicine).

246. Ascertain whether EMDR (eye movement desensitization response) helps people lessen negative emotional reactions related to disturbing cognitions and stimuli.

247. Ascertain whether EMDR (eye movement desensitization response) helps separate cognitions and disturbing stimuli from associated emotional reactions in Stimulus-and-Root Sequences.

248. Develop methods that can lessen irritability, anger, and desire for retaliation.

249. Identify Psychological Roots that aid long-term memory and whether modifying those factors can aid people with dementia.

250. Ascertain whether Psychological Roots such as evaluation criteria and problem-solving strategies affect people's executive functioning.

251. Ascertain whether constructively modifying Psychological Roots that facilitate effective evaluating can aid people's executive functioning.

252. Ascertain how alcohol and drugs (such as prescription medicines, heroin, and marihuana) lessen distress, such as by affecting internal reactions or the evaluative function.

253. Ascertain the biological and psychological reasons why cigarettes help people cope.

254. Develop a program to help people overcome the biological and psychological reasons why people smoke cigarettes.

255. Ascertain whether feeling overwhelmed by distress produces biochemical changes similar to those related to depression (e.g., serotonin and dopamine levels).

256. Assess whether modifying depressed clients' distress-oriented Psychological Roots and stimulus conditions improves their serotonin and dopamine levels.

257. Ascertain whether distress-prone Psychological Roots and stimulus conditions are associated with some serious medical conditions, such as

heart disease, stroke, high blood pressure, diabetes, and inflammation, including psychological aspects that foster resistance to prevention and lifestyle change. Also identify the psychological internal reactions associated with medical illnesses, such as anxiety and depression.

258. Identify the psychological internal reactions (including resistance to change) associated with medical illnesses.

259. Ascertain the degree to which distress-prone Psychological Roots and stimulus conditions are associated with headaches, and the degree to which migraine headaches are triggered by stress.

260. Ascertain how to distinguish between stress headaches and migraines.

261. Ascertain Psychological Roots, stimulus conditions, and internal reactions in medical disorders whose causes have not been identified effectively (e.g., fibromyalgia, chronic fatigue, auto-immune diseases, allergies). An example of a Psychological Root that might be involved is a low threshold for emotional arousal.

262. Ascertain whether having a strong drive (e.g., regarding short- or long-term goals) aids health and longevity (i.e., boosts vitality and prolongs life).

263. Ascertain the Psychological Roots that contribute to social popularity and shyness.

264. Ascertain if the core Psychological Roots of people in different cultures delays assimilation into a different culture.

265. Ascertain if discrimination against immigrants diminishes to the degree to which those individuals acquire the host culture's psychological roots.

266. Develop a training program for diplomats that can help them understand the Psychological Roots of people in other societies.

267. Develop a training program for diplomats that provides instruction in how to create win-win solutions, with special emphasis on interaction with other societies (see Chapters 20 - 23).

268. Ascertain what strategies contribute to effective problem-solving ability (e.g., strategies that aid in solving challenges involving tasks, concepts, and relationships).

269. Ascertain whether paper-and-pencil measures of behavior are more highly correlated with behavior than paper-and-pencil measures of internal reactions.

270. Ascertain whether measures of internal reactions measures are more predictive of behavior than measures of Psychological Roots owing to internal reactions being more directly related to behavior in Hidden Sequences.

271. Ascertain if combined measures of Psychological Roots, internal reactions, and behavior patterns are more highly correlated and predictive of actual behavior than the individual measures.
272. Ascertain whether modifying distress-prone Psychological Roots in advance helps prevent psychological disorders in individuals thought to be at high risk for those disorders.
273. Ascertain if acquiring skill in non-absolute thinking lessens states of uncontrollability and whether that skill aids people's ability to extricate themselves from those states.
274. Ascertain whether self-affirming statements (e.g., "I'm worthy") can become conditioned to thereby continually override negative roots such as low self-esteem.
275. Ascertain whether clusters of distress-prone Psychological Roots are involved in many instances of post-traumatic stress disorder, especially regarding treatments of PTSD that are slow or ineffective.
276. Ascertain whether successfully treating post-traumatic stress disorder requires constructively modifying clusters of distress-prone Psychological Roots, not just a few Psychological Roots.
277. Ascertain whether borderline personality disorder and bipolar disorder-2 are the same disorder or whether they are similar. If somewhat similar, how do they differ?
278. Ascertain whether phobias that result from single incidents occur because of impacting the genetic need for safety and possibly also the genetic need for stability.
279. Ascertain the relative frequency of phobias due to hidden psychological aspects vs. due to overt stimuli (see Nell's phobia in Chapter 28).
280. Ascertain if lack of interest in challenges and acquiring knowledge are signs of mental decline and encroaching dementia.
281. Identify and categorize a large number of distress-prone and eustress-prone Psychological Roots.
282. Develop ways that people, in general, can readily acquire eustress-prone roots and lessen their distress-prone roots.
283. Develop methods that help people in general successfully modify some of their deep Psychological Roots.
284. Develop a program to instruct people how to extricate themselves from various states of uncontrollability.
285. Develop a training program for couples that can help them understand one another's Psychological Roots and then create compatible solutions.
286. Develop a training program for potential parents that can help children acquire effective social strategies and create compatible solutions based

on Psychological Roots' effects on evaluations, thoughts, emotional reactions, decisions, and behaviors.

287. Develop effective programs that help prevent and correct uncivil behavior (e.g., antisocial, angry, and hostile) based on Psychological Systems Theory.

288. Develop school programs to help students improve their lives and society by acquiring civilizing Psychological Roots regarding relationships, occupations, income, leadership, and productivity.

289. Ascertain whether Psychological Systems Theory concepts can bolster artificial intelligence regarding reasoning, problem-solving, evaluating, and decision-making (e.g., regarding robots).

290. Develop intangible reinforcements based on Psychological Roots for use in behavior modification.

291. Ascertain whether a reason for backsliding to a previous viewpoint after initially changing is due to that change being inconsistent with a Psychological Root somewhere in a person's network of roots.

292. Ascertain whether strengthening a change helps reduce the likelihood of that person backsliding and thereby help maintain the changed viewpoint.

293. Ascertain whether separate ratings of factors involved in an upcoming decision produces results comparable to a single overall rating of the alternatives (e.g., on a -10 to + 10 scale).

294. Ascertain whether human learning is aided by utilizing Psychological Systems Theory concepts such as pre-scanning of new information, skill in identifying key aspects (extraction ability), and linking with Psychological Roots.

295. Ascertain whether students' acquiring practical strategies related to Psychological Systems Theory (such as self-comprehension activities, thematic analysis, and strategies for taking tests) improves their learning, thinking, problem-solving ability, cooperativeness, personal lives, and grades.

296. Ascertain whether students' use of strategies related to Psychological Systems Theory improves their ability to think complexly and solve problems.

297. Ascertain the Psychological Roots that contribute to being an effective student.

298. Ascertain the Psychological Roots that contribute to being an effective teacher.

299. Ascertain whether the teaching strategies of more effective teachers coincide with Psychological Systems Theory concepts (e.g., self-

comprehension learning, linking with students' Psychological Roots, and the three-stage communication and persuasion methods).

300. Ascertain whether students' interest in learning improves when schools use Psychological Systems Theory concepts (e.g., self-comprehension, appealing forces, and decreased use of repelling forces).

301. Ascertain whether learning, a likelihood of entering college, and graduation rate are aided by learners utilizing strategies related to Psychological Systems Theory (such as self-comprehension activities, thematic analysis, identifying key aspects among the themes, and linking of new information with their Psychological Roots).

302. Develop programs based on Psychological Systems Theory that can bolster teaching effectiveness.

303. Develop programs based on Psychological Systems Theory that can bolster students' scholastic success.

304. Ascertain whether teaching non-absolute thinking in schools can broaden students' perspectives, aid understanding concepts and problem-solving ability, and facilitate creating win-win solutions.

305. Ascertain whether having a strong tendency to think in absolutes creates difficulty in being able to uncouple expectations from goals.

306. Develop methods that help people lower their expectations while retaining their high goals.

307. Develop methods that help people raise their goals even higher than ordinarily while maintaining low expectations or having no expectations.

308. Ascertain whether the drive to achieve goals is powerful enough to keep dying people alive for a short while longer (e.g., long enough to achieve an important aspiration).

309. Develop a strategy to lessen impatience (e.g., extended time to achieve a goal, lowered expectations).

310. Ascertain whether there is a strong negative emotional reaction if the drive for closure is not satisfied (e.g., frustration when delays occur, such as when physical obstacles or other people block attainment of a goal).

311. Ascertain whether there are biological effects if the drive for closure is not satisfied (e.g., headaches, high blood pressure).

312. Ascertain whether an unfulfilled drive for closure may occur in some psychological conditions such as obsessive-compulsive disorder, anxiety, depression, bipolar disorder, and borderline personality disorder.

313. Ascertain the Psychological Roots that are involved in violent acts such as murder, serial killings, and Jihad, and what distinguishes between engaging in such acts and not doing so.

314. Ascertain whether intense conflicts, violence, and war are more likely for people who have a strong tendency to think in absolutes.

315. Ascertain whether concordance of researchers' findings and correlation of multiple items that assess the same Psychological Roots is an effective reliability and validity test of Psychological-Root questionnaires.

316. Test whether role-playing particular Psychological Roots can produce results similar to those of studies that use experimenter-introduced stimulus conditions that impact actual Psychological Roots.

317. Develop an adult-oriented standardized measure for distress-prone Psychological Roots that contribute to disorders (e.g., low threshold for negative arousal, hard-to-meet expectations, and narrow acceptability range).

318. Develop a teen-oriented, age-appropriate standardized measure for distress-prone Psychological Roots that contribute to disorders (e.g., low threshold for negative arousal, hard-to-meet expectations, and narrow acceptability range).

319. Develop a child-oriented, age-appropriate standardized measure for distress-prone Psychological Roots (e.g., low threshold for negative arousal, hard-to-meet expectations, and narrow acceptability range).

320. Create an early childhood screening program that can identify children at risk (e.g., due to parenting issues, abuse, deprivation) that includes Psychological Systems Theory aspects.

321. Develop an early childhood prevention program using aspects of Psychological Systems Therapy.

322. Ascertain the extent to which distress-prone Psychological Roots exist in the general population (e.g., using standardized fixed-alternative questionnaires).

323. Develop measures of Psychological Roots related to terrorism and the stages that lead to becoming a terrorist, joining a terrorist group, and engaging in terrorist acts.

324. Develop measures of the Psychological Roots that lead to, joining a terrorist group vs. being a "lone wolf".

325. Create methods to assess distress-prone internal reactions quantitatively (e.g., feeling vengeful, unloved, or jealous).

326. Create methods to quantitatively assess modifiers (amplifiers and diminishers) such as emotionality, threshold for emotional arousal, and absolute thinking.

327. Ascertain whether measures of distress-prone Psychological Roots and stimulus conditions relate to causality, such as predicting the occurrence of psychological disorders (e.g., depression and anxiety).

328. Develop a standardized measure of borderline personality disorder based on Psychological Roots, internal reactions, and behaviors.
329. Develop measures of cues indicating cumulative build-up in various psychological conditions.
330. Develop a standardized measure of appealing forces.
331. Develop a standardized measure of repelling forces.
332. Develop a standardized measure of social strategies based on Psychological Systems Theory.
333. Develop a standardized measure of problem-solving skills and problem-solving effectiveness based on Psychological Systems Theory.
334. Develop a standardized measure of resistance to change based on Psychological Systems Theory.
335. Develop a standardized measure of persuasiveness and also persuasibility based on Psychological Systems Theory (see Chapters 25 and 26).
336. Develop a standardized measure of happiness based on Psychological Roots, internal reactions, and behaviors.
337. Ascertain the Psychological Roots underlying strong political beliefs (e.g., the foundation of liberal and conservative philosophies, also non-political orientations).
338. Ascertain the psychological reasons why people have difficulty resolving their disagreements.
339. Ascertain whether people's tendency to engage in leadership or followership is related to the hierarchical structure of the brain and also Psychological Root hierarchies.
340. Ascertain whether factors contributing to an authoritarian philosophy include strong drives for stability and closure, also impatience, focus on tangible aspects, and thinking in absolutes.
341. Develop methods based on Psychological Systems Theory that help people acquire information that can improve their general health and well-being.
342. Ascertain whether people's answers to simple, direct questions about their psychological condition (e.g., depression, anxiety, anger) correlate with the results obtained through standardized tests.
343. Compare the long-and short-term effectiveness of Psychological Systems Therapy with other psychotherapies whose primary focus is on internal reactions or behavior (e.g., CBT, acceptance and commitment therapy, mindfulness therapy, rational-emotive therapy, gestalt therapy, psychoanalytic therapy, behavior modification, relaxation, meditation, hypnosis, and yoga).

344. Compare the long-and short-term effectiveness of Psychological Systems Therapy with biological treatments such as medication and electro-cortico therapy.
345. Ascertain whether some biological effects that have psychological effects (e.g., depression and loneliness) occur because they set the stage for acquiring distress-prone Psychological Roots and those roots lead to the psychological effects.
346. Ascertain whether working constructively with Psychological Roots can help improve extreme behavior, including behavior that had not been under control previously.
347. Ascertain whether a Psychological Roots approach works with people of limited intellectual capability.
348. Ascertain whether a Psychological Systems approach offers a successful alternative when other treatments are not successful.
349. Ascertain when each type of psychotherapy (mentioned above) is most useful alone or when utilized in combination with another therapy.
350. Ascertain the Psychological Roots that contribute to hostility and violence, including the Psychological Roots that would help differentiate among perpetrators of the four different types of hate crimes identified by McDevitt, Levin, & Bennett (2002).
351. Ascertain the Psychological Roots underlying typologies in the psychological and sociological literature.
352. Ascertain whether thinking in absolutes is more likely to occur with non-familiar aspects than with familiar aspects.
353. Ascertain whether training in non-absolute thinking can lessen extremism and violence.
354. Ascertain whether a belief that is not inherently dysfunctional can nevertheless lead to a psychological disorder it. (For example, having a strong sense of responsibility could lead to anxiety, guilt, and depression at times; having high expectations can be inappropriate at times).
355. Ascertain whether there are conditioned patterns regarding Psychological Roots such as goals, beliefs, and expectations (e.g., being responsible for others, a desire to lead, control, exert power, be analytical, or remained focused on tasks or other tangible aspects), not just with internal reactions and behaviors.
356. Ascertain whether some Psychological Roots and internal reactions can contribute to personality traits that seem to characterize a person (e.g., typically being upbeat, generous, caring, impatient, in a down mood, or irritable).

357. Ascertain whether there is a conditioned tendency to enter some states of uncontrollability (e.g., panic, depression, apathy, ecstasy, or rage), and to enter precursors to those states.

358. Ascertain whether improving students' liking of teaching and school improves their learning, maturity, grades, a likelihood of entering college, graduation rate, and willingness to obtain further training as an adult (e.g., after a job or occupation ends).

359. Ascertain whether students can do well if goals are high and expectations low.

360. Ascertain whether expectations or beliefs need to be acquired surreptitiously or subconsciously as in the Rosenthal & Jacobson (1968) Pygmalion study to be effective, or what counts is that the teacher believe that students can improve.

361. Ascertain whether students' acquiring academic problem-solving strategies improves their learning and liking of school. (Academic strategies include learning how to study, write cohesive reports, and answer exam questions effectively.)

362. Ascertain whether level of achievement is closely related to the level at which goals are set.

363. Ascertain whether the effective teaching of social skills and other applied psychological aspects, including non-absolute thinking, improves life for people and society, and increases the chances of peace rather than war.

364. Ascertain whether Thaler's (1991) concepts of the endowment effect, the hot hand fallacy, and loss aversion are explained by Psychological Roots related to Psychological Systems Theory such as a strong sense of responsibility, selective attention, and negative emotional reactions being stronger than positive reactions.

365. Ascertain whether taking ownership of an issue creates or boosts a sense of responsibility for that issue.

366. Ascertain whether having ownership of something or a sense of responsibility contributes to making changes to improve it.

367. Ascertain whether the most likely cause of psychological disorders is rooted in psychology and the most likely cause of biological disorders is rooted in biology, as the concept of Hidden Sequences suggests.

368. Ascertain whether the most prominent causes of anxiety, depression, obsessive-compulsive disorder are psychological rather than biological. Also ascertain whether psychological causes are also important in addiction, bipolar disorders 1 and 2, borderline personality disorder, post-traumatic stress disorder, and attention deficit disorder.

369. Ascertain Psychological Roots that contribute to post-traumatic stress disorder.
370. Ascertain whether the treatment of choice for frequently occurring psychological disorders such as anxiety, depression, obsessive-compulsive disorder is psychological. Also ascertain whether psychological treatments are also important for addiction, bipolar disorders 1 and 2, borderline personality disorder, post-traumatic stress disorder, and attention deficit disorder.
371. Ascertain whether there is a tendency for people to focus on relieving symptoms more than on addressing hidden causes.
372. Ascertain whether overtly irrational behavior makes logical sense when the relevant underlying aspects are unearthed, in other than abnormal circumstances such as brain damage, disease, or poisoning.
373. Ascertain whether having a strong commitment to thinking positively might facilitate developing a mental block about some negative things. Also ascertain whether thinking negatively might facilitate having a mental block about some positive things.
374. Ascertain whether young children's desires (e.g., for candy or a toy) are experienced as needs by them rather than just desires.
375. Ascertain whether a tendency to think in absolutes, desire simplicity, and have strong internal reactions increases the likelihood of having generalized prejudices and holding them strongly and rigidly.
376. Ascertain whether negative reactions are likely to be easily aroused and last longer than positive emotions, and whether negative prejudices might have a particularly long life.
377. Ascertain whether the more credible, familiar, and tangible a negative statement is, and the more readily it fits a recipient's Psychological Roots, the more likely it is to be accepted by the recipient. Also ascertain whether these aspects are why some people are especially likely to accept conspiracy theories.
378. Ascertain the length of time that genetic and acquired Psychological Roots can be over-ridden (e.g., by will-power, relaxation, meditation, hypnosis, medication, psychotherapy, and self-statements).
379. Ascertain whether Psychological Roots help explain the results of prior basic and applied research studies.
380. Ascertain whether there are more and stronger distress-prone Psychological Roots in chronic depression than in situational depression, also fewer and weaker eustress-prone roots.
381. Ascertain whether filtering and shaping are ways that the brain uses to help make sense of new things.

381. Ascertain if the programs mentioned in this book intended to help improve people's functioning accomplish the objectives (e.g., improved relationships and lessened psychological disorders).
382. Ascertain whether non-human creatures can experience states of uncontrollability (e.g., the dogs that seemed helpless in Klein, Fencil-Morse, & Seligman's, 1976, learned helplessness research).
383. Ascertain whether much wider acquisition of civilizing Psychological Roots by humans throughout the world, including leaders, helps create a better world.
384. Ascertain whether psychological disorders might intensify and be prolonged because of negative outcomes related to them that continue to occur.
385. Identify the biological structures of Psychological Roots, hierarchies, and Hidden Sequences.
386. Develop practical applications based on Psychological Systems Theory in addition to those mentioned in the above list.
387. Improve Psychological Systems Theory and its practical applications.

Factor analysis and multiple regression
Finding a solution to problems is aided by identifying the cause. Many factors may be involved and it can be essential to identify those that are the most important, also which combination of factors produces the strongest effect after eliminating the amount of overlap among the various factors. Understanding of this sort can be obtained with two statistical methods, multiple regression and factor analysis.

Multiple-regression identifies the most important individual factors and the total effect of those factors. For example, in tuberculosis, the most important causal factor is Mycobacterium tuberculosis; the best medications are isoniazid and rifampicin; the most useful diagnostic tests are a tuberculin skin-test, a Gram-stain blood analysis, and chest X-rays that can identify the signature pattern of tuberculosis; and the most important additional circumstances are particular sanitary, nutritional, and living conditions. Those aspects individually and together can pinpoint specific solutions for tuberculosis.

Factor-analysis is useful when the objective is to identify general themes, that is, the clusters of factors that are involved, also the potency of each cluster. For example, in tuberculosis, the most important general groupings related to tuberculosis are: there is a pathogenic cause, there are living conditions that affect whether that disease is contracted or not, and there are diagnostic tests that can identify that disease.

When the objective is to pin down specific elements – such as the particular Psychological Roots that most account for depression or anxiety – multiple-regression is the method of choice. However, when the objective is to ascertain the broad themes that are important and their relative significance, factor-analysis is useful.

415

Chapter 39. EPILOGUE

Psychological research presents many challenges, in large part because mental processes are largely invisible. Nevertheless, a huge amount of knowledge has been obtained in the less than 150 years that psychology has been a discipline. That extensive understanding provides a foundation for acquiring still more trenchant information. This chapter touches on some of these aspects.

Comprehending the human psyche
     Seeking to identify the many hidden psychological processes in humans is an intriguing challenge. Many of those subconscious components operate simultaneously, either individually or in combination, and need to be understood separately as well as jointly. Complicating the issue is that the same outcome can result from many causes, for example, anxiety can stem from a need for safety, a low threshold for negative arousal, difficult-to-meet expectations, and still other factors. Conversely, one cause can produce different outcomes, for example, hard-to-meet expectations can lead to frustration, anger, aggression, depression, anxiety, or crying. Also, a specific outcome can result from a single Psychological Root, a combination of roots, or a stimulus condition that impacts more than one root. Still another complication is that some psychological outcomes originate from biological causes.
     Because psychological processes are hidden, some people believe that psychology is not real ("Psychology is what people make up"), not important ("Psychology is fluff"), or not strong enough to cause serious problems. Some people believe that psychological processes cannot be tested scientifically or that what counts is only what is observable (e.g., behaviors, emotional reactions, or conscious thoughts).
     The lack of psychological knowledge has led some people to rely on their intuition, (e.g., "I do what seems logical to me", "I go where my emotions take me", "Everyone is a psychologist"). Some people rely substantially on self-help books and articles, and some rely on sayings (e.g., "People do what's in their own best interest", or conversely, "People do *not* do what's in their own best interest"). Some individuals act in accord with rigid formulas or aspects they learned from their parents (e.g., "Spare the rod and spoil the child", "Children should be seen and not heard"). Some persons subscribe to a particular theory while others disdain any abstract perspective.
     Lack of effective psychological knowledge greatly affects people's lives. For example, many people believe that their using facts, logic, or criticism will

persuade other people, even when their experience in doing so has often been unsuccessful. Some people try to get other people to change by making demands, complaining, or giving unasked-for advice (e.g., "Get over it", "Just do it", "Just say no") despite getting negative responses when doing so. Many people quarrel even though that makes things worse. Some people believe that punishment, such as prison and beatings, are effective ways to change people notwithstanding its counterproductive results. Many people make resolutions to change and try to use will-power even though their doing so in the past has not succeeded.

One reason why people continue to engage in unsuccessful behavior is that nature gears us to resist change and to focus on what is tangible, which makes it difficult to grasp hidden aspects such as subconscious psychological processes. A better understanding of psychology might bring people more success, less distress, and fewer psychological disorders.

If and when people are more effective psychologically, some indications might be that:

1. People understand a great deal about psychology and use it constructively.
2. Individuals, groups, and nations use win-win solutions to resolve conflicts.
3. Nations around the world work together on constructive common goals.
4. Vulnerable individuals around the world are safe.
5. Nations focus on improving the welfare of all of their citizens.
6. Living conditions improve around the world and are the norm, not an exception.
7. A large majority of people around the world have a reasonable level of prosperity.
8. People accept responsibility for their mistakes and improve, instead of blaming others.
9. People do not believe that only their viewpoint should prevail.
10. Bigotry is uncommon and people with different characteristics are valued.
11. People everywhere care about others and support people who are in need.
12. Strife rarely occurs and almost everyone gets along well with one another.
13. People frequently solve their problems effectively, including psychological difficulties.
14. Anti-social behavior, criminality, and violence rarely exist.
15. Most people are good at prevention and do not ignore potential problems.
16. People readily improve themselves and do so frequently.
17. People are effective learners and retain a great deal of what they learn.
18. Instructors frequently use self-comprehension activities in their teaching.
19. Students enjoy school.
20. People are good at thinking abstractly and coping with complex issues.

21. People do not revere absolutes and readily think in a non-absolute manner when useful to do so.
22. Couples are skilled at creating win-win solutions to resolve their conflicts.
23. People are skilled at choosing an effective mate and maintaining good relationships.
24. Parents are effective at helping their children acquire civilizing Psychological Roots.
25. People are creative problem solvers and choose leaders who excel at doing so.
26. Harmful addiction rarely occurs because people use constructive methods for lessening their distress.
27. Transformative ideas are welcome and many people are innovative.
28. People do work that is appropriate for them and they enjoy doing so.
29. Managers of people are skilled in obtaining their employees' liking, respect, and effectiveness.
30. People who have a psychological disorder readily improve and are not stigmatized.
31. Much research, thinking, and writing is highly innovative and goes well beyond what is already known.

The future

Psychological knowledge has advanced greatly in the relatively short time since Freud demonstrated the importance of the subconscious. With that as a foundation, a much deeper understanding of psychology continues to occur and with it, better ways to improve lives around the world.

SECTION III. AUXILIARY INFORMATION

ACKNOWLEDGEMENTS
AN ADDITIONAL COMMENT
ABOUT THE AUTHOR
A LONGER LIST OF KEY WORDS
REFERENCES
GLOSSARY
INDEX

***

ACKNOWLEDGEMENTS

No human enterprise is entirely the work of a single individual because, as is well known, we stand on the shoulders of those who have come before us and those who currently assist us. I owe a deep debt of gratitude to many people.

My late parents, Esther and Jacob Greenwald, deserve special recognition for overcoming enormous obstacles and for their generous labors on behalf of their children and others. You will always be dear to my heart. I am especially indebted to my family, particularly my wife, Nina (Dr. Nina Greenwald), who has encouraged me throughout the many salt-mine years of my trying to ascertain what makes people tick psychologically. Nina has remarkable knowledge about teaching, learning, creativity, critical thinking, social relations, and childhood development. She is my go-to person for input and evaluation, the principal editor of this book, and my major support. Thank you, Nina, for your tremendous comments, ideas, and guidance, as well as this book's title.

My esteemed professor at Columbia University, Dr. William J. McGuire, was a genius who changed my life as he did for others as well. I am also indebted to my colleagues who I cannot thank enough for their comments, comradeship, and time, including Dr. James Scroggs, Dr. Carl Gustafson, Dr. Paul Lapuc, Carlos Raposo, and Dr. T. Berry Brazelton. My thinking has also been greatly aided by my three sons and their wives – Dan and Kim Greenwald, Ken and Kristin Greenwald, and Josh and Jodi Greenwald. They have been a sounding board for my ideas, have greatly helped this book become a reality, and most importantly are terrific people, as are their children – Cam, Mia, Emily, Megan, and Alex; Isabel and Jacob; and Max and Ian, respectively. Dan designed the cover of this book, Ken helped with computer issues, and Josh provided feedback in his use of Psychological Systems Theory's concepts in business. I am also beholden to my many clients, students, and research aides whose names I cannot mention because of privacy issues.

I am also fortunate that my family and friends are special. These individuals include my sister, Barbara Kaplan, and her children – Drs. Gary, Scott, and Todd Kaplan and their families, and my brother-in-law David Lebowitz and his wife, Fran. My wife's deceased parents, Raymond and Anna Lebowitz deserve much gratitude. I am indebted to the friendship I have received from many people such as Dr. Jack Levin and his wife Flora, Miriam and Herb Kronish, Whitney Wright and his bride Britt Magneson, and Peter and Debbie West. I am also grateful to Dr. Sherman Eisenthal and his late wife, Susan, Drs. Leonard and Fran Solomon, Dr. Fred Tirrell and his wife Julie, and Drs. David and Susan Martin. I owe a special debt to my faculty colleagues at Bridgewater State University, such as Dr. David Richards and his wife Karen, and Dr. James Scroggs and his wife, Emily. I have also gained a great deal from my relationship with my clinical colleagues at Allied Health Providers, including Dr. Carl Gustafson, Dr. Paul LaPuc, Dr. Geoffrey Cohen, Dr. John McHale, Dr. Paul Goldring, and counselors Judi Bari and Paula Fabyan. Counselors Elizabeth Vigliotti and Dr. Joanne Hager have also been helpful. My editors – my wife Dr. Nina Greenwald and Dr. Susan Martin – are exceptional people who greatly helped improve my writing. Any problems with the writing are entirely my responsibility.

There also are a great many other people too numerous to mention, including many brilliant people throughout the distinguished history of psychology whose insights and efforts help us understand important psychological processes. Especially prominent for me is Dr. Kurt Lewin whose insights, unique perspective, understanding of social psychological processes, ingenious research designs, and the inspiration he gave others, resonate strongly with me and continue to guide my thinking.

I have been fortunate to meet and learn an enormous amount from many people in all walks of life. Kindly accept my gratitude. If I have not mentioned someone, please accept my apologies.

***

AN ADDITIONAL COMMENT

How do we make the world a better place? Where should we start? For me, the place to begin is psychology since almost everything humans do originates in the mind. Trying to fathom that substantial mystery is a powerful challenge especially because of the hidden nature of psychological processes. Many people are involved in adding useful knowledge through their research, clinical work, theoretical analyses, discussions, assessment, and educated guesses.

Together with other psychologists and quite possibly the reader as well, I am intrigued by the compelling challenge of trying to figure out what exists "behind the curtain". The result has been a fascinating journey that transformed my life and this book presents my understanding of that complexity. I hope that you find the ideas in this book useful to you as they have been for my clients, family, and me.

Sincerely,

Herbert J. Greenwald, PhD
BS (Columbia University), BA (Columbia University), MA (Columbia University), MS (Long Island University), Ph.D. (Columbia University), and Post Doctoral Fellowship (Duke University)

P.S. I would like to hear from you.
My email address is: hgreenwald@comcast.net
My current web site is: https://doctorgreenwald.wordpress.com

***

ABOUT THE AUTHOR

Herbert J. Greenwald, Ph.D., is a psychologist with over 30 years of clinical experience. Dr. Greenwald has BS and BA degrees from Columbia University, MA degree from Columbia University, MS degree from Long Island University, and Ph.D. from Columbia University, plus a postdoctoral fellowship at Duke University.

Dr. Greenwald has been a professor at Duke University, University of North Carolina, Boston University, and most recently Massachusetts State University at Bridgewater. He has published research articles in leading professional journals, written two books on couple relations, six textbooks, and has received numerous honors, including Outstanding Professor, Outstanding Alumnus, and Distinguished Service Awards. Some of Dr. Greenwald's future books will address strategies for bolstering interpersonal skills, resolving conflicts, parenting, solving problems, teaching effectively, and coping with difficult people.

A LONGER LIST OF KEY WORDS

absolute thinking
acceptable range
adaptive range
addiction
alerting threshold
alignment effect
amplifiers
anxiety
appealing forces
behavior
behavior modification
beliefs
borderline personality disorder
centrality principle
civilizing factors
closure
clusters
communication
conditioning
conflict resolution
core personality factors
countervailing factors
cumulative build-up
decision-making
deep roots
defense effect
depression
diminishers
distress-prone
emotional reaction
eustress-prone factors
evaluation
evaluation criteria
executive function
expectations
flow-down effect
goals
Hidden Sequences

intensity curve
intermediate Psychological Root
internal reaction
interests
intolerable range
learning
linking
long-term memory
modifiers
needs
negative emotional center
obsessive-compulsive disorder
   (OCD)
originating causes
ownership
panic
persuasion
positive emotional center
post-traumatic stress disorder
   (PTSD)
precipitating causes
precursors
prediction of psychological
   disorders
prejudice
preparedness
prevention
proximal causes
psychological homeostasis
Psychological Root hierarchy
Psychological Roots
Psychological Systems Theory
psychotherapy
rage
repelling forces
Root Sequence
resistance to change
selective attention

REFERENCES

Abeler, J., Falk, A., Goette, L., & Huffman, D. (2011). Reference Points and Effort Provision. *American Economic Review. 102* (2), 470-492. doi: 10.1257/are.101.2.470. ISSN 0002-8282

Abnagale, F. W. & Redding, S. (1980). *Catch Me If You Can*. Broadway Books. ISBN-10: 0767905385, ISBN-13: 978-0767905381

Adamson, G. (1972). An Emotional Reunion Between Man and Lion. *YouTube*. https://www.youtube.com/watch?v=yHhnOcR843c also https://www.youtube.com/watch?v=fl1y9IOHof8

Adler, A. (1927). *The Practice and Theory of Individual Psychology*. New York: Harcourt. ISBN-10: 1631822152, ISBN-13: 978-1631822155

Ainsworth, M. D. S. (1991). Attachment and other affectional bonds across the life cycle. In C. M. Parkes, J. Stevenson-Hinde, & P. Marris (Eds.), *Attachment Across the Life Cycle*. New York, NY: Routledge.

Akagi, H., & House, A. O. (2001). The epidemiology of hysterical conversion. In P. Halligan, C. Bass, & J. Marshall (Eds.) *Hysterical Conversion: Clinical and Theoretical Perspectives* (pp. 73–87). Oxford: Oxford University Press. doi:org/10.1017/s0033291703228774

Allport, G. W. (1937). The Functional Autonomy of Motives. *American Journal of Psychology, 50*, 141-156. doi.org/10.2307/1416626

Allport, G. W., & Postman, L. (1948). *The Psychology of Rumor*. New York, NY: Holt. ASIN: B000JD9IDS

Amabile, T. (1983). *The Social Psychology of Creativity*. New York: Springer-Verlag. ISBN-10: 1461255352, ISBN-13: 978-1461255352

Arango, V., Huang, Y. Y., Underwood, D. D., & Mann, J. J. (2003). Genetics of the serotonergic system in suicidal behavior. *Journal of Psychiatric Research, 37* (5), 375-386. doi.org/10.1016/s0022-3956(03)00048-7 PMID: 12849930

Azrin, N. (1967). Pain and aggression. *Psychology Today*. May, 27-33.

Bandura, A. (1977). Self-efficacy: Toward a unifying theory of behavioral change. *Psychological Review*, 84, 191-215 dx.doi.org/10.1037/0033-295X.84.2.191

Beck, A. T. (1991). Cognitive therapy: A 30-year retrospective. *American Psychologist, 46*, 368-375. doi:10.1037/0003-066X.46.4.368

Beck, A. T. (2008). The evolution of the cognitive model of depression and its neurobiological correlates. *American Journal of Psychiatry, 165*, 969-977. doi:10.1176/appi.ajp.2008. 08050721

Beck, A.T., Steer, R.A., & Brown, G.K. (1996). *Manual for the Beck Depression Inventory-II*. San Antonio, TX: Psychological Corporation.

Beck, A. T., & Ward, C. H. (1961). Dreams of depressed patients: Characteristic themes in manifest content. *Archives of General Psychiatry*, 5, 462-467. doi:10.1001/archpsyc.1961. 01710170040004

Berne, E. (2015). *Transactional Analysis in Psychotherapy: A Systematic Individual and Social Psychiatry*. Eastford, CT: Martino Fine Books. ISBN-10: 161427844X, ISBN-13: 978-1614278443

Bigos, S. J., Bowyer, O. R., Braen, G. R., Brown, K., Deyo, R., Haldeman, S., Hart, J. L., Johnson, E. W., Keller, R., Kido, D., Liang, M. H., Nelson, R. M., Nordin, M., Owen, B. D., Pope, M. H., Schwartz, R. K., Stewart, Jr., D. H., Susman, J., Triano, J. J., Tripp, L. C., Turk, D. C., Watts, C., & Weinstein, J. N. (1994). Acute low back problems in adults. *Clinical Practice Guideline* No. 14, *AHCPR Publication* No. 95-0642. Rockville, MD: Agency for Health Care Policy and Research, Public Health Service, U.S. Department of Health and Human Services.

Billings, A. G., Cronkite, R. C., & Moos, R. H. (1983). Social-environmental factors in unipolar depression: Comparisons of depressed patients and nondepressed controls. *Journal of Abnormal Psychology*, 92, 119-133. doi:10.1037/0021-843X.92.2.119

Blanch, A. K., Shern, D. L. & Steverman, S. M. (2014) Toxic Stress, Behavioral Health, and the Next Major Era in Public Health. *Mental Health America*.

Boucsein, W. (2012). *Electrodermal Activity*. Springer Science & Business Media. p. 2. ISBN 978-1-461-41126-0. doi.org/10.1007/978-1-4614-1126-0

Bowlby, J. (1983). *Attachment: Attachment and Loss*, vol 1 (2nd ed.). New York City, NY: Basic Books. ISBN-10 0465005438, ISBN-13 978-0465005437.

Brazelton, T. B. & Sparrow, J. (2006). *Touchpoints: Birth to Three: Your Child's Emotional and Behavioral Development*. 2nd rev. ed. Cambridge, MA: Perseus Publishing.

Brehm, J. W. (1956). Post-decision changes in desirability of alternatives. *Journal of Abnormal and Social Psychology. 52,* 3, 384-389. doi:10.1037/h0041006

Brehm, M. L., Back, K. W., & Bogdonoff, M. D. (1964). A physiological effect of cognitive dissonance under stress and deprivation. *Journal of Abnormal and Social Psychology*, 69 (3), 1964, 303-310. doi: doi.org/10.1037/h0041671

Brehm, S.S. & Brehm, J.W. (1981). Psychological reactance: A theory of freedom and control. New York: Academic Press. ISBN-10: 148326625, ISBN-13: 978- 148326629

Briggs Myers, I., McCaulley, M. H., Quenk, N. L., Hammer, A. L., & Mitchell, W. D. (2009). MBTI Step III Manual: Exploring Personality Development

Using the Myers-Briggs Type Indicator. *Consulting Psychologists Press* (3rd Ed.) ISBN 0-89106-130-4

Bu, Z. & Callaway, D. J. (2011). Proteins MOVE! Protein dynamics and long range allostery in cell signaling. *Advances in Protein Chemistry and Structural Biology*, 83, 163-221. doi: 10.1016/B978-0-12-381262-9.00005-7. ISBN: B978-0-12-381262-9. PMID: 21570668

Bureau of Justice Statistics Recidivism of Prisoners Released in 1994. (2002). Ojp.usdoj.gov. 2002-06-02.

Burgoon, J. K., Guerrero, L. K., & Floyd, K. (2009). *Nonverbal Communication.* London, UK: Routledge. ISBN-10: 0205525008, ISBN-13: 978-0205525003

Burns, D. D. (1989). The Feeling Good Handbook: Using the New Mood Therapy in Everyday Life. New York, NY: W. Morrow. ISBN 0-688-01745-2

Butler, A. C., Chapman, J. E., Forman, E. M. & Beck A. T. (2006). The empirical status of cognitive-behavioral therapy: A review of meta-analyses. *Clinical Psychology Review*, 26, 17–31. doi:10.1016/j.cpr.2005.07.003

Carmon, Z. & Ariely, D. (2000). Focusing on the Forgone: How Value Can Appear So Different to Buyers and Sellers. *Journal of Consumer Research.* 27, 3, 360-370. doi:10:1086/317590

Cattaneo, L. & Rizzolatti, G. (2009). The mirror neuron system. *Archives of Neurology.* 66, 5, 557-560. doi: 10.1001/archneurol.2009.41

CDC (2008). Prevalence of post-partum depressive symptoms. *MMWR Weekly*, April 11, 2008. 57, *14*, 361-366.

Choca, J. P. (2012). *The Rorschach Test: An Interpretive Guide For Clinicians,* 1st ed. Washington, D. C.: American Psychological Association. ISBN-10: 1433812002, ISBN-13: 978-1433812002,

Chomsky, N. (1957). *Syntactic Structures.* The Hague, Netherlands: Mouton. ISBN 10: 1614278040, ISBN 13: 978-1614278047

Ciompi, L. & Panksepp, J. (2005). Energetic effects of emotions on cognitions: complementary psychobiological and psychosocial findings. In Ralph D. Ellis & Natika Newton (Eds.), *Consciousness & Emotion: Agency, Conscious Choice, and Selective Perception.* Amsterdam, Netherlands: John Benjamins, pp. 23-55. ISBN-10: 1588115966, ISBN-13: 978-1588115966

Coch, L. & French, Jr., J. R. P. (1948). Overcoming resistance to change. *Human Relations, 1*, 4, 512-532. doi.org/10.1177/001872674800100408

Conrad, K.L., Ford, K.A., Marinelli, M., & Wolf, M.E. (2010). Dopamine receptor expression and distribution dynamically change in the nucleus accumbens after withdrawal from cocaine self-administration. *Neuroscience.*169:182–194. doi:10.1016/j.neuroscience.2010.04.056.

Cousins, N. (1981). *Anatomy of an Illness: As Perceived by the Patient – Relflections on Healing and Regeneration.* New York City, NY: Bantam Books. ISBN 10-0553014919, ISBN-13: 978-0553014914

Coyne, J. C. & Gotlib, I. H. (1983). The role of cognitions in depression: A critical appraisal. *Psychological Bulletin,* 94, 472-505. doi:10.1037/0033-2909.94.3.472

Crowne, D. P. & Marlowe, D. (1960). A new scale of social desirability independent of psychopathology. *Journal of Consulting Psychology,* 24(4) 349-354. doi: 10.1037/h0047358.

Cullen, J. B., Cullen, F. T., Hayhow, V.L., & Plouffe, J. T. (1975). The Effects of the Use of Grades as an Incentive. *Journal of Educational Research.* 68, 277-279. doi: 10.1080/00220671.1975.108884770

Dawson, D.A. and Room, R. (2000). Towards agreement on ways to measure and report drinking patterns and alcohol–related problems in adult general population surveys: The Skarpo Conference overview. *Journal of Substance Abuse,* 12, 1–21. doi.org/10.1016/j.drugpo.2014.11.004.

deBerker, A. O., Rutledge, R. B., Mathys, C., Marshall, L., Cross, G. F., Dolan, R. J., & Bestmann, S. (2016). Computations of uncertainty mediate acute stress responses in humans. *Nature Communications,* 7, 10996. doi: 10.1038/ncomms10996

deGraaf, L. E., Roelofs, J., & Huibers, M. J. H. (2009). Measuring dysfunctional attitudes in the general population: The dysfunctional attitude scale (Form A) revised. *Cognitive Therapy Research,* 33 (4), 345–355. doi:10.1007/s10608-009-9229-y, PMCID: PMC2712063125

Delgado, J. M. R. (1969). *Physical Control of the Mind: Toward a Psychocivilized Society.* New York, NY: Harper & Row. ISBN-10: 0060110163, ISBN-13: 978-0060110161

Dewey, J. (1938). *Experience and Education.* Kappa Delta Phi. New York, NY: Touchstone Edition, Simon and Schuster, 1997. ISBN 0-684-83828-1.

Drachman, D. (2005). Do we have brain to spare? *Neurology,* 64, 12, 2004-2005. doi:10.1212/01.WNL.0000166914.38327.BB PMID 15985565

Edebol, H., Lars H., & Norlander, T. (2013). Measuring adult Attention Deficit Hyperactivity Disorder using the Quantified Behavior Test Plus. *PsyCh Journal,* 2, 1, 48-62. doi:10.1002/pchj.17

Ellis, A. & MacLaren, C. (2005). *Rational Emotive Behavior Therapy: A Therapist's Guide,* 2nd Ed. Atascadero, CA: Impact Publishers. ISBN-10: 1886230617, ISBN-13: 978-1886230613

Erikson, E. H. (1963). *Childhood and Society.* New York, NY: Norton. ISBN-10: 039331068X, ISBN-13: 978-0393310689

Exner, J. E. *(2002). The Rorschach: Basic Foundations and Principles of Interpretation: Volume 1. Hoboken, NJ:* John Wiley & Sons. ISBN 0-471-38672-3

Falvey, M. A., Forest, M., Pearpoint, J., & Rosenberg, R. L. (2000). *All my Life's a Circle. Using the Tools: Circles, Maps & Paths.* Toronto: Inclusion Press. ISBN-10: 1895418262, ISBN 13: 978-1895418262

Feldman, G. C., Joormann, J., & Johnson, S. L. (2008) Responses to Positive Affect: A Self-Report Measure of Rumination and Dampening. *Cognitive Therapy Research, 1,* 32 (4), 507–525. doi: 10.1007/s10608-006-9083-0, PMCID: PMC2847784, NIHMSID: NIHMS183393

Festinger, L. (1957). *A Theory of Cognitive Dissonance.* Stanford University Press. ISBN-10: 0804709114, ISBN-13: 978-0804709118

Fisher, S. & Lubin, A. (1958). Distance as a determinant of influence in a two-person serial interaction situation. *Journal of Abnormal Psychology, 56,* 2, 230-238. doi:10.1037/h0044609

Fiske, D. W., & Maddi, S. R. (1961). *Functions of varied experience.* Homewood, Il: Dorsey Press. ASIN: B002AALBV0

Flavell, J. H. 1966). *The Developmental Psychology of Jean Piaget.* New York: Van Nostrand. ASIN: B000GWHSJS

Fox, J. A. & Levin, J. (2015). Extreme Killing: Understanding Serial and Mass Murder. Thousand Oaks, CA: Sage. ISBN 10:148335072X, ISBN 13:978-1483350721

France, C. M., Lysaker, P. H., & Robinson, R. P. (2007). The "Chemical Imbalance" Explanation of Depression: Origins, Lay Endorsement, and Clinical Implications. *Professional Psychology: Research and Practice, 38,* 4, 411-420. doi.org/10.1037/0735-7028.38.4.411

Freud, S. (1990). An Outline of Psycho-analysis (The Standard Edition) (Complete Psychological Works of Sigmund Freud). Peter Gay and James Strachey (Eds.) New York, NY: Norton. ISBN-10: 0393001512, ISBN-13: 978-0393001518

Gao, J., Davis, L. K., Hart, A. B., Sanchez-Roige, S., Han, L., Cacioppo, J. T., & Palmer, A. (2016). Genome-Wide Association Study of Loneliness Demonstrates a Role for Common Variation. *Neurosychopharmacology* advance online publication. Doi: 10.1038/npp.2016.197

Garcia, J. & Koelling, R. A. (1966). The relation of the cue to consequence in avoidance learning. *Psychonomic Science, 4,* 123-124. doi.org/10.3758BF03342209

Gardner, H. (1983). *Frames of Mind: The Theory of Multiple Intelligence.* BasicBooks. ISBN-13: 978-0465024339, ISBN-10: 0465024335

Gibbons, M. (2002). *The Self-Directed Learning Handbook: Challenging Adolescent Students to Excel.* San Francisco, CA: Jossey-Bass, Wiley. ISBN-10: 0787959555, ISBN-13: 978-07878959555

Goleman, D. (2005). *Emotional Intelligence: Why It Can Matter More Than IQ.* New York, NY: Bantam Books. ISBN-10: 055338371X, ISBN-13: 978-0553383713

Gordis, E. (1992). Alcohol Alert. *National Institute on Alcohol Abuse and Alcoholism.* 18 PH 357.

Gottman, J., & Silver, N. (2015). *The Seven Principles for Making Marriage Work: A Practical Guide from the Country's Foremost Relationship Expert* (2nd ed.). New York, NY: Harmony ISBN-10: 0553447718, ISBN-13: 978-0553447712

Gough, H.G. (1987) California Psychological Inventory Administrator's Guide. Palo Alto, CA: Consulting Psychologists Press.

Greenwald, H. J. (1964). The involvement controversy in attitude change research. Unpublished doctoral dissertation, Columbia University.

Greenwald, H. J. (1968). The basic assumptions of dissonance theory. *Psychological Reports, 22,* 3, 888. doi.org/10.2466/pr0.1968.22.3.888

Greenwald, H. J. (1969). Dissonance and relative versus absolute attractiveness of decision alternatives. *Journal of Personality and Social Psychology, 11,* 4, 328-333. doi.org/10.1037/h0027369

Greenwald, H. J. (2001). Inner motivations associated with emotional deprivation. Talk presented at the Center for the Advancement of Research and Teaching, Bridgewater State University, Bridgewater, MA.

Greenwald, H. J. (2014). Psychological Roots associated with depression. Unpublished study, Bridgewater State University, Bridgewater, MA.

Greenwald, H. J. (2017). *The Psychological Brain.* Barnstable, MA: Essential Concepts Press. ISBN-10: 1544077521, ISBN-13: 9781544077529

Guilford, J. P. (1967). *The Nature of Human Intelligence.* New York, NY: McGraw-Hill. ISBN-10: 0070251355, ISBN-13: 978-0070251359

Gutnik, L.A., Hakimzada, A. F., Yoskowitz, N. A., & Patel, V. L. (2006). The role of emotion in decision-making: A cognitive neuroeconomic approach towards understanding sexual risk behavior. *Journal of Biomedical Informatics, 39,* 6, 720-736.

Hare, B. & Woods, V. (2013). *The Genius of Dogs: How Dogs Are Smarter Than You Think.* New York, NY: Plume. ISBN-10: 0142180467, ISBN-13: 978-0142180464

Harlow, H. F. (1961). The development of affectional patterns in infant monkeys. In B. M. Foss (Ed.), *Determinants of Infant Behavior.* London, UK: Methuen.

Hartley, E. L. (1946). *Problems in Prejudice.* New York, NY: King's Crown.

Hauslohner, A., Achenbach, J., & Nakashima, E. (2016). Investigators said they killed for ISIS. But were they different from 'regular' mass killers? *Washington Post*, September 23.

Hebb, D. O. (1955). Drives and the C.N.S. (conceptual nervous system). *Psychological Review. 62*, 243-254. doi.org/10.1037/h0041823

Hetherington, M. J. & Weiler, J. D. (2009). *Authoritarianism and Polarization in American Politics.* New York City, NY: Cambridge University Press. ISBN-10: 052171124X, ISBN-13: 978-0521711241

Hoffer, E. (1951). *The True Believer.* New York, NY: Harper & Brothers. ASIN: B00AYTHML2

Horowitz, A. (2009). *Inside of a Dog. What Dogs See, Smell, and Know.* New York, NY: Scribner. ASIN: B002NT3B52

Hull, C. L. (1952). *A Behavior System.* New Haven, CT: Yale University Press. ASIN: B000JVIA4I

Iacoboni, M. (2009). Imitation, empathy, and mirror neurons. *Annual Review of Psychology. 60*, 653-670. doi: 10.1146/annurev.psycho.60.110707.163604

Imperato, A., Puglisi-Allegra, S., Casolini, P., & Angelucci, L. (1991). Changes in brain dopamine and acetylcholine release during and following stress are independent of the pituitary-adrenocortical axis. *Brain Research, 538*, 111-117. doi:10.1016/0006-8993(91)90384-8

Janis, I. L. & Feshbach, S. (1953). Effects of fear arousing communications. *Journal of Abnormal and Social Psychology, 48*, (1), 78-92. doi.org/10.1037/h0060732

Jannis, S. (2017). Slide 9, www.alz.org/braintour. Alzheimers Associates. Chicago, Il.

Jarcho, J. M., Berkman, E. T., Lieberman, M. D. (2010). The neural basis of rationalization: cognition dissonance reduction during decision-making. *Social Cognitive Affective Neuroscience, 6*, 460-467. doi:10.1093/scan/nsq054.

Jeffery, R. W., Epstein, L. H., Wilson, G. T., Drewnowski, A., Stunkard, A. J., & Wing, R. R. (2000). Long-term maintenance of weight loss: Current status. *Health Psychology, 19* (1, Suppl.), 5-16. doi.org/10.1037/0278-6133.19.Suppl1.5

Jones, D. E., Greenberg, M., & Crowley, M. (2015). Early Social-Emotional Functioning and Public Health: The Relationship Between Kindergarten Social Competence and Future Wellness. *American Journal of Public Health, 105*, 11, 2283-2290. doi:10.2105/AJPH.2015.302630

Jung, C. G. (1953). The psychology of the unconscious processes. In *Collected Works*, Vol.7: *Two Essays on Analytical Psychology* (R. F. Hull, Trans.). London, UK: Routledge and Kegan Paul. doi.org/10.1515/9781400850891

Kahneman, D., Knetsch, J. L., & Thaler, R. H. (1991). Anomalies: The Endowment Effect, Loss Aversion, and Status Quotient Bias. *The Journal of Economic Perspectives*. *5*, 1, 193-206. doi.org/10.1257/jep.5.1.193

Kahneman, D. & Tversky, A. (1979). Prospect Theory: An Analysis of Decision Under Risk. *Econometrica*. *47*, 2, 263. doi:10.2307/1914185.

Kandel, E. R. (2006). *In Search of Memory: The Emergence of a New Science of Mind.* New York, NY: Norton. ISBN-10: 0393329372, ISBN-13: 978-0393329377

Kirsch, I., Deacon, B. J., Huedo-Medina, T. B., Scoboria, A., & Moore, T. J. (2008). Initial Severity and Antidepressant Benefits: A Meta-Analysis of Data Submitted to the Food and Drug Administration. *PLoS Medicine, 5*, 2. doi:10.1371/journal.pmed.0050045

Kirsch, I. (2009). *The Emperor's New Drugs: Exploding the Antidepressant Myth.* London, England: The Bodley Head. B003XKM98U

Klein, D. C., Fencil-Morse, E., & Seligman, M. E. (1976). Learned helplessness, depression, and the attribution of failure. *Journal of Personality and Social Psychology*. *33*, 5, 508-516. doi.org/10.1037/0022-3514.33.5.508 ISSN 0227514

Kühn, S., Romanowski, A., Schilling, C., Lorenz, R., Mörsen, C., Seiferth, N., Banaschewski, T., Barbot, A., Barker, G. J., Büchel, C., Conrod, P. J., Dalley, J. W., Flor, H., Garavan, H. Ittermann, B., Mann, Know, Martinot, J-L., Paus, T., Rietschel, M., Smolka, M. N., Ströhle, A., Walaszek, B., Schumann, G., Heinz. A., & Gallinat, J. (2011). The neural basis of video gaming. *Translational Psychiatry, 1*, 53. doi:10.1038/tp.2011.53

Kurzweil, R. (2005). *The Singularity Is Near. When Humans Transcend Biology.* New York: Viking Press. ISBN: 0-670-03384-7 ISBN 13: 978-0-670-03384-3

Lacasse, J. R., & Leo, J. (2005). Serotonin and Depression: A Disconnect between the Advertisements and the Scientific Literature. *PLOS Medicine*. doi:10.1371/journal.pmed.0020392

LaFrance, A. (2015). America's top killing machine. *The Atlantic*, January 12. http://www.theatlantic.com/technology/archive/2015/01/americas-top-killing-machine/384440/.

Lah, M.I. (1989). Sentence Completion Tests. In C.S. Newmark (Ed.), Major psychological assessment instruments, Vol. II (pp 133-163). Boston: Allyn and Bacon. doi.org/10.1007/978-1-4615-1185-4_7

LaPiere, R. T. (1934). Attitudes vs. actions. *Social Forces, 13*, 230-237. doi: 10.2224/sbp.1989.17.1.9 ISSN 1179-6391

Leavitt, H. J. (1951). Some effects of certain communication patterns on group performance. *Journal of Abnormal and Social Psychology, 46*, 38-50. doi.org/10.1037/h0057 189

Leshner, A.I. (1997). Addiction is a brain disease, and it matters. *Science, 278,* 5335, 45-7. PMID: 9311924

Lewin, K. (1947). Group decision and social change. In T. M. Newcomb & E. L. Hartley (Eds.), *Readings in Social Psychology.* New York, NY: Holt, Rinehart and Winston, pp. 197-211. ASIN: B002ESQV7C

Lewis, O. (1966). *La Vida: A Puerto Rican Family in the Culture of Poverty* – San Juan and New York. New York, NY: Random House. ISBN-10: 0394450469, ISBN-13: 978-0394450469

Lilly, J. C. (1956). Mental effects of reduction of ordinary levels of physical stimuli on intact, healthy persons. *Psychiatric Research Reports. 5,* 1-9.

Linehan, M. M. (1993). *Skills Training Manual For Treating Borderline Personality Disorder.* New York: Guilford. ISBN-10: 0898620341, ISBN-13: 978-0898620344

Loewenstein, G. (2010). Insufficient emotion: Soul-searching by a former indicter of strong emotions. *Emotion Review, 2,* 3, 234-239. doi.org/10.1177/1754073910362598

Lorenz, K. (1971). Studies in animal and human behaviour. England: Methuen. ISBN-10: 0416418201, ISBN-13: 978-0416418200

Mann, J. J., Arango, V., & Underwood, M. D. (1990). Serotonin and suicidal behavior. *Annals of the New York Academy of Science, 600* (1), 476-484. doi.org/10.1111/j.1749-6632.tb16903.x

Mann, L., Janis, I. L. & Chaplin, R. (1969). Effects of anticipation of forthcoming information on predecisional processes. *Journal of Personality and Social Psychology, 11,* 1, 10-16. doi.org/10.1037/h0026967

Manninen, S., Tuominen, L., Dunbar, R., Karjalainen, T., Hirvonen, J., Arponen, E., Hari, R., Jasskelainen, I. P., Sams, M., & Nummenmaa, L. (2017.). Social laughter triggers endogenous opoid release in humans. *Journal of Neuroscience,* 0688-16. doi : 10.1523/JNEUROSCI.0688-16.2017

Martel, B. (2006). Storms payback from God, Nagin says. Associated Press, in the *Washington Post,* January 16, 2006.

Maslow, A.H. (1954). *Motivation and Personality.* New York, NY: Harper. ASIN B0006ATW94

Mayer, J. D., Salovey, P., Caruso, D. R., & Sitarenios, G. (2003). Measuring Emotional Intelligence With the MSCEIT V2.0. *Emotion, 3,* 1, 97-105.2003, Vol. 3, No. 1, 97–105. doi: 10.1037/1528-3542.3.1.97

McCauley, C. & Moskalenko, S. (2017). Understanding Political Radicalization: The Two-Pyramids Model. *American Psychologist, 72,* 3, 205-216.

McCall, R. J., Holtzman, W., Thorpe, J.S., Swartz, J. D., & Herron,W. (1961). *Inkblot Perception and Personality: The Holtzman Inkblot Technique.* American Journal of Psychology, *77*, 4, 687. doi.org/10.2307/1420794

McDevitt, J., Levin, J., & Bennett, S. (2002). Hate Crime Offenders: An Expanded Typology. *Journal of Social Issues, 58*, 2, 303-317. doi: 10.1111/1540.00262

McKinley, J. C, & Hathaway, S. R. (1944). A multiphasic personality schedule (Minnesota): V. Hysteria, Hypomania, and Psychopathic Deviate. *Journal of Applied Psychology, 28*, 153-174. doi.org/10.1037/h0059245

McNay, D. (2012). *Life Lessons From the Lottery: Protecting Your Money in a Scary World.* Richmond, KY: RRP International, Eugenia Ruth. ISBN-10: 0979364426, ISBN-13: 978-0979364426

Merton, R. K. (1963). *Social Theory and Social Structure.* Glencoe, IL: Free Press. ASIN: B0007K77W2

Miller, N. E. (1944). Experimental studies of conflict behavior. In J. McV. Hunt (Ed.), *Personality and Behavior Disorders*, New York, NY: Ronald Press.

Miller, W. R. & Rollnick, S. (1991). *Motivational Interviewing: Helping People Change* (3rd ed.). New York, NY: Guilford Press. ISBN-10: 1609182278, ISBN-13: 978-1609182274

Moehringer, J. R. (2012). *Sutton.* Thorndike Press. ISBN-10: 14010312683, ISBN-13: 978-14010312688

Moffitt, T. E., Caspi, A., Taylor, A., Kokaua, J., Milne, B. J., Polanczyk, G., & Poulton, R. (2010). How common are common mental disorders? Evidence that lifetime prevalence rates are doubled by prospective versus retrospective ascertainment. *Psychological Medicine, 40*, 899-909. doi:10.1017/S0033291709991036

Monroe, S. M. & Harkness, K. L. (2011). Recurrence in major depression: A conceptual analysis. *Psychological Review, 118*, 655-674. doi:10.1037/a0025190

Moos, R. H. & Moos, B. S. (2006). Rates and predictors of relapse after natural and treated remission from alcohol use disorders. *Addiction. 102*, 2, 211-222. doi: 10.1111/j.1360-0443.2006.01310.x

Morewedge, C. K., & Gibliin, C. E. (2015). Explainations of the endowment effect: an integrative review. *Trends in Cognitive Sciences. 19*, 6, 339-348. PMID 25939336 doi:10.1016/j.tics.2015.04.004

Morgan, C. L. (1903). *An Introduction to Comparative Psychology.* (2nd ed.). London: W. Scott. doi:org/10.1037/13701-000

Mowrer, O. H. (1950). *Learning Theory and Personality Dynamics.* New York, NY: Ronald Press. ISBN-10: 0826064256, ISBN-13: 978-0826064257

Muller, M.J., Bosy-Westphal, A., & Heymsfield, S. B. (2010). Is there evidence for a set point that regulates human body weight? F 1000 *MedicineReports. 2*, 59. doi 10.3410/M2-59

Murray, H. A. & collaborators (1938). *Explorations in Personality.* New York, NY: Oxford. ISBN-10: 019530506x, ISBN-13: 978-0195305067

Murray, H. A. (1943). Thematic Apperception Test manual. Cambridge, MA: Harvard University Press.

Nation, P. & Waring, R. (1998). Vocabulary size, text coverage, and word lists. In N. Schmitt & M. McCarthy (Eds). *Vocabulary: Description, Acquisition, Pedagogy.* New York City, New York: Cambridge University Press, 6-19. ISBN-10: 0521585511, ISBN-13: 978-0521585514

Navarro, G., Quiroz, C., Moreno-Delgado, D., Sierakowiak, A., McDowell, K., Moreno, E., Realize, W., Cai, N., Aguinaga, D., Howell, L. A., Hausch, F., Cortés, A., Mallol, J., Casadó, V., Lluís, C., Canela, E. I., Ferré, S., & McCormick, P. J. (2015). Orexin–Corticotropin-Releasing Factor Receptor Heteromers in the Ventral Tegmental Area as Targets for Cocaine. *Journal of Neuroscience, 35,* 17, 6639-6653. doi:10.1523/JNEUROSCI.4364-14.

Nezu, A. & Wilkins, V. (2005) Problem solving-depression. In Stephanie H. Felgoise, ed. (with Arthur Freeman, Arthur M. Nezu, Christine M. Nezu, and Mark A. Reinecke). *Encyclopedia of Cognitive Behavior Therapy,* New York, NY: Springer, pp. 298-301. ISBN-10: 030648580X, ISBN-13: 978-0306485800

Nickerson, R. S. (1998). Confirmation Bias; A Ubiquitous Phenomenon in Man Guises. *Journal of Personality and Social Psychology. 43,* 1, 22-34. doi:10.1037/0022-3514.43.1.22. ISSN 1939-1315

Nyhan, B. & Reifler, J. (2006). When corrections fail: The persistence of political misperceptions. Paper presented at the *American Political Science Association.*

Orpinas, P. & Frankowski, R. (2001). The aggression scale: A self-report measure of aggressive behavior for young adolescents. *Journal of Early Adolescence, 21,* 1, 50-67. doi:10.1177/0272431601021001003

Otis, J. D. (2007). Managing Chronic Pain: A Cognitive-Behavioral Therapy Approach Workbook. New York, NY: Oxford University Press. ISBN-10: 0195329171 ISBN-13: 978-0195329179

Parker, G., Anderson, I. M., & Haddad, P. (2003). Clinical trials of antidepressant medications are producing meaningless results. *British Journal of Psychiatry, 183,* 102-104. doi: 10.1192/bjp.183.2.102

Pavlov, I. P. (1927). Conditioned Reflexes: An Investigation of the Physiological Activity of the Cerebral Cortex. Translated by G. V. Anrep.

London: Oxford University Press. ISBN-10: 1614277982, ISBN-13: 978-1614277989

Penfield, W. (1975). *The Mystery of the Mind: A Critical Study of Consciousness and the Human Brain.* Princeton, N.J.: Princeton University Press, 1975. ISBN-10: 069108159X, ISBN-13: 978-0691081595

Perls, F. (1973). *The Gestalt Approach and Eyewitness to Therapy.* Palo Alto, CA: Science & Behavior Books. ASIN: B0085O67LO

Petries, A. (1978). *Individuality in Pain and Suffering,* 2nd ed. Chicago, IL: University of Chicago. ISBN-10: 0226663477, ISBN-13: 978-0226663470

Premack, D. (1959). Toward empirical behavior laws: I. Positive reinforcement. *Psychological Review,* 66, 219-233. doi.org/10.1037/h0040891

Regolin, L., Rugani, R., Pagini, P., & Valiortigara, G. (2005). Delayed search for social and nonsocial goals by young domestic chicks, Gallus Gallus Domesticus. *Animal Behaviour, 70,* 4, 855-864. doi.org/10.1016/j.anbehav.2005.01.014

Rogers, C. (1951). *Client-Centered Therapy.* Boston, MA: Houghton Mifflin (1951). ISBN-10: 0395053226, ISBN-13: 978-0395053225, ASIN: B0006ASPJ2

Rosenthal, R. & Jacobson, L. (1968). Pygmalion in the classroom: Teacher expectation and pupils' intellectual development. New York: Holt, Rinehart & Winston. ISBN 10: 1904424066, ISBN 13: 9781904424062

Rotter, J. B. (1966). Generalized expectancies for internal versus external control of reinforcement. *Psychological Monographs, 80* (1, Whole, No. 609). PMID:5340840

Rubinstein, J. S., Meyer, D. E. & Evans, J. E. (2001). Executive Control of Cognitive Processes in Task Switching. *Journal of Experimental Psychology: Human Perception and Performance.* 27, 4, 763-797. doi.org/10.1037/0096-1523.27.4.763

Schaefer, J. D., Caspi, A., Belsky, D. W., Harrington, H., Houts, R., Horwood, L. J., Hussong, A., Ramrakha, S., Poultin, R., & Moffitt, T. E. (2017). Enduring mental health: Prevalence and prediction. *Journal of Abnormal Psychology, 126* (2), 212-224. doi.org/10.1037/abn0000232

Schuman, H. & Johnson, M. P. (1976). Attitudes and behavior. *Annual Review of Sociology, 2,* 1, 161-207. doi.org/10.1146/annurev.so.02.080176.001113   ISSN 03600572

Schwartz, B. (1974). On going back to nature: a review of Seligman and Hager's *Biological boundaries of learning. Journal of Experimental Analysis of Behavior, 21* (1), 183-198. doi: 0.1901/jeab.1914.21-183

Segal Z. V., Bizzini, L., & Bondolfi, G. (2005). Cognitive behaviour therapy reduces long term risk of relapse in recurrent major depressive disorder. *Evidence Based Mental Health, 8*, 38. PMID: 15851801

Seligman, M.E.P. (1971). Phobias and preparedness. *Behavior Therapy, 2,* 307-320. doi.org/10.1016/S0005-7894(71)80064-3

Seligman, M.E.P. (1975). *Helplessness: On Depression, Development, and Death.* San Francisco, CA: W.H. Freeman. ISBN-10: 0716707527, ISBN-13: 978-0716707523

Seligman, M.E.P. & Hager, J. L. (1972). *Biological Boundaries of Learning.* New York, NY: Appleton-Century-Crofts. ISBN-10: 0130771724, ISBN-13: 978-0130771728 doi.org/10.1037/e400472009-006

Seligman, M.E.P. & Maier, S.F. (1967). Failure to escape traumatic shock. *Journal of Experimental Psychology, 74,* 1, 1-9. doi.org/10.1037/h0024514

Selye, H. (1978). *The Stress of Life.* 2nd ed. New York, NY: McGraw-Hill. ISBN-10: 0070562083, ISBN-13: 978-0070562080

Sharot, T., DeMartino, B., & Dolan, R. J. (2009). How choice reveals and shapes expected hedonic outcome. *Journal of Neuroscience, 29,* 12, 3760-3765. doi:10.1523/jneurosci.4972-08.2009

Sherif, M. (1958). Superordinate goals in the reduction of intergroup conflicts. *American Journal of Sociology. 63,* 349-356. dx/doi.org/10.1086/222258

Shettleworth, S. J. (2009). Cognition, Evolution and Behavior (2nd ed.). New York, NY: Oxford. ISBN-10: 0195319842, ISBN-13: 978-0195319842

Silverman, J. S., Silverman, J. A., & Eardley, D. A. (1984). Do Maladaptive Attitudes 'Cause' Depression: Misconception of Cognitive Theory-Reply. *Archives of General Psychiatry, 41,* 28-30. PMID: 6691782

Skinner, B. F. (1974). *About Behaviorism.* New York, NY: Knopf. ISBN-10: 0394716183, ISBN-13: 978-0394716183

Smith, C. L. & Zielinski, S. L. (2014). The Startling Intelligence of the Common Chicken. *Scientific American, 310,* 2, 60-65. doi.org/10.1038/scientificamerican0214-60

Snell, W. E., Jr., Gum, S., Shuck, R. L., Mosley, J. A., & Hite, T. L. (1995). The Clinical Anger Scale: Preliminary reliability and validity. *Journal of Clinical Psychology, 51,* 215-226. doi.org/10.13072/midss.627

Souter, C. R. (2016). Election cycle analyzed by political psychologist. *New England Psychologist,* July 1, p. 3.

Sternberg, R. J. (Ed.) (1988). *The Nature of Creativity: Contemporary Psychological Perspectives.* New York, NY: Cambridge University Press. ISBN-10: 0521338921, ISBN-13: 978-0521338929

Sternberg, R. J. (1996). *Successful Intelligence, How Practical and Creative Intelligence Determine Success In Life.* New York, NY: Simon & Schuster. ISBN-10:0452279062, ISBN-13:978-0452279063

Stockmeier, C. A., Shapiro, L. A., Dilley, G. E., Kolli, T. N., Friedman, L. & Rajkowska, G. (1998). Increase in serotonin-1A autoreceptors in the midbrain of suicide victims with major depression – postmortem evidence for decreased serotonin activity. *Journal of Neuroscience, 18* (18). 7394-7401.

Takayanagi, Y., Spira, A.P., Roth, K.B., Gallo, J.J., Eaton, W.W., & Mojtabai R. (2014). Accuracy of reports of lifetime mental and physical disorders: results from the Baltimore Epidemiological Catchment Area study. *JAMA Psychiatry, 71*, 3, 273-80. doi:10.1001/jamapsychiatry.2013.3579.

Taub, A. (2016). *The Rise of American Authoritarianism.* http://www.vox.com/2016/3/1/11127424/trump-authoritarianism

Taylor, J. A. (1953). A personality scale of manifest anxiety. *Journal of Abnormal and Social Psychology, 48*, 2, 285-290. doi: 10.1037/h0056264

Templin, C., Ghadri, J.R., Diekmann, L. et al. (2015). Clinical features and outcomes of Takotsubo (stress) cardiomyopathy. *The New England Journal Of Medicine, 373*, 929-938. doi: 10.1056/NEJMoa1406761

Terman, L. M. & Merrill, M. A. (1960). *Stanford-Binet Intelligence Scale: Manual for the Third Revision Form L-M with Revised IQ Tables by Samuel R. Pinneau.* Boston, MA: Houghton Mifflin. ASIN: B000MBC2WQ

Thibaut, J. & Kelley, H. H. (1959). *The Social Psychology of Groups.* New York: John Wiley & Sons. ASIN: B00KQ8WBXU

Visick, K. L. & Fuqua, C. (2005). Decoding microbial chatter: cell-cell communication in bacteria. *Journal of Bacteriology, 187*, 16, 5507-5519. doi:10.1128/JB.187.16.5507-5519, 2005

Warren, L. W. & McEachren, L. (1983). Psychosocial correlates of depressive symptomatology in adult women. *Journal of Abnormal Psychology, 92*, 151-160. doi:10.1037//0021-843X.92.2.151

Wechsler, D. (1981). *WAIS-R: Manual: Wechsler Adult Intelligence Scale-Revised.* New York, NY: Harcourt-Brace-Jovanovich. ASIN: B0006YQQPS

Wicker, A. (1969). Attitude versus actions: The relations of verbal and overt behavioral responses to attitude objects. *Journal of Social Issues, 25*, 4, 41-78. doi.org/10.1111/j.1540-4560.1969.tb00619.x ISSN 00224537

Widom, C. S. (1989). The cycle of violence. *Science, 244*, 160-166. doi: 10.1126/science.2704995

Wikipedia (2014). Aviation accidents and incidents. https://en.wikipedia.org/wiki/Aviation_accidents_and_incidents

Wolpe, J. (1958). *Psychotherapy By Reciprocal Inhibition.* Stanford, CA: Stanford University Press. ASIN: B011ME1Y2A

Young, J. E., Klosko, J. S., & Weishaar, M. (2006). *Schema Therapy: A Practitioner's Guide.* New York, NY: Guilford. ISBN-10: 1593853726, ISBN-13: 978-1593853723

Zeigarnik, B. (1967). On finished and unfinished tasks. In W. D. Ellis, (Ed.) *A Sourcebook of Gestalt Psychology.* New York, NY: Humanities Press. ASIN B000P8AMSM

Zachs, J. M., Kurby, C. A., Eisenberg, M. L., & Haroutunian, N. (2011). Prediction Error Associated with the Perceptual Segmentation of Naturalistic Events. *Journal of Cognitive Neuroscience, 23,* 12, 4057-4066. doi.org/10.1162/jocn_a_00078

GLOSSARY
Concepts, words, and phrases particularly utilized in Psychological Systems Theory

Ability – A particularly strong capability that is genetically wired into a person such as art, mathematics, and verbal reasoning. Extensive Psychological Roots are involved, some that are genetically wired-in and some that are acquired (strong psychological-root complexes). An ability can be further developed through tutoring, experimentation, motivation, practice, support, and opportunity to engage in those things. An ability is not as substantial as a talent or a gift. (See talent, gift, skill, strong psychological-root complex.)

Abnormal – (See discussion of normal.)

Absolute thinking. Thinking in all-or-nothing terms (e.g., either-or, friend-or-enemy, right-wrong), such as the use of terms such as always, never, all or none. (Synonyms: thinking that is black-and-white, all-nothing, either-or, dichotomy, categorical.) (See non-absolute thinking.)

Accelerating gradient – Increased intensity between a comfort zone and an extreme upper limit. As intensity increases toward the upper emotional extreme, there might be an increasing tendency to experience agitation, disturbance, irritability, or annoyance, which becomes very strong at the extreme. Those states are often noticeable and signal that the tipping point is near. (See decelerating gradient.)

Acceptable range – A range of aspects along a Psychological Homeostasis continuum that a person considers agreeable. The acceptable range lies between the comfort range and the tolerable range along the continuum. When a reference is made to people a person knows, the intolerable range pertains to people with whom there is no desire to have contact. (See wide adaptive range, comfort range, concentric social circles, unacceptable range.)

Accommodation –Piaget's term (see Flavell, 1966) for a change that happens after acquiring new knowledge. Accommodation is a flow-down effect in Psychological Systems Theory. (See linking, alignment effect, defense effect, flow-down effect, assimilation.)

Acquired core Psychological Roots – Psychological Roots obtained through experiences that are key parts of a person's personality. (Synonym: acquired inner motivations.) (See genetic core Psychological Roots, linking.)

Acquired inner motivations – (See acquired Psychological Roots.)

Acquired necessity – A requirement that is not genetically wired-into an organism and arouses a negative reaction if not met, but a positive reaction when met. Acquired necessities include responsibilities, standards, requirements, and expectations. (See acquired needs, Psychological Root.)

Acquired Psychological Roots – Psychological Roots obtained through experiences rather than being genetically wired-in. Initially acquired Psychological Roots link to genetic Psychological Roots. Everyone's Psychological Roots differ which makes each person unique, including identical twins, because everyone's experiences are different. Genetic Psychological Roots are analogous to computer hardware and acquired Psychological Roots are analogous to software. (Synonym: acquired inner motivations.) (See linking and genetic Psychological Roots.)

Action cascade – (See multiple Hidden Sequences.)

Acting out – An out-of-control behavior, often anti-social and counterproductive for the individual and others.

Active conflict – A conflict that is currently occurring and is the focus of attention. (See conflict.)

Active Psychological Root – (See pertinent Psychological Root.)

Adaptive range – (See adaptive zone.)

Adaptive zone – A portion of a continuum in which an organism functions well and feels comfortable. (Synonyms: adaptive range, comfort zone, desirable range.) (See wide adaptive range, narrow adaptive range.)

Addiction – A strong habit that occurs automatically or semi-automatically in which a person feels compelled to engage. Addictions often result from a way of coping with distress.

Adlerian – Ideas promulgated by Alfred Adler, an associate of Sigmund Freud, who recognized the relevance of beliefs. (See Psychological Roots.)

Alerting threshold – A point at which a signal occurs, which indicates that a threshold has been crossed (e.g., at the upper and lower limits of an adaptive range). A person might not respond to the signal. (See threshold, warning signal, adaptive range, Psychological Homeostasis.)

Algorithms – A series of steps in which different actions are triggered depending on the evaluation that takes place at each step, for example, if A occurs, then do X; if not A occurs, then do Y. Examples include infection triggering white blood cell responses, achieving a goal triggering positive emotions, and not meeting expectations triggering negative emotions. The executive function uses algorithms. (See executive function.)

Alignment effect – The consistency of all Psychological Roots within a particular hierarchy, which stems from all roots having to be aligned with the genetic Psychological Root at the foundation of each hierarchy and all subsequently acquired roots. (See: defense effect, flow-down effect.)

Alignment with a Psychological Root – Something that consistent with a Psychological Root, for example when someone agrees with a belief of yours. Alignment is pleasing. (See non-alignment with a Psychological Root.)

Alternation solution – (See sequential solution.)

Alzheimer's disease – A type of memory loss and loss of control of other functions, resulting in death. It starts with loss of short-term memory due to biological changes such as a build-up of beta-amyloid plaques and clumping of tau proteins. Alzheimer's disease accounts for about 75% of senile dementia and can be difficult to differentiate from other types of dementia, such as Lewy body dementia.

Ambiguity, ambiguous – Vagueness, lack of clarity.

Amplifier – A factor that increases an effect (e.g., high emotionality increases the likelihood of behavior associated with it; see Petries, 1978, for a discussion of augmenters). Some aspects are capable of either amplifying or reducing depending on the situation, such as thinking in absolutes. (Synonym: intensifier.) (See diminisher.)

Amygdala – A pair of almond-shaped small organs in the diencephalon ('old brain') which houses the center of awareness, also fear and hostility when a threat is perceived. (See awareness.)

Analysis – Breaking things down into smaller parts to aid understanding it. (See synthesis.)

Anger –Antagonistic feelings toward someone or something. (See hostile, rage.)

Anhedonia, anhedonic – Relating to having no positive emotion. That circumstance can be disturbing and generate a negative emotional reaction. (See also dysthymia.)

Anxiety – Fear due to a circumstance that is emotionally disturbing but unlikely to cause physical harm, such as being anxious about an upcoming exam or a job interview. (Synonym: tension.) (See panic.)

Apathy – Feeling no emotion, positive or negative. A bland circumstance can generate a negative emotional reaction feel and be distressing.

Appealing force – Something that generates a positive emotional reaction. Examples of appealing forces are positive reinforcement (Skinner, 1974) and unconditional positive regard (Rogers, 1951). The cessation of unpleasantness (negative reinforcement, Skinner, 1974, or the end of a repelling force) can be an appealing force. (See positive reinforcement, unconditional positive regard, negative reinforcement, repelling force.) (Synonym: toward force.)

A priori experiment – An experiment in which the researcher introduces the experimental treatment. (Synonym for *a priori*: before the fact. Synonym for *a priori* study: experimenter-introduced treatment, experimenter-introduced independent variable study.) (See *post hoc* study.)

Art therapy – Helping clients tap their inner feelings and thoughts through artistic expression.

Assimilation –Piaget's term (see Flavell, 1966) for the acquisition of new knowledge. Assimilation is followed by accommodation – a change in behavior in accord with what has been acquired. (See linking, accommodation, alignment effect, defense effect, flow-down effect.)

Attention deficit disorder – Great distractibility that impedes focusing, persevering on a given task, and completing those tasks. This problem interferes with being effective in school and is often first noticed as an important issue by teachers. (See attention deficit hyperactive disorder.)

Attention deficit hyperactive disorder – Distractibility accompanied by hyperactivity with a resulting impediment with regard to focusing, persevering on tasks, and completing projects. This condition interferes with effectiveness in school work and teachers are often the first to notice it. (See attention deficit disorder.)

Attribution – Identifying something as a cause of something else.

Auditory – Pertaining to hearing.

Auditory cortex – Part of the cerebral cortex that decodes and interprets auditory stimuli, allowing hearing to occur. It is on both sides of the cortex, not far from the ears.

Automatic behaviors – Internal reactions and behaviors that occur without conscious control, for example, biological reflexes. (See semi-automatic behaviors.)

Autonomic nervous system – A part of the central nervous system that triggers excitation and inhibition that typically happens without conscious control. Examples of aspects that are affected include emotional reactions (e.g., fear, anger, feeling like a failure), biochemical changes (e.g., in serotonin and dopamine), and gastro-intestinal reactions (e.g., stimulation of the intestinal tract). (See skeletal nervous system.)

Awareness – Being conscious of something. Awareness is mediated by a small portion of the amygdala in the diencephalon (see Penfield, 1975). Thus, we are aware of perhaps $1/100^{th}$ of what goes on in our brain.

Background distress – Distress that is not salient. That distress can be short-lived or exist for a long time without being noticed, contributes ongoing unpleasantness, and is an impediment to pleasure and happiness. Some of it is due to low self-esteem and low self-confidence, unmet goals and expectations, and unpleasant stimulus conditions such as difficult people, unresolved difficulties, and nagging medical problems. (See eustress.)

Background Psychological Root – a Psychological Root not currently involved in a situation, remaining dormant in the background until a stimulus interacts with it to create a Stimulus-and-Root Sequence. It is dormant, passive, and inactive (e.g., a belief that does not apply to a current situation), awaiting a stimulus that may or may not come that might temporarily transform it into a pertinent Psychological Root. (Synonym: passive Psychological Root.) (See Psychological Root, active Psychological Root, pertinent Psychological Root.)

Behavior – Observable action that is mediated by the skeletal nervous system. It is preceded by an internal reaction. (See Hidden Sequence.)

Behavioral psychology – A psychological discipline that focuses on observable behavior exclusively, such as by using positive reinforcement to obtain desired behavior in children and mentally-delayed individuals. Subconscious processes are not addressed because of the difficulty in doing so, with the belief that it is not necessary to do so to control behavior. Skinner (1974) was a major proponent. (See operant conditioning, classical conditioning, positive reinforcement, negative reinforcement.)

Behavioral research – Research that is conducted on behavior in which the experimenter introduces stimuli to observe their effect on behavior. (See operant conditioning, classical conditioning, Skinnerian).

Belief – Something that is considered to be true or correct by an individual or group. A belief is a Psychological Root. (See Psychological Root, expectation, goal.)

Below the surface – Aspects hidden from what is observable, including mental processes in the subconscious. (See subconscious, awareness.)

Benign – Something mild, and not distressing or harmful.

Bifurcate – Split into two parts.

Bigot, bigotry – Obstinately intolerant. Bigotry is not just ordinary disagreement.

Biochemical changes – changes in biochemistry such as in the brain (e.g., in serotonin and dopamine levels), in glandular outputs (e.g., secretions of hormones), and in smooth muscle activities (e.g., involving constriction of blood vessels or gastro-intestinal muscles).

Biological box – A biological state of uncontrollability, difficult to be extricated from, such as a serious infection, cancer, or loss of a limb. (See psychological box, state of uncontrollability.)

Biological Homeostasis – A genetically wired-in feedback system that helps keep biological processes stable when instability occurs by aiding a return to an adaptive range. When a condition is sufficiently extreme and exceeds a continuum extreme, a state of uncontrollability occurs (such as hypothermia regarding temperature), at least temporarily ending a system's ability to return to the adaptive zone. A state of biological uncontrollability puts an individual in a 'biological box'. (See adaptive range, biological box, Psychological Homeostasis.)

Biological reflex – An automatic reaction that occurs when a stimulus impacts a sensory nerve, for example, an eye blink when dust hits an eye.

Biological state of uncontrollability – (See state of uncontrollability.)

Bipolar disorder 1 – (See manic-depression, cyclothymia.)

Bipolar disorder 2 – Counterproductive interpersonal behavior to the point where it makes the person difficult to be with, "like walking on egg shells". Such individuals often have an especially low threshold for psychological injury, defensiveness, and verbal aggression, and sometimes a cumulative build-up of distress physical aggressiveness Some other psychological factors include feeling emotionally deprived and needy, egocentricity, and difficult-to-meet expectations. Some other characteristics include an unwillingness to be wrong, blaming others, and resistance to improving themselves. They may also have a poor ability to understand people and a desire to control others. These are similar characteristics to people who have borderline personality disorder, which has led to the hypothesis that the two diagnoses refer to the same condition. (See borderline personality disorder.)

Bipolar scale – A scale with opposite values at each end (e.g., choices of like or dislike, yes or no, plus or minus), including a continuum with many alternatives such as -10 to + 10). (See unipolar scale, magnitude scale, continuum.)

Borderline personality disorder (BPD): counterproductive interpersonal behavior that makes a person difficult to be with, needing to "walk on egg shells" when with them. (The term 'borderline' refers to angry or explosive episodes that sometimes happen to a person who might appear on the surface to function normally otherwise.) Part of the cause of their disorder for some BPDs is trauma (e.g., sexual or emotional abuse). The author has found that many BPDs have a "victim mentality" and might say such things as "Why me?". They have difficulty accepting being wrong and easily triggered irritability. They have a tendency to blame others rather than taking responsibility for their actions. Many have difficult-to-meet expectations, are impatient, act impulsively, try to control others, and cross interpersonal boundaries. They might point out others' flaws, be verbally aggressive, be irritated for long periods, hold grudges. They might be vindictive, create turmoil, and be explosively angry, and physically aggressive. Some have paranoid tendencies or are oppositional, and some have multiple lawsuits and court cases. As a consequence, many people may dislike them. BPDs may feel emotionally deprived, be egocentric, not understand other people, not understand why people dislike them, and want to control others. They may be depressed or suicidal and as a consequence may be diagnosed as such, rather than as having borderline personality disorder.

Branch – A Psychological Root hierarchy that branches out from an existing hierarchy by links to a Psychological Root in that hierarchy. It becomes the foundation of a separate hierarchy, for example, a person's interest in mathematics might lead to a career in physics and then a particular aspect of physics, then a specialization in a particular aspect of physics such as string theory. Each branch permits Psychological Roots to be acquired that are associated with it, which can lead to the creation of many trees of Psychological Roots. The multiplicity of branches and sub-branches creates an ever-growing forest of Psychological Roots. (Synonym: Psychological Root branches) (See Psychological Roots, Psychological Root hierarchies.)

Bridging – (See successive approximations to the goal.)

Categories – A number of psychological clusters with a common theme. (See clusters.)

CBT – (See cognitive behavioral therapy.)

Centrality principle – One or a few core aspects form the foundation of what is seen on the surface. (See Chapters 27 - 30 on psychotherapy.)

Cerebral cortex – A portion of mammals' brains between the diencephalon and the cranium. The cerebral cortex contains control centers for many automatic and semi-automatic activities, such as skeletal muscles, senses, executive function, and long-term memory. (Synonym: new brain). (See diencephalon.)

Characterizing trait – A personality style that seems to characterize a person such as generally being upbeat, friendly, irritable, or rigid. A characterizing trait might be due to a strong cluster of Psychological Roots, such as those related to positive or negative social strategies.

Chemical imbalance – Changes in brain biochemicals – such as a decrease in the neurotransmitter, serotonin – have been found in people who suffer from depression (e.g., Stockmeier, Shapiro, Dilley, Kolli, Friedman, & Rajkowska, 1998). That correlation has led many people to believe that biochemical changes cause depression, an idea that has been challenged (e.g., France, Lysaker, & Robinson, 2007, and in this book). Also, psychological aspects change biochemical levels (e.g., Imperato, Puglisi-Allegra, Casolini & Angelucci (1991). And antidepressant medications that attempt to correct those biochemical changes have an only limited effect (e.g., Parker, Anderson, & Haddad, 2003) and studies have found that psychotherapy does as well or better than antidepressants (e.g., Beck, 2008). So, while biochemical changes may occur, a number of findings plus issues discussed in this book raise the possibility that biochemical changes *result* from psychological causes and lead to internal reactions and psychological disorders such as depression, rather than being the originating cause.

Chronic depression – Frequent depression. In Psychological Systems Theory, depression is thought to be substantially due to distress-prone Psychological Roots, such as a low threshold for negative arousal, pessimism, and poor problem-solving strategies. Stressful stimulus conditions may also be present. (See situational depression, depression, Psychological Roots, stimulus conditions, Hidden Sequences.)

Civilizing factors – Psychological Roots, internal reactions, and overt behaviors that generate civilized behavior without which humans might be savages. Some types of anti-social, violent, or sociopathic behavior may be due to not acquiring civilizing Psychological Roots, having poorly formed modifiers, intentionally bypassing civilizing Psychological Roots and modifiers, a state of uncontrollability, or brain damage. (See modifier, Psychological Root, Modified Root Sequence, Modified Root and Stimulus Sequence.)

Classical conditioning – When a previously 'neutral' stimulus becomes a cue that triggers a genetically wired-in response (e.g., when Pavlov's dog salivated at the sound of a bell). The dog expected food after the bell had sounded many times immediately before food had been presented to the dog. Classical conditioning is possible with the autonomic nervous system. Psychological Roots are involved (e.g., expectations and beliefs). (Synonym: respondent conditioning.) (See operant conditioning.)

Clinical condition – A physical or psychological state that interferes with effective functioning for more than a short time (e.g., heart disease, depression, anxiety, general irritability). (Synonym: disorder.)

Close-minded – A narrow range of acceptability, greatly reducing openness to ideas other than one's own. Close-mindedness occurs in people who are prejudiced, have unyielding convictions, think they know it all, or cannot tolerate being wrong. (Synonyms: narrow comfort zone, narrow acceptability range, low tolerability, wide unacceptable range.) (See open-minded, narrow comfort zone.)

Closure drive – A strong impetus for something to end, such as finishing a task, achieving a goal, ending discomfort, or finding out how a story ends.

Cluster – (See Psychological Root cluster.)

Cognition, cognitive – Information or information processing in the frontal lobe of the cerebral cortex, with some aspects possibly in the hippocampus (e.g., short-term memory).

Cognitive behavioral therapy (CBT) – Aaron Beck's (1991) therapy for psychological disorders in which clients are helped to change their dysfunctional attitudes, beliefs, thoughts, and behaviors (e.g., realizing that there are some positive aspects in their life instead of believing the opposite). CBT addresses some aspects that in Psychological Systems Theory are considered intermediate or surface Psychological Roots such as dysfunctional beliefs) in people with psychological disorders. (See Psychological Systems Theory.)

Cognitive dissonance, cognitive dissonance theory. (See dissonance theory.)

Cognitive internal reaction – A thought, concern, evaluation, or decision in a Hidden Sequence that occurs as a result of a Psychological Root itself or Psychological Root having been impacted by a stimulus. Another type of internal reaction is an emotional reaction, such as pleasure or unhappiness. (See internal reaction, emotional internal reaction, Hidden Sequence.)

Cognitive significance – Something cognitive (such as knowledge, thought, or idea) with great meaning for a person (e.g., as an aid for solving problems, or a special proverb, poem, phrase).

Cognitive state of uncontrollability – A thought that controls a person's thinking and behavior because it is held to an absolute degree, strongly resists being changed, and greatly influences a person's thinking. (See emotional state of uncontrollability.)

Combination solution – A conflict resolution in which the conflicting alternatives or substantial portions of them are joined (e.g., when one person wants to buy a cake, the other ice cream, they can get ice cream on a cake). If a combination solution is viewed as a sacrifice, it is a compromise. (See win-win solution, sequential solution.)

Comfort range – A range of aspects along a Psychological Homeostasis continuum with which a person feels especially comfortable, between the positive extreme and the acceptable range. An intolerable range pertains to those for whom there is no desire to have any contact. (Synonym: desirable range.) (See comfort zone, adaptive zone, wide adaptive range, unacceptable range, concentric social circles.)

Comfort zone – A portion of a continuum in which a person functions well and feels comfortable. (Synonyms: adaptive range, desirable range.) (See wide adaptive range, narrow adaptive range.)

Common factors – Some Psychological Roots (e.g., hard-meet-expectations, low threshold for negative arousal, poor problem-solving strategies, pessimism) are present in more than one psychological condition (e.g., depression, anxiety, OCD, bipolar disorder)

Common goal – A goal held by more than one person. Hence, each person's effort to achieve the goal helps everyone, which can lead to viewing those others in a positive way and thereby lessen hostility (e.g., Sherif, 1958). This circumstance often happens in effective sports teams. (See compelling common goal.)

Common sense – An idea a person believes to be held by people in general, often with the implication that it is obvious, practical, and effective. A problem is that each person can believe that *his/her* viewpoint is common sense even though it differs from everyone else's ideas.

Compatible solution – A solution that is acceptable to those who are in a conflict. (See win-win solution, compromise, conflict.)

Compelling common goal – A common goal that each party strongly wants and therefore generates an appreciation of others who help achieve the goal.

Complex web – (See web.)

Compromise – A compatible solution that is arrived at by sacrificing something to achieve that solution, making it a lose-lose situation. Compromise is unpleasant and may be viewed as surrendering, so may be resisted. (See lose-lose solution, win-win solution, hard conflict, soft conflict.)

Compulsive behavior, compulsivity – Behavior that someone feels compelled to engage in, for which there may not be an objective rationale for doing so. (See obsessive-compulsive disorder.)

Concentric social circles – A visual depiction of different degrees of emotional closeness to other people. People with whom a person is very connected are in the center or rings close to the center, with less emotional closeness the further away the rings are from the center. In the outermost ring are people for whom a person has no desire to have any contact. (See Intolerability range.)

Concurrently opposed factors – Aspects that directly oppose one another. When factors pushing in one direction are more powerful than those in the opposite direction, the net result favors the more powerful factors. (e.g., negatives generally are far stronger than positives).

Concurrent shaping - New information that is changed as part of the process of its being assimilated, according to Piaget (Flavell, 1966). If alterations also occur during accommodation, it would be another example of concurrent shaping. (Synonym: simultaneous shaping.) (See assimilation, accommodation, pre-shaping, post-shaping, flow-down effect).

Confidence – Belief that something will succeed. Lack of confidence is a belief that something will not succeed. (See self-confidence, optimism, pessimism.)

Conflict – Competing alternatives when a choice is to be made among them. Selecting an alternative resolves the conflict. Thus, a conflict exists until a decision is made. (See win-win solution, hard conflict, soft conflict, compromise.)

Consciousness – Awareness of something. Awareness aids problem-solving, however simultaneous awareness of more than one aspect can impede effectiveness. Awareness of what goes on inside ourselves is limited (less than $1/100^{th}$ of what goes on in our brain, see Penfield, 1975).

Continuum, continua – A range of alternatives along a dimension. Examples include inches on a ruler, different points between 0 and 10 on a numerical scale, different viewpoints between total agreement to total disagreement, different musical notes, and the large number of different electro-magnetic wavelengths. (Synonyms: spectrum, range, multiple alternatives). (See absolute, relative.)

Conversion disorder – When something psychological triggers a physiological illness (e.g., when blindness results from no longer being able to handle distress).

Core acquired Psychological Root – An acquired Psychological Root that is part of a person's basic personality (e.g., a goal, belief, expectation,). It is likely to be hard to change and long-lasting. (See core Psychological Root, genetic Psychological Root, foundation root.)

Core personality – The Psychological Roots that form the foundation of a person's personality. (See foundation root, core acquired Psychological Root, genetic Psychological Root.)

Core personality factor – A Psychological Root that is part of the core personality. (See foundation root, core acquired Psychological Root, genetic Psychological Root.)

Core Psychological Root – A Psychological Root that is part of a person's basic personality. It can be a genetic Psychological Root or a core acquired Psychological Root and is likely to be long-lasting and hard to change. (See core acquired Psychological Root, genetic Psychological Root, foundation root.)

Countervailing factors – Aspects that oppose one another. Those aspects and their potency can vary from moment to moment. Countervailing factors can be simultaneously opposed or sequentially opposed. (See simultaneously opposed factors, sequentially opposed factors.)

Covert – Hidden aspects that often can be discerned upon analysis (e.g., thoughts and feelings that do not show on the surface but can be tapped via discussions and questionnaires). (Synonyms: covert indications, covert signals, covert symptoms.)

Creativity – An ability to develop something new. Psychological Systems Theory postulates that there is a genetic drive for new experiences, which can lead to developing new things, such as problem-solving inventions. There are individual differences ranging from being extremely creative to being largely uncreative. There can be creativity in one field (e.g., music), not another (e.g., mechanical things.).

Criterion – A basis for evaluation, such as success or failure.

Criterion for failure – A basis for judging when failure occurs. (Synonyms – requirement, necessity, need, standard, high or low bar, responsibility, expectation.) Goals can be consciously separated from expectations to avoid having to be 100% successful to avoid feeling like a failure. (See executive function, goal.)

Criterion for success – A basis for judging whether or not success has occurred. (Synonyms – aim, aspiration, desire, want, goal.) Goals can be consciously separated from expectations to avoid needing to be 100% successful so as not to feel like a failure. (See executive function, goal.)

Cumulative build-up – An additive accumulation such as increases in anxiety that ratchet up tension. If build-up continues, the result could be extreme enough to pass a tipping point into a state of uncontrollability (e.g., a panic attack). An increasing sense of failure could reach a tipping point where people can be so overwhelmed by failure that they plunge into depression. (See tipping point, state of uncontrollability, Psychological Homeostasis.)

Curriculum – A number of courses that are intended to improve knowledge of a particular subject matter, such as the courses offered by a school.

Cybernetic – Automatic feedback from an outcome that provides an opportunity for a process to be modified. Cybernetic processes are self-adjusting.

Cycles – A repetition of something such as when ruminating occurs.

Cyclothymia, cyclothymic – Frequent mood alternations that occur for non-obvious reasons. Extreme cyclothymic intensity occurs in bipolar disorder 1/manic-depression. (See bipolar 1.)

Darwinian – Pertaining to Darwin's theory.

Darwin's theory of evolution – Some genetic mutations that spontaneously occur are particularly well suited for environmental conditions and thereby aid survival of that particular species, while other organisms become extinct ("survival of the fittest"). For example, white-winged moths resting on soot-covered trees in Great Britain were easy pickings for birds, while moths with darker wings survived, which eventually led to that species having black-colored wings. Lamarck's theory is the opposite: that the environment triggers genetic changes. The evidence favors Darwin's theory. (See Lamarck's theory of evolution.)

Debilitation – Weakening, such as due to fatigue or illness.

Decelerating gradient – Decreased intensity as an extreme lower limit is approached. That decrease might lead to decreased apathy, lethargy, boredom, fatigue, or anhedonia. Such states are often noticeable and signal that the tipping point is near. (See accelerating gradient.)

Decision – The selection of an alternative among the available choices. There always are at least two choices since even when there is only one alternative, that alternative might or might not be chosen.

Deconditioning – Lessening of a conditioned response. Deconditioning can result from non-reinforcement or an aversive stimulus. A fully de-conditioned response is said to be extinguished. (See extinction.)

Deductive reasoning – Deriving something specific from something general, such as wanting to use an appealing force and then choosing to compliment someone's performance. Another example is saying that a particular insult is an example of a repelling force. (See inductive reasoning.)

Deep learning – When new information links with a recipient's deep Psychological Roots. That contributes to long-term learning. (See Psychological Roots, long-term learning, emotional significance, cognitive significance, long-term cognitive significance, short-term learning.)

Deep motivation – A Psychological Root at or close to the core of a person's personality, such as people's values, genetic needs, and long-term goals.

Deep Psychological Roots – Psychological Roots (e.g., values) at or near the foundation of psychological hierarchies, hence a major part of a person's basic personality. (Synonyms: high-order Psychological Roots, Early Psychological Roots.) (See Early Psychological Roots, Hidden Sequences.)

Deep psychology – Psychological aspects at or near the core of a person's personality including the way a person thinks, analyzes, and draws hypotheses. (See insight psychology, behavioral psychology.)

De-escalation point – The inflection point along a gradient of decreasing intensity at which the level of intensity takes a sharp decrease (e.g., 1.5 on a 0-10 scale). (See escalation point, intensity curve.)

Defense effect – An attempt to maintain consistency in a Psychological Root hierarchy when a stimulus creates a problem with a Psychological Root, by defending what has taken place, such as by making excuses. (See: alignment effect, flow-down effect, Hidden Sequence.)

Dementia – Pathological loss of memory such as Alzheimer's disease and Lewy Body dementia. Causes include disrupted brain functioning, poor nutrition, limited blood supply, and brain damage.

Demographic data – Information that pertains to observable aspects in a population (e.g., gender, age, income). (See sociology.)

Depression – A state of uncontrollability characterized by a severe down mood, lethargy, overwhelming gloom, hopelessness, failure, loss, disappointment, or rejection, and feeling helpless to change it. Psychological contributors can include difficult-to-meet expectations, weak problem-solving strategies, poor social strategies, impatience, rigidity, absolute thinking, surface orientation, and sense of vulnerability. The proximal cause of depression is a chemical imbalance, such as a low level of the brain neurotransmitter serotonin. Psychological Systems Theory postulates that everyone is capable of becoming depressed if they go past the extreme negative end of an emotional continuum, such as feeling like a total failure with no way out.

Desensitization – A form of de-conditioning in which a person becomes less reactive to a stimulus. In Wolpe's (1958) systematic desensitization method, a mild stimulus is increased in gradual steps until it coincides with the threat, with the client learning to relax at each step. In eye-movement desensitization (EMDR), the client follows a therapist's rapidly moving finger while recalling disturbing aspects. (See sensitization, habituation.)

Desirable range – A portion of a continuum that is particularly comfortable (Synonym: comfort zone.) (See acceptable range, tolerable range, unacceptable range, intolerable range.)

Disorder – A long-lasting extreme internal reaction or behavior.

Drive for closure, desire for closure – (See closure drive.)

Desire for stability – A desire for things to remain as they have been. Many things contribute to stability, such as a genetic need for safety, aversion to negative arousal, and hierarchies of Psychological Roots.

Detoxification – A method of lessening an addiction by abstaining from an addictive behavior or by switching from one habit to another. (Synonyms: detox, rehabilitation, rehabilitate.) Alcoholics Anonymous (AA) helps people with an alcohol problem to voluntarily abstain from using it.

Developmental stages – Different phases that living creatures are genetically programmed to go through (e.g., human infants initially behave in a global manner, are egocentric, and think "concretely", but as they grow, they become increasingly differentiated and able to think abstractly). Among the best known developmental theories are those proposed by Jean Piaget (see Flavell, 1966) and Erik Erickson (1963).

Didactic – Information communicated to recipients by a presenter, such as by a teacher talking to students. (See: self-comprehension learning.)

Diencephalon – A part of mammals' brains between the top of the spinal cord (medulla oblongata) and the bottom of the cerebral cortex. Many creatures that came before mammals have a diencephalon and top of the spinal cord but no cerebral cortex, such as reptiles (e.g., snakes, alligators, lizards), amphibians (e.g., frogs, turtles), fish, and insects. The diencephalon contains control centers for many automatic activities, such as emotional reactions, short-term memory, and hormonal stimulation. (Synonym: old brain). (See cerebral cortex.)

Diminisher – A factor that decreases an effect, for example, high confidence decreases the likelihood of anxiety (See Petries, 1978, for a discussion of reducers). Some aspects are capable of either amplifying or reducing depending on the circumstance (e.g., thinking in absolutes). (See amplifier.)

Discrimination – Distinguishing between aspects. Discrimination that involves prejudice against people refers to acting negatively toward those individuals. (See generalization.)

Disorder – (See clinical condition, mental illness.)

Displacement – Expressing a pent-up emotion on something other than what caused that emotion, such as slamming a book after having been criticized by a boss rather than acting against the boss. The substitute object is often that can be acted against safely. (Synonym: emotional spillover.)

Dissociation – Detachment from reality, such as unawareness of what is happening in the immediate environment (e.g., being "spaced out" from using a drug, being panicked, and being so focused on what one is doing or thinking as not to be aware of surroundings ["absent-minded professor"]).

Dissonance, dissonance theory – Festinger's (1957) theory that subconscious efforts are made to lessen discomfort that arises after a decision is made. There are two postulates (Greenwald, 1968): 1) that dissonance occurs after a decision is made, and 2) that the greater the importance of the circumstance the greater the dissonance. This theory has spawned much interest and many studies, including some findings that support the study and some that do not (e.g., Greenwald, 1969).

Distal – Something that is far from the point of reference (e.g., an experience that occurred in early childhood is a distal stimulus condition). (See proximal.)

Distraction – A shift of attention away from something. Hence, tasks do not get finished, which often happens for people with attention deficit disorder (A.D.D.). Distraction can occur because of lack of interest; when A.D.D. are interested, they can often focus for a long time

Distress – Bothersome stress. Some stress is pleasurable and healthful ("eustress"). (See distress-prone Psychological Roots, eustress.)

Distress-prone Psychological Roots – Some psychological factors directly generate distress (such as low self-esteem and pessimism) or upon impact of a stimulus condition (e.g., an unmet expectation). Distress-prone Psychological Roots can be assessed with questionnaires. (Synonym: negative Psychological Root.)

Distress-prone stimulus conditions – Some stimulus conditions (e.g., being criticized, insulted, or failing) generate distress because they generate negative emotions such as by being inconsistent with Psychological Roots.

Domain – A category, such as each of the various types of elements in a Hidden Sequence (stimulus condition, Psychological Root, internal reaction, and observable behavior). (See primary domain, Hidden Sequence.)

Dominance – Overshadowing, controlling, or overpowering other entities. Deep Psychological Roots dominate intermediate and surface Psychological Roots.

Domino effect – (See flow-down effect.)

Drive – Energy directed toward achieving a goal. The drive to avoid or escape negatives is stronger than the drive to acquire positives since negatives are stronger than positives. (Synonym: motivation.)

Dysthymia – A down mood that lasts more than a month. In Psychological Systems Theory, dysthymia is a strongly experienced down mood (8-10 on a 10-point scale) that can be a precursor to depression. (See precursor, anhedonia.)

Early Psychological Root – A Psychological Root at or near the foundation of a Psychological Root hierarchy (e.g., genetic Psychological Roots such as needs for safety and connecting with others, and acquired roots such as values obtained early in life such as believing in working diligently and taking personal responsibility). Early Psychological Roots may be a part of an individual's core personality and likely to be more general and less tangible than Later Psychological Roots. (Synonym: high-order Psychological Root, deep Psychological Root.) (See later Psychological Root.)

Easily triggered irritability – A condition in which a person is readily annoyed, like "walking on egg shells" when being near them. This counterproductive social behavior can be a precursor to borderline personality disorder. (See precursor.)

Egocentric, egocentricity – (See narcissism.)

Elixir of cordiality – Appropriate use of appealing forces and non-use of repelling forces. (See: appealing forces, repelling forces, positive reinforcement, negative reinforcement, punishment, social strategies.)

Emotion – A positive or negative reaction produced by the positive or negative emotional center in the brain's limbic area. Extreme emotions can trigger a state of uncontrollability such as depression or euphoria. (See comfort zone.)

Emotional connectedness – Feeling a strong emotional bond with someone or something.

Emotional deprivation – Feeling a lack of emotional support from someone important to the person, such as a parent. Lack of support can have a long-lasting negative emotional effect and might contribute to borderline personality disorder (e.g., Greenwald, 2001).

Emotional intelligence – Social effectiveness. Emotional intelligence (EI) may be essential for success in life (see Goleman, 2005). EI is aided by using appealing forces effectively and not using repelling forces. (See: appealing forces, repelling forces, positive reinforcement, negative reinforcement, punishment, social strategies, elixir of cordiality.)

Emotional internal reaction – An emotional reaction that occurs in a Hidden Sequence as a result of a Psychological Root alone or a Psychological Root that has been impacted by a stimulus condition. A cognitive reaction – such as a thought, evaluation, or decision – is another type of internal reaction. (See internal reaction, cognitive internal reaction, Hidden Sequence.)

Emotional nerve – Something in a person that produces a strong emotional reaction (e.g., a Psychological Root).

Emotional significance – Something that generates a strong emotional reaction for a person, such as an important childhood experience that causes pleasure or discomfort.

Emotional spillover – Expressing a pent-up emotion on something other than what caused that emotion, such as slamming a book after having been criticized by a boss rather than acting against the boss. The substitute object is often something safe to act against. (Synonym: displacement.)

Emotional state of uncontrollability – An emotional state that is so extreme (less than 0 or beyond 10 on a 0-10 scale) that it controls a person's behavior, such as depression, panic, rage, and addiction. It is analogous to excess water spilling over the rim of a glass. It is often difficult to rebound from that state. (See emotional takeover, cognitive state of uncontrollability.)

Emotional takeover – When an emotion is so strong that it controls a person's behavior.

Escalation point – The inflection point along a gradient at which the level of intensity sharply increases (which might be about 7.5 on a 0-10 scale of emotion). (See de-escalation point, intensity curve.)

Eustress – Positive stimulation. Eustress can be healthy and beneficial, whereas distress is bothersome and unhealthy. (See eustress-prone Psychological Roots, distress.)

Eustress-prone Psychological Roots – Psychological Roots that generate eustress (such as high self-esteem and optimism) or do so when impacted by a stimulus condition (e.g., achievement of a goal). (Synonym: positive Psychological Root.)

Excitatory nervous system – Part of the autonomic nervous system that produces activation. It counterbalances the inhibitory nervous system. (See inhibitory nervous system.)

Executive function – Portions of the brain's frontal cortex that affect judgment, such as evaluation and decisions (e.g., judging success and failure).

Expectation – Anticipation that something will happen and if not, generates a sense of failure, triggering a negative emotional reaction. The mind links expectations with goals, so some people believe that expectations are the same as goals, even though goals are criteria for success while expectations are criteria for failure. It is possible to lessen distress by consciously separating expectations from goals. (See goal, Psychological Root.)

Experiential learning – (See self-comprehension learning.)

External motivation – (See stimulus condition.)

Extinction – The elimination of a conditioned response so that the cue that once elicited that response no longer does so. (See de-conditioning.)

Extraction ability – The ability to identify the key aspect in a large amount of information. (Synonym: extraction skill.)

Extreme high end of negative emotions – The tipping point into a negative state of uncontrollability – such as depression, panic, rage – according to Psychological Systems Theory (e.g., -10 on a 0 to -10 scale). (See state of uncontrollability.)

Extreme high end of positive emotions – The tipping point into a positive state of uncontrollability – such as love, euphoria, ecstasy, mania – according to Psychological Systems Theory (e.g., +10 on a 0 to +10 scale). (See state of uncontrollability.)

Extreme lack of emotion – Psychological Systems Theory postulates that no emotion is a state of uncontrollability such as boredom, apathy, disinterest, or anhedonia. (See anhedonia.)

Extreme threshold – The tipping point into a state of uncontrollability, in Psychological Systems Theory.

Factor analysis – A statistical procedure that sorts data into a limited number of underlying groupings.

Fear message – A message intended to persuade by informing people that they would be harmed by doing what the message alludes to. Fear messages are repelling forces and therefore tend not to persuade.

Failure zone – The gap between a goal and the starting point, which creates stress as a result of viewing the goal as a criterion for failure.

Filtering, filtration – The discarding of new information that does not align with an existing Psychological Root.

Fixed-alternative questionnaire – A questionnaire in which respondents answer by choosing one alternative among those that are provided (e.g., "yes or no", 0-10). Use of numbers facilitates quantifying the answers, which aids computations and precision. (See respondent, questionnaire item, open-ended questionnaire, magnitude scale, bipolar scale, unipolar scale, continuum.)

Flash point – The point along a continuum into a state of uncontrollability according to Psychological Systems Theory. At the flash point, emotions fully take over (e.g., panic, depression, rage). (See tipping point.)

Flooding – A form of desensitization that uses a large input of an aversive stimulus with the aim of increasing the recipient's ability to handle adverse conditions (See desensitization, habituation.)

Flow-down effect – A domino effect in which Psychological Roots subsidiary to a modification that occurred earlier in a psychological hierarchy also change in order to be aligned with that modification (e.g., the placebo effect, in which a benign pill brings actual relief because internal reactions change to be in accord with that belief). (Synonyms: trickle-down effect, domino effect, post-shaping, post-adjustment). The flow-down effect is related to Piaget's concept of accommodation, which occurs after assimilation (i.e., behavior changes to be in accord with newly assimilated information; Flavell, 1966). (See: assimilation, accommodation, alignment effect, defense effect.)

Focus – Attention to something. Focusing on something causes other aspects to fade into the background, which diminishes distractions and aids problem-solving. Something unpleasant can be kept out of focus by procrastinating. (See absolute thinking, distraction, multi-tasking.)

Foundation root – A genetic Psychological Root that forms the base of a root hierarchy. Acquired roots in a given hierarchy are consistent with the foundation root. (See genetic Psychological Root, core Psychological Root, core acquired Psychological Root.)

Frame of reference – A perspective shaped by a Psychological Root or domain that is limited to what is within those boundaries, for example, judging people by their religion, ethnicity, or belief.

Freudian – Pertaining to Freud's ideas. (See psychoanalytic theory and Freud, 1990.)

Full goal – The full amount of what is aimed for. (See goal, sub-goal, minimum goal.)

Functional autonomy – Allport's (1937) idea that adult motives and behavior can continue to occur on their own, apart from additional reinforcement or the original reason they were engaged in.

Generalization – A broad concept encompassing a number of aspects that blurs distinctions among the included aspects (e.g., "westerners", "white collar workers", "Americans"). (See discrimination.)

General Psychological Roots – Psychological Roots that are likely to be held by a large percentage of the population, such as needs for safety and stability, expecting others we know well to be true to their word and meet their responsibilities, and having a desire to live and be regarded well by others.

Genetic core Psychological Roots – Psychological Roots that are wired-into a person and provide a foundation for a person's basic personality structure (e.g., needs for safety, stability, and emotional connectedness with others). (See genetic Psychological Roots, acquired core Psychological Roots.)

Genetic inner motivations – (See genetic Psychological Roots.)

Genetic Psychological Roots – Wired-in Psychological Roots (e.g., needs for safety, stability, and emotional connections with other humans). Everyone has the same general Psychological Roots, with variations. Genetic Psychological Roots are analogous to computer hardware, while acquired Psychological Roots are analogous to software. (Synonym: primary Psychological Roots.) (See acquired Psychological Roots.)

Gift – An even stronger ability than a talent that is genetically wired into an individual (e.g., in art, concepts, mathematics). Psychological Systems Theory postulates that there is an especially strong drive to use one's gifts, with discomfort if that drive is not pursued. A person who has a special gift might have an exceptionally strong Psychological Root complex with well-developed and extensive sub-categories, clusters, and sub-clusters of Psychological Roots (strong psychological-root complexes). A gift can be further developed through tutoring, experimentation, motivation, practice, support, and opportunity. (See ability, talent, skill, strong psychological-root complex.)

Goal – What is aimed for, hoped to be achieved, and if attained, triggers a positive emotional reaction. This attribute makes a goal a threshold for positive emotional stimulation. A goal provides a focus for what is to be accomplished and generates a drive to achieve it. Goals may be confused with expectations because the mind links them, however goals are criteria for success whereas expectations are criteria for failure, hence it is possible to separate goals from expectations to lessen distress. (See expectation, full goal, sub-goal, Psychological Root.)

Gradient - An increase or decrease over a period of time (e.g., increases or decreases in temperature, intensity, or liking). A gradient in one direction is monotonic when graphed; a gradient that changes directions (e.g., first going up, then down) is a non-monotonic function. (See monotonic, non- monotonic.)

Habituation – A lessened reaction due to a raised threshold. Habituation to background stimuli permit awareness of other aspects, such attention to a problem or to finishing a task. (See sensitization.)

Happiness potential – A quantitative index of the likelihood of being happy. One index is the difference between a measure of positively- and negatively-oriented Psychological Roots (those that are eustress-prone compared to those that are distress-prone). Another measure is the ratio of positive to negative Psychological Roots. Measures can be weighted to reflect the stronger influence of negatives compared to positives. (See distress-prone and eustress-prone Psychological Roots.)

Hard conflict – A conflict that is difficult to resolve. (See conflict, soft conflict, win-win solution.)

Hedonic – Relating to pleasure. (See anhedonia.)

Here and now orientation – Focus on the present rather than the past or future.

Heuristic – Something that provides an opportunity to obtain a new perspective.

Hidden Sequence – Aspects that lead to an internal reaction (e.g., a thought or feeling), and perhaps also an observable behavior. A Root Sequence starts with a Psychological Root (e.g., low self-esteem), whereas a Stimulus-and-Root Sequence starts with a stimulus condition (e.g., failure) that impacts an existing Psychological Root (e.g., low self-esteem, or a desire to be effective). Trying to change observable; behavior directly is unlikely to have much effect if the originating Psychological Roots are not modified (Synonym: underlying sequence.) (See: Root Sequence, Stimulus-and-Root Sequence, modified root sequence, modified Stimulus-and-Root Sequence, stress cascade.) (Synonyms for Hidden Sequences are *'subconscious sequences'* and *'underlying sequences'*).

Hierarchical tree – A Psychological Root hierarchy with branches and clusters of Psychological Roots. (See Psychological Roots, Psychological Root hierarchies.)

Hierarchy – (See Psychological Root hierarchies.)

Higher-order inner motivation – (See higher-order Psychological Root.)

High-order Psychological Root, higher-order Psychological Root – A genetic or acquired Psychological Root at or somewhat near the foundation of a hierarchy. Higher-order Psychological Roots are likely to be more general than Later Psychological Roots. Very Early Psychological Roots are likely to be a part of the core personality structure of an individual. (Synonym: deep Psychological Root, early Psychological Root.) (See later Psychological Root, lower-order Psychological Root.)

Hostile, hostility – Anger directed at someone or something, often with intent to harm. (See anger, rage.)

Homeostasis – (See Biological Homeostasis, Psychological Homeostasis.)

Homeostatic continuum – (See psychological homeostasis.)

Humanistic psychology – Theories and concepts that are substantially concerned about people and interpersonal relationships. Some humanistic theorists are Adler, Horney, Fromm, Sullivan, Maslow, and Rogers.

Hyperactivity – A person's exceptionally high activity that seems to control him/her. It might lead to impulsivity, impatience, or interrupting others, and interferes with maintaining socially acceptable behavior. (See attention deficit hyperactive disorder.)

Hypnosis – A method for introducing ideas with a low likelihood of the recipient filtering them out. It may be that hypnosis occurs during the alpha state between waking and sleeping, in which the executive function is not as strong as ordinarily. Hypnosis has been used as an aid for sleep, tapping memory, and solidifying desired changes (e.g., to try to stop cigarette smoking or overeating).

Hypothesis – An educated guess. Scientific research is based upon testing hypotheses, such as hypothesizing that a stimulus generates a particular behavior. Hypotheses are more specific than theories and often are derived from theories. (Synonyms: guess, estimate, idea, belief). (See theory.)

Impatience – Desire for something to occur rapidly, often with frustration about the delay. (See patience.)

Impulsive behavior, impulsivity – Acting without careful prior evaluation. Impulsive behavior is often difficult to control or change.

Inductive reasoning – Deriving a general idea from something specific (e.g., viewing a compliment as an appealing force). (See deductive reasoning.)

Inflection point – The place where the intensity level changes on a curve (e.g., from a gradual change to a sharp incline). In Psychological Systems Theory, inflection points are thresholds that at which change occurs. (See threshold, escalation point, de-escalation point, intensity curve.)

Inhibitory nervous system – Part of the autonomic nervous system that limits activity and counterbalances the excitatory part of the autonomic nervous system. (See excitatory nervous system.)

Initial interaction – A stimulus impacting a Psychological Root to start a Stimulus-and-Root Sequence. (See Stimulus-and-Root Sequence, Hidden Sequence, stimulus condition.)

Inner motivation – (See Psychological Root.)

Inner motivation hierarchy – (See Psychological Root hierarchy.)

Insight psychology – Any psychotherapeutic method that identifies the cause of behavior in subconscious aspects, such as beliefs, goals, drives, needs, expectations, and fears.

Instinct – A semi-automatic behavior that is genetically wired into a species, such as a tendency to attack when injured. An instinct consists of an intermediate cognitive neuron between a sensory neuron and a motor neuron, which offers an opportunity to evaluate and modify or stop the programmed behavior. A biological reflex does not offer an opportunity to stop the behavior this way because there is a direct connection of a sensory neuron with a motor neuron (e.g., dust in an eye triggers an eye blink). Some people do not believe that humans have wired-in instincts and automatic reflexes.

Intangible – Something our wired-in senses are unable to make us aware of, such as Hidden Sequences.

Intelligence – Ability to solve problems, aided by intellectual skills (e.g., reasoning, analysis, synthesis, association, generalization, discrimination, deductive and inductive reasoning, extraction ability, identifying causality, non-absolute thinking, perceptions, and observations). (See problem-solving, intelligence test.)

Intelligence test – A quantitative evaluation of a person's intelligence. A single test does not measure the many different aspects of intelligence.

Internal motivation – (See Psychological Root.)

Intensifier – A factor that increases an effect (e.g., high emotionality increases anxiety; see Petries, 1978, for a discussion of augmenters). Intensity and thinking in absolutes can increase or lessen an effect. (Synonym: amplifier.) (See diminisher.)

Intensity curve – The level of intensity increases as it approaches the upper end of an emotional continuum, according to Psychological Systems Theory. Past that point is a state of uncontrollability, such as panic, depression, rage, or shock regarding negative emotions. States of uncontrollability with positive emotions include euphoria, ecstasy, and amazement. The point at which the intensity level changes (e.g., from gradual to a sharp incline or decline) is a threshold. (See threshold, escalation point, de-escalation point, intensity curve, state of uncontrollability. Synonym: equilibrium curve.)

Intermediate inner motivation – (See intermediate Psychological Root.)

Intermediate Psychological Roots – Psychological Roots that exist between deep and surface Psychological Roots in psychological hierarchies. (See

Psychological Root hierarchy, early Psychological Root, deep Psychological Root, later Psychological Root, surface Psychological Root.)

Internal motivation – (See Psychological Root.)

Internal reaction – An emotional, glandular, hormonal, neuronal, biochemical, or cognitive outcome that is part of a Hidden Sequence. Examples of cognitive outcomes are thoughts, evaluations, and decisions. Examples of biochemical outcomes are changes in neurotransmitter levels such as in serotonin, dopamine, and acetylcholine. Indications of internal reactions can sometimes be manifested overtly, such as emotional exuberance or salivation (e.g., Pavlov's dog).

Interpersonal – A social connection with someone else.

Intolerable range – A range of disliked, unwanted, or not tolerated aspects along a continuum. The intolerable range includes people for whom there is no desire to contact. (See narrow adaptive range, adaptive zone, unacceptable range, comfort range, acceptable range, tolerable range, concentric social circles.)

Intrapersonal – Aspects operating within a person (e.g., beliefs, drives, and personal expectations).

IQ – Intelligence quotient. A numerical index of a person's intelligence derived from an intelligence test. (See emotional intelligence.)

Jargon – Specialized vocabulary or shorthand. Jargon is often used in specialized occupations, disciplines, practices, schools of thinking, theories, and groups (e.g., 'displacement' is jargon that refers to taking out frustrations on something other than the cause of the frustration).

Jungian – Pertaining to Carl Jung's ideas, theory, and perspective.

Key root – The most potent pertinent Psychological Root in a circumstance. Satisfactorily addressing the key roots aids resolving Psychological problems (e.g., distress-prone roots in depression). (Synonym: key pertinent root.) (See pertinent root, non-salient pertinent root, background Psychological Root.)

Kinesthetic – Muscle movement (e.g., athleticism and fluidity) and senses that detect muscle movement.

Lamarck's theory of evolution – Lamarck's belief that the environment triggers physiological changes in an organism (e.g., giraffes acquired long necks to eat leaves at tree tops). Lamarck's theory is the opposite of Darwin's idea that genetic mutations spontaneously occur, with those changes that aid a parent's survival being passed along to subsequent offspring. Organisms that do not adapt can become extinct ("survival of the fittest"), for example, the change of white-winged moths in Great Britain to black wings because darker wings are less visible against soot-covered trees. The evidence strongly favors Darwin's theory. (See Darwin's theory of evolution.)

Lamarckian – Pertaining to Lamarck's theory.

Later Psychological Root – A Psychological Root added to a Psychological Root hierarchy later than existing Psychological Roots (e.g., desire to learn a new computer application). Later Psychological Roots are likely to be less general than Early Psychological Roots. (Synonym: later Psychological Root, surface Psychological Root.) (See higher-order Psychological Root, early Psychological Root, intermediate Psychological Root.)

Learned helplessness – A condition in which an individual learns to feel powerless. It is a state of uncontrollability and may contribute to depression. (See state of uncontrollability.)

Learned safety – A condition in which an individual learns to feel safe. (See learned helplessness.)

Learning – Acquiring new information (e.g., by linking with a Psychological Root). It can remain briefly (short-term learning) or for a long time (long-term learning). (See short-term learning, long-term learning, linking.)

Lethargy – Slowness, such as due to a lack of energy or motivation, or to fatigue or illness.

Lewinian – Pertaining to the ideas, research, and theories of Kurt Lewin, a social psychologist. (See quasi-stationary equilibrium, three-stage theory of attitude change.)

Lewy body dementia – A pathological loss of memory due to deteriorating brain neurons that accounts for about 25% of senile dementia and eventuates in loss of life. Losing motor neurons impedes muscle movement, such as in Parkinson's disease. (See dementia, Alzheimer's disease.)

Limbic system – Part of the brain's diencephalon (the "old brain") that contains centers for positive and negative emotions. The negative emotional center is well defined and discernible to the naked eye, while the positive emotional center fades into surrounding tissue. The negative emotional center appears to have originated after the positive center, consistent with negative emotions being more powerful than positive emotions.

Linking – Attaching of a Psychological Root with another Psychological Root, bringing new information and beliefs, etc., according to Psychological Systems Theory. Initial Psychological Roots are genetically wired-in (e.g., needs for safety and connecting with others), then new Psychological Roots link to those genetic Psychological Roots, and then additional roots link to those acquired roots. (See Psychological Root, Psychological Root hierarchy, Psychological Root cluster, assimilation. Synonyms: associating, connecting, attaching, adhering, bonding, binding, and absorbing.)

Logic – The consistency of one idea with another, such as stating that you will drive to work in your car, whereas it would be illogical to say that you will drive to work by walking or running.

Long-term change – Change that remains a long time. (See short-term change, long-term memory, emotional significance, cognitive significance, long-term cognitive significance, deep learning.)

Long-term cognitive significance – Information that has long-term utility for a person (e.g., information that aids an important relationship or job effectiveness. (See cognitive significance.)

Long-term emotional significance – An emotional reaction that remains for a long time, such as love for a marital partner, child, or parent, or a particular occupation, sport, or food.

Long-term learning – Acquisition of new information that remains a long time, such as by linking with deep Psychological Roots. Long-term learning is aided by special cognitive or emotional significance for the recipient. (See short-term learning, linking, genetic Psychological Roots, higher-order Psychological Roots, core personality Psychological Roots, deep learning.)

Long-term memory – Memory that remains for a long time, in some cases a lifetime, such as basic values or significant experiences (e.g., childhood enjoyment or abuse). Long-term memory is aided by cognitive or emotional significance and linking to a deep Psychological Root. (See short-term memory, emotional significance, cognitive significance, long-term cognitive significance, deep learning.)

Long-term state of uncontrollability – A state of uncontrollability that lasts for can last from several months to years. Examples include depression, obsessive-compulsive disorder, and addiction. (See state of uncontrollability, short-term state of uncontrollability, temporary state of uncontrollability, moderate-term state of uncontrollability.)

Lose-lose solution – A compatible conflict. It is likely to be viewed as surrendering and therefore resisted. (See compromise, win-win solution, hard conflict, soft conflict.)

Lower-order inner motivation – (See lower-order Psychological Root.)

Low-order Psychological Root, lower-order Psychological Root – A Psychological Root acquired much later in a Psychological Root hierarchy than Early Psychological Roots (e.g., desire to acquire a new appliance). Low-order roots are likely to be less general than Early Psychological

Roots. (Synonym: surface Psychological Root, later Psychological Root.) (See higher-order Psychological Root, early Psychological Root.)

Magnitude scale – A scale with a number of positions (e.g., degrees, small to large, 0 – 10). (See bipolar scale, unipolar scale, continuum.)

Malaise – Discomfort, often vague rather than specific and may be hard to pinpoint. Malaise might occur at the onset of a disorder or an illness.

Mania, manic – Hyperactivity, grandiose statements, wildly excessive frivolity, or other out of control behavior that seems unattached to reality.

Manic-depression, manic-depressive – Extremely emotional reactions, either positively (such as manic behavior or euphoria) or negatively (such as anger, depression, or gloom). Mood change can be rapid and unpredictable, without an apparent reason. (Synonym: bipolar 1.) (See cyclothymia.)

Manifest, manifestation – What is apparent. The origin may not be apparent, such as Psychological Roots.

Meaningful experience – Something that has either cognitive or emotional significance. (See cognitive significance; emotional significance.)

Memorizing by rote – Trying to remember something by repeating it (e.g., re-reading it or using flash-cards). Rote memorization is likely to produce short-term memory because it ends after no longer being needed (e.g., forgetting what has been studied after an exam is over). Rote memorization does not require understanding and therefore may not be as useful as comprehending it.

Mental illness – A psychological state that interferes with effective functioning for more than a short time (e.g., depression, anxiety). Much mental illness originates for psychological reasons, but some can be due to physiological causes (e.g., autism, schizophrenia, mental retardation.) (Synonym: mental disorder.) (See clinical condition.)

Mental incubation – The brain's self-engaging in an issue below awareness, often when not consciously focused on that problem (e.g., during showering, taking a break, or vacationing).

Metacognitive activities – Thinking about thinking.

Mindfulness – Focusing on something to the exclusion of other things (e.g., paying particular attention to the present). Mindfulness lowers the threshold of awareness for what is focused on (*sensitization*) and raises the threshold of awareness for what is not, thus diminishing notice of other aspects (*habituation*). It can help to focus on future circumstances, not necessarily what is going on at present.

Minimum goal – The lowest level of a goal or series of sub-goals. If the minimum goal is not met, no portion of the goal is met so is a criterion for failure.

Moderate-term state of uncontrollability – A state of uncontrollability that can last a week to several months). (See state of uncontrollability, short-term state of uncontrollability, long-term state of uncontrollability.)

Modified Root Sequence – An altered Root Hidden Sequence such as by knowledge, experience, method, skill, or strategy. The components are **Psychological Root → internal reaction + modification** (and in some instances resulting in **observable behavior** as well). (See Root Sequence, Stimulus-and-Root Sequence, Modified Stimulus-and-Root Sequence, modifier.)

Modified Stimulus-and-Root Sequence – An altered Stimulus-and-Root Sequence such as by knowledge, experience, method, skill, or strategy. The components are **stimulus + Psychological Root → internal reaction + modification** (and in some instances resulting in **observable behavior** as well). (See Root Sequence, Modified Root Sequence, Stimulus-and-Root Sequence, modifier.)

Modifier – An aspect that alters internal reactions or overt behavior, such as aiding self-control of counterproductive actions (e.g., by using knowledge or focus on tangibles). Civilized behavior is aided by having civilizing modifiers and Psychological Roots (civilizing factors). Some anti-social behavior may be due to poorly formed or intentionally bypassed civilizing modifiers and states of uncontrollability. Modifiers that are beliefs (e.g., methods and strategies) are Psychological Roots. (Synonym: modifying factors.) (See: Hidden Sequence, Root Sequence, Stimulus-and-Root Sequence, absolute thinking, amplifier, diminisher, tangible, civilizing Psychological Root, civilizing modifier, displacement).

Modifying factor – See modifier.

Multiple Hidden Sequences – More than one Hidden Sequence that occurs shortly after one another. (See Hidden Sequences, sequential multiple Hidden Sequences, simultaneous multiple Hidden Sequences.) (Synonyms: action cascade, hidden cascades, motivational cascades, multiple underlying processes, multiple psychological sequences, and multiple sequences.)

Multi-tasking – Shifting one's focus back and forth from one task to another. Multi-tasking is easier with uncomplicated tasks, such as talking or listening to a radio while driving in low traffic, rather than with tasks that require much concentration or thoughtfulness (e.g., when driving in a potentially dangerous situation). (Synonym: serial tasking). (See focus, distraction, absolute thinking.)

Multiple regression – A statistical analysis that identifies variables that account for much of a phenomenon (e.g., difficult-to-meet expectations, pessimism, giving up quickly regarding depression, the author has found.) Hence, a therapy that addresses the major factors multiple regression identifies can be particularly effective.

Music therapy – A technique a musician can use to help people with their hidden feelings.

Mutually beneficial solution – (See win-win solution.)

Mutually satisfactory solution – (See win-win solution.)

Narcissism – Focus that is largely on oneself. Narcissistic individuals may think they are superior to others or might feel vulnerable underneath. (Synonym: egocentrism, self-centered, self-promotional.)

Narrow adaptive zone – (See narrow comfort zone.)

Narrow comfort zone – A small range along a continuum in which an organism functions well and feels comfortable. (Synonyms: narrow adaptive range, narrow comfort zone.) (See closed-minded, unacceptable range, intolerable zone, adaptive range, wide adaptive range, open-minded.)

Narrow tolerance – (See narrow comfort zone.)

Natural phenomenon – What occurs in nature, such genetic programming (e.g., human beings are thought to be genetically programmed to have Psychological Homeostasis and states of uncontrollability such as panic, rage, and anhedonia, according to Psychological Systems Theory).

Need – A necessity which, if not met, arouses a negative reaction. Some genetically wired-in biological needs are for air, food, water, shelter, reproduction, and acceptable temperature; some psychological needs are for safety, stability, stimulation, connection with others, communicating, and closure. Some needs are acquired such as responsibilities, standards, requirements, and expectations. Biological needs are biological roots; psychological needs are Psychological Roots. A need has a stronger drive compared to a want because the need to avoid a negative is stronger than the desire to acquire a positive. (Synonyms: goal, aim, aspiration, desire.) (Synonym: necessity, requirement.) (See acquired needs, Psychological Root.)

Need for safety – A genetically programmed need to avoid harm and escape from it. (See need.)

Need for stability – A genetically programmed need to remain within an acceptable range. It is aided by Biological and Psychological Homeostasis, also by countervailing factors and absolute thinking. (See need, Psychological Homeostasis, countervailing factors, absolute thinking.)

Negative build-up – An accumulation of negative emotional intensity that can reach a tipping point (e.g., into depression, panic, rage). Many factors can contribute to the build-up (e.g., illness, pain, and worry). Negative emotional reactions are strong, easily aroused, and long-lasting, so are more likely to build-up than positives. (See cumulative build-up, positive build-up.)

Negative emotion – Distress, tension, anxiety, disappointment, loss, failure, embarrassment, frustration, anger or another displeasing emotional reaction that results from arousing the negative emotional center. Such emotions are disliked unless desired to be used, such as for self-protection or revenge.

Negatively-keyed questions – Questions that people with a particular trait (e.g., stress) are likely to disagree with and therefore receive a low score. (See positively-keyed questions.)

Negatively-oriented Psychological Roots – Psychological Roots that generate negative emotions, (e.g., low self-esteem and pessimism). Some Psychological Roots do so when impacted by distress-prone stimuli, such as unmet expectations and poor social strategies. Negatives overshadow positives so even a small amount of negative arousal can dim a person's mood. (See positively-oriented Psychological Roots.)

Negative Psychological Root – See distress-prone Psychological Root.

Negative reaction potential – A quantitative index of how likely a person is to have negative reactions such as distress or displeasure. It could include an assessment of negative Psychological Roots, stimulus conditions, feelings, and behaviors. The index could contribute to an index of the potential to be unhappy. (See distress-prone Psychological Roots, eustress-prone Psychological Roots.)

Negative reinforcement – Something that can strengthen a behavior because it ends unpleasantness (e.g., turning off electric shock, see Skinner, 1974) and can therefore be a substitute for direct positive reinforcement. Negative reinforcement has the opposite effect of punishment. (See positive reinforcement, appealing force, repelling force, punishment.)

Negative solution – A resolution to a conflict in which one or more individuals give up something they do not want to, such as in a compromise. (Synonym: lose-lose solution, distasteful solution.) (See: positive solution.)

Negative stimulus condition – A stimulus that a recipient dislikes and to which it responds unfavorably (e.g., being criticized, failing, being rejected). (See positive stimulus condition.)

Network – Interconnections. (See Psychological Root networks, web.)

Neuron – A nerve fiber that carries an electrical message (e.g., a pain nerve that transmits a signal from the afflicted part of the body to the brain). The brain then addresses that part, including by bringing awareness to it.

Neurotransmitter – A biochemical that permits an electrical signal to jump from the end of one neuron to the beginning of another neuron (e.g., serotonin, dopamine, acetylcholine). Some neurotransmitters in the brain are associated with emotions, such as serotonin.

Non-absolute thinking – Thinking that does not involve absolutes (e.g., taking into account multiple possibilities, tentative conclusions, and a combination of components). (Synonym: relative thinking.) (See absolute thinking.)

Non-alignment with a Psychological Root – Inconsistency with a Psychological Root (e.g., disagreeing with someone). It produces a negative reaction. (See alignment with a Psychological Root.)

Non-salient pertinent root – Pertinent roots that are not the key roots in a particular situation (See pertinent root, key pertinent root, background Psychological Root.)

Normal – The 95% of a distribution surrounding the center of a bell curve (e.g., an IQ score between 85 and 130). Thus, an extremely bright person is abnormal as are multi-billionaires and U.S. presidents. Normal does not necessarily mean healthy (e.g., 1/3 of the U.S. population is very overweight). (Synonym: normal distribution.)

Normal continuum – The baseline along which a representative population is a measured.

Normal distribution – (See discussion of normal.)

Nutritional programs – Diets that aid health (e.g., the Feingold diet for attention deficit hyperactive disorder, low-salt diet for high blood pressure, low-fat/low cholesterol diet for heart disease.)

Obsessive-compulsive disorder (OCD) – Rigid adherence to a behavior pattern, such as frequently washing hands, scrubbing with germicides, and superstitions (e.g., not stepping on sidewalk cracks). Such behaviors are typically repetitive, intense, and out of control. Causes include anxiety, low threshold for emotional arousal, desire to ward off unpleasantness, and difficulty dealing with setbacks.

Occipital cortex – An area at the rear of the cerebral cortex that decodes visual stimuli from electric signals sent from the retina of the eye through the optic nerve. (Synonym: visual cortex.)

Open-ended questionnaire – A questionnaire in which respondents answer by using their own words rather than selecting among choices. Answers can be quantified by grouping them by their meaning, thereby permitting statistical analyses, scientific research, and drawing conclusions. (See questionnaire item, fixed-alternative questionnaire, magnitude scale, bipolar scale, unipolar scale, continuum, respondent.)

Open-minded, open-mindedness – Having a wide range of acceptability, which aids receptivity to other people's thoughts and behavior. It is characteristic of people who are flexible, do not think they know it all, tolerate being wrong, and are not prejudiced. (Synonyms: wide comfort zone, wide acceptability range, high tolerability.) (See wide adaptive range, close-minded, narrow comfort zone.)

Operant conditioning – A type of conditioning in which an initially voluntary skeletal muscle behavior is triggered by an appropriate stimulus (e.g., automatically shaking hands upon introducing oneself; see Skinner, 1974). (Synonym: instrumental conditioning.) (See classical conditioning.)

Opposition defiant disorder – Behavior that is characterized by resistance, argumentativeness, anger, defiance, aggressiveness, and vindictiveness, which causes significant problems at home, school, or work, and continues for at least six months.

Optimism – Belief that good things will happen. (See confidence, self-confidence, pessimism.)

Originating cause – The initial starting point of an outcome. In psychological matters, the originating cause often is a Psychological Root and functions subconsciously (e.g., an argument might appear to be about money, but may be about one party feeling disrespected and the other party feeling controlled). (See precipitating factor, proximal cause, Psychological Root.)

Overt behavior – Behavior that is observable, such as talking, moving, standing still, and observable manifestations of internal emotional reactions.

Overt signs – Observable indications of something going on covertly below the surface.

Overt symptoms – Observable indications of something going on covertly below the surface (e.g., illness).

Over-the-counter medication – Medicine that can be purchased without a prescription from a physician, such as headache tablets, cough medicines, and antibiotic skin creams.

Ownership – Feeling a personal connection with something and responsibility for taking care of it.

Panic, panic attack – When anxiety is beyond the furthermost extreme and enters a state of uncontrollability. Some psychological factors can be low threshold for emotional arousal, pessimism, weak problem-solving strategies, impatience, rigidity, high emotionality, absolute thinking, and belief of vulnerability. (See anxiety, fear.)

Paranoia, paranoid – A person's belief that he/she is under threat from something or someone.

Passive conflict – A conflict that exists in the background, manifesting little intensity, emotionality, or consequences, but which can become an active conflict. (See conflict, active conflict.)

Passive Psychological Root – (See background Psychological Root.)

Pathogen – The cause of a disorder (e.g., in medical circumstances it could be harmful bacteria).

Pathogenic – Something that causes harm.

Patience – Acceptance of a delay without tension or frustration. Putting a clamp on negative feelings is not patience, but rather an attempt to keep impatience under control (See impatience.)

Pattern recognition - The brain's identification of a pattern. Pattern recognition aids the brain to make sense out of otherwise confusing circumstances.

Pattern seeking - The brain's wired-in drive attempt to identify patterns.

Pedagogical – Instruction-oriented, something that is associated with teaching.

Perfectionism – A desire to be totally correct, often with an unwillingness to settle for less than the best.

Permanence – Long-lasting Psychological Roots, such as values acquired in early childhood.

Pertinent Psychological Root – A Psychological Root that contributes to an internal reaction or behavior. Some pertinent roots are key while others are in the background (Synonym: active Psychological Root.) (See key pertinent root, non-salient pertinent root, background Psychological Root.)

Pessimism – Belief that bad things will happen. (Synonym: negative anticipation.) (See optimism, confidence, self-confidence.)

PET scan – (See positive emission tomography.)

Physical therapy (PT) – A form of therapy primarily focused on helping clients improve their muscular movements, such as after surgery, trauma, stroke, or vertigo.

Physiological reaction – An internal reaction mediated by the autonomic nervous system. Examples are emotional reactions (e.g., feelings, disappointment, pleasure), biochemical changes (e.g., serotonin and dopamine levels in the brain), glandular outputs (e.g., secretions of hormones), and smooth muscle activities (e.g., constriction of blood vessels, movement of gastro-intestinal muscles). (See autonomic nervous system, sympathetic nervous system, para-sympathetic nervous system, neurotransmitter, skeletal nervous system.)

Piagetian – Pertaining to ideas promulgated by Jean Piaget (e.g., developmental life stages, assimilation, and accommodation; see Flavell, 1966) developmental stages, assimilation, accommodation.)

Positive build-up – An accumulation of positive emotion that if it continues can reach a tipping point into a state of uncontrollability such as euphoria, an orgasm, or joyful hysteria. The buildup can be due to many factors (e.g., having a good day at work, feeling close to someone special). Music can swell to a crescendo and comedians can string laughs together until the audience is engulfed in laughter. Positive emotional reactions are less likely to build-up than negatives because they do not last as long. (See cumulative build-up, negative build-up.)

Positive emission tomography – A radioactive method for measuring the amount and location of chemicals in the body. Substances used by the body, such as glucose or dopamine, can be made radioactive and injected into the blood stream, then a Geiger counter tracks where those substances move to in the body and the amount used at those spots. Brain functioning can be assessed this way after giving subjects particular tasks (e.g., reading, watching a comedian or a drama, or doing word problems). Other uses are detecting weaknesses or blockage in the heart and the effect of different medications. (Synonym: PET scan).

Positive emotion – Pleasure, happiness, amusement, ecstasy, joy, contentment, serenity or other pleasant results after the positive emotional center is stimulated. People seek such effect unless there is a reason for not doing so, such as distraction, expense, or self-protection. (See negative emotions.)

Positively-keyed questions – Questions that people high in a particular trait (e.g., happiness) are likely to agree with and therefore receive a high score. (See negatively-keyed questions.)

Positively-oriented Psychological Roots – Psychological Roots that generate positive emotional reactions. Some positive emotional reactions occur when Psychological Roots are impacted by eustress-prone stimuli (e.g., praise, emotional support). (See negatively-oriented Psychological Roots.)

Positive Psychological Root – See eustress-prone Psychological Root.

Positive solution – A resolution to a conflict in which every person's concerns are satisfied without anyone experiencing a sacrifice, providing a win-win outcome for everyone. (Synonym: win-win solution, mutually satisfying solution.) (See: negative solution.)

Positive stimulus condition – A stimulus condition that the recipient of it likes and to which it responds favorably. (See negative stimulus condition.)

Post hoc study – A study in which assessments are made after a circumstance has occurred, such as in astronomy and some psychological questionnaires. (Synonym for *post hoc*: after the fact. Synonym for *post hoc* study: response variable study.) (See *a priori* study.)

Post-shaping – When subsidiary Psychological Roots are altered to be in alignment with the modification of a Psychological Root in a flow-down effect. An example is modifying one's perspective to accept the defeat of one's favored candidate after an election. (Synonym: Psychological Root modification.) (See shaping, pre-shaping, concurrent shaping, flow-down effect.)

Post-traumatic stress disorder (PTSD) – An upsetting psychological result of a disturbing event. Examples include anxiety-inducing flashbacks and strong reactions to a circumstance that reminds a person of a disturbing past experience.

Potential for happiness – (See happiness reaction potential.)

Potential for negative reaction – (See negative reaction potential.)

Potential for positive reaction – (See positive reaction potential.)

Pre-adjustment – (See pre-shaping.)

Precipitating cause – What triggers an outcome. A precipitating cause might not be the originating cause, even if observable (e.g., it could be "the straw that broke the camel's back"). (Synonym: precipitating factor.) (See originating cause, proximal cause.)

Precursor – A circumstance that can lead to a state of uncontrollability (e.g., dysthymia before depression, anxiety before panic, easily triggered irritability before borderline personality disorder). (See predisposition, Psychological Root, distress-prone Psychological Root, eustress-prone Psychological Root, intensity curve.) (Synonym: precursor range, precursor condition.)

Predisposition – A circumstance that can lead to being in a precursor range (and from there to a state of uncontrollability), such as Psychological Roots that are distress-prone (e.g., pessimism, difficult-to-meet expectations) or eustress-prone (e.g., optimism, easy-to-meet expectations). (See precursor, Psychological Root, distress-prone Psychological Root, eustress-prone Psychological Root, intensity curve.)

Prejudice – A pre-developed belief, like, dislike, or other judgment about something (e.g., people, food, ideas). There can be a prejudice without any direct experience with the object of that prejudice.

Premature closure – When striving ends before a conclusion occurs. One way it can occur is when a belief arises that there is no good solution to a problem or that everything possible has been tried.

Preparedness – The innate ability of an organism to engage in a particular behavior to a stimulus.

Pre-shaping – Adjustment of new information to make it fit a Psychological Root so that linking can occur. Types of pre-shaping include re-interpreting, ignoring, and modifying (e.g., some religionists accept Darwin's theory of evolution by viewing earth's creatures as having evolved after they were created by God; modifying one's perspective to accept someone.). (Synonym: pre-adjustment). (See shaping, post-shaping, concurrent shaping, flow-down effect.)

Primary domain – A category of principal concern, interest, or focus (e.g., a community's concern regarding education, budget, police actions). (See domain.)

Primary Psychological Roots – (See genetically wired-in Psychological Roots.)

Problem-based learning – A type of self-comprehension learning in which students develop a solution to an ambiguous task. This educational method helps students learn how to raise significant questions and develop problem-solving strategies.

Problem-solving – An effort that overcomes an impediment. Creatures who solve the problems of their circumstances increase their chances of surviving. Psychological Systems Theory considers problem-solving ability to be a major factor in intelligence and postulates a wired-in drive to work on problems (one of the reasons challenges are engaged in such as exploration, mountain climbing, puzzles, experimentation, and science). (See intelligence.)

Problem-solving strategies – Methods that aid the solving of problems (e.g., plans, strategies, knowledge, task and social strategies). Strategies are beliefs and therefore are Psychological Roots. Methods are tactics that often are behaviors.

Process – A step-wise series of steps (e.g., the steps in Hidden Sequences.)

Profiling – Evaluating people on the basis of tangible characteristics (e.g., skin color, accent, appearance).

Programmed depression – Depression that is genetically wired to occur upon reaching the tipping point at the end of a negative emotional continuum, according to Psychological Systems Theory. (Synonym: genetically programmed depression)

Proximal – Something close to a reference point (e.g., a stimulus that preceded a behavior). (See distal.)

Proximal cause – What is believed to be the cause since it occurred shortly before an observable outcome (e.g., anger before committing violence). (See originating cause, precipitating factor.)

Psychiatric nurse – A nurse with professional training in psychiatric conditions who assists psychiatrists in treating clients with a mental illness.

Psychiatrist – A medical doctor trained in psychiatry, who treats clients with a mental illness.

Psychoanalysis – Psychotherapy in which the therapist analyzes the cause of a person's psychological problems – with particular attention to early childhood, parental relationship, and sex – by having the person say whatever comes to his/her mind (see Freud (1990, and psychoanalytic theory.)

Psychoanalytic theory – Freud's explanation of the human psyche, such as the "id" (basic drives, including animalistic urges), the "superego" (the conscience), and the "ego" (an agency that resolves conflicts between the id and the superego; see psychoanalysis).

Psychologic – Subjective reasoning, thinking, logic, or opinion. A person's psychologic may differ from objective logic, evidence, facts, & other individuals, since it originates from his/her own particular Psychological Roots.

Psychological box – Feeling psychologically trapped, with difficulty extricating oneself (e.g., a state of uncontrollability such as panic, obsessive-compulsive disorder, addiction). (See biological box.)

Psychological disorder – A behavior pattern that is intense, such as a state of uncontrollability (e.g., panic, rage, mania). (Synonym: mental disorder.) (See mental illness, clinical disorder.)

Psychological driving force – (See Psychological Root.)

Psychological guiding factor – (See Psychological Root.)

Psychological Homeostasis – A feedback system that aids maintaining a steady psychological state. Alerting thresholds signal when the boundaries of an adaptive range are exceeded (e.g., malaise, agitation, dysthymia),

according to Psychological Systems Theory. That signal permits a
conscious decision whether or not to return to the comfort zone. An
individual may elect not to do so, such as when angry. Homeostasis no
longer functions in a state of uncontrollability (e.g., depression), and
rebounding from it may not be easy, keeping the individual in a
'psychological box'. One Psychological Homeostasis system involves
emotions (such as happiness, sadness, and displeasure); another system
involves cognitions (such as beliefs, goals, and expectations).
Psychological Homeostasis is a psychological cognate of Biological
Homeostasis. (See biological homeostasis, adaptive range, psychological
box.)

Psychological lens – Filtering due to Psychological Roots that affects
perception, thinking, evaluation, and decisions. Aspects consistent with
Psychological Roots are positive, while those that are inconsistent with
Psychological Roots are negative. (See Psychological Roots.)

Psychological Root – A psychological factor that drives reactions and affects
perception and understanding. Psychological Roots operate below
awareness, but can be identified (e.g., when actors discuss a character's
motivation they are addressing Psychological Roots). Examples of
cognitive Psychological Roots are goals, beliefs, and expectations;
examples of non-cognitive Psychological Roots are inherited needs and
thresholds. (Synonyms: inner motivation, psychological driver,
psychological driving force, driving force, psychological seed,
psychological guiding factor.)

Psychological Root category – A number of conceptually related Psychological
Root clusters. (See Psychological Root cluster.)

Psychological Root cluster – A group of related psychological aspects (e.g.,
beliefs associated with a particular discipline such as science or ideology).

Psychological Root hierarchy – A chain of linked Psychological Roots whose
foundation is a genetic Psychological Root (e.g., need for safety).
Subsidiary Psychological Roots are aligned with the genetic foundation
root and each other as well. (See Psychological Root, linking, early & late
Psychological Roots, alignment, defense, & flow-down effects.)

Psychological Root network – Extensive and complex web-like connections
among different hierarchies, branches, and clusters owing to
Psychological Roots' ability to link with each other. (Synonym: web.) (See
Psychological Root cluster, Psychological Root hierarchy.)

Psychological state of uncontrollability – (See state of uncontrollability.)

Psychological Systems Theory, (PST) – Greenwald's general theory of
psychology in which mental processes are considered to be subconscious

systems such as Psychological Homeostasis, Psychological Roots, Hidden Sequences, countervailing factors, positive and negative emotional centers, evaluation, and absolute thinking. The theory suggests ways to facilitate persuading, creating win-win solutions, teaching, and learning. The theory also leads to the idea that a continuum exists between normal and abnormal psychological functioning and offers a new approach for psychotherapy. (See Psychological Homeostasis, Psychological Roots, Hidden Sequences, countervailing factors, positive and negative emotional centers, evaluation, absolute thinking, and Psychological Systems Therapy.)

Psychological Systems Therapy – Greenwald's treatment for psychological disorders that addresses what it considers the originating causes of disorders (e.g., Psychological Roots and the stimulus conditions), derived from Psychological Systems Theory (PST). The therapy seeks subconscious causes followed by modifying, satisfying, or overriding distress-prone Psychological Roots and stimulus conditions that lead to states of uncontrollability and their precursors. The treatment uses methods for teaching, persuading, and resolving conflicts derived from Psychological Systems Theory. (See Psychological Systems Theory.)

Psychological warning signal, psychological warning sign – An indication of something extreme should a particular direction continue, allowing a person to decide what to do. It can be difficult to extricate oneself after entering a state of uncontrollability. (See alerting threshold.)

Psychologist – A person trained in sub-surface psychological processes (e.g., evaluating, decision-making, emotional reactions) and resolution of intra- and inter-personal problems. There are over 50 sub-disciplines in psychology, each with its own concepts and style of research. (Synonym: warning signal.)

Psychopath – A person who harms others owing to mental illness, often planful, manipulative, and client, compared to sociopaths who are impatient, impulsive, and aggressive. (See mental illness.)

Psychotherapeutic – Pertaining to psychotherapy. (See psychotherapy.)

Psychotherapy – A therapy that helps lessen psychological problems. (See Psychological Systems Therapy, cognitive behavioral therapy, psychotherapeutic.)

Psychotropic medications – Medicines that affect psychological behavior by acting on brain functions.

Qualitative – Pertaining to a particular type or quality of something. (See quantitative.)

Quantitative – Pertaining to a numerical amount of something. (See qualitative.)

Questionnaire item – A question in a questionnaire (e.g., asking how much a thing applies to the person).

Rage – A state of uncontrollability due to extreme anger. (See anger, state of uncontrollability.)

Rebound – Extrication from a state of uncontrollability. (See state of uncontrollability, Psychological Homeostasis.)

Reflex – (See biological reflex.)

Reframing – Creating a different perspective such as viewing something that is disturbing in a less disturbing way by finding something positive in it.

Relative deprivation – Feeling deprived due to unmet expectations as distinguished from actual deprivation (Merton, 1963). That frustration can trigger riots, explosions, deaths, and revolutions.

Relaxation therapies – Methods of relaxing (e.g., breathing slowly and deeply, visualizing disturbing thoughts exiting oneself, warm baths, massage, meditation, hypnosis, distraction, vacations, spas, and sequentially relaxing muscles throughout the body [the Jacobson method]).

Reliability – A statistical estimate of the likelihood that a finding will recur at least 95 times out of 100.

Repelling force – Something that triggers a negative emotional reaction (e.g., failure, insult, disappointment), including an expected appealing force that does not happen (e.g., being overlooked, not being greeted, not being invited). (See appealing force.) (Synonym: away force.)

Respondent – Anyone who answers a question. (See questionnaire item, fixed-alternative questionnaire, open-ended questionnaire, subject.)

Respondent conditioning – (See classical conditioning.)

Rogerian – Pertaining to Carl Rogers' ideas (e.g., non-directive psychotherapy in which the counselor sets the stage for the client to solve his/her own problems.) (See Rogers, 1951; Socrates.)

Root category, root categories – (See Psychological Root category.)

Root cluster, root clusters – (See Psychological Root cluster.)

Root hierarchy, root hierarchies – (See Psychological Root hierarchy.)

Root network – (See Psychological Root network.)

Root Sequence – An internal reaction (e.g., a thought or emotional reaction) – and perhaps a behavior – that starts with a Psychological Root). The components of a Root Sequence are **Psychological Root → internal reaction** (*& perhaps* **observable behavior**). (See Modified Root Sequence, Stimulus-and-Root Sequence, Modified Stimulus-and-Root Sequence.) (Synonym: Psychological Root Sequence.)

Rote memorization – (See memorization by rote.)

Rumination, ruminating – Repeatedly dwelling on the same thing without resolution or stopping. That issue can be pleasing (e.g., a spectacular sports play) but more likely disturbing (e.g., while depressed, anxious, or angry).

Salience – Something prominent, so has a high chance of being selected, reacted to, or paid attention to.

Scanning – Rapid skimming of a large amount of information to identify some of the major aspects.

Secondary Psychological Roots – Psychological Roots in a Hidden Sequence that are not primary roots.

Selective attention – Focus on what is being attended to while other aspects fade into the background out of attention.

Self-affirmation – (See self-statement.)

Self-comprehension learning – Learning by self-processing information (e.g., by solving problems), which thereby has a chance to connect new information with a person's deep Psychological Roots in the learner's own way. Self-comprehension is likely to be more effective than information presented by someone else (e.g., a teacher), or rote memorization. (Synonyms: self-discovery learning, self-directed learning, problem-based learning). (See Socratic teaching, rote memorization, didactic.)

Self-confidence – A person's belief that he/she will succeed. (See optimism, pessimism, lack of confidence.)

Self-directed learning – (See self-comprehension learning.)

Self-discovery learning – (See self-comprehension learning.)

Self-efficacy – Believing that you can be effective. (See self-confidence.)

Self-esteem – Self-evaluation. High self-esteem is believing oneself to be worthwhile, valued, and worthy of respect. A person with low self-esteem believes the opposite.

Self-fulfilling prophecy – When something occurs as a result of a person believing that it will happen (e.g., you believe that someone is nice and he is because you treated that person well). A self-fulfilling prophecy is consistent with the idea that behavior is in accord with beliefs.

Self-statement – Something people say to themselves that can help them change a thought or behavior, for example, "I'm a good person", "Don't take this personally". Uplifting Self-statements are self-affirmations.

Semi-automatic behaviors – Reactions or behaviors that occur automatically but can be consciously controlled and extinguished (e.g., conditioned responses and instincts). (See automatic behaviors.)

Sensitization – A low threshold, permitting a strong reaction to occur. (See habituation, desensitization.)

Sequence – A series of steps (e.g., sub-goals, Hidden Sequences, the three-stage attitude change model).

Sequentially opposed factors – When an aspect oppose another subsequently (e.g., the inhibitory nervous system's opposing an excitatory nervous system's effect, and when people argue). (Synonym: sequential countervailing factors.) (See simultaneously opposed factors, countervailing factors.)

Sequential multiple Hidden Sequences – Hidden Sequences that shortly follow one another (e.g., a thought triggers another). (See hidden sequence, multiple Hidden Sequences, simultaneous Hidden Sequences, initial sequence.)

Sequential solution – One part of a solution occurs first, another later (e.g., both people doing what Mary wants first, then both doing what Jon wants later). If a sequential solution is viewed as a sacrifice, it is a compromise. (See win-win solution, compromise.)

Series of steps – (See sequence, successive approximations to the goal.)

Series of sub-goals – Step-wise effort to achieve a goal by resolving smaller goals along the way.

Set – A grouping or category (e.g., ten repetitions of an exercise).

Shaping – When something new is modified, such as when new information is re-interpreted, altered, added to, or subtracted from. Shaping may be a way the brain makes sense of things. (See pre-shaping, post-shaping, concurrent shaping, flow-down effect).

Short-term change – Change that does not last long (e.g., when it involves an upcoming goal and therefore lasts only as long as that goal exists). (See short-term memory, long-term change.)

Short-term learning – Learning that does not remain long (e.g., due to attachment to a short-term goal, thus lasts only as long as that goal exists). (See long-term learning, linking, lower-order Psychological Roots, deep learning.)

Short-term memory – (See short-term learning.)

Short-term state of uncontrollability – A state of uncontrollability that lasts a second to a few days. Examples include crying, hysteria, laughter, and rage. (Synonym: temporary state of uncontrollability.) (See state of uncontrollability, a short-term state of uncontrollability, long-term state of uncontrollability.)

Simultaneous multiple Hidden Sequences – Hidden sequences occurring about the same time (e.g., when a stimulus condition impacts more than one Psychological Root, such as when a compliment satisfies a desire for emotional support but also touches a belief that the person does not deserve to be complimented). The result is a mixture of responses. (See hidden sequence, multiple Hidden Sequences, sequential Hidden Sequences.)

Simultaneously opposed factors – Aspects that oppose one another at the same time rather than sequentially (e.g., pro and con considerations regarding a decision). The outcome is the net balance of all the underlying factors. (Synonym: simultaneously opposed countervailing factors, simultaneous countervailing factors). (See sequentially opposed countervailing factors, countervailing factors.)

Situational depression – Depression thought to be caused entirely by a distressing stimulus. However, situations have an effect because they impact Psychological Roots. Not knowing the Psychological Roots involved can lead to believing that stress alone causes depression. (See chronic depression, depression, Psychological Roots, stimulus conditions, Hidden Sequences.)

Skeletal nervous system – A part of the central nervous system that moves bones and the tongue. Skeletal muscles respond to a conscious direction (e.g., speaking, writing, fighting).

Skill – An acquired capability. Acquisition of a skill is aided by an associated genetic ability, motivation, experimentation, tutoring, practice, support, and opportunity to do these things. (See ability, talent.)

Skinnerian – Pertaining to B. F. Skinner's ideas regarding operant conditioning. (See Skinner, 1974.)

Social influence – Persuasion by a person or group of people. (See the three-stage method of persuading.)

Social strategies – The ability to get along well with others. Interpersonal skill is aided by using appealing forces, effective communication, and compatible solutions, and especially by not using repelling forces since negatives far outweigh positives. (See: elixir of cordiality, appealing forces, repelling forces, positive reinforcement, negative reinforcement, punishment, win-win solutions.)

Social work – Help for others by people professionally trained to use community resources or counseling.

Social worker – People professionally trained to help others using community resources or counseling.

Sociology – A discipline that studies societal patterns. (See demographic information.)

Socratic teaching – A teaching method used by used by Socrates in which he asked successive questions until students discovered the answer themselves. (See self-comprehension learning; Rogerian.)

Soft conflict – A conflict with no harshness or pressure. (See conflict, hard conflict, win-win solution.)

Solidifying a change – The third stage of the three-stage persuasion model in which a change is strengthened (e.g., by using it or learning more about it). (See three-stage model of attitude change.)

S-O-R – Mowrer's (1950) stating that a stimulus (S) interacts with an organism (O) to produce a response (R). That interaction is with a Psychological Root, according to Psychological Systems Theory.

Specific Psychological Roots – Psychological Roots that exist in only a small percentage of the population or are unique to just one individual, for example, believing that they have a system that can beat gambling odds, an ailing person wanting to stay alive long enough to see a child born, or believing that the world will end at a soon-occurring date.

Spectrum – An array of aspects along a continuum. (Synonym: range, continuum.)

State of uncontrollability – A changed circumstance that occurs when a tipping point is exceeded either at the high or low end of a homeostatic continuum. At the high end the intensity is so strong that it takes control (e.g., depression, panic, rage, ecstasy, or addiction), and at the low end the lack of energy takes control. Either way, the person is controlled and there no longer is homeostatic regulation and ability to return to an adaptive state. A state of uncontrollability can last for a period of time that is short, moderate, or long. (Synonyms: psychological box, biological box, dissociation.) (See long-term state of uncontrollability, short-term state of uncontrollability, temporary state of uncontrollability, psychological homeostasis, biological homeostasis.)

Step ladder – (See successive approximations to the goal.)

Stimulus – (See stimulus condition.)

Stimulus condition, stimulus conditions – Something that produces a reaction. A stimulus in a Hidden Sequence impacts a Psychological Root, resulting in an internal reaction, which may produce an observable behavior. The term 'stimulus condition' is preferred to "stimulus" because there can be a mixture of aspects affecting more than one Psychological Root. Stimulus conditions can be outside the body (e.g., what people say) or inside (e.g., serotonin), and difficult to identify when mixed with other factors. Some stimulus conditions have a long-lasting effect (e.g., significant childhood experiences).

Stimulus condition-Psychological Root interaction – (See stimulus condition.)

Stimulus-and-Root Sequence – An internal reaction (e.g., a thought or emotion) – and perhaps also a behavior – that starts with a stimulus that impacts a Psychological Root. The components of a Stimulus-and-Root Sequence are **stimulus + Psychological Root → internal reaction** (and perhaps **observable behavior**). (See Root Sequence, Modified Root Sequence, Modified Stimulus-and-Root Sequence, modifier.) (Synonyms: Stimulus Sequence, Stimulus-and-Psychological Root Sequence.)

Strategy – An idea or plan believed capable of solving a problem. A strategy is a belief and therefore a Psychological Root. (See problem-solving strategies.)

Stress cascade – (See Hidden Sequence.)

Strong psychological-root complex – An extensive set of categories, sub-categories, and clusters of Psychological Roots regarding a particular aspect. (See ability, weak psychological-root complex.)

Sub-category – A category within a larger category (e.g., a category of beliefs about what constitutes being a good neighbor within a larger category of what constitutes being a good citizen.)

Sub-cluster – A cluster within a larger cluster (e.g., beliefs about what constitutes appropriate church attendance within a larger cluster about what constitutes religious observance.)

Subconscious – Below awareness. The subconscious is vast (see Penfield, 1975), which aids giving conscious attention to a single focus but does not permit being aware of our psychological and biological processes. (Synonym: sub-surface.)

Sub-goal – Part of a goal. Sub-goals can provide stepping stones toward a full goal. (See full goal.)

Subject – What is studied when research is conducted, such as a person or other object of attention.

Subliminal – Something that occurs below awareness. (See consciousness.)

Subsidiary Psychological Roots – Psychological Roots that are involved with a particular behavior, but are not the primary factors that lead to that behavior.

Substrate – What a stimulus interacts with (e.g., a Psychological Root.) (See stimulus condition.)

Sub-surface – Below awareness (e.g., Psychological Roots and Hidden Sequences that operate subconsciously). (Synonym: subconscious, sub-aware.)

Successive approximations to the goal – Small steps toward a goal. The result might not have occurred otherwise (e.g., a pigeon hitting a small bowling ball by moving its head sideways rather than forward). (See operant conditioning, positive reinforcement, negative reinforcement.) (Synonyms: baby steps, bridging, step ladder.)

Successive insights – Obtaining greater understanding because of sequential steps that might not have occurred otherwise. New experiences have the potential to produce successive insights.

Surface Psychological Roots – Psychological Roots that are at the tangible end of psychological hierarchies (e.g., beliefs about socially appropriate behavior). (Synonym: low-order Psychological Roots, Later Psychological Roots.) (See Later Psychological Roots, Early Psychological Roots, deep Psychological Roots, intermediate Psychological Roots, Hidden Sequences.)

Surrogate – A substitute, such as a person who takes the place of biological mother.

Synthesis – Combining things to create something new. (See analysis.)

System – Components that interact in a unified manner.) (See Psychological Systems Theory.)

Talent – A very strong genetic ability (e.g., in art, mathematics, athletics). There is a strong Psychological Root complex and drive to use it, and can be developed with motivation, practice, experimenting, tutoring, support, and opportunity. A gift is even more substantial. (See ability, gift, skill, strong psychological-root complex.)

Tangible, tangibility – Something material that can be noticed using typical senses. Some highly tangibly- oriented people disdain abstract concepts, such as hidden psychological processes.

Temporary state of uncontrollability – Being in a state of uncontrollability for a relatively short time (e.g., ecstasy or panic). (See state of uncontrollability, short-term state of uncontrollability, long-term state of uncontrollability.)

Tension – A state of psychological intensity or unrest that can be due to stress. (See anxiety.)

Theory – A possible explanation (e.g., Galileo's theory of earth's solar system, Einstein's theory of relativity, Darwin's theory of evolution, and Freud's theory of psychology). A general theory is hard to prove definitively since every possible instance cannot be tested, but evidence for or against can be gathered to support or detract from it. (Synonyms: concept, idea, guess). (See hypothesis.)

Three-stage method of communicating – *Preparing* (e.g., obtaining receptivity and identifying the recipient's Psychological Roots), *Presenting* (e.g., being consistent with the recipient's Psychological Roots and not using repelling forces), and *Solidifying* (e.g., a review of the main points and the recipient's use of the new idea).

Three-stage method of persuading – *Preparing* (e.g., obtaining receptivity and identifying the recipient's Psychological Roots), *Presentation* (e.g., showing how the message solves a problem the recipient has without using repelling forces), and *Solidifying* (such as a review of the main points and the recipient's use of the idea).

Three-stage method of psychotherapy – *Preparing* (e.g., obtaining receptivity and identifying the recipient's Psychological Roots), *Presentation* (e.g., showing how the message solves a problem the recipient has without using repelling forces), and *Solidifying* (such as a review of the main points and the recipient's use of the idea).

Three-stage method of resolving conflicts – *Preparing* (e.g., obtaining receptivity and identifying the recipient's Psychological Roots), *Presentation* (e.g., showing how the message solves a problem the recipient has without using repelling forces), and *Solidifying* (such as a review of the main points and the recipient's use of the idea).

Threshold – The point at which change takes place (e.g., a criterion for evaluating success or failure). A threshold acts as an on/off switch (e.g., when the end of a homeostatic continuum is crossed, a state of uncontrollability results). (Synonym: switch point, tipping point.) (See tipping point, flash point.)

Tipping point – The point along a continuum at which a major change occurs, according to Psychological Systems Theory (e.g., crossing the endpoint of an emotional continuum into abnormality). A small difference can thereby create a major change. (See flash point.)

Tolerable range – A range along a homeostatic continuum that is tolerable but not desirable, between acceptable and intolerable ranges (e.g., people who are tolerated but not well liked). (See narrow adaptive range, adaptive zone, concentric social circles, unacceptable range.)

Tradeoff – When the parties in a conflict give up something qualitatively different (e.g., one spouse agrees to give up alcohol, and the other spouse relinquishes cigarettes). (See compromise, win-win solution.)

Trickle-down effect – (See domino effect, flow-down effects, post-shaping.)

Unacceptable range – An undesired range along a Psychological Homeostasis continuum, between tolerable and intolerable (e.g., people there is no desire to be in contact with). (See narrow adaptive range, concentric social circles, acceptable range, tolerable range, intolerable range, comfort range.)

Unconditional positive regard – Accepting and approving a person without his/her having to earn it (see Rogers, 1951) and is related to the use of Psychological Systems Theory's concept of appealing forces. Positive reinforcement differs from unconditional positive regard because the recipient must do something to acquire something positive. (See appealing force, positive reinforcement.)

Underlying sequence – (See Hidden Sequence, Root Sequence, Stimulus-and-Root Sequence).

Understanding drive – A drive the brain has to make sense out of circumstances, such as identifying patterns, making associations, drawing conclusions, and solving problems.

Unipolar scale – A scale that ranges from low to high along a single dimension such as positive (e.g., happy), or negative (e.g., sad). (See bipolar scale, magnitude scale, continuum.)

Validity – Something that is valid, accurate, correct, or truthful.

Values – Strongly held beliefs that are part of a person's basic personality and function as a person's core principles, guiding a person's thinking, reacting and behaving (e.g., believing in fairness, kindness, & being responsible).

Victim mentality – Feeling vulnerable, victimized, defensive, taking things personally, complaining frequently, often saying "woe is me" or "why me?". (See borderline personality disorder.)

Visual cortex – (See occipital cortex.)

Want – Something desired. A want has a weaker drive compared to a need because the desire to acquire a positive is weaker than the need to avoid a negative. (Synonyms: goal, aim, aspiration, desire.)

Warning signal, warning sign – (See psychological warning signal.)

Weak psychological-root complex – A sparse number of clusters or categories of Psychological Roots involving a particular aspect. (See strong psychological-root complex, ability, talent.)

Web – An extensive interconnection of Psychological Roots across different hierarchies and clusters. That complex network aids making associations, reasoning, drawing on information, finding solutions, and staying within guidelines. Psychological Root webs can grow throughout life. (See Psychological Root network.)

Welcome intermediary – A person who is well liked and respected by everyone in a conflict and who is willing to help resolve the conflict between those individuals. (Synonym: go-between.)

Wide adaptive range – (See wide adaptive zone, open-minded.

Wide adaptive zone – A wide psychological range in which an organism is comfortable and functions well. (Synonyms: wide adaptive range, wide comfort zone.) (See open-mindedness, closed-mindedness, adaptive range, wide and narrow adaptive range, unacceptable range, intolerable zone.)

Wide comfort zone – (See wide adaptive zone.)

Wide tolerance – Acceptance of a large range of aspects. (Synonyms: wide adaptive range, wide comfort zone.) (See open-mindedness, closed-mindedness, adaptive range, wide adaptive range, narrow adaptive range, unacceptable range, intolerable zone.)

Will-power – The exertion of conscious control over something. Some people believe that will-power is all that it takes to stop something undesirable in a person, such as an addiction.

Win-win solution – A compatible solution to a conflict in which each of the parties is satisfied without feeling that they are making a sacrifice. By contrast, a compromise is a lose-lose compatible solution in which one or more of the parties must give up something and feels that they have made a sacrifice.

Xenophobia – Fear or hatred of people who are different than oneself or one's sub-group.

Zeigarnik effect – Unfinished tasks are remembered more than completed tasks, evidence of the drive for closure.

Zone of acceptable positions – A range of acceptable aspects. The comfort zone is particularly acceptable. (See comfort zone, adaptive zone, zone of failure.)

Zone of failure – An unacceptable range of aspects. (See comfort zone, acceptable zone, tolerable zone.)

INDEX

Below are concepts, words, and phrases that have particular application in Psychological Systems Theory. These aspects occur frequently throughout the book; this index identifies some of their most prominent locations in the book.

Series of sub-goals, 165, 166, 469, 483
Set point, 16, 436
Shaping, 48, 70, 126, 130, 131, 132, 208, 217, 218, 219, 220, 388, 389, 451, 460,
    476, 477, 483, 488
Short-term change, 467, 483
Short-term learning, short-term memory, 453, 466, 467, 483
Short-term state of uncontrollability, 467, 469, 483, 485, 487
Simultaneous multiple Hidden Sequences, 469, 483
Simultaneously opposed factors, 452, 483, 484
Situational depression, 307, 308, 349, 387, 414, 448, 484
Skill, 30, 49, 96, 140, 142, 147, 149, 150, 187, 206, 236, 242, 265, 269, 301, 322,
    368, 369, 371, 372, 375, 407, 408, 441, 459, 461, 469, 484, 487
Social influence, 4, 65, 76, 77, 127, 137, 151, 184, 268, 275, 279, 284, 289, 296,
    316, 372, 401, 484
Social skill, social strategies, 40, 44, 49, 55, 104, 140, 142, 150, 205, 352, 404,
    407, 411, 447, 454, 457, 471, 477, 484
Soft conflict, 450, 451, 462, 467, 485
State of uncontrollability, 2, 7, 8, 17, 18, 20, 21, 22, 23, 25, 26, 28, 29, 31, 33,
    34, 35, 36, 37, 38, 39, 40, 42, 52, 71, 196, 197, 224, 232, 235, 323, 324, 330,
    331, 337, 342, 363, 391, 395, 399, 401, 402, 425, 446, 448, 449, 452, 454,
    457, 458, 459, 460, 464, 466, 467, 469, 474, 475, 476, 477, 478, 479, 480,
    481, 483, 485, 487, 488
Step ladder, 485, 487
Stimulus condition-Psychological Root interaction, 486
Stimulus-and-Root Sequence, 58, 59, 61, 64, 71, 88, 208, 213, 307, 445, 462,
    463, 469, 481, 486, 489
Strong psychological-root complex, 140, 441, 461, 486, 487, 489
Sub-category, 486
Sub-cluster, 138, 486
Subconscious, 8, 10, 14, 15, 45, 64, 75, 87, 91, 159, 163, 185, 186, 188, 189, 191,
    192, 203, 218, 223, 227, 281, 291, 292, 294, 301, 314, 315, 316, 317, 323,
    324, 328, 329, 333, 335, 337, 338, 340, 343, 345, 383, 386, 416, 417, 418,
    425, 445, 456, 462, 464, 479, 480, 486
Sub-goal, 165, 166, 460, 461, 486
Subsidiary Psychological Roots, 124, 130, 268, 281, 388, 389, 476, 479, 486
Sub-surface (see subconscious), 10, 37, 49, 60, 75, 87, 92, 95, 96, 142, 175, 182,
    184, 262, 291, 292, 341, 348, 354, 358, 480, 486
Successive approximations to the goal (see bridging), 287, 447, 483, 485, 486
Successive insights, 134, 425, 487
Surface Psychological Root, 60, 425, 465, 466, 468

95873947R00283

Made in the USA
Middletown, DE
28 October 2018